Classical Archaeology

BLACKWELL STUDIES IN GLOBAL ARCHAEOLOGY

Series Editors: Lynn Meskell and Rosemary A. Joyce

Blackwell Studies in Global Archaeology is a series of contemporary texts, each carefully designed to meet the needs of archaeology instructors and students seeking volumes that treat key regional and thematic areas of archaeological study. Each volume in the series, compiled by its own editor, includes 12–15 newly commissioned articles by top scholars within the volume's thematic, regional, or temporal area of focus.

What sets the *Blackwell Studies in Global Archaeology* apart from other available texts is that their approach is accessible, yet does not sacrifice theoretical sophistication. The series editors are committed to the idea that useable teaching texts need not lack ambition. To the contrary, the *Blackwell Studies in Global Archaeology* aim to immerse readers in fundamental archaeological ideas and concepts, but also to illuminate more advanced concepts, thereby exposing readers to some of the most exciting contemporary developments in the field. Inasmuch, these volumes are designed not only as classic texts, but as guides to the vital and exciting nature of archaeology as a discipline.

FORTHCOMING

Classical Archaeology

Edited by

Susan E. Alcock and
Robin Osborne

Blackwell
Publishing

BLACKWELL PUBLISHING
350 Main Street, Malden, MA 02148-5020, USA
9600 Garsington Road, Oxford OX4 2DQ, UK
550 Swanston Street, Carlton, Victoria 3053, Australia

First published 2007 by Blackwell Publishing Ltd

2   2008

Library of Congress Cataloging-in-Publication Data

Classical archaeology / edited by Susan E. Alcock and Robin Osborne.
    p. cm. – (Blackwell studies in global archaeology ; 10)
  Includes bibliographical references and index.
  ISBN 978-0-631-23418-0 (hardback : alk. paper)
  ISBN 978-0-631-23419-7 (pbk. : alk. paper)
1. Classical antiquities.   2. Greece–History–To 146 B.C.   3. Rome–History.   I. Alcock,
Susan E.   II. Osborne, Robin, 1957–

  DE86.C58 2007
  938–dc22
                                                                      2006032271

A catalogue record for this title is available from the British Library.

Set in 10 on 12.5 pt Plantin
by SNP Best-set Typesetter Ltd, Hong Kong
Printed and bound in Singapore
by Markono Print Media Pte Ltd

The publisher's policy is to use permanent paper from mills that operate a sustainable forestry
policy, and which has been manufactured from pulp processed using acid-free and elementary
chlorine-free practices. Furthermore, the publisher ensures that the text paper and cover board
used have met acceptable environmental accreditation standards.

For further information on
Blackwell Publishing, visit our website:
www.blackwellpublishing.com

Contents

List of Figures

Notes on Contributors

Susan E. Alcock is Director of the Artemis A.W. and Martha Sharp Joukowsky Institute for Archaeology and the Ancient World, Joukowsky Family Professor of Archaeology and Professor of Classics at Brown University. Her research interests include the Hellenistic and Roman Eastern Mediterranean, landscape archaeology, and the archaeology of imperialism. She has been involved with several regional archaeological projects in Greece, and has recently begun fieldwork in southern Armenia.

Bettina Bergmann is Helene Philips Herzig '49 Professor of Art at Mount Holyoke College. Her research concerns the Roman art of landscape, domestic space, and the reception and reconstruction of ancient houses and villas.

John F. Cherry is Professor of Classics at Brown University, where he teaches in the Artemis A.W. and Martha Sharp Joukowsky Institute for Archaeology and the Ancient World. His fieldwork has mainly involved surveys in Greece and Italy, but he is currently co-directing a project in Armenia. He is an Aegean prehistorian, whose current research interests include the archaeology of islands, landscape archaeology, lithic analysis, and reception studies of Alexander the Great.

Penelope J. E. Davies is Associate Professor in the Department of Art and Art History, College of Fine Arts, University of Texas at Austin. Her research focuses on the roles of state art and architecture in the political life of Rome during the Republic and the Empire.

Jack L. Davis is Carl W. Blegen Professor of Greek Archaeology at the University of Cincinnati. His research interests include landscape archaeology, Greek prehistory, and the rural history of Ottoman and Venetian Greece. He has directed or co-directed several regional archaeological projects in Greece and Albania, and is currently excavating a Greek temple at Apollonia and studying unpublished finds from the Palace of Nestor at Pylos in Greece.

Hamish Forbes is Senior Lecturer in Archaeology at Nottingham University. His main research interests lie in the study of recent and modern Mediterranean landscapes and their communities and how they impact on our understanding of the archaeological and historical records.

Lin Foxhall, Professor of Greek Archaeology and History in the School of Archaeology and Ancient History, University of Leicester, was educated at Bryn Mawr College, University of Pennsylvania and the University of Liverpool. She has also held posts at Oxford University and University College London. She has published extensively on gender in classical antiquity, as well as on agriculture and the ancient economy.

Jonathan M. Hall is the Phyllis Fay Horton Professor in the Humanities, Professor and Chair of Classics, and Professor of History at the University of Chicago. His research interests include ethnic and cultural identities in Greek antiquity, issues of historical method in Greek protohistory, and the relationship between history and archaeology.

Tonio Hölscher is Professor of Classical Archaeology and Director of the Seminar of Classical Archaeology at the University of Heidelberg, Germany. His main research field is Greek and Roman figurative art in political, social and religious contexts; this embraces studies of urbanism as well as aesthetic theory. His current research projects include political monuments in the ancient world and the use of images in social practice.

Henry Hurst is Reader in Classical Archaeology at the University of Cambridge. His main research interest is urban archaeology and he is currently involved with publishing work on the Santa Maria Antiqua complex in Rome. He also continues to be involved in the archaeology of Carthage and Roman Britain, where he worked previously.

Martin Jones is George Pitt-Rivers Professor of Archaeological Science at the University of Cambridge. His field of interest is bio-archaeology and the spread and development of agricultural practices and crops.

Martin Millett is Laurence Professor of Classical Archaeology at Cambridge University and a Fellow of Fitzwilliam College. His principal interests are in the social and economic archaeology of the Roman empire. He has run field surveys and excavations in Britain, Spain, Portugal and Italy.

Sarah P. Morris is a classicist and archaeologist in the Department of Classics and the Cotsen Institute of Archaeology at UCLA, where she was named the Steinmetz Professor of Classical Archaeology and Material Culture in 2001. Her teaching and research interests include early Greek literature (Homer, Hesiod, and Herodotus), Greek religion, prehistoric and early Greek archaeology, ceramics, Greek architecture and landscape studies, and Near Eastern influence on Greek art and culture. She has excavated in Israel, Turkey, and Greece, and is currently co-director of a new project in Albania.

Lisa Nevett is Associate Professor of Greek Archaeology at the University of Michigan, Ann Arbor. Her research involves using interdisciplinary approaches to the built environment as a way of addressing large-scale questions about Greek and Roman society. To date, her main focus has been on domestic space which she has used to explore the rise of the Greek city-state, gender relations and acculturation in the Roman empire.

Robin Osborne is Professor of Ancient History at the University of Cambridge. He has published widely on topics in Greek archaeology, art, and history, including *Classical Landscape with Figures* (London, 1987), *Greece in the Making, c. 1200–479 B.C.* (London, 1996) and *Archaic and Classical Greek Art* (Oxford, 1998).

Nicholas Purcell is Fellow and Tutor in Ancient History at St John's College, Oxford, and Lecturer in Ancient History at Oxford University. He works on ancient social, economic and cultural history and is also interested in the history of the Mediterranean over the longer term.

Christopher Smith is Professor of Ancient History at the University of St Andrews. His research interests include early Rome, ancient religion and ancient rhetoric and historiography. He has recently completed a book on the Roman *gens*.

Anthony Snodgrass was Laurence Professor of Classical Archaeology at the University of Cambridge from 1976 to 2001. He has worked for many years primarily on the archaeology and history of pre-Classical Greece, more recently also on the intellectual and disciplinary background of Classical Archaeology. He has a long-standing involvement in intensive field survey in Greece.

Nicola Terrenato is an Associate Professor of Classical Archaeology at the University of Michigan at Ann Arbor. He has conducted extensive fieldwork in and around Rome and in Northern Etruria. His research interests include Roman imperialism and colonialism, field survey methods and early Roman landscapes.

Andrew Wallace-Hadrill is Director of the British School at Rome and Professor of Classics at the University of Reading. His work lies in the area of Roman social and cultural history, from imperial ideology to domestic space. He is involved in various projects in Italy, and directs a project of conservation and research at Herculaneum.

Jane Webster is Lecturer in Historical Archaeology at the University of Newcastle-upon-Tyne (UK), where she teaches and researches on colonial archaeology in both the Roman and early modern periods. A former Caird Senior Research Fellow at the National Maritime Museum, Greenwich, she is currently working on a study of the material culture of slave shipping.

Introduction

Robin Osborne and Susan E. Alcock

Why *Classical Archaeology?*

Unlike "Mesoamerican Archaeology," "North American Archaeology" or "The Archaeology of Mediterranean Prehistory," "Classical Archaeology" is a title with strong, and not entirely positive, connotations. The title "classical" carries with it a claimed value judgment that is quite absent from the geographical or period titles of other volumes in this series. In fact, the "classical" of "classical archaeology" does not directly apply to the archaeology—"classical archaeology" is not the archaeology of material that has acquired "classic" status. It applies rather to the "Classical World," that is, the world that has left us the literature that has acquired "classic" status in western civilization. This is the world inhabited by Greeks and Romans between the eighth century B.C. and the fourth century A.D. "classical archaeology" is the archaeology of that world.

It is not difficult to envisage an archaeological guide that treated Greece with its Near Eastern neighbors or one that subsumed imperial Rome into the early Christian world. Our decision to treat Greek and Roman civilization as a single "classical" whole is traditional but it is neither innocent nor inconsequential. It is a decision that both reflects and perpetuates the claims that have been made by Europeans and their descendants repeatedly since the Renaissance for the unique status of the ancient Greek and Roman worlds. The intellectual understanding of the world and how to live in the world, and the literary expression of that understanding achieved in Greece and Rome, have been hailed as the necessary basis for civilized life. It has been the spreading of this "classical" understanding of the world which, along with the spreading of Christianity, has underpinned, and served to justify western imperialism. The imperialism of our own day, with its stress on democracy, continues to draw a significant amount of its power from the claim that democracy was invented by the ancient Greeks.

Why, then, have we persisted with the title "Classical Archaeology" rather than using, for example, "The Archaeology of the Iron Age Mediterranean"? Precisely because it is important to acknowledge that the archaeology of the Greek and Roman worlds has a history. All scholarship builds upon the work of previous scholars in the field: not for nothing do doctoral theses regularly begin with a "survey of past literature." Yet in the archaeology of the Greek world and the archaeology of the Roman world that past literature carries a burden that extends beyond the particular substantive discoveries and insights that it records. The material culture of Greece and Rome has been uniquely freighted with moral value, and has come to play an ongoing role in the formation of western sensibilities. It is simply not possible to revisit the material world of the Greeks and the Romans as a disinterested observer: whether we as westerners like it or not, this material has been privileged in our own formation, and it has been privileged as *our* past. The archaeology of Greece and Rome has been given a role in our intellectual formation which is not rivaled by the archaeology of Celts, Germans, Iberians or Gauls—even for inhabitants of Britain, Germany, Spain and France. The more we find the imperialism of the "classical world" a political and moral embarrassment, the more vital it is to understand it and the basis for it.

What Sort of Classical Archaeology?

If the choice of "Classical Archaeology" in the title is a traditional and thereby conservative one, the organization and contents of this volume are far from traditional. The organization reflects an acknowledgment that the unity implicitly claimed for the Greek and Roman worlds and for the whole of a period of more than a thousand years by subsuming it as classical archaeology obscures important differences. Each of the topics discussed in the book (except the natural environment) is discussed from two angles, broadly Greek and Roman. This division is in part a chronological one: the focus of Greek archaeology has been the period from ca. 700 to ca. 100 B.C., the focus of Roman archaeology the period from ca. 200 B.C. to ca. A.D. 500. (The period 323–30 B.C., known as the "Hellenistic" period, is variously discussed in "Greek" or "Roman" sections, as appropriate to each topic.) In part, however, the division is geographical: the focus of Greek archaeology lies in the Greek peninsula and the eastern Mediterranean, the focus of Roman archaeology in the Italian peninsula and in western Europe. Since the political history of western Europe and of the eastern Mediterranean has been very different over the past millennium, that geographical difference has resulted in the ongoing use of the classical heritage being very different, and political differences continue to affect the conditions in which archaeology can be carried out today. By exploring our chosen themes from both Greek and Roman angles we hope to alert the reader not simply to the different material available for discussion in the later Roman west from that available from the earlier Greek east, but also to the ways in which that different inheritance affects the approaches which archaeologists take, the questions that they ask, and the answers with which they are satisfied.

The themes which we have chosen to explore also mark this volume out as breaking with tradition. Classical archaeology, as Snodgrass explains in his contribution to chapter 1, has been "a discipline devoted to the archaeology of objects," "governed and organized . . . by classes of material." A guide to classical archaeology might therefore be expected to be itself organized by classes of material—pottery, metalwork, sculpture, architecture. Many well-established introductions to periods or regions within classical archaeology are organized in that way. R. G. Collingwood and I. A. Richmond's *The Archaeology of Roman Britain*, a revision published in 1969 of a book first published in 1930, starts with roads, goes on through military camps, forts, and frontier works to towns, villas, temples, and tombs, and ends up with inscriptions, coins, fine and coarse pottery, brooches and weapons. William Biers's *Introduction to Greek Archaeology* (1996) divides itself by period, but within the periods discussion proceeds by artifact type; Nicolas Coldstream's *Geometric Greece* (1977) organizes itself by period and region but within the region by artifact type. And the same would be true of many period-specific guides. Even the recent German collection *Klassische Archäologie: eine Einführung*, edited by Borbein, Hölscher, and Zanker (Borbein et al. 2000) includes a section with separate chapters on towns, architecture, sanctuaries, and graves.

This volume is not organized by classes of material. This is partly a practical matter. It is indeed hard to see how any guide to classical archaeology within the space of a single volume could offer any helpful introduction to the rich, various, and swiftly changing types and styles of artifact produced and used in the Greek and Roman worlds over this millennium. It is partly a matter of what can be done on the printed page and what can be done only in the field or the museum. A short amount of time handling artifacts or seeing on the ground the traces of ancient buildings and settlements introduces one to material much more efficiently than much time spent with the printed page—or in a lecture room. But it is also a matter of what archaeology is about.

What we know about classical archaeology has come about through people's curiosity about objects which have survived from antiquity or been discovered, whether by chance or by planned excavation. It is because people have wanted to know "What is this?" that we are able to date artifacts and interpret sites. There is still a lot that we do not know about particular artifacts and classes of artifact from the Greek and Roman world, and there are still occasional sites which those who excavate them find it hard to classify. But in general our knowledge of the material culture of the Greek and Roman worlds is now so firmly based that we can readily answer the question of what an object, an assemblage, or a site is. The hard questions which classical archaeology still has to face up to are questions about how objects relate to each other and above all to people. What patterns of human behavior are indicated by the artifacts, assemblages, and sites available for study? How can we convert collections of grave goods, or dumps of votives, or the buildings of a civic center into witnesses to the social, religious, and political life of Greek and Roman communities? When we find an object made in one place being deposited in a different place, can we reconstruct the reasons why and means by which it traveled? What does the spread of an artistic motif, or a fashion for building in a particular type of stone, tell us about the interactions of communities within and across political boundaries?

Studying classical archaeology by studying and specializing in particular types of material does not merely fail to address and to answer these interpretative questions. It frequently also assumes answers to these questions, answers that are drawn not from any feature of the artifacts themselves but from the modern world. Classical archaeologists have often been shy of, and resistant to, archaeological theory. Theory has been held to be unconnected to the real concerns of the archaeologist in the field, and to dress itself up in impenetrable jargon. But "theory" is not an optional extra for the archaeologist, since all who attempt to say anything about objects which survive from antiquity do so on the basis of a body of assumptions. Archaeological theory is about making the assumptions explicit, whether those assumptions are assumptions about how an object came to be in the place where it was found, about whether it is or is not "typical," or whether those assumptions are about the sorts of connections one object may have with another, either in terms of their origin or in terms of their "biography." The more different the society being studied archaeologically is from our own society, the more essential is the clear articulation of assumptions, and the more essential is archaeological theory.

This book explores classical archaeology as a discipline that is concerned with the interpretation of the material culture of classical antiquity. It is concerned with the sorts of artifacts which, because of their intrinsic merits and because of their influence on western civilization since the Renaissance, attract discussion in their own right. But it is also concerned with the sort of artifacts whose banality and lack of aesthetic merit mean that no one would spend time on them in their own right. So, it is concerned with works of art—sculptures, buildings, and paintings—but it is also concerned with broken shards of coarse pottery, the stone beds of oil and wine presses, lumps of slag from mining and metalworking, and so on. It is the mix of such items in the archaeological record that enables us to recreate some picture of the nature of Greek and Roman communities, their values, their way of life, and their expectations. It is only on the basis of such an understanding that we can come to comprehend how classical Athens sustained a democratic constitution in which all Athenian adult males could participate in political decision-making, or how the Romans conquered the Mediterranean between the end of the third century B.C. and the beginning of the first century A.D. It is only by such an understanding that we can come to comprehend also those literary, philosophical, and artistic developments which have been so fundamental to the subsequent self-understanding of the West.

The Archaeology of an Alien World

There is no doubt that in many respects the Greeks and Romans were remarkably like us. The very status of classical literature in modern western education has ensured that in important ways we share the same heritage and moral, social, and political expectations with the classical world. The extent to which the agenda of western philosophy was set by Plato is a mark of the degree to which modern western puzzles about the world run along much the same lines as ancient Greek puzzles about the world. But it is equally the case that Greeks and Romans were in other respects quite unlike us. The polytheism which they shared was based on expectations about the natural world and about the moral order of the world which are quite foreign to a civilization built on the Judaeo-Christian tradition. The economic base of the western world was transformed by the invention of a mechanical substitute for human and animal labor which brought about the Industrial Revolution; that revolution utterly changed production per man-day, not simply in the manufacture of artifacts but in agriculture also. Rapid and reliable communications over long distances, such as only became regular in the 20th century, radically alter the nature of relationships between individuals and communities far separated in space.

No scholar studying the Greek and Roman world is ignorant of such differences, but it is nevertheless hard to keep assumptions born in the modern world out of interpretations of ancient material unless attention is directly and explicitly focused on questions of interpretation. Fully to realize the importance of this, consider the following examples, one socio-economic and one socio-political.

In the modern world most goods move through trade. Most of what most people own in the western world today was purchased by them for money. Some will have been bought direct from the producer, but most will have been bought from a middleman, a retailer. Few who buy from them have any personal knowledge of the retailer or manufacturer involved. A small number of items owned by individuals today will have been given to them, either by the person who made them or by someone who bought them, whether from their producer or from a middleman. For some periods of classical antiquity we believe the situation to have been very different all over the Greek and Roman world, and for other periods to have been very different in at least some areas of those worlds. In those periods and places, most of the, generally much smaller, number of items owned by someone would have been acquired other than by money purchase. They would be gifts or acquired in exchange for goods or services. Even where objects were money purchases, the purchaser will generally have known, and have been known to, the seller. Interpreting objects, particularly objects found distant from their place of manufacture, depends crucially on what we think to have been the dominant nature of exchange in the world in which they were produced and used.

The expectation that pots or everyday goods will have been traded for money comes naturally to us since we ourselves expect to purchase equivalent items, but there are plenty of past societies in which it has been gifts or bartering which have dominated the exchange of goods. The challenge to the archaeologist is to detect features of the material record which may offer clues as to the exchange relationship in question. In looking for these clues, it is not facts about the object itself, the technique by which it was produced, the ascription to a particular manufacturer or absolute date, which are likely to be most important, but rather the nature of the context in which the item was found, what other objects it was found with, whether other similar objects are rare or abundant in the vicinity of the find-spot, what the pattern of distribution of this particular object is, and so on. Of course, classifying the object accurately and precisely is vital, but it is a preliminary to the major task of interpretation, not a substitute for such interpretation.

If the dissemination of goods was often by quite different means in Greek and Roman antiquity, the dissemination of verbal and visual information was almost always by different means. For hundreds of years now the West has been used to the possibility of mass reproduction of texts and images. "The Gutenberg Revolution" made it possible to put the same written text into the hands of thousands of people over a wide area in a short space of time. Today's instant beaming of words and images across the world has taken this revolutionary development several steps further on, but the significance of the invention of the very possibility of mass reproduction of the same text or image was fundamental.

In the Greek and Roman worlds there were simply no ways to reproduce extensive texts or images. There was indeed essentially only one way of mass reproducing any text or image, and that was through coinage. Stamping the same image and brief text on coins was the only way of getting a written message or particular image into the hands of significant numbers of people with any rapidity. And disseminating coins was a state monopoly.

The impossibility of getting the same written text to any significant number of people has all sorts of consequences. It has political consequences. Government decisions cannot be put into the hands of those who are affected by them as written texts. People have to be encouraged to come to the texts instead. Hence, for example, the Athenians made the statues in the Agora of the ten heroes after whom their tribes were named the place where public notices were put up. But there are cultural consequences too. A song that catches on in Rome cannot be dispatched to the other cities of the empire except by sending out people who will sing it. Cultural fashions can only sweep across the Mediterranean through individuals traveling and passing on their enthusiasms. And although scholars sometimes talk about "school texts" in antiquity, the labor of copying texts meant that there was no way that every pupil in the Roman empire could ever have the same text in his hands to learn from. The reach of the state was severely restricted by the absence of the technology for textual reproduction, and in these circumstances regional variation was bound to thrive.

The consequences of not being able to disseminate images is, however, even more important. Texts could, after all, be spread in oral form. The six thousand Athenian citizens at a meeting of the Athenian Assembly only had to talk to ten others on their way home and the whole citizen body would have the news of what had been decided. But there was no oral way of conveying a visual image. Those who caught sight of Boudicca, the queen of the tribe known as the Iceni who led a rebellion against the Romans in 60 A.D., could convey her striking appearance only in words ("long auburn hair down to her hips and a large golden torque," according to the much later Roman writer Dio Cassius [62.2.4]). Most inhabitants of the Roman empire would never know what the consuls for any particular year looked like, and beyond the local community the only person with whose image they would be familiar, precisely because it was reproduced on coinage, was the emperor.

The difficulties of conveying visual images directly impacted on their power. Rather than a world in which people expect to recognize anyone of any public prominence because they will have seen their picture, the classical world was one where names normally carried no image with them, and where it was recognizing a person, not failing to recognize a person, that was shocking. The impact of recognition added to the power of the individual. It did so not least because the widespread adoption of the same "types" for images of the gods meant that one of the few sets of images that were widely recognizable were images of the gods.

Yet if the power of the image reflected back on the individual whose image it was, it reflected also on the individual who made the image. The fantasy of the artist who carves a statue that comes to life, most famously exemplified by the myth of Pygmalion, reflects upon the ability of the artist to "bring to life" distant figures who would otherwise simply be names. And once more, this ability to overcome distance applied not simply to making recognizable persons who were physically distant but also to making recognizable those who were metaphysically distant—the gods.

Classical archaeology distinguishes itself in part as the archaeology of societies rich in texts. Yet whereas most texts in the modern world are best treated as having no particular objective status, the texts of the ancient world are importantly not just all objects, but all individual objects in their own right, neither mass produced nor identical. The scholar in the famed library at Alexandria, in which the first Ptolemies attempted to make a systematic collection of Greek literature, might be able to emulate the modern student, able to access a world of written data without interacting with any other human being. But for all but the extremely few such scholars, acquiring information and learning about literature meant talking to others and committing to memory literary and dramatic performances that they had heard.

The invention of the "art of memory" was attributed in antiquity to the fifth-century poet Simonides, from the island of Keos. In its classic form the art of memory involved "placing" what had to be remembered, for instance, the different parts of a speech, onto a familiar building, so that they could be retrieved by calling to mind the building and recalling what was in each doorway, window, niche, or whatever. Studies of memory have shown that it is precisely those things which simultaneously evoke multiple senses (color, feel, sound) that are most clearly and vividly recalled. The absence of ready ways of recalling the appearance of persons or objects once seen but now no longer in view arguably ensured that visual appearances made a particularly striking impact, and hence made it entirely appropriate to "hang" texts upon a visual framework.

The archaeological consequences of the differences between classical and modern dissemination of goods and of texts and images are profound. In both cases the differences mean that very much more was invested in objects in the classical world. Objects that were exchanged had an important life, what Appadurai has called "the social life of things" (Appadurai 1986). Texts and images too carried rich material associations. In all cases, the particular object mattered. Context was all-important for ancient producers and consumers, and context has to be to the fore when we study what it was that they produced and consumed.

How This Guide to Classical Archaeology Is Organized

In this book we attempt to provide readers with what they need to know in order to understand the material culture of classical antiquity. Readers will not come away from this book able to put a date on a piece of classical sculpture, identify the hand of the painter responsible for the scenes painted on a vessel of fine Athenian pottery, able to distinguish "real" Arretine pottery from imitations made in Gaul or Britain, or ascribe a marching camp to the campaigns of a particular Roman emperor. The classical archaeologists whom this book aims to create will be classical archaeologists with a number of distinctive traits. First and foremost, they will use texts along with material archaeology, offering both a context for archaeology and an indication of areas of material culture ideologically understated or repressed. They will be aware of the tradition within which all classical archaeologists operate and write, and will understand the sorts of archaeological fieldwork which are and have been possible in classical lands, and the constraints which have determined and still determine what can and cannot be done in the field. They will see the physical environment not in terms of unchangeable conditions which Greeks and Romans had to endure, but in terms of a dynamic ecological relationship which patient fieldwork and judicious use of ethnography enable us to understand. Their picture of how that environment was inhabited, whether in rural settlements or towns, and of the quality and dominant concerns of country and civic life will draw on sociology and the importance of representation, as well as upon dots on the map. They will be conscious of the range of particular ways in which individuals related to each other directly, both in the household and in public life, secular and sacred, and indirectly through the exchange of goods, and of the ways in which they presented themselves to others and represented others to themselves. And we hope that, in consequence, they will reflect upon the ways in which they themselves engage with, and are encouraged by the ways in which the media present the classical world to engage with, this particular past, and on the oscillation between idealist and realist visions of classical antiquity which mark all studies, scholarly and popular.

We open with "What is Classical Archaeology?," two discussions of the way in which classical archaeology has been practiced, and of its scope and range. These studies focus upon the subject as a whole, as manifested above all in what is published. They are complemented by "Doing Archaeology in the Classical Lands," two studies of what it is to practice classical archaeology in the field, studies which reveal the ways in which the vagaries of real life, including international politics, impinge upon the field archaeologist, but which also reflect something of the excitement that accompanies the exploration not just of new sites or countrysides but of new archaeological methods.

The nature of the countrysides that have been increasingly the focus of classical archaeologists' concerns over the past quarter century is further explored in the following studies. The first of these, "Human Ecology and the Classical Landscape," concerns the reconstruction of both the natural and the agricultural environment, the uncovering of the physical conditions within which life was lived, and because it is the natural world that is at issue, Greek and Roman worlds are discussed together. The following pair, "The Essential Countryside," concern what was made of the countryside—the ways it was exploited and settled and the forms of social life betrayed by its monuments.

The two chapters that follow turn respectively from countryside to city ("Urban Spaces and Central Places"), and from the interaction of households to interactions within the household ("Housing and Households"). Urban life developed particularly characteristic forms in classical antiquity, with highly developed communities devoting extensive resources to public facilities both for secular purposes of mutual defense and self-government (meeting places, offices for magistrates, law courts) and for the worship of the gods. Greek and Roman patterns of urban life, and in particular the importance attached to central places, emerge as highly distinctive. Public life, and in particular secular civic life, were throughout antiquity dominated by men, and it is to the household that attention must be turned if we are to understand the place and condition of women. The rich evidence of surviving domestic housing has only recently begun to be intensively investigated, and to reveal a much less uniform set of living practices than classical literary texts had led scholars to expect.

The religious side of civic life and the personal side of civic politics are investigated in the next two chapters, "Cult and Ritual" and "The Personal and the Political." The most distinguished examples of classical architecture belong to religious buildings, but these have been more regularly analyzed as buildings than inserted into their religious context. Similarly, commemorative statuary, whether honoring the living or the dead, has been regularly inserted into the history of sculpture rather than seen as part of the political self-presentation of those who had or aspired to power. These two chapters take these familiar classes of evidence and show the ways in which they look different when seen as parts of a functioning system.

The final two substantive chapters look at how the communities which have been examined individually or as types in early parts of the book interacted with each other. The two studies in "The Creation and Expression of Identity" explore the ways in which whole communities projected particular identities, signaling to others the values which they held to be particular to them. The two further studies in "Linking with a Wider World" look at how such signaling was received and what was reflected back, as they look at the exchange of representations that went with the exchange of goods, and explore the ways in which the classical world as we know it was constituted by this exchange of goods and ideas.

In "Prospective," a reflective conclusion to the volume, we encourage readers to engage both with the construction of the classical world which they are offered by film, newsprint, and popular books and on the construction which they have been offered in this volume.

REFERENCES

Appadurai, Arjun 1986 The Social Life of Things: Commodities in Cultural Perspective. Cambridge: Cambridge University Press.

Biers, William R. 1996 The Archaeology of Greece: An Introduction. 2nd edn. Ithaca: Cornell University Press.

Borbein, Adolph H., Tonio Hölscher, and Paul Zanker, eds. 2000 Klassische Archäologie: eine Einführung. Berlin: Reimer Verlag.

Coldstream, J. Nicolas 1977 Geometric Greece. London: Benn.

Collingwood, R. G., and I. A. Richmond 1969 The Archaeology of Roman Britain. London: Methuen.

1

What is Classical Archaeology?

Introduction

More than any other branch of archaeology, classical archaeology has a history. It is not simply that people have been concerned with the material culture of Greek and Roman antiquity for a very long time now, and that attempts to put the remains of Greek and Roman sculpture and architecture into some sort of order go back to the 18th century. It is also that what scholars do with that material culture today is in dialogue not just with the Greek and Roman past but with the history of its own scholarship.

It is for this reason that this volume opens with two discussions of the nature and tradition of classical archaeology that have a strongly historical focus. Understanding what questions classical archaeologists have asked, why they have asked these questions, and why some questions have raised and continue to raise particular scholarly sensitivities depends upon understanding the history of the discipline.

Part of the peculiar position of classical archaeology arises from the way in which it is both a branch of archaeology and a branch of Classics. Interest in the material culture of Greek and Roman antiquity has arisen not simply through the intrinsic interest of the material but through interest in the relationship between the material world and the world of classical texts. At the same time, the wealth of classical texts offers classical archaeologists a resource not available to prehistoric archaeology. Yet the way in which the questions asked by classical archaeologists, and the sites which they investigate, have been determined by classical texts has often been seen as a weakness, rather than a strength. Archaeologists working in prehistory have frequently found themselves impatient with what they see as the reduction of material culture to providing illustration to texts. They have been impatient too with classical archaeology's tendency to pay attention to certain classes of artifact (above all to "works of art") and to ignore other classes of artifact. For them, classical archaeology has too often seemed to be a treasure hunt where the clues are provided entirely by texts, in the tradition of Schliemann digging at Troy with Homer in hand.

Our two discussions of the nature of the subject are drawn from scholars who come from the opposite ends of classical archaeology. One is a specialist in Greek and the other a specialist in Roman archaeology. Yet more importantly in this context, one is a scholar whose primary training was in Classics, whose first publication was an artifact study (of arms and armor), and whose university positions were always associated with departments of Classics. The other is a scholar whose training was in archaeology and who until recently had held positions entirely in archaeology departments. The very different perspectives offered from these different backgrounds offer a comprehensive foundation for understanding the classical archaeology to which they and the rest of this volume serve as a guide.

I (a)
What is Classical Archaeology?

Greek Archaeology

Anthony Snodgrass

A book like this, and especially a chapter like this, must have it as its prime aim to describe and not to prescribe, however strong the temptation to become pre-scriptive may be. This is all the harder when disagreement prevails, as we shall see that it does today, over any final definition of classical archaeology. The task of this first contribution is to address the question from the point of view of Greek archaeology: it will incorporate certain approaches that are not explicitly confined to ancient Greece, but which would be quite differently formulated in a Roman context.

The first task might be to set out, in simplified outline, some different and rival positions taken today on this issue of definition. The positions are not as mutually incompatible as this simplified form may suggest; they have already co-existed for some years, and direct confrontations between them do not happen that often—thanks partly to the fact that in many cases they prove to divide along the bound-aries of nationality and language. Yet we can take the analysis one step further by trying to identify the (often implicit) issues which divide the groups from each other. In first putting together a list of specimen answers to the question "What is classical archaeology?" and concentrating on those approaches that are essen-tially characteristic of the Greek branch of the subject, I hope we can give a fair spectrum of the views commanding the most support among the practitioners of Greek archaeology, without excluding the beliefs, accurate or distorted, of the educated general public. The list should be not merely an abstract, but also an operational or behavioral one, in the sense of conforming to what classical archae-ologists actually *do*. With this preamble, we can attempt our listing:

1. Classical archaeology is by definition a branch of archaeology. It is the term used to denote that branch of the subject which concerns itself with ancient Greece and Rome; it can employ not only the entire range of methods used in archaeology at large, but also some additional ones of its own.

2. Classical archaeology is a branch of Classical studies; its objective is to use material evidence to throw light on the other, non-material cultural achievements of the ancient Greeks and Romans, preserved for us mainly through the medium of written texts. For this reason, it can hardly participate in the aims, the theories or the debates of archaeology as a whole, which cannot possibly share the same objective.

3. Classical archaeology is essentially a branch of art history, directed at discovering and establishing, in the arts of antiquity, a visual counterpart for the intellectual achievements of the ancient Greeks and Romans. Because its subject matter is more fragmentary than that of many later periods of art history, it must use certain peculiar techniques of discovery and reconstruction; but its aims are not essentially different.

4. Classical archaeology is none of the above. It is an autonomous discipline operating according to its own principles, and pursuing aims which are palpably different from those of non-classical archaeology, non-archaeological Classics, post-Classical art history, or indeed any other discipline. Its overriding concern is the purely internal one of imposing order on the vast body of material with which it must deal. One has only to look at its output to see the truth of this.

The first three of these are more "idealist" positions than the fourth, though their supporters usually turn out to practice what they preach. No. 1, in particular, purports at the outset to be little more than a tautology; but it may prove to conceal at least as strong a prescriptive element as Nos. 2 and 3. The latter more openly embody an agenda, each presenting the Greeks and Romans as readily separable from all other prehistoric or ancient peoples, with cultural and especially artistic achievements that require special treatment (less obviously, they are also responses much more likely to come from a Greek than from a Roman specialist). No. 4 differs in being a confessedly operational definition, derived from observation of actual practice and telling us nothing about the nature of the subject: as such, it can hardly be adopted as a program, but its supporters might argue that it is nevertheless tacitly accepted by the great majority of Greek archaeologists, even when they protest their allegiance to one of the other three. As already hinted, any suggestion of irreconcilable differences of outlook within Greek archaeology would be an exaggeration. In the end, these are indications of priorities rather than absolute positions: few if any classical archaeologists would embrace any one of them to the total exclusion of the others. But the modern history of the subject is the history of the reciprocal ebb and flow between these four fundamental viewpoints, or combinations of them.

There are certain key issues which tend to determine the individual's choice of position and, explicitly or more often implicitly, to divide this position from the others. The most important of these relates to the surviving ancient texts, or "sources" as they are often called in historical circles—slightly misleadingly, since the majority of them date from centuries later than the events, or works, which they describe. The ancient texts explicitly lie at the heart of the argument of position No. 2 above: it is they which have preserved most of the "other . . . cultural achievements" of the Greeks and Romans, and according to this view, the function of classical archaeology is to supplement them with the evidence derived from material remains, on which the texts have much less to say. Even so, there is often some information to be found in the texts which has at least an indirect bearing on the material record: a statue may perhaps be connected with a known work, attributed by some ancient author to a known artist; a deposit at an identifiable site may perhaps be connected with a documented event in the history of that site. It will clearly be a source of satisfaction if the material evidence is found to be compatible with the textual account, and much ingenuity is spent, by the upholders of this view, in trying to reconcile them.

Less obviously, textual evidence is almost as important a factor for the supporters of position No. 3, who concentrate on the products of Classical (and especially Greek) artists. Although unaided archaeological discovery, at first haphazard and later systematic, would in due course have brought to light the magnitude of the Greek achievement in the visual arts, the historical fact is that, long before most such discoveries were actually made, they were confidently anticipated on the basis of the ancient texts. The pioneering work of Johann Joachim Winckelmann in the mid-18th century (see below, p. 17) was directly inspired by his knowledge of the ancient (especially the Latin) sources for Greek art, and characterized by his deference to them; his model for the phases of development of Greek art was directly based on a pattern much earlier adopted for Greek poetry. Many of Winckelmann's most illustrious successors have retained similar attitudes, and almost all later narratives of Greek art have accepted (though with a very different terminology) the skeleton of his outline for its development.

As a consequence, this general position can reasonably be claimed as the "founding definition" for Greek (but only for Greek) archaeology. Already while Winckelmann was studying the collections of ancient art works in Rome, excavations at the Italian provincial sites of Herculaneum and Pompeii were actively under way; but Winckelmann took a disparaging view of these and their potential value. Greek art history had been pointed on a course which it was long to follow: one which distanced it from field archaeology and assimilated it to philological scholarship. More importantly, this approach was to prove so fruitful and so satisfying that, for many of its exponents, Greek archaeology *became* Greek art history, and nothing more.

This discussion of texts may be briefly extended in a different direction. Ancient writings survive not only in the manuscripts of authors, but in the lettering which may occur on the material objects revealed by archaeology, often in association with works of art: on the pedestals of statues, beside painted figure- or relief-scenes in ceramics, very commonly on coins and occasionally on buildings, but above all on stones which have been inscribed in their own right, as records of events or transactions. The study of such writings belongs mainly to two sub-disciplines, epigraphy and numismatics, which are often distinguished from archaeology, though occasionally subsumed within it. Here, the former alternative will be followed: partly on pragmatic grounds (many distinguished archaeologists do not possess these skills, while most of their own exponents do not also practice archaeology), partly on theoretical: the raw material for these disciplines may often be brought to light by archaeological discovery, but their training and methods, their interests and goals, from that point on proceed according to quite separate principles.

If attitudes to the ancient Greek texts do not create a clear division between positions Nos. 2 and 3 above, then nor does the valuation of Greek art. Its primacy may be made explicit in position No. 3, but study of actual practice suggests that its pre-eminence may equally be taken for granted by No. 2. Throughout the universities of the western world, Classical courses have existed for a century and more in which the study of Greek literature, history, and thought is combined with that of art, but not of any other aspect of Greek archaeology. Book-length studies of Greek art abound, ranging from simple text-books to high-level works of synthesis (Robertson 1975 still stands out among these for its combination of broader insight and close detail); whereas comparable treatments of Greek archae-ology as a whole have been few and recent (Etienne and Etienne 1992[1990] is invaluable as an historical summary; Snodgrass 1987 and Whitley 2001 analyze current positions). All this suggests a strong belief in the educational value of Greek art, to supplement if not to match that of literature—just as a brief study of Renaissance art has featured in many a course devoted to early modern Euro-pean history. What distinguishes position No. 2 is that it does not explicitly privi-lege art history: for the purposes of research at least, if not of teaching, it keeps its door open to the whole range of material culture. The guiding principle here is one dictated by the accompanying study of history: material discoveries, of a non-artistic kind, have repeatedly been used to throw light on historical events, or to reflect the processes of documented history. Thus, no account of the Persian Wars would be complete without mention of the archaeological discoveries made at Marathon or in the destruction deposit on the Athenian Acropolis; the monu-ments of the Periclean building program could hardly be omitted from a narrative of the growing centralization of the Athenian Confederacy, or the tombs at Vergina from the study of the rise of Macedon. The status of positions Nos. 2 and 3 can be summed up as embracing, between them, the more traditional approaches to Greek archaeology.

The "operational" definition of classical archaeology in position No. 4, by its rejection of all such high-sounding programmatic pronouncements, keeps both these approaches at arm's length. The risk is that, in doing so, it lapses into cyni-cism: from focusing on the activities of the army of solitary scholars producing a corpus of brick-stamps or terracotta revetments, bronze safety pins or iron weapons, or assembling and publishing the undecorated pottery, the lamps or lead weights from a given excavation, it reaches the ostensibly reasonable conclusion that classical archaeologists are making no measurable contribution either to Clas-sical studies or to the history of art. Nor do their activities any longer have a true counterpart in world archaeology as practiced today, as position No.1 might seem to imply. They are simply "doing their own thing." This argument ignores the pedagogical and instrumental function of these apparently mundane activities, as a training for higher things. Many of those undertaking such research would rather be dealing with broader issues, and have every intention of moving on to such activity; those who are in university posts must already do so in their teaching.

But this position has the merit of having incidentally uncovered a more profound truth about classical archaeology: that it is a discipline devoted to the archaeology of objects, one which is traditionally governed and organized, not by competing objectives or theories, approaches or models, but by classes of material. Individual practitioners have for long made their reputations as experts on a given class of artifact, sometimes more than one. Any large library of classical archaeology proclaims this, if not by its subject-headings, then by the titles of the books within them: monographs devoted to categories and sub-categories of arms, bronzes, gems, stone reliefs, terracottas, vases, and many other types of artifact; or multi-volume excavation reports which are divided up according to a similar scheme. It is difficult to find another discipline, in the 21st or even the later 20th century, which remains similarly dominated by taxonomy and typology. This is the basis for the criticism that classical archaeology has become a self-contained, even hermetically sealed, branch of scholarship whose activities and findings are of only intermittent interest even to its most closely related sister subjects, and of none at all to the wider intellectual community.

Such attitudes, however, traduce traditional classical archaeology and present a caricatured version of it. Certainly there are also more positive things to be said about it. We may briefly look back to the time when the subject first came into existence. Though it would be misleading to try to identify this with a precise historical moment, the nearest approach to such a landmark, for Greek archaeology, is certainly to be found somewhere in the mid-18th century, when Johann Joachim Winckelmann was compiling his ground-breaking works on Greek art (between 1755 and 1767: abridged translations in Irwin 1972), and when James Stuart and Nicholas Revett were measuring and drawing the most important surviving buildings of Athens (Stuart and Revett 1762, 1787, 1794, and 1816). Such a dating reinforces the status of the study of Greek art as the "founding definition" of the subject, as embodied in position No. 3 above. What is often forgotten, however, is that Winckelmann's pioneering work was essentially laying the foundations, not just for the study of Greek art, but for the whole discipline of art history, of all periods. So central was the position that classical archaeology once occupied.

The contribution of the excavation and study of the surviving material remains on the ground was only to come much later. An awkward fact, but one to be assimilated into any history of field archaeology as applied to Classical Greece, is that its great period of flowering, from about 1875, came about largely in response to the challenge from Aegean prehistory, and specifically to the discoveries of Heinrich Schliemann at Troy, Mycenae, and elsewhere (Aegean prehistory is itself excluded from this account because of the quite distinct, and increasingly divergent, course which it has followed). Yet the wide popular interest aroused by the revelation of the Bronze Age civilizations of Greece had convinced the Classicists that they must offer something similar of their own. The result was a whole series of large-scale, long-running excavation projects, some of them continuing with little interruption for well over a century, concentrated on major sanctuary sites. Like much else in Greek archaeology, they have no real parallel anywhere else in the world (Whitley 2001:32–36 gives a good summary of them).

Their relevance here is that, for a period of about two generations' length, the discipline which they represented was generally seen as occupying the heartland of archaeology as a whole. Until the rapid rise of prehistoric world archaeology in the 20th century, public perception of the nature of archaeology was dominated by the Mediterranean lands in general and Greece in particular. When, for example, the Archaeological Institute of America was set up in 1879, its founders took it for granted that Greece would be its main focus of interest; many archaeologists with other interests, especially those centered in the New World, withdrew from the Institute. The establishment of an American School of Classical Studies in Athens followed soon after (1881) and the first large-scale American excavation in Greece, at the Argive Heraion, in 1892 (Dyson 1998:37–60, 82–85). Several European countries were meanwhile following a parallel path. This era saw the peak of prominence for classical archaeology (Figure 1.1); since then, a decline in scale and in profile has been, for most countries in the world, an inescapable fact. To maintain the goals and methods which had once brought such success, though perhaps a natural human reaction to such an experience, is hardly the answer.

But it is time for something more constructive and less pessimistic. Some may believe, like the present writer, that a way forward can be found through a more

Figure 1.1 The heyday of the "great sanctuary excavation": Archaic sculptures unearthed at the Sanctuary of Artemis, Corfu, 1911

explicit association with non-classical archaeology, as intimated in position No. 1 above; but they have to admit that they may still be in a minority. Yet to identify the distinctive fields of activity in classical archaeology, and its unique strengths, it is not necessary to embrace this or any other prescriptive position: achievements of enduring value can be found in the past more easily than in the present, and in many different areas of the discipline.

Connoisseurship

This field is, by common verdict, the first place to look for such achievements. This is "connoisseurship" in its stricter sense: the close study of works of art with a view to attributing them to an individual artist or workshop. This was a product of the subject's coming of age, long after the time of Winckelmann; its first main application was to Greek sculpture, and to the lost masterpieces of its greatest artists. Adolf Furtwängler (1853–1907) (Figure 1.2) argued in effect that, if one brought together all the references in ancient literature which described a given work of Classical sculpture—a task already accomplished before his time—and assembled all the copies of Roman date which appeared to derive from one and the same Greek original—his own achievement—then it was reasonable to expect the two classes of evidence, on occasion, to meet up: the lost masterpiece of the texts (the more mentions, the greater its presumed fame) and the lost original of the copies (the more copies, the wider its presumed impact) might sometimes, if there were no contradictory feature, turn out to be one and the same. Nothing could bring the original back into existence, but much that was new could be learned about it and, more important, about its creator (Furtwängler 1895[1893]). His declaration of faith, in the Preface to his best-known book, makes striking reading:

> It may be further objected that it is not yet time, while we are still so behindhand in the knowledge of the general development of the separate forms, to inquire into the individualities of the several artists. The study of these forms, however . . . is inseparable from—nay, even identical with—the inquiry into the individualities to whom precisely this or that particular development of form is due. (Furtwängler 1895:ix)

Armed with such respect for the Great Artist as initiator of every important "form," Furtwängler (who held that even copies of works by Raphael or Michelangelo would be more valuable than any number of originals by lesser contemporaries) would set Classical art history on a new path: the pursuit, not just of art or even of great art, but of the Great Artist. He could (and still can) be credited with a huge, if still provisional, extension in our knowledge of the favored styles of Myron, Pheidias, Alkamenes, Polykleitos or Praxiteles: it is easy enough to criticize him for pushing his evidence too far, often writing of the lost original as if he had it actually in front of him; harder to demonstrate an instance where he

Figure 1.2 Adolf Furtwängler, 1853–1907

was wrong. This is in part because even today, more than a century later, our knowledge of the great age of Greek sculpture, in the fifth and fourth centuries B.C., remains a shifting, uncertain quantity: further discoveries have brought to light a steady trickle of major originals, but an invariable accompaniment to such finds has been the disarray of the experts, as they seek to assimilate them into existing knowledge by attributing them to one or another great name.

A very different application of connoisseurship followed soon afterwards; and, as with Furtwängler, it is inseparably associated with the name of a single scholar, J. D. Beazley (1885–1970) (Figure 1.3). Beazley devoted almost his whole working

Figure 1.3 Sir John Beazley, 1885–1970

life to the study of Athenian painted pottery. Here was a class of material which offered two great advantages over Greek sculpture: it consisted, to all appearances, entirely of original work, and it vastly exceeded surviving sculpture in sheer quantity. The disadvantages were less absolute: there was virtually no ancient literary evidence to deploy in this case and, more problematically, the artistic status of even the finest painted pottery was perhaps open to question. Yet, long before Beazley, scholars had noted that decorated Athenian vases, at their best, embodied drawing and composition of a standard that had never been matched in this medium; and had speculated that these works could reflect, at a distance, the vanished contemporary masterpieces of another attested field of Greek art, contemporary wall- and easel-painting. A few had gone further and, making use of the occasional survival of painters' signatures, had put together groups of works which seemed to come from the hand of a named individual.

Beazley carried this last activity to a much higher level. Working his way through a good proportion of the tens of thousands of Athenian black- and red-figure vases in the world's collections, he was able to assemble them into groupings, which could in each case be associated with the hand, the group, the circle, the manner, or the following of an individual painter (Beazley 1956 and 1963, his canonical works, present catalogues of such attributions). Unlike his predecessors, Beazley did not turn first to the signed pieces: he was looking for subtler criteria. When a body of paintings showed a similar level of anatomical knowledge and technical skills, with other linkages to suggest that they must be of broadly the same date, then how could they be apportioned among individual hands? His answer lay, not in those overall effects for which the painters were consciously striving, but in the trivial differences of rendering which they unconsciously, yet regularly, observed: in their drawing, for example, of the ear or the nose, the knee-cap or the ankle. The analogy with handwriting has been well suggested—with Beazley as a master graphologist. There is plenty of supporting evidence from other media to strengthen the belief that such differences of detail can and do reveal different hands: the most relevant is perhaps that from Renaissance painting where, in the previous generation, Giovanni Morelli had applied a closely similar method, and to a wide measure of acceptance. But Beazley's attributions won a measure of unanimity that was unmatched. During and after his time, too, Beazley's methods have been applied, with varying but generally reasonable success, to other classes of Greek pottery from outside Athens or of earlier date.

Debate in recent years has nevertheless arisen, not in the main about the validity of Beazley's work, but about its value (for a fierce defense of both, see Boardman 2001:128–138). The expected difficulty of securing unanimity, after Beazley's death, over the attribution of new works did not really materialize: the vast range covered by his own attributions could simply absorb them. Instead, some younger classical archaeologists have treated Beazleyan attribution as a closed book, and have tried to put this same body of material to different, and to them more interesting, uses. Sometimes, as in its application to chronology (below, pp. 26–28), there has been a hidden dependence on Beazley's system. But other new fields of study have grown up which appear to owe less and less to him: the epigraphy and the significance of the various kinds of painted or scratched inscription on Athenian vases; the whole question of the economic importance (or lack of it) of their production and distribution; above all, the choices of subject in the paintings, their iconography, their meaning and the light that they throw on the cultural patterns, whether universal and enduring or time- and place-specific, of Greek society. This last, the most fruitful of these approaches, sometimes referred to as *iconologie*, has been especially associated with French-speaking countries: one work in particular, *La Cité des images* (Bérard et al. 1989 [1984]—a book which uses Beazley only for purposes of reference) has become an indispensable aid to modern study.

A much more direct and radical confrontation with Beazley came with the arguments brought together in Vickers and Gill 1994. Here was an attempt to undermine the very corner-stone of Beazley's work, his belief in the vase-painter as artist and in his work, at its best, as "High Art"—a belief to which he had largely converted the professional world, and which the art market had long taken for granted. Vickers and Gill argue that high esteem for Greek pottery is a purely modern construct, not shared by contemporaries, who reserved their admiration for the vessels in gold and silver, of which black- and red-figure pots are cheap copies; that even the most exquisite of the drawings, on which Beazley had expended such effort and insight, were themselves no more than copies of original designs on lost work in precious metals. This venture has received a chilly reception: it threatens not only Beazley's achievement, but the whole underpinning of the subject, at least as practiced in the 20th century. The search for the individual behind the work of art had become the crowning endeavor of the discipline: what if the largest known group of "creative artists" of ancient Greece proved to be nothing of the kind? Of what use was the scrupulous and scientific attention to detail in vase-painting studies, if central elements of that detail turned out to have been irrelevant? If and when the threat recedes altogether (many would hold that it already has), it will still leave the memory of a moment of fleeting awareness that perhaps even the work of Beazley, and much more obviously that of other attribution studies in Greek art, has not advanced beyond the status of the highly convincing hypothesis.

Greek Architecture

To nominate this as the next field of achievement will doubtless cause surprise in some quarters: notably in Britain, where as a branch of study and teaching, it is today in rapid retreat, in Classical courses as in schools of architecture. But, to illustrate a point made at the outset about national differences, the same by no means applies to France, Germany, Greece, or the United States: in these and several other countries, the subject is still pursued assiduously. One reason for this is pragmatic: without continued expertise in the identification and interpretation of Greek architecture, it would be quite impossible for these countries to maintain their long-standing field projects at such sites as Olympia, Delphi, the Acropolis, or the Agora of Athens. These are sites which constantly bring their explorers face to face with major remains of Greek (and Roman) architecture: they are places where "marble rules" (note the anecdote in Whitley 2001:57 and the title of Dyson 1998).

If, in this kingdom of marble, Greek sculpture had always claimed precedence, it is architecture that holds the advantage in other ways. Its symmetry and precision make it obviously more susceptible of accurate measurement, and therefore of restoration on paper or in the round. Unlike sculpture (and like painted pottery), it is largely free of the pitfalls posed by ancient copying: Greek buildings have seldom been mistaken for anything else. The ancient sources offer relatively little, nearly all of it in small, isolated pieces of testimony: the one continuous text that survives, the *Ten Books* of Vitruvius, belongs to a time and place too far removed from the heyday of Greek architecture to be a genuine "source." Indeed, the modern study of the subject can be more or less dated from the time when it broke free of dependence on Vitruvius. What grew up instead was a uniquely mathematical, even "scientific," branch of classical archaeology, and this probably has something to do with its current lack of academic popularity.

But there is another unusual dimension to the study of Greek architecture: its influence on later practice, which has excelled that of Greek sculpture in cross-cultural diffusion and in sheer duration, if not in the power to arouse the passions. The Classical, it has been well said, is the only universal style in architecture, and Greek temple building stood at its heart. Its influence extends, with interruptions, through time, via Roman architecture, the Italian Renaissance, Palladio and Inigo Jones, into Neo-Classicism and the specific "Greek revival" of the 1780s, and across huge geographical distances. Even in the practice of today, its reign cannot be said to be over in the same sense, or to the same degree, as can that of Classical Greek sculpture.

The drawings of Stuart and Revett (above, p. 17) began a tradition of learned investigation which can match that of any branch of the subject. For, despite many appearances of repetition and homogeneity, Greek temple architecture, in particular, embodies frequent, subtle variations (Coulton 1977 is the most accessible account). These are carried to an extreme level in the Parthenon (447–432 B.C.) which, despite repeated protestations of its untypical quality, continues to exemplify Greek architecture for most people. As has been known for some time, the deliberate deviations from the horizontal and the vertical in the Parthenon mean that, for example, every one of the 46 external columns differs from every other one; but during the current program of restoration, it was also found (summer 2002) that each of the hundreds of rectangular blocks that made up its inner walls is also unique, and has only one placement in a correct reconstruction. The expertise required for analyzing such complexities today is considerable; but it is dwarfed by respect for the mathematical and engineering skills of its original builders. The author of the most learned and detailed handbook of the 20th century, William Bell Dinsmoor (Dinsmoor 1950, with earlier editions) also presided over the construction in the 1920s of the millimeter-accurate reproduction of the Parthenon in Nashville, Tennessee.

Topography and Regional Survey

For our third example, we turn to an aspect which has a long and honorable tradition, but which has also taken a new lease of life in the past three decades. At its origin there lay the notion of *mapping* the Greek landscape of antiquity: of drawing on to the largely blank outline of a modern physical map the cities and villages, rivers and mountains, frontiers and routes of the Classical world. If the ancient sources, yet again, provided the starting point for this endeavor, they proved to be defective in more ways than usual: geographical texts are few and impressionistic, with sparing use of distances and bearings and virtually no description of the landscape; maps are largely displaced by itineraries; historical sources, preoccupied with the urban and religious scene, tend to ignore not only rural settlements, but even such features as physical relief. The results can be seen in the small-scale, sparsely lettered "modern" atlases and maps of Classical Greece, some of which were reproduced without change for nearly a century, until their welcome replacement by the Barrington Atlas (Talbert 2000); only for a few select regions (Curtius and Kaupert 1881–1900, for Attica and other contemporary work, also mainly German, elsewhere) was a fuller coverage achieved.

The pioneering age of this activity had begun very soon after 1800: for all the distinction of early French work in the Peloponnese (the *Expédition Scientifique de Morée*), it became and for a time remained a specialty of British travelers, with their propensity for rural rides and small-boat sailing (see Whitley 2001:44–47, for a convenient summary). They took as their prime task the location of the documented sites of Greek history, but even this limited aim encountered many obstacles: genuine survival of ancient toponyms was relatively uncommon, relief features—ignored by the ancient texts—intruded, and the actual 19th-century landscape differed in every way from their often false and idealized visions of its ancient counterpart. Many of the more important problem cases of identification were still solved, though a few have survived to divide scholarly opinion right up to the present day.

On the foundation of these tireless labors, the late 20th century was to build a new kind of archaeological concept: regional surface survey. Although not perhaps explicitly conceived as an alternative to excavation, that is what it rapidly became. Economic factors, with the growth in the cost of funding an excavation team and its accessories, played a part here; but there was also a methodological dimension, almost an ideological one. If excavation, at its best, could only recover the detailed sequence of deposits in a limited sample of a single site, then might not more be learned from discovering a lot less about a much larger area? Excavators of towns and cities had long since recognized that any conclusions that they drew, as to the population, the prosperity, the occupations, the rise and decline, the external contacts, or any military involvement, and consequent damage of their site, were no more than inferences, based on an assumption that the excavated sample had been representative; and that it was, at the very least, a useful check on these findings to examine the whole surface of the unexcavated parts of the site to see if any discordant evidence were visible there.

Now this kind of ancillary activity was to become an end in itself, but with a marked change of direction. Attention was diverted from urban sites to the open country. This meant relinquishing the aid of the ancient sources, which had little or nothing to contribute on the rural sector. The existing political map of the ancient world was to be supplemented by an economic one. The previous focus on known and identified sites was replaced, first, by investigating any location with the characteristics known to have been favored in certain periods—naturally fortified hilltops, for instance; later, by a completely open-ended search of an entire sector of the landscape, without any preconception of what might be found. By the 1980s, this last practice, known as intensive survey, was prevailing all over the Greek world and beyond: region after region was traversed by teams of fieldwalkers, spaced evenly across the fields. From the start, there were surprises: none greater than the general density of the finds which could be picked up on any piece of cultivated terrain. But this material was unevenly spread, in space and in time: the small but dense concentrations, which sometimes occurred at intervals of only a few hundred meters, were widely interpreted as marking the locations of farms or other agricultural structures. It was a further surprise to find that these reached their peak of frequency in certain relatively short historical periods; and that, in many regions, the Classical and earlier Hellenistic era (the fifth to third centuries B.C.) had witnessed the high point of this exploitation of the cultivated landscape in the whole of its 5,000-year-long history from Neolithic times to the present day. For the first time, the ancient city had been given a local context: its imagined history, as an island of habitation in the otherwise empty territory on which it depended for its maintenance, had to be re-written. Classical archaeology had also been able to draw on one of its most priceless assets: the huge quantity and density of finds, and the availability of vastly larger samples than in most areas of world archaeology.

Chronology

No account of Greek archaeology would be complete without brief discussion of this, the intermittent concern of every archaeologist, working on anything from the early hominids to the recovery of a recent murder victim. Classical archaeology can achieve a precision in its dating which, at least if taken in proportion to the distance in time, is probably as high as anywhere in the world. This is not merely because, for much of the period between 500 and 100 B.C., a documented history exists with fairly close calendar datings of events: it also results from the nature of the material evidence. With painted pottery and buildings, in particular (to say nothing of coins), a whole series of contexts have been found which link the surviving materials with the calendar dates. In rare cases, this can be both direct and datable to the year: for example, the inscribed building accounts of the Parthenon and a few other temples survive, enabling us to date their completion exactly, thanks to our knowledge of the sequence and dating of the annually-elected magistrates at Athens; while a series of late Athenian black-figure pots (Panathenaic amphoras of between 379 and 312 B.C.) actually carry the name of the magistrate for that year.

Most other fixed points for Greek archaeology are more indirect and inferential. It is, for instance, an exceedingly probable conjecture that the Athenian burials in the mound at the battlefield of Marathon, with their associated pottery, date from immediately after the battle in September, 490 B.C.; it is a much less trustworthy assumption that every one of the works of art found damaged and buried in pits on the Athenian Acropolis was a victim of the Persian destruction of the city in 480 B.C. From this level downwards, there is a gradation from near-certainty to probability to reasonable likelihood, and from datings to the year to approximations of about a generation. The historical sources may give only a rough guide; the identification of an historical event or individual may be uncertain; and allowance has often to be made for human propensities, such as the retention of old objects for several generations (to take an uncomfortable instance, both the Marathon mound and the Acropolis deposit contained works by a vase-painter, Sophilos, who is reckoned to have been at work getting on for a century earlier).

The framework of chronology for Greek antiquity, gradually built up by scholars during the 20th century, was tested towards its end by two new and radical proposals for revision. One of these (James et al. 1991) affected only the later prehistoric and protohistoric periods of Greece, leaving later eras undisturbed: its result, by way of an adjustment of the Egyptian chronology, would have been to bring down the date of the fall of the Mycenaean palaces from about 1200 to about 950 B.C. Even so, if only about five hundred years, rather than eight hundred, intervened between the Greece of Agamemnon and that of Pericles, this would not be without its effects on broader Classical studies. The other project (Francis and Vickers 1983, with a series of later articles) took over in time more or less where the first left off, addressing historical times down to and including the earlier fifth century B.C.; again, the proposal was for the lowering of dates, in this case by the less drastic margin of some two generations. While neither attempt has convinced more than a handful of scholars, both have had the salutary effect of focusing attention on the framework of superimposed conjectures which makes up much of the traditional chronology, and of inculcating a more flexible attitude to it.

Such flexibility will undoubtedly be needed when, in the not too distant future, it becomes possible to apply the more accurate scientific dating methods to the historical period of Greek and other Mediterranean civilizations. Obstacles to this have persisted: the radiocarbon determinations for the first millennium B.C. are, for technical reasons, too imprecise to offer any improvement on traditional means. Tree-ring (dendrochronological) dates are potentially of an unmatched precision, but Greece offers few appropriate settings for long-lived species and, so far, the long sequences of tree-rings and closely datable episodes have only been established for locations and periods at some distance from the Classical world. Meanwhile, both these methods have proved applicable to the Aegean Bronze Age where their results, when confronted with the much looser conventional chronology adopted for that era, have created some disarray. It is surely only a matter of time before a datable tree-ring sequence emerges for historical Greece, or for some region in close enough touch with it to produce a match of archaeological sequences, and it would be folly to expect that, when this happens, the traditional datings will be confirmed at every point.

Before we leave this topic, there is an important link to be established with our earlier discussion. In the material record of ancient Greece, it is above all to the pottery sequence that we turn for dating purposes. Pottery can be depended upon for two vital assets, full seriation and quantitative profusion. In relative terms, the Athenian and a few other series can be followed without a break for more than half a millennium, with enough historical fixed points to make up a credible absolute chronology as well. And it is pottery which, more than any other kind of artifact, can be relied on to occur in whatever context is being investigated, not excluding the surface finds of the fieldwalker. Yet when we ask on what foundations the dating and continuity of the series rest, the answer is often a surprising one: for in many cases, it is not from observation of stratified sequences in excavations, still less from association with dated historical events, but from the practice of connoisseurship. By building up a sequence of painters' careers, one is also (thanks to the limited duration of any individual's working life) building up a series of chronological phases. A long-lived painter may be represented in more than one such phase, but this will merely increase the chance of synchronisms with the work of others; by the end, the network will retain its collective validity even if attributions are questioned. Yet even beyond the realm of painted pottery, in areas where attribution can hardly operate, we can find some at least of the same potential: the plain black wares, produced in the later historical period by many Greek cities, have also proved susceptible of detailed seriation (Rotroff 1997 is a good example of what can be done with it).

Conclusion

Our selective survey of four topics has, it is hoped, fairly represented both the traditional and the more recent activities within the archaeology of Greece. Several connections between them, some unexpected, have emerged. Connoisseurship, for instance, widely seen as an "extreme" development within the subject, taking it further and further away from the practices of other archaeologies, has turned out to be vital even in strictly archaeological fields: not only for chronological studies, but also for modern surface survey, which depends heavily on such museum-based research for the understanding of the damaged and fragmentary materials with which it must operate. It could be added that, even in architectural studies, there are many buildings which, though provisionally dated by means of historical texts, have acquired a more detailed and sometimes conflicting chronology through the excavation of pottery and other artifacts which underlie their foundations.

Returning for a moment to the four representative positions with which we began, we find that each of them makes a continuing contribution to the progress of the subject: classical archaeology needs them all, provided that none is allowed to usurp the whole discipline. If position No. 1, with its insistence that classical archaeology is a kind of archaeology, has now become the ruling principle in some quarters, it will never reach the point of eliminating the study of the ancient texts and works of art, championed respectively by positions Nos. 2 and 3. The more cynical attitude displayed in position No. 4 has proved to embody only a part of the truth: the archaeology of Greece *is* a discipline which can speak to others, and can be expected to do so more and more widely in the future.

NOTE

The references for this chapter are on pp. 48–50.

I (b)
What Is Classical Archaeology?

Roman Archaeology

Martin Millett

Definitions and Perceptions

To understand classical archaeology we need to appreciate something of its history and also to have some knowledge of its changing status. As a long-established discipline, the origins of which can be traced back to at least the 18th century, it sometimes seems to be unchanging and conservative in nature. I hope to demonstrate that both these impressions are false. Before considering this, we need to define the scope of the subject. Broadly, there are two current approaches that can perhaps be characterized by distinguishing "Classical Archaeology" from "the archaeology of the classical world" (with a deliberate difference in the capitalization used).

"Classical Archaeology" tends to be used by those who think that the material evidence from the Greek and Roman worlds (including architecture, works of art, coinage, etc.) has particular and individual characteristics which set their study entirely apart from any other discipline. The skills required are refined and they provide classical archaeology with a unique toolbox which enables the Greek and Roman worlds to be studied through material culture—but only if deployed by those immersed in the full range of evidence about Greece and Rome. This sets classical archaeology apart from the archaeology of other periods and places. From this perspective, the subject is seen not as a sub-discipline within archaeology but rather as a distinctive and specialist branch of Classics, employing methodologies largely founded in long-established traditions of detailed empirical study based on generations of past work.

In contrast, "the archaeology of the classical world" can be seen as a broadly based discipline, rooted in the social sciences, that shares with the archaeology of other periods methodologies developed to enable us to "read" the material culture of past societies. These methodologies are generic and, although each individual society studied through archaeology has distinctive characteristics and used objects in different ways, the approach to each is similar and the archaeology of the Classical world is thus the adaptation of archaeological methods to another particular place and time. Hence, the study of Greek painted pots or figured Roman mosaics benefits from the application of approaches developed for the analysis of objects from other periods and places. So too methods developed in classical archaeology can be deployed in the study of other human societies.

I would suggest that in contemporary classical archaeology we should be moving towards a new integration drawing on both these traditions, building on their strengths and aiming to create a "contextual classical archaeology." This recognizes the separate and distinctive contribution that classical archaeology can make to our understanding of the world of Greece and Rome through its own material-based agenda. Equally, it acknowledges the contribution that the archaeology of the Classical world can make in broader debates, not simply in providing another data set for analysis, but instead in helping to develop ideas that have broad relevance to the archaeology of other periods and places.

Historical Perspectives: Origins

To understand the development of the subject we need to place it within a broader historical and political context. The roots of classical archaeology lie much further back in time than is often acknowledged since a familiarity with, and interest in, the artifacts associated with the Classical past are deeply entrenched in the self-definition of the peoples of Europe. Appreciating the centrality of objects to the definition of cultural identity is essential if we are to understand the role of archaeology in western society. The Romans appropriated art objects from the Greek world, bringing them to Italy and copying them as part of the process whereby they appropriated Greek culture in order to legitimate their own cultural dominance (Strong 1973). They did not confine their interest to the Greeks, taking a profound interest also in the past of other areas like Etruria or Egypt, and it is significant that sculpture and works of art became central to the display of status in the private sphere as well as the public. Objects were thus of key importance, and references to the past were a central feature of cultural definition.

An example of this phenomenon is the way in which the Emperor Constantine removed objects from ancient sanctuaries like Delphi and set them up in his newly founded capital at Constantinople (Figure 1.4). Some objects from Constantinople, like the great quadriga now on the porch of St Mark's in Venice or the porphyry statue of the Tetrarchs, were later transferred to Venice after the sack of Constantinople in the Fourth Crusade in 1204 (Favaretto and Da Villa Urbani 2003:188–189, 192–193). Here they were again used to decorate the buildings of the new Mediterranean power, providing appropriate linkages back to the Classical—specifically to the imperial Roman—past.

Figure 1.4 Snake Column dedicated at Delphi, later taken to Constantinople (Istanbul). Photo: author

This process of using objects to create and legitimate imagined historical links long continues as a key theme. It is within this old-established tradition that we should place Napoleon's transfer of antiquities from Rome (and elsewhere) to Paris as part of his creation of the cultural identity of his empire (Gould 1965). Similarly, the modern trend for rich collectors to buy antiquities looted from Classical sites is part of a continuing obsession with owning and controlling objects from the past in order to define status in the contemporary world. The centrality of Classical material in this process is because—until very recently— the Greek and Roman past has been essential to the self-definition of civilization both in the Latin Christian west and the Orthodox Christian east. An exclusive interest in the Classical world is arguably changing now as Christianity becomes less central to the definition of western society and as the fashions in collecting have become broader and cultural looting has spread to exploit other centers of past civilization across the globe.

The physical evidence of the Classical past can thus be seen to have been widespread in European society throughout the Middle Ages. The systematization of the study of objects also has a deep history, although it is customary to see its roots in that reawakening of interest in the past referred to as the Renaissance. The whole of this concept of a "Renaissance" is questionable, not least since it is certain that the Church maintained an awareness of the Classical past in all its guises throughout the Middle Ages. This is well illustrated by the persistent reuse of classical sculpture, inscriptions, and so on in church buildings in Italy and elsewhere long before the 14th century (Greenhalgh 1989). The process of reworking Classical material nevertheless did become much more widespread, especially from the 15th and 16th centuries.

This increased fashion for ancient material brought about, first, a considerable interest in the aesthetics of ancient art—itself deeply bound up with the creation of new works of art. This was followed by two parallel trends: first, the wish to understand the material better and, second, the desire to find more of it. This process intensified during the 18th century as the connections between Italy and Northern Europe developed. On the one hand, the interests of those who traveled south to see and collect antiquities stimulated further exploration and systematization of knowledge since this helped define social and class identities at home. At the same time, such a demand arguably enhanced the status to be gained from knowledge of and ownership of classical objects. It is against this background that we see a burgeoning of the study of Classical antiquities. This is represented both by the collectors and those who worked for them, acting as clerks and agents in collecting and also in ordering and researching the objects (Schnapp 1996:258–266). The development of this knowledge and its dissemination represent the birth of classical archaeology in the modern sense. This knowledge was closely associated with the ruling classes in Europe, with royalty closely associated with the early exploration of Pompeii and with Vatican control equally important elsewhere in Italy. Significantly, in the new American Republic, there was a parallel interest, specifically in Roman styles, stimulated in part by the perceived political relevance of the Roman Republic. This is reflected in the active adoption of

Classical architectural styles in public building and the use of Greek and Roman models for public iconography (Dyson 1998:7–8).

Although we should not underestimate the knowledge accumulated by earlier generations of scholars, those who characterized the second half of the 18th century made a considerable new contribution in applying the ideas that were evolving in other branches of knowledge to further the systematic study of antiquities. In this sense, Winckelmann, whose formulation of a framework within which ancient sculpture could be understood and related to Classical texts, should perhaps be seen not only as the father of art history but also as the first theoretical archaeologist (Leppmann 1971). It is in any case notable that this tradition—of the systematic study of objects—was certainly developing in advance of the tradition of artifact classification in European prehistory (Gräslund 1987; Trigger 1989:38–39).

Of equal importance to the development of classical archaeology in this period was the growth in the scale of printing, with the production and dissemination of engravings of antiquarian topics and ancient buildings effectively internationalizing knowledge and stimulating further interest (Salmon 2000). This fed back to stimulate the exploration of monuments not only in Italy at sites like Pompeii and Herculaneum, but from the onset of the Napoleonic Wars also in the Ottoman world (especially in what is today Greece and Turkey). Previously, excavations of this period have not been viewed as very systematic and those writing histories of archaeology too often consider that proper excavation techniques developed only much later. However, it is increasingly evident that, when considered in their proper context, excavations undertaken to obtain antiquities in this period were well recorded (Bignamini 2004); we have a wealth of publications that describe sites and objects, making sense of them in relation to ancient texts and especially emerging topographic knowledge. Through these processes of travel, exploration, study, and publication, classical archaeology emerged as a distinctive branch of learning connected with antiquarianism as closely as with other branches of Classical learning.

One of the perceptible changes that characterized the growth of classical archaeology during the 19th century is its increasing association with the creation of contemporary political identities. This has already been noted in the United States where the relevance of Rome to the new republic was clear. Paradoxically, another early example is offered by the Emperor Napoleon and his systematic exploration of the buildings of Rome during that city's French occupation. A deliberate association was created between ancient Rome and Napoleon's empire so the physical remains of the past were given considerable and careful attention (Ridley 1992). Later, the newly unified states of Italy and Greece also looked back to the past to create their own individual national identities in the present. In Italy, archaeological exploration and display of imperial monuments were key instruments in creating Rome as the capital of the new state. In Greece, a parallel process involved defining a particular golden age—the great age of Pericles—as a symbol of national identity at the expense of later periods of "foreign occupation," the evidence of which came to be deliberately cleared away (Beard 2002:49–115). Although from a contemporary perspective this clearly distorts the evidence, creating nothing more than a modern myth, it remains politically powerful, as witnessed in the manipulation of the Classical past for the opening ceremony of the Athens Olympics in 2004. Nationalism has undoubtedly provided an important impetus to the systematic exploration of the past.

The most extreme example of such a use of classical archaeology comes from Mussolini's Italy in the 1930s and 1940s when an ideal of the Roman past was central to the construction of the political ideology of the present. This stimulated the large-scale excavation of Roman sites and the presentation of archaeological remains for public display: examples include the Ara Pacis and the Roman Forum. Not only were objects and excavated sites in Italy and overseas used in this process but the whole grammar of architecture and urban planning in Rome was remodeled to help recreate this imagined past through the construction of such monuments as the Via dei Fori Imperiali and the Piazza Augusto Imperatore (Barbanera 1998:119–154).

A major trend during the 19th century was the desire of the northern European powers and the United States to develop active interests in the archaeology of the Classical world, arguably as a cultural extension of their own rivalries. Learning about the Classics was central to the education of the elites who governed the European powers, largely as a development of earlier medieval systems of learning that were based within the framework of Christianity. This educational tradition was also replicated to a lesser extent in North America in the 18th and 19th centuries. With the growth of increased competition between these various powers, interests in the ownership of antiquities spread, together with the increased association of both collecting and excavating to promote national interests. Involvement with the cultural property of the Classical world became a matter of pride both for powerful individuals (such as Heinrich Schliemann and Arthur Evans), independent archaeological societies (such as the Archaeological Institute of America) and also nation states. The acquisition of material like the Pergamum altar in Berlin brought prestige to museums in the main cities of the great powers. Thus, international rivalries were played out through the development of museum collections and through the sponsorship of great excavations. For instance, Olympia became symbolic of German interests, Delphi with the French, and Knossos the British. Similarly, it was essential for the great powers to establish cultural bases in Greece and Italy to mark their established links with the origins of western civilization. The French Academy was founded in the mid-17th century but the others were primarily late 19th-century creations, albeit growing out of earlier institutions. In Rome, the German Archaeological Institute was constituted in 1871, the British School opened in 1900, and the American Academy was created in 1905.

Given the centrality of such connections with the past and in particular the key role of the study of Classics in the education and self-definition of the ruling elites of Europe, these developments should occasion little surprise. Although some would stress how conscious parallels were drawn and the Roman empire was used as a model for the British and other empires (Hingley 2000), this probably underestimates the way in which the Classical past was implicitly central to the whole perception of those in power (Freeman 1996). This is clearly the case in the United States of America where the impetus for exploration was much more loosely associated with the political establishment (Dyson 1998).

Historical Perspectives: Development

One of the consequences of the growth of economic prosperity and political capital within both the United States and Britain from the second half of the 19th century up to World War I was an expansion of and investment in higher education. In Britain, since the Classics were at the center of elite education, one of the consequences was the growth in the provision for classical archaeology. In Cambridge, the curriculum reforms of 1879 went hand in hand with the growth of the collection of sculptural casts while the first appointment to teach classical archaeology came in 1883 (Beard 1999). Similarly, in Oxford, the Chair of Classical Archaeology was created in 1883. Although such an expansion was also seen in the United States, the pattern of development was different, first, because of the strong influence of German scholarship and, second, through an increased trend towards graduate programs (Dyson 1998:95–102). Nonetheless, on both continents, this period marks the beginning of the widespread academic study of the subject.

It is interesting to note how the development of the subject in Cambridge was initially concerned with broad interdisciplinary approaches encompassing domains such as mythology and anthropology rather than archaeology in any narrow sense. By contrast, the traditions that became dominant in the United States and Germany tended to be concerned more with the systematic study of Classical art. The development of classical archaeology in universities went side by side with the growth of excavations and of research on objects by scholars working in museums and those of independent means. Despite the broad perception of the subject by some, however, a narrower and largely empirically based approach came to dominate the subject and by the last decade of the 19th century its boundaries seem to have become defined both geographically and in terms of subject matter.

Some insight into this is provided by the definition used for the Professorship of Classical Archaeology at Oxford in 1883. Arthur Evans wrote:

> I understand that the Electors . . . regard "archaeology" as ending with the Christian Era. . . . Further it appears that a knowledge of Semitic or Egyptian antiquities is to be admitted: anything in short Oriental, but Europe, except for Europe of a favored period and a very limited area (for I take it that neither Gaul, Britain or Illyricum were ever "classical" in Jowett's sense) is to be rigorously excluded! (Evans 1943:261)

It is clear from this that the boundaries of classical archaeology had—at least in Oxford—been fairly closely defined by this stage as relating solely to the core areas of Greece and Rome. It is perhaps ironic that Evans served with distinction at the Ashmolean Museum and led the major excavations at Knossos which produced such spectacular evidence for the flowering of Bronze Age Crete and the use of the writing system known as Linear B. The decipherment of this script in 1953 and the demonstration of its importance in the development of the Greek language ensured, of course, that Bronze Age Aegean archaeology has subsequently become central to the discipline of classical archaeology.

Despite the incorporation of the Aegean Bronze Age, the limits of the subject defined in the late 19th century have continued to be widely accepted. However, one present trend is to use a broader definition that encompasses the lands the Greek and Roman worlds controlled and those with whom they had close contacts. For the study of Roman archaeology the origins of this trend lie in the late 19th century. Those trained in Classics in northern Europe had often taken a keen interest in the archaeology of the countries where they lived, although understandably these areas never attracted serious attention from those living in the United States. With the increasing systematization of archaeological knowledge, such study was drawn more into the mainstream. This is perhaps nowhere clearer than in the study of the frontiers of the Roman empire. The empire-wide collation of inscriptions for the *Corpus Inscriptionum Latinarum* (initiated in Berlin in 1863) included the frontier provinces like Germany and Britain, and a growing interest in the Roman army led to systematic campaigns of excavation designed to understand monuments such as Hadrian's Wall in the years just before and after World War I. Although some of the scholars engaged on this work were parochial in their interests, others like F. Haverfield, E. Birley and I. A. Richmond came to take an empire-wide view of the issues raised.

This established a continuing trend that now enables us to understand Greece and Rome better within the context of the sophisticated but non-literate societies with whom they interacted (for instance, in the Iberian peninsula). Equally it opens up the whole subject of cultural change and interaction, in particular the ways in which classical culture spread across Europe away from the Mediterranean. Thus, the archaeology of the Roman provinces has to some extent become subsumed within the broader domain of classical archaeology.

The range of subject matter incorporated within classical archaeology is, therefore, clearly diverse. This can be illustrated by some of the different interests of those who have worked within the Faculty of Classics at Cambridge since the 1880s, developing a variety of particular and specialist methodologies vital to the study of ancient societies. These include the study of Greek religion and its material manifestations, Greek and Roman architecture, Greek, Etruscan and Roman art history and iconography, Greek pottery, Greek and Roman numismatics, and epigraphy (including the analysis of Linear B tablets). In addition, others have deployed fieldwork skills through excavation at key sites such as Mycenae, Carthage, and Rome, as well as survey in Italy, Greece, the Iberian peninsula, and Britain. In some ways, this range of activity well characterizes the practice of classical archaeology, although it still has a much stronger connection with art history than other areas of archaeology.

Contrasting Social Contexts:
Britain and the United States of America

In Britain, academia was not protected from what Harold Macmillan called the "wind of change" that blew through the world in the decades following World War II. While Classics lost its dominant position in the education of the elites, new disciplines like archaeology rose in popularity, especially with the expansion of university education from the 1960s onwards.

The manner in which Classics lost its position in British education is complex and has many facets, but the underlying trends are associated with the social revolution connected with the loss of empire and world economic dominance and with the decline in international influence that took place in the middle of the 20th century. The association of Classics, especially education in the Greek and Latin languages, with the traditional elites who had run the empire undoubtedly contributed to the subject's changing position within society. Such social changes lay behind its rejection as politicians sought greater emphasis on subjects of "relevance" within the curriculum of state education.

The development of archaeology in Britain during the same period contrasts greatly with the story of Classics. Before the late 1960s, it was almost absent from university teaching and considered a subject only appropriate for post-graduate study. Two things altered this situation radically. Post-war economic development, particularly the rebuilding of cities and later the construction of motorways, resulted in a boom in field archaeology in Britain. Increased expenditure on rescue excavations followed from political campaigning about the consequence of development for the historical environment and there was thus a huge rise in demand for trained archaeologists. Second, the growth in university education that was a product of 1960s political initiatives drew in students from a broad social range. This stimulated a diversification in provision of courses in new and attractive subjects including archaeology. These two changes fed off each other to ensure that a new generation of people came into the subject which had obtained a certain "alternative" cachet, at least in the late 1960s and early 1970s. Through a complex combination of circumstances, many of the newly created university archaeology departments were also successful in taking advantage of the funding roller-coaster that characterized the public sector in Britain in the last decades of the 20th century. The result was that while Classics suffered a decline, archaeology thrived with a massive increase in staff and student numbers.

The boom in archaeology brought many people into contact with the archaeology of the Roman world through first-hand experience of excavation. At the same time a number of the academics working in the new archaeology departments developed field projects, giving students from a wide social range their first experience of the Classical world. This changed the face of classical archaeology as many, trained in archaeology departments rather than in Classics, developed interests in the subject. This had a social significance, as well as academic consequences, since many of these incomers were beneficiaries of the 1960s widening of access to university education and did not come from the same socio-economic groups as those who still received a Classical education. In that sense, in Britain, the archaeology of Greece and particularly Rome, became democratized. Also significant was the way in which these changes led to a diversification of approach, while the development of a new disciplinary self-confidence has meant that archaeology is less often the "handmaiden of history" and has taken a lead in defining new intellectual approaches.

The story of post-war classical archaeology in the United States provides something of a contrast, for the period represents one of increasing economic prosperity and cultural self-confidence. Equally, while in Europe the study of the Classical world was in inevitable decline, in the United States it had only ever been a specialized interest and its development after 1945 shows strong elements of continuity with the earlier part of the century. However, increased resources became available to support it; not only was there a strong tradition of private philanthropy which continued to fund archaeological work, but there was institutional growth in the universities for which new government research funding became available.

Classical archaeology also benefited from the increased global influence of the United States of America, as it became the country to which others looked as a center of academic power. Links with European countries increased and a number of refugees from pre-World War II Germany, who had made their homes in America, became significant academic leaders. These influences broadened the base of classical archaeology as resources were found for the continuance of major field projects in the Mediterranean. These were, initially, mainly excavations following the models set earlier in the century, with a focus on important sites like the Athenian Agora. New projects were also begun, however, such as the American Academy at Rome's important excavations at Cosa. These endeavors may be characterized as representing a fairly conservative tradition of excavation but the resources were available on a scale that was the envy of many in Europe and as a result there was a continuing strong tradition of field training. Similarly, the resources available to major museums at home ensured a continuing strength in the traditions of art historical scholarship (Dyson 1998:217–285).

Classical archaeology in America was at first relatively insulated from some of the new theoretical ideas that came to dominate other branches of the subject during the 1960s. This was partly because of institutional structures through which classical archaeology commonly remained separate from both contract archaeology and the academic discipline of Anthropology—which included prehistoric archaeology. However, it was also a product of self-confidence in its academic traditions and the economic circumstances which enabled it to prosper while the discipline in Europe suffered contraction. It is perhaps a paradox that these circumstances of prosperity provided less scope for the cross-fertilization of ideas than was seen in Britain in the 1970s.

A New Classical Archaeology

The first wave of disciplinary change in classical archaeology in Britain is closely associated with people such as my predecessor at Cambridge, Anthony Snodgrass. He and others did much to integrate classical archaeology into the mainstream of the broader discipline (e.g. Snodgrass 1980; see chapter 1[a], this volume). In particular, there was a concern with the deployment of contemporary archaeological methodology to address a range of key social issues regarding the emergence and operation of the Greek polis, or city-state. Comparable wide-ranging work also happened in the United States, particularly among those who turned to large-scale field survey as a result of these new ideas. Comparable work in prehistoric periods was pioneered also by Michael Jameson and others at Franchthi Cave in the Greek Argolid, where a full range of the techniques of environmental archaeology were used to understand an exceptionally long habitation sequence (Dyson 1998:252–253).

The genesis of both approaches lies in the "New Archaeology" or "processual archaeology" of the 1970s, but the success of integration is shown by the way in which classical archaeology has since become more central to methodological and theoretical debates, making contributions to various schools of thought and approach. Furthermore, through the development of field practice in archaeological survey, classical archaeology has also made a distinctive and original contribution to the repertoire of the broader archaeological discipline, while at the same time setting its own agenda of historical questions to be addressed in Classics as a whole.

This development needs to be put in context with increasing methodological sophistication of work on the archaeology of the Classical world. Although conventional skills in object analysis and description remains vital, the framework within which they are discussed is now more open. Equally, contemporary classical archaeology routinely deploys an enormous range of techniques drawn from the natural sciences as well as more traditional disciplines. For instance, archaeobotany aids in the understanding of agrarian systems; geomorphological and soil studies contribute to our knowledge of the processes of environmental change; the chemical analysis of clays provides new dimensions to our knowledge of pottery production and distribution. At the same time, approaches drawing on other social sciences have provided insights into topics such as the evolution of houses and have encouraged provocative rethinking about issues of cultural identity.

These changes have resulted in something of a blurring of the boundaries that once seemed to separate our subject from the rest of archaeology. At the same time there has been an increasing interaction between archaeologists and those working on other aspects of the Classical world. This has been characterized by a greater readiness on the part of both ancient historians and archaeologists to learn from each other, to respect each other's approaches and to use information in a genuinely interdisciplinary manner. In both these respects, the field has arguably

become more difficult to categorize, and it would seem we are increasingly concerned with a mixture of approaches to the archaeology of the classical world
rather than with classical archaeology as such. In many ways this takes us back
to the interdisciplinary ideal of Cambridge Classics in the late 19th century.

Classical Archaeology Today

Within what is now a diverse and vibrant discipline it is difficult to identify particular trends as being of especial significance. Instead I would like to pick out a
series of issues which interest me, simply to illustrate something of the character
of the contemporary subject. This approach is arguably itself typical of the move
in contemporary archaeological theory away from broad generalizing, or processual, approaches towards an interest in the way material culture is deployed by
human societies in historically particular contexts. Through this shift in theoretical perspective, it is notable that the tradition of context-specific and interdisciplinary archaeological study of the Classical world has become increasingly
relevant to the broader discipline. The particularly rich and diverse sources of
evidence available to us, together with the supply of developed and sophisticated
studies of other data sets, mean that it is possible to approach the historically
contingent circumstances of the Classical world with unusual subtlety. The examples I am going to explore are related to my own research on the Roman world,
but there is an enormous range of other research in other areas on which I could
have drawn.

One core theme has been the attempt to understand cultural change within
the Roman provinces. I believe that classical archaeology more generally has much
to learn from the experience of Roman provincial studies which, by their very
nature, rely much more heavily on material evidence than on texts. It is notable
that, although the Roman empire was a large and long-lived political structure,
its archaeology displays both common characteristics and enormous diversity.
Indeed, far from the standardized and culturally uniform entity that is sometimes
portrayed, the empire's development and operation have wide interest and broad
contemporary relevance. There has long been a realization, through study of the
provinces, that the Roman empire was not monolithic but rather—given the slow
speed of communication and the strengths of local traditions—that it was a het-
erodox grouping of societies under a single political structure. More recently there
has been an increasing appreciation of the *bricolage* that comprised Roman identity
itself and the broad mix of influences that created the metropolitan character of
the empire.

An illustration of these issues concerning the character of empire can be provided with reference to the very northwest of the Iberian peninsula, a zone far
from Italy that was only finally incorporated by Augustus. Here, a strong and
independent pattern of cultural identity was emphasized in particular by the
establishment of distinctive fortified hilltop settlements known today as *castros*.
These seem to have formed the foci for close-knit social groups who had a

reputation as warriors. The houses in these settlements were distinctive, stone-built, round houses, very different from the traditions of the Classical Mediterranean. Following the Roman conquest of this area, we see the successful incorporation of these people into the imperial system. A particular contribution of the region came from the soldiers recruited to serve Rome as auxiliary troops—indeed, the people of the region contributed one of the largest numbers of soldiers in the western empire. This form of service certainly represents integration into the empire, but the region does not show strong evidence for the adoption of the new forms of building and settlements that are generally seen as typical of Roman cultural identity. Instead, there is a very strong pattern of continuity of sites and traditional forms of building, with only some modification at the margins. Although some castros were abandoned, they seem to have remained central to the perceptual geography of the region with rural sites carefully placed to be able to see them (Millett 2001). Some would certainly see this as evidence for some form of cultural resistance to Roman imperialism, but such explanations are too simplistic—as illustrated by the way in which at the castro site of Citânia de Briteros, Latin inscriptions are added to the door lintels of some houses (Figure 1.5). Neither the form of the inscriptions nor the names recorded suggest particularly Roman characteristics while the decoration and house form are strongly traditional. However, the very act of adopting Latin and inscribing it illustrates an internalization of Roman ideas within a distinctive traditional context.

Brilliant historical work has been done on issues such as these, drawing on archaeological evidence, especially in Gaul (Woolf 1998). Archaeology has a unique contribution to make as it provides voices for the many peoples of the empire who have left no literature and who are represented now only by the anonymous evidence of their settlements, possessions, rubbish, and graves. It is thus important that the archaeological methodologies followed are not determined simply by an agenda derived from textual sources. Such work has recently been pioneered by Louise Revell (1999) in an examination of the construction of identities in the Roman provinces. In such endeavors, archaeology has different strengths at two particular scales of analysis.

First, archaeology is the only source of evidence for life at the local scale, from which we can establish something of the rhythms of everyday existence in the domestic sphere and how they changed. Archaeological excavation and associated artifact studies provide an array of techniques through which we can establish patterns of development of houses themselves and explore how the households who lived in them were structured and how they evolved through time. Both in the Mediterranean and in the provinces, we now possess interesting syntheses assessing the character of architectural development and its social implications, but the exploration of individual households provides fascinating insights into the complexities of people's lives and into how both individuals and groups used artifacts to create their identities within the broader context of Roman power structures (Wallace-Hadrill 1994; cf. Nevett 1999).

An instance of this type of approach in a far-flung province is provided by work on a small block of landscape in eastern Yorkshire. Here at one excavated site,

Figure 1.5 Lintel inscription from Citânia de Briteros, Portugal. Photo: author

Shiptonthorpe, we see the construction of a fairly standard form of house replacing an earlier type built in a distinctively local tradition (Figure 1.6). The house is adjacent to the Roman road and, in contrast to other settlements nearby, seems to have adopted a full range of the material culture associated with Roman hegemony in Britain—even down to the use of waxed wooden writing tablets. Although by no means sophisticated by continental standards, the lives of its occupants, presumably a family of the aspirant "middling sort," certainly seem to have bought into the culture of Roman Britain. The only markedly distinctive feature of their way of life lay in the way that the whole settlement was peppered with burials, both of neonatal infants and of a range of animals. These were not randomly

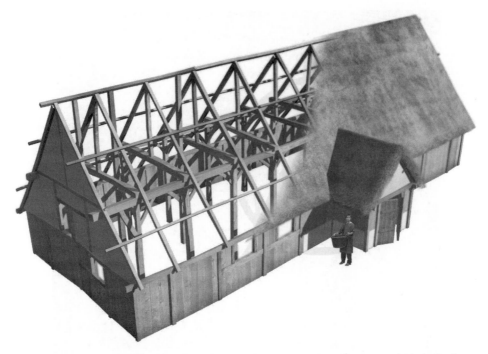

Figure 1.6 Hall reconstruction, Shiptonthorpe, East Yorkshire. Courtesy of Mark Faulkner, based on architectural analysis by Martin Millett

distributed across the site; indeed a careful study of their distribution has enabled us to identify the social rules which seem to have governed their burial. It is very difficult to establish whether this behavior was determined by traditional religious beliefs or represents something else, but the grammar of their burial certainly moves debate about these people's lives beyond established discussions about any so-called Romanization (Millett 2006). In this way the interrogation of archaeological evidence is raising new questions, forcing us to address cultural change in a different way. Some other more wide-ranging social analyses using burial evidence are beginning to emerge, especially in the study of Roman provincial society (Pearce 2000; Gowland 2001).

Archaeologists in the Roman provinces have been rather successful in developing approaches for understanding sites in the provinces through the excavation and the analysis of patterns of artifact use and distribution, both locally and regionally. They have been less successful in using similar approaches for the detailed understanding of the much larger-scale settlements that typify the center of the empire and where monumental art and architecture could also contribute. The problems are understandable as the sheer scale of the sites and the quantities of finds make the task daunting, but progress on understanding local patterns of society in the core of the empire demands that we rise to this challenge.

The enormous scale of the Roman empire also defies approaches which are based on the small scale alone. This does not imply that its investigation should attempt to write grand narratives based on simplified explanatory frameworks. Nevertheless, it seems very important to acknowledge the role of the unintended consequences of the growth of imperial power on indigenous societies. This means that we have to take approaches that acknowledge the agency of individuals but also pay due attention to the powerful overarching forces that shaped their worlds and with which they had to interact. Thus, for instance, the historical events that led to Roman military expansion into northeast Spain during the Second Punic War created new circumstances for the peoples who lived at Cesse. The selection of their settlement, Tarraco (now Tarragona), as a Roman base and its subsequent choice by Augustus as his center of operations during the Cantabrian Wars changed the circumstances within which they lived (Keay 1997). This is not to deny that individuals influenced the shape of the settlement that developed, only to emphasize that bigger events had consequences, like the creation of major communication links and the stimulation of large-scale movements of goods and people, which must be understood if the complexities of the empire are to be understood.

At a practical level, this involves moving above the level of the site to appreciate the broader development of the landscape in all its dimensions. Archaeological survey has long been used to map rural landscapes. While these methods have made a significant contribution to understanding the broad patterns of landscape change through the whole of the Classical period and beyond, they are not without their limitations. Recently there has been much discussion of the methodological limitations of survey and how these can be mitigated (e.g. Francovich and Patterson 2000). These debates represent an increased maturity of approach to survey archaeology but can be rather inward-looking. Equally important issues are often overlooked, including whether the scale of analysis and the level of chronological resolution are appropriate for making comparisons at the supra-regional level and thus for understanding changing imperial systems. Although there has been some success in making comparisons across broader areas, these issues have too rarely been given the attention they deserve.

Another form of larger-scale work is also important if we are to understand the Roman empire. Large individual sites, particularly cities and towns, characterize the empire and are presently far too poorly understood. While there has been a long and productive tradition of excavation on ancient urban sites, even the largest campaigns of excavation can only examine a tiny proportion of an urban landscape. Thus, with the exception of a small number of sites, like Pompeii, our evidence for towns is derived from "keyholes" which give an immense amount of detail about very small samples of the site—forming a doubtful basis for broad generalization. One product of this is a heavy reliance on more extensively excavated sites combined with composite generalizations derived from a mosaic of limited excavations in a variety of towns. Given the current emphasis on local variation and particular local histories, this is clearly unsatisfactory.

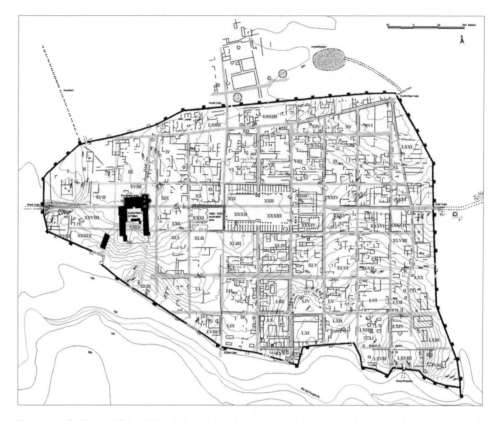

Figure 1.7 Plan of Falerii Novi, based on the results of geophysical survey. Copyright British School at Rome, reproduced with permission of The British School at Rome

One answer to this lies in the deployment of new technologies for understanding whole towns. An example of this type of work is taking place in the Tiber valley around Rome where we are attempting to examine the variability in Roman urban settlements. This work exploits basic modern technologies to map large areas, allowing us to look at varying urban forms of entire sites rather than the small samples that can be examined by excavation. The main technique is geophysical survey, principally magnetometry, which is widely used in rescue archaeology in Britain and enables a rapid survey to provide a plan of buried archaeological deposits. Such work can offer some spectacular and surprising results although whether it works depends on the characteristics of the soil. At Falerii Novi we were able to produce a good and detailed plan of most of the town (Figure 1.7) using this technology (Keay et al. 2000). Although the level of detail produced is variable and the complexity of the development of a site is not revealed in its entirety, it is wrong to suggest that the method can only be used in conjunction with excavation. The detailed analysis of the plan of Falerii Novi, combined with the addition of surface survey and topographic detail, provided an overall understanding of the site's development that would have been impossible without very extensive excavation. While it is true that some of these hypotheses can only be tested with further work—either different forms of survey or excavation—the same is invariably also true of excavation results; we must learn to value such urban survey work in its own right rather than thinking of it always as an *hors d'œuvres* to digging. Most important is the scale at which geophysical survey can operate. For example, my colleagues and I have recently completed a new survey of the Portus, the port of imperial Rome at the mouth of the Tiber River. The fieldwork here has covered in excess of 175 ha. At this scale, it has become possible to provide new perspectives on a key imperial monument at the center of the empire in a way that would have been simply inconceivable through excavation (Keay et al. 2005). Such work is providing new perspectives on Roman Italy which should be extended to other parts of the empire in future.

Prospects

It should be clear from this review of the discipline that an integration of classical archaeology into a broader discipline is the product of historical trends and that we are consequently seeing something of a renaissance in the subject. Contemporary classical archaeology should continue to develop, forming a fine bridge between Classics and archaeology. We should not allow it simply to be a structure that is scarcely visible yet functional; rather, it ought to develop its own distinctive engineering and elegant architecture. This will transform classical archaeology into a laboratory for investigating the use of material culture in literate and proto-literate societies alike. In creating this laboratory and developing this subject, we will combine the sound use of traditional methods of study with the best innovations from the contemporary world.

One of the unique aspects of archaeology is its ability to discover new evidence through fieldwork and finds analysis. Discovery is not enough, re-thinking meaning is also vital. It is the constant process of discovery, combined with the questioning, re-envisioning, and expanding of horizons, that makes classical archaeology so invigorating and absorbing a subject.

ACKNOWLEDGMENTS

This chapter is a modified version of my inaugural lecture as Laurence Professor of Classical Archaeology in Cambridge, entitled: "After the Ark: A Classical Archaeology for Our Time," delivered on 30 April 2002.

REFERENCES

Barbanera, Marcello 1998 L'archeologia degli italiani. Rome: Editori Riuniti.

Beard, Mary 1999 The Invention (and Re-invention) of "Group D": An Archaeology of the Classical Tripos, 1879–1984. *In* Classics in 19th and 20th Century Cambridge: Curriculum, Culture and Community. Christopher Stray, ed. Pp. 95–134. Cambridge Philological Society Supplementary Vol. 24. Cambridge: Cambridge Philological Society.

——2002 The Parthenon. London: Profile.

Beazley, John D. 1956 Attic Black-Figure Vase Painters. Oxford: Clarendon Press.

——1963 Attic Red-Figure Vase Painters. 2nd edition. Oxford: Clarendon Press.

Bérard, Claude, et al. 1989[1984] A City of Images: Iconography and Society in Ancient Greece. D. Lyons, trans. Princeton: Princeton University Press.

Bignamini, Ilaria 2004 British Excavations in the Papal States during the Eighteenth Century: Written and Visual Sources. *In* Archives and Excavations: Essays on the History of Archaeological Excavations in Rome and Southern Italy from the Renaissance to the Nineteenth Century. I. Bignamini, ed. Pp. 91–108. Archaeological Monograph of the British School at Rome 14. London: British School at Rome.

Boardman, John 2001 The History of Greek Vases. London: Thames & Hudson.

Coulton, J. J. 1977 Greek Architects at Work: Problems of Structure and Design. London: Paul Elek.

Curtius, E., and J. A. Kaupert 1881–1900. Karten von Attika. Berlin: D. Reimer.

Dinsmoor, William B., Sr. 1950 The Architecture of Ancient Greece. 3rd, rev. edition. London: B. T. Batsford.

Dyson, Stephen L. 1998 Ancient Marbles to American Shores. Philadelphia: University of Pennsylvania Press.

Etienne, Roland, and Françoise Etienne 1992[1990] The Search for Ancient Greece. A. Zielonka, trans. London: Thames & Hudson and New York: Harry N. Abrams.

Evans, Joan 1943 Time and Chance: The Story of Arthur Evans and his Forebears. London: Longmans, Green and Co.

Favaretto, Irene, and Maria Da Villa Urbani, eds. 2003 Il Musei di San Marco. Venice: Marsilio Editori.

Francis, E. D., and Michael Vickers 1983 Signa priscae artis: Eretria and Siphnos. Journal of Hellenic Studies 103:49–67.

Francovich, Ricardo, and Helen Patterson, eds. 2000 Extracting Meaning from Ploughsoil Assemblages. Oxford: Oxbow Books.

Freeman, Philip 1996 British Imperialism and the Roman Empire. *In* Roman Imperialism: Post-Colonial Perspectives. Jane Webster and Nicholas Cooper, eds. Pp. 19–34. Leicester Archaeological Monograph 3. Leicester: University of Leicester, School of Archaeological Studies.

Furtwängler, Adolf 1895[1893] Masterpieces of Greek Sculpture. E. Strong, trans. London: William Heinemann.

Gould, C. H. M. 1965 Trophy of Conquest: The Musée Napoleon and the Creation of the Louvre. London: Faber and Faber.

Gowland, R. 2001 Playing Dead: Implications of Mortuary Evidence for the Social Construction of Childhood in Roman Britain. *In* TRAC 2000: Proceedings of the Tenth Annual Theoretical Roman Archaeology Conference. G. Davies, A. Gardner and K. Lockyear, eds. Pp. 152–168. Oxford: Oxbow Books.

Gräslund, Bo 1987 The Birth of Prehistoric Chronology: Dating Methods and Dating Systems in Nineteenth-Century Scandinavian Archaeology. Cambridge: Cambridge University Press.

Greenhalgh, Michael 1989 The Survival of Roman Antiquities in the Middle Ages. London: Duckworth.

Hingley, Richard 2000 Roman Officers and English Gentlemen. London: Routledge.

Irwin, David G., ed. 1972 Winckelmann: Writings on Art. London: Phaidon.

James, Peter, with I. J. Thorpe, Nikos Kokkinos, Robert Morkot, and John Frankish 1991 Centuries of Darkness. London: Jonathan Cape.

Keay, Simon J. 1997 Urban Transformation and Cultural Change. In The Archaeology of Iberia. Margarita Díaz-Andreu and Simon J. Keay, eds. Pp. 192–210. London: Routledge.

——, Martin Millett, L. Paroli, and K. D. Strutt 2005 Portus: An Archaeological Survey of the Port of Imperial Rome. London: British School at Rome.

——, Martin Millett, Sarah Poppy, Julia Robinson, Jeremy Taylor, and Nicola Terrenato 2000 Falerii Novi: A New Survey of the Walled Area. Papers of the British School at Rome 68:1–93.

Leppmann, Wolfgang 1971 Winkelmann. London: Victor Gollanz.

Millett, Martin 2001 Roman Interaction in North-west Iberia. Oxford Journal of Archaeology 20:157–186.

——2006 Shiptonthorpe, East Yorkshire: Archaeological Studies of a Romano-British Roadside Settlement. Yorkshire Archaeological Society, Roman Antiquities Section Monograph.

Nevett, Lisa 1999 House and Society in the Ancient Greek World. Cambridge: Cambridge University Press.

Pearce, John 2000 Burial, Society and Context in the Provincial Roman World. In Burial, Context and Society in the Roman World. John Pearce, Martin Millett and Manuella Struck, eds. Pp. 1–12. Oxford: Oxbow Books.

Revell, L. 1999 Constructing Romanitas: Roman Public Architecture and the Archaeology of Practice. In TRAC 98: Proceedings of the Eighth Annual Theoretical Roman Archaeology Conference, Leicester 1998. P. Baker, C. Forcey, S. Jundi and R. Witcher, eds. Pp. 52–58. Oxford: Oxbow Books.

Ridley, Ronald T. 1992 The Eagle and the Spade: The Archaeology of Rome during the Napoleonic Era. Cambridge: Cambridge University Press.

Robertson, Martin 1975 A History of Greek Art. Cambridge: Cambridge University Press.

Rotroff, Susan 1997 Hellenistic Pottery: Athenian and Imported Wheelmade Table Ware and Related Material (2 vols.). The Athenian Agora 29. Princeton: American School of Classical Studies at Athens.

Salmon, Frank 2000 The Impact of the Archaeology of Rome on British Architects and Their Work, c. 1750–1840. In The Impact of Italy: The Grand Tour and Beyond. Clare Hornsby, ed. Pp. 219–243. London: British School at Rome.

Schnapp, Alain 1996 The Discovery of the Past. London: British Museum Press.

Snodgrass, Anthony 1980 Archaic Greece: The Age of Experiment. London: Dent.

——1987 An Archaeology of Greece. Berkeley and Los Angeles: University of California Press.

Strong, D. E. 1973 Roman Museums. In Archaeological Theory and Practice. D. E. Strong, ed. Pp. 247–264. London: Seminar Press.

Stuart, James, and Nicholas Revett 1762–1816 The Antiquities of Athens, vols. i–iv. London: John Haberkorn (vol. i, 1762), John Nichols (vols. ii and iii, 1787 and 1794), T. Bensley (vol. iv, 1816).

Talbert, Richard J. A., ed. 2000 The Barrington Atlas of the Greek and Roman World. Princeton: Princeton University Press.

Trigger, Bruce G. 1989 A History of Archaeological Thought. Cambridge: Cambridge University Press.

Vickers, Michael, and David Gill 1994 Artful Crafts: Ancient Greek Silverware and Pottery. Oxford: Clarendon Press.

Wallace-Hadrill, Andrew 1994 Houses and Society in Pompeii and Herculaneum. Princeton: Princeton University Press.

Whitley, James 2001 The Archaeology of Classical Greece. Cambridge: Cambridge University Press.

Woolf, Greg 1998 Becoming Roman: The Origins of Provincial Civilization in Gaul. Cambridge: Cambridge University Press.

2

Doing Archaeology in the Classical Lands

Introduction

How does one become a classical archaeologist? What goes into the training of such an individual? How does this vary between countries (e.g., United States versus United Kingdom) or between particular chronological interests (e.g., prehistoric Aegean versus historic archaeology)? What kinds of archaeological fieldwork are going on today in the classical lands, and how do they differ from past practice? This chapter is designed to present two perspectives on these issues, addressed through the personal experiences of the authors.

What also emerges from these accounts is the disparity between the experiences of the field archaeologist when compared to the stereotypical image of the library-bound academic. Setting off to do research bearing suitcases stuffed with cash may sound peculiar (or romantic), but such practicalities are frequently the norm for those who work in the field, be it in archaeology or other disciplines. Archaeological fieldwork is further complicated by the fact that it is almost never a solo operation; teams of people, endowed with various forms of expertise, must be gathered (usually from a number of countries), housed, fed, watered, and kept happy. Project directors can end up playing a variety of roles outside the intellectual sphere, including budget manager, labor arbitrator, psychologist, and cruise director.

Any impression that archaeological research is performed in a kind of sterile "bubble" is also dashed by the realities of working in what are, for many classical archaeologists, foreign countries. The past possesses paramount significance in the national identity of most Mediterranean lands, and in many nation states it is the "Classical past," so attractive to classical archaeologists, that overshadows all other periods. Not surprisingly, local reactions to the sight of outsiders (however well funded and well meaning) investigating and in some way controlling that past are frequently equivocal; imperialist and colonialist legacies weigh heavily here. From the other side, frustrations arising from difficulties experienced in obtaining official permits to carry out fieldwork, or reverses in hoped-for research designs, are recounted in this chapter, as are more positive situations in which genuine collaboration and mutual trust have been achieved. How best to "do" archaeology in the Classical lands is very much still a work in progress; in many ways, things appear to have become more, rather than less, difficult. Cooperation across nationalist, linguistic, and disciplinary boundaries, working to resolve the political (and emotional) tensions that underlie the practice of archaeology, appears an increasingly key priority.

2 (a)
Doing Archaeology in the Classical Lands

The Greek World

Jack L. Davis

This part of chapter 2 is written from the perspective of an American professor of classical archaeology who has organized several research projects in the eastern Mediterranean, in parts of the ancient Greek world within and outside the borders of the modern Greek state. Unlike Henry Hurst, author of the other half of this chapter, most of my own fieldwork has consisted of surface archaeology; I was trained in America in the field of Classics (i.e., the study of Greek and Roman languages, literature, art history, history, and archaeology); and my initial specialization was in prehistory, rather than historical archaeology. I have here focused on my own experiences in the discipline of classical archaeology, some of which no doubt are more typical of scholars of previous generations than of those today, especially in the United Kingdom. Still, the more things change, the more they stay the same, and I will suggest that a student in classical archaeology will still find much that is familiar in my adventures over the past three decades and will come to appreciate something of the challenges and rewards of doing archaeology in lands where archaeology and politics remain closely intertwined.

Learning to Do Classical Archaeology: An American Perspective

Unless he or she is extremely lucky, a foreign student's first opportunity to participate in fieldwork in lands that were part of the ancient Greek world is likely to come as a graduate student. Classical archaeology in this regard is completely different from many other archaeologies: early training in the crafts of excavation and field survey is rarely a fundamental component of undergraduate education.

My own career course was not atypical for an American who chose to specialize in the archaeology of ancient Greece. In a public secondary school in the rural Midwest, I had become interested in Greco-Roman antiquity largely through the study of Latin. At a large second-tier state university, the University of Akron in Ohio, I decided to study ancient Greek in fulfillment of an undergraduate language requirement and eventually chose Classics as my major discipline. I was fortunate to have found myself in a department where a broad approach to the study of antiquity was emphasized.

At many universities in North America, Classics can be defined so narrowly as to consist largely of the study of language and literature, perhaps with a flavoring of art history. My professors at Akron firmly believed, however, that the material culture of the Greeks and Romans had a unique contribution to make to the study of the Greek and Roman civilizations—that archaeology was of more use than as a source of illustrations for ancient texts. In the year prior to the receipt of my Bachelor of Arts degree, I began for the first time seriously to explore the possibility of pursuing a career in archaeology. I soon saw that my options were limited if I wanted to maintain my focus on the ancient Mediterranean, and the Greek world in particular. In the first place, in North America, there were only a few programs outside Classics that would permit me to do that, and most of these were biased toward instruction in the history of art. I wanted to find a program that emphasized fieldwork and that treated the analysis of all categories of artifacts from excavations with respect. It was also important for me to choose a department that offered significant support to its students in the form of scholarships. Financial constraints all but ruled out application to departments of archaeology in the United Kingdom, and led me directly into a graduate program in Classics at the University of Cincinnati in the United States.

What I did not realize at the time was the extent to which language training was emphasized in graduate programs in Classics. My first years of graduate school were occupied with developing greater competence in ancient Greek and Latin, and in reading modern scholarly languages, especially French and German. I received no particular encouragement from my supervisors to begin study of modern languages of the eastern Mediterranean (such as Greek or Turkish), the acquisition of which seemed to me to be essential were I to pursue a career in Greek archaeology.

All students were expected to study ancient history and to subscribe to the maxim that "archaeology is the handmaiden of history." I received no formal instruction in the methods of archaeological fieldwork or in the actual analysis of archaeological finds from archaeological contexts. I was told that this was something I would learn by doing in the field, after I had proven myself in the classroom. But we were taught formal methods of art historical and typological analysis, and were expected to acquire the ability to recognize artistic styles of particular periods and hands of particular artists. I learned that for many of my teachers and fellow students, classical archaeology was nearly synonymous with the history of ancient art: sculpture, painting (both murals and the decoration of ancient vases), and civic architecture.

Doing Mediterranean Archaeology At Last

In the spring of my second year of graduate school I was invited to join members of an excavation team from my own department. They had been excavating for some 15 years the ruins of a prehistoric town that had been founded in the 3rd millennium B.C. on a small peninsula called Ayia Irini (Figure 2.1), inside a capacious harbor on the Greek island of Keos (Caskey 1971; 1972). The project was directed by my advisor, John L. Caskey, and had been initiated in 1960. The archaeology of the Greek islands, particularly that of those central Aegean islands known as the Cyclades, was then in a very confused state. Earlier excavators had, with few exceptions, concentrated on the exploration of the cemeteries that were so characteristic of the island landscapes in the latter half of the 3rd millennium B.C. (in the Early Bronze Age). The graves in the cemeteries, for the most part, small boxes built of stone slabs, had been veritable treasure troves for looters and archaeologists since the 19th century, both groups encouraged by the popularity in the international art market of the characteristic marble female sculpted figures that were sometimes deposited with the dead (Gill and Chippindale 1993).

Emphasis on the exploration of cemeteries in the Cycladic islands had resulted in the neglect of study of contemporary settlements and, indeed, of time periods

Figure 2.1 The peninsular site of Ayia Irini (inside the bay at center) on the island of Keos in Greece. Excavated from 1960–1974 with financial support from an endowment established by Louise Taft Semple, one of the wealthiest citizens of Cincinnati. Courtesy of the Department of Classics, University of Cincinnati

when cemeteries were not common. The only major excavations of settlements in the Cycladic islands had occurred years before, when archaeological techniques of excavation were still rudimentary. Caskey set out to alter this picture.

As I prepared for that first summer, I became increasingly puzzled by the extent to which those who had lived in the settlement at Ayia Irini appeared to have responded to influences from the culture of Crete. What were the processes that had led to the adoption of so many elements characteristic of the Minoan civilization in a place like Ayia Irini, several days sail to the north of Crete and previously, it seemed, largely isolated from that island? I became fearful that I would lack the necessary skills to answer these questions when I was confronted with the archaeological evidence in the field.

On arrival on Keos, I was thrown immediately into the fray. Caskey assigned me to study excavated materials from the end of the Middle Bronze Age (ca. 1700 B.C.). I accepted the task in part because it fulfilled a graduate student dream. It gave me the opportunity to control my own "room in the mansion of knowledge," advice that had been given by Colin Renfrew to some of his graduate students. I would be an expert in the archaeology of the Cycladic islands! On the other hand, I realized that such a specialization might give me the chance to try to explain why the material culture of the people who had lived at Ayia Irini had changed so dramatically in the years when they began to interact frequently with the Cretans.

I had become interested in explaining the reasons why material culture changes, not through any training that I had received in Classics, but through exposure to the New Archaeology of the early 1970s. Although I and my fellow graduate students were discouraged by our professors from enrolling in classes in anthropology, I had read seminal papers by Lewis Binford (e.g., 1962), Kent Flannery (e.g., 1973), and others, and I was convinced that their writings could supply me with the vision of archaeology that I sought. The problem-oriented type of deductive reasoning that these anthropological archaeologists espouse—defining a concern, advancing a hypothesis to explain it, and then collecting data—made sense to me. Especially influential was the scholarship of Colin Renfrew, in whose *Emergence of Civilisation* (1972) I found examples of how the ideas and methods of analysis espoused by North American anthropological archaeologists might be applied to problems that were of concern to me as a Mediterranean archaeologist. Renfrew's own interests in the explanation of changes in material culture offered potential models for my own work on Keos (Renfrew 1973).

My first week in Keos was a baptism by fire. I found myself expected to reconstruct from old notebooks what excavators had done years before. I was supposed to make decisions about the dating of pottery and other artifacts of types that I had never seen before "in the flesh." My second week went from bad to worse when I was assigned to conduct test excavations with the help of two workmen with whom I could not communicate, when I myself had virtually no excavation experience.

Eventually, however, I managed to complete a PhD dissertation and to publish it in a revised edition in the series of hard-covered volumes dedicated to explicating the discoveries of our fieldwork (Davis 1986). The result was not in my eyes entirely satisfactory. Caskey's own view was that the obligation of an archaeologist in what was commonly known as a "final publication" was to present an objective view of what had been found: "tell the people the facts." But I had come to doubt that there could be such a thing as one single, final publication of Ayia Irini or any other site, when it was the implicit or explicit decisions of the excavator that determined what was worthy of publication and what was not. My own view was that any decision about what to publish should largely be based on the relevance of the finds to questions asked about them and that consequently many different publications of a site were theoretically possible, none of them in any way final.

The Institutions of Archaeology in the Eastern Mediterranean

In the autumn after that first summer in the field I begin a two-year stint living in Athens, Greece, as a student at the American School of Classical Studies—probably the most influential academic experience of my career (Figure 2.2). ASCSA, as it is known, was founded at the end of the 19th century by a consortium of universities on the east coast of the United States, but now has 175 member institutions (American School of Classical Studies; n.d.). It offers students from member institutions a program of academic instruction; it organizes and funds its own excavations in the ancient marketplace of Athens (the Agora) and in the center of the ancient Greek city-state of Corinth; and it reviews proposals from archaeologists at its member institutions who want to conduct other fieldwork in Greece.

ASCSA is one of more than 15 national schools of archaeology in Greece that have been established since the foundation of the first, the École Française d'Athènes, in 1846. The most recent is the Georgian Institute at Athens, established in 1997. From the beginning there was considerable national competition among these schools for archaeological concessions, i.e., the exclusive rights to excavate at significant sites (e.g., Dyson 1998:72–74, concerning competition for the Sanctuary of Apollo at Delphi). Many ancient sites in Greece today continue to be the preserve of particular nationalities: e.g., ancient Corinth is "American," Delphi is "French," Olympia is "German," and Knossos in Crete is "British." These concessions are zealously guarded against infringements by other groups of foreign archaeologists and, at times, even against "incursions" by archaeologists in the service of the Greek state.

Each foreign school in Greece is currently allowed to sponsor three excavations or surveys each year, and to cosponsor three additional projects in cooperation with members of the archaeological service of Greece. Proposals for fieldwork must be submitted by the foreign school to the Greek government on an annual basis. An archaeological council operating under the auspices of the Ministry of Culture of Greece then reviews these proposals and may grant permission. All foreign archaeological research must be conducted under the auspices of the appropriate national school. It is often difficult to acquire the sponsorship of a

Figure 2.2 Loring Hall, residence hall for the American School of Classical Studies at Athens, first occupied in 1929. Named in honor of Judge Caleb Loring, Justice of the Supreme Court of Massachusetts and President of the Board of Trustees of ASCSA. Courtesy of the Department of Classics, University of Cincinnati

foreign school, particularly in the case of a large country with many universities such as the United States.

Greece is among those nations that impose the tightest restrictions on archaeological fieldwork, almost certainly because its antiquities have played such a central role in nationalist projects of western nations and of the nation-state of Greece itself (e.g., Hamilakis and Yalouri 1996; Yalouri 2001). Virtually all countries of the eastern Mediterranean have, however, enacted legislation that forbids the exportation of antiquities beyond their borders without explicit permission. In many, there are rules that encourage or require foreign teams to include in their projects local archaeologists and archaeological students. In most, archaeologists, foreign and native, are required to conform to reasonable deadlines within which reports of discoveries will be published, if permits are to be renewed. Directors also may be obligated to demonstrate that funds are available for the conservation of sites, once excavated.

Foreign archaeological projects represent, however, only a tiny fraction of all archaeology that is conducted in Greece. Most archaeology is in the charge of the Greek Archaeological Service, an organ of the Ministry of Culture of Greece. It maintains more than 75 regional offices, 38 of which are entrusted with managing the prehistoric and classical archaeological heritage of a particular region, and 28 with Byzantine and later archaeology; there are also offices concerned with underwater archaeology and paleoanthropology and speleology (Hellenic Ministry of

Culture; n.d.). Under their auspices, hundreds of excavations are conducted each year, the majority of these emergency projects initiated to salvage antiquities that are threatened by modern construction or have been endangered by illicit looting. Greek universities sponsor some 20 additional field projects. Private Greek institutions, such as the Hellenic Institute of Maritime Archaeology, organize still more. The most significant private patron of archaeology in Greece has, however, long been the Archaeological Society of Athens, which was founded in 1837 and currently funds more than a dozen projects annually.

Foreign schools have, however, rarely encouraged their students to seek participation in Greek projects. And, although an increasingly large number of foreign projects have included Greek archaeologists and students of archaeology on their staff, interaction between most Greek and foreign archaeologists is limited. The result is an unfortunate situation in which the activities of local archaeologists and those of foreigners are largely segregated.

Directing Fieldwork in the Mediterranean for the First Time

Shortly before finishing my dissertation, I had taken the first steps to cut the umbilical cord that still tied me closely to my graduate professors. An opportunity arose to participate in Colin Renfrew's excavations on the island of Melos, a Cycladic island that lies between Keos and Crete (Renfrew and Wagstaff 1982). There, for the first time, I met a significant number of archaeologists who were "doing" archaeology in Greece, but were not based in Classics departments. Renfrew and his colleagues were practicing the sort of problem-oriented archaeology that I had admired as a student. Although excavations were limited to a single settlement (a prehistoric town known as Phylakopi), a field survey had been organized by John F. Cherry, a student of Renfrew's, to explore the remainder of the island in the belief that the siting of centers of population and power on the island will have changed through time in response to influences external to Melos. Phylakopi was imagined to be a part of a larger system of settlement, one that in turn related to economic and social systems that embraced a large part of the ancient Aegean. To comprehend the processes that provoked changes at Phylakopi required an understanding of how the island in the past had been exploited by the outside world.

In the early 1980s, after completion of fieldwork at Phylakopi, Cherry and I developed a plan for a survey of the island of Keos, similar to that of Melos. Our purpose was in part to create a context for Caskey's excavations at Ayia Irini, so that the patterns of settlement on Keos could be reconstructed in their totality— ultimately permitting comparison with those of Melos. Thus it was that in my early thirties (unusually young for a foreigner or a Greek), I first had the opportunity to organize archaeological field research.

Other projects of this sort were already underway in Greece. A survey sponsored by Stanford University had been investigating the Argolid district (Jameson et al. 1994), while another organized by the British School at Athens was

examining the countryside in parts of the district of Boiotia (Bintliff and Snodgrass 1985). We planned the systematic examination of large parts of the island
of Keos by putting into the field each day three teams of archaeologists and students of archaeology who would walk side-by-side through designated fields,
inspecting the ground for evidence of ancient remains, according to techniques
that had been developed for such purposes by Cherry and others (as described
by Alcock and Terrenato in chapter 4).

Finding the financial resources to support the 25 members of our team was
relatively simple compared to the logistical problems that we faced once we arrived
on the island. Keos in the early 1980s was still a relatively isolated place: tourism
was just beginning to be developed and the island had only recently been discovered by the urban population of Athens to be a close and desirable venue for the
construction of weekend and summer retreats. Although an owner of a grocery
store offered limited facilities for changing currency, there was not even a bank.
John and I arrived on Keos with an attaché case literally stuffed with stacks of
Greek currency, which we then divided into piles and hid under mattresses until
the money was needed to pay for room and board. Transportation was another
critical problem for us, since, unlike an excavation, our project required that we
drive our teams each day into the countryside, often to a considerable distance
from our base camp. The nearest car rental agencies were in Athens, and supplies
of gasoline were limited. If winds were strong, the ferryboats that serviced the
island could not sail, tanker trucks did not arrive, and everyone could be reduced
to walking. Fortunately, however, we found comfortable quarters in rented rooms
that had been built by a Greek-Australian family in anticipation of the tourist
onslaught that had yet to arrive.

It took two attempts on our part to acquire permission from the Ministry of
Culture of Greece to conduct fieldwork. I naively imagined that the officials who
approve such requests would be captivated by the brilliance of our research plan
and would agree that our work would be invaluable to Greek archaeologists in
designing programs of cultural-resource management for the island and in protecting its archaeological remains from the inevitable dangers that would eventually follow in the wake of increased tourism. They instead were justifiably suspicious
of our motivations in wanting to investigate the entire island; archaeologists in
Greece, foreign and native, had sometimes argued that their prior topographical
investigations in an area later gave them rights to conduct more detailed fieldwork
there.

We were not the only archaeologists who had thought of initiating new research
on Keos, although we were blissfully unaware of this when we started. As so often
in archaeology, our plans, much discussed among ourselves and even published
in advance, thus needed to be adjusted "on the fly." Another of our original intentions was to examine parts of the territory of each of the four city-states that had
existed on Keos in antiquity. We thought we would compare the historical growth
and development of these city-states with a view towards determining why two
had ceased to exist as independent political entities by the end of the first millennium B.C. Yet the terms of the permit that we were granted required us to limit

our research to the territory of just one city-state, so as not to encroach on parts of the island being studied by others. We needed to jettison our designs to sample randomly the archaeological remains in environmental zones representative of all parts of the island. We instead adopted a strategy that emphasized what has come to be called "full-coverage" survey. But in so doing, we lost the ability to draw, as fully as we had hoped, comparisons and contrasts between the four city-states of Keos.

Our project on Keos remains one of only a handful of archaeological expeditions that have involved Greek and foreign archaeologists in fieldwork in a partnership. Eleni Mantzourani, a professor at the University of Athens, and a group of her students, equal in number to those from our own universities, joined the expedition. Our research was a genuinely international collaboration, consisting of archaeologists of a half-dozen different nationalities (although predominantly Greek, British, and American), operating under a permit granted to the American School of Classical Studies at Athens. Our teams were led by Greeks, as well as foreigners.

For five years after the conclusion of fieldwork we prepared the publication of our discoveries. Members of the project composed reports that described the date and nature of our finds and examined the spatial distribution of artifacts and sites of particular periods of the past (Figure 2.3). We also commissioned scientific

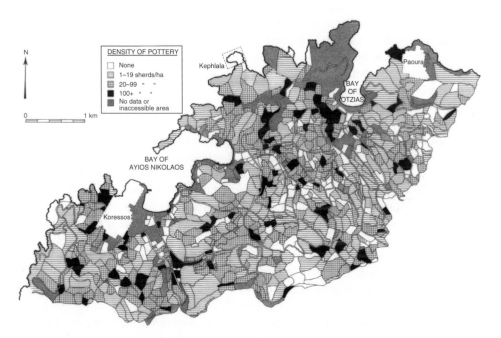

Figure 2.3 Densities of broken pieces of ancient and medieval pottery in the area surveyed on the island of Keos. This graphic represents one of the first attempts in Greece to map ancient artifacts found on the surface of the earth in an entire region. After Cherry, Davis and Mantzourani 1991: figure 3.3. Courtesy of John F. Cherry

analyses and historical syntheses of documentary evidence (among them, a study by Robin Osborne, one of the editors of this volume). The job of John, Eleni, and myself, as directors of the archaeological fieldwork now turned editors, was to integrate these disparate threads of evidence into a coherent whole. Some 17 authors ultimately contributed to a book that is more than 500 pages in length (Cherry et al. 1991).

Fin de Siècle Classical Archaeology in Greece

In the 20 years since our research on Keos I have been fortunate to have the opportunity to participate in the organization *de novo* of two still larger programs of fieldwork in Greece. In the mid-1980s several of my collaborators from Keos and I joined Jim Wright of Bryn Mawr College to field a particularly ambitious archaeological expedition that would investigate the history of the Nemea Valley in the northeastern Peloponnese through archaeological survey, excavation, and ethnographical research. Excavations of the Sanctuary of Zeus at the head of the valley, like Delphi one of the international pan-Hellenic sanctuaries of ancient Greece, had already been conducted with sponsorship by the University of Cincinnati and ASCSA (1924–27) and, more recently, by the University of California at Berkeley. In Antiquity, city-states had dispatched representatives to the sacred precinct every four years to participate in a religious festival and in athletic and musical competitions. Our objective was not, however, further to explore the Sanctuary of Zeus, but to document the ebb and flow of settlement in the valley over the past millennia from the time that the area was first settled until the modern period (Wright et al. 1990).

In the 1990s, some of us who had worked at Nemea and on Keos joined forces once again to investigate those parts of western Messenia centered on the "Palace of Nestor," the best-preserved administrative center of the Mycenaean civilization of the later 2nd millennium B.C. (Blegen and Rawson 1966). Carl Blegen (Caskey's professor) had begun excavations there in 1939. On the very first day of excavation, Blegen's workmen uncovered the first of hundreds of clay tablets with inscriptions in an early form of the Greek language. These documents record the transactions of an elaborate bureaucracy that administered a kingdom ruled by a king who lived in this palace. They mention the names of many smaller settlements, some of which appear to have been capitals of districts into which the kingdom was divided.

Blegen himself understood the potential value of these texts: archaeologists might locate the places mentioned in them. One member of his team, Bill McDonald, later the founding father of the Minnesota Messenia Expedition, the first interdisciplinary regional archaeological project in Greece, rose to the challenge. McDonald combined his own observations with extensive local knowledge concerning the locations of antiquities to compile an enormous catalogue of archaeological sites. With a colleague, Richard Hope Simpson, he eventually extended the scope of his research to include all of the modern province of Messenia (McDonald and Rapp 1972), and then chose one of the likely provincial capitals of the kingdom for excavation.

But McDonald and Hope Simpson's techniques came to be criticized in the 1970s and 1980s by a younger generation of field archaeologists as being too "extensive" in comparison to the more systematic "intensive" methods that we had, for example, employed on Keos and at Nemea (e.g., Cherry 1983). One major objection was that McDonald and Hope Simpson tended to look for archaeological sites only in particular places in the landscape that conformed to preconceived notions about where and where not sites would be found; another that their fieldwork was systematically biased toward the discovery of sites of the prehistoric, rather than historical, periods. If this were true, then it would be impossible for historians or prehistorians to put any faith in the patterns revealed by their fieldwork. In large part, it was for this reason that we believed a reinvestigation of the Pylos area was necessary.

The Pylos Regional Archaeological Project (Davis 1998), as we called it, was an enormously complex undertaking that involved delegation of responsibilities among a group of co-directors (including Sue Alcock, the other editor of this book) based in the United States, England, Switzerland, and Greece. At times, more than 60 individuals were in the field. Several geologists studied the topography of the area with a particular view to determining how its appearance had been altered since antiquity through erosion, the deposition of alluvial soils by streams, and vacillations in the levels of the sea relative to the height of the coasts. A paleobotanist drilled cores in a lagoon in order to retrieve fossilized remains of pollen; he then used these to determine the types of vegetation that grew around the lagoon in the past. Meanwhile our survey teams mapped daily the surface archaeological remains that they discovered in the landscape and brought many of them to our workrooms to be examined and dated by a team of experts.

One of my own special interests in Pylos was the reconstruction of patterns of settlement in the early modern period (from the 16th century until the independence of Greece was declared in 1821), when nearly all of the territory that now constitutes the modern nation of Greece belonged to the Ottoman empire. This is a period that has in many ways been more poorly known archaeologically than prehistoric times, and my colleagues, John Bennet and Fariba Zarinebaf, and I have struggled to write a local history for the Pylos area, based on the artifacts found by our teams and a rich store of Turkish documents (including tax registers) that we have mined in Istanbul.

The particular challenge in directing PRAP was, however, to provide for the daily needs of so many people on the cheap, a task that I accomplished only with a great amount of help from Panayiotis Petropoulos, the mayor of Hora, the village in which we lived. The municipality allowed us to use classrooms in an elementary school as dormitories and laboratories, and Petropoulos pointed us to several houses in the town and an abandoned restaurant that could be rented at reasonable prices. With the addition to our staff of a cook, our parsimonious purchasing agent managed to feed and house everyone for only a few dollars a day—with only occasional grumbling about living conditions from a good-spirited team.

Doing Classical Archaeology in Albania

In the mid-1990s, my program of fieldwork took an unexpected turn, after the last bastion of Communism in Europe, Albania, declared itself a democracy and opened its borders to the outside world for the first time since World War II. Many parts of the ancient Greek world had been isolated from the West under Communism: e.g., much of the coast of the Black Sea lay within the borders of the Soviet Union and Bulgaria, while the northeastern coast of the Adriatic Sea belonged to Yugoslavia; but Albania was the most difficult to access. In trips to northern Greece as a student of ASCSA I had dreamt of traveling there, but for an American an entry visa was impossible to obtain. Enver Hoxha, the Stalinist dictator of Albania from 1944 until his death in 1985, had demonized the United States in his propaganda. At the same time the movements of Albanians themselves had been tightly controlled within their country and very few had the opportunity to travel abroad.

Prior to World War II there existed a vigorous program of classical archaeology in Albania—one, however, that was almost exclusively dominated by foreigners who focused their efforts on investigations at significant centers of Greek and Roman civilization and competed among each other to control archaeological resources. Systematic archaeological investigations had been initiated in the 1930s by Leon Rey, representing the École Française d'Athènes, at Apollonia, a Greek colony many believed was founded in the early 6th century B.C. (Figure 2.4). At about the same time, Luigi Ugolini, funded by Mussolini's fascist government, began excavations at Buthrotum, a city traditionally said to have been established by Trojan refugees following the fall of Troy. Albania had not, however, become the focus of intense research by foreign teams, and its archaeology remained peripheral to that of Greece in the minds of most classical archaeologists. No foreign schools of archaeology existed there. There were also few Albanian archaeologists, little in the way of an organized antiquities service, and archaeology was not (and is still not) taught as a discipline at the principal university of the country in its capital, Tirana.

Under Communism, local archaeology grew considerably in significance and came to play an important role in the creation of an ideology of national unity and identity for the country (Miraj and Zeqo 1993). The focus was on the native population of Albania in antiquity, the "Illyrians," a people sometimes mentioned in Greek and Roman literary sources but imperfectly known (Wilkes 1992). The "Illyrians" were argued to be the ancestors of the modern Albanian people, some of whom, through trading, marriage, and other co-mingling with Greeks who had settled on the coast at places like Apollonia, came to adopt many aspects of Greek culture, including urban lifestyles, dining habits, architectural styles, and, in some instances, also burial customs. One significant goal of archaeology in the time of Hoxha was to document the essential continuity of the Albanian population from earliest until recent times by describing changes in the material culture of the native populations—a task that had been of little interest to the foreign archaeologists who had previously worked in Albania.

Figure 2.4 View of the ancient city of Apollonia in Albania and of the medieval monastery, a peaceful oasis only a half hour west of the city of Fier, the center of the country's oil industry. Courtesy of the Department of Classics, University of Cincinnati

The opening of its borders in 1990 had dramatic repercussions for Albania. Tens of thousands of its citizens left almost immediately to seek work abroad. Its industries ground to a halt. Even the ability of the country to feed its population with locally grown produce was at times impaired. As a succession of new governments struggled to repair a domestic infrastructure crippled by years of neglect, archaeological activities, formerly so essential to the nationalist program of the socialist state, ceased to hold a high priority. Archaeologists of the Institute of Archaeology, like other governmental employees, went unpaid for long periods of time; little funding was available in support of fieldwork or publication. Some local archaeologists began to look to foreign collaborations for an escape not only from financial difficulties but also for opportunities to familiarize themselves and their students with archaeological practice outside Albania.

It was in this social and economic context that I, my wife Sharon Stocker, and John Cherry, spent some days in the summer of 1996 in the company of the distinguished Albanian prehistorian Muzafer Korkuti. After visiting many archaeological sites in the central part of the country with him, we reached agreement that in the coming summer we would cooperate in mounting an intensive surface survey around Apollonia. But a wave of violence hit Albania in the spring of 1997, when pyramid banking schemes collapsed and many Albanians were defrauded of their life savings. Government munitions warehouses were sacked and the nation was in chaos. Our plans were cancelled.

Finally, in 1998, Stocker and I were able to begin work, and Mike Galaty of Millsaps College assumed responsibilities as field director of the project. Two of Korkuti's colleagues in the archaeological service of Albania filled out our group of six co-directors. Albanian law does not permit independent foreign projects. For me organizing an archaeological project in Albania was consequently an experience totally unlike any I had earlier had in Greece. We were on our own without the bureaucratic safety net provided by ASCSA—this in a country where it was then impossible to rent a car or to purchase many of the supplies that were essential to an archaeological expedition. We ourselves were totally responsible for any negotiations we might have with the archaeological authorities in Albania. And again, as on Keos two decades earlier, I found myself carrying suitcases of money into the field in order to pay for our daily expenses.

Archaeology in Albania remains on a much smaller scale than in Greece, and we quickly became part of a community that embraced all archaeologists, regardless of nationality. Following our first season, we presented our results in Tirana to locals and foreigners, and in subsequent years we have come to know personally many, even most, Albanian archaeologists. In turn, more than a dozen Albanian university students have learned the methods of intensive survey while participating in our project; one has completed an advanced degree at my university. We and our Albanian colleagues have shared research facilities in Tirana and Cincinnati.

Closer relations have also been developed with foreign archaeologists who are working in Albania. At Apollonia, we have been fortunate to enjoy living quarters in an archaeological center built jointly by the French and Albanian governments. We ourselves have helped to improve facilities for the study of archaeological finds there by providing the financial support that has permitted parts of the medieval monastery at the site to be remodeled. In Albania, exclusive concessions to particular sites are not awarded to teams of archaeologists, whether local or foreign, and several different groups may well be involved in the investigation of different parts or different aspects of the same site or region. Nor is there any sharp division between archaeologists who teach at the universities of Albania and those in the state archaeological service: many of the same individuals are, in fact, employed in both capacities.

Once agreement between foreign and Albanian colleagues is reached on a matter of archaeological policy, little in the way of additional governmental bureaucracy impedes action. Integration of archaeological enterprises at the personal level in Albania has eliminated much of the "us vs. them" mentality that understandably lingers in some other areas that were part of the ancient Greek world. The countries of the eastern Mediterranean, particularly those that were part of the Ottoman empire, have long been the victims of colonial and cultural domination by the West (Shaw 2003). Many have seen their significant archaeological monuments removed to foreign lands. The legacy of such checkered histories can be a lack of trust, and the exportation of even the smallest samples of antiquities for scientific analysis abroad is sometimes a complicated process.

But other challenges for foreign archaeologists do exist in Albania precisely because it is such a new democracy and because its political and cultural infrastructure is still in the process of being shaped. There is an obvious enormous imbalance between the financial resources available to local and foreign archaeologists—and the latter always control the purse strings. The foreign archaeologists also control academic capital, at least in international arenas. They can provide Albanian students with opportunities to study abroad. They can offer access to specialists and to expensive hardware that has been commonly employed in the West, but is still unfamiliar in Albania. They have libraries of a caliber that do not exist in Albania. They are familiar with modes of thinking about the interpretation of archaeological evidence from which Albanian archaeologists were almost completely isolated under Communism.

There is a real danger that such inequalities between foreigners and local archaeologists, if they are allowed to become institutionalized, will soon lead to resentments of the sort that similar imbalances of power have provoked elsewhere in the eastern Mediterranean. And there have already emerged situations where the "best" interests of archaeology in Albania, as defined by foreign archaeologists, have been viewed by some sectors of the Albanian population as being in conflict with the general welfare of the Albanian people (e.g., Pluciennik and Drew 2000): for example, how much of the unspoiled countryside around an archaeological site should be preserved as park, and how much should be opened to private tourism developments? Enormous sums of money are potentially at stake.

There is reason to be hopeful that the fossilization of imbalances of power can be avoided. It is especially encouraging that an international center for Albanian archaeology has been established in Tirana with funding from the Packard Humanities Institute of the United States. This center is managed by Albanian archaeologists and, although still small, offers facilities and support for all archaeologists working in the country. It also provides access for Albanians to advanced technology in support of their own field research without the necessity of foreign collaborations.

Doing Archaeology in the New Millennium

The practices of governmental and educational institutions continue to exercise a profound influence on the nature of archaeological research in the eastern Mediterranean. In some countries, such as Greece and Egypt, opportunities to participate in fieldwork for anyone who is not a representative of the governmental archaeological services are even more restricted than when I was a graduate student in the early 1970s. In Greece, surface surveys of the sort that John Cherry and I were able to conduct on Keos are now as highly regulated as excavations and competition for permits is keen. Bureaucratic decisions may force research designs to be altered in ways that we never imagined three decades ago. In Egypt, authorization to begin new projects in the Nile Valley is almost impossible to obtain. The unpredictability of permits can hamper efforts to find funding for fieldwork since financial backers require guarantees that research will be completed within a specified time frame.

But all is by no means gloom and doom. The future of classical archaeology in the eastern Mediterranean can be as bright as its past. Impediments to doing classical archaeology in the eastern Mediterranean need to be viewed in their historical context and steps taken to avoid mistakes of the past. I have already suggested that neocolonial attitudes and past practices have conditioned the present policies that governments in the eastern Mediterranean have established to control the activities of foreigners. If this is so, then there is hope that in the future it will be possible to construct alternative models for archaeological field-work that emphasize integration rather than segregation of efforts, and coopera-tion rather than national competition.

Meanwhile, although opportunities for new excavations and surveys may be limited in many parts of the eastern Mediterranean, prospects for doing other types of archaeology in these places may not be. In the past, classical archaeolo-gists have often been rather better about conducting their fieldwork than in publishing their results. As a consequence masses of artifacts that were once painstakingly retrieved now molder in museum storerooms. There are real oppor-tunities here for archaeologists of any age. Hollywood may want us to believe that the fame and glory of archaeology lie in excavation and exploration, but major scientific contributions to our field continue to be made by those scholars who have the imagination and perseverance to interpret discoveries and to communi-cate them to our colleagues. Opportunities to study older, unpublished archaeo-logical finds often are abundant, and these discoveries may well be of greater significance than any that an archaeologist is likely to be so fortunate as to make today, at much greater expense.

ACKNOWLEDGMENTS

In writing this section of the chapter, I am grateful for discussions I have enjoyed with colleagues about "doing archaeology" in parts of the Mediterranean with which I am not familiar personally. These include Joseph Greene, Lynn Meskell, Brian Rose, and Gisela Walberg. I thank the editors of this volume for their remarks on various drafts of my text, and Jeffery Kramer for assistance in the preparation of illustrations.

NOTE

The references for this chapter are on pp. 85–88.

2 (b)
Doing Archaeology in the Classical Lands

The Roman World

Henry Hurst

This discussion will be mostly about fieldwork and its publication, thinking especially about the problem of how new discoveries are related to the existing body of knowledge—though "doing classical archaeology" could also mean library or museum study or laboratory analysis. Paired as I am with a specialist of the Greek world and of surface survey, I shall stay mostly within the Roman world and use excavation as the main example of "doing."

There is at once an identity problem. In fieldwork, "Classical" cannot be done in isolation: walk across any field or subject it to remote sensing, dig any hole, and the results will invariably not be confined to any one short period of the human past. There is a further paradox over the collective term Classical: as a "doing" archaeologist, I might call myself an excavator, an urban archaeologist, a Roman archaeologist, a Mediterranean archaeologist, but it has never occurred to me to put the adjective Classical in front of my activities, and I do not think that is atypical of colleagues who work in the archaeology of the Roman world, or of many (though perhaps not quite all) archaeologists of ancient Greece. Yet I am based in the Classics Faculty of a university with a post in Classical Archaeology.

So does classical archaeology have any meaning except in the university setting, where there is a special way we talk about its results, to fit within the discourse of Classics as a whole? In its broadest sense that question is better answered by other contributors to this volume (see especially the essays in chapter 1). My personal response would be to remember the remark of Moses Finley, that there is no such subject as Classics: Classical literature is a part of literature, Classical philosophy is a part of philosophy, and so on. I think that applies to archaeology, but, as I shall try to show, not quite totally.

Classical archaeology is, of course, a branch of historic archaeology in the sense that the Classical past belongs to that relatively short stretch of human history for

which we have written records—and in this case an exceptionally rich and prestigious documentation in the eyes of later generations. Knowledge of relevant
documentary material is therefore essential. Yet such knowledge alone, however
profound, without an ability to read the material results of human activity in an
archaeological way, does not equip one to do useful classical archaeology. This
ability, incidentally, is not a requirement in order to be famous. It could be fun
to list examples going up to the present time, but let us fall back on Heinrich
Schliemann, the Father of Aegean Archaeology. He misread Classical texts and
applied that misunderstanding in an archaeologically destructive pursuit of what
(partly) never existed, incidentally making notable discoveries for later generations
to salvage as best they could (Traill 1995, for a biography of Schliemann). Lesser
Schliemanns, more learned but mostly without his roguish panache, are still to
be found within classical archaeology: we all have a bit of this tendency, so that
in that sense he might truly be seen as the father of our subject.

How archaeologists handle the particular types of textual evidence we have for
the Classical world is, therefore, a special characteristic of doing classical archaeology. This is a central issue in the subject—in my view, the only methodological
issue by which a distinctive "classical archaeology" can be defined—so that is my
answer to the question posed about the identity of the subject. The distinctiveness
arises from the nature of the documentation of the Classical world by comparison
with other literate cultures studied by archaeologists. What marks it out is the
weight of literature, in a "high-cultural" sense, in forming our overall picture.
Although thousands of non-literary documents survive from ancient Greece
and Rome, our picture of those cultures is constructed to a quite exceptional
extent from the writings of educated Greeks and Romans, with all the slanting
of the picture towards the thought of this rather limited sector of society
which might be expected from such sources. Not only that, but given that these
writers established the framework for our own idea sets in the fields of literature,
philosophy and historical writing, their writings are irresistibly tenacious in our
thought. Westerners do not have this relationship with the documentation of any
other literate culture or period studied in archaeology: for a start, far less literature
usually survives, as for example, with ancient Egypt or Mycenaean Greece, or
when it does survive, as in medieval and early modern Europe, there is such a
wealth of non-literary documentation of closer relevance for archaeological purposes, like property deeds, rent rolls and the like, that literary documents are
relatively less important. We will come back to examples of how this affects the
character of the subject by looking at some case studies, but first it may be helpful
to proceed a little further with considering "doing classical archaeology" as simply
a part of archaeology.

At the risk of another statement of the obvious, let us assert that archaeology
is research. This needs saying because when it is qualified by an adjective such
as "salvage" or "contract," the suggestion is sometimes made that it is something
else. In much contract archaeology "research" is explicitly excluded from project
designs, to the point where in Sweden there is actually legislation to introduce a
research component into such work (one day per week!; Carver 2002). Seeing

operatives on developer-funded archaeological projects mechanically recording data they are discouraged from trying to understand while "the suits" keep the enterprise on (non-archaeological) schedule, within budget and on message for public relations purposes, one can understand the confusion about their aims. Research such work nevertheless is: compromised, certainly, but its ultimate value is as a contribution to knowledge. "Doing archaeology," then, is doing research, wherever you are in the spectrum between what is called a "research project" and work done in response to various forms of non-archaeological considerations (for further discussion, see Carver 2003).

Research, of course, can only be "done" in a social and political context and if done collaboratively is liable also to be an intensely human experience. These sometimes neglected aspects are where I think the discussion of doing any sort of archaeology should begin.

How Is Research Generated?

Within the concrete walls of a university faculty, the intellectual side of archaeological fieldwork rightly receives most emphasis—the prevalent state of knowledge of a topic in academic study, the type of research project which might address important questions in that field of study, the appropriate methodology of study, and the relevant techniques. Elements at least of that thinking are present in every piece of successful research in classical archaeology over the past few decades, yet it would be true to say that a purely or predominantly intellectual agenda has been the determining factor of only a small minority of the projects which have made major contributions to the subject. An example of this for Roman archaeology would be the project directed by Andrea Carandini on the Roman villa at Settefinestre. Here was an archaeologist who, on the one hand, was excited by the potential of a range of archaeological techniques which until that time (the mid-1970s) had only been applied in a relatively limited way on Classical sites in Italy and, on the other, had a social-historical research agenda which he felt could be tested against the material evidence of archaeology (Carandini and Settis 1979, and Carandini 1988, for the agenda; Carandini 1985, for full publication of the site). Settefinestre and its publication made a big impact, in part directly, by training a generation of archaeologists, but also in the type of information the publication contained. Whether or not one agreed with the exact conclusions, the potential of archaeological information and the types of argument which it allowed were brought to the attention of those studying Classical Italy in a manner which changed the subject.

It could be argued that an equally, or perhaps more, influential study for Classical Italy over the past two and a half decades has been Tim Potter's book, *The Changing Landscape of South Etruria* (1979), and the fieldwork which preceded it, since this has in many ways led what today is a huge area of activity in Italian regional studies. The circumstances in which this study came about were totally different from those of Settefinestre, in that this involved no initial problem-orientation, but was a rationalization during and after the event of a set of opportunities created by non-archaeological circumstances—in this case, the effects of deep plowing over the landscape in the 1950s and 1960s, bringing to the surface an abundance of archaeological material (while, sadly, also doing irreparable damage to sites). An initial "recover as much as possible" approach evolved into a series of structured studies focused on localities defined in terms of their Classical identity (the Ager Veientanus, Ager Faliscus, etc.); the techniques for recovering and presenting information in such a manner as to allow comparison between different such localities were also developed. Potter's book was, however, a further rationalization after the event, in that he drew on publications of specific areas, which had not necessarily been designed with wider comparison in mind, or he used hitherto unpublished information.

These two examples set parameters. The second—an essentially responsive approach to a situation determined at least partly by non-academic factors—is the more common framework for most archaeological fieldwork. The South Etruria study shows that a contribution of major academic importance can be generated in this way and that, within archaeological work, there are opportunities for problem-formulation and resolution (in an academic sense) at stages after the moment of initial conception of the project. There is also, a difference of intellectual approach in these two studies, reflecting two intellectual traditions: loosely speaking, an agenda-driven Latin (in the modern sense) approach versus one more in the Anglo-Saxon empirical tradition. This, to me, however, is a less significant point than the role of non-archaeological factors in research formulation.

Organizing a Project: Thoughts Between the Lines

The scale, as well as the type of work done, might be thought to be determined by the nature of the academic questions asked, but we must ask ourselves what questions and how generated? Perhaps this is cynical, but academically competent archaeologists can make a persuasive case for almost any sort of research on any scale. Classical archaeology, like any other branch of the subject, has a mass of open research agendas—for me, this is one of its most engaging characteristics. In this respect, perhaps it has liberated itself over the past two or three decades, since two alternative scenarios are of recent memory: one of a subject where the questions to be asked seemed to be rather confined and most of them already answered, as in Roman Britain—or, for that matter, Greek Art—in the 1960s, and one of a subject affected by a "missionary" phase of theory and its application, sometimes verging on the authoritarian (as with processual approaches in the 1970s; for a general account, see, for example, Trigger 1989). All this led to a certain amount of verbal aggression about classical archaeology, not in itself a problem (and not wholly unjustified); and, as is the way with classical archaeologists, a substantial proportion of them remained not only unaffected but also unaware. The harmful effect comes when large amounts of the same type of unimaginatively conceived, and rapidly dated, research is the result.

When one looks at the actual proposals set for archaeological projects, they of course are a response to academic concerns in the subject, but non-academic factors are powerfully present, not least purely human ones. It requires a special sort of personality allied to a certain level of academic status to conceive, conduct, and bring to a conclusion a project involving as many other individuals as Settefinestre, and so it simply would not occur to many scholars to pose as a research target the questions which Settefinestre addressed. It is much easier to do research on your own or with small numbers of collaborators, and the over-whelming majority of publications reflect that reality. It is also easier to conduct responsive rather than proactively formulated research, as the South Etruria example shows. This is in no way to belittle the fine achievement of Potter in drawing many disparate strands together, but this was essentially study done on his own, for all that it drew upon the work of many.

To this human dimension can be added institutional and financial aspects. There are, of course, many collaborative projects, which may be organized at an institutional level, like the South Etruria Survey or its current counterpart, the Tiber Valley Survey, both organized by the British School at Rome (for the latter, Patterson 2004), or many university and inter-university expeditions. They may also be the initiatives of a regional authority or a national government, or be an international enterprise, like the UNESCO Save Carthage campaign (Ennabli 1992) or the European Union's Mediterranean desertification and land-use project (Brandt and Thornes 1996). The larger the project, more or less as a logical con-sequence, the broader its defined purpose (up to the point of meaninglessness!) and the looser the links between its internal components: many large projects are in effect umbrellas for a whole series of smaller pieces of research, in turn often single-person enterprises. Both academic and non-academic motives can be seen in organizing such projects. There may be an academic objective or set of objec-tives which might require interdisciplinary study, or (as is often the reality) a series of studies in different disciplines, or a challenge may be posed (which again might be academic) requiring a multiplicity of excavation groups working at the same time, as at Carthage, Beirut or Zeugma, before the site is developed or flooded. But in many cases such projects also exist to justify the continuing existence of the institutions, and that, rather than any inherent academic need, is why they are on the scale they are; the institution's finance-raising and spending capacity is placed on view.

All of the above is permeated by the big and small politics of our response to the past. Big politics—the willingness of governments to finance, or encourage others to finance, archaeological research, frequently at the cost of manipulating the results, or their refusal—often occupies the driver's seat in classical archaeol-ogy. Mussolini's Augustan Rome perhaps remains the purest expression of this phenomenon (Scobie 1990; Benton 1995), but for many countries, especially those with a recent colonial history, the manner in which the Greeks and Romans are handled is a live issue. The impact is erratic, as three examples will show.

Figure 2.5 Politics and archaeology: a portrait of Hannibal in front of a reconstruction of the Carthaginian naval harbor on a Tunisian banknote

The Libyan Valleys Survey was an exception to the general rule in post-revolutionary Libyan archaeology, of keeping quiet about the Roman period, for the sole reason that it was thought that some practical utility—learning how Roman-period inhabitants farmed in what is now desert—might derive from the results. This project delivered information as intended (Barker 1996), even if it was possibly not very helpful for today's purposes. In neighboring Tunisia, the intended archaeological script was somewhat pushed aside. A government seeking to underpin its authority by promoting certain aspects of the country's history made a delicate choice: the Romans were like the colonial French, while too much emphasis on the Islamic period could also prove troublesome. The Punic period therefore seemed a good focus for a national identity, with a "repatriated" Hannibal as a Big Name (Figure 2.5; despite his having spent no more than six unhappy years of his life there). The economic logic of tourism, however, favors the Romans, and Roman remains are consequently the dominant "popular" image of the Tunisian cultural heritage. Finally, in Rome during the 1980s, a move to give the imperial fora a post-Mussolini image by excavating away the Fascist Via dei Fori Imperiali (driven right through the ancient fora) ran into an alliance of the car and environmental lobbies: where would the traffic on this main artery go? What would have to be sacrificed to traffic instead (*Roma, conti-nuità* . . . 1981)? Mussolini's triumphal way stayed, but excavations were done on both sides. The excavated remains at the present time (the project is not completed) are displayed indecisively, in a manner which renders them partly incomprehensible even for archaeologists, but so neatly expresses the project's politics: in places, the Roman imperial levels are exposed, elsewhere the early medieval remains, elsewhere the houses demolished to make the Duce's road in 1933.

Archaeologists usually have no impact on big politics, though it may be the determining factor behind their work, and they may be deeply corrupted by it. Small politics is the archaeologist's daily fare. It means everything in doing archaeology: from acquisition of funds and permissions, encounters with the local municipal and antiquities authorities or the embassy, all aspects of local employment and other local dealings, through to interaction with other team members. To be a successful archaeologist in the field, small political skills are vital, archaeological ones are desirable. If you cannot get on with your team or fall out with the local Antiquities czar, the only option is to give up—but you can usually get somebody else to work the total station or fill in the context sheets.

Drawing together the ends in this discussion of project-formation, non-academic considerations shape every piece of work done, and even where there is an avowedly "academic" approach it is possible to see the impact of non-academic factors. The message from this is emphatically not to belittle the need for asking academic questions of research—we go nowhere at all unless we ask questions, and a major element of research lies in formulating them, however flawed they might turn out to be—but to press the case for flexibility. There is an almost infinite spectrum of possible archaeological research situations and so there should be of responses (a broader expression of these views is the "go with the flow" line of Hodder 1999).

Doing Specifically Classical Archaeology: Three Case Histories

A more extended look is now taken at the issue of how the archaeologist's work is affected by the types of written documentation about the Classical world which are available to us. Comments have already been made about the dominance of high literature in forming our image of this world. In other periods of "historic" archaeology, there is nothing quite to compare with, say, the influence of Pliny and Pausanias on the study of Classical art and architecture, of Varro and Columella on agriculture and its social basis in Italy, of Varro on the topography and physical history of Rome, or of the Classical historians (such as Herodotus, Thucydides, Livy and Tacitus) for giving what we might almost call a Braudelian view of the times they wrote about, combining the widest view of humankind with thoughtful observation of the structures and forces at work in human society, together with the events, leading personages and their motivations. So, for topics where this rich documentation combines with archaeology—military history and archaeology, any form of social archaeology, indeed most imaginable forms of archaeology—the impact of this literature is powerful. Although the Classical world also yields countless non-literary documents (from thousands of inscriptions on stone or coins to residues of more ephemeral documentation such as many papyri, ostraka, writing tablets or the graffiti on walls or objects), typically these play a secondary role in determining the dominant character of a field of study—for example, for Roman military history, one thinks of Polybius and Tacitus before the Vindolanda tablets or documents from Dura Europus.

Such is the power and prestige of this literature, and of the generations of scholarly study devoted to it, that it exerts the most tenacious hold on any field of study in the Classical world. This makes archaeology difficult, since one is torn between the Scylla of imposing one's own conception of literary meaning onto archaeological data and the Charybdis of ignoring literary information which could render one's archaeological study at best deficient in a contextual sense—if not plain wrong. To illustrate this difficulty, and to explore some of the issues it raises, it seems useful to turn to three case studies and here, apologetically, I will use examples drawn from my own experience, with the excuse that these are topics I have had to think about.

Case study 1: Roman military archaeology and history

Roman military archaeology typifies the conjunction of abundant material evidence in the remains of Roman military sites and artifacts, with ancient written documentation, both literary and in many types of inscriptions (building, dedicatory, epitaphs, diplomata, etc.), and visual representations ("historical" relief sculpture, tombstones, and various other media) which can be encountered in classical archaeology. There are, indeed, huge areas of specialized and technical study, in the evolution and character of all kinds of material remains from frontier systems down to belt buckles, but the challenge might be posed of what types of contribution to knowledge, other than to such technical studies, might be expected from field projects on Roman military sites.

A generation ago, in the English-speaking literature especially, the construction of historical narratives was an overriding concern (Webster 1970, for the military conquest of Roman Britain, and Salway 1981, more generally for the "history" of the province, are illustrations of this approach). My personal involvement was through employment as an archaeologist for the city of Gloucester, where there was a succession of Roman military sites covering a span of some fifty years or so from the Roman invasion of Britain to the conversion of the former legionary fortress at Gloucester into a civilian settlement (*Colonia Nervia Glevensis/ium*), peopled with veteran soldiers and their families. Recognition of the nature of various military installations, first at Kingsholm (slightly north of the later city center) and then at the city center and the establishment of a chronology for their development, might seem to be straightforward archaeological tasks, and I was indeed concerned to build on the work of my predecessors toward these ends. But this work could not be done "innocently," as it were, of what both then and now seems to me to be a misguided reading of a Classical text and misdirection of research. The text is Tacitus, *Annals* 12.32, where he talks about the campaigns of the second governor of Roman Britain, Ostorius Scapula, in pursuit of the rebel British leader Caratacus, who—after being defeated in southeastern England—established himself with the Silures, a group located in southern Wales, across the river Severn from Gloucester. "Neither clemency nor force could hold down the Silures," said Tacitus, "so they needed suppressing by a legionary camp (*castrisque legionum premenda*)." It seems reasonable to infer that Tacitus, based in

Rome and constructing his history entirely from secondhand information fifty years after the situation he was describing, was here making a general statement about Roman strategic thinking, without having any particular location or military unit in Britain in mind.

This was not, however, how that passage was read by historians and archaeologists of Roman Britain. An association between the Roman wall at the city center of Gloucester and a legionary fortress was made as early as 1877 (Bellows 1877); at some point after that Gloucester became "the legionary fortress Tacitus says was built to suppress the Silures"; by the 1970s, following the archaeological demonstration that military occupation at Gloucester city center dated no earlier than the mid-60s A.D., and confirmation that Kingsholm was earlier, more elaborate interpretative structures were being built. For example, *castrisque legionum*, in the view of Webster (1970:186, n. 44) showed that more than one legion was involved; and Manning (1981:35) suggested that they might have been combined in vexillation formations (for my disagreement, see Hurst 1985:119–22). These structures were fitted into a narrative of early Roman Britain, whose objective was to locate military units in the province year-by-year and campaign-by-campaign. There was emphasis on making everything "work" in a tidy tactical way.

A further application of this thinking—which was already feeling the strain of its contradictions in the 1970s—was set out as recently as 1999, in the argument that the *colonia* at Gloucester, whose official title, *Nervia*, is likely to refer to the reign of the Emperor Nerva (from A.D. 96–98), was really founded under his predecessor Domitian and its title subsequently changed following the *damnatio memoriae* after Domitian's death. The reason was that there would be "no need for" a legionary fortress there from ca. A.D. 75, when the base of the Second Legion at Caerleon in South Wales was established; the authorities would have to do something with the site, and so the colonial foundation "must be" earlier (for a debate on this, see Hassall and Hurst 1999).

At issue is not whether the narrative is in the end right or wrong but whether it is an appropriate objective in this particular branch of Classical—or, more widely, historical—archaeology. Inappropriate is my view: this crosses the boundary from history into historical fiction and it was a waste of archaeological resources when sites were dug with such an agenda. There are archaeologically attainable and more interesting objectives in digging up early Roman imperial military sites: for example, looking at the relationship between soldiers and where they were stationed in all its dimensions or looking at all aspects of military organization (Figure 2.6). One consequence of these misapplied objectives has been a swing in recent years against the whole field of Roman military archaeology in English-speaking scholarship. Outside of Britain there has always been a more sociocultural approach to Roman military studies (admittedly partly because it was based more on the study of inscriptional evidence than the remains of military sites) and consequently the field has seen less of an upheaval (James 2002, for a review and discussion of British military archaeology; Le Bohec 1994, for a general study of the Roman army from a French viewpoint).

This example, then, shows that, to operate effectively in dealing with the archaeology of an historic period, the archaeologist has to be both a critical

Figure 2.6 Tombstone of a soldier of the XXth legion, found at Wotton, Gloucester, which could be used in constructing a "history" of the Roman military occupation of Britain. It records the personal story of a man born at Eporedia (modern Ivrea) in the Italian Alps, who ended his days in southern England. Reproduced with permission of McCarthy & Stone, CgMs Consulting. Photograph courtesy of Oxford Archaeology

historian and a technically competent archaeological fieldworker. In the end, a synthesis is made: the Roman archaeologist cannot "unknow" the historical framework which, however indirectly, has influenced his/her thinking, and if s/he pretends to do so, the results are invariably absurd. So the issue is how to control the relationship.

Case study 2: Religion in Roman North Africa: the Tophet at Carthage

Religion, and its manifestations in material remains, is a challenge throughout all archaeology—partly because, at a simple level, there are so many ambiguities but also because, in this internally constructed world of the human mind, we have perhaps traveled furthest from our ancestors. Yet, with a rich textual base in classical archaeology, starting with the references to deities of the Linear B tablets and proceeding through very full and rich expressions of religious thought, and with a wealth of imagery to refer to, surely we can overcome many of these difficulties?

The case study is the Roman use of an area of Carthage which had served as a sacrificial precinct—commonly known as the Tophet. Here from the eighth century B.C. probably until the destruction of Carthage in the second century B.C. thousands of sets of cremated human and animal remains had been buried in the ground, with stone stelae set up as markers. There were varying proportions of humans and animals both spatially within the precinct and chronologically, with a higher proportion of human remains, mostly infants from 2–3 years down to neonatal, in the later levels. Many of the latest stelae (which were not found *in situ*) had dedications in the Phoenician script using a standard expression "To Ba'al Hamon and Tanit face of Ba'al" for the dedicatees (Brown 1991; Lancel 1995). From the Roman period, over the same area, were found: a series of remains of monumental structures with walls of Roman concrete (*opus caementicium*) dating them in the second century A.D. or later; a small number of stelae with Latin dedications to Saturn; some fragments of statuary, including a head of Saturn; and a mosaic floor probably of fifth-century A.D. date, showing female winged seasons with Venus-like attributes. The prevailing interpretation was that the monumental Roman buildings were store buildings of the docks, the Saturn stelae and head represented a small cult to Saturn and the mosaic may have represented a wealthy house or market building attached to the port (Charles-Picard 1965: chapter 2).

The work done was: a resurvey and detailed plot of all visible Roman structures after cleaning but not, except on a very minor scale, excavation of the site (which had been dug at various times between the 1920s and the 1980s); a reconsideration of all publications on the site, focusing especially on the reports of Roman and later discoveries; and a re-examination of the surviving parts of the mosaics and architectural remains from the site. From the resurvey it was inferred that there were at least three monumental Roman buildings: a series of vaulted terraces; a differently-aligned building, which partly followed the clearance of the stelae with dedications to Saturn (the stelae were probably first–second century A.D. and the building not earlier than the late second century); and a third building, apparently in courtyard form with a curving side wall of the courtyard and a range of rooms at its west end. The mosaic with the Venus-like winged seasons seemed to be located at a point where the second and third buildings abutted each other. It was noted that the terraces and second building were located where sacrificial remains overwhelmingly of infant humans had been found in pre-Roman levels; the courtyard building was where sacrificial remains of a more varied sort were discovered, and the iconography of the earlier Punic stelae also differed from those on the site of the terraced building.

My interpretation was that, far from being converted into Roman docks, this area had retained its pre-Roman religious identity. The second building was a temple to Saturn (following the identification of the stelae); and the third building might have been a temple to Venus-Astarte reflecting the cult in this area in Punic times. One detail about the mosaic was that the surviving two seasons (Summer and Autumn) were seated in landscapes beside columns on which there were, respectively, a dove and a lotus flower (both attributes of Astarte); freestanding columns were also a common iconographic type of the Punic stelae from this area. Tanit is usually equated with the Roman Caelestis, as Ba'al is with Saturn, so—in view of the dedications to Ba'al Hamon and Tanit face of Ba'al on the stelae seemingly associated with human sacrifices—I inferred that this was also a cult area of Caelestis. This made me think of the account by the fifth-century A.D. Christian bishop Quodvultdeus describing the former temple of Caelestis at Carthage, which had fallen into disuse at the end of the fourth century A.D. (this account had been considered but rejected as irrelevant by earlier interpreters of the area). Influenced also by Apuleius' *Metamorphoses*, on the cult of Caelestis and the conception of her divinity as capable of taking a thousand forms, as well as by (principally) inscriptional evidence showing the merging of Caelestis with many other deities, my final suggestion was that the temples identified in the area were all of attributes of Caelestis: Caelestis-Saturn, corresponding to Tanit face of Ba'al, and Caelestis-Venus, corresponding to Tanit-Astarte (and there were other attributes suggested by additional loose finds). The focus of the Caelestis worship was suggested to be the summit of a man-made hill some 12 meters high, on whose lower slopes the remains described were located (Figure 2.7; Hurst 1999).

Again, the exact story and its veracity or otherwise are less our concern than the nature of its construction. One small point may first be made about the fieldwork—that it was entirely re-examination of what had been previously exposed: this is an important and still underrated side of re-evaluating important Classical sites. The confection here—established from a mixture of structural remains, iconographic evidence, and documents ranging from Phoenician and Latin stelae inscriptions to the texts of Apuleius and Quodvultdeus—is elaborate. In the previous case study, restraint over the synthesis between history and archaeology was urged, with the implication that such a synthesis should be done only at a rather high or general level. In this case, by contrast, I actively made direct and "low-level" syntheses between structural remains, documentary and iconographic

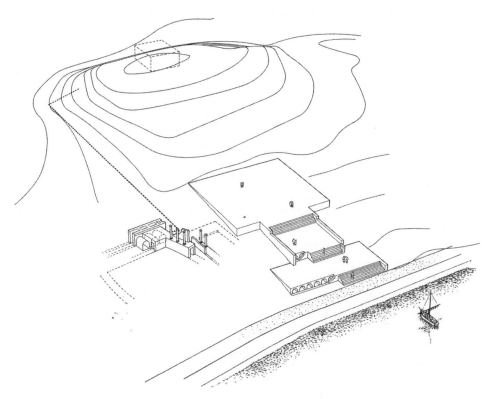

Figure 2.7 A reconstructed sacred landscape in Roman Carthage showing the slopes of a man-made hill suggested to have been dedicated to the cult of Caelestis (Carthaginian Tanit), with the harbor edge in the foreground and parts of possible temples to Venus and Saturn to the left of the main terraced approach. The dotted line shows the possible course of the city wall and sanctuary boundary. Reproduced from Hurst 1999: fig. 18, by permission

evidence and so they perhaps should be subject to the same kind of criticism. The central question, as with the other two case studies, is: what type of reconstruction of the past do we want to attempt? If we are led to believe from a reading of Quodvultdeus that there was a particularly notable temple of Caelestis at Carthage, and from general knowledge that Caelestis is a Romanized Tanit, and Tanit was the principal deity of Carthage, and if we have before us the remains of a major sanctuary to Tanit with monumental Roman constructions in the same area—then is there any realistic prospect that we could just "read" the material remains and not think about our ultimately document-based picture of the cults of Tanit and Caelestis? And if we did that, would it have any value as a contribution to knowledge? We are almost inevitably led into making guessed connections, which are only in an indirect and slow-moving way likely to be susceptible to further demonstration or refutation. In other words, we are led into a certain type of non-scientific, "humanistic" manipulation of data, which any classical archaeologist, from Bronze Age Greece through to Late Antiquity, will recognize as characteristic of their field of study.

Case study 3: Topography in the city of Rome

Appropriately enough, the archaeology of the city of Rome and the mode of its study are exceptional within classical archaeology. Here the documentary record is particularly rich, because, in addition to all the categories already encountered, many of the ancient authors who wrote in Latin whose works have survived lived in Rome, so their writings abound with incidental references to localities within the city based on personal familiarity. And, in Varro, for example, we encounter pedantic learning which is not that far removed from modern topographical scholarship. Iconographical study here is exceptionally rich through the buildings represented on coins and in monumental sculpture, and there is the unique resource of the Severan Marble Plan of Rome. Despite its depredations, Rome the Eternal City has a remarkable survival of physical remains and of images of ancient buildings going back to medieval times; and, finally, apart from the many precise dates given through historical references, for the first and second centuries A.D. in particular, many buildings have more or less precisely dated tags on them, in the form of imperial brick-stamps. The result has been the synthesis of history and archaeology we know as topography: a partly completed puzzle in which every named building of any date will ultimately be pinned on the map of Rome—or so the approach would suggest. (Such a map is the Forma Urbis Romae, established by Rodolfo Lanciani and published in eight fascicles between 1893 and 1901, Lanciani 1990 is a republication at reduced scale. Work over the last century has refined and added to this map and an electronic version is under preparation at the present time. There is also a tradition of topographical "dictionaries" to sites or buildings named in ancient texts, giving verbal accounts of literary references and archaeological finding: Platner and Ashby 1929 and Steinby 1993–2000 are the best known. For a recent set of introductory essays in English on archaeological work in Rome, see Coulston and Dodge 2000).

It might be thought that this is a classic case of losing the wood for the trees, that what we really want to know about are the broader pictures of the urban dynamics of Rome, of how its population, both rich and poor, lived and were buried, of Rome as the great consumer of resources, and so on. The topographers' answer to this could be (though mostly it would not be) that this was precisely their concern: if we could locate, say, Cicero's house on the Palatine in some physical reality, the gain would be not just a famous name on a domestic site, but all the socio-economic literary baggage that Cicero's house carries of being in the "right" part of the city for a leading public figure, of being the residence of a "novus homo" ("self-made man"), of Cicero's taste in art and architecture, and so on. So there would be a contribution to these broad historical pictures: multiply that addition of information many times and a topographical knowledge will give us an insight into the urban character and dynamics of Rome which could be achieved no other way. In a way this echoes the wider debate in archaeology of recent years between processualist and "post-processualist" approaches (Trigger 1989; Renfrew and Bahn 2000:465–72; Hodder 1999:2–3, for the basics of this debate). In its methodology Roman topography is about as "un-processualist" as it would be possible to be; so whereas twenty or thirty years ago it was utterly alien to the mainstream of archaeologists' thinking, one could now repackage it as a coming area of post-processualist thought.

On doing archaeology in this setting, if there was an innocence problem in establishing the archaeological chronology of a Roman military site in Britain, this is as nothing for anyone who puts a trowel into the soil of Rome. What material remains seem to be, or have been thought for a long time to be, are liable to be converted into something quite different when the weight of topographical learning is applied. For example, major streets whose line we thought had been established for the last century can be diverted, like the Via Sacra, or moved altogether, like the Via Nova; what we thought was the core of one of the imperial palaces, the Domus Tiberiana, can become the basement of the platform for the Temple of Divus Augustus, to name just two current areas of attention (Cecamore 2002 and Carandini 2004, for the Via Sacra; Hurst and Cirone 2003 and Wiseman 2004a, for the Via Nova; Cecamore 2002 for Divus Augustus). Discussion on such questions of identity can be fierce, and differing views have been used as instruments in the definition of rival "schools" of scholarship in Rome. It could be said quite easily that this partly reflects an imbalance between library learning and archaeological knowledge. The scholarly tradition is heavily weighted towards the former and it is, indeed, amazing how much there still is to discover by simply looking at the material remains (one reason is that many of the prestigious buildings of central Rome are published poorly, or not at all at the straightforward level of archaeological description). Also techniques of modern urban archaeology, taking for granted an ability to unravel complex stratification and record poorly preserved remains, came late to Rome and to this day are not routinely established, though there have been many fine examples of urban archaeology (among which the work on the Crypta Balbi is outstanding: Manacorda 2001). But, even with such techniques under one's belt, the problem of objectives remains.

Perhaps the best illustration of this in recent years has been the work of Andrea Carandini's team on the lower northern slopes of the Palatine Hill, next to the Forum Romanum. This has been an excavation of superlative quality and scale, revealing huge amounts of new information about the evolution of a central area of the city from the eighth century B.C. onwards. Were this excavation to have been done in nearly any historic city other than Rome, the presentation of results in straightforward archaeological terms ("this was what we found in the eighth-century level," and so on) would be, as it were, the main story. Such a presentation is offered in this case, but implicit in the way it is put forward is the impression that on its own it is not enough. Instead it is overlain by a dialogue with documented information and a reinterpretation of the whole—the Romulean walls, the *domus* of Tarquinius Superbus and of the Regis Sacrorum, the early *lucus Vestae* (the sacred grove of Vesta), and so on—and this is offered in support of a revised view of the emergence of Rome as a city (Carandini and Carafa 2000, for the site; Carandini 1997, for the view of Rome; Carandini 2004 and various authors in Workshop di archeologica classica, Vol. 1, for interpretation of the monuments and topography). The revised view is controversial, as is the interpretation of some of the archaeological discoveries, so a debate on familiar, mostly irresolvable grounds has followed, with relatively little attention having been paid so far to the actual discoveries made (see Cornell 1995, for a more "consensual" version of early Rome; Wiseman 1995; 2004b, for a radically different approach to the interpretation of early Roman myths; and Carandini 2000:88–93, for a response to critiques of his approach). For the excavator not to engage with the documentary "big picture" when presenting these results would not be a realistic option in the sense that, while the primary archaeological report might in theory (but probably not in practice) keep itself "pure," the moment it was published, the information would be manipulated by others, often from rather superficial knowledge. Better then to be realistic about the context, and to try to give a steer to interpretation from first-hand knowledge? The troubling and, in my own mind, only partly-resolved thought, is that, once one accepts that one is going to engage with the documentary "big picture," how does one manage the impact that it has on what one actually "does" archaeologically?

Conclusion

While I see classical archaeology in most aspects as simply part of a wider archaeology, I have argued for it having a distinctive character in the relationship between the study of material remains and documented information. After general, and I hope mildly anarchic, comments about setting up projects—that it is up to the individual(s) and the context in which they are working as to how they proceed, and broadly anything goes—a look was made at three types of research project which had increasingly complex relationships between material remains and documentary evidence. With the study of the Roman army, it is relatively easy to see that, while there is complementarity between historical and archaeological evidence, a synthesis directed at a history of "events" rapidly tends to fiction; other directions appear more promising. For religion in Roman Carthage, the construction of a cult model from a mixture of material, documentary and iconographic evidence seems a more central, so less resistible, task, but it ends with suggestions of the unprovable. For the topography of Rome, the very scope of the study was fixed by synthesis of observation of surviving material remains with documentary and iconographic information. This way, there is a small potential of being "right" in the sense of fitting a piece into a jigsaw, but a much larger one of being wrong; either way, the nature of the image captured in the jigsaw is under constant discussion for its wider, as well as more limited, implications. The discussion is as a rule more revealing than whether the piece is in the right or wrong position—and that seems an appropriate last thought on "doing" classical archaeology.

REFERENCES

American School of Classical Studies at Athens, n.d. The American School of Classical Studies at Athens. Electronic document, http://www.ascsa.edu.gr/.

Barker, Graeme, ed. 1996 Farming the Desert: The UNESCO Libyan Valleys Archaeological Survey, vol. 1. Synthesis. London: Society for Libyan Studies.

Bellows, J. 1877 On the Ancient Wall of Gloucester, and Some Roman Remains Found in Proximity to It, in 1873. Proceedings of the Cotteswold Naturalists' Field Club 6:154–240.

Benton, Tim 1995 Rome Reclaims its Empire. In Art and Power: Europe under the Dictators 1930–45. Dawn Ades et al. Pp. 120–129. London: Hayward Gallery.

Binford, Lewis R. 1962 Archaeology as Anthropology. American Antiquity 28:217–225.

Bintliff, John L., and Anthony M. Snodgrass 1985 The Cambridge/Bradford Boeotian Expedition: The First Four Years. Journal of Field Archaeology 12:123–161.

Blegen, Carl W., and Marion Rawson 1966 The Palace of Nestor at Pylos in Western Messenia. Princeton: published for the University of Cincinnati by Princeton University Press.

Brandt, C. J., and John B. Thornes, eds. 1996 Mediterranean Desertification and Land Use. Chichester: John Wiley & Sons, Ltd.

Brown, Susanna Shelby 1991 Late Carthaginian Child Sacrifice and Sacrificial Monuments in their Mediterranean Context. JSOT/ASOR Monograph 3. Sheffield: JSOT Press for the American Schools of Oriental Research.

Carandini, Andrea, ed. 1985 Settefinestre: Una villa schiavistica nell'Etruria Romana, 3 vols. Modena: Edizioni Panini.

——1988 Schiavi in Italia. Rome: La Nuova Italia Scientifica.

——1997 La nascità di Roma. Dei, lari, eroi, uomini all'alba di una civiltà. Turin: Einaudi.

——2000 Giornale di Scavo. Pensieri sparsi di un archaeologo. Turin: Einaudi.

——2004 Palatino, Velia e Sacra Via. Paesaggi urbani attraverso il tempo. Workshop di Archeologia Classica, Quaderni 1. Rome: Edizioni dell'Ateneo.

——, and Paolo Carafa, eds. 2000 Palatium e Sacra Via I. Prima delle mura, l'età delle mura e l'età case archaiche. Bolletino di Archeologia 31–33 (text) and 34 (plates) for 1995. Rome: Istituto Poligrafico e Zecca dello Stato.

——, and Salvatore Settis 1979 Schiavi e Padroni nell'Etruria Romana. Bari: de Donato.

Carver, Martin 2002 The Future of Field Archaeology. In Quo Vadis Archeologia? Whither European Archaelogy in the 21st Century? Z. Koblinski, ed. Pp. 118–132. Warsaw: European Science Foundation.

——2003 Archaeological Value and Evaluation. Mantua: Società Archeologica Padana.

Caskey, J. L. 1971 Investigations in Keos. Part I: Excavations and Explorations 1966–1970. Hesperia 40:359–396.

——1972 Investigations in Keos. Part II: A Conspectus of the Pottery. Hesperia 41:357–401.

Cecamore, Claudia 2002 Palatium. Topografia storica del Palatino tra III sec. a.C. e I sec. d.C. Bolletino della Commissione Archeologica Comunale di Roma, supplementi 9. Rome: L' "Erma" di Bretschneider.

Charles-Picard, Gilbert 1965 La Carthage de Saint Augustin. Résurrection du passé 12. Paris: Fayard.

Cherry, John F. 1983 Frogs Around the Pond: Perspectives on Current Archaeological Survey Projects in the Mediterranean Region. In Archaeological Survey in the Mediterranean Area. Donald R. Keller and David W. Rupp, eds. Pp. 375–415. Oxford: British Archaeological Reports.

——, Jack L. Davis, and Eleni Mantzourani 1991 Landscape Archaeology as Long-term History: Northern Keos in the Cycladic Islands from Earliest Settlement until Modern Times. Los Angeles: UCLA Institute of Archaeology.

Cornell, Tim 1995 The Beginnings of Rome: Italy and Rome from the Bronze Age to the Punic Wars (c. 1000–264 BC). London and New York: Routledge.

Coulston, Jon, and Hazel Dodge, eds. 2000 Ancient Rome: The Archaeology of the Eternal City. Oxford University School of Archaeology Monograph 54. Oxford: Oxford School of Archaeology.

Davis, Jack L. 1986 Ayia Irini: Period V. Mainz on Rhine: Philipp von Zabern.

——, ed. 1998 Sandy Pylos: An Archaeological History from Nestor to Navarino. Austin: University of Texas Press.

Dyson, Stephen 1998 Ancient Marbles to American Shores: Classical Archaeology in the United States. Philadelphia: University of Pennsylvania Press.

Ennabli, A., ed. 1992 Pour sauver Carthage. Exploration et conservation de la cité punique, romaine et byzantine. Paris and Tunis: UNESCO/INAA.

Flannery, Kent V. 1973 Archaeology with a Capital "S." In Research and Theory in Current Archaeology. Charles L. Redman, ed. Pp. 47–53. New York: John Wiley & Sons, Ltd.

Gill, David W. J., and Christopher Chippindale 1993 Material and Intellectual Consequences of Esteem for Cycladic Figures. American Journal of Archaeology 97:601–659.

Hamilakis, Yiannis, and Eleana Yalouri 1996 Antiquities as Symbolic Capital in Modern Greek Society. Antiquity 70:117–129.

Hassall, Mark, and Henry R. Hurst 1999 Soldier and Civilian: A Debate on the Bank of the Severn. In The Coloniae of Roman Britain: New Studies and a Review. Henry R. Hurst, ed., Pp. 181–190. Journal of Roman Archaeology Supplementary Series 36. Portsmouth, R.I.: Journal of Roman Archaeology.

Hellenic Ministry of Culture, n.d. Hellenic Culture. Electronic document, http://www.culture.gr/

Hodder, Ian 1999 The Archaeological Process: An Introduction. Oxford: Blackwell.

Hurst, Henry R. 1985 Kingsholm. Gloucester Archaeological Reports 1. Cambridge: Gloucester Archaeological Publications.

——1999 The Sanctuary of Tanit at Carthage in the Roman Period: A Reinterpretation. Journal of Roman Archaeology Supplementary Series 30. Portsmouth, R.I.: Journal of Roman Archaeology.

——, and Dora Cirone 2003 Excavation of the Pre-Neronian Nova Via, Rome. Papers of the British School at Rome 71:17–84.

James, Simon 2002 Writing the Legions: The Past, Present and Future of Roman Military Studies in Britain. Archaeological Journal 159:1–58.

Jameson, Michael H., Curtis N. Runnels, and Tjeerd H. van Andel 1994 A Greek Countryside: The Southern Argolid from Prehistory to the Present Day. Stanford: Stanford University Press.

Lancel, Serge 1995 Carthage: A History. Antonia Nevill trans. Oxford: Blackwell.

Lanciani, Rodolfo 1990 Forma Urbis Romae. With an introduction by Filippo Coarelli. Rome: Quasar.

Le Bohec, Yann 1994 The Imperial Roman Army. London: B. T. Batsford.

Manacorda, Daniele 2001 Crypta Balbi: archeologia e storia di un paesaggio urbano. Milan: Electa.

Manning, William H. 1981 Report on the Excavations at Usk 1965–1976: The Fortress Excavations 1968–71. Cardiff: University of Wales Press.

McDonald, William A., and George R. Rapp, Jr., eds. 1972 The Minnesota Messenia Expedition: Reconstructing a Bronze Age Regional Environment. Minneapolis: University of Minnesota Press.

Miraj, Lida, and Moikom Zeqo 1993 Conceptual Changes in Albanian Archaeology. Antiquity 67:123–125.

Patterson, Helen, ed. 2004 Bridging the Tiber: Approaches to Regional Archaeology in the Middle Tiber Valley. Archaeological Monographs of the British School at Rome 13. London: British School at Rome.

Platner, Samuel Ball, and Thomas Ashby 1929 A Topographical Dictionary of Ancient Rome. London: Oxford University Press.

Potter, Tim W. 1979 The Changing Landscape of South Etruria. London: Elek.

Pluciennik, Mark, and Quentin Drew 2000 "Only Connect": Global and Local Networks, Contexts, and Fieldwork. Ecumene 7:67–104.

Renfrew, Colin 1972 The Emergence of Civilisation: The Cyclades and the Aegean in the Third Millennium B.C. London: Methuen.

——, ed. 1973 The Explanation of Culture Change: Models in Prehistory. Pittsburgh: University of Pittsburgh Press.

——, and Paul Bahn 2000 Archaeology: Theories, Methods and Practice 3rd edition. London: Thames and Hudson.

——, and Malcolm Wagstaff, eds. 1982 An Island Polity: The Archaeology of Exploitation in Melos. Cambridge: Cambridge University Press.

Roma, continuità . . . 1981 Roma, Continuità dell'Antico: i fori imperiali nel progetto della città. Milan: Electa.

Salway, Peter 1981 Roman Britain: The Oxford History of Britain 1A. Oxford: Clarendon Press.

Scobie, Alex 1990 Hitler's State Architecture: The Impact of Classical Antiquity. College Art Association Monograph. 45. University Park and London: Pennsylvania State University Press.

Shaw, Wendy M. K. 2003 Possessors and Possessed: Museums, Archaeology, and the Visualization of History in the Late Ottoman Empire. Berkeley: University of California Press.

Steinby, Eva Margareta, ed. 1993–2000 Lexicon Topographicum Urbis Romae, 6 vols. Rome: Quasar.

Traill, David A. 1995 Schliemann of Troy: Treasure and Deceit. London: John Murray.

Trigger, Bruce G. 1989 A History of Archaeological Thought. Cambridge: Cambridge University Press.

Webster, Graham 1970 The Military Situations in Britain between AD 43 and 71. Britannia 1:179–199.

Wilkes, John 1992 The Illyrians. Oxford: Basil Blackwell.

Wiseman, T. P. 1995 Remus: A Roman Myth. Cambridge: Cambridge University Press.

——2004a Where Was the *Nova Via*? Papers of the British School at Rome 72:167–184.

——2004b The Myths of Rome. Exeter: Exeter University Press.

Wright, James C., John F. Cherry, Jack L. Davis, Eleni Mantzourani, Susan B. Sutton, and Robert F. Sutton, Jr. 1990 The Nemea Valley Archaeological Project 1984–1987: A Preliminary Report. Hesperia 59:579–659.

Yalouri, Eleana 2001 The Acropolis: Global Fame, Local Claim. Oxford: Berg.

3

Human Ecology and the Classical Landscape

Introduction

Art and artifacts tell us a great deal about people, but how can we understand those people unless we know something about the physical world in which they lived? And how can we know anything about the physical world when the best we have are organic residues?

Until comparatively recently, archaeologists had little choice but to assume that the physical environment of the past was like the physical environment of the present or to speculate about major episodes of climatic or vegetational change. Dramatic fantasies of massive deforestation were traded against conservative pictures that held that if there had ever been significant change in the landscape, it had happened long before the classical period.

Initial advances in our understanding of the changing environment came from geomorphology. Geomorphological change is a prerequisite of excavation: without the accumulation of soil on top of archaeological sites, there would be no stratigraphy, no possibility of sorting out different phases of occupation. In an early example, 19th-century excavations of the site of Olympia, which lies at the confluence of two major rivers, the Alpheus and the Cladeus, in the western Peloponnese, alerted archaeologists to a major episode of alluviation in late antiquity. In the 1970s, the geographer Claudio Vita-Finzi investigated similar episodes of major alluviation across the Mediterranean, and argued that the more or less simultaneous laying down of thick layers of alluvium over a wide area indicated a significant climate change. Since then, much work has been devoted to better understanding these episodes and the relative role of human action and climatic factors in bringing them about, and few today would endorse Vita-Finzi's universalizing picture.

One major advance that has contributed to a better understanding of the processes of geomorphological change has come from the work of palynologists, studying pollen preserved in waterlogged environments, and from the recovery through sieving of assemblages of seeds and other plant remains from archaeological sites. Together pollen cores and botanical analysis have offered windows onto local environments and indications of the part changing agricultural practices have played in transforming the plant communities among which human and animal communities live and upon which they depend.

Making sense of the data produced by experts in the identification of pollen and seeds, however, depends upon understanding the ecosystem more generally, and this can come only from the study of contemporary ecosystems. Our knowledge of the classical landscape is directly dependent upon our understanding of plant communities and their interaction with agricultural and other human activities today. Just as anthropology is sometimes seen as a "present past" which can serve as a laboratory in which what was possible in the past can be experimentally determined, so the contemporary environment and understanding of traditional agriculture within that environment serve as a laboratory against which our claims about the environment of classical antiquity must be tested. This chapter takes up the challenge not simply of describing the natural environment but of exploring the human ecology, the changing and in some aspects distinct ways in which Greek and Roman societies related to and interacted with that environment.

3

Human Ecology and the Classical Landscape

Greek and Roman Worlds

Lin Foxhall, Martin Jones and Hamish Forbes

The classical world brings together two societies linked by text and ideas, and the considerable influence of one upon the other. This chapter looks at human ecology—the modes of engagement of Greek and Roman societies with their respective environments. We are here using "ecology" in its precise sense as the study of the interaction between an organism and its environment, in other words, not the direct study of an external world of nature, but more specifically of modes of engagement with that world. The texts that survive from both Greek and Roman sources portray an ecological stance that has persisted in subsequent western intellectual traditions. It is one in which control and mastery of nature are emphasized, and these in turn underpin the central notion of "civilization": aspects of the environment over which humans could not exercise control, such as weather conditions were conceptually allocated to the realm of the supernatural, being associated with the gods.

These two societies brought that notion of control and mastery to a common environmental context, the "Mediterranean region," a region whose ample ecological resources are fragmented through space and time by abrupt topography and marked seasonality. Much of their means of controlling nature entailed the connecting and combining of these fragments to form a coherent whole as the annual agrarian cycle unfolded. It involved ameliorating, containing and slowing down the abrupt distribution of rainfall on the ground by careful management of soil and small plots, and judicious use of trees. It entailed an exploitation of altitudinal variation for different forms of woodland and different seasons of grazing. It required a selection of plant and animal domesticates which themselves were adapted to the spatially and temporally fragmented nature of Mediterranean ecology.

However, the two cultures also display marked ecological differences. This is immediately evident from the geography of their sites. Classical Greek sites are concentrated in regions that would, in broad climatic and topographic terms, be described as "Mediterranean." It has been observed that the florescence of Greek society and the olive tree, a species often used to delineate the Mediterranean region, are broadly coincident. Roman settlements also have a strong Mediterranean epicenter, but their range is quite different. During the imperial period they spread extensively across Atlantic Europe in modern-day Spain, France, and Britain, and in the south, penetrated into desert regions of Africa. The political and military dimensions of these differences in pattern are well known; the ecological dimension is becoming clearer as textual evidence is increasingly being augmented by environmental archaeology. In this chapter we explore that ecological dimension, and in particular the contrast between a Greek society whose mastery of nature entailed the negotiation with one particular environmental region, the Mediterranean, and Roman society, whose style of mastery was in part transferable to some quite contrasting environmental zones.

The Mediterranean Context of Greek Society

By the beginning of the fifth century B.C., the Greek heartland, the territory which now comprises mainland and island Greece and the west coast of modern Turkey, was only a small portion of the Greek world. From the eighth century onward Greeks had established communities spreading east–west across the Mediterranean from the Levant to southern France and Spain, and north–south from southern Russia to North Africa. In the course of this great diaspora, Greeks encountered numerous other cultures, from which they borrowed some elements and to which they donated others in the course of adapting to these new places. Although most of these Greek communities, especially those which had dispersed from the Greek heartland, were set in environments which were broadly "Mediterranean" in terms of their climate, geography, and vegetation, and Greek culture only rarely ranged beyond this zone, there is a huge range of local variation even over very short distances. The consequence is that though some practices were common over a wide area, Greeks exploited the environments they inhabited in many different ways, depending on both local traditions and local conditions.

In both the northern and southern hemispheres, all areas with Mediterranean-type climates are on or close to the 35° latitude lines and bordering the sea (Grove and Rackham 2001:11 and figure 1.2). Ancient Greek settlement in fact ranged somewhat beyond the fringe of land surrounding the Mediterranean Sea. Often the limits of the olive's cold tolerance are perceived as defining the extent of the Mediterranean zone, though this is something of an over-simplification (Grove and Rackham 2001:11). Certainly it is true that the olive and Greek culture have flourished in most of the same places. Although Mediterranean climates are often said to be characterized by cool, wet winters and hot, dry summers, variability is its most obvious characteristic: Europe's driest and wettest places are both found in this zone. Landforms are equally varied, but a rugged, often mountainous topography in conjunction with a diverse land–sea interface is particularly characteristic. This is primarily the result of recent tectonic activity, which has also been responsible for the relative fertility of soils in comparison to those of other Mediterranean-type environments. Although frost-free areas are the exception, at least in Mediterranean Europe, only the high mountains regularly experience intense frosts (Grove and Rackham 2001:25, 28, 37–44, 47). The combined effect is that—while the basic ingredients of life (sunshine, water, and soil-nutrients) are for the most part plentifully available—they are discretely packaged in space (altitude) and time (seasons). Negotiation with altitude and season has thus been central to Mediterranean ecological strategies. Summers are largely sunny with temperatures often over 30°C, and in many areas at altitudes under 200 meters above sea level even dew is rare. Summer temperatures are generally cooler at higher altitudes, and places only a few kilometers distant from each other but differing by several hundred meters in altitude can differ perceptibly in temperature.

Precipitation in the Mediterranean is characterized by its unpredictability, and this has important implications for agriculture in the region. Generally the bulk of the year's rainfall occurs between mid-September and April and rainfall events may be very unevenly distributed over this time. Even over the summer, occasionally a sudden, violent thunderstorm may result in flash floods or damaging hailstorms. In addition, rainfall in any particular area may vary dramatically from year to year. And, often over short distances, especially over changes in altitude and aspect (the direction a place faces and to which it is exposed), rainfall can vary quite substantially from one place to another. Generally, precipitation increases (and the length of the dry season decreases) with altitude, although the degree of increase with altitude varies greatly according to other factors (Grove and Rackham 2001:26). It also varies in relation to rain-bearing winds. West-facing locations such as the island of Kerkyra (modern Corfu) are usually wetter than east facing ones such as Attica and the Cyclades. Absolute amounts of annual precipitation rarely exceed 1000 mm except in the more northerly parts of the region, and at high altitudes. In most parts of southern Greece, Italy, and Spain, average annual rainfall ranges between 400–650 mm, though in some significant places this figure is lower. Athens averages 385 mm per year, Thera (modern Santorini) in the Cyclades, 357 mm (Grove and Rackham 2001:24–28). These low rainfall figures place Attica and the Cyclades close to the limits for non-irrigated cereal cultivation. In addition, areas with the lowest average precipitation have the greatest inter-annual variability, hence the greatest risk of serious crop failure. In these areas, therefore, cereal agriculture depended particularly heavily on drought-tolerant barley, rather than wheat (see below, p. 102).

Having a rainfall regime characterized for the most part by relatively low annual rainfall and a prolonged summer drought, the Mediterranean basin contains few substantial permanently flowing rivers. Some of the exceptions to this rule include the Tagus in Iberia, the Tiber and Po in Italy and the Eurotas in Greece. Many so-called rivers and streams in the region have always been at best seasonal, flowing only through the winter months. Others only flow during, and immediately following, storms. Small springs, therefore, tend to be particularly important as reliable sources of water. Since these are heavily dependent on the existence of suitable impermeable strata in the geology, their distribution is highly irregular.

Where permanent rivers or springs do not exist, an area's inhabitants have been dependent on underground supplies of water. The history of well-digging in the Mediterranean has been little studied. In the Athenian Agora wells went in and out of use from the Mycenaean period onwards, although extravagant claims have sometimes been made about the significance of well-digging activity (Camp 1979, 1982) and two fountain houses there, one built in the sixth century B.C. and one in the fourth century B.C., exploited water piped in from nearby springs for public use. The origins and development of underground cisterns as a means of storing winter rainwater are even less well understood, but both were known by the Archaic and Classical periods in Greece and the bottle-shaped cistern became an established feature of Athenian houses by the fourth century B.C. (Camp 1982:12).

The lack of large, permanently flowing rivers comparable to the Nile in Egypt or the Tigris and Euphrates in the Middle East meant that virtually all agriculture in the ancient Greek world was rainfall-dependent: only after the establishment of their rule in Egypt in the late fourth century B.C. were Greeks interested in irrigation agriculture. Tree crops, vines, and even summer field crops (see below) were therefore dependent on the application of careful cultivation techniques to ensure effective rainwater penetration of the soil during the winter, and to minimize soil moisture losses during the summer. Unlike the Romans, the Greeks do not seem to have had a developed technology for raising water from lower levels for irrigation, at best only using a swipe (*shaduf*)—a counterbalanced lever—to ease the lifting of buckets from shallow wells. Irrigation therefore tended to depend on diverting water from springs where this could be managed, or to be very small-scale pot-irrigation from wells or even cisterns, probably only useful for small gardens.

Greeks used large amounts of water for some industrial processes, such as in the ore-washeries at Laurion in Attica, but they did not use the force of running water to power machinery such as grain mills or olive mills. Their failure to do so was probably one of outlook, not simply a result of the lack of suitable water supplies: in medieval and later Greece, seasonal streams were used to provide the motive force for a variety of operations, milling grain, processing olives and processing textiles included. By contrast, the Romans were prepared to exploit the natural force of running water in a number of ways. Water mills for grinding cereals are well attested, and the Roman writer Vitruvius mentions *noria*, a water-powered machine for lifting water for use in irrigation on a substantial scale. The latter may well have been initially developed by Middle Eastern societies, but as with the moldboard plow (see below), the Romans saw its potential and introduced it elsewhere. The Romans' predilection for machinery to replace human-powered operations also led to their use of the *saqiya*—an animal-powered water-lifting device used for irrigation—and to the development of the donkey-mill, as seen at Pompeii, for grinding grain. In their attitudes towards the forces of nature, there seems to have been a fundamental difference between the Greeks and the Romans: Greeks attempted to domesticate them while the Romans tried to subjugate and harness them.

The present Mediterranean climate has existed barely longer than the first appearance of agricultural communities some 8,000 years ago, so it is incorrect to consider present plant communities as highly climatically adapted (Grove and Rackham 2001:45). Even before this time, environments were exploited by hunters and gatherers, and by 6,000 years ago agriculture was widespread. Hence the Mediterranean ecosystems that we observe today are, for the most part, creations of human culture. It is therefore impossible to point to pristine "natural" environments unaffected by human activities. Plant communities are highly diverse, with a key variable being the ability to withstand conditions of drought, high evaporation levels, and thin soils. It is, nonetheless, still possible to discern an altitudinal zonation that would broadly correspond to climatic "climax vegetation," insofar as such a term is appropriate in such an intensely modified landscape. Along coasts and at lower altitudes, evergreen woodland of Aleppo pines and evergreen oaks persist in those few areas not entirely transformed by clearance, settlement, and agriculture. Above the Mediterranean "olive line," the sharp Mediterranean seasonality is in places ameliorated so that a range of deciduous trees can flourish, such as chestnut, ash, and deciduous oak. These deciduous woodlands tend to have a long history of economic exploitation. At higher altitudes still, beech woods may flourish, and in many places the constrained growing season once again favors evergreen woodland; fir and pine prevail up to the tree line.

Millennia of human action have modified this altitudinal zonation in four principal ways. First, it may have completely cleared and replaced it with settlement and farmland, particularly at lower altitudes. Second, the deciduous woodlands in particular have been continuously managed for nuts, leafy fodder, building material, and fuel, transforming both their composition and form. Third, a range of extensive forms of exploitation, particularly grazing, has shifted the altitudinal positions of each of the zone transitions, up to and including the tree line. Fourth, a similar range of exploitation, and also cycles of abandonment, have stimulated a distinct range of vegetation forms, variously described around the Mediterranean as *maquis* and *garrigue* (France), *macchia* and *garriga* (Italy), *thamnoi* and *phrygana* (Greece). *Maquis/macchia* refers to a diverse composition of low growing, mostly evergreen shrubs, which are primarily tree species reduced to a low height via anthropogenic factors such as cutting and grazing. *Garrigue/garriga* refers to an equally diverse community of low-growing, tough, and often spiny aromatic herbs, generally determined by low rainfall, thin soil, and largely impenetrable bedrock (Grove and Rackham 2001:48–59).

The Mediterranean zone has probably never seen a simple altitudinal zonation of climatically determined woodlands, as both the diversity of bedrock types, and the contingencies of rapid climatic and tectonic events in a rugged terrain have always ensured a complex mosaic of woodland, scrubby vegetation, and bare rock.

However, the complexity of that variation has undoubtedly been enhanced, and exploited by human action.

Adaptations to the Mediterranean in the Classical Greek World

In the Greek texts, as in the later Roman texts, the land holdings of wealthy farmers are inevitably far better attested than those of small-scale farmers. One of our most important documents for demonstrating the scattered landholdings of rich Greek men is the so-called "Attic Stelae" of fifth-century B.C. Athens. These Athenian inscriptions (*Inscriptiones Graecae*, I³ 420–430; Pritchett 1956; Amyx 1958) record the auctioning of the property of some of Athens' wealthiest and most eminent citizens and metics (resident aliens) implicated in the major religious and political scandals of 415 B.C. (Thucydides 6.27–29, 60–61). The culprits had ample warning of their impending arrest and most appear to have disposed of or hidden as much of their property as possible before they fled Attica. Therefore, it is likely that the imperfectly preserved lists represent only the relatively worthless items or property which they could not hide (some of which is plainly quite valuable), not the full extent of their estates. Even so, it is possible to catch a glimpse of the wide range of agricultural and other property which a wealthy citizen might own, and its geographical spread.

The texts summarized in Tables 3.1 and 3.2 show the property listed under the names of two different men, Adeimantos, son of Leukolophides of Skambonidai, and Axiochos, son of Alcibiades of Skambonidai. Adeimantos owned land in at least two different parts of Attica, and it appears to have been divided into a minimum of six different plots. He also owned land abroad in Thasos, which itself may well have been divided into smaller plots. Axiochos owned land in at least seven different places in Attica (and some of these holdings must have consisted of several separate plots), as well as land overseas in Abydos, Klazomenai, and elsewhere. However imperfect our knowledge of the full range of their property, it is clear that in both these estates, agricultural land and enterprises were extremely important sources of wealth and income for these men, and that the range of their agricultural activities was diverse, and covered a wide range of different environments. But, despite the fact that these were some of the richest men in Athens, their properties are miniscule in scale compared to the vast provincial estates of wealthy Romans.

Managing Soils: Terracing and Drainage

In ancient Greek, the word *chora* meant a piece of land of any size from the entire territory of a *polis* to a tiny field. Today and in the recent past, the agrarian landscapes of Greece and many other parts of the Mediterranean are characterized by fields in small areas of plains land, combined with a patchwork of terraces on the hill slopes (Figure 3.1). However, it is not clear that the fields of classical

Table 3.1 Surviving possessions in the Attic Stelae: Adeimantos son of Leukolophides of Skambonidai

Source		Possessions
IG I³ 422	187–190	4 shadufs and a large trough on land in Xypete
	182–186	land (specifications and location lost)
	178–181	land (specifications and location lost)
IG I³ 426		[skilled slaves and equipment—prices missing]
	10–39	Phrygian man
		a man, Apollophanes
		Charias, *obeliskopoios* [spit or nail maker]
		Aristarchos, *skutotomos* [leather worker]
		his equipment: small table, 2 couches, table, sleeping pallets, building timber, and 8 unpreserved and unidentified items
		Satyros, *skutotomos* [leather worker]
		[3 lines missing and 3 lines that seem to have been equipment]
	44–51	[Thasian farm specializing in vines]
	44	man, Aristomachos [bailiff?]
	45–46	land and *oikia* in Thasos in I–
		large numbers of good and bad pithoi with lids
		590 (?) amphoras of wine (capacity: 3 *choai*)=8.64 liters each = 5,098 liters of wine total
	106–107	income from rents on land that had been owned by Adeimantos (cf. line 100): 1632 dr., 4 ob. [if a rent of around 8% of the capital value is assumed, this makes for a capital value of about 3 T, 2408 dr]
	142	something unidentifiable worth 520+ dr.
IG I³ 430 a	1–4	"oakery" and "pinery" and *oikia* in B–, 8 pithoi in the *oikia*, and Kudimachos, slave of Adeimantos [who presumably managed the "oakery" and "pinery"]
	10–12	harvested crops [cereals or other arable?], worth 50 dr., from land in Ophryneion
	27–28	Satyros [slave], 170 dr.

Note: T = talents, dr. = drachma, ob. = obol.

Greece were farmed in the same way. Among the few descriptions that we have in ancient literature and inscriptions of ancient fields, there are no unambiguous references to terraces or terrace walls (Foxhall 1996). In contrast, there are numerous references to other techniques for soil management on steep slopes. Although several scholars claim to have discovered terraces dating to the classical period (Bradford 1956; 1957; Lohmann 1992), the chronological evidence for most of these is insecure. The most convincing are the carefully excavated classical terraces on the island of Delos (Brunet 1999). Indeed, it is not certain, except in very unusual circumstances, that an agricultural terrace from classical times would easily survive to the present day. Mediterranean hillsides are landscapes which have been repeatedly re-sculpted by a combination of the people who

Table 3.2   Surviving possessions in the Attic Stelae:
Axiochos son of Alcibiades of Skambonidai

Source		Possession
IG I³ 422	194–204	[slaves]
		Arete, Thracian woman (361 dr., for all 3?)
		Grulion, Thracian man
		Habrosune, Thracian woman
		Dionysios, Scythian bronze smith (155 dr.)
		income from rents on fields (*choria*) in Tho—which had been owned by Axiochos, 150 dr. [if a rent of around 8% of the capital value is assumed, this makes for a capital value of 1875 dr.]
IG I³ 424	10–16	apartment house
		total of houses [*oikiai*]—large sum of money not preserved
		foreign agricultural land—details not preserved
IG I³ 426	101–102	income from rents on land owned by Axiochos
	108–111	1633 dr. 2.5 ob. [if a rent of around 8% of the capital value is assumed, this makes for a capital value of about 3 T, 2417 dr.]
		item not preserved, more rents? 250 dr.
		item not preserved, more rents? 162 dr, 4 ob.
IG I³ 427	52–85	[equipment and fittings from a country house]
		5 *phidaknai* [small pithoi]: 9 dr; 11 dr.; 4 dr., 4 ob.; 4 dr., 3 ob; 4 dr.
		funnel [no price, goes with next item?]
		lead pipe 2 dr., 2 ob.
		written board/picture 60 dr.
		another small one 6 dr., 4 ob.
		painted (?) picture 5+ dr.
		land that had belonged to Axiochos ... [further details missing]
		[poorly preserved entry] 2040 dr. (?)
		[poorly preserved entry] 1590 dr. (?)
		area of land (in *plethra*) with *oikia* in the country site, another at Emporia [no price]
		3 *plethra* arable land with vines 1900 dr. [goes with last item?]
		oikia in the countryside [*agroi*]
		another piece of arable land, with olives (?), 3 *plethra* 6100 dr.
		[something unidentifiable] with vines; [something unidentifiable] in Abydos 310 dr.
		[something unidentifiable] in Klazomenai 200 dr.
IG I³ 430	6–7	a man, Olas 195 dr.
	8–9	Messenian man 130 dr.
	24–25	Keph– [slave] 195 dr.
	33–35	crops in the field (?) 20 dr.

Note: T = talents, dr. = drachma, ob. = obol.

Figure 3.1 Terraced landscape in modern Methana. Photo: Hamish Forbes

worked the fields and natural forces such as tectonic activity, forest fires, floods, wind, erosion, and alluviation. Terraces are therefore inherently unstable anthropogenic features in an unstable landscape, which are continuously being built and re-built, even in more recent periods.

The main purposes of terracing are to get rid of the rocks, hold soil in place, create a level area for cultivation and, critically, both to ensure the drainage of the erratic rainfall into the soil and reduce the amount of potentially erosive run-off flowing downhill. Many of these aims can be achieved by other means. In the absence of terraces, many hill slopes were planted with trees and vines (Theophrastos, *De Causis Plantarum* 3.6.7). The trees themselves helped to hold the soil in place. Wealthy farmers who had slave labor available were able to dig trenches around trees, shaped like basins sloping in towards the trunk, which caught precious rainwater and kept it where it would most benefit the tree. In areas where drainage was a problem in winter, these basins around trees could be connected by ditches dug across the slope (Theophrastos, *De Causis Plantarum* 3.6.3–4). Repeated digging around trees also removed weeds which would compete for moisture and nutrients, and kept the top layer of soil dry and crumbly, thus reducing the loss of water from lower soil levels via capillary action and evaporation. Theophrastos, writing about plants in the fourth century B.C., was clearly familiar with this practice and recommended a regime of regular digging around trees three times throughout the year (Theophrastos, *De Causis Plantarum* 3.12.2;

3.16.2, 3). The practice is also stipulated in land leases (Rhodes and Osborne 2003:no.59, from Amorgos; see also Osborne 1987:42–43). Indeed, repeated plowing and digging were considered the best way to work land for arable crops as well as for trees, though this would have needed much labor, possibly more than a poorer household could manage on its own without the help of slave labor.

Cultivation Technologies and Techniques: Plows and Plowing

The tools of ancient Greek farming were basic. Simple ard plows were appropriate for the shallow soils of the Mediterranean region: deep digging can be counter-productive and can damage the soil structure in these environments. Harrows and wooden mallets were used for breaking up clods after plowing. Mattocks and wide-bladed hoes were important for digging on small plots and around trees (the Greeks did not have spades or shovels). With sickles, axes, and adzes, pruning knives, winnowing forks, and baskets, and sometimes basic threshing sledges, this comprised virtually the entire repertoire. Very little metal was used in their manu-facture, and even implements such as plows might be almost entirely made of wood. Though sickle blades were sometimes made of metal, the teeth could also be triangular flakes of obsidian (volcanic glass) set in a wooden haft—even stone tools still had their place. Transport and other motive power were supplied by cattle, donkeys and mules. Much of the agricultural machinery of classical times, such as wine and oil presses, was simple and modular—assembled for the job in hand then taken apart so that the components could be used for other tasks (Figure 3.2).

Crops were generally grown in a two-year rotation system: cereals were grown on the field in alternate years. It is generally assumed that in the year following a crop nothing was grown and the land was left fallow. In temperate regions, fal-lowing is used primarily to conserve and restore soil fertility, and to prevent the build-up of pests and diseases. This would also have been the case in the ancient Mediterranean, but in addition, fallow land with weeds growing on it could also be an important resource for grazing. In the dryer parts of the Mediterranean multiple plowing of fallow land in spring and summer was sometimes practiced to conserve soil moisture. Plowing ensured that weed growth did not consume moisture trapped in the soil from the winter rains, the broken top levels of soil acting as a blanket to stop the loss of water by capillary action and evaporation.

On occasions, however, land was not left fallow in the year following a wheat or barley crop. A number of types of winter-sown leguminous (pulse) crops were known in antiquity (Isager and Skydsgaard 1992:42). It is likely that these were sometimes alternated with cereals. Greeks and Romans recognized the abili-ties of some leguminous crops to replace nitrogen in the soil. In addition, a range of spring-sown crops, such as chick peas and millet (see below, p. 103) could be grown unirrigated in plowed fallow land as well as a limited range of summer vegetables.

(a)

(b)

Figure 3.2 (a) Beam press, probably for wine; (b) Installation for treading grapes located in the Methana countryside. Photo by Lin Foxhall; (c) (Overleaf) Reconstruction of an ancient olive press. Drawing: Hamish Forbes; (d) Wine presses from the imperial Roman villa at Settefinestre, Toscana

(c)

(d)

Figure 3.2 *Continued*

The most important cereal in much of the Greek world was barley. It is more tolerant of drought, alkaline and slightly saline conditions than wheat. Although it is sensitive to frost, this is not generally a relevant factor in lowland Mediterranean environments where low rainfall is commonest. The drawbacks are, first, that most types of barley grown in classical Greece had hulls which took considerable pounding to remove (although they protected the kernel from pests in storage) and second that it is not well suited to bread-making, at least to the styles of bread becoming popular. Wheat was considered a much more desirable cereal by Greeks, because of its bread-making qualities, and many varieties were grown in classical antiquity. Because it does not produce as prolifically in less than optimal conditions, it was something of a "luxury" cereal—perhaps not eaten as an everyday food by poorer people. One variety of wheat was spring sown, and was sometimes used as an emergency crop if the autumn rains had been inadequate. In areas with deep, water-retentive soils, broomcorn and foxtail millets (sown in the spring) were also grown, though they were not as important as wheat and barley. In addition to winter- and spring-sown legumes (see above, p. 100), other field crops regularly grown included sesame, fenugreek, and in damp areas with good soil, flax for both linseed and for rope and textiles.

For arable crops the field was plowed and sown in the autumn, after the onset of the winter rains had sufficiently softened the ground. The sower would walk in front of the plowman scattering the seed broadcast, while the plow breaks up the soil and covers it over. Cereals sown at higher altitudes and/or in colder locations need up to two months more growing time than those planted at lower altitudes and/or in warmer locations. This is where the Greek habit of holding fragmented plots could be advantageous: farmers could spread out the work of the busy sowing and harvest seasons by having plots in both cooler, wetter, higher places and warmer, dryer lower ones. This also incidentally spread the risks of crop failure: in dry years grain on damper plots grew better, while in wet years dryer plots might produce more.

Important by-products of arable crops included chaff and straw which were used for animal fodder, and in the latter case also for stable bedding. Grain was normally harvested close to the ear, so the straw left in the field was generally quite long. This could be gathered separately, or it could have been used for grazing as stubble. The haulms (stalks) of leguminous crops also made nutritious fodder. Unsuccessful crops of cereals or legumes might be harvested early for fodder or hay, though sometimes crops, such as vetch, were grown specifically for hay.

Arboriculture

Although polycropping, growing trees with arable crops in between, has regularly been practiced in the recent past in the Mediterranean, it may have been less common in classical antiquity, at least on the plots of wealthy farmers, because of the habit of trenching around trees. Theophrastos certainly understood that repeated digging around trees throughout the year, to direct water to the roots, retained soil moisture and eliminated weed growth, improving the productivity of the tree. In consequence, he did not generally recommend polycropping.

Olives, vines, and figs, like most fruit trees, do not grow true to type from seed. The Greeks propagated them vegetatively using cuttings, ovules (growths at the bases of old olive trees), and grafting. Theophrastos (*De Causis Plantarum* 1.6.1–10) has a long and detailed discussion of grafting techniques, which farmers clearly used with considerable sophistication. Sometimes farmers used the wild forms of olives, figs, or pears as rootstock because they were vigorous and well adapted to drought conditions, and grafted choice domestic varieties onto them.

Beyond the primary output of fruit, there were many important by-products of arboriculture. Branches pruned, or leaves collected from, olives, vines, and other fruit trees were an important source of fodder for animals (Foxhall 1998). When all the leaves had been eaten, the branches could then be cut and stored for fuel. Vine prunings in particular made excellent fuel for kilns and ovens. Fallen fruit (e.g., maggot-infested figs, olives which fell prematurely) and almond husks were also important supplements for animals in late summer and early autumn when grazing was scarce. The residue from the pressing of grapes made nutritious fodder, and the residue from olive pressing could be used for either fodder or fuel. Details of arboricultural practice are now coming to light through extensive archaeobotanical analyses of such sites as the Hellenistic farmsteads at Kompoloi and Tria Platania in Southern Macedonia (Margaritis and Jones in press).

Gardens

The Greeks were enamored with plants and flowers, and grew them ornamentally in gardens (Osborne 1992). Unlike Roman or modern gardens, Greek gardens were not attached to houses, but were simply small, accessible plots of land, often situated along roads and surrounded by trees. They also differed from our gardens in that they were based on trees and contained mostly "economic" plants, but grown in an ornamental way. Just as Greeks were partial to grid-planned towns and rural landscapes where this was possible, they also preferred grid-planned gardens: timber or fruit trees arranged in orderly rows, sometimes with vines or other climbing plants growing up them and flowers growing in between, protected by the shade from the burning summer sun. Flowers, such as roses, violets, and lilies, also had economic uses, for perfume, garlands, and flavoring.

Small garden plots were one of the few settings in which small-scale irrigation might have been possible, using a spring, well, or cistern, perhaps in combination with some kind of water lifting device, such as the shadufs mentioned in the Attic Stelae. This would have allowed the cultivation of cucumbers, flax, greens, and other vegetable crops over the hot summer. However, judicious use of plowed fallow on deep soils would allow the summer vegetables to exploit two years of rainfall, if planted far apart and constantly weeded (Figure 3.3). Theophrastos (*Historia Plantarum* 2.7.5; *De Causis Plantarum* 3.16.3, 4) describes the technique of "dusting" dry-farmed summer vegetables, which seems to be similar to the dry gardens (*xerika bostania*) of modern Greek farmers.

Pastoralism, Transhumance, and Seasonality

The role of livestock in Greek farming regimes has been much debated (Hodkinson 1988; Skydsgaard 1988; Forbes 1995). Certainly it is clear that the keeping of animals was closely integrated with other agricultural activities, and animals

Figure 3.3 Dry garden (*xeriko bostani*) for summer vegetables in Methana, photo taken in the 1980s. Photo: Lin Foxhall

exploited resources which humans could not otherwise use directly, such as plant growth on fallow and uncultivated land and agricultural by-products. The evidence is scanty for specialized transhumance, that is, the movement of flocks seasonally from one environmental and/or climatic zone to another, as subsequently described by the Latin author Marcus Varro for southern Italy in the first century B.C. Some scholars (Hodkinson 1988:51–58) think that it was not widely practiced in Classical Greece. Certainly the kinds of long-distance transhumance routes found in later periods in some parts of the Mediterranean world seem inherently unlikely, given the territoriality of classical Greek *poleis*, and the relatively constrained sizes of their territories (Hodkinson 1988:53). In areas where borders were relatively clear-cut, shepherds would have been unlikely to graze animals or walk them through land that was not deemed to be part of their own *polis*: epigraphic examples of the problems of shepherds and animals from one polis moving across boundaries into the territory of another exist (Osborne 1987:48, 50–52). In more mountainous areas, however, where territories might be less well defined, the situation might have been different (see below p. 107 for a discussion of Tegea).

On the other hand, there are indications that the movement of flocks over short distances from winter lowland grazing to upland summer grazing was regularly practiced. The Vari House in southern Attica is one of only a few excavated rural houses, sited on the road up to a remote rural sanctuary (the Cave of Pan, a god

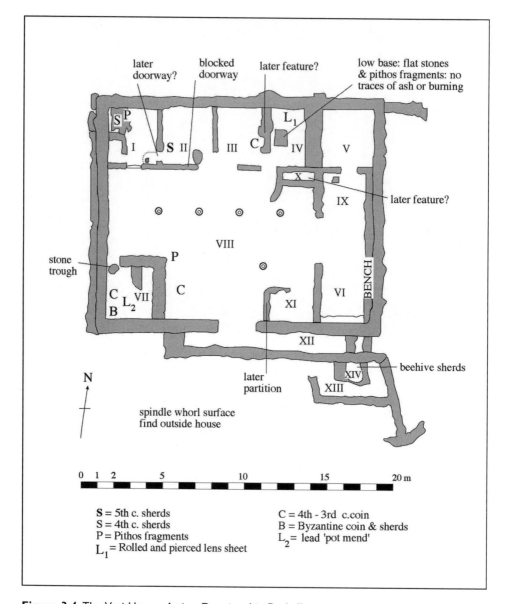

Figure 3.4 The Vari House, Attica. Drawing: Lin Foxhall

special to shepherds and their flocks) on Mount Hymettos, above the ancient deme village of Vari (Figure 3.4; Jones et al. 1973; see chapter 4 [a], this volume). Though the main period of the house dates to the early fourth century B.C., there was earlier fifth-century occupation on the site. This is a relatively small courtyard house with a tiled roof, and there is some limited evidence for agrarian activities. The range of finds is close to those of the rural sites discovered in archaeological survey and is significantly different from the archaeological assemblages of urban houses. The house is set within a large enclosure wall, probably because livestock (most likely sheep or goats) were kept in the yard. The surrounding area is highly suitable for summer grazing. The beehive sherds found near the door in the yard suggest that the occupants kept bees on the thyme-covered slopes of Mount Hymettos, famous for its honey from antiquity to the present. Keeping bees by the back door seems highly unlikely and rather dangerous, and the broken bee-hives must have been thrown into the yard for the animals to lick once the honey had been removed. Grazing in the mountains and bee keeping are both summer-time activities so it is probable that the occupants lived here only for part of the year, at the time when the sanctuary would have been most regularly visited. As is the case for many farmers today, tourists might have provided a welcome stream of customers for honey, cheese, and other farm products. In winter, the occupants probably moved themselves and their animals down to the coast to where the ancient village of Vari was located.

From the Temple of Athena Alea, located in the mountains of the central Peloponnese near Tegea, an early fourth-century B.C. inscription (*IG* V.2, see also Osborne 1987:49) lays out the regulations for grazing livestock on both the land owned by the sanctuary and land within the sacred precinct. Certain officials of the temple are allowed grazing rights for restricted numbers of animals. However, there also seems to be provision for people who are not citizens of Tegea, to stop overnight at the sanctuary with their flocks while moving animals from one area to another. This could imply that the sanctuary was located on a well-established transhumance route in the broken upland landscapes of Arkadia.

The animals most commonly kept were sheep and goats, well adapted as they are to the rugged landscapes and the harsh, dry conditions. Flocks were probably relatively small—generally 50 animals or fewer—because of high mortality rates from disease and parasites in the absence of modern veterinary medicine. They were versatile and were exploited for wool, milk, and meat, though it is clear that a number of specific breeds were recognized. Contrary to popular belief, goats are particular about their diet, but both can survive on rough Mediterranean grazing when desperate in the dearth of mid-summer, even consuming desiccated, prickly thistles and the leathery leaves of shrubs. Nonetheless, they must have considerable amounts of water to survive.

Cattle were important as traction and transport animals, but are more difficult to maintain in the drier parts of the Mediterranean as they need good quality grazing and/or browsing as well as very large amounts of water, far greater than the quantities needed by sheep and goats. Beef was a luxury as only small numbers of cattle were kept, except in localities where appropriate resources were available, such as marsh lands. Pigs were useful in areas of upland forests, as they could be left to forage for acorns, beech mast, arbutus, and cornel fruits and a wide range of other foods. Sows and piglets could be kept in pens, but boars may have been too wild and dangerous to keep as domestic animals. Chickens arrived in Greece in the eighth century B.C. and were ubiquitous by classical times.

Equids—horses, donkeys, and mules (the latter a sterile hybrid between a mare and a male donkey)—were not generally eaten but were important as beasts of burden. Horses, which required high quality grazing, such as that in marsh lands, and supplementary grain rations when working, were normally owned only by the elite, who rarely used them for agricultural purposes. Donkeys and mules, which were less demanding in their dietary requirements, were widely used as pack animals as well as to pull light carts.

Contrasting Ecological Strategies of the Greek and Roman Worlds

For Greeks, taming the landscape was the first step toward civilization: the Athenians claimed cultural superiority over other Greeks because, according to the myth of Eleusis and the Eleusinian Mysteries, they had served as the intermediaries through whom Demeter had bestowed on humans the divine gifts of cultivating cereals and enacting her mysteries. The Greeks saw themselves as human masters of the natural world around them, and exploited their landscapes, especially the lowlands, intensively. The spatial scale of interaction was, however, relatively local. A farmer might move between different holdings to perform different seasonal tasks, and move the grazing animals around the landscape in a similar way, but all on a rather local scale reflecting the similarly localized dynamics of the polis. As such, the human ecologies of the Greek world constituted a diverse patchwork of adaptations to a rich landscape that was nevertheless characterized by abrupt changes in climate, season, and topography. The dynamics of Roman engagement with nature started from a similar Mediterranean environment, but proceeded in a different direction.

Composed in the middle of the second century B.C., Cato the Elder's Latin text *De Agri Cultura* incorporates many familiar elements of Mediterranean practice: cereals, olives, vines, timber cutting, manuring, milling, and fruit-pressing, perhaps drawn from contemporary practice in Latium and Northern Campania. White (1970) makes the observation that the most orderly and precise sections of the work are not those dealing with working the land directly, which in places are haphazard and incoherent. They are instead the sections dealing with the organization and management of the estate, and in particular, the technological requirements of a production line in oil and wine. The emphasis is on the profitable management of a slave-run estate, in which investment, sale, and export are key. The human ecology of the Roman world goes on to have a spatial reach, extended by imperial expansion and trade which differentiates it from the polis-based ecology of the Greek world. Many similar activities were undertaken, but facilitated by the movement of materials, crops, livestock, and human beings on a much enlarged scale and linked to each other within the hierarchal framework of the Roman empire. The prudent management of large commercial estates supplying oil, wine, and other goods, remains the focus of subsequent agricultural authors, notably Marcus Varro (first century B.C.) and Lucius Columella (first century A.D.). Organization, management, living styles, and networks of distribution are central to the ecological agency of the particular style of Roman farming documented in these texts.

These concerns manifested in the literature have a clear archaeologically visible correlate in the architecturally elaborate farm or "villa." Terrenato (chapter 4 [b], this volume) has emphasized that the unifying aspect of these villas is a common style of consumption, in terms of architecture, personal adornment, and hygiene, as well as food and drink, rather than any common practice of agricultural production. It is, however, those styles of consumption that very conspicuously spread north and south from the Mediterranean itself, to those contrasting environmental regions that would go on to form the arena for the diverse ecologies of the Roman world.

Northern Expansion

North of the Alps within temperate Europe, the environmental challenges faced by farmers were significantly different from those faced in the Mediterranean. While the annual level of sunshine is lower in more northerly latitudes, peaks of sun and rain are no longer segregated to separate seasons; indeed, neither water nor the unevenness of its supply continue to be factors limiting biological productivity. This has significant implications for animal husbandry, particularly the large water-demanding animals such as horse and notably cattle. There is much archaeological evidence for prehistoric traditions of cattle husbandry on a variety of scales in Europe north of the Alps, sometimes indicating large herd sizes. There is furthermore growing evidence for long traditions of secondary bovine products such as milk and butter.

Temperate Europe is characterized by much larger expanses of plains and gently rolling topographies than the Mediterranean. Rather than gardens and terraces (van der Veen 2005), the emphasis was upon extensive fields, growing a diverse range of cereal and legume crops. While small enclosures and paddocks are widespread, we know of no clear evidence of what might be described as a "garden" in prehistoric temperate Europe. As we move north and east across Europe, the limiting factors to growth in these fields were depressed sunlight hours, and constraints upon either end of the growing season by late spring frosts and late summer storms. The winter and spring frosts in particular were ameliorated on the Atlantic face of Europe by the Gulf Stream, and significantly, it was along the Atlantic face of Europe—in Spain, France, and Britain—that the Roman empire proved ecologically able to extend furthest beyond the Mediterranean. There is now clear evidence that mixed farming with cattle and cereal agriculture is attested in many parts of prehistoric temperate Europe. However, the imperial *limes* only stabilized where cereals were not simply *grown*, but were already being *mobilized* as surplus on at least a local scale. Rather than being attached to a particular set of farming practices and environmental resources, the ecology of Roman farming was instead attached to a style of living and of agrarian management, and, critically, an exchange network to which these were attached. In Germany, the Netherlands, and Northern Britain, that ecological pattern fluctuated around the limits of its sustainability, ultimately settling along the

Rhine Valley and the line of Hadrian's Wall (Van der Veen 1992; Zachariasse 2003).

The earliest indications of a Mediterranean engagement with these Northern Atlantic regions all concern styles of consumption, first of wine, bodily adornment, and hygiene (Hill 1995). It may also be that the Iron Age northern chieftains whose graves are well furnished with amphoras also consumed Mediterranean food. It is certainly the case of the first military elite to land in Britain, whose meals included figs, grapes, olives, and dates (Murphy 1992). Within a generation, Roman architectural styles are seen in the form of rural "villa" architecture. However, Hingley (1989) has argued that such architectural styles do not penetrate deep into the underlying structure of the traditional compounds of the local elite. Archaeobotanical evidence from this period of temperate Europe also suggests a continuity of traditional agrarian practice, of extensive field agriculture using the same crops that had been grown in the region for centuries, and the same farming techniques. Styles of consumption, networks of exchange, military appropriation, and rural villa architecture all spread north as part of imperial expansion, and expansion initially built on existing local traditions of ecological engagement, quite distinct from Mediterranean practice. With time, however, these styles of ecological engagement were themselves transformed.

The first discernible transformation was in the use of metal. Iron production was greatly stimulated by the imperial process, and unprecedented quantities of the hitherto scarce resource were distributed around the imperial network. Some of that was used to fashion a new generation of harvesting tools, which have been interpreted as hay scythes (Rees 1979). The harvesting equipment attested in prehistory would have been poorly suited to gathering herbaceous hay, which can only be effectively harvested with a much longer blade than was available to prehistoric farmers. There is scattered evidence that branches of leafy fodder, that can be harvested with more modest blades, was the prevailing winter-feed of livestock (Jones 1991). The long iron blades that appear in the early Roman empire allowed the plant community we know as hay meadows to proliferate. They may even have led to their original genesis as distinct plant communities (Jones 1991). Although their first appearance seems linked to Roman expansion, the Roman favorites of pork, chicken, and oysters, are little augmented by the maintenance of hay meadows. This novel ecological product of metal technology, the hay meadow, was of more relevance in the sustenance (and especially the winter survival) of those essentially northern symbols of prestige and wealth, horses, and cattle.

Otherwise, the clearest indications of change in food are to do with handling and mobilization on an unprecedented scale. Within the limes forts along Hadrian's Wall are a series of vast granaries storing cereals in unprecedented quantities, and the traces of mechanical mills that could transform their contents into flour. More valuable and transportable foods were traveling across the empire and beyond (Bakels and Jacomet 2003). The peppercorns that have been recovered from a number of sites in Roman Britain may well have traveled from the

Malibar coast in southern India, entering the imperial network at the African port of Berenice (Cappers 1999; see chapter 10 [b], this volume).

Southern Expansion

Archaeology has recently cast considerable light on the ecology of the Roman empire in its most southerly reach. Egypt's Eastern Desert (around 25° north), where Van der Veen's work has demonstrated that mixed agriculture was flourishing, is and was a far more hostile environment than northern Britain around 55° north. The Eastern Desert is best known as a trading route to the port of Berenice, and a source of quarried stone, at Mons Claudianus and Mons Porphyrites. A combined study of textual fragments of ceramic *ostraca*, and archaeological analysis has allowed Van der Veen to construct an ecological picture of life within the parched stone quarries. She has shown that, not only did Roman styles of food consumption spread with the southern *limes* much as they did with the northern *limes*, but that some elements of small-scale production also traveled to this hostile region. The presence of such green vegetables as cabbage, chicory, cress, and lettuce bears witness to the vegetable gardens that flourished in this arid zone (Figure 3.5 [a–c]).

The means of transferring ecological agency to this most hostile part of the empire was that ultimate symbol of classical mastery over nature—the *hortus*, or garden, the small plot in which every feature of the environment is closely managed, often in spite of the prevailing climate and topography. While in a field we see economic plants and animals arranged in harmony with the dynamics of nature, in a garden, we see them arranged in harmony with the aesthetics of culture. Just as gardens had been a prominent feature of the Greek Mediterranean world, they became a recurrent mark of Romanization along the diverse *limes* of the empire.

Meadows, Gardens, and Moldboard Plows

Ornamental gardens had appeared in conjunction with the earliest villas and "palaces" within the northern *limes*, notably attested at Fishbourne in Sussex (Cunliffe 1971). We are not sure to what extent, if at all, they had a strictly economic dimension, just as we are unclear whether the hay meadows attested by hay scythes and fragments of the hay itself were of widespread ecological significance or something specifically for raising prestigious animals. From the late third century A.D. onwards, however, there is recurrent evidence, from villa plans, planting pits, "dark earths," and the diversification of subsidiary food plants, that an economic garden was becoming a recurrent feature of the northwest provinces (Jones 1989). This was also a period in which the balance of investment between the town and the countryside was shifting; the imperial margins, both in the north and the south, were witnessing a surge in conspicuous rural wealth. In

(a)

(b)

Figure 3.5 (a) View of the Roman site at Mons Claudianus, Egypt; (b) Remains of artichoke from the Roman site of Mons Claudianus; (c) Remains of garlic from the Roman site of Mons Porphyrites. All photos courtesy of Professor M. Van Der Veen

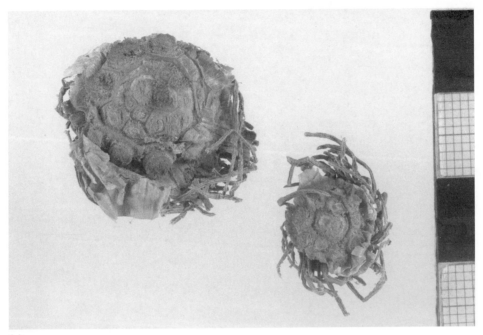

(c)

Figure 3.5 *Continued*

the northwest provinces, this provided the context for a highly significant ecological shift. This shift was the consequence of a fusion between the core elements of temperate European agriculture: adequate water, gentle topography, deep soils, and a long tradition of cattle management, and the core elements of Roman agrarian ecology, particularly the ease of mobilization and exchange of goods, materials, and investment. Just as with the earlier hay scythes, a crucial material that was mobilized was iron.

Three iron implements that recur on Romano-British sites of the late third and fourth centuries A.D. are the long harvesting scythe, the coulter, and the asymmetrical plowshare (Rees 1979). All three can be linked to the intensification of cereal production, and the latter two to the moldboard plow, designed to cut deep into the soil and invert the furrow (Jones 1981). Contemporary inverted furrows have also been found with the buried soil at the north German site of Feddersen Wierde (Körber-Grohne 1967). Like some of the metalwork finds, this latter site lies beyond the *limes* of the empire itself, an indication that moldboard plowing arose from a fusion between ecological traditions rather than as a simple introduction. Furthermore, the moldboard plow was developed to deal with environmental conditions specific to Europe north of the Alps—the simple ard, which did not invert the soil and was associated with shallow tillage, continued as the cultivation implement of preference in much of the Mediterranean until the 20th century A.D. (Figure 3.6 [a, b]). Interestingly, Körber-Grohne (1967) has interpreted

(a)

(b)

Figure 3.6 (a) Cross-cultivation with a wooden ard in contemporary Nepal. The bidirectional cultivation, while tearing up and aerating the weedy vegetation, does not invert it; (b) A recent moldboard plow, with cutting blade or "coulter" clearly visible in front of the metal edge of the moldboard itself, which completely overturns and inverts the weedy vegetation, leaving a deeply cultivated, plant-free surface

some of the economic plant remains from Feddersen Wierde as deriving from what were essentially managed "gardens" within the settlement. The crop repertoire also shifts with the spread of deep moldboard plowing, with a particular emphasis upon bread wheat in the western regions of temperate Europe, and rye in the east, both crops favored by deep cultivation.

The full impact of deep plowing and bread wheat cultivation came after the end of the Classical period, though it was a key element of the late Classical world of Christianity, that would take bread wheat and the plow, first across Europe, and then across the world, as hallmarks of the new faith, and in the process raising bread wheat to the status of the primary food source of the human species. The early roots of that process lie in a particular style of Roman ecology, that emphasized control, management, and distribution, rather than over-stamping or eradicating any existing agrarian practice.

Contrasts in the Ecology of the Classical World

Two literate and closely intertwined societies that emerged from a common Mediterranean environment ultimately proceeded along distinct ecological paths. The difference involved scale and a sense of place. Greek ecological practice embodied a wide diversity of detailed environmental knowledge about the Mediterranean region, the potential and challenges it offered. Those challenges were met by diverse practices and a certain degree of mobility, but mobility primarily on the local scale of the polis. Mobility beyond the polis was primarily focused on the widespread network of *poleis* scattered across the islands and the littoral zones of the Mediterranean. As a consequence, the Greek world displayed a patchwork mosaic of the diversity of responses to one particular topographic climatic region. Roman ecological practice also arose in the Mediterranean region, but was less grounded within it. The emphasis within a succession of agricultural authors is instead upon estate management, investment, and export, within a transferable model of farming that could follow imperial expansion to a succession of contrasting regions. Within those regions, there was a certain amount of introduction and agrarian imposition, but a substantial degree of exploitation and larger-scale mobilization of what was already there. It was the fusion between those new scales of mobilization, and existing ecological practice, that generated some of the most significant ecological legacies of the classical world (Horden and Purcell 2000).

REFERENCES

Amyx, D. A. 1958 The Attic Stelai, III: Vases and Other Containers. Hesperia 27: 163–310.

Bakels, Corie, and Stephanie Jacomet 2003 Access to Luxury Goods in Central Europe during the Roman Period: The Archaeobotanical Evidence. World Archaeology 34:542–557.

Bradford, John 1956 Fieldwork on Aerial Discoveries in Attica and Rhodes, II. Antiquaries Journal 36:172–180.

——1957 Ancient Landscapes: Studies in Field Archaeology. London: Chivers.

Brunet, Michèle 1999 Le paysage agraire de Délos dans l'antiquité. Journal des Savants 1999:1–50.

Camp, John 1979 A Drought in the Late Eighth Century B.C. Hesperia 48:397–411.

——1982 Drought and Famine in the 4th Century B.C. In Studies in Athenian Architecture, Sculpture and Topography: Presented to Homer A. Thompson. Hesperia Supplement 20. Pp. 1–17. Princeton: American School of Classical Studies at Athens.

Cappers, René 1999 Trade and Subsistence at the Roman Port of Berenike, Red Sea Coast, Egypt. In The Exploitation of Plant Resources in Ancient Africa. Marijke Van der Veen, ed. Pp. 185–197. New York: Kluwer Academic.

Cunliffe, Barry 1971 Fishbourne: A Roman Palace and its Garden. London: Thames and Hudson.

Forbes, Hamish 1995 The Identification of Pastoralist Sites within the Context of Estate-based Agriculture in Ancient Greece: Beyond the "Transhumance versus Agropastoralism" Debate. Annual of the British School at Athens 90:325–338.

Foxhall, Lin 1996 Feeling the Earth Move: Cultivation Techniques on Steep Slopes in Antiquity. In Human Landscapes in Classical Antiquity: Environment and Culture. Graham Shipley and John Salmon, eds. Pp. 44–67. London: Routledge.

——1998 Snapping Up the Unconsidered Trifles: Agricultural By-products and Animal Husbandry in Classical Antiquity. In Fodder: Archaeological, Historical and Ethnographic Studies. Michael Charles, Paul Halstead, and Glynis Jones, eds. Pp. 35–40. Environmental Archaeology 1. Oxford: Oxbow Books,.

Grove, A. T., and Oliver Rackham 2001 The Nature of Mediterranean Europe: An Ecological History. New Haven: Yale University Press.

Hill, Jeremy 1995 The Iron Age in Britain and Ireland, c. 800 BC–AD 100: An Overview. Journal of World Prehistory 9:47–98.

Hingley, Richard 1989 Rural Settlement in Roman Britain. London: Seaby.

Hodkinson, Stephen 1988 Animal Husbandry in the Greek Polis. In Pastoral Economies in Classical Antiquity. C. R. Whittaker, ed. Pp. 35–74. Cambridge Philological Society Supplement 14. Cambridge: Cambridge Philological Society.

Horden, Peregrine, and Nicholas Purcell 2000 The Corrupting Sea: A Study of Mediterranean History. Oxford: Blackwell.

Isager, Signe, and Jens Erik Skydsgaard 1992 Ancient Greek Agriculture: An Introduction. London and New York: Routledge.

Jones, J. E., A. J. Graham, and L. H. Sackett 1973 An Attic Country House below the Cave of Pan at Vari. Annual of the British School at Athens 68:355–452.

Jones, Martin 1981 The Development of Crop Husbandry. In The Environment of Man: The Iron Age to the Anglo-Saxon Period. Martin Jones and Geoffrey Dimbleby, eds. Pp. 95–127. Oxford: British Archaeological Reports.

——1989 Agriculture in Roman Britain: The Dynamics of Change. In Research on Roman Britain, 1960–1989. Malcolm Todd, ed. Pp. 127–134. Britannia Monograph 11. London: Society for the Promotion of Roman Studies.

——1991 Agricultural Productivity in the Pre-documentary Past. In Land, Labour and Livestock: Historical Studies in European Agricultural Productivity. Bruce Campbell and Mark Overton, eds. Pp. 78–93. Manchester: Manchester University Press.

Körber-Grohne, Udelgard 1967 Geobotanische Untersuchungen auf der Feddersen Wierde. Wiesbaden: Franz Steiner.

Lohmann, Hans 1992 Agriculture and Country Life in Classical Attica. *In* Agriculture in Ancient Greece: Proceedings of the Seventh International Symposium at the Swedish Institute at Athens, 16–17 May, 1990. Berit Wells, ed. Pp. 29–57. Skrifter utgivna av Svenska institutet i Athen 4°, 42. Stockholm: Svenska Institutet i Athen and Göteborg: Paul Åströms Förlag.

Margaritis, Evi, and Martin Jones, in press. Beyond Cereals: Crop-processing and *Vitis vinifera* L. Ethnography, Experiment and Charred Grape Remains from Hellenistic Greece. Journal of Archaeological Science.

Murphy, Peter 1992 Environmental Studies, Culver Street. *In* Excavations at Culver Street, the Gilberd School and Other Sites in Colchester, 1971–85. Philip Crummy, ed. Pp. 273–287. Colchester: Colchester Archaeological Trust.

Osborne, Robin 1987 Classical Landscape with Figures: The Ancient Greek City and its Countryside. London: George Philip.

——1992 Classical Greek Gardens: Between Farm and Paradise. *In* Garden History: Issues, Approaches, Methods. John Dixon Hunt, ed. Pp. 373–91. Washington, DC: Dumbarton Oaks.

Pritchett, W. K. 1956 The Attic Stelai, II. Hesperia 25:178–317.

Rees, Sian 1979 Agricultural Implements in Prehistoric and Roman Britain. Oxford: British Archaeological Reports.

Rhodes, Peter J., and Robin Osborne 2003 Greek Historical Inscriptions 404–323 BC. Oxford: Oxford University Press.

Skydsgaard, Jens Erik 1988 Transhumance in Ancient Greece. *In* Pastoral Economies in Classical Antiquity. C. R. Whittaker, ed. Pp. 75–86. Cambridge Philological Society Supplement 14. Cambridge: Cambridge Philological Society.

Van der Veen, Marijke 1992 Crop Husbandry Regimes: An Archaeobotanical Study of Farming in Northern England, 1000 BC–AD 500. Sheffield Archaeological Monographs 3. Sheffield: J. R. Collis.

——1999 The Food and Fodder Supply to Roman Quarry Settlements in the Eastern Desert of Egypt. *In* The Exploitation of Plant Resources in Ancient Africa. Marijke Van der Veen, ed. Pp. 171–183. New York: Kluwer Academic.

——, ed. 2005 Garden Agriculture. World Archaeology 37.2.

White, K. D. 1970 Roman Farming. London: Thames and Hudson.

Zachariasse, Fiona 2003 Lowland Farming: A Comparative Study of Agricultural Variation and Change in the Netherlands during the 1st Millennium A.D. Ph.D. dissertation, University of Cambridge.

4

The Essential Countryside

Introduction

Essential is a strong word, yet it is entirely appropriate in this context. First and most obviously, without the agricultural production of the countryside to feed local populations, Mediterranean cultures would never have achieved their eventual levels of power and sophistication. Beyond such pragmatics, however, the life of the countryside wove through all dimensions of ancient society: its everyday politics, its social hierarchies, its cultic practices, and its military stances.

One would never know this from the subject's treatment throughout much of the history of classical archaeology. Classicists by and large disregarded the countryside, the rural landscape, in their exploration and reconstruction of Mediterranean societies. While this neglect was more pronounced in the Greek world than in the Roman, in both cases, archaeologists were guided by the urban and "high elite" predilections of most ancient textual authorities. The prevailing form of archaeological investigation—stratigraphic excavation—also made it difficult to see how best to explore something as fuzzy and unbounded as "countryside."

Significant, late 20th-century trends in the discipline of classical studies as a whole, not least a developing interest in the ancient economy and a growing concern for non-elite social actors, increasingly highlighted the problem of this past neglect of the rural landscapes of classical antiquity. The introduction of new archaeological methodologies, in particular regional field survey, aerial photography, and satellite imagery, offered an unprecedented opportunity to redress the situation. As a result, from the 1970s onward, systematic, regional surveillance of landscapes all over the Mediterranean basin and beyond has provided a new and rapidly growing dataset testifying to human occupation, utilization, and perception of the ancient countryside.

Much of the initial interpretation of these results revolved around what (at first) appeared straightforward, practical questions. How many people lived in the countryside? Did they live in isolated farms, or in hamlets and villages? How much land did they farm? What did they grow? What quickly emerged, however, is that such questions immediately open out into larger debates, not just about the ancient economy, but about such things as structures of local authority, household organization, and regional interaction. Moreover, as survey archaeology became more confident in its methodologies, more nuanced data and interpretations appeared. The discovery of traces of ritual and mortuary activity, for example, provides much-needed insight into the symbolic force and emotional weight invested in the rural landscape by the peoples of the ancient Mediterranean.

As the previous chapter outlined, the nature of "the countryside" varied immensely across the Mediterranean basin (not to mention the expansion by the Hellenistic and Roman empires into other geographic and climatic zones). Yet differences in the patterning of landscape elements—farmsteads, villages, shrines, and tombs (as well as walls, aqueducts, terraces, quarries, wells, and dozens of other rural components)—clearly also reflect variable political formations and social choices over time. As this chapter details, key developments, such as the rise of the *polis* or the growth of empire, are marked in landscapes transformed to accommodate the new order. From being a "blank space" on the map, the essential countryside thus becomes an alternative lens through which to view and consider the workings of the ancient world at large.

4 (a)

The Essential Countryside

The Greek World

Susan E. Alcock

It is more than likely that, 50 years ago, a chapter such as this would not have appeared in any standard work on classical archaeology. The countryside was long considered a blank zone, a mere empty space between the cities and sanctuaries that attracted the bulk of scholarly attention. This blindness has well-established and authoritative roots for it can be traced back to the attitudes of the ancients, particularly the Greeks, themselves. To them, what merited written comment and detailed consideration was what happened in civic or religious centers, in places where people came together and important business, or significant thinking, took place. With such a set of priorities and objectives, the countryside remains essentially "silent" in our remaining textual sources (Osborne 1987:13–26).

The irony of this, of course, is that the rural landscape was essential to the formation and endurance of the complex societies of classical antiquity. First and most fundamentally, food came from the countryside, notably in the form of the "Mediterranean triad" of olives, vines, and cereals, to which legumes and other vegetables, as well as various modes of animal husbandry, should be added (for a discussion of the Greek environment and its agricultural capabilities, see chapter 3). While marine resources could contribute a component to certain diets (especially for those living close to the sea), and while imported foods were always signs of luxury, the bulk of what a community ate would have been drawn from its own terrestrial hinterland. The ownership of land was also key to the social organization of classical societies, with personal wealth and elite status measured by the possession of large estates. Land ownership could determine an individual's political status and military role as well. For example, in fifth-century B.C. Athens, citizens in the wealthiest census classes (such as the *hippeis*) were knights who provided the cavalry; next down came the *zeugitai*, those in possession of sufficient land to pay for their own military equipment and who were enrolled as hoplites; the poorest among the citizens, *thetes*, received no income from the land and fought mainly in the navy (Hanson 1995). Finally, the role played by this essential rural landscape was not merely economic and pragmatic; far from being a blank slate, the countryside was full of a very wide range of special, and frequently sacred, places.

The Greek *Polis*

There is an additional irony to the silence of this landscape. Aristotle once famously observed that man is a "political animal" (*Politics* 1253a 1–3), by which he meant that man is a creature who lives in a *polis*. Modern understandings of the term "political" have led many to assume this refers only to urban-based, civic life. But in the ancient Greek world (and as exported to its colonial domains), the polis unit in fact involved country as well as town. The polis, rather like an egg with white and yolk, was comprised of the *astu* (town) and *chora* (countryside) to form a relatively seamless whole. At the time of the widest distribution of the polis, in the fifth and fourth centuries B.C., it is thought that there were over a thousand of such units on the Greek mainland and islands, distributed over the highly dissected topography of this land. Most poleis, not surprisingly, were quite small; in this regard, as in so many others, Athens and its extensive territory of Attica is a wildly atypical example.

The question of where people actually lived within the polis unit is further addressed below (p. 126). The short answer, however, is that the majority of people would have lived in the astu, in or near the urban center. Athens with its great size, again, is unusual in having numerous *deme* (village) communities, some 139 in all, scattered throughout Attica (as well as within the walls of Athens itself; Camp 2001:271–318). Even then, Athens was always the dominant population center of the polis, being bolstered by a higher proportion of resident foreigners (known as *metics*) and slaves. What this nucleated dwelling necessitated, of course, was a constant flow of movement between town and country, as workers of various status (citizen farmers, tenant farmers, hired laborers, slaves) moved out to tend their fields, and back in to return home (Jameson 1992). Whenever life in the Greek polis is envisioned, this constant movement of people needs to be remembered; through this habitual action, town and countryside would have been constantly connected.

A polis was held together in a number of other ways as well. Roads, for example, extended out from the urban center through its territory. Although these were never as well developed or as highly engineered as their Roman successors, they were nevertheless major achievements and vital to military movements. Lesser routes and pathways split off to connect different parts of the chora. Sanctuaries in the countryside were attended by those who resided in the city, just as rural dwellers would travel to the city for religious festivals, as well as to participate in civic and political duties (see chapter 5). The borders of a polis were marked in various ways, though never by any formalized barrier or wall. Statues of Hermes (herms), god of crossings and boundaries, appear to have been erected as signals that travelers were passing from one territory to another; small forts and towers sometimes marked other crucial points (Whitley 2001:395–399). That such boundaries were clearly acknowledged and highly sensitive is apparent from the accounts of inter-polis friction set off by their violation, for example, by raiding of crops or livestock. Warfare between these small units was endemic, a fact with intermittent negative implications for life in the countryside and for the stability of its agricultural base (Osborne 1987:137–164).

Exploring the Chora

The lack of ancient evidence for the Greek countryside has already been mentioned; with a few notable exceptions (such as Hesiod, *Works and Days* or Xenophon, *Oeconomicus*), few texts address the topic directly and some that do, such as the plays of Aristophanes, generally caricature countrymen as rustics or boors. Nor is monumental architecture or what we would consider "fine art" much help. Athena's sacred olive may have been tended on the Acropolis near the Erechtheion and represented on the east pediment of the Parthenon, but depictions of the rural countryside were not an artistic priority, even in the plentiful visual testimony of Attic black- and red-figure pots. A few scenes of rural life appear (olive harvesting, plowing) but these are very rare (for one example, Boardman 1974: no. 186).

In other words, when it came to the countryside, classical archaeology by and large lacked its traditional sources of evidence. Moreover, few in the discipline thought much about the economic base of ancient society, at least until the latter part of the 20th century. These two factors long combined to stymie any significant investigation of the chora. Yet under pressure from historians of other periods and cultures, and (especially) from developments in archaeology elsewhere, that status quo became increasingly unacceptable. Classicists increasingly came to perceive the unlikelihood that cities could be magically fed from an invisible countryside, and at least some classical archaeologists recognized their research should involve "the detailed and systematic study of regions that can be expected to have supported cultural systems" (Binford 1964:426). These realizations paved the way for the introduction to Greece of a technique fostered in Mesopotamia, Mesoamerica and the southwestern United States—systematic regional survey.

Regional survey is an archaeological methodology that, as its name suggests, adopts a regional (not single site-based) focus, and that relies, not on excavation, but on surface reconnaissance to locate traces of past human activity. In some ways, survey had been conducted in Greece (and in the Mediterranean at large) for decades; archaeologists often took Sunday picnics out into the countryside, or undertook healthy hikes, sometimes replicating military routes or episodes related in the ancient sources, sometimes following the description of Greece offered by the Roman traveler Pausanias (p. 128). Such casual exploration often led to the discovery of sites, numerous of which could be identified by their ancient names and some of which were later excavated. More rigorous, but still largely unsystematic work, was extended over larger regions in the 1950s and 1960s; the most famous project in this vein was the University of Minnesota Messenia Expedition, often called the "grandfather of Greek survey" (McDonald and Rapp 1972).

This type of "extensive" survey is certainly useful, but it possesses significant bias towards larger and more famous sites, belonging to only certain, more illustrious periods in Greek history. As a result, the study of the Greek countryside—both in terms of chronological coverage and the full range of human activity within it—remained badly hampered. To counter this problem, from the 1970s to the 1990s, numerous projects instituted the practice of diachronic, intensive and systematic survey in Greece (Cherry 2003; for essays illustrating the different stages of modern survey in Greece, see chapter 2 [a]; Davis 1998:163–166, 302–306). The majority of recent Greek surveys are multi-period in focus, taking an interest in objects ranging from the Palaeolithic to the Early Modern periods. While the precise methodologies of these projects varied from case to case, in general, they involved the systematic pedestrian coverage of designated study regions, with fieldwalkers spaced between 15 and 25 meters apart (Figure 4.1). Such a research design allows a fairly intensive reconnaissance of the ground surface by survey teams charged with looking for all traces of past human activity. Fieldwalkers count any artifacts visible and (in most cases) collect potentially diagnostic pieces, as well as recording any features of note. Unlikely as the presence of such surface material may seem, artifacts are routinely brought up from buried deposits below through a variety of processes, both anthropogenic (plowing is especially efficacious) and natural (such as erosion).

Figure 4.1 Fieldwalkers in action on the Cycladic island of Keos. Note the agricultural terracing on the slopes above. Photo: John F. Cherry

By far the most common artifacts observed are potsherds which, if not entirely indestructible, survive such post-depositional movement better than more fragile objects. Roof tiles are another common discovery, as are stone tools; it should be noted that lithic artifacts, far from being confined to prehistoric periods, were used well into historic times in Greece. Other possible finds include agricultural equipment such as presses or mills, architectural elements such as blocks or (more infrequently) column fragments; rock cuttings for foundations or graves are also to be observed. Rarer finds include inscriptions, votives such as figurines or miniature pots, glass or metal fragments, and coins.

All artifacts collected are studied, dated, categorized, and recorded by project specialists. Dating of surface ceramics is rarely very refined; indeed, a sizable proportion of what is found by surface reconnaissance remains unidentifiable and undatable. But better-preserved or more easily recognizable types of artifacts can be assigned to defined periods, usually several decades, or even centuries, in length. The most frequently used chronological categories in Greek survey are the following: Archaic (ca. 750–480 B.C.), Classical (ca. 480–323 B.C.), Hellenistic (ca. 323–31 B.C.) and Roman (ca. 31 B.C.–ca. A.D. 500). In some instances, these periods can be subdivided into "Early", "Middle", or "Late" phases, and artifacts pinned down more closely in time. Apart from chronological assignments, study of (usually unattractive) surface remains can provide much other information. For example, the presence of imported materials (fine wares, amphoras that suggest the importation of wine or other luxuries, or non-local marbles) can attest to a region's connection with the wider world and to a desire for status display. Utilitarian objects such as millstones or spindle whorls would point to certain types of economic activities, while votives or column fragments provide an indication of ritual behavior.

Much (though not all) of this surface material comes from localized concentrations of artifacts found in the course of fieldwalking. The chief units of analysis in Greek survey are these concentrations, usually termed "sites." From the location, size, and composition of these surface concentrations, functional identifications (village? farmstead? sanctuary? tomb?) can be made, as shall be seen. Some caution is necessary here: many of the sites located through Greek survey are long-lived in nature, and a site that is a sanctuary in one period might well be converted into a farmstead in another. Moreover, given the crudity of much ceramic dating, the exact life-span of any individual site is frequently hard to determine: the presence of Classical pottery, for example, does not mean a site survived for the entirety of that period (in survey terms, ca. 480–323 B.C.). For all these caveats, however, what survey allows—through the study, identification and mapping of its data—is a reconstruction of the structure and organization of the Greek countryside, on a period-by-period basis.

When the results of intensive survey projects first began to appear, it was, for numerous scholars, as big a bombshell as had hit classical archaeology in many a decade (see, for example, the Boeotia Project, Bintliff and Snodgrass 1985; the Argolid Exploration Project, van Andel and Runnels 1987). Instead of an empty, silent countryside, intensive survey revealed a truly unexpected degree of rural activity, with patterns of site types and distribution that varied greatly over time. Much of this variety revolved around the appearance and disappearance of a class of very small sites with pottery finds suggesting a range of domestic activities; these were dubbed "farmsteads" (see below, p. 126). Even more remarkable, apart from such concentrations, many surveys discovered an almost continuous carpet of individual finds, termed "background noise" or (and better) "off-site scatter" (for a map that illustrates this phenomenon, see Figure 2.3). Such light scatters appear to reflect traces of low-level rural activity (including the practice of field manuring with ordure collected from human settlements); their patterning too revealed differences from period to period (Alcock et al. 1994). In other words, the countryside was not only far from empty, but it clearly altered in organization and structure over time. Explaining these diachronic transformations became a priority for archaeologists and ancient historians alike. This in turn required the development of other archaeological strategies, such as the extension of survey techniques to the study of large settlements, including *poleis* centers; this type of "urban" or "large-site" survey allows movements of people and activity across the entire polis (astu and chora) to be brought into direct correlation (Bintliff and Snodgrass 1988).

Survey has been practiced in an impressive range of regions in the Greek peninsula and the islands; indeed, this is the one of the most intensively examined portions of the Mediterranean, if not of the world. Many Greek projects are now published, or nearing final publication; others are still in progress. The data set is not without its problems, not least in terms of comparability of results from project to project—not everyone follows the same chronological periodizations, not everyone defines "sites" in the same fashion. Nevertheless, what all these results allow is a number of glimpses into the long-term operation of ancient Greek society. Combined and compared, they can build up a broader picture of life in the Greek countryside, which can then be contrasted with developments in other parts of the Mediterranean, such as Cyprus, Spain or Magna Graecia. Much of this work still remains to be done, but it is one of the most promising directions in classical archaeology today.

What Is Found in the Countryside?

Some of the results and insights from regional survey in Greece are reviewed in the remainder of this chapter. First, it makes sense to outline the range of types of finds and categories of site—in other words, the pieces of the puzzle—to give a sense of the activities in play within this rural infrastructure. Second, a summary overview of patterns in rural settlement and land use, from Archaic (ca. 750–480 B.C.) through Late Roman (ca. A.D. 300–500) times, will be presented. While most regions do follow the same general trajectory over this time span, it should be appreciated that this summary does elide certain regional distinctions.

Most consideration and interpretation of survey results have tended to revolve around settlement sites in the countryside; ritual sites such as shrines and burials too are receiving increasing attention. Both these categories will be further discussed below. Yet other, if often more exiguous, traces of human use and modification of the countryside can also be discovered. A simple list of "special-purpose" sites might give some impression of this diversity. Regional surveys in Greece have noted the presence of wells, threshing floors, kilns, mills, caves, quarries, terraces, dumps, cisterns, agricultural processing sites, bridges, mines, lithic knapping-floors, check-dams, drainage ditches, and sheepfolds, or other animal pens. Many of these special-purpose sites can be very small and in certain cases difficult to date. But their importance to the overall performance, particularly the agricultural and pastoral functioning, of the countryside cannot be denied.

Where did people live?

For the period of classical antiquity considered here, as already stated, most people, and certainly the wealthy movers and shakers of society, would have lived in their polis centers. "Commuting farmers" would have been a common phenomenon, one fostered by an environment marked by great local variation and by a system of partible inheritance: both factors that encourage the scattering of a family's agricultural holdings, making central residence a sensible course (Halstead 2002; Forbes 1976; see chapter 3). One of the revelations of regional survey, however, was a greater degree of rural dwelling than had previously been appreciated. This is most securely attested by the appearance of villages (komai) in the countryside, a class of settlement that appears as well in many ancient textual sources. Survey has now explored a number of these satellite communities, which usually lie some distance from the astu and presumably allowed closer access to fields and other resources. A famous example of such a village is Hesiod's hometown of Askra, in the Valley of the Muses, Boeotia. The Boeotia Survey has intensively explored this community, which is some 10 hectares in extent, placing it within a broader network of small sites that occupied the hinterland of the dominant nearby polis of Thespiae (Bintliff and Snodgrass 1988).

The most commonly found category of site in most surveys, however, is that of the farmstead. Although diverse "archaeological signatures" have been proposed for the classical farmstead, in general, these tend to be small concentrations (less than 0.5 hectare in extent and usually much smaller), with finds including ceramic wares for cooking, eating and storage, occasionally other signs of domestic activity such as loom weights or spindle-whorls, and almost always tiles, indicating the presence of a roofed structure (Pettegrew 2001). Such sites begin to appear, as we shall see, in the Archaic period and were normally most prevalent in the Classical (often later Classical) and early Hellenistic periods (see below, p. 131).

Very few farmstead sites in Greece have been excavated, the most famous of which are the Dema House and the Vari House in the Attic countryside (Figure 3.4; Jones et al. 1973; Whitley 2001:377–378). These houses possessed a range of domestic wares, a roofed structure and a courtyard. The size and well-built nature of these excavated farmhouses suggest, however, that they would probably

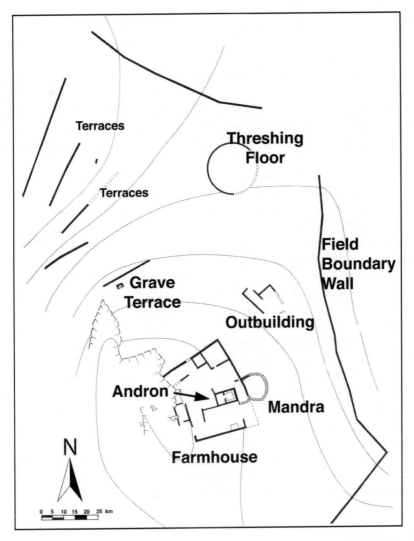

Figure 4.2 Plan of the classical farmhouse at Legrena: Palaia Kopraisia (LE 16) After Lohmann 1993: figure 34

have been more imposing than many of our survey examples, indicating the likely existence of a hierarchy of rural dwelling types in the Archaic to Hellenistic periods. This would have been a modest hierarchy; only in Roman times would a significantly outstanding style of rural dwelling, the elaborated villa, appear (see below, p. 136). One very well-preserved farm complex, discovered by survey in southern Attica near the deme of Atene, is Legrena: Palaia Kopraisia (Figure 4.2; Lohmann 1993:165–167; 513–515). This farm is itself unusual in its possession of an *andron* (see chapter 6 [a]); otherwise, its outbuilding, terraces, threshing floor, and field boundary wall are apparently fairly common rural elements.

When these farmstead sites were first identified, they were assumed to be the permanent residence of a portion of the polis' population: presumably citizen farmers working their own independent holdings. Living on the land would allow more intensive cultivation, leading to the higher yields especially necessary for smaller landholders (Garnsey 1988:43–68). That identification seems quite sensible; what has been questioned is just how permanent these dwellings were. Present-day field-shelters (*spitakia* in modern Greek), used only periodically at the busy farming times of sowing or harvesting but with an archaeological "footprint" much like an ancient farmstead, have been offered as an alternative model (Whitelaw 2000).

It might be asked why choosing between these options would potentially be a vexed question. In many ways, it is not: most scholars today would accept the uncertainty over whether farmsteads were permanent homes or part-time structures for those who lived primarily within the astu or in a satellite village; the use of the term farmstead in this chapter likewise accepts that ambiguity. The bottom-line argument—that the existence of farmstead sites suggests that people were more intensively cultivating their own properties from a rural base—remains the same. What *is* affected is our ability to estimate population numbers from survey data, for example, by extrapolation from site numbers and sizes. For example, in one early major study, farmsteads were assigned five persons each; survey appeared to offer a new way to "crack" the problem of estimating the size of ancient populations and their demographic fluctuations (Bintliff and Snodgrass 1985:140–145). Historians have now backed off considerably from such claims, noting not only the danger of double-counting mobile people, but also the likelihood that not all farmsteads were in use contemporaneously. Moreover, even where many farmsteads were found, the total number of people associated with them would have been so small as to be nearly meaningless in the assessment of overall poleis sizes (villages are a different matter, but there, at least, a more stable population can be assumed). All in all, the utility of survey to ancient demographic estimations must be approached with caution (Osborne 2004).

Tombs and shrines

The final major category of things found in the countryside takes us into other dimensions of human existence, those of burial and religious ritual. Here we do have a very detailed accounting of the Greek landscape, that of the traveler Pausanias who personally journeyed through most of mainland Greece in the second century A.D. While he is, on the whole, as silent as any other ancient commentator on the agricultural or quotidian aspects of rural life, he is an enthusiastic recorder of antique (and, in some cases, even extinct) sanctuaries, shrines, sacred places, and tombs. His *Periegesis* ("description" or "guide book" as it is sometimes translated) is a most valuable resource, but it does pose some problems of interpretation. First and foremost, it was written in the context of the early Roman eastern empire, emerging from the general classicizing atmosphere of the rhetorical and literary phenomenon known as the "Second Sophistic" (Habicht 1985; Elsner 1992). It would be a mistake unthinkingly to project back in time the Roman religious landscape Pausanias sketches; on the other hand, many of the places and patterns he notes can be archaeologically demonstrated to have existed in earlier times.

According to Pausanias, tombs were found in rural locations, especially those of mythical figures or heroes, for example, that of Aeneas' father Anchises (Pausanias 8.12.8–9). The normal location of Greek cemeteries for more mortal populations, of course, was on the penumbra of the city proper, or around major villages (see chapter 5 [a]). Rural graveyards, associated with family properties, did exist, however; some leases of agricultural land formally prohibit such burials (Osborne 1987:42–43). The typical modest burials of the classical epoch are difficult to detect through surface reconnaissance, as are the tombs of the poor in all periods. Nevertheless, survey projects have sometimes been able to note grave terraces (as in southern Attica, at Palaia Kopraisia, Figure 4.2), chamber tombs or the remains of built or rock-cut graves; occasionally, small and delimited concentrations of material, consisting only of a very few fine-ware vessels, have also been identified as burials. More ostentatious rural tombs had been known in the Bronze Age Mycenaean period (mid- to late second millennium B.C.)—for example, the well-known "beehive," or tholos, tombs—but such massive structures do not occur in the Greek countryside again until Roman times.

Those prehistoric tombs, however, did come to serve as one focus of rural cult activity in historic times. A pattern of tomb cult is visible in certain parts of Greece (including Attica, Boeotia, the Argolid and Messenia), most frequently in Archaic and Classical times (de Polignac 1995:128–149). This ritual involved the return of later populations to the tomb (or its visible remains), the offering of votives, and the communal consumption of food. The rite is usually interpreted as revealing a desire to communicate with an ancestral presence and to claim their interest and influence in present-day affairs: hence the selection of unequivocally ancient tombs. It has been debated whether these rites were led by the community elite (those who might claim direct descent from heroic ancestors) or rather celebrated a more communal ethos; these are, of course, not mutually exclusive possibilities. In certain cases (as at Eretria on Euboea), the tomb cult was celebrated just outside a polis center, but, in most cases, the tombs were in the countryside and would have necessitated a kind of rural pilgrimage, however brief.

As for rural shrines, Pausanias would have us believe that they were everywhere in the countryside: on mountaintops, near springs, on hills, in groves. There seems little reason to doubt his general point (Osborne 1987:165–192). Agricultural or fertility deities such as Demeter or Artemis may lead the parade (Cole 2004), and others take their expected place (Zeus on mountain summits, Pan on mountain slopes and in caves, nymphs at springs), but on the whole, according to Pausanias, a remarkable range of gods and heroes make an appearance in the countryside. Rural shrines also varied in size and scale, from major, well-documented complexes to tiny, insignificant locales. To augment the *Periegesis*, regional survey projects have discovered a number (admittedly a small number)

of such shrines, identified on the basis of architectural elements, votive dedications, and fine ceramics. Such a spectrum of sacred places clearly would attract
different levels of patronage and types of audience. Significant strategic sanctuaries could call forth an entire population in polis-wide rituals; smaller shrines
might have been in the care of a village, or even of just a local family and passers-
by. The power of rural sanctuaries in articulating political relationships is discussed further below (p. 136).

Social positions and relationships, too, were monitored and guided through the
sacred landscape. A rural location was essential for certain rituals, not least those
of rites of passage. For example, the pre-pubescent females of Athens would travel
to the sanctuary of Artemis Brauronia (in the deme of Brauron), there to enact
various rituals that prepared them for marriage and adult socialization. Dressing
up and dancing like *arktoi* ("little bears") seems to have been an element in this
performance (Camp 2001:276–281). In Sparta, male youths aspiring to Spartiate
(i.e. full citizen) status were tested in various ways, one of which was the *krypteia*,
in which young men were sent out into the countryside, with little equipment, to
live off the land and (we are told) to kill any troublesome helots, the dependent,
serf-like populations of Laconia and Messenia, the territories controlled by Sparta.
The precise character and implementation of this ritual are debated, but the
requirement to leave the city (representing culture and civilization) to journey
into nature and the wild is clear enough (Vidal-Naquet 1986).

The Countryside through Time: The Archaic to Late Roman Periods

From a combination of sources, especially the evidence of regional survey, it is
now possible to sketch a general account of diachronic developments in the Greek
countryside. No single summary can do justice to its full complexity, and new
evidence will continually modify the story we can tell; but some revealing trends
can nevertheless be traced over time. To set the scene, this overview can begin in
the so-called "Dark Age" (ca. 1000–750 B.C.), the period following the collapse
of the Mycenaean palaces and of the state-level system of government that supported them. That collapse extended into the structure of the Bronze Age countryside, which had been closely tied to palatial organization. The "Dark Age"
witnessed a sharp decline in any rural presence, notably a scarcity of settlements.
Population decline in the wake of political chaos, and a turn at least in part to
pastoral activity (leaving fewer permanent traces in the countryside), have been
employed to explain survey's inability to locate many signs of activity during this
epoch.

Around 750 B.C., with the inception of what is known as the Archaic period,
that situation begins to alter. Population levels, as indicated by the number of
graves, appear to rise dramatically, although this remarkably sharp increase may
reflect changing burial practices as well as an undoubtedly growing population.
This picture is most fully apparent in Attica, but can be observed in other
areas as well (Snodgrass 1980:21–24; Morris 1987). Related to this development,

settlement, in the form of villages and smaller sites, returns to the countryside in Archaic times, arguing for a reversion as well to a predominantly agrarian economy. This rural patterning, and that of the other periods discussed below, are illustrated here by reference to the results of the Argolid Exploration Project, in the Southern Argolid peninsula of the Greek Peloponnese (Figure 4.3 [a]).

The Archaic period, of course, is also the time of the "rise of the polis" in many (if by no means all) regions of Greece; the era witnessed the creation of male citizen bodies, the generation of the astu–chora bond, and the definition of precise territorial boundaries. The mix of forces that brought about this phenomenon is much debated (Osborne 1996; Whitley 2001:165–194). What is clear is that the countryside both reflected and fostered these changes. Citizenship, tied to the ownership of land among other indices, is of course discussed in our textual sources, with one archaeological correlate now visible in the appearance of small-scale, independent farmsteads. The inception of tomb cult in this period has also been traced to an increasing need to mark and consolidate land ownership, through appeals to past authority (Snodgrass 1980:37–40, 74–75; Antonaccio 1995). The unity of town and country, and the boundedness of the polis entity, were also ritually celebrated in the Archaic period. Rural sanctuaries, practically unknown in Dark Age times, reappear. Most significantly, major extra-urban sanctuaries develop such as, for example, the Argive Heraion (dedicated to Hera), on the edge of the Argive plain about 10 kilometers from the astu of Argos itself. Ancient testimonia describe civic rituals here in which a procession from the city wound out to the sanctuary, bringing the citizen body together in a single act and—by their very passage—claiming the territory over which they moved. Although it now seems unlikely that this ritual dates to the very beginning of the Argive polis, it certainly reinforced that entity's existence and power (de Polignac 1995).

The Classical period (ca. 480–338 B.C.) experienced an intensification of what the Archaic period had begun, with a more densely inhabited and utilized countryside (Figure 4.3 [b]; Whitley 2001:382–391). In the course of this period, Athens began, of course, to follow a highly individual political trajectory, not least with the inception and expansion of its imperial Delian League and its long-term struggles with Sparta in the Peloponnesian War (431–404 B.C.). Both the wealth introduced by the former, and the crises instigated by the latter, have implications for the rural landscape (Garnsey 1988:89–164).

The ascendancy of Athens in the decades after the Battle of Marathon (490 B.C.) led to the celebration and ornamentation of the city, the fifth-century monuments that long mesmerized practitioners of classical archaeology (Camp 2001:59–160). Attic marbles were used in this beautification project, not least the white stone of Mount Pendele, northeast of the city, which was employed in the construction of the Parthenon. Quarry sites, in Attica or elsewhere (such as Mount Hymettos or the island of Paros), had been exploited before the Classical period, but the period again witnessed an intensification of their use. Greece possessed a range of other natural resources, including minerals and metals; the most famous of the latter are the silver mines of Attic Laurion, a resource which worked

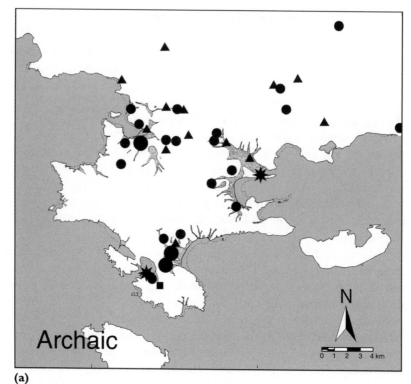

(a)

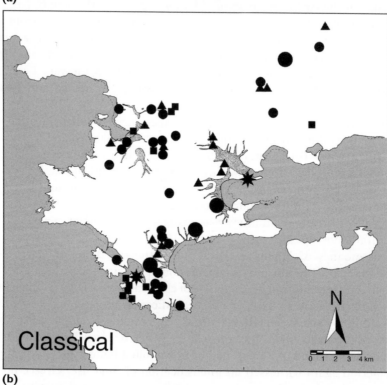

(b)

Figure 4.3 Distribution of survey sites discovered in the Southern Argolid. Large, medium and small sites are shown as circles of different sizes; sites of unknown size as squares; sites of uncertain date as triangles. Stars indicate the location of polis centers. (a) Archaic; (b) Classical; (c) Late Classical/Early Hellenistic; (d) Hellenistic; (e) (Overleaf) Early Roman; (f) Late Roman. After Jameson et al. 1994: figures 4.21–25. 4/27

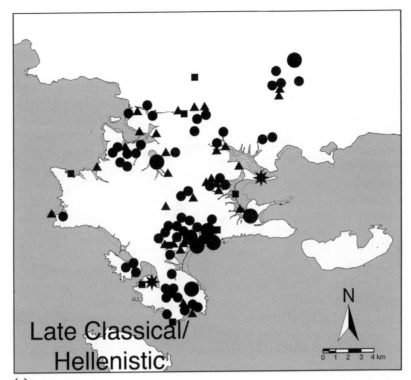

(c)

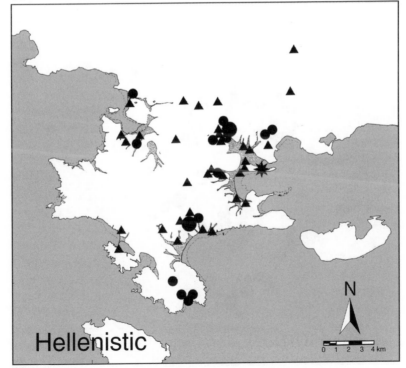

(d)

Figure 4.3 *Continued*

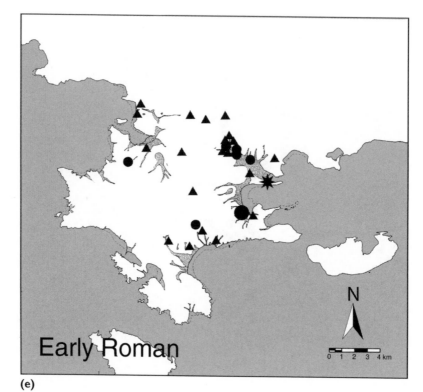

Figure 4.3 *Continued*

to support Athenian imperial ambitions (Camp 2001:310–315). Exploitation of these mines in the fifth century, for example, allowed Athens to coin their prized currency of silver "owls" (named after the bird associated with the city's patron deity, Athena). Quarrying and mining facilities, and the resulting need to feed a specialist (in some cases, slave) work force, directly influenced the organization of the surrounding countryside, a phenomenon seen in the Roman world as well, and on a grander scale (Osborne 1987:75–92; Whitley 2001:377–382; for the Roman world, see Greene 1986:142–155).

As for the Peloponnesian War, invasion and raiding by Spartan forces were a constant feature of the conflict; for a long time the negative long-term effects of such actions were over-estimated, and the "ruin" of Attica by the end of the war was assumed. Although such depredations were hardly pleasant, the ultimate resilience of the countryside and its crops has now been soundly argued (Hanson 1998). The most remarkable thing about this particular countryside at war, however, was its abandonment. In 431 B.C., Pericles summoned the Attic rural population into the city, where, thanks to the protection of the "Long Walls" extending from Athens to the port of Piraeus, the dominant Athenian navy could feed the city. The strategic ability to cut off a population from its rural base could only have happened in Athens, although one ultimate consequence of the urban crowding was a deadly plague that struck the city and killed many, including Pericles himself (Thucydides 2.47–55).

If one had to select the period in which the Greek countryside was at its "busiest"—the most sites, the most individual finds, the most traces of human activity—the answer would be the Classical and Early Hellenistic period (in some survey data sets, the Late Classical and Early Hellenistic period (ca. 350–250 B.C.; Figure 4.3 [c]). In the majority of cases, this expansion involved movement onto previously under- or unutilized land in less desirable, more marginal terri-tory. The explanation for this remains uncertain and may have varied from one region to the other, although population increase, with the concomitant need to feed more mouths and to provide holdings for more families, is one possibility. Another argument, made for the Southern Argolid peninsula in particular, was that the period saw an increasing availability of distant markets interested in the export of olive oil. The efflorescence of small sites in the peninsula, into areas suitable for olive cultivation, was thus seen as the result of external economic incentives (Figure 4.3[c]; Runnels and van Andel 1987; Jameson et al. 1994:383–394). Until recently, models for the ancient economy downplayed such trade and market forces, emphasizing above all the need to satisfy local subsistence require-ments (Finley 1973). That substantivist interpretation of ancient economic behav-ior is now under attack, and the role of exchange and a desire for profit allowed more significance (Scheidel and von Reden 2002). Such a stimulus can be hypoth-esized at work here behind the increasingly busy pattern of this rural landscape.

What happens next is a dramatic change, perhaps one of the most radical in the long-term human occupation of Greece. From that dynamic countryside of Classical and Early Hellenistic times, the Hellenistic (ca. 323–31 B.C.) and Early Roman (ca. 31 B.C.–A.D. 300) periods saw a sharp drop-off in all the indicators of human activity we have been considering (Figures 4.3 [d], 4.3 [e]). Relatively few rural sites, either settlements or special-purpose sites, have been found. Given the correspondence of this phenomenon with the troubled politics of the period (with various military conflicts involving Rome and eastern powers, many of which took place on Greek soil), it was assumed to reflect the population down-turn and poverty associated with "bad times." Warfare and turmoil may have been one part of the rural shift, but other factors too must be considered, espe-cially for Greece during the early centuries of the *Pax Romana*, when Greece and the islands were converted into the Roman province of Achaia.

One more deep-seated factor behind this transformation can be traced to that altered position of Greece, now lodged within a wider imperial system. Roman authorities bolstered the power of local magnates, who did much of the adminis-trative work of empire in their stead. Such central favor and support facilitated the growing control of political capital and economic resources by the elite fami-lies of the eastern Roman empire. One result visible in the countryside is a shift in land ownership, namely a move away from widespread holdings by citizen farmers towards the concentration of land into fewer, more prosperous hands. Such a development would help explain the apparent "clearing out" of the rural landscape. This should not be taken to suggest that there were never inequities in property holding, nor a lack of dominant landowners in classical Greece, nor that all of Roman Greece was divided up in *latifundia* (large, unified estates; fragmented holdings appear to have continued as the norm). Nonetheless, the magnitude of this political and economic reconfiguration cannot be denied, and it is also marked by the appearance in the countryside of more ornate, imposing rural residences, usually called villas, and of elaborate rural tombs. Both phenom-ena indicated distinctions of wealth and authority, and acted as social markers in the countryside on a scale not seen since Bronze Age times.

Those families left with smaller holdings, or none at all, would work the fields of others, as tenants or paid labor, and might well turn to other forms of employ-ment as well. For all of these strategies, a more central, urban residence made sense. Any such decision to dwell in nucleated settlements contributes to explain-ing the emptiness of the rural landscape, although it must be remembered that "empty" would by no means have meant ignored and uncultivated. People no doubt continued to commute out to tend their fields. Pausanias testifies to the continued presence of major, markedly venerable rural sanctuaries, the kinds of places no doubt supported by the urban-based elite. By contrast, more grassroots ritual activity seems to come to an end, with the contemporary disappearance of most minor, survey-attested rural shrines. All in all, it would seem that, in this period, something significantly altered in the relationship of people to the land.

Activity returns to the countryside in Late Roman times (ca. A.D. 300–500), with the re-emergence of numerous small sites (often on the same locations as their classical predecessors) (Figure 4.3 [f]). Several explanations may account for this rejuvenation, such as the proximity of the new imperial capital of Con-stantinople, which now required to be fed from nearby sources. Changes in social relationships and legal privileges, benefiting the elite, also played their part; in

Late Roman times, tenants became more firmly bound to the lands, and the bidding, of their masters. With the re-peopling of the landscape came a return to at least some classes of rural sanctuary, for example, mountain-top shrines to Zeus (Langdon 1976)—locales which would, however, gradually be annexed by the new official religion of Christianity. The countryside may eventually have become a refuge for pagan practices; caves of Pan in Attica, for example, have been suggested as safe places to worship, out of sight of interfering Christians.

This narrative, for the sake of coherence, has stressed similarities in regional patterning. Any scratching of the surface would lead to a multiplicity of variations on these basic themes. It would be especially interesting to compare regions where poleis were predominant with those constituted in league (*ethnos*) structures (such as Aetolia and Achaea); a relative lack of intensive work in such areas, however, makes this still somewhat difficult. One anomalous zone that has been explored is Messenia, conquered (we are told) by the Spartans in the Archaic period and held in thrall until the region's liberation in the early fourth century B.C. Inhabited by helots who farmed and worked for Spartan masters, Messenia enjoyed no independent political life until that time. The rural landscape of subject Messenia signals this unusual status, for example, through a lack of the small farmstead sites so commonly associated with self-sufficient small landowners elsewhere. Nucleated dwelling is more the norm in Messenia, which may reflect a desire on the part of the Spartans to keep the helots "corralled" and under control, or it may instead stem from the helots' own choice to cope with their hard lot by living and working in communal fashion. Either way, only after liberation does settlement in Messenia assume a more "normal" course (Alcock 2002:132–175). The centrality of the countryside to Greek life, and its ability both to reflect and reproduce social and political relationships and conditions, are thus manifest as much in the differences visible in Messenia, as in the shared developments of other parts of Greece.

Outside Greece: The Hellenistic World

With the conquests of Alexander the Great (d. 323 B.C.), and the dynasties that followed him, the "Greek world" extended far beyond the mainland peninsula and Aegean islands that have been the subject of discussion so far. It is impossible to cover this vast and topographically variable expanse in any kind of detail, not least because regional survey has not been systematically carried out in all parts of it. We can, however, make a few very basic observations. First, while the polis, with its symbiotic unity of town and country, was exported to certain parts of the Hellenistic world, it was by no means the norm. Major urban centers, with supporting but also subordinate village structures, were common in Asia Minor and the Near East; temples owned large estates (as they did in Greece, on a more moderate scale), which again were often worked from a village base. Second, the political and cultural transformations that accompanied the career of Alexander and its subsequent fall-out have visible corollaries in Hellenistic countrysides: few landscapes remain unchanged. On the whole, as far as available data can show, developments tended towards an intensification of land use and a rise in settlement numbers, suggesting an increase in population, in economic prosperity, or in financial pressures (for example, from royal taxation). Some combination of these, as well as other more local factors, would need to be deployed to explain rural developments at this time (Alcock 1994; Alcock et al. 2003).

Notwithstanding these signs of change, it is equally clear that this epoch did not signal a total departure from previous patterns of life and activity; the "coming of Alexander" did not mark the beginning of a new and superior era, as was long assumed in the hellenocentric models of earlier generations (Kuhrt and Sherwin-White 1987). Aï Khanoum in Bactria (modern-day Afghanistan and Tajikistan)—a Greek urban foundation at the farthest extent of the Hellenistic world—is one fine example of this. A sophisticated irrigation system, with channels and levees, surrounds this city, making possible its ability to flourish in a dry and unpromising environment. At first hailed as a sign of "Greek genius," it is now apparent that the irrigation system, and settlement in the area, long predated the Greek presence (Gardin and Lyonnet 1978/79). That observation by no means detracts from the remarkable character of Aï Khanoum, a place most famed for its Hellenic cultural features, including a theater, a gymnasium, and an inscription recounting Delphic maxims (Figure 8.3; Green 1990:332–335; Holt 1999:37–47). Yet there are aspects to Aï Khanoum of more local origin, not least its domestic and public spaces, which equally require recognition and interpretation. Integration of the countryside into analyses of this city would help to balance these various elements, and to reinforce the point that Hellenistic developments must be viewed in the context of previous political regimes and pre-existent cultures.

All the countrysides discussed here of course—from Greece itself to distant Bactria—were ultimately annexed or their development impacted by Rome, or by the enemies of Rome such as Parthia. That leads to the second part of this chapter, which considers the parallel landscapes of Italy and the Roman world.

NOTE

References for this chapter are on pp. 156–161.

4 (b)
The Essential Countryside

The Roman World

Nicola Terrenato

Among pre-modern cultures, the Roman is the one traditionally most often credited with having left the largest and the most indelible footprint on its landscapes. In regions as geographically and environmentally disparate as the Libyan desert, the hills of Tuscany, or the British Fens a massive human impact is often directly attributed to the Romans (see chapter 3). The legions, the land surveyors, the colonists, the owners of villas, and the slaves building roads and digging channels are some of the main characters in a grandiose historical *tableau* depicting Man's industrious triumph over nature and savagery. Generations of scholars have added to a picture that was really a product of the nationalist views of the early 19th century, effectively creating an autonomous disciplinary discourse within classical archaeology. It is only in recent years that some of the basic assumptions and straightforward interpretations about Roman landscapes have finally been radically challenged. A major role in this has been played by the development of new methodologies of field survey, as illustrated in chapter 4 (a). As a result, a review of the Roman countryside reveals today a very different picture from the one that has been current for centuries.

Chronological Development

A reconsideration of what the Romans did with their land must necessarily take as its chronological baseline the situation in Central Italy during late prehistory. It is with the emergence of fortified hilltop settlements during the Middle and Late Bronze Age that some sites destined to a long life in Roman (and occasionally post-Roman) times begin their existence. Even aside from future major urban sites such as Veii, Caere, Vulci or Tarquinii, there are a number of smaller settlements in central Italy that started out as villages towards the end of the second millennium B.C. and remained occupied for the following one, two or even three thousand years, such as Saturnia or Otranto. Recent work on abandoned Late and Final Bronze Age sites such as Luni sul Mignone (Hellström 1975) has shown the presence of a warrior elite controlling a village composed of several dozen huts and which included at least one large building. Evidence for isolated farms or other residences is by contrast rather scarce. Associated graveyards also suggest a permanently stratified society, although one in which social differences are not overly emphasized through burial rituals (Peroni 1996). In the Final Bronze Age (known as Proto-Villanovan), a handful of these hilltop sites begin to expand in surface, and, by the beginning of the Iron Age, a strong trend towards centralization and nucleation is clearly discernible in Southern Etruria (Pacciarelli 2000). Many village sites are abandoned, and the inhabitants apparently resettle in the immediate adjacency of the few growing ones. This typically happens on the vast volcanic plateaus on which the larger south Etruscan cities would develop in the following centuries.

While the concentration of settlement in the centers is fairly clearly attested, there is an ongoing debate on how much this impacted the rest of the landscape. Quite a few hill forts, especially in the immediate surroundings of the main South Etruscan cities, are actually abandoned, but many more go on undisturbed. Furthermore, it has been pointed out how it would be unsustainable in agricultural terms to have all the population concentrated in the centers (Rendeli 1993). Regional variability is probably the key to the issue, with different areas responding differently to the new tension between the budding cities and the traditional villages, which will remain a long-term trait for the rest of the ancient period. In regions such as South Etruria, where the emerging urban centers are packed together closely enough to function effectively as agro-towns, the process may even result in a dramatic decrease in the number of surrounding villages. But where urban centers are spaced much further apart, as they are in North Etruria, or are altogether absent, as in Samnium, hill forts remain the predominant settlement type for a much longer time (Barker 1995).

The picture starts changing already in the Archaic period, when smaller isolated farms make their appearance in a number of contexts (Cifani 2002). They have been found around Rome and in Latium, as well as in some parts of Southern Etruria. The few excavated examples, like the one at Tartuchino, in the Albegna valley, show simple structures with half a dozen rooms at most, often arranged around a courtyard (Figure 4.4; Attolini and Perkins 1992; Perkins 1999). There is very little architectural sophistication and dry stone rubble masonry is the typical building technique employed in these farms. Their distribution, as far as we can determine it, seems to concentrate in the densely urbanized regions where hill fort abandonment had been stronger in the early Iron Age. This could be explained by a need to resettle the countryside as well as by a tighter control by the cities over their territories, which reduces the need for defensible positions. In areas where cities are much further apart, however, there is no sign of small isolated farms till much later. It may be also worth noting that in the territories of some Greek colonies in southern Italy, such as Metapontum, there is also in

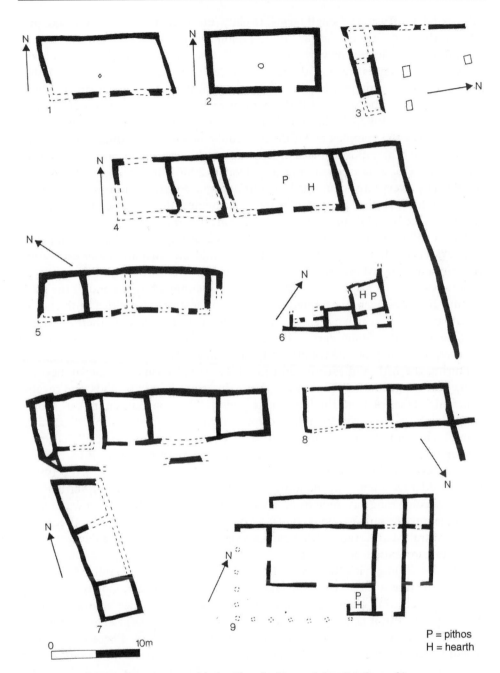

Figure 4.4 Archaic farms in central Italy. After Perkins and Attolini: figure 21

this period a diffusion of small farms, usually interpreted as the original assigna-tions to the new settlers (Carter 2000; Thompson 2004).

Another conspicuous new trait of archaic landscapes is the appearance of luxu-rious elite residences, frequently referred to as palaces. Only one example has been extensively explored, but insufficiently published, that of the site at Murlo (Phillips 1993). The site is still the subject of an extremely active debate (e.g. De Grummond 1997; Turfa and Steinmayer Jr. 2002). On the one hand, the excavators see the complex at Murlo as a public or sacred building of some sort, while, on the other, most experts in Etruscan architecture interpret it as the offi-cial residence of a petty local king (e.g. Donati 2000). Its expansive plan, char-acterized by a very large courtyard surrounded by wooden columns on three sides, finds very few parallels anywhere in Italy, although it does bear a strange resem-blance to Late Republican square porticoes (*quadriportici*). While the specific case of Murlo will only be resolved after a fuller excavation report of the site appears, more evidence is being provided by further palatial sites that are under excavation in Etruria and elsewhere, strongly suggesting a greater diffusion of these excep-tional sites. The fact that several of them were abandoned by the end of the sixth century B.C. has been interpreted as evidence of a stronger political influence of the urban centers, which are less willing to tolerate buffer states at their boundar-ies (Torelli 1981). Some early villa sites recently discovered, discussed below, however, may carry on the tradition of elite residences.

During the fifth and fourth centuries B.C., small farms very slowly become thicker on the ground, until they are the main actors in a true landscape revolu-tion, which takes place in the Hellenistic period. The slow buildup to this is only visible in those areas that they had colonized in the Archaic period. Excavated examples are practically unknown, but survey evidence seems especially clear for Latium and the southernmost parts of Etruria for the fifth century B.C. (*Crise et transformation des sociétés archaïques de l'Italie antique au Ve siècle av. J.-C.* 1990). Fairly suddenly, starting in the fourth and third century B.C., these settlements now were colonizing vast regions on an absolutely massive scale. What was a local phenomenon of limited proportions now becomes a global trend that affects the entire central Mediterranean and causes what is in most cases the deepest land-scape transformation of antiquity.

Scholars dealing with Roman landscapes originally saw the capillary diffusion of small farms as a direct consequence of the Roman conquest, mostly because it was first observed in central Italy in areas where Rome expanded at an early stage (Potter 1979). But it is now clear that the process happens everywhere roughly at the same time, regardless of the date of the Roman conquest. There seems to be little difference between the spread of farms in the *ager Veientanus* (conquered in the early fourth century B.C., Kahane et al. 1968) and in the *ager Volaterranus* (conquered in the first century B.C.), in most of southern Italy and even in many mainland Greek landscapes that would not be conquered until the second century B.C. (Figure 4.5, and see the previous part of this chapter).

As field survey upon field survey comes up with similar patterns, the spread of small farms emerges as an issue key to the understanding of the whole Hellenistic

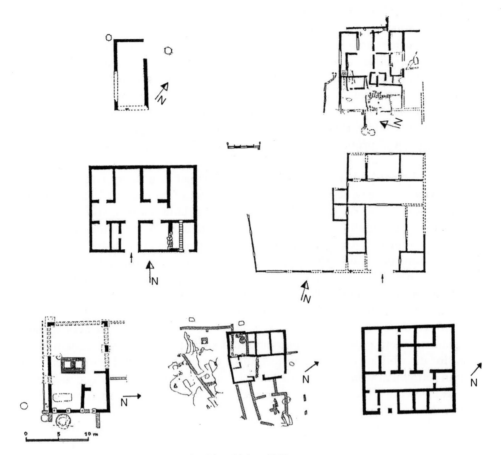

Figure 4.5 Hellenistic farms in Italy. After Volpe 1990

world. While population growth, the spread of arboriculture, social and political changes have all been called into question as potential causes, the phenomenon is still in need of a convincing global explanation. For central Italy, there is some evidence to connect these farms with the social developments attested for instance by the Licinian-Sextian laws (367 B.C.), which finally put an end to the struggle of the orders. The plebeians, according to some scholars, would finally be able to hold land in private property instead than as a temporary assignation (Capogrossi Colognesi 1994). Similar processes may be gleaned in Etruria from changes in the onomastic system and from other textual evidence (Torelli 1987). Small farmers, in this perspective, would acquire the legal rights and the social status necessary to build more permanent residences on the land they had been cultivating.

A part of this radical transition may also have been represented by the much stronger interest that elites now have for urban life (see chapter 5 [b]). It is enough to consider the vast increase in urban size, public buildings and projects or suburban mausolea to realize that the center of gravity for aristocrats in Italy had suddenly shifted to the urban side of things. While unfortunately most mid-Republican urban architecture remains highly problematic for us, there is little doubt that elites were at this point much less interested in residing in the countryside, in villages or in isolated palaces, and this may have had a social impact on the locational choices of the commoners as well. Elite conurbation may be another key factor in how the landscape is perceived by everybody. At any rate, in many parts of Italy, this dual transformation set the stage for the Roman conquest, which was probably facilitated somehow by the changes in aristocratic priorities.

In simple terms, what was traditionally described as a direct consequence of the conquest can now be viewed as a process that often preceded and prepared it. It is of course still true that Roman colonization, land reforms, and other forms of land distribution all contributed to further changes in the landscape, but, in most cases, they end up having an impact that is not as great as that of the pre-conquest transformation. Although large numbers of army veterans are recorded to have received land in Italy and elsewhere, the material traces left by the event are often very hard to find (Bradley and Wilson 2005). In many cases, it is quite likely that the assignees immediately sold or leased the land back to its occupants. In other cases, considerable pains were taken not to dislodge farmers without adequate compensation. Reclaimed land and vacant estates were frequently targeted for distributions in order to minimize the disruption and resentment that veteran settlement would otherwise cause. Colonies too should not necessarily be seen as involving a revolution in settlement patterns. It is becoming progressively clearer that local people had a considerable role in the makeup of the new citizen body. Centuriation (discussed below) entailed a rationalization of land tenure patterns, but one in which pre-existing structures could still find a place.

All these trends are becoming very apparent in peninsular Italy. Etruscan and Greek landscapes often found a way of surviving conquest, colonization, and centuriation, at least in part. The same seems to be true of those areas, like the Narbonensis, SE Spain, Sicily or North Africa where a Hellenistic farm system was already well established before the Roman conquest (Keay and Terrenato 2001). Elsewhere, as in the Po plain, things might have been different. It is only in the relatively few areas where a capillary network of small farms was not already there that a new landscape organization seems to have accompanied the early years after the conquest (Chevallier 1983). And even these few instances tend to take place in environmentally suitable areas. In mountainous Liguria, for example, the conquest, even if it probably involved a massive use of violence and even forced relocations, left very little material trace. In short, Roman impact on the rural landscape in the decades following the conquest seems confined to a limited number of surgical reorganizations in areas that simply could not be integrated the way they were.

The situation is different for the second wave of colonial foundations and land distributions in the late second and first centuries B.C. Here the effects are much more visible, at least in some areas. They should however be seen as part of the internal renegotiation of power that characterizes the period, and of which the Social War is the most blatant sign (Mouritsen 1998). While new farm systems, and occasionally even villas, are discernible in some areas (such as coastal Campania or South Etruria), it is still not the revolution that has sometimes been envisaged. Passive resistance, feet dragging, false compliance, and finally open war ensured that the rights of the Italians who were traditionally controlling the land were never completely trampled. It is significant here that the otherwise omnipotent Late Republican dictators trod much more lightly and went out of their way to mitigate the discontent caused by the settling down of their veterans (Keppie 1983).

The same developments perceptible in terms of rural settlement can also be traced in the record of productive activities. Another key element of the multifaceted revolution that takes place in the early Hellenistic period is the increase of agricultural surplus exported over long distances. Italian wine and oil were traded across the Mediterranean in much greater quantities than before beginning the late fourth century and peaking in the second–first century B.C. (Tchernia 1986). So-called Graeco-Roman amphorae are the key indicator in reconstructing the remarkable size and range of this trade. Slightly less clear is which kinds of rural sites were actually involved in producing the surplus. Down to at least the mid-second century B.C., the only possibility is represented by medium-sized farms such as the site 11 at the Via Gabina (Widrig 1987), or Posta Crusta (Volpe 1990). Only a handful of villas are known to have been occupied in the Middle Republic, and virtually all of them had been built much earlier.

Thus, while agricultural intensification is well attested in many areas, the connection traditionally upheld with the emergence of Roman villas is much less sure. And indeed a very active controversy has centered in recent years upon the origins of villas. The mainstream view, developed in the 1970s and 1980s was that villas, albeit modest and plain ones, were already in existence by the late third century B.C. Archaeological fieldwork, however, has so far failed to produce a convincing example of these early villas, unless they be the same thing as the Hellenistic farms that are discussed above. What has been found instead, near Rome and possibly in Southern Etruria, are villas that have a monumental phase as early as the fifth or fourth century B.C., clearly attested at the Auditorium site (Terrenato 2001) and very probably at the Villa delle Grotte near Grottarossa (Becker 2006). At the Auditorium, there is an expansive structure firmly datable to the early fifth century B.C., with about fifteen rooms articulated around two spacious courtyards (Figure 4.6). These are clearly elite residences from the start, built in first-rate ashlar masonry and decorated with architectural terracottas. However, they are unlikely to have played any major part in the Hellenistic agricultural expansion, given that they did not increase in number, size or productive capability in the third or second century B.C. They remained instead isolated examples of grandiose luxury and probably constitute the architectural models for the villas that would suddenly boom as a settlement type in the first century B.C.

Indeed, it is only starting in the 80s B.C. that a vast number of villas were built throughout the peninsula and beyond. They explicitly imitated the architecture

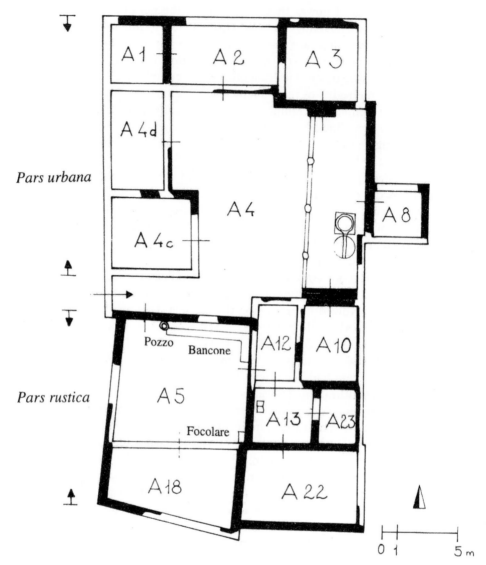

Figure 4.6 The Auditorium site in the fifth century B.C. After Carandini, et al. 1997

of earlier palaces such as the Auditorium, and became a very familiar and common trait of the Roman countryside everywhere in the empire. The peak of villa construction seems to date between 50 B.C. and 100 A.D. (Carandini 1989). To the early part of this period are attributable the classic examples of Settefinestre (Carandini and Ricci 1985) or Francolise (Cotton and Métraux 1985). Most often, they have extensive residential parts whose architecture represents a variant of the standard domus layout. Being less constrained by space, the emerging building type generally has expansive peristyles in lieu of the atrium, and tends to be much wider than its urban counterpart. The décor is fully in line with other elite residential spaces, as the Vesuvian examples lavishly illustrate (D'Arms 1971).

While the stylistic and architectural discourse is clearly the same in Italy and in some of the Mediterranean provinces, the social, productive and economic context of villas is much less susceptible of a single explanation. It is certainly true that some Late Republican villas were fully integrated within the investment agriculture that had been active at least since the mid-third century B.C. The mass production of Dressel 1 amphorae is often tightly connected with these settlements and clearly attests to the sheer size of the phenomenon. Literary evidence, mainly from Varro's and Columella's agronomic treatises, provides us with a sense of the cultural context in which villa owners operated in central Tyrrhenian Italy and in a few other regions. Epigraphic material, mostly in the form of stamped amphora handles, has even on occasion allowed detailed reconstructions of trade networks, down to the level of the individual wine or oil producer.

It is important to remark, however, that this level of integration and synergy is only seen within specific areas, such as Southern Etruria, coastal Campania or Apulia, and it would be questionable to extend this model to the rest of Italy or to the provinces. Outside of the core productive areas, in fact, villas were much fewer and they seem to have a predominantly residential, as well as symbolic, function. This is typically seen in the hinterlands of big cities and in some pleasant coastal areas. Elsewhere, even if villas were not purely residential, they showed little sign of being linked with a slave-driven productive intensification, be it agricultural or otherwise. This is indicated by the absence of amphora production and of any other evidence of long-distance trade relationships. It is not unusual, in some of these cases, to find descendants of non-Roman elites as owners of villas in their traditional areas of provenance. Northern Etruria is a particularly good case in point, revealed by the peculiar Etruscan onomastic systems (Terrenato 1998). Similar processes can be observed in at least some of the provinces, where distinctive architectural traits were probably associated with vernacular housing concepts (Millett 1990; Smith 1997). All things considered, it seems unwise to consider the remarkable diffusion of Late Republican villas as evidence of a new and all-pervasive mode of production. More than anything else, villas represent fashionable status symbols that elites, old and new, Roman and non-Roman, generally coveted. They were occasionally part of a well-conceived investment plan, sometimes a front to give respectability to fortunes made otherwise, and in yet other cases a materialization in new forms of traditional and well-established dominant positions. The primary trait they seem to have in common is their strong association with the self-representation and image of the owner and of his ancestry (Bodel 1997).

The first century A.D. by and large witnesses a further intensification of the phenomenon. More and more villas were built throughout Italy, with residential parts that progressively became larger and more ornate. Many Vesuvian villas provide perfect examples of the trend, with their extensive formal gardens and lavish sunrooms overlooking the sea. Villas made their appearance also in more recently annexed provinces, such as Britain or Egypt. The case of Fishbourne, traditionally seen as a post-conquest Romanized palace, but now shown to be still very much linked to the local context and possessing earlier phases, further illustrates the paradigm shift that is changing our understanding of Roman villas (Creighton 2001).

The surprising popularity of these sites at the beginning of the Principate should be seen as another cultural item on which a vast number of disparate affluent families converge for different reasons. Far from showing assimilation or restructuring, villas are yet another example of the multiplicity of meanings that similar material artifacts can have in different contexts (Dyson 2003). Indeed, such apparent paradoxes and ambiguities ended up being an important element of cohesion for the whole empire. In this perspective, villas can be seen as part of a broader cultural phenomenon that characterizes the Augustan period in many ways. Between the late first century B.C. and the early first century A.D., a considerable ripple runs through the whole empire and its effects are very visible in most landscapes. New architectural models become fashionable at all levels, in parallel with a universal adoption of brick and mortar as the default building technique. As with the Gracchan/Sullan transition, it is worth underlining again that it does not seem appropriate to frame the Augustan transition in terms of straightforward Rome-driven acculturation either, even if the chronological proximity to the conquest in some of the western provinces has tempted some scholars to do so. Like the Hellenistic transition some three centuries before, this was mostly a shift in tastes, fashions, and models, than one in cultural and or ethnic identities. In the same way, the fad for Egyptian themes in the visual arts does not indicate a cultural dominance of that new imperial province (if anything, it is a sign of the opposite). Augustan classicism and exaltation of *humanitas* (inasmuch as they touched the rural contexts) are best seen as a new image of how rural life should be, rather than as a radical structural shift in local power networks and settlement systems (Woolf 1998). At least as far as the peninsula was concerned, a key plank in the Augustan policy of consensus-building clearly entailed that the symbiotic link between the local aristocrats and their peasants would be left largely undisturbed.

The rural extravaganzas of early imperial elites could not be sustained for long. The double burden of urban public munificence and rural private splendor soon started pulling aristocrats under. Fashionable villa-hopping produced a proliferation of rural residences which was simply not viable in most regions, and especially in Italy where, for a variety of reasons, investment villas were ceasing to return meaningful profits. Italian amphora production went into an unstoppable decline in the mid-second century A.D., as Spanish and African imports were increasing in volume all the time (Panella and Tchernia 1994). Even more significantly, urban munificence lagged behind, as the political role of cities became progressively smaller. In many regions of the empire, aristocrats seem to have had fewer resources and less interest in local politics. Villas were abandoned in considerable numbers (and especially those mainly geared towards the long-distance wine and oil trade, Carandini 1988). No global, pervasive crisis can be demonstrated, but in many areas there is a perceptible thinning out of elite residences (Patterson 1987). This is a phenomenon that began in Italy in the second century A.D. and slowly spread to most of the western empire, till by the sixth century A.D. there were virtually none of these sites left with their original function.

At the same time, in an apparent contradiction, many villas were redeveloped, expanded and monumentalized around the same period, or shortly thereafter. It looks as if many elites were concentrating on a smaller number of residences, in which they would now spend longer periods than before. They retreated from the cities (as the sharp drop in the number of votive dedications and other forms of urban munificence shows), as well as from city-oriented agricultural production, to the comfort and solidity of traditional rural social relationships. This is best reflected by the frequent addition to mid-imperial villas of expansive bath complexes and other amenities, such as fancy dining halls, sunrooms or stadia (Sfameni 2004). The villa designed and built by the emperor Hadrian at Tibur is a hyperbolic example of the redefinition the settlement type is undergoing in this period. Extravagantly appointed with countless fancy-shaped courtyards, vaulted pavilions and pools, set in a richly landscaped park, it will become the archetype for future imperial villas (such as the Villa of Maxentius on the Via Appia), as well as for lesser elite residences (Adembri 2000; MacDonald and Pinto 1995). Another interesting phenomenon, which should be studied more extensively, is the increase in the number of rural mausolea associated with villas. They are an attestation that elites spent more time on their estates, retired to them in their old age and, more importantly, that they were again keen on investing in their local image, perhaps emphasizing a sense of family continuity.

This subtle transition, although more elusive than many others, is crucial, because it activates a long-term trend that will eventually lead to Late Roman and Early Medieval landscapes. The villas that survived the Antonine age and the rest of the Middle Empire progressively became more monumental, more continuously occupied and more of a social, cultural and economic focus for their local communities. Crafts and local productions were at this point frequently clustered around the residence, and a real village community sometimes clustered around the site (Carandini 1994). As exemplified by the Younger Pliny's letters, aristocrats now re-engaged in a serious way in the local life and wanted to reinforce their positions, since there was less that could be done in this sense in the cities. Although in the modern literature on this period the finger is often pointed at very large estates (*latifundia*), which would be characterized by non-intensive production, poor management, and absentee landlords (*Du latifundium* 1995), there is considerable evidence of a renewed interest for rural life. A possible exception may be represented by imperial estates, which are probably expanding in size. However, they often seem densely populated and in good working order, even if the actual landlord is almost always not in residence.

During the third and fourth centuries A.D., the trend towards a renewed strengthening and structuring of rural life continues, as cities, plagued by frequent political unrest, became less and less attractive (Ward-Perkins 1984). Villa architecture grew even more flamboyant and impressive (Figure 4.7), even as

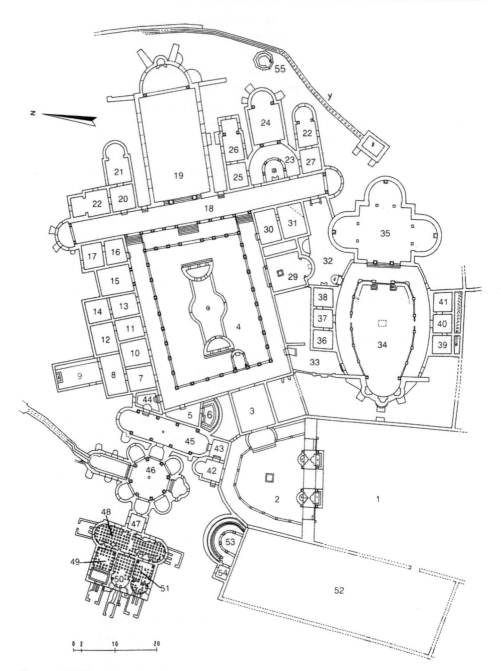

Figure 4.7 The Villa at Piazza Armerina in the fifth century A.D.

more villa sites were abandoned. Small farms continued their symbiotic integration with villas, but villages appeared, once again, to find a new role. These processes took place in a general context of prosperity in some regions, such as Sicily, which had in part missed out on earlier developments. There seems to be an "oriental" model in the Mediterranean, in which the strongest investments in the rural sphere were made from the Middle Empire onwards, as shown by Greece, North Africa, and other oriental provinces (Bintliff 1997; see the previous part of this chapter). Sicilian villages are good examples of the direction in which, in different ways, the system was moving (Wilson 1990).

As we move into the fifth and sixth century A.D., our understanding of Roman landscapes becomes much less clear, because of the quality of the evidence. Pottery is much less easy to date accurately, and architecture and building techniques are less likely to survive and less easy to characterize. It seems indubitable that villas and farms were still being abandoned at the same slow pace, but it is none the less remarkable how many of them were able to survive the collapse of the western Roman empire. Large villas such as San Giovanni di Ruoti (Small 1994) were still going strong and show more and more signs of self-sufficiency and local integration. It is only some way into the sixth century that many of the less defensible sites in Italy and elsewhere (especially in the NW empire) were deserted in a massive way (Bowden et al. 2004). In Italy, this was clearly a result of catastrophic events such as the Gothic war, which made it extremely unsafe for a local community to inhabit anything other than an eagle's nest. Elsewhere in the empire, and especially in the East and in North Africa, rural sites fared much better, as the long continuity of Maghrebine oil-producing villa shows clearly. Amphora production and circulation were also on the rise in many areas of the Eastern Mediterranean. In any case, there is no real evidence of a wholesale reversion to simple, egalitarian landscapes, as some scholars have suggested (Francovich and Hodges 2003). Elites are still visible through their donations and through the occasional inscription, especially in the context of rural religious buildings, such as churches and monasteries. They have simply ceased to consider villas as viable residences. While most villas were abandoned altogether, some seem to be morphing into something new, i.e. into rural sites that are part of the ecclesiastic structure, such as agricultural estates (*curtes*) owned by the pope or by bishops, or even monasteries (Volpe 2002; Sfameni 2004).

Villages too have a part in all this. Some were still conveniently located on hilltops and could be easily converted in fortified communities. Other persisted in open positions for a little longer, perhaps as curtes or similar settlements, and then moved up to castle positions. In general terms, there was a severe contraction in the numbers of Roman rural settlements, which may appear worse than it is because of our reduced ability to date materials produced in this period. The sites that did continue or were created in this period, however, were very robust and would provide the backbone for the medieval settlement system. Indeed, many of them became full-blown castles by the late eighth–ninth century A.D., completing the return to hilltops from which settlement increase and expansion had originated in the Early Iron Age.

Some Thematic Elements

A chronological survey that focused primarily on settlements would necessarily omit some extremely important traits of Roman and pre-Roman landscapes. Perhaps more than any other ancient culture, what the Romans do between settlements is at least as important as the settlements themselves. Road building and centuriation figure very prominently in our perceptions of the Roman expansion, often to the detriment of those infrastructures that were there before. Italy has been characterized, ever since the Middle Bronze Age, by a network of transhumance routes that facilitated the seasonal transport of large herds of sheep and goats. Even if they do not usually involve a massive impact, they forever changed the topology of the landscapes; some are still in use today. Early lines of communication took long, winding detours to negotiate the hilly relief of Italy and this is particularly a problem in west central Italy, where deep valleys separate flat volcanic plateaus. It is in this context that the Etruscan roads show the first signs of engineering solutions that involve substantial modification of the morphology. In the Archaic period, these roads were usually short and typically only connected the major cities with their extraurban graveyards. As they approached cities on plateaus such as Caere or Tarquinia, however, they needed to cut into the edges of these formations for wheeled vehicles to be able to negotiate the slope, creating deep incisions known as *tagliate*.

The technology developed in this period provided an important foundation for the far-reaching landscape modifications that will characterize the Roman road network. Even in terms of their actual courses, it is important to realize that many of the major Roman trunk roads, such as the Aurelia and the Salaria, had had a series of predecessors. Overland travel, especially along the coast and the main river valleys, had always been possible. Roman roads, more than anything else, changed the social and cultural context of traveling, even before facilitating it. The Roman empire offered precisely the kind of federal control that was necessary to establish, maintain and secure reliable connections between existing city-states. As always, technological innovation followed the practical necessity. The late third-century B.C. Via Flaminia required spectacular cuttings and bridges to overcome the natural obstacles that had always made crossing the girth of Italy problematic. These engineering *tours de force*, not always absolutely indispensable, were repeated all over the empire, advertising Roman dominion over natural constraints as well as the great rewards of global centralization and cooperation (Laurence 1999).

Another linear feature that is associated with the Roman impact on landscapes is centuriation. The checkerboard reorganization of land units is an empire-wide phenomenon that is often seen as a hallmark of total control and power by the conquerors. While there is no doubt that some human landscapes were completely redesigned in this process, recent studies suggest more caution. In most cases, the alleged traces that centuriation left in modern field boundaries and rural roads are very hard to demonstrate convincingly. It seems that a real reapportioning of

Figure 4.8 The centuriation around the Via Aemilia in the Po Plain. After Chevallier 1983

land took place on a massive scale primarily in areas where this was politically and environmentally appropriate, such as the Po plain (Figure 4.8). Here, pre-Roman individual parcel boundaries were vague or non-existent and the flat alluvium was ideal for an orthogonal grid. Elsewhere, centuriation appears to have had a much more moderate impact, modifying the existing pattern only where necessary or even just serving as a convenient cadastral tool.

Hydraulic works are yet another celebrated element of Roman landscapes. Once again, pre-Roman antecedents are not hard to identify, especially in Etruria. Extensive systems of drainage channels and tunnels (*cuniculi*) dating back to the Archaic period have been found underneath and around major settlements such as Veii or Caere. They appear to drain the volcanic plateaus as well as to channel water for various uses. They seldom extend far from the settlements they serve, but they reveal a considerable understanding of water dynamics and hydraulic engineering. After the Roman conquest, again the scale and impact of these works escalated by several orders of magnitude. Like roads, Roman aqueducts were built soon after the conquest and can be seen as federal infrastructural projects that could not be realized before the unification (Hodge 1993). They too, like roads, were connected with specific social and political conditions. In conceptual terms, they could only function within the context of global control and policing of the landscape as well as of conciliation of local identities and needs. As soon as the countryside reverted to its "natural" role as an arena for conflict and violence, roads and aqueducts, even if they materially survived for a while, became obsolete and unviable, from the social and cultural point of view (Coates-Stephens 1998).

Having looked at settlements and at the infrastructures that connect them, it is now time to turn to other, less palpable aspects. Roman landscapes are, like most others, a rich palimpsest made up of a variety of markers. They are all, in one way or another, part of a discourse about power and memory that every generation contributes to embed on the ground. Perhaps the most common examples of this are elite rural tombs and residences. Ever since the Archaic period, large tombs had been strategically placed on the landscape as symbols of the control clans have over it. These artifacts simultaneously engaged memory (through the cult of ancestors), power (through their location), and prestige (through the luxury of their construction and fittings).

Few examples of this are clearer than Etruscan tumuli. Aside from those located in the suburban necropoleis, they were clearly used to stake out portions of the landscape to which elite families laid claim (Zifferero 1991). Topped with stone markers, or even large statues of deified ancestors (for instance, at Casale Marittimo), they eloquently symbolized the long continuity and the local social dominance of the aristocrats who had set them up. In association with Etruscan palaces, their magnificence is a constant reminder of elite privileges in terms of surplus extraction and accumulation.

While tombs progressively decline as landscape markers with the approach of the Hellenistic period, elite residences carry on and expand their role. Early and Middle Republican villas, such as the Auditorium site, clearly suggest a local discourse of dominance which hails back to the Archaic royal palaces like Murlo (Terrenato 2001). In the meanwhile, Hellenistic mausolea tend to cluster around cities and along consular roads and away from individual estates, implicitly severing the reference to a specific landscape of power. Elite residences, on the other hand, become the standard form through which power takes on a material form in the rural context, and most elites deploy them in the areas they control. This will always remain a key function of this settlement type throughout its long history (Pearce et al. 2001). In a sense, a direct parallel can be established with Early Medieval castles, which are another form of elite residence imbued with a very high symbolic value. When framed in the context of what comes before and after it, Roman landscapes appear as part of a discourse about power, which becomes materialized in different ways in different periods, but which has a similar goal of reinforcing the prevailing social structure.

A related but different layer of meaning is imposed on the landscape by religious and ritual elements (see, further, chapter 7 [b]). Shrines, temples, and altars are all visible signs of a broader involvement of the gods with rural life. While at some level elites once again play a key role in shaping and maintaining this cultural sphere, commoners have more of a chance to make a contribution of their own than they do in the social and political landscapes. Institutionalized religion has a clear vested interest in reinforcing the established order. It is enough to recall the sacredness of land boundary markers, or the idea that property boundaries are divinely ordained. Major rural sanctuaries also often have an explicit political meaning, such as the definition of an area of influence by a city, a clan or even an ethnic group. Such" "boundary sanctuaries" formed a sort of crown around the earliest territory controlled by Rome, the *Ager Romanus Antiquus* or marked the limits of Campanian influence (Pearce and Tosi 1998: 177–258).

But, all the while, in the religious landscape there was room for other forms of power dialectics. Some sanctuaries had a federal role, joining together different communities, such as that of Juppiter Latiar, others provided a convenient commercial interface for different cultures, such as the trading shrines at Gravisca, yet other mediated large-scale conflict, such as the Samnitic ones (Strazzulla 1971). While the spread of the Roman empire made these kinds of rationales less pressing concerns, many rural sanctuaries can be seen to continue some version of their original function long into the empire. Small-scale shrines can sometimes be associated with the lower classes and even with slaves. Rock altars, small votive deposits, *aediculae*, sacred trees, pools, and streams have all been shown to have been the focus of non-elite ritual activities, which often involved magic. They allowed commoners to shape and modify their immediate religious surroundings. In this way, even if the general cultural map was traced by elites, and appropriately marked on the ground, everybody else had a chance of modulating it locally to make it more suited to their needs. Here we have one of the very few ways to access the level of past landscape perceptions. We can see how different groups tried to impose a certain view on large or small portions of the landscape, while others tried to contest, negotiate, or blur it.

Religious features on the landscape tend to have long lives and to become the focus of collective memories, whether real or imagined. The origins of cult places are often forgotten, and they can easily come to symbolize continuity with a very distant past. In other cases, reuse even after long periods of abandonment can have a specific cultural meaning of reconnection with an ancestral world. Such is clearly the case of Sardinian Bronze Age nuraghi, which were often reused as cult places in the Hellenistic period and even later, possibly as a form of resistance to the new imperial religious forms (Van Dommelen 1998). Similar instances are also common in the provinces, where pre-Roman shrines can serve a variety of new purposes in the new order, from the exaltation of synergy and assimilation to the expression of the bitterest resistance (Millett 1995). Controlling memory is one of the forms that power takes and it is not surprising to find it continuously contested and redefined in Roman landscapes.

Perhaps the other main focus of memory in rural landscapes is represented by tombs. Very early elite tombs that are still visible can often become objects of cult and be re-functionalized for new political and cultural purposes, for instance through identification with heroic burials (such as the Tomb of Aeneas at Lavinium). Family tumuli can be revisited (and even used again) by descendants to emphasize the long-standing tradition of a local lineage. In a way, the return of mausolea in Middle Imperial landscapes is again a form of shaping of local memories, and the same trend is even clearer in Early Christian graveyards, where the proximity to the burials of martyrs became crucial (significantly the tomb of Peter and Paul on the Via Appia was called *Memoria Apostolorum*).

Conclusion

Like many other landscapes, Roman landscapes can be seen as arenas in which complex power interactions and struggles over memory and means of production, ritual and routes are played out. But it would of course be limiting to see this as a closed system, i.e. to ignore the ever-changing challenge posed to it by the city. Well-structured landscapes of power exist before and after urbanization, as the Early Iron Age and the Early Middle Ages illustrate. Indeed, it is likely that cities first emerge as common meeting places agreed upon by feudal lords. But they soon take on a life of their own and begin to play havoc with traditional rural stability. Throughout the first millennium B.C., elites abandoned the countryside for the city in waves, unbalancing the social contract they had with their dependent farmers. As Archaic and Hellenistic urban centers assume a growing political importance, both regionally and globally, their attraction becomes harder and harder to resist.

And yet, rural life always maintains an undying fascination at all levels. The idealization of the countryside is a by-product of the stresses induced by the urban centripetal motion. Elites and commoners alike did their utmost to resist being completely uprooted and to maintain a share in the traditional system of values. Thus when, by the Middle Empire, the trajectory of Roman urbanism had begun its descending arc, it came naturally to return to a predominantly rural worldview. In many places, the traditional social structures had survived enough to be still functional, and old and new rural dwellers of all classes could rediscover the comfort of a tightly-knit, face-to-face community. When feudalism, in the strict historical sense of the word, eventually rolls along, it can build on a long, if patchy, tradition of conservatism in Roman landscapes.

REFERENCES

Adembri, Benedetta 2000 Hadrian's Villa. Milan: Electa.
Alcock, Susan E. 1994 Breaking Up the Hellenistic World: Survey and Society. *In* Classical Greece: Ancient Histories and Modern Archaeologies. Ian Morris, ed. Pp. 171–190. Cambridge: University Press.
——2002 Archaeologies of the Greek Past: Landscape, Monuments, and Memories. Cambridge: Cambridge University Press.
——, John F. Cherry and Jack L. Davis 1994 Intensive Survey, Agricultural Practice and the Classical Landscape of Greece: *In* Ancient Histories and Modern Archaeologies. Ian Morris, ed. Pp. 137–170. Cambridge: Cambridge University Press.

——, Jennifer E. Gates, and Jane E. Rempel 2003 Reading the Landscape: Survey Archaeology in the Hellenistic *Oikoumene*. *In* A Companion to the Hellenistic World. Andrew Erskine, ed. Pp. 354–372. Oxford: Blackwell.

Antonaccio, Carla 1995 An Archaeology of Ancestors: Tomb Cult and Hero Cult in Early Greece. Lanham, MD: Rowman & Littlefield Publishers, Inc.

Attolini, Ida, and Philip Perkins 1992 The Excavation of an Etruscan Farm at Podere Tartuchino. Papers of the British School at Rome 60:1–76.

Barker, Graeme W. W., ed. 1995 A Mediterranean Valley. London: Leicester University Press.

Becker, Jeffrey A. 2006 The Rediscovery of the Villa delle Grotte at Grottarossa and the Prehistory of Roman Villas. Journal of Roman Archaeology 19:213–20.

Binford, Lewis 1964 A Consideration of Archaeological Research Design. American Antiquity 29:425–441.

Bintliff, John L. 1997 Regional Survey, Demography, and the Rise of Complex Societies in the Ancient Aegean. Core-periphery, Neo-Malthusian, and Other Interpretive Models. Journal of Field Archaeology 24:1–38.

——, and Anthony M. Snodgrass 1985 The Cambridge/Bradford Boeotian Expedition: The First Four Years. Journal of Field Archaeology 12:123–161.

——, and —— 1988 Mediterranean Survey and the City. Antiquity 62:57–71.

Boardman, John 1974 Athenian Black Figure Vases. New York: Oxford University Press.

Bodel, John 1997 Monumental Villas and Villa Monuments. Journal of Roman Archaeology 10:5–35.

Bowden, William, Luke Lavan, and Carlos Machado, eds. 2004 Recent Research on the Late Antique Countryside. Leiden and Boston: Brill.

Bradley, Guy, and John-Paul Wilson, eds. 2005 Parallels and Contrasts in Greek and Roman Colonisation: Origins, Ideologies and Interactions. London: Duckworth.

Camp, John M. 2001 The Archaeology of Athens. New Haven and London: Yale University Press.

Capogrossi Colognesi, Luigi 1994 Proprietà e signoria in Roma antica I. Rome: La Sapienza.

Carandini, Andrea 1988 Schiavi in Italia. Rome: La Nuova Italia Scientifica.

——1989 La villa romana e la piantagione schiavistica. *In* Storia di Roma, vol. 4. Pp. 101–200, Torino: Einaudi.

——1994 I paesaggi agrari dell'Italia romana visti a partire dall'Etruria. *In* L'Italie d'Auguste à Dioclétien. Pp. 167–74. Rome: Ecole Française.

——1997 La nascità di Roma. Dei, lari, eroi, uomini all' alba di una civiltà. Torino: Einaudi.

——, and Andreina Ricci, eds. 1985 Settefinestre. Modena: Panini.

Carter, Joseph Coleman 2000 The Chora and the Polis of Metaponto. *In* Die Ägäis und das westliche Mittelmeer. Beziehungen und Wechselwirkungen 8. bis 5. Jh. v. Chr. F. Krinzinger, ed. Pp. 81–94. Wien: Österreichische Akademie der Wissenschaften.

Cherry, John F. 2003 Archaeology Beyond the Site: Regional Survey and its Future. *In* Theory and Practice in Mediterranean Archaeology: Old World and New World Perspectives. John K. Papadopoulos and Richard M. Leventhal, eds. Pp. 137–159. Los Angeles: Cotsen Institute of Archaeology, University of California, Los Angeles.

Chevallier, Raymond 1983 La romanisation de la celtique du Po: essai d'histoire provinciale. Rome: Ecole française de Rome.

Cifani, Gabriele 2002 Notes on the Rural Landscape of Central Tyrrhenian Italy in the 6th–5th Centuries B.C. and its Social Significance. Journal of Roman Archaeology 15:247–260.

Coates-Stephens, Robert 1998 The Walls and Aqueducts of Rome in the Early Middle Ages, A.D. 500–1000. Journal of Roman Studies 88:166–178.

Cole, Susan Guettel 2004 Landscapes, Gender, and Ritual Space: The Ancient Greek Experience. Berkeley: University of California Press.

Cotton, M. Aylwin, and Guy P. Métraux 1985 The San Rocco Villa at Francolise. Rome: British School at Rome.

Creighton, John 2001 The Iron Age-Roman transition. *In* Britons and Romans: Advancing an Archaeological Agenda. Simon James and Martin Millett, eds. Pp. 4–11. York: Council for British Archaeology.

Crise et transformation des sociétés archaïques de l'Italie antique au Ve siècle av. J.-C. Actes de la table ronde, 1990. Rome: Ecole française de Rome.

D'Arms, John H. 1971 Romans in the Bay of Naples. Boston: Harvard University Press.

Davis, Jack L., ed. 1998 Sandy Pylos: An Archaeological History from Nestor to Navarino. Austin: The University of Texas Press.

De Grummond, Nancy T. 1997 Poggio Civitate: A Turning Point. Etruscan Studies 4:23–40.

Donati, Luigi 2000 Civil, Religious and Domestic Architecture. *In* The Etruscans. M. Torelli, ed. Pp. 313–34. Milan: Bompiani.

Du latifundium au latifondo: un héritage de Rome, une création médiévale ou moderne? 1995. Actes de la table ronde internationale du CNRS organisée à l'Université Michel de Montaigne-Bordeaux III, les 17–19 décembre 1992. Paris: Diffusion De Boccard.

Dyson, Stephen L. 2003 The Roman Countryside. London: Duckworth.

Elsner, Jaś 1992 Pausanias: A Greek Pilgrim in the Roman World. Past and Present 135:3–29.

Finley, M. I. 1973 The Ancient Economy. Berkeley: University of California Press.

Forbes, Hamish A. 1976 "We Have a Little of Everything": The Ecological Basis of Some Agricultural Practices in Methana, Trizinia. *In* Regional Variation in Modern Greece and Cyprus: Toward a Perspective on the Ethnography of Greece. M. Dimen and E. Friedl, eds. Pp. 236–250. New York: The New York Academy of Sciences.

Francovich, Riccardo, and Richard Hodges 2003 Villa to Village: The Transformation of the Roman Countryside in Italy, c. 400–1000. London: Duckworth.

Gardin, J.-C., and B. Lyonnet 1978/79 La prospection archéologique de la Bactriane antique. Bulletin de l'Ecole Française de l'Extrême Orient 66:1–29.

Garnsey, Peter 1988 Famine and Food Supply in the Graeco-Roman World: Responses to Risk and Crisis. Cambridge: Cambridge University Press.

Green, Peter 1990 Alexander to Actium: The Hellenistic Age. London: Thames and Hudson.

Greene, Kevin 1986 The Archaeology of the Roman Economy. London: B. T. Batsford Ltd.

Habicht, Christian 1985 Pausanias' Guide to Ancient Greece. Sather Classical Lectures 50. Berkeley: University of California Press.

Halstead, Paul 2002 Traditional and Ancient Rural Economy in Mediterranean Europe: Plus Ça Change? *In* The Ancient Economy. Walter Scheidel and Sitta von Reden, eds. Pp. 53–70. Edinburgh: Edinburgh University Press.

Hanson, Victor Davis 1995 The Other Greeks. New York: Free Press.

——1998. Warfare and Agriculture in Classical Greece. Rev. edition. Berkeley: University of California Press.

Hellström, P. 1975 Luni sul Mignone 2, 2. The Zone of the Large Iron Age Building. Stockholm: Svenska institutet i Rom.

Hodge, A. Trevor 1993 Roman Aqueducts and Water Supply. London: Duckworth.

Holt, Frank L. 1999 Thundering Zeus: The Making of Hellenistic Bactria. Berkeley: University of California Press.

Jameson, Michael H. 1992 Agricultural Labor in Classical Greece. *In* Agriculture in Classical Greece. Berit Wells ed. Pp. 135–146. Stockholm: Paul Åströms Förlag.

——, Curtis N. Runnels, and Tjeerd H. van Andel 1994 A Greek Countryside: The Southern Argolid from Prehistory to the Present Day. Stanford: Stanford University Press.

Jones, J. E., L. H. Sackett, and A. J. Graham 1973 An Attic Country House Below the Cave of Pan at Vari. Annual of the British School at Athens 68:355–452.

Kahane, A., L. M. Threipland, and John B. Ward-Perkins 1968 The Ager Veientanus, North and East of Rome. Papers of the British School at Rome 36:1–218.

Keay, Simon J., and Nicola Terrenato, eds. 2001 Italy and the West: Comparative Issues in Romanization. Oxford: Oxbow.

Keppie, L. J. F. 1983 Colonisation and Veteran Settlement in Italy, 47–14 B.C. London: British School at Rome.

Kuhrt, Amélie, and Susan Sherwin-White 1987 Hellenism in the East. London: Duckworth.

Langdon, Merle K. 1976 A Sanctuary of Zeus on Mount Hymettos. Princeton: American School of Classical Studies at Athens.

Laurence, Ray 1999 The Roads of Roman Italy: Mobility and Cultural Change. London and New York: Routledge.

Lohmann, Hans 1993 Atene: Forschungen zu Siedlungs- und Wirtschaftsstruktur des klassischen Attika. Teil I: Text; Teil II: Fundstellenkatalog. Köln: Böhlau Verlag.

MacDonald, William Lloyd, and John A. Pinto 1995 Hadrian's Villa and its Legacy. New Haven: Yale University Press.

McDonald, William A., and George R. Rapp, Jr., eds. 1972 The Minnesota Messenia Expedition: Reconstructing a Bronze Age Regional Environment. Minneapolis: The University of Minnesota Press.

Millett, Martin 1990 The Romanization of Britain: An Essay in Archaeological Interpretation. Cambridge: Cambridge University Press.

——1995 Re-thinking Religion in Romanization. *In* Integration in the Early Roman West. J. Metzler, M. Millett, N. Roymans, and J. Slofstra, eds. Pp. 93–100. Luxembourg: Musée National d'histoire et d'art.

Morris, Ian 1987 Burial and Ancient Society: The Rise of the Greek City-State. Cambridge: University Press.

Mouritsen, Henrik 1998 Italian Unification. London: Institute of Classical Studies.

Osborne, Robin 1987 Classical Landscape with Figures: The Ancient Greek City and its Countryside. London: George Philip.

——1996 Greece in the Making: 1200–479 BC. London and New York: Routledge.

——2004 Demography and Survey. *In* Side-by-Side Survey: Comparative Regional Studies in the Mediterranean World. Susan E. Alcock and John F. Cherry, eds. Pp. 163–172. Oxford: Oxbow Books.

Pacciarelli, Marco 2000 Dal villaggio alla città: la svolta protourbana del 1000 a.C. nell'Italia tirrenica. Firenze: All'insegna del giglio.

Panella, Clementina, and André Tchernia 1994 Produits agricoles transportés en amphores. L'huile et surtout le vin. *In* L'Italie d'Auguste à Dioclétien. Pp. 145–165. Collection de l'Ecole française de Rome 198. Rome: Ecole française de Rome.

Patterson, John R. 1987 Crisis? What Crisis? Rural Change and Urban Development in Imperial Apennine Italy. Papers of the British School at Rome 55:115–146.

Pearce, John, Martin Millett, and Manuela Struck, eds. 2001 Burial, Society and Context in the Roman World. Oxford: Oxbow.

Pearce, Mark, and Maurizio Tosi, eds. 1998 Papers from the EAA Third Annual Meeting at Ravenna 1997, vol. 1. Pre- and Proto-history. Oxford: Archaeopress.

Perkins, Philip 1999 Etruscan Settlement, Society and Material Culture in Central Coastal Etruria. British Archaeological Reports International Series 788. Oxford: Archaeopress.

Peroni, Renato 1996 L'Italia alle soglie della storia. Rome: Laterza.

Pettegrew, David 2001 Chasing the Classical Farmstead: Assessing the Formation and Signature of Rural Settlement in Greek Landscape Archaeology. Journal of Mediterranean Archaeology 14.2:189–209.

Phillips, Kyle Meredith 1993 In the Hills of Tuscany: Recent Excavations at the Etruscan Site of Poggio Civitate (Murlo, Siena). Philadelphia: University Museum, University of Pennsylvania.

Polignac, François de 1995 Cults, Territory and the Origins of the Greek City-State. Trans. Janet Lloyd. Chicago and London: University of Chicago Press.

Potter, Timothy W. 1979 The Changing Landscape of South Etruria. London: Elek.

Rendeli, Marco 1993 Città Aperte. Rome: GEI.

Runnels, Curtis N., and Tjeerd H. van Andel 1987 The Evolution of Settlement in the Southern Argolid: An Economic Explanation. Hesperia 56:303–334.

Scheidel, Walter, and Sitta von Reden 2002 The Ancient Economy. Edinburgh: Edinburgh University Press.

Sfameni, Carla 2004 Residential Villas in Late Antique Italy: Continuity and Change. *In* Recent Research on the Late Antique Countryside. *In* W. Bowden, L. Lavan, and C. Machado, eds. Late Antique Archaeology, vol. 2. Leiden: Brill.

Small, Alastair 1994 The Excavations at San Giovanni di Ruoti. Toronto: University of Toronto.

Smith, John Thomas 1997 Roman Villas: A Study in Social Structure. London: Routledge.

Snodgrass, Anthony 1980 Archaic Greece: The Age of Experiment. Berkeley and Los Angeles: University of California Press.

Strazzulla, Maria José 1971 Il santuario sannitico di Pietrabbondante. Rome: Deutsches Archäologisches Institut in Rome.

Tchernia, André 1986 Le vin de l'Italie romaine: essai d'histoire économique d'après les amphores. Rome: L'Ecole française de Rome.

Terrenato, Nicola 1998 Tam firmum municipium: The Romanization of Volaterrae and its Cultural Implications. Journal of Roman Studies 88:94–114.

——2001 The Auditorium Site and the Origins of the Roman Villa. Journal of Roman Archaeology 14:5–32.

Thompson, Stephen 2004 Side-by-Side and Back-to-Front: Exploring Intra-regional Latitudinal and Longitudinal Comparability in Survey Data. Three Case Studies from

Metaponto, Southern Italy. *In* Side-by-Side Survey: Comparative Regional Studies in the Mediterranean World. Susan E. Alcock and John F. Cherry, eds. Pp. 65–85. Oxford: Oxbow.

Torelli, Mario 1981 Storia degli Etruschi. Bari and Rome: Laterza.

——1987 La società etrusca. Rome: NIS.

Turfa, J. M., and A. G. Steinmayer, Jr. 2002 Interpreting Early Etruscan Structures: The Question of Murlo. Papers of the British School at Rome 70:1–28.

Van Andel, Tjeerd H., and Curtis N. Runnels 1987 Beyond the Acropolis: A Rural Greek Past. Stanford: Stanford University Press.

Van Dommelen, Peter 1998 On Colonial Grounds: A Comparative Study of Colonialism and Rural Settlement in First Millennium BC West Central Sardinia. Leiden: Faculty of Archaeology, University of Leiden.

Vidal-Naquet, Pierre 1986 The Black Hunter. Baltimore: Johns Hopkins University Press.

Volpe, Giulio 1990 La Daunia nell'età della Romanizzazione. Bari: Edipuglia.

——, ed. 2002 San Giusto: la villa, le ecclesiae. Bari: Edipuglia.

Ward-Perkins, Bryan 1984 From Classical Antiquity to the Middle Ages: Urban Public Building in Northern and Central Italy, AD 300–850. Oxford and New York: Oxford University Press.

Whitelaw, Todd 2000 Reconstructing the Classical Landscape with Figures: Some Interpretive Explorations in North-West Keos. *In* Extracting Meaning from Plough-soil Assemblages. The Archaeology of Mediterranean Landscapes 5. R. Francovich, H. Patterson and G. Barker, eds. Pp. 227–243. Oxford: Oxbow Books.

Whitley, James 2001 The Archaeology of Ancient Greece. Cambridge: Cambridge University Press.

Widrig, W. M. 1987 Land Use at the Via Gabina Villas. *In* Ancient Roman Villa Gardens. E. B. MacDougall, ed. Pp. 223–260. Washington, DC: Dumbarton Oaks.

Wilson, Roger John Anthony 1990 Sicily under the Roman Empire: The Archaeology of a Roman Province, 36 BC–AD 535. Warminster: Aris & Phillips.

Woolf, Greg 1998 Becoming Roman: The Origins of Provincial Civilization in Gaul. Cambridge: Cambridge University Press.

Zifferero, Andrea 1991 Forme di possesso della terra e tumuli orientalizzanti nell'Italia centrale tirrenica. *In* The Archaeology of Power. E. Herring, R. Whitehouse, and J. Wilkins, eds. Pp. 333–350. London: Accordia.

5

Urban Spaces and Central Places

Introduction

Civic life is one of the features of classical antiquity which, since the Renaissance, the West has sought to emulate. Involvement in a civic community is assumed by the writers of the literary texts which survive from classical antiquity, and the organization of the participatory civic community dominates the epigraphic record. Archaeology has concentrated its urban excavations on city centers, and the agora of the Greek town and forum of the Roman town are among the best-known and best-understood parts of the human landscape of classical antiquity. It is the Forum at Rome and the Agora at Athens that tourists most readily call to mind after the iconic temples of the Parthenon and Pantheon.

The familiarity of the modern visitor with the civic centers of Greek and Roman towns and cities can easily obscure, however, the peculiarity of these places. Modern towns and cities separate buildings for national or local decision-making (town halls, parliament buildings) from buildings for the judiciary, and separate both from religious buildings and from commemorative monuments. However, the Greek and Roman civic center not only concentrated into the same space council chambers, law courts, temples, and commemorative monuments (statues of benefactors, monuments celebrating military victories), it often made that space also the center of its commercial transactions, petty as well as major. The ancient civic center was indeed a center, a place around which all aspects of community life revolved. That physical proximity of activities which we would regard as distinct and even disparate both reflected and enabled intensive links between politics and religion, public deliberation, and private initiative.

Greek and Roman civic centers were neither identical to one another, nor were they unchanging. The much more centralized political arrangements in Republican and Imperial Rome led to the development of a particular style of center, whose replication was politically required. In both Greek and Roman urban centers certain distinctive building types were developed (like the Roman basilica) or adapted (like the Greek stoa) for the civic center. Within the Roman empire even if there was no identikit model of what a forum should look like, there were very clear expectations of what would be found there. The configuration of civic space varied from town to town and varied over time. Areas which had been left free to enable flexible use in archaic and classical Greek towns came to be filled with permanent monuments of defined function. In Rome itself, the very size of the city, and the ambition of emperors, caused the Republican Forum to be duplicated in the imperial period, its functions divided between different sites. But these changes should not be seen either as merely the chance products of particular local decisions or as the result of some natural evolution. As the spaces changed, so what was and could be done in those spaces changed also, and equally as what was done in the spaces changed, so also the configuration of those spaces changed. The archaeological challenge which this chapter addresses is of turning the material record of the history of changing buildings into not merely the history of the changing hustle and bustle of this lively focus of human encounters but the history of changing ways of conceiving the world.

5 (a)
Urban Spaces and Central Places

The Greek World

Tonio Hölscher

Urban Spaces: Conditions and Mirrors of Social Life

In the fifth century B.C., public life within the city of Athens became so concentrated and intense that the Athenians were forced to change the fundamental structure and organization of their urban spaces (Hölscher 1991; 2005). Population estimations are controversial, but the assumption for Attica of around 200,000 inhabitants (including 30,000 male citizens), one-third of them living in Athens itself, should be approximately right. Forty times a year, that is every nine days on average, the people's assembly was called together, with a quorum of 6,000 participants. The day before (normally) the council of the Boule with its 500 members from all parts of Attica came together in the Bouleuterion in the *agora*. All this must have caused many hundreds of male citizens to set out for the capital from the countryside in order to join their urban fellow-citizens early in the morning, all of them suspending their normal activities and gathering in the common assembly space. In the Tholos, a round building next to the Bouleuterion, 50 *prytaneis*, the executive committee of the council, were permanently on duty. In addition, there was the old council of the Areopagus with its approximately 150 members, although this group, with its powers restricted to trying homicide cases and some religious offenses, rarely met. Even more important, the number of public law courts around the agora increased rapidly to perhaps five in number, involving more and more of the 6000 potential members of juries and trying judicial cases for perhaps 200 days a year. Apart from all this, state religious festivals, several of which included large processions through the streets, sacrifices, and banquets in the main polis sanctuaries, were celebrated on some 30 days of the year (see Thompson and Wycherley 1972; Millett 1998; Hölscher 2005).

All this activity would have affected public life enormously, with mass movements of people often overcrowding the streets. The agora in particular seems to have been disrupted from its everyday functions with increasing frequency. It was not only the political and juridical institutions, the gatherings of the people's assembly, of the council and the prytaneis, which disturbed normal routines there. Other events and manifestations took over this space, above all the numerous rituals and spectacles of great religious festivities watched by a multitude of citizens from the surrounding porticoes, as well as from temporary stands. Processions moved from the periphery to urban sanctuaries, to the temples of Athena on the Acropolis and of Dionysus on its south slope; conversely they set out from the city to far-away places such as Eleusis or Delphi. The music contests and even the athletic games of the Panathenaia were celebrated in the agora, with a short racetrack at its center and the finish of a longer racecourse for horses in one of its corners. Theater performances at the festival of the Great Dionysia originally had their place on the agora. It becomes no wonder that, in the course of time, some of these functions would be transferred to other sites. From the early fifth century B.C., for example, the theater festival was held near the sanctuary of Dionysus to the south of the Acropolis. At approximately the same time the people's assembly was installed on the Pnyx hill, although ostracism—the casting of ballots to exile a political figure for ten years—continued to take place in the agora. Athletic games had to wait until later in the fourth century B.C. with the construction of a stadium near the Ilissus River.

Generally speaking, the structured spaces of societies and their forms of cultural life are interdependent. Specific forms of life require specific spaces, and conversely these spaces determine the forms taking place therein. Societies form these spaces according to what they require for their conception of life, and these self-created spaces in their turn condition societies in their mode of living. Since the time when Greeks conceived and established themselves as polis communities, urban spaces had become the primary condition of communal life. Civic life formed urban space, and urban space formed civic life.

Historical changes to cultural spaces, therefore, are crucial indicators of changes in cultural life. In the specific case of Athens, the increasing concentration and intensification of space for political activities testify to an increasing politicization of the Athenian citizen-body. The subsequent relocation of specific functions from the agora to other areas both mirrored and actively promoted the growing autonomy of specific cultural realms: religion, politics, economy, theater, sports, education, and so forth.

The Origin of the Polis in the Eighth and Seventh Century B.C.: Structuring Social Spaces

A Greek polis was a kind of city-state. It normally consisted of a central "urban" settlement and its territory—a plain of fertile farmland, possibly with smaller dependent settlements, and surrounding marginal areas of uncultivated pasture, woods and mountains. The geological conditions of Greece favored the emergence of such separate political entities, without ultimately determining their size. Yet a definite step towards conceptualizing the polis was taken only during the eighth century B.C. (Osborne 1996:70–136, 197–202).

In Athens, Argos, and Corinth, the separation of burial grounds from the area of urban residence between 750 and 700 B.C. has been observed (Morris 1987:62–69, 183–196). From that time onwards cemeteries were placed outside the living spaces, betraying a clear conceptual division between an urban "inside" and the world "outside." City walls, which protect and at the same time define the space inside, have only rarely been definitely identified in this early period, mainly on the Aegean islands. The concept of a walled city, however, is found both in the Homeric epics and in local myths, and at Eretria the entrance of the main country road into the city was marked by a great protective hero sanctuary (Altherr-Charon and Bérard 1980). At the same time, in Athens, the Acropolis was defined as the central cult place of the community, both by new sorts of votive offerings and by marking the borders of the city-goddess Athena's property within which no human dwelling was permitted. Moreover, a first civic meeting place, an "old agora," must have originated within the same period in an area whose location remains hotly debated (Robertson 1998; *contra* Hölscher 2005). This early date is suggested by the fact that, by the first half of the sixth century, the "old agora" had obviously become too cramped and was replaced by a new one (Camp 2005). An analogous structural differentiation of communal spaces can be recognized or at least supposed, with greater or lesser plausibility and for more or less similarly early periods, at Argos, Corinth, Sparta, and Eretria.

These public spaces of early Greek cities were often connected to each other by a main street that also served as a "sacred axis" (Hölscher 1998b:74–83). In Athens, as well as at Eretria, the most important road connecting the settlement with other parts of Greece was bordered by the most important necropolis, for which it may also have served as a racecourse for funeral games. This road led to the main city gate, separating inside and outside, where religious rites of entrance and exit were performed. It then continued to the agora and to the main cult center of the polis. At great religious festivals, processions advanced along these axes from the periphery to the center, and vice versa. In Athens, the procession of Dionysus passed along this road from the Academy to the god's urban sanctuary, and part of this route was also taken by the procession of the Panathenaic festival, leading from the entrance to the city at the Dipylon Gate and ending on the Acropolis; at Miletus, a comparably important procession passed from the urban precinct of Apollo Delphinios to the extra-urban sanctuary of Didyma. In all such cases, the citizens came to experience for themselves the structured space of their polis.

Last but not least, the territories of these emerging *poleis* were increasingly conceived as, and formed into, structured concentric areas of human culture, with the urban center as its core, surrounded by an intensely used peri-urban zone, the arable land in the extra-urban zone, and the wildness of the "edge-land" (*eschatia*) with its mountains, pastureland and woods. This wider territory was conceptually occupied by sanctuaries and appropriated by the urban and rural population alike in regular festivals and rituals (de Polignac 1995).

The same structure underlies the cities of the Homeric world, displayed in the *Iliad* and the *Odyssey*. We should see these poems not as descriptive reproductions of existing urban situations but as cognitive "urban" concepts of the eighth century B.C. Homeric men live in a structured cosmos called the polis, which means not only an organized community but also a significantly defined space (Hölkeskamp 2002). Thus, the "ideal" polis of Scheria is said to have been set up by erecting a wall around the polis, building houses for men, erecting temples for the gods, and distributing the fields (Homer, *Odyssey* 6.7–10). Normally, Homeric cities contain an agora and a main sanctuary, are protected by a city wall, and possess a territory of fertile farmland, surrounded by a girdle of pasture, forests and wild mountains.

In other cities, founding myths confirm this concept. At Megara, the hero Alkathoos had first to kill a dreadful lion before he founded the city by erecting a great defensive wall (Pausanias 1.39–44; Bohringer 1980). Cities were conceived as islands of safety, surrounded by a zone of relative security, within a wilderness of permanent potential danger. Plato says that the first cities were founded for protection against wild beasts (Plato, *Protagoras* 322a–b). This concept of human cultural space is most clearly described on the fictional shield made by Hephaestus for Achilles (*Iliad* 18. 478–608; Schnapp 1996:122–129). Here two cities are depicted, misleadingly dubbed by scholars "the city in peace" and "the city in war"; they are, in fact, an "inside" and an "outside" city.

Particularly clear and fascinating examples of Archaic cities have been preserved and excavated in the area of Greek colonization, above all in Southern Italy and Sicily. Megara Hyblaia, founded in 728 B.C., is a surprisingly early example of a large-scale regular grid of streets (not yet orthogonal but parallel to each other) which, planned and laid out at the beginning, defined equal plots for houses, and left a free area for the agora (Mertens 2006:63–72). Similarly, in these colonies the territory was regularly divided into equal pieces of farmland and assigned to each of the colonists. Altogether, this is an impressive conception of a totally new community devising its communal spaces according to radically rational, egalitarian categories (Castagnoli 1971:10–54; Hoepfner 1994:1–10; Greco 1996).

In the old cities of mainland Greece, which had grown over centuries, such urban and rural divisions would have been hard to realize. The experience of colonization has sometimes therefore been perceived as a decisive stimulus behind a new conception of the city. However, it seems rather romantic to suggest that these colonists—forced to leave their home cities after years of social struggle and crossing, in inexperienced fashion, the sea with its incalculable dangers—might have invented totally new concepts of society and urban spaces. And, indeed, we have already seen that Homer, around 700 B.C., describes the mythical foundation of Scheria by Nausithoos as containing all the essential aspects of this concept: city walls, houses, temples, and an organized distribution of arable land. Obviously, these ideas and ideals were developed in the old centers of mainland

Greece where, however, such concepts were difficult to push through within the
time-honored structures of society and settlement. In the vacuum of the new
world, by contrast, old wishes and hopes could be transferred into reality. This is
in fact the contribution of the newly founded colonies: to testify more clearly than
the old-established centers the way in which all Greeks conceived their living
spaces.

Early Iron Age Greece may have been unique among ancient Mediterranean
and Near Eastern cultures in these developments. A certain caution is required,
however, since the urban centers of the city-states of Phoenicia have not yet been
sufficiently explored. One may ask whether, beside the local rulers and their residences, communal institutions with corresponding communal spaces existed in
those cities too. However that may be, it was in Archaic Greece that the polis with
its public spaces developed its specific form.

A basic aspect of this new urban (and at the same time social) structure was
the intentional separation of what we define, not quite adequately, as "public" and
"private." The crucial fact about the origin of the Greek polis was the emergence
or, rather, the creation of "public" spaces. Such spaces served as communal areas
for the communal activities of inhabitants, who only through this process developed a specific political coherence and who thereby became a polis community.

These public spaces were destined for the three main elements of this conceptual community, those comprising the basic forces of the polis: (1) the agora for
the (male, adult) citizens; (2) the sanctuaries for the gods of the polis; and
(3) the cemeteries for the dead ancestors. Each of these spaces had its own functional focus, and their increasing separation appears to have been a dominant
feature in the political development of Archaic Greece (Altherr-Charon and
Bérard 1980; Hölscher 1998b).

In cities where the major sanctuary of the polis deities was situated on a steep
acropolis, as in Athens, Megara or Cyrene, the installation of the agora in a
separate area was imposed by necessity (Martin 1951; 1974:266–275; Hölscher
1998b:29–45; Kenzler 1999). The same phenomenon is represented at Rome,
with the Capitoline Hill as a sacred citadel, crowned by the temples of Jupiter
Optimus Maximus and Juno Moneta, and the forum at its foot (Hölscher 2005).
On other sites, the main sanctuary seems to have developed from early times near
or at the border of the agora. In very early settlements like Zagora on the island
of Andros and Emporio on Chios, the sanctuary location may have been determined by the development of a ruler's palace, with a meeting place adjacent to a
communal sanctuary (Mazarakis Ainian 1997:171–176, 197–198). At Dreros on
Crete, the agora developed beside the temple of Apollo, and at Argos the sanctuary of Apollo Lykeios was situated at the northern edge of the agora area (Hölscher
1998b:50–52).

Nevertheless, there was always a clear distinction made between the political
center of the agora, where the people's assembly was held, and the cult center of
the main poliadic divinity. The agora was not a secular space; it could contain
numerous and various cult places, particularly for political gods such as Zeus
Agoraios or local city heroes (Martin 1951:174–186). In Athens, for example,

water basins set at the entrance for ritual purification protected the agora, and proceedings like the people's assembly were inaugurated by a purificatory sacrifice. But the agora as such was never a sanctuary of a specific god or goddess, and the political activities carried out there comprised no religious service.

This distinction between the realms of cult and of policy was a basic feature of the Greek polis (Hölscher 1998b:43–45, 49–62). The agora, on the one hand, was the space where the political members of the community, the adult male citizens, deliberated on questions of communal interest. This was a space of debate and contest, controversies and conflicts, and final decisions. The main poliadic sanctuary, on the other hand, was a space where the whole community came together, united in religious rituals, celebrating unanimously their common god or goddess. This was a space where the controversial decisions of the agora were fixed by inscriptions and sanctioned by divine authority, where the instability of policy was counterbalanced by the stability of religious cults. Only in the newly founded Roman cities, from the fourth and third century B.C. onwards, was the main temple of the Capitoline Triad (Jupiter, Juno and Minerva) firmly combined with the forum, testifying to the powerful religious foundation of the Roman empire on the basis of a common state cult (Lackner in press).

In this context, the cemeteries, as the third realm of a certain "public" significance, were the space of the exemplary power of the ancestors. Regularly evoked by sepulchral rites, the great forefathers represented models of behavior and values, merit and glory, for the present generation (Morris 1992). Somewhere between the eternal greatness of the gods and the efforts and struggles of living men there was the unquestionable ideal of the ancestors.

These public spaces imply also three aspects of "cultural time": (1) the unstable political present in the agora; (2) the timeless eternity of the gods in the sanctuaries; and (3) the normative memory of the past in the burial grounds.

In historical reality, we find that such concepts were realized in a great variety of ways according to specific natural conditions and/or human decisions (Greco and Torelli 1983). In cities like Athens, Megara, and Cyrene, the agora was placed in a flat area, separated from the acropolis, where roads from various surrounding regions came together. In other places, such as Miletus and Iasos on the Ionian coast, Thasos in the Northern Aegean, and probably also Naxos in Sicily, it was situated near the harbor, again far away from the main sanctuary or sanctuaries which might be placed at the center or even at the opposite end of the urban area.

Particularly interesting are some newly founded cities where no compelling landscape features influenced the installation of public spaces (Greco and Torelli 1983). Eretria, founded in the eighth century B.C. on a coastal plain, had its main sanctuary, dedicated to Apollo, in the center of the settlement, while the agora was installed (in the sixth century) in a separate area towards the sea. A similar situation is met at Olbia, on the north coast of the Black Sea. At Megara Hyblaia in Sicily, also founded on level ground, the agora consists of an irregular space left free in an area where three systems of parallel streets met (Figure 5.1); the partially recovered sanctuary or sanctuaries of the deities of the polis were

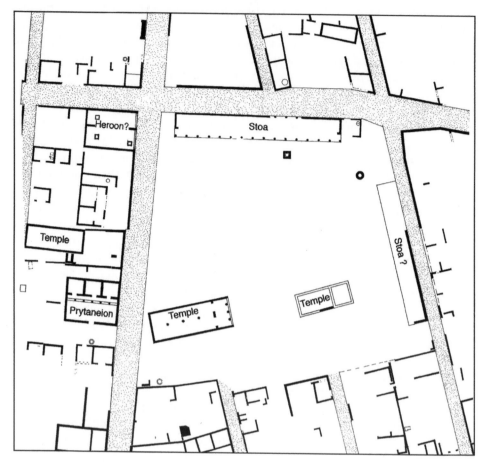

Figure 5.1 Plan of the agora area of Megara Hyblaia

probably dispersed in various other areas near the northern city wall and along the seaside (Gras and Tréziny 1999). Better known is the situation in Selinus, a daughter colony of Megara Hyblaia, where the agora was again situated in the center (where city quarters met at different orientations), while the great urban sanctuary was situated at the edge of a plateau looking towards the sea, allowing the greatest possible visibility for arriving ships from the east (Mertens 2003; Mertens 2006:175–89).

Even more complex is the situation at Akragas with its old sanctuaries of Zeus and Athena on a cliff, an agora on the gentle slope of a valley at the city's center, and a series of classical temples on the steep edge of the city towards the large coastal plain, overlooking the city wall. These temples provided a magnificent urban façade for those who approached the city from the harbor or who passed by on the main coastal road from Selinus to Gela (Mertens 2006:261–66, 317–8). Last but not least, in various cities the main urban sanctuaries and the agora were installed one beside the other. Thus, at Argos, the agora, in the center of the city, had the sanctuary of Apollo Lykeios at its northern side; likewise, at Syracuse, the agora and the main temple precinct lay side by side in the urban center on the island of Ortygia (Di Vita 1996:268–274). Particularly impressive is the situation in the city center of Poseidonia-Paestum where the Greek agora is framed by two large sanctuaries, the twin temples of Hera to the south and the temple of Athena to the north (Mertens and Greco 1996:248–252). Otherwise, at Himera, the agora and the adjacent temple area were placed immediately after the entrance to the city from the harbor plain (Di Vita 1996:290–292), while, at Metapontum, the agora, together with the major sanctuary of Hera and Apollo, was situated opposite the main entrance from the harbor (Mertens 1985; Mertens 2006:157–63).

In most of these places—and particularly impressively at Athens, Miletus, Syracuse, and Selinus—a "sacred axis" connects, in various constellations, these public spaces not only with each other, but moreover with the main entrance/exit of the city, often in connection with the main necropolis beyond the city walls.

In the case of Athens, the agora was the most dynamic center of the city, undergoing a rapid development from Archaic to Hellenistic and Roman times (Figures 5.2 and 5.3). At the beginning, Greek agoras were essentially large open areas, lacking in elaborate architecture, and therefore difficult to explore by archaeological methods (Greco 1998). Their primary role was to provide space for all kinds of public gatherings: people's assemblies, athletic and musical games, commercial activities, and so forth.

As at Athens, specific facilities seem to have been rare in agoras. Most important were circular installations within these areas, described in Homer as a *hieros kyklos* (sacred circle) and attested by excavations in various cities, being sometimes surrounded by temporary wooden stands (Kolb 1981:10–19, 53–58; Kenzler 1999:243–248). One of their functions was as a meeting place for assemblies, with the speaker in the center, the elder noblemen seated in an inner circle, and the other men of the community standing around them. Their names, however— *orchestra* at Athens, *choros* at Sparta—suggest that they were also used as places for religious manifestations. At Athens, we know of theater performances; at Sparta, we hear of dances of young men and women. In the same context must be seen the racecourses for athletic contests, found in the agoras of Athens, Argos, and Corinth. For longer foot or horse races, the major street leading from outside the city into the agora must have been used, as is known from Athens and Elis. The explanation for the central significance of such phenomena is that they were not merely events of collective entertainment, but also played a crucial role in the constitution of the civic community. Dances of youths and maidens were presentations of their beauty and nobility, and not least of their readiness for marriage, while athletic contests served as a trial run for wooing. At Sparta, the main street leading to the agora had allegedly been the racecourse for the wooers of Penelope, and similar myths are known from Argos (Marchetti and Kolokotsas 1995:221–266). Thus, the earliest installations of the agora served the councils of the political community, presided over by the elders, and the festive rituals of the younger generation, on whom lay the hopes for the polis' future.

Figure 5.2 Plan of the classical agora at Athens, as it was ca. 500 B.C.

The surroundings of the agora seem at first to have been constituted chiefly by private houses. At the foundation of Megara Hyblaia a division of the urban space into equal private plots was carried out all around the open area of the agora; only later were some of these estates turned into public property to be used for public buildings (Gras and Tréziny 1999).

Civic Density and Monumentalization of Public Spaces in Archaic Times

In the course of time, agoras were conceived, planned, and realized in a more and more monumental form. In Athens, as noted, an "old agora" of uncertain location and increasingly inadequate size, was replaced or succeeded in the second quarter

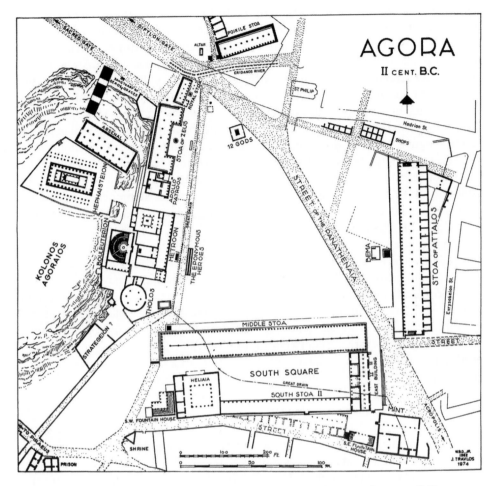

Figure 5.3 Plan of the classical agora at Athens, as it was in the second century B.C.

of the sixth century by a new public area of larger dimensions (Camp 2005). At approximately the same time at Rome, a small meeting place in front of the senate house was extended by the king Tarquinius Priscus into a large forum between the Palatine and the Capitoline Hill (Carafa 1998). Contemporaneously, at Selinus, a first great agora was planned at the beginning of the sixth century, one generation after the colony's foundation (Mertens 2003; Mertens 2006:175–83).

Within and around these areas, various architectural installations were designed, resulting step-by-step in a certain monumentalization of the civic centers of Archaic cities (Martin 1951; Kenzler 1999:304–321). At Megara Hyblaia, two or three temples for unknown divinities and a hero sanctuary were built in the agora, at Cyrene, a cult place of the founder hero Battos. Somewhat later, at Athens, the classical agora acquired sanctuaries for Zeus, who elsewhere was often named *Agoraios*, and Apollo, as well as a sanctuary of the Twelve Gods that served as the central meeting point of all the roads of Attica. The first large stoas, or porticoes—providing an open area with shelter from heat and rain—were erected Samos and at Megara Hyblaia in the later seventh century B.C.; at Athens, the Stoa Basileios ("Royal Stoa") was later built as the office of the Archon Basileus ("King Archon"), a magistrate with religious duties. Particularly impressive is the enormous agora at Selinus which is the most distinguished example of the public center of an important Archaic polis. Here, excavations have shown that the entire eastern side was designed according to a homogeneous plan which created regular plots for house units, determined a uniform series of shops along the entire front (to be rented out to merchants and craftsmen), and provided special spaces for a sanctuary and a banquet house (Mertens 2003; Mertens 2006:177–83). This gives us a concrete notion of the contemporary installation of two series of shops (*tabernae*) along the long sides of the Roman forum by Tarquinius Priscus mentioned by literary texts.

In most cities, however, the monumentalization of the agora in Archaic times can only be traced by a few indications, since public centers were particularly exposed to intensive building activities in later centuries. The most extraordinary transformation has been observed at Metapontum where, in the late seventh century B.C., within the open area of the agora, a first meeting place was equipped with wedge-shaped wooden stands. In the second half of the sixth century these were replaced by a large installation of amphitheater-like form, heaped up with earth and enclosed by a circular wall of no less than a 62-meter diameter, with a small sanctuary of Zeus Agoraios at its side. This magnificent setting for public meetings was again, after a period of abandonment, succeeded in the late fourth century by an extraordinary theater-like building which must have served the same multifunctional purposes (Mertens 1985). In other cities, where such an overwhelming occupation of the agora may have appeared less tolerable, from the fifth century B.C. onwards theater buildings for assemblies and other mass gatherings were placed more at one side of the area (as at Mantineia and Morgantina), or even in definite separation from the agora (as at Argos, Sparta, and Athens).

Many further examples of early monumentalization are suggested by literary sources, above all by Pausanias, although their actual origin in Archaic times is often a matter of hypothesis which only future excavation can confirm or deny. All in all, however, there can be no doubt about the general development of urban centers towards monumental architectural forms: not only in the primarily functional buildings of the agora but also in the sanctuaries where the deities of the polis were represented and worshipped. From Samos to Athens, Corinth to Corcyra, Metapontum to Selinus, the Archaic period—and above all the first half of the sixth century B.C.—was an era of widespread monumental temple building.

Historically, this urban development towards architectural monumentality testifies to a strong desire to lavish great economic wealth and much skilled manpower to enhance the splendor of the city. The ideological and ethical connotations may be recognized in Herodotus' famous story about the agora with its new council house on Siphnos, both dating to around 530 B.C. and both built entirely of resplendent white marble. This was at one and the same time a matter of great pride and an outrageous display of wealth—punished immediately afterwards by a pirate raid (Herodotus 3.57). Often such monumental public and sacred buildings are considered by scholars to be typical enterprises of megalomaniac tyrants. This view, however, depends both on overrating the status of Archaic "tyrants" (who were, in fact, not autocrats imposing their will without question on their subjects) and on underrating the ambitions of aristocratic communities to present themselves, in full view of the entire Greek world, as rich, magnificent, and mighty poleis. Indeed, in Athens, the phase of monumental temple building on the Acropolis and by the River Ilissus began in the early sixth century B.C., and the new laying-out of the agora was achieved in its second quarter, while the first attempt of Peisistratus at tyranny (ca. 561 B.C.) failed, and his final success happened only in 546 B.C. Obviously, therefore, in Athens, it was not the monarchic will of an autocratic ruler, but the collective power and mentality of the citizen-body and its aristocratic leaders that created such buildings as an expression of their political ambitions. The decades around 600 B.C. were a period in which Greek cities developed a greater political density and civic coherence, partly under the influence of political reformers like Solon in Athens. Far from annihilating this coherence, tyrants promoted it by founding their power on the middle classes. Thus, the progressive monumentalization of public spaces resulted from, and at the same time forcefully advanced, the growth of "political communities" in their proper sense.

These spaces were where communal life developed into highly intensive forms of living together. "Face-to-face" was not only a given precondition but was in most cities a central conceptual factor of social and political life. Even in larger states like Athens, where local communities played an important role, political affairs were a matter of direct civic interactions. Increasingly, people came together for more and more common activities and interests. In the agora, citizens' assemblies, although still of limited power, must have become more numerous. Likewise, the council of elder citizens assembled with increasing frequency. Jurisdiction was more and more institutionalized in public places. At Athens, the first law-courts must have not only involved hundreds of jurors but also attracted many spectators. Lavish festivals, with dances, theater performances, religious processions and banquets, were enacted more and more in the area of the agora. Again at Athens, the Panathenaic festival must have transformed the newly established agora for several days into a crowded and vivid urban center. Moreover at Athens, as also elsewhere, the solemn funeral processions to the Kerameikos cemetery must have crossed the agora, where they may have been observed and admired by numerous spectators as manifestations of influential families—a situation that in Rome was later turned into the famous ritual of public funerals in the forum. Growing wealth too must have promoted increasing commercial activities in and around the agora. And last but not least the increasing leisure time of the upper classes encouraged people to come together, here and elsewhere, to meet friends and fellow-citizens in an atmosphere of lively discussion and entertainment.

The Political Activation of Public Centers in Classical Times

In fifth-century Athens, on its way towards a democratic manner of government, the enormous increase of a "civic presence" in the agora, as described in the introduction, was due to the augmentation of old and the institution of new functions, entailing new purpose-built structures (Camp 1986:61–150). A new large council house, a circular building for the council's permanent representatives (the *prytaneis*), new law courts, and several porticoes with public functions all strongly emphasized the political character of the area. The great achievement of Cleisthenes, the initiator of these reforms, was summed up in the general statement that he "brought the Athenians together."

Symptomatically, it was in this period that the political character of the agora was first visually emphasized by political monuments in the strict sense (Hölscher 1998a; 1998b:84–103). The earliest sculptural monument with primarily political associations erected in the public space was the group of Harmodius and Aristogeiton, who had assassinated Hipparchus, son of Peisistratus. At the edge of the meeting-place for the people's assembly, they represented the ideal models of "democratic" behavior to be imitated by all living citizens. Two or three generations later, a large monument for the eponymous heroes of the ten Athenian tribes, ideal representatives of the citizen-body of Athens, was erected in the agora as well, and came to serve as a public notice board for the city's increasing population. A splendid Painted Portico (Stoa Poikile) was built, containing a cycle of paintings depicting Athens' mythical and historical deeds of glory, above all the Battle of Marathon against the Persians. Such monumental self-celebration served to define the collective identity of the polis within the community, as well as against its arch enemy. Later, individual political ambitions competed more and more through the erection of honorary statues for contemporary politicians. A whole set of rules, norms, and laws regulated the dedication of such statues, covering issues such as for what sort of person, at what point in their life or after death, in what more or less visible location, near which other famous monuments, at what cost to the state or the dedicant, and so forth. All this testifies to the highly competitive character of the political center of the polis: such monuments are not only mirrors reflecting political reality but are forceful factors in political practice itself. Monuments become weapons, to be used in the political space of the city.

The significance of this phenomenon is made clear by the Athenian orator Lycurgus who claims that, while other cities had statues of athletes in the agora, at Athens there stood great statesmen and the tyrant-slayers (Lycurgus, *Against Leokrates* 31). Similarly, Vitruvius reproaches the people of Alabanda in Asia Minor because they had set up images of lawyers in the gymnasium, but of discus-throwers, runners, and ball-players in the agora (Vitruvius 7.5.6). The polis' political center, if rightly conceived as such, was defined as a political space by monuments of policy and images of politicians. By implication, this demonstrates that the realm of politics had by now obtained a certain autonomy, with its own rules, requirements, and modes of behavior.

The intellectual conception of social space that underpins this development appears to have had Hippodamus of Miletus as its most prominent representative (Aristotle, *Politics* 1268a; McCredie 1971; Gehrke 1989). To this individual are ascribed the most ambitious city designs of classical Greece: the layout of Miletus after its destruction by the Persians in 494 and its liberation in 479 B.C.; Athens' newly founded harbor city, the Peiraeus, between 479 and ca. 450 B.C.; and the Athenian colony of Thurii in South Italy in 444 B.C. The ascription to him of the 408 B.C. plan of Rhodes remains doubtful (Hoepfner 1994:17–67; 1999:201–315). The proverbial "Hippodamian lay-out" of cities, which is a matter of constant controversy, is difficult to deduce from what remains of these cities. It cannot have been, as was long thought, the orthogonal grid plan, which in fact had already been adopted in colony foundations of the Archaic period. Rather, his great achievement was a rational distribution (*diairesis*) of functional spaces. The territory surrounding the polis was to be divided into: one third for meeting the costs of the state's sacred institutions, one third for paying the warriors, and one third for "private" farming. Obviously, these same principles cannot have been adopted for the city area, but some analogous categories may well be supposed, such as sacred, political and residential areas, each set into functional relation to the other. Moreover, without any recognizable relation to his division of urban space, Hippodamus devised, in a theoretical essay, an almost utopian, and again tripartite, concept of an ideal society consisting of warriors, farmers, and craftsmen. He is an outstanding exemplar of a new type of high-flown intellectualism that developed during the fifth century B.C., the clearest expression of which is given by the philosopher Xenophanes:

> Not from the beginning did gods give all things to mortal men,
> But in the course of time men themselves found by searching the better. (B18)

The far-sighted character of such town planning may be recognized by the fact that at Miletus, in the (re-)founding of 479 B.C., large areas were defined and reserved for public spaces—to be "filled out" only in Hellenistic times by architectural enterprises such as surrounding porticoes and the like (Hoepfner 1994:17–22; 1999:207–212).

Visualizing Public Order and Political Identity in Late Classical and Hellenistic Times

Late Classical and Hellenistic towns display a wide variety of concepts regarding public spaces. The most prominent feature is that the cityscape now is consciously conceived and shaped as a visual context, explicitly expressing the basic principles of its public order and presenting the crucial elements of its collective memory and identity. Cities become self-referential images of their own ideal and ideological significance.

There are five main features to this new visualization of urban spaces. First, on the level of urban planning, comes a rational configuration of the main public places and buildings. Second, on the level of architectural typology, is the creation of clearly defined and widely adopted functional devices, particularly for theaters, bouleuteria, prytaneia, gymnasia, etc. with significant façades emphasizing the building's public importance. Third, in terms of architectural design, there develops a system of unifying façades surrounding public and religious spaces in long porticoes, integrating other buildings and forming large rectangular layouts of agoras and urban sanctuaries. Fourth is a more and more widely diffused practice of decorating such spaces with significant public monuments, representing the divinities and heroes of the community, recording the glorious past of the city, and celebrating the leading members of the citizen-body. Fifth, and finally, appears an increasing orientation towards a citizen audience participating in collective festivals and observing public rituals and events, as well as of foreign visitors admiring the grand tradition and glory of the city. This visual self-celebration and self-reflection became the main motor behind the development of public spaces in late Classical and Hellenistic cities in Greece.

To begin with an old traditional place, at Athens, the agora—which had been a conglomerate of heterogeneous political buildings, juridical installations, sacred areas, and public monuments—was transformed by large unifying porticoes along its sides (Camp 1986:153–180). Typically, foreign kings (particularly the Attalids of Pergamon who ideologically claimed the heritage of Athens' cultural traditions) took the most impressive initiatives. These rulers framed the agora with a monumental two-storied portico at the east side and a smaller portico in front of the sanctuary of Meter at the west side, and they concentrated all viewpoints on a high pillar monument dedicated to the royal donor. Since political activities were more and more transferred to other places, especially the theater, and since a stadium was built in the Ilissus valley for athletic games in the later fourth century B.C., the agora became more and more a place for public monuments, recording the glorious memory of the city. Moreover, it was transformed into a place where the citizens came together to enjoy that atmosphere of historical greatness, and a place where philosophers of the Stoic school continued the great intellectual tradition of Socrates, Plato, and Aristotle, and a place where tourists admired the age-old center of Greek culture.

Towards the middle of the fourth century B.C. the ancient city of Priene in Asia Minor was re-founded according to a totally new, "modern" plan, including an orthogonal street grid, despite its irregular site on the slope of Mount Mykale which caused a considerable unevenness of perpendicular streets (Rumscheid 1998). Under these peculiar conditions, all traditional requirements of Greek cities were fulfilled by a rational design, clearly separating all essential functions: at the center the agora, aligned with the main street axis and, perpendicular to it, the two hubs of culture and education—the theater above and the gymnasium below. The steep rock above the city, being almost inaccessible, was used mainly as a citadel, a kind of military acropolis, while the main sanctuary of the polis goddess, Athena, was integrated on a lower ridge within the street system as a sacred acropolis. The agora was from the beginning conceived as a political center, later giving access to a bouleuterion and a prytaneion, and with a separate market place beyond its western edge. In the course of time, this place was more and more shaped into a closed area of political representation: framed by regular, unifying portico buildings, with a stage-like space for ceremonies and performances, bounded by the honorific monuments of leading citizens, linked by a stepped terrace with an adjoining portico for spectators, and—finally—marked by an elegant entrance arch at the eastern exit. Compared with the vivid multifunctional character of the Athenian agora in the fifth century, this is a solemn visual monumentalization of civic identity.

More ambitious was Megalopolis, founded in 369 B.C. in the middle of the Peloponnesus as the capital of a new league of Arcadian cities. Megalopolis had two focal areas, opposite to each other on both sides of the River Helisson (Lauter 2002). To the north, the civic center of the agora has a multifunctional architectural complex on its western side, containing buildings for the three main political institutions of the city. These were the council (*boule*), its executive committee (*damiourgoi*), and the military commander (*polemarchos*), as well as a sanctuary of Zeus, the god of these political institutions. Large winged porticoes gradually framed the northern and eastern sides. Opposed to this is the magnificent complex of the theater, the greatest in Greece, and the adjoining Thersileion, a highly innovative hypostyle hall, both serving the league's assemblies. As at Priene, public areas were set in relation to each other according to clear principles of spatial opposition.

The most challenging task, however, was of course the design of the new metropoleis of the Hellenistic monarchies, with the royal palaces as new centers of gravity. Around 400 B.C., King Archelaus IV of Macedonia, fueled by great ambitions, transferred his residence from Aigai to Pella. There he started to build, according to the rules of "modern" Greek urbanism, his new city, which then was realized on an even greater scale by Philip II (Siganidou and Lilimbaki-Akamati 1997; Akamatis 2001). Their main concern was the configuration of palace and polis, and this resulted in an antithetic structure, bringing the king's dominance clearly to the fore. The palace was erected on a steep hill, while the city expanded at its feet in a large regular grid of orthogonal streets, the center of which was occupied by the agora. This magnificent public place consisted of a wide, almost square, open area, surrounded by uninterrupted unifying porticoes. Two main doorways on the east and west sides, opening towards the main street of the city, provided access to this space, as did two minor passageways on both northern angles. Within the porticoes regular series of shops were installed, for foodstuffs and handicrafts, while the more distinguished northern wing probably served public functions. Further excavations are needed to determine whether some monument marked the center of the agora. Whatever the case, major public architecture, political or religious, seems to be lacking: a sanctuary of Aphrodite and Meter as well as a peristyle building, perhaps a public archive, are situated nearby, but beyond the surrounding porticoes. The agora itself appears primarily as a secular zone of civic intercourse and public trade.

At the same time, the old Macedonian residence of Aigai was transformed into a ceremonial residence for dynastic rituals like weddings and burials. Here too the palace, mainly consisting of large and lavish banquet halls, was built on a mountain slope, in a dominant position over the city area. Between these two poles, some conspicuous links were installed. On the edge of the agora, a sanctuary of Eukleia was embellished with rich votive-offerings from Queen Eurydike, thus demonstrating the royal presence in this cult of public significance. Moreover, between the palace and the agora, as a "hinge" between the ruler and his people, a theater served as a space of public ceremonies—for example, the conspicuous royal wedding at which Philip II was murdered.

The unsurpassed zenith of Hellenistic city building was Alexandria, initiated by Alexander the Great himself, and designed by Ptolemy I as the future capital of Egypt (Hoepfner 1994:235–256; 1999:455–471; Grimm 1998). The orthogonal plan had three main streets: one longitudinal (where the main public buildings and facilities were aligned), and two perpendicular. One of these led to the island of the gigantic Pharos lighthouse, one of the Seven Wonders of the World, the other to the royal palace quarter. As at Priene, the urban center was still the agora with its law court and other public buildings, but this was surrounded by additional public facilities that hitherto had been placed more at the fringes of Greek cities. There was, for example, a famous gymnasium, center of Greek education, and a public park, probably of sacred character and containing an artificial hill (with a sanctuary of the god Pan) that offered a magnificent view over the whole city. On the other hand, the palace quarter too had a public face, turned towards the city, with buildings and monuments of highly official and ideological character. These included a monumental peristyle construction for the reception of foreign guests, a sanctuary of the Muses with the fabulous royal library, and probably also the tomb of Alexander, the founder hero of the city and of Ptolemaic rule over Egypt. Thus, in Alexandria, the two main forces of the capital, royal and civic, are inextricably interconnected with each other in the city's topography.

The same holds true, under very different conditions, for Pergamon, where a small local citadel was expanded into the capital of the Attalid kings (von Hesberg 1996; Radt 1999). The most striking feature of this place is the installation, on the acropolis, of a coherent complex of palace buildings in close connection with monumental state sanctuaries: the precinct of Athena, with famous monuments of victories over the Gauls, the monumental altar building for Zeus, and the theater with an adjoining temple of Dionysus, who was worshipped in Pergamum as a "leader" of the rulers' dynasty. In early Hellenistic times, the area between the palace-fortress and the still restricted residential quarters seems to have been occupied by a sort of agora (Rheidt 1992). Later, when the city grew to a veritable metropolis, a new, rectangular agora of "modern" type was founded at a greater distance, while a heröon-like building for the ruler-cult was established at the border between the palace area and the city. As in Pella, the separation of the palace area, and the corresponding independence of the city from the palace, seem to have been clearer than in Alexandria, where a more assertive concept of the ruler led to a stronger domination of the city by the king's presence.

It was this concept of political monumentality and forceful kingship with which Rome had to compete when it aimed for a dominant political position over the

Greek world. But it was not until the time of Augustus that such urban plans were transferred, on a grand scale, to Rome where they were adopted and further developed in order to establish and strengthen the power of Roman emperors.

ACKNOWLEDGMENTS

I am very grateful to Susan Alcock and Robin Osborne for correcting and anglicizing my text, as well as for their useful comments, criticism, and suggestions.

NOTE

The references for this chapter are on pp. 198–202.

5 (b)

Urban Spaces and Central Places

The Roman World

Nicholas Purcell

Introduction

Imperial Rome specialized in centrality. This chapter must tend the opposite way to its pendant piece. It does not so much explore fecund and responsive variety, unshaped by orthodox order, as describe the repeated patterns of the attempted organization and imposition of plan and system through reference to the imperial center.

Autocratic monarchies always focus intently on the person of the ruler. Emperors often have capitals: the despot and the city where he is enthroned reinforce each other's glory. Rome was no exception. As the emperor's base, Rome was enriched and embellished in proportion to the size of the empire. It acquired monuments which excelled all other cities of the Roman world, in their number, the conspicuous cost of building them, the technical virtuosity of their design and execution, and, above all, their vast dimensions.

The Roman state under the emperors also functioned in ways which allowed, indeed necessitated, symbolic emphasis on the center to counter the devolution of power unavoidable in so far-flung a polity. Ideology, supporting both military loyalty and the acquiescence in the system of the wealthy of the empire's hundreds of cities, needed strong, simple messages of unity. Regional government was relatively weak, to ensure that administrators would find it hard to think about rivalry with the center. The emperor needed monopolies of control over money, movement, status, religion, and attempting to manage these monopolies added to the standing of the center (Millar 1977). At the same time, this was a society in which levels of mobility were high, the economy diverse and vigorous, and a sense of opportunity widespread—linked above all with the emperor and his power. The splendor of the emperor was not isolated. It was meant to be seen and admired, and floods of people were to be expected wherever he traveled. At Antioch in A.D. 115, when the emperor Trajan made the great city his base for war against the Parthians, "many soldiers and private individuals had come together there— for lawsuits, on missions to the emperor, for commerce, or sightseeing" (Dio 68.24). So, when a massive earthquake wrecked the place, "it was as if the whole world under Roman domination was stricken."

This city was the emperor's winter-quarters on campaign. The effect was much more marked with his regular capital. Constant movements in and out of all these types of traveler, and the maintenance of the capital as a setting for a huge and fluid population added still further to the sense of centrality experienced at Rome.

But the emperors were not the whole story of Roman urban centrality.

Centrality—Without Really Trying

"Where is the middle of things?," is a piece of elementary psychological geometry. Thinking of the world as a body—what other easy, physical metaphors are there for thinking about complex wholes?—the Greeks looked for the navel, the *omphalos*, and located it at Apollo's sanctuary at Delphi (among other places: a second-century orator also uses this expression of the Athenian acropolis, the harbor at Smyrna, Cyzicus, and the Roman province of Asia; Müller 1961). Thinking of the world geographically, as the assemblage of seas and continents which is more abstract, more geographical, and more familiar to us, does not mean abandoning the question "where's the middle?" Ways were found of going on answering the question with Delphi. But information poured in from all points of the compass, and the layout of the lands looked more complicated all the time. Halfway between north and south was quite an easy one to cope with: that meant half-way between hot and cold, and the inhabitants of the Mediterranean had some reason to think that their homes fitted that climatic definition. Halfway between east and west was more difficult, as the east reached ever further into Asia in the Hellenistic period. The Romans came up with a brilliant solution. Cut off the east, as generally alien and inferior, and take the Mediterranean world, the world of the "Sea near Us" as the Greeks called it, as what mattered. Then work out what is in the middle of the Mediterranean—dividing the eastern from the western basins of the Inland Sea—bingo, Italy! And what is in the middle of Italy, halfway down the more fertile, more accessible western coast? The Tiber mouth and the city of Rome.

> Since all other peoples are made diverse with uneven physical characteristics, it is in the true centre of the space of the whole circle of lands and of the layout of the physical world that the Roman people owns its territory . . . the Divine Intellect has established an outstanding city and a finely-balanced location for the Roman people, to enable it to assume the hegemony of the earth. (Vitruvius 6.1.10–11)

This account was written under and for the emperor Augustus, but while no doubt winning approval in the court circles, this is the thinking that reinforced imperial power through the specialness of Rome, and not the other way round (Nicolet 1991).

Now these grandiloquent visions are not as self-deluding as they might seem. Rome undoubtedly did owe a good deal to a practical centrality which was not its inhabitants' invention. Tyrrhenian Italy is a very well networked node within the Mediterranean, and the centrality of the Italian peninsula within the Mediterranean basin as a whole is an advantage which Italian communities have enjoyed at many periods. The Tiber, navigable in antiquity far above Rome, was a major routeway within the Italian peninsula. Its crossing points were key to movements from the wealthy agricultural regions of the south to the flourishing cities of the Etruscan northwest. The earliest community on the site of Rome, indeed, can only have grown because of such advantages, as the immediate region of the city, until the end of the fifth century a political territory not much more than 20 kilometers across, is not especially fertile, and must from the first have been insufficient for supporting a city any larger than the numerous city-lets which dotted the Latin plain and hill country to the south. Rome did take off because of centrality. Confirmation of that is to be found in many places: in the Roman insistence on the importance of the ancient wooden bridge across the Tiber; in the oldest Roman road, the Salt Road, which carried this vital commodity for the upland pastoralists of central Italy inland from the lagoons of the Tiber delta; in the archaeological evidence of trade with far-flung parts of the Mediterranean in the river-harbor of Rome from the sixth century B.C.; and in the contacts of west central Italy with Greeks and Carthaginians which are attested from the same period in inscriptions and in the literary tradition (Smith 1996).

There are two further signs that Rome had early grown out of being a largely self-supporting market-center and secure residence for the laborers of a productive countryside. The Romans told a story of their origins which was heavily concerned with wanderers, outsiders, and the gathering of a vagabond population—an unusually self-effacing foundation-saga, on the face of it. And the early open spaces of Rome were rather different from those of Greek cities in being concerned more explicitly with economic activities. The center of the city was a public square like an agora, the Forum Romanum, and it is overwhelmingly likely, given the rapid development at the same time of the nearby river-harbor, that a principal function of the early Forum was economic. Later tradition provides echoes of that in the Etruscan Street, and a Potter's Quarter, suggesting craft specialization of the sort found in the Kerameikos of contemporary Athens. There were from a quite early date specialized retail outlets, secure *tabernae* or shops, on both sides of the Forum piazza. Nearer the river though, and of equal venerability, were two more Fora, known as Vegetable and Cattle Markets. In later years Rome counted its citizens with care. It is not very likely that the figures alleged for the end of the archaic period (the sixth century B.C.) are based on real evidence, but they indicate a population for Rome and its territory considerably larger than Athens at the same date, while the physical extent of the city nucleus at Rome was also rather greater. It is likely in both cases that we are witnessing states which grew rapidly through attracting immigration of many different kinds, and which supported populations much larger than the average carrying capacity of the region through the earnings of specialized economic activities.

Centrality—Thinking Very Hard About It

So Romans experienced a practical, organic centrality from archaic times—the Greek community of that age which was most comparable was Corinth, with its unrivalled topographical centrality in the Greek peninsula. The Romans were certainly in close contact with the Corinthians overseas, as with other mobile peoples in the archaic Mediterranean, and they were fully familiar with contemporary developments in the world of the *polis*.

From the same period come the first signs that the Romans consciously built on, adapted, and enhanced their centrality as an ideology, that—it is scarcely too strong a word—they theorized it.

The first sign was the development of a focal public space, closely analogous to the first agoras which are known from seventh- and sixth-century B.C. Greek cities. The Forum was an open space, ritually delimited, at the meeting of carefully laid out major streets, equipped with numerous sacred sites and shrines (but not, before the end of the sixth century, actual temples in the familiar architectural sense) onto which faced buildings of public significance, including the homes of the first citizens (Tagliamonte 1995). This space was integral enough to Roman self-consciousness to be referred to with the people's name, obvious though that might be thought to be: it was the Forum Romanum, not just the public space at the heart of Rome, but much more distinctive and special with regard to the non-Roman peoples around. This space was paved already by the end of the seventh century B.C., and was the site of important new cult-places at the beginning of the fifth, when the Temples of Saturn and the very substantial Temple of Castor and Pollux were built on the south side, traditionally in the first years of the Republican state (founded in 509 B.C.).

The Romans thought of this as originally a market place, as we have seen, but alongside the commercial function there was from an early date an elaborate symbolic centrality. This also took forms familiar from elsewhere in the Mediterranean world: the city had a hearth here, the shrine of Vesta, goddess of the hearth-fire, as well as a house (known as the Regia) which was described as the abode of a first citizen, the emblematic primary house of the city. The Romans linked this structure with an extended period of political kingship in their early history (753–509 B.C.) which is not especially unlikely but hardly demonstrable. At the other end of the Forum was a place for political assemblies and what would have been called in a Greek town of the time a *bouleuterion*, a meeting-place for the council of elders of the community. The third great function of early agoras, spectacle and competition, was a feature of the Forum in later times, and it is not unreasonable to retroject that to the archaic period. Certainly the two religious spectacles which the Romans themselves regarded as immemorially ancient both used the Forum as part of their stage (Purcell 1995).

These spectacles were: the *Ludi Romani*, the Roman Games, the festival which was, like the Forum, called by the name of the people; and the triumph, the commemoration of Victory in war. This pair of public occasions introduces us to two other foci of the Roman theory of centrality (and at the same time to a characteristic feature of Roman ideology—overkill. If centrality is good, it is worth over-specifying it, with multiple, repeated, overlapping centers.)

The first of these other foci is a very early spectacle-facility which the Romans called Circus Maximus—the "Very Big Round." Essentially the valley between two hills, this was another center of early shrines and commemorations, and another major focus of the city's space (Humphrey 1986:60–67). Beyond the two festival processions, the Circus also housed horse-races and chariot races in the Greek manner. Apart from this open ground and that of the Forum, the city had no purpose-built permanent structures for watching festival competitions before 55 B.C.—an absence which the Romans regarded with puritan pride. The Circus was linked to the Forum by the processional route followed by the images of the Gods at the Ludi Romani, and by the victorious troops at the triumph. But these pomps started and finished at the most important Roman center of all—the Capitolium.

The rocky crag at the western end of the valley of the Forum Romanum, the Capitoline Hill or the Capitol, was a sanctuary and a stronghold from very early in Rome's urban history. This routine centrality was overwhelmed in new significance when the community decided to invest in a gigantic temple on its highest point. Tradition ascribed the decision to two of the last kings; archaeology (especially new excavations since 1995: Mura Sommella 2000 and 2003) confirms the approximate date of the second half of the sixth century B.C. It also leaves no doubt as to the scale of the original plan, for which a huge platform of tufa blocks was built, an investment of manpower and of wealth which can hardly not at some level represent awareness of and competition with the very large temples which certain Greek communities (Ephesus, Samos, Athens, and nearer at hand, Selinous and Akragas in Sicily) were building at this time (Figure 5.4). The cult was grandiose, ambitious and original. The sixth-century Romans adapted the most popular city-protecting deities of the contemporary Greek world, pairing Athena (Minerva) and Hera (Juno), and adding to them the overarching authority of Zeus (Jupiter), to form the Capitoline Triad. Rome's city gods combined the best patrons of powerful Greek cities with the supreme ruler of Gods and men, whose domain was the whole Hellenic world. Olympian authority—the authority of Olympos and of Olympia—was invoked at Rome from then on, and the Ludi Romani, the festival of the deities of the Capitol, at some point came to draw on the Olympic Games for its imagery and reputation.

It is hard to imagine what can have been going on at Rome at the time this cult was established, but what matters for this survey is that the result was a "reading" of many contemporary ways of establishing hierarchical order with reference to

Figure 5.4 Plastico di Roma, showing the Capitol above the Forum. This model of imperial Rome shows the rebuilding of the Capitoline Temple by the emperor Domitian, but its dominant central role in the city's landscape went back to the sixth century B.C.

symbolic centrality. The huge temple, the Capitolium, was one; the daring modification of the hilltop with the enormous platform was another. The theology of Zeus and the Olympian theme already suggested a cosmic imagining of the significance of the cult. But the centrality was not only of the mind. Topographical centrality is most frequently articulated through human action and especially movement. The great shrine of the Capitol was the setting for *rites de passage* such as coming of age, as well as some of the most solemn religious ceremonial of the year—it was, as befitted Jupiter, especially concerned with the calibration of passing time. The open porch at the front of the temple was a political space itself, used for meetings of the Senate. But the open space in front of the Capitoline temple, the Area Capitolina, was highly important too as the site of political assemblies and of the military levy, while the opening of the new, gently sloping paved road up the side of the hill from the Forum made possible the great processions which we have already mentioned. Just as the architectural and landscape works were intended to astonish, so the carrying of heavy images of the gods on ponderous vehicles which were almost—but not quite—too heavy to be hauled up the slope onto the hill was a demonstration of capability, sophistication and power.

There are parallels for this management of civic space at various points in the Greek world, including the sixth-century developments at the pan-hellenic sanctuaries of Delphi and Olympia, but the closest point of reference is Athens. The transformation of the Acropolis from fortress to civic sanctuary, and its opening up with an access road which made possible both the building of the great monuments of the hilltop, and the processions which punctuated the festival year, uniting the acropolis with the lower civic assembly-place, are close enough parallels on the physical plane: but the novel way in which the Athenians expressed a new Athenian identity in their political and religious institutions, and especially in the idea of a Panathenaia, may help us understand the political and social project of the late archaic Capitol too (Hurwit 1999). An important difference, however, is that the Romans practiced their public and religious life hand-in-hand on the Capitol and in the Forum—there was no separation of sacred and secular spaces whatsoever. Just as the Acropolis forms the inevitable backdrop to the Athenian agora, so the Capitol does for the Forum. But the Capitoline temple dominated the precinct below in a way that the Acropolis temples never did, and the visual pairing of Capitol and temple high above and forming the unavoidable focus of the public square is one which the Romans reproduced in scores of their cities.

The Capitol matters, not just because of its curious but spectacular precocious appearance in a generally obscure phase of western Mediterranean history, but because of its continuing, always refreshed and reinterpreted significance to the invented centrality in which ancient Rome ever afterwards specialized. It has to be admitted that there is a gap. There can now be no doubt about the date of the centralizing transformation of late archaic Rome. But little else can be said for 150 years about the centrality which it must have been intended to promulgate.

Effects of the Center on its Periphery: Territoriality and Space

In the fourth century B.C., however, further impressive landscape architecture projects enhanced the Capitoline Hill, at the beginning of a period in which the Roman state first developed a number of political behaviors which were to become characteristic. One of these was the establishment of daughter-settlements (Salmon 1969). It was a feature of Roman new towns from the first that they were more dependent on the mother-city than was normal with the offshoots of Greek *poleis*, and a variety of institutional and symbolic means was elaborated to express their participation in a larger polity—and their subordination to Rome. The rhetoric of centrality was a natural addition to this portfolio of aggressive interventions—since we must not lose sight of the fact that any civilizing aspects of these transformations were very secondary indeed to the demonstration of the implacable will and overwhelming superiority of the Roman state.

There were several different types of dependent settlement which expressed their allegiance to Rome in different ways. There seems to have been a regularity of spatial organization, and an architectural homage to the layout of the capital; cults echoed those of the center, and monuments replicated those of the Forum in Rome; on a perhaps less formal level toponyms within the city were often echoes or memories of features of the capital. A difficulty in assessing all this for the phases of Roman settlement which go back to the fourth century is that many of these themes were recognized with enthusiasm by later Romans and deliberately propagated in later phases of the relationship between Rome and the daughter-towns, especially after the beginning of the principate. We should probably not read too much system and too highly organized a plan into the first phases. But the effect is a real one, and enhanced by interventions which certainly do go back to the middle Republican period (von Hesberg 1985).

Of these the most striking is the invention of the Roman road. The Appian Way was built in 311 B.C. to link Rome and Capua, and exhibits much that is characteristic of the Roman Republican road (Humm 1996). First, it is—as the Capitol had been two centuries before—a virtuoso display of engineering and technical expertise. One section ran straight for more than 60 kilometers; the general direction as far as Tarracina was a close approximation to the shortest possible route; the project was conceived as a statement of Roman superiority in relation to the independent but potentially troublesome Campanians; and it was explicitly linked with the allocation to Roman agriculturalists of large tracts of high-quality land along its route. And these tracts of land were surveyed and measured and distributed with the same showy technical ability that went into the building of the road (Figure 5.5; Campbell 2000). The land was also improved through the management of water-resources, and nearer Rome it was in the same period that the same benefactors saw to the provisioning of the city with its first long-distance water conduits, or aqueducts.

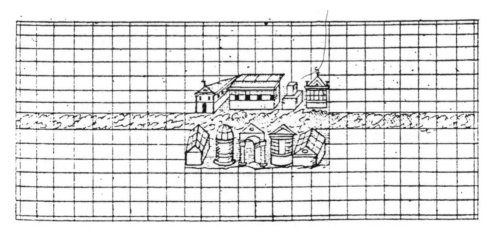

Figure 5.5 Agennius Urbicus' treatise, Illustration 37. From Campbell 2000:285. This original illustration from a Roman treatise on how to allot land shows a stylized Roman city on a road bisecting a completely regular planned landscape

Figure 5.6 The allotted landscape of the *ager Campanus*. Notice how the grid is highly central-
ized, but avoids a focus on the ancient city of Capua, in disgrace when this grid was laid out.
Since this map was drawn it has been demonstrated that the grid also extended north of the
River Volturnus seen in the upper left of this image

The land-divisions were carried out in a characteristically Roman way. From
the distant past, Roman religious expertise seems to have been a source of pride.
One technique which seemed to later Romans to be especially arcane and archaic
was the science of augury, in which trained experts divided the sky into conceptual
zones so as to assess the meaning of the behavior of birds. The land beneath was
also schematized in this way, and it is clear that the layout of both towns and
agrarian landscapes was conducted according to this lore. The second-century
land divisions of the extremely fertile territory of Capua, for instance, are aligned
precisely on the cardinal points (Figure 5.6). The position of the observer, in such
a system, was pivotal, and the land-allotments created centers—where the main
axes crossed—as much as the roads, joining central places as they did (Torelli
1966). Implicit behind the whole system was naturally the centrality of Rome
itself, where the augurs' principal lookout was on the Capitol (of course); and a
revealing and related story came to be told about the building of the great temple
just described.

While the temple's foundations were being laid, a bleeding human head was discovered deep in the excavations. Ambassadors were sent to the wisest seer of the time, an Etruscan who lived in Veii. They drew a sketch plan in the dust to show where the head had turned up. The clever sage pointed to the ground and asked: "Did you say it was found here?" The Roman team were ahead of him. "No, it was found at Rome, on the Capitol." What the sage had been attempting to transfer to Veii was the sign and demonstration of nothing less than "throne and headship of all the lands" (Florus 1.1).

Such stories and their articulation in monument and institution were a gradual process of deposition. By the second century B.C. the effect had become regular and developed. The innovative politician Gaius Gracchus made a particular point of improving access to Rome with better quality roads, marked with milestones expressing precise distances to the center (Plutarch, *Lives of the Gracchi* 28; Laurence 2004). Augustus made a point of road-building explicitly "so that Rome could be reached easily from every direction." He took on personal responsibility for the re-working of the all-important highway to the north, the Via Flaminia (Figure 5.7). The distances were measured from a central feature where the Forum abutted the Capitol, the Golden Milestone (Mari 1996).

City foundation and land allotment proceeded at a faster rate than ever before. As Roman political and military power in the Mediterranean expanded, Greek theorists were quickly found who were eager to enrich the store of symbolic messages which the Romans had been accumulating, and express the centrality of the victorious city in ever more grandiloquent terms—terms which continued to draw on and to elaborate the ancient themes which we have mentioned. "She dwells upon earth upon holy Olympus, ever unshaken," said Melinno in her *Hymn to Rome*; "shut the Gates of Olympus, Zeus, and mount guard over the holy acropolis of the aether," says another poet—sea and land are under the sway of Rome and only Heaven is still unapproached (Alpheus of Mitylene, *Anthologia Palatina* 9.526). Significantly, this Republican age saw the first attempts to imitate Rome, a flattery and a homage, but one which is telling. Rome came to be understood as template and model, in a way which Greek cities had not been.

Centrality and the Ideology of the Roman Town

To the modern observer, this expression of the dominance of the Roman core is most apparent in the cities of the Roman world founded in the late Republic and the early empire. The Greek historian Polybius (6.26.10) had noted the regularity of Roman military planning. The Romans themselves would not have thought that the military sphere was unusual in that respect. Template-thinking was apparent in law and in administration in the civilian world too, as was hardly surprising in a society in which the military was still an aspect of the citizen

Figure 5.7 Augustus' arch at Rimini. The great Italian highway, the Via Flaminia, was like a huge building or public space, with one end at the gate of Rome, the Porta Fontinalis on the slopes of the Capitol, and the other at the *colonia* of Ariminum. The monumental entry to this road survives at Rimini. The inscription (*ILS* 84) says "The Senate and People of Rome dedicated this to the emperor Augustus when he had rebuilt the Via Flaminia and all the busiest roads of Italy according to his own plans and at his own expense." Reproduced with permission of Deutsches Archäologisches Institut, Rom

ideology. The truth of Polybius' observations is apparent in the archaeology of the siege works of Numantia (133 B.C.) in northern Spain (Johnson 1983:224–227), but becomes a celebrated feature of Roman culture under the empire, when the regular forms of a centralized military culture can be studied through an abundant archaeological record from Egypt, Syria and Romania to Morocco, and Britain. Soldiers were citizens (or potential citizens) under arms and the regularity of their bases was reflected in the regularity of the cities in which they were settled when they were discharged from active service. Drawing on the long history of daughter-settlements, these new towns became ever more faithful to a model, in the institutional charters with which they were set up, and in the architecture with which they were equipped. The design of the headquarters building was a calque on the design of a forum, or vice versa. But Polybius perhaps did not see how much the architecture which the Romans made into a system was an adaptation of city-forms which were current in the Greek kingdoms of the eastern Mediterranean. The towns of Italy, Roman and non-Roman alike, became thoroughly Hellenistic during the second century B.C.

The first new cities to form a patterned sequence of this kind, however, were the veteran settlements of Italy of the very end of the Republican period, and in the north the remains of Aosta and Turin show vividly how close to military planning the foundations of the emperor Augustus could be. But the regularity was somewhat older. Gaius Gracchus tried to build a Roman city in the ruins of Carthage, and wanted to appropriate the great protecting goddess of the Carthaginians, Tanit, for his new foundation—but in the form she was worshipped on the Capitol at Rome, as Juno. Julius Caesar had given new titles to the Roman communities which were chartered all over Rome's dominion in Spain, and the point is constantly to echo the institutions, and especially the sacred institutions, of the ancient heartland of the Roman people. Thus, we hear of Obulco of the High Priest; Sacili of the People of Mars; Hispal the city of Romulus; Lucurgentum "Divine Spirit of Julius"; Venus' own Nabrissa; Hasta of the Kings; Urso of the Family Tradition, city of people from the City (Pliny, *Natural History* 4.6–17). It is no surprise that it is in this age that we first certainly hear of the setting up in towns like these of temples which actually replicated the core of Roman centrality, religion, the Capitolium. In Roman daughter-settlements, cults characteristic of Rome had long been practiced, but now there was an attempt to produce a literal imitation of the distant capital—a reflection evoked also in the names of the districts of some of the cities. An imperial writer referred to *coloniae* as "miniature Romes" (Aulus Gellius 16.13.9).

This was the symbolic language which Augustus found ready for use when he came to shape Rome's public institutions around his own power. He made his mark emphatically on all the focal monuments and spaces of the capital—Capitol, Forum, Circus, all became stages for the expression of his messages. He also developed an architectural language suitable for the claim to centrality which he so enhanced. The initiatives which he took at Rome were zealously picked up by benefactors in Roman cities of Italy and the provinces, who had often benefited from imperial patronage through service of the state in military or civilian posts, and who could now be relied on to spread Augustan messages in their home communities (Zanker 1988).

The Forum with which Augustus extended the Forum Romanum was thus copied at faraway Mérida, Emerita Augusta, a *colonia* in western Spain. The portico which his wife Livia built in the elite residential quarter of Rome was copied for a public building by a lady benefactor of Pompeii, Eumachia. Inscriptions show a rash of buildings called Augustan (or Julian) Aqueduct, Augustan Law court, Augustan Council house, in towns like these across the empire. One vivid example is what the Romans did to the ancient city of Corinth. Razed to the ground in a display of Roman might in 146 B.C., Corinth was refounded by Julius Caesar. Its central feature, where the agora of the Greek city had stood, was an unmistakably Roman Forum. It was dominated at one end by Roman-style temples on an elevated terrace (Schowalter and Friesen 2005). Around it were porticoes with *tabernae*. Behind these there were purpose-built structures called Basilicae, like the buildings which housed the law courts in Rome itself. The colonia at Corinth was laid out on a strict grid-plan like the military camps of Rome, and it came to include a building for the distinctively Roman spectacle of gladiatorial combat, the amphitheater.

Corinth was a typical foundation of the late Republic or early empire. The status of citizen colony changed over the imperial period, and the homage of imitation now became possible for many rich and important cities which could not claim the Roman credentials of the chartered towns. It was still the great imperial benefactions of the center which acted as the prototypes, but these were now the awe-inspiring amphitheaters, as at Corinth, or imperial bath-complexes. The distribution of the distinctive plan of metropolitan bath complexes, a huge block of buildings in a great precinct, all arranged in a deliberately prodigal way on a symmetrical plan, tracks the aspirations of cities to be a local capital like Ephesus or Carthage—or the process of devolution by which emperors moved for long or short periods to a provincial center. That was how Trier acquired the "Kaiserthermen," one of the most lavish bath complexes outside Rome (Ward-Perkins 1980:442–449). In this age, moreover, Capitolia (temples dedicated to the Capitoline Triad) too become part of the common currency of an imperial architecture which never ceased to recognize the imperial center—they turn up in towns which had little or no claim to be Roman in any special sense. Finally, when Hadrian added a further term to Rome's theological pushiness in building his remarkable temple of All Gods, the Pantheon, this wonder of Rome too became something which could be imitated on a deferentially smaller scale, across the empire: in the sanctuary of Asclepios at Pergamum, for instance.

Rome under the empire extended the application of its centralizing templates far beyond the citizen community. In the west, each non-Roman community recognized by the institutional planners was encouraged to develop its own Roman form, so that Britain and Gaul were dotted with centralized local capitals such as Cirencester or Paris, often the result of the forced replacement of a secure hilltop fortification with a new settlement on the Roman communications network of roads and rivers. In the older cities of the east, monumental styles derived from Roman cities and expressing pride in Roman-guaranteed communications flourished. The acropolis at Pergamum and the agora at Ephesus were dominated by Roman-style monuments, while harbors, gates, colonnaded streets, and fountains at the end of aqueducts, all identified with an essentially Roman set of urban expectations.

On Roman Imperial Space

The cities of the Roman empire were therefore shaped by a tradition which reached back to the age of the Roman conquest of Italy. That age, as we saw, was also one in which the territories of cities were transformed, with allotment schemes, and with the building of more and more permanent and spectacular roads and aqueducts (even harder to survey and engineer than roads and allotted landscapes because of the problems of relief and gradient: Hodges 1992:171–214). Both these reinforced centrality—an ideological centrality through reference to the source of the expertise and the wealth, and a topographical one, in that both planned landscapes and linear features led to the neighboring city whose power and status they expressed.

Roman authorities were well aware of this effect, and ensured that the cities whose status they wished to recognize in the order of the provinces were reflected by planned territories as redolent of Roman power as the monuments of the city centers. Two cities of the Roman West may serve as examples. Carthage, whose history had been close to that of Corinth, became the capital of Africa after its re-foundation by Caesar and Augustus. Its giant territory, the *pertica*, was divided up into geometrical lots, crossed by roads joining Carthage to the other cities of the province. And an aqueduct of more than 80 kilometers brought water across the plain from the magnificent nymphaeum at Zaghouan. Almost contemporary, Lugdunum (Lyon), the seat of the governor of most of Gaul, again a colonia, was also supplied by spectacular aqueducts. But Lugdunum illustrates also a further kind of centrality which was to be important in Roman imperial behavior.

In 10 B.C., Augustus' step-son Drusus set up in the plain below Lugdunum an altar dedicated to the goddess Rome and to Julius Caesar, on whose orders the city above had been established. The cult involved a festival in which all the constituent peoples of the province of Gaul were to participate. Its priesthood was held in rotation by the magnates of these Gallic subject peoples, at considerable expense. The festival involved games for which an amphitheater was provided alongside the sanctuary. The setting was not just beside the residence of the governor—the plain below Lugdunum was the confluence of two of the great rivers of the region, the Saône and the Rhône, both major arteries of communication—but summed up the centrality of the Roman capital city in a geographical language of the rivers and mountains, the physical features of the earth's surface, which is how the Romans had come to conceptualize their power in the world (compare Vitruvius' remarks on the Divine Intellect, above p. 183; Purcell 1990). When Drusus himself died, his cenotaph was built beside a great Roman legionary base in Germany, which it was still hoped at that date would be the center of a new Roman province. The peoples of the area were commanded to participate in an annual religious festival in honor of their conqueror, and a Roman-style spectacle building was provided. The location echoed Lugdunum: the cenotaph was high on a hill overlooking the confluence of the Rhine and the

Main, or Moguntia to the Romans, after which the place was called Moguntia-cum, today Mainz.

A template was thus set up for the centralization of Roman provinces, which we can see in action in other areas too. In Spain, milestones along the road from Cordoba to Lisbon record their distances as "between the Arch of Augustus on the River Baetis and the Ocean" (*Inscriptiones Latinae Selectae* 102: the arch must have resembled that of Augustus at Ariminum, see Figure 5.7). Cordoba, *Colonia Julia Patricia*, its Caesarian title evoking the dictator's patrician family and the status system of the old Republic, was the capital of Baetica, the province named for the River Baetis, today the Guadalquivir. Roman power now joined that great geographical feature to the river of Ocean which marked the outer boundary of the world. In Lycia, when Claudius added the region to the provincial empire, a monument was set up at the capital and principal port Patara, in which Claudius' great contribution to peace and security in annexing the province was proclaimed—and the distances to all the towns of the province by road given in long columns of names and figures (Jones 2001). Similar ways of thinking about the space of the region were to be found all over the Roman empire.

Rome in Context: The City to Which All Roads Lead

We began with the movements generated by the Roman emperor. Although those movements helped make Rome of the imperial period more conspicuously central than it had ever been before, the emperors were themselves mobile, and indeed, during the second and still more the third centuries A.D., resided more and more in subsidiary capitals across the empire: Trier, Milan, Thessalonica, Nicomedia, and eventually Byzantium, which was to be the New Rome. And this roving centrality had a long tradition behind it. Much in Roman imperial monarchy descended from the paradigmatic royalty of west Asia from the second half of the second millennium B.C. on, the kingdoms which we call Neo-Assyrian and Neo-Babylonian, and the Persian state which followed. These kings had also formed the living heart of the gigantic polities, and they had moved their bases, converting ancient cities into their own capitals, founding monumental cities with (deliberately) prodigal carelessness, and abandoning them within decades. What is so conspicuous about imperial Rome against this background, then, is that it acted as an imperial capital for so long, and that even when the emperors were seldom there, it retained so much of the charisma of a political capital. That must be attributed to the liveliness and potency of a constantly re-invigorated and ever more venerable historical tradition, and to the efficacy of the symbolic centrality with which the city had equipped itself even before Augustus created the imperial monarchy.

The centrality of Rome continued to be expressed in a unique legal and institutional position, in which it was universally recognized that the city which had

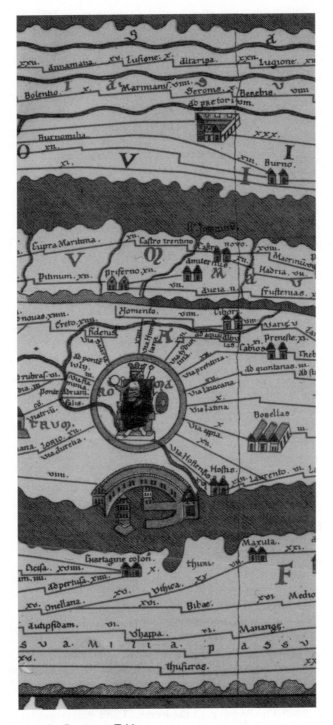

Figure 5.8 Rome on the Peutinger Table

conquered the world deserved to reap the benefits of victory in an unrivalled supply of all the necessities of life and of every kind of luxury and wonder too. This unquestioned centrality combined with the continuation of the economic functions, which Rome as a central place had fulfilled for a millennium, to allow the accumulation and maintenance of a very substantial population, normally comprising several hundred thousand people, despite the appalling living conditions which were the inevitable accompaniment (Morley 1996; Purcell 1996; 2000). Rome became a precocious and spectacular example of a certain sort of "giant city," a swollen center with over-developed centrality, which is familiar from other phases of pre-modern Mediterranean history (Pleket 1993; Nicolet et al. 2000).

The remarkable status of the city continued to be a given long after the emperors had ceased to reside there. The spoils of empire, the records of conquest, and the architectural heritage of 1200 years of urban history helped underscore this position. On the late Roman road map, the Peutinger Table, Rome's centrality to the road network is vividly visible (Figure 5.8). Rome was the Cosmopolis, in which all the nations of the world could be found (Edwards and Woolf 2003).

But just as it had been religion which first articulated the centrality of the city, so it was in religion that Rome's centrality went on being proclaimed longest. The authority and charisma of the emperors were passed to Rome's Christian bishops, and the centrality of their see to Christian topography was expressed in forms which were directly continuous with the symbolic language of the Roman past. Constantine renounced the ancient cults of the Roman Capitolium during his first triumph: but he did not demote the city which it had represented. And when he created his own new Mediterranean super-city, Constantinople, to be the center of the East for another millennium, even though he did not dedicate it to Jupiter, he made sure to build a Capitol.

REFERENCES

Akamatis, Ioannis 2001 Agora Pellas 1994–1999. Egnatia 5:257–281.

Altherr-Charon, Antoinette, and Claude Bérard 1980 Erétrie: l'organisation de l'espace et la formation d'une cité grecque. In L'archéologie aujourd'hui. A. Schnapp, ed. Pp. 229–249. Paris: Hachette Litteratures.

Bohringer, François 1980 Mégare: traditions mythiques, espace sacré et naissance de la cité. L'Antiquité classique 49:1–22.

Camp, John M. 1986 The Athenian Agora. London: Thames and Hudson.

——2005 The Origins of the Classical Agora. In Teseo e Romolo. Le origini di Atene e Roma a confronto. Emanuele Greco, ed. Pp. 197–209. Athens: Scuola Archeologica di Atene.

Campbell, Brian 2000 The Writings of the Roman Land Surveyors: Introduction, Text, Translation and Commentary. London: Society for the Promotion of Roman Studies.

Carafa, Paolo 1998 Il Comizio di Roma dalle origini all'età di Augusto. Rome: L'Erma di Bretschneider.

Castagnoli, Ferdinando 1971 Orthogonal Town Planning in Antiquity. Cambridge, MA: Massachusetts Institute of Technology Press.

Coarelli, Filippo 1983 Il Foro Romano, vol. 2. Rome: Quasar.

Di Vita, Antonino 1996 Urbanistica della Sicilia antica. *In* I Greci in Occidente. Giovanni Pugliese Carratelli, ed. Pp. 263–308. Milan: Bompiani.

Edwards, Catharine, and Greg Woolf, eds. 2003 Rome the Cosmopolis. Cambridge: Cambridge University Press.

Gehrke, Hans-Joachim 1989 Bemerkungen zu Hippodamos von Milet. *In* Demokratie und Architektur. Wolfgang Schuller, Wolfram Hoepfner, and Ernst-Ludwig Schwandner, eds. Pp. 58–68. Munich: Deutscher Kunstverlag.

Gras, Michele, and Henri Tréziny 1999 Megara Iblea. *In* La città greca antica: istituzioni, società e forme urbane. Emanuele Greco, ed. Pp. 251–267. Rome: Donzelli.

Greco, Emanuele 1996 La città e il territorio. *In* I Greci in Occidente. Giovanni Pugliese Carratelli, ed. Pp. 233–242. Milan: Bompiani.

——1998 Agora eumegethes. L'espace public dans les polis de l'Occident. Ktema 18:153–158.

——, and Mario Torelli 1983 Storia dell'urbanistica. Il mondo greco. Rome and Bari: Laterza.

Grimm, Günter 1998 Alexandria. Die erste Königsstadt der hellenistischen Welt. Mainz: Philipp von Zabern.

Hodges, A. Trevor 1992 Roman Aqueducts and Water Supply. London: Duckworth.

Hoepfner, Wolfram 1994 Haus und Stadt im klassischen Griechenland. Munich: Deutscher Kunstverlag.

——ed. 1999 Geschichte des Wohnens I:123–608. Stuttgart: Deutsche Verlags-Anstalt.

Hölkeskamp, Karl-Joachim 2002 *PTOLIS* and *AGORE*. Homer and the Archaeology of the City-State. *In* Omero tremila anni dopo. F. Montanari, ed. Pp. 297–342. Rome: Edizioni di storia e letteratura.

Hölscher, Tonio 1991 The City of Athens: Space, Symbol, Structure. *In* City-States in Classical Antiquity and Medieval Italy. Anthony Molho, Kurt Raaflaub, and Julia Emlen, eds. Pp. 355–380. Ann Arbor: University of Michigan Press.

——1998a Images and Political Identity: The Case of Athens. *In* Democracy, Empire, and the Arts in Fifth-Century Athens. Deborah Boedeker and Kurt A. Raaflaub, eds. Pp. 153–183. Cambridge, MA: Harvard University Press.

——1998b Öffentliche Räume in frühen griechischen Städten. Heidelberg: Universitätsverlag C. Winter.

——2005 Lo spazio pubblico e la formazione della città antica. *In* Teseo e Romolo. Le origini di Atene e Roma a confronto. Emanuele Greco, ed. Pp. 211–283. Athens: Scuola Archeologica di Atene.

Humm, Michel 1996 Appius Claudius Caecus et la construction de la Via Appia. Mélanges d'archéologie et d'histoire de l'Ecole Française de Rome 108:693–746.

Humphrey, John H. 1986 Roman Circuses: Arenas for Chariot-Racing. London: B. T. Batsford.

Hurwit, Jeffrey M. 1999 The Athenian Acropolis. Cambridge: Cambridge University Press.

Johnson, Anne 1983 Roman Forts of the 1st and 2nd Centuries AD in Britain and the German Provinces. London: A. & C. Black.

Jones, Christopher P. 2001 The Claudian Monument at Patara. Zeitschrift für Papyrologie und Epigraphik 137:161–168.

Kenzler, Ulf 1999 Studien zur Entwicklung und Struktur der griechischen Agora in archäischer und klassischer Zeit. Frankfurt am Main: Peter Lang.

Kolb, Frank 1981 Agora und Theater, Volks- und Festversammlung. Berlin: Gebrüder Mann.

Lackner, Eva-Maria, In press Republikanische Fora. Munich: Biering und Brinkmann.

Laurence, Ray 2004 Milestones, Communications and Political Stability. In Travel, Communication, and Geography in Late Antiquity: Sacred and Profane. Linda Ellis and Frank Kidner, eds. Pp. 41–58. Burlington, VT: Ashgate.

Lauter, Hans 2002 "Polybios hat es geweiht . . ." Antike Welt 33:375–386.

Marchetti, Patrick, and Kostas Kolokotsas 1995 Le nymphée de l'agora d'Argos. Paris: De Boccard.

Mari, Z. 1996 Miliarium Aureum. In Lexicon Topographicum Urbis Romae, Vol. 3. Eva Margareta Steinby, ed. Pp. 250–251. Rome: Quasar.

Martin, Roland 1951 Recherches sur l'agora grecque. Paris: De Boccard.

——1974 L'urbanisme dans la Grèce antique. Paris: A. & J. Picard.

Mazarakis Ainian, Alexander 1997 From Rulers' Dwellings to Temples: Architecture, Religion and Society in Early Iron Age Greece (1100–700 B.C.). Jonsered: Paul Åströms Förlag.

McCredie, James R. 1971 Hippodamos of Miletos. In Studies Presented to George M. A. Hanfmann. David G. Mitten, John G. Pedley, and Jane Ayer, eds. Pp. 95–100. Mainz: Philipp von Zabern.

Mertens, Dieter 1985 Metapont. Ein neuer Plan des Stadtzentrums. Archäologischer Anzeiger:645–671.

——2003 Die Agora von Selinunt. Mitteilungen des Deutschen Archäologischen Instituts Römische Abteilung 110:389–446.

——2006 Städte and Bauten der Westgriechen. Munich: Hirmer.

——, and Emanuele Greco 1996 Urbanistica della Magna Grecia. In I Greci in Occidente. Giovanni Pugliese Carratelli, ed. Pp. 243–262. Milan: Bompiani.

Millar, Fergus G. B. 1977 The Emperor in the Roman World. London: Duckworth.

Millett, Paul 1998 Encounters in the Agora. In Kosmos: Essays in Order, Conflict and Community in Classical Athens. Paul Cartledge, Paul Millett, and Sitta von Reden, eds. Pp. 203–228. Cambridge: Cambridge University Press.

Morley, Neville 1996 Metropolis and Hinterland: The City of Rome and the Italian Economy, 200 B.C.–A.D. 200. Cambridge: Cambridge University Press.

Morris, Ian 1987 Burial and Ancient Society: The Rise of the Greek City-State. Cambridge: Cambridge University Press.

——1992 Death-Ritual and Social Structure in Classical Antiquity. Cambridge: Cambridge University Press.

Müller, Werner 1961 Die heilige Stadt: Roma Quadrata, himmlisches Jerusalem und die Mythe vom Weltnabel. Stuttgart: W. Kohlhammer.

Mura Sommella, Anna 2000 Le recenti scoperte sul Campidoglio e la fondazione del tempio di Giove Capitolino. Rendiconti della Pontificia Accademia Romana di Archeologia 70 (1998–99):57–80.

——2003 Notizie preliminari sulle scoperte e sulle indagini archeologiche nel versante orientale del Capitolium. Bullettino della Commissione Archeologica Comunale in Roma 102 (2001):263–264.

Nicolet, Claude 1991 Space, Geography, and Politics in the Early Roman Empire. Ann Arbor: University of Michigan Press.

——, Robert Ilbert, and Jean-Charles Depaule, eds. 2000 Mégapoles méditerranéennes: géographie urbaine retrospective. Rome: L'Ecole française de Rome.

Osborne, Robin 1996 Greece in the Making. London: Routledge.

Pleket, Henri W. 1993 Rome: A Pre-industrial Megalopolis. In Megalopolis: The Giant City in History. Theo Barker and Anthony Sutcliffe, eds. Pp. 14–35. New York: St. Martin's Press.

Polignac, François de 1995 Cults, Territory, and the Origins of the Greek City-State. Chicago: University of Chicago Press.

Purcell, Nicholas 1990 Maps, Lists, Money, Order and Power: Review Essay on C. Nicolet, L'inventaire du monde. Journal of Roman Studies 80:177–182.

——1995 Forum Romanum, Republican and Imperial Periods. In Lexicon Topographicum Urbis Romae, vol. 2. Eva Margareta Steinby, ed. Pp. 325–342. Rome: Quasar.

——1996 The City of Rome under Augustus and his Successors. In Cambridge Ancient History X². Alan Bowman, Edward Champlin, and Andrew Lintott, eds. Pp. 782–811. Cambridge: Cambridge University Press.

——2000 Rome and Italy. In Cambridge Ancient History XI². Alan Bowman, Peter Garnsey, and Dominic Rathbone, eds. Pp. 405–443. Cambridge: Cambridge University Press.

Radt, Wolfgang 1999 Pergamon: Geschichte und Bauten einer antiken Metropole. Darmstadt: Primus.

Rheidt, Klaus 1992 Die Obere Agora. Zur Entwicklung des hellenistischen Stadtzentrums von Pergamon. Istanbuler Mitteilungen 42:235–282.

Robertson, Noel 1998 The City Center of Archaic Athens. Hesperia 67:283–302.

Rumscheid, Frank 1998 Priene. Istanbul: Ege Yayinlari.

Salmon, Edward Togo 1969 Roman Colonization under the Republic. London: Thames and Hudson.

Schnapp, Alain 1996 Città e campagna. L'immagine della polis da Omero all'età classica. In I Greci in Occidente. Giovanni Pugliese Carratelli, ed. Pp. 117–163. Milan: Bompiani.

Schowalter, Daniel N., and Steven J. Friesen, eds. 2005 Urban Religion in Roman Corinth: Interdisciplinary Approaches. Cambridge, MA: Harvard Theological Studies, Harvard Divinity School.

Siganidou, Maria, and Maria Lilimbaki-Akamati 1997 Pella. Athens: Archaeological Receipts Fund, Direction of Publications.

Smith, Christopher 1996 Early Rome and Latium: Economy and Society, c. 1000 to 500 B.C. Oxford: Oxford University Press.

Tagliamonte, Gianluca 1995 Il Foro Romano fino alla prima età repubblicana. In Lexicon Topographicum Urbis Romae, vol. 2. Eva Margareta Steinby, ed. Pp. 313–325. Rome: Quasar.

Thompson, Homer A., and R. E. Wycherley 1972 Excavations in the Athenian Agora, vol. XIV: The History, Shape and Uses of an Ancient City Center. Princeton: American School of Classical Studies at Athens.

Torelli, Mario 1966 A templum augurale of the Republican Period at Bantia. Reprinted in Studies in the Romanization of Italy. Helena Fracchia and Maurizio Gualtieri eds. Pp. 97–127. Edmonton: University of Alberta Press (1995).

——1999 Tota Italia: Essays in the Cultural Formation of Roman Italy. Oxford: Oxford University Press.

von Hesberg, Henner 1985 Plangestaltung der coloniae maritimae. Rheinisches Museum 92:127–150.

——1996 Privatheit und Öffentlichkeit der frühhellenistischen Hofarchitektur. *In* Basileia, die Paläste der hellenistischen Könige. Wolfram Hoepfner, ed. Pp. 84–96. Mainz am Rhein: Philipp von Zabern.

Ward-Perkins, John 1980 Roman Imperial Architecture. New York: Penguin Books.

Zanker, Paul 1988 The Power of Images in the Age of Augustus. Ann Arbor: University of Michigan Press.

6

Housing and Households

Introduction

That people had to live somewhere is a seemingly simple observation, but one not always heeded in classical archaeology's past emphasis on monumental urban spaces and public central places. The detailed study of ancient housing began only in the latter part of the 20th century; evolving profoundly since then, it is now one of the more flourishing subfields in the discipline.

In its early stages, not surprisingly, the analysis of domestic structures (from *domus*, Latin for "house") relied greatly on issues and clues provided by textual evidence. In the Greek world, for example, this led to focused attempts to identify and delimit separate "male" and "female" spaces in the home (an expectation based on testimony from the fourth-century B.C. law court speeches). The interest of ancient philosophers in the link between city plan and social structure also led to an emphasis on the degree to which Classical house plans appeared identical and egalitarian. In the Roman world, the writings of the first-century B.C. architect, Vitruvius, dictated a largely uniform interpretation of house composition and organization. Modern preconceptions, such as the assumption of an unambiguous division of public versus private, also held sway.

Such initial approaches have rapidly been outgrown or expanded, in part thanks to the realization that ancient written sources—while they can "re-people" the past in lively fashion—are not the best representative of the diversity of house design and human behavior over time. Instead, the material evidence of house construction and organization is today taken more seriously in its own right. The reasons for this are numerous, but the growing theoretical sophistication of "domestic studies" in the archaeology of other regions and time periods has unquestionably played a part. So too, in the Greek world especially, has the expansion of the available sample, though excavation of domestic architecture still lags woefully behind that of more major, public structures.

The issue of sample size and quality, of course, marks a significant difference in the study of Greek and Roman houses. In the Greek world, the best evidence comes from the city of Olynthos, abandoned in the fourth century B.C., but here the departing inhabitants seem to have taken most movable items with them. By contrast, the eruption of Vesuvius, near the Bay of Naples, captured and preserved an astonishing range of domestic architecture and artifacts in communities such as Pompeii and Herculaneum. The combination of standing architecture, wall paintings, and interior furnishings, allowing us to envision the experience of living and moving through these spaces, generates a richness of interpretation that is nearly impossible elsewhere. Pompeii, however, does not answer all questions about Roman-period housing: it cannot represent the entire empire, or all social classes, or all periods. How to employ the evidence of these "lost cities" the most wisely is a major question today in wider studies of Roman domestic architecture.

What makes the study of *houses* most compelling, perhaps, is that it is just as much a study of *households*. The physical space and furnishings of any house—its potential combination of domestic artifacts, doors, courtyards, corridors, furniture, hearths, mosaics, rooms, wall paintings, and windows—shape and reflect the behavior of the full range of its inhabitants, their internal relationships as well as their points of contact with "outsiders." The sheer variety of ancient household formations, and their sensitivity to the broader social and political formations in which they subsisted, emerges clearly in this chapter. The household becomes an ever more provocative unit to consider, as house studies continue to reveal its continuing transformations in the ancient Mediterranean world.

6 (a)
Housing and Households

The Greek World

Lisa Nevett

Introduction

Today the word "house" carries with it assumptions about the architectural form
of a building, the range of activities taking place inside, and the relationships
between its different occupants. But a closer look at individual examples of houses,
even within a single culture, reveals almost infinite variation in the structures
themselves, in the range of functions they perform, and in the identities of their
inhabitants. In the context of the ancient world there has been a tendency for
scholars to generalize about the appearance of houses and about the ways in which
they were used. Yet here, too, more detailed examination reveals great variety in
the form taken by individual dwellings, and in the ways in which they served as
settings for social life. This section of chapter 6 discusses some specific examples
of Greek houses from different periods in order to explore some of the ways in
which both their symbolic and their functional roles were defined and re-defined
through time. By highlighting similarities and differences between buildings and
taking a long-term perspective, it becomes clear that the influence on domestic
life of various cultural dimensions such as wealth, status, and gender, waxes and
wanes through time, changing in response to external social and political
factors.

Domestic Space in the Early Iron Age: Defining a "House"

The first step in our investigation is to explore what we mean by a house in the
ancient Greek context, and this is less straightforward than it might at first appear.
Archaeological evidence shows that the architecture of the small, relatively egalitarian communities of the pre-literate Early Iron Age (tenth to eighth century B.C.)

was comparatively unsophisticated in construction materials and techniques, and in plan. In southern mainland Greece a common form of structure was the apsidal building, which had an elongated rectangular shape but with one curved end (Figure 6.1 [a]). The walls were unfired mud brick on a shallow stone footing, with a timber and thatch roof. Inside, the floor consisted of earth which was beaten and packed down to give a hard, flat surface. Because these materials are not very durable, such buildings are frequently poorly preserved, so that elements of the organization of individual examples, and the range of functions they served, are sometimes open to debate. For example, one such building, Unit IV.5 at Nichoria in Messenia, occupied during the ninth century, has been interpreted in two alternative ways, either with a small roofed area and adjoining open enclosure (Coulson 1983:51), or as a larger, fully roofed building (Mazarakis Ainian 1992:82) (Figure 6.1 [a]).

Even where such buildings are relatively well preserved, they contain few of the kinds of fixtures and fittings which would give visitors to a modern western house some ideas about what kinds of activities took place inside, and about how those activities might have been organized. In a similar, slightly earlier, building from Nichoria, Unit IV.1, the only surviving architectural feature to give away anything about the activities taking place is a large, central hearth. A closer look can, nevertheless, tell us something about what people did in such buildings: there, some of the objects found show that storage, preparation, and consumption of foodstuffs (including lentils, meat, and drink), and weaving of cloth took place. Doubtless, in these buildings groups of people carried out many of the chores which today would be associated with the life of a household. Nevertheless, space would have been relatively cramped, and instead of being divided up into separate rooms, the only partition walls were used to create a porch at the front and a small room at the rear, in the apse. Despite this, there seems to have been some orderliness in the way in which the inhabitants used their space: in Unit IV.1 an assortment of utensils, together with some foodstuffs, were stored in the apse room. Broken crockery in the area around the central hearth suggests that this was where eating and drinking took place. Further storage and cooking implements in the porch seem to indicate the use of this area for preparing meals. Lack of technology suitable for producing translucent materials during this period must have meant that any "windows" would have been simple openings in the walls and were probably small and high up, serving for ventilation rather than to let in light. Nevertheless the absence of partitions would have enabled daylight to penetrate much of the interior from the doorway and perhaps from an opening in the roof above the hearth. The large interior space could also have been heated and lit from the central hearth. Members of such households would have had to share such spaces day and night, achieving little privacy from their fellows. But how many people would have lived in this kind of building? What was their relationship to each other? And what was the full range of activities carried out here? In short, how similar was the role of this structure to what we think of as a "house" today?

Despite careful analysis of the objects found at Nichoria (Mazarakis Ainian 1992), these questions are difficult to answer. In an effort to count the occupants

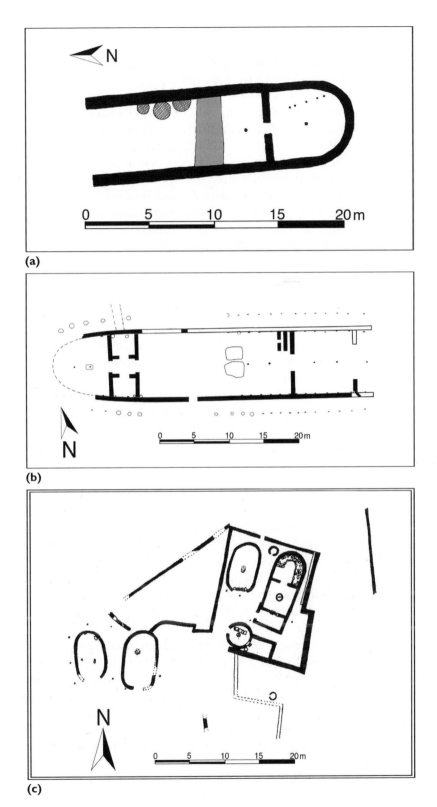

Figure 6.1 (a) Unit IV.5, Nichoria. After Coulson et al. 1983: figure 2–27; (b) Heroon building, Lefkandi, Euboea. After Popham and Sackett 1993: plate 5; (c) Skala Oropos, Attica, central sector. After Mazarakis Ainian 2002: figure 68, Phase 5

we could try to calculate how many people could be supported by the amount of food stored here, but how long were those stores supposed to last? Alternatively, we could look at the number of broken vessels in order to assess how many people would have been served at one time. But how often did such breakages happen? And did individuals customarily share a single communal vessel, or did they use different ones for different purposes? We might guess that a family group was accommodated here, but even this assumption raises further questions: was this a nuclear family (just parents and children) or an extended one (including grand-parents, uncles and aunts and other, more distant, relations)? Might there even have been some other form of "family," perhaps comprising one man with several wives and their offspring? Exploring the full range of activities taking place in this building is also a challenging task, since the archaeology preserves only a selection of the less perishable items with which it was once furnished. At the same time, activities may have taken place here which required little or no special-ized equipment and which therefore left no trace.

There is, then, a limit to the conclusions which can be drawn on the basis of a single structure. But if we broaden the scope of our inquiry, comparing different buildings, we can improve our understanding of the way in which they were used, and gain insight into the nature of the society which constructed and occupied these houses. The famous tenth-century apsidal building at Lefkandi in Euboea used similar materials to the Nichoria houses, but it is more carefully built and on a much larger scale, covering an area of around $500\,m^2$ and comprising several separate rooms as well as a colonnade around the exterior (Figure 6.1 [b]: the central section was not preserved). The precise function of the building, and the exact circumstances of its construction and destruction are debated (it may never have been completed). The same area was also used for numerous burials, including those of a man and woman placed in a shaft under the floor of the building itself, and further tombs dug into a mound which was raised over the top of the building's remains (Popham and Sackett 1993). At nearby Eretria, a cluster of similar apsidal buildings, dating to the eighth century and on the site of the later Apollo sanctuary, seems to have a variety of functions: while one of these was later replaced by a rectangular hekatompedon, a "hundred foot" long temple, and may therefore have served as a cult building, the finds from buildings nearby reveal that iron-working took place in one, while domestic activities were carried out in several others.

By comparing the evidence from Nichoria, Lefkandi, and Eretria it becomes possible to identify certain trends and distinctions. If the Lefkandi building was a house at all, its size suggests that it may have been occupied by an extended family group. The comparatively large scale and careful construction may indicate that it functioned as a marker of the high status of the man and woman buried under its floor, and it may have also have served as a relatively luxurious dwelling for them during their lifetime, and/or as a heroon or monument for commemorat-ing them after their deaths. Despite its relatively early date and the limitations of the building materials, architecture was being used here in a specific manner which drew a distinction between this and other contemporary structures and marked it out as more than an ordinary house. Thus, while the form is similar to Nichoria Unit IV.5 and buildings like it, the function of the building was probably somewhat different. This can also be seen at Eretria, where distinctions between the types of objects found inside the various structures show that there may have been some specialization, with different buildings serving domestic, craft, or perhaps also religious functions.

In sum, while the identification of a house might at first seem to be straight-forward, the reality is actually more complex. The range of roles potentially per-formed by a domestic structure is broader than we may assume based on modern, western practice, and buildings may share a single form while fulfilling contrast-ing purposes. Nevertheless, comparison between different structures and their associated furnishings demonstrates the way in which a single, relatively straight-forward architectural form was already starting to be adapted to a range of specialized purposes, as well as to serve as a symbolic marker.

Eighth-century Housing: Social Revolution?

A different way of organizing space can be seen at Skala Oropos on the Attic coast opposite Euboea, and at Zagora on the Cycladic island of Andros, both of which were occupied during the eighth century B.C. At Skala Oropos, a cluster of build-ings is built in a similar technique to the Nichoria houses. The group sits within an enclosure wall which seems to define them as belonging together as a complex (Figure 6.1 [c]). Whereas the scale of a building like Nichoria Unit IV.5 suggests that it may have been home to a nuclear family, it has been suggested that the complex of Oropos buildings should be interpreted as representing a single com-posite dwelling belonging to some form of extended family group. Whatever the reason, it seems that here what was required—rather than a single large space like that at Nichoria—was a set of separate, smaller "rooms," probably to provide dif-ferent locations for various people and/or activities.

A similar development can be seen at the settlement of Zagora in the Cycladic islands (Cambitoglou et al. 1971; Cambitoglou et al. 1988) (Figure 6.2 [a], showing two, apparently separate, domestic units). Like many excavated ancient Greek houses, these were lived in for a long period, perhaps as long as one hundred years. During this time families may have come and gone, or a house may have been occupied by several generations of a single family. The archaeological evi-dence shows two separate phases of use, indicating how, through time, small houses were expanded to provide more living space. Superficially the Zagora structures look quite different from those we have seen so far: they are built com-pletely of stone slabs forming small, rectilinear rooms, and complexes that are apparently independent units share party walls with their neighbors. These dif-ferences may well result from the use of stone as the principal building material (a necessity in the island environment where timber to support a mud brick struc-ture would have been in short supply). If we look at the organization of space, the constructions of the earlier phase bear some resemblance in plan to Nichoria

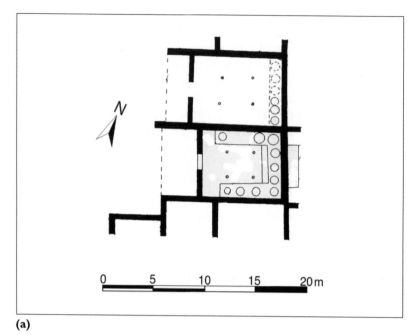

(a)

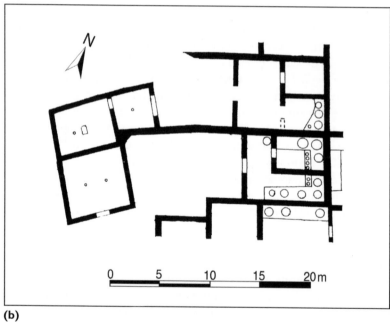

(b)

Figure 6.2 (a) Zagora, Andros, units H24/25/32, phase 1. After Cambitoglou et al. 1988: plate II; (b) Zagora, Andros, units H24/25/32, phase 2. After Cambitoglou et al. 1988: plate II

Unit IV.5, with a large interior room and smaller porch area, although the space available in each of the Zagora units is more limited (around 60 m²). During the second phase the original large room was subdivided in each case, and a further unit was built on the other side of an open space (Figure 6.2 [b]). The organization of these different parts suggests that they functioned together as a single unit, while the addition of specific features which repeat from unit to unit suggests that they played a relatively standardized role: stone benches in the original nucleus of each one seem to have served as stands for storage vessels, and a hearth was included in the newly-constructed area. Again, a range of domestic functions seems to be represented.

In this case, the organization of space has led to the development of more detailed hypotheses about one particular aspect of the lives of the inhabitants of the site, namely relations between male and female family members. Athenian textual sources of the fifth century give the impression that within a single house men and women would have led largely separate lives, and this has often been interpreted literally as implying that different living quarters were provided for each (for example, Walker 1983). The binary structure of the Zagora houses, together with the central open area at the center, which resembles the courtyard of the later, Classical, house (see below), has been taken as evidence of a conceptual differentiation between male and female activities and areas at this early date (Morris 2000:280–286). Such a distinction is difficult to prove convincingly, however, and Zagora is, as far as we know, unique. It therefore seems preferable to see the layout of these buildings as resulting from the way in which living space was expanded through time, rather than as indicating such social ideals.

Nevertheless, what we can see clearly at Zagora, and perhaps also at Skala Oropos, is a trend towards the partitioning off of spaces serving different purposes. This movement towards functional specialization in architecture is characteristic of the period in general and can also be seen at a larger scale in the increasing creation of a variety of buildings for specific uses: in particular, those serving a more communal function, for example, temples, began to look different from domestic buildings (Mazarakis Ainian 1997). Both trends suggest a new conception of architectural space as a means of providing separate areas for different activities. This kind of specialization becomes more pronounced through the Archaic and into the Classical periods when we see both an increased variety of structures, and deliberate differentiation between them by using specific constructional and decorative features (such as exterior columns), which act as visual clues as to their purpose (see chapter 5).

The Fifth and Fourth Centuries: Spatial Organization and Social Control

The later sixth and earlier fifth centuries B.C. seem to have been a time of rapid change in the organization of domestic space in Greece. The exact timing and the detailed progression of that change are difficult to examine in detail because excavated houses of this period are relatively rare. Many small settlements like Zagora had failed and were abandoned by this time. Others, like Athens, went on to flourish, becoming *poleis* or city-states, with larger populations and complex social and political institutions. Where such expansion took place, later structures tend to have obscured or destroyed much of the evidence of the earlier housing. From the late fifth century onwards, however, examples of domestic buildings are more plentiful, and they highlight some of the radical changes in individual households that accompanied these larger-scale social developments.

A cluster of fifth-century houses from the Areopagos at Athens, for example, reveals variation in living conditions between Athenian families during this period (Figure 6.3). Like the earlier buildings, the main construction material is mud

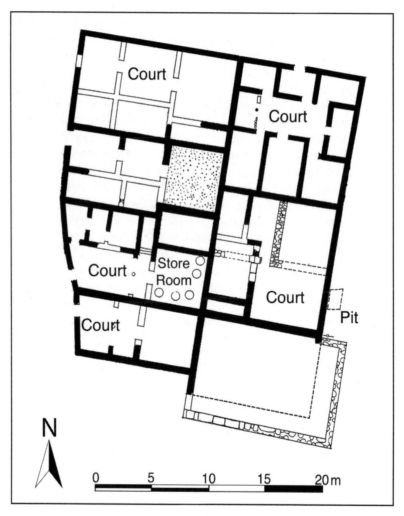

Figure 6.3 North shoulder of Areopagos group. After Thompson and Wycherley 1972: figure 42

brick, supported on a stone base or socle, although the roof is now covered with tile rather than with thatch or clay. Inside, most of the floors are still simply beaten earth. The shape and size of the small houses on the western side of the block follow a pattern which is seen from the sixth century onwards, with individual units of only a few rooms leading from an open, outer courtyard, space. But those on the eastern side show that among some households there had been a radical change in the conception of what a house should be, and how it should be organized to fulfill the needs of its occupants. These two houses are comparable in scale to Nichoria Unit IV.5, but the organization of interior space is very different. In each case, a single entrance leads into a central open courtyard, surrounded by a number of separate rooms which can only be reached from the courtyard itself and which, in most cases, do not interconnect. What are the implications of this new pattern of organization? How were the lives of the families occupying this house different from those of their predecessors? What kind of lifestyle were these, and houses like them, designed to facilitate?

Most obviously, the subdivision of the interior into separate rooms must have meant that in these houses a range of spaces was available for use by different members of the household and for different tasks. A possibility exists here for a kind of privacy which is not seen in a house like that at Nichoria, and at first sight this might seem to support the idea, mentioned above, that men and women occupied separate areas. But are these rooms quite as private as they first appear? And do they really suggest a binary division of space? In fact, the house is not divided into two halves which might accommodate male and female family members. Instead, a variety of rooms radiate from the central space of the courtyard suggesting somewhat different conclusions about relationships between the inhabitants (Nevett 1999:70–73). Such an arrangement would have meant that there could not have been too many secrets in these houses: while individuals occupying different rooms were out of sight of each other, as soon as they wanted to move between rooms, they would have had to pass through the court, and their movements must therefore have been very clear to anyone sitting or standing there, or looking in from one of the rooms. The same is also true of anyone entering or leaving the house itself: again, any visitor would have had to pass through the single street door and into the courtyard in order to reach one of the interior spaces, and would therefore also have been exposed to view.

In practice, therefore, there would have been great potential for individuals to keep an eye on each other, and to be involved in each other's business. Some of the Athenian texts of this period suggest that there was a strong obligation on individuals to demonstrate their legitimate parentage in order to avoid challenges to their right to inherit property and claim citizenship. The pattern of spatial organization in these houses, and others like them, may have been a response to such social pressures, keeping outsiders separate from female family members and ensuring that surveillance of individual family members was relatively easy. It is possible that the families of citizens were under more pressure to conform to ideal patterns of behavior than those of non-citizens, and this, as well as inequalities in wealth, may help to explain the disparity between houses seen in this block (compare Nevett 1999:167).

We do not know much about what the rooms of the Areopagos houses were used for, since we lack information on the objects found in them, and—like the earlier structures—there seem to have been few substantial architectural features which would have dictated the use of different spaces. Nevertheless, there are similar houses for which we do have such information. An example is an early fourth-century house, Avii 4, from the city of Olynthos in northern Greece, which is representative of some of the main features found in approximately one hundred houses partially or fully excavated at the site (Cahill 2002:103–108) (Figure 6.4 [a]). Again, an entrance leads from the street into a central open court which gives access to the different rooms. The building may once have boasted an upper storey, although the superstructure of unfired mud bricks and timber did not survive and its arrangement and function are unknown. But the rooms of the lower storey reveal much about the lives of the people who once occupied it. Fragments of table vessels and loomweights from the court may be the residue of activities taking place in the open air, or alternatively could be rubbish, moved here for disposal. To the north of the courtyard, a covered portico, or *pastas*, shelters the entrances to the largest of the rooms. Objects found in this space include fragments of bronze and terracotta table vessels, storage jars, and weights from scales, suggesting that the pastas was used for a variety of household chores or, at least, for storing items used for those activities. Indeed, a collection of metal bosses which are probably from a piece of wooden furniture, long since decayed, may suggest that some of these items were kept here in some sort of wooden chest or cupboard. In the northeast corner, a three-room complex (rooms C, D and E) seems to have served a combination of functions. Traces of ashy, burned material may indicate that a tall narrow space (D) may once have been occupied by a fire which is likely to have been used both for cooking and for heating water. Room C is one of the few rooms given a hard, water-resistant floor, made of cement. A gap in the floor marks the position where a small, terracotta hip-bath once stood, although no plumbing was provided: instead, the bather had to bring (or ask someone else to bring) water to the bath, jar by jar, perhaps heated on the fire in the adjacent space. Room E seems to have been one of the main domestic areas: here, a stone mortarium would have assisted in the production of flour, and a variety of tablewares also associate the room with serving food.

Houses like this were not only places to live, but also centers for processing and manufacturing the essentials on which the household depended, and so shop or workshop areas were sometimes included. This is likely to have been the function of room H, which has its own separate entrance from the street. Fragments of large storage jars found in room G and in the space to its east, show that agricultural produce such as grain, olives, and grapes, would be brought here from the fields to be stored. At the same time, terracotta weights from looms show that essentials, such as textiles for clothes and furnishings, would also have been produced within the household.

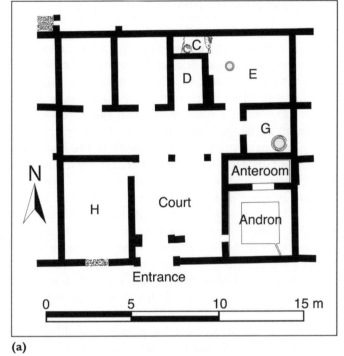

(a)

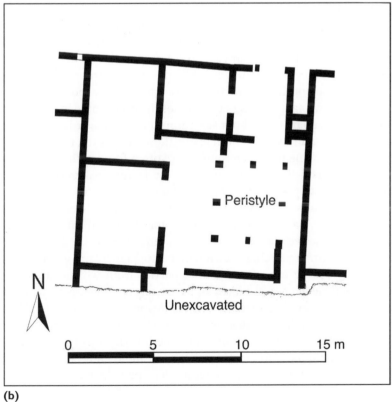

(b)

Figure 6.4 (a) Olynthos Avii 4. After Robinson and Graham 1938: plate 99; (b) Olynthos A3. After Robinson and Graham 1938: plate 89

Into the Hellenistic Period: Housing as Status Symbol

A number of the other areas of the Olynthos house provide only limited evidence to suggest how they were used. But one further space has characteristic features which indicate that it served a very specific purpose (although of course, other activities may have taken place there as well). In the southeast corner there is a square chamber, approached through a small outer room or antechamber (Figure 6.4 [a]). In both, the walls show traces of plaster colored with red, white, black and yellow pigments. Unlike the other rooms in the house, the doorway is not placed centrally but instead sits to one side. There are other unusual features, too: the floor is a durable and waterproof mortar surface, with a raised border once colored yellow. In some houses the floors of comparable rooms are set with small, black and white, or occasionally colored, pebbles forming geometric patterns or even figured scenes—an early form of mosaic. The hardness of the floor surface made it easy to clean, so that almost no objects have been recorded, either from this room, or from the many like it that are known at Olynthos and at other contemporary Greek settlements. But a variety of texts and images surviving from this period suggest what the purpose of this room may have been: a central element of the social lives of Greek men during this period seems to have been the *symposium*, at which the man of the house entertained his friends at home. Together the participants would have reclined on couches placed along the walls of the room and drunk wine.

Our square room fits perfectly the requirements of a space used for such an occasion, known in the texts as an *andron*: if wine were drunk, and spilled, here, the cement floor would have been easy to clean, and was even furnished with a drain so that it could be washed down, while the raised borders mark the position of the couches. The antechamber would have isolated this room from the rest of the house: its door was at right angles to that of the inner room, so that even when it was open, the occupants could not see out into the courtyard, and no-one elsewhere in the house could see in. In many of these houses the andron preserves a stone threshold, showing that such rooms were often fitted with solid doors which would have acted as a barrier to sound. These features suggest that particular care was taken here to ensure that activities taking place in the andron were kept separate from what was going on elsewhere in the house. It seems that one of the aims of this design was to provide privacy for visitors from the members of the household not actively entertaining them, and vice versa. There is probably some degree of distinction being drawn here between men and women, given that the room was probably used for drinking parties from which—surviving texts suggest—respectable women are likely to have been excluded. Nevertheless, more importantly there is a differentiation between members of the household and visitors coming from outside: it is these outsiders who are being kept separate from the rest of the household, isolated and contained within this room.

The andron would have provided a private setting to entertain visitors, but the relatively elaborate decoration here suggests that it also played another role, as a place more gracious or pleasing to spend time in than the other, undecorated, rooms of the house. Perhaps the colored walls and floor simply contributed to the comfort of the space and to the overall atmosphere of the occasions taking place here. But it seems likely that such decoration was also a way for the house owner to convey a message to his visitors: their sparing use suggests that these were relatively costly, but their presence in one room may have indicated that the family could afford to spend money on elements which were not strictly functional. Other houses of this date feature additional architectural elements which are also decorative. In another example from Olynthos, house A3 (Figure 6.4 [b]), the pastas has been extended so that it surrounds the open court on all four sides, making a peristyle. The colonnaded effect must have been reminiscent of the public buildings of Greek cities during this period, such as the elongated stoas of the agora or the sanctuary, and perhaps they even evoked the colonnades of temple façades. Again, the result may have been to convey a sense of importance and luxury to visitors entering the house, who would have had to pass through this area. What we appear to see here, therefore, is the use of the house as a symbol, to convey something about the wealth and status—or aspirations—of the family living inside. Such features are likely to have been intended as indications of their owners' good taste, elegance, and wealth.

These relatively spacious houses appear to provide generous accommodation both for the necessary activities of daily living and also for relaxation and entertainment. If the open courtyard space is included, the houses from Olynthos, with a ground area of nearly 300 m² each, offer more living space than many families have today, even in affluent western European towns. Nevertheless, these are not by any means the largest Greek houses known. An example of a late-fourth century house from the northern Greek city of Pella is constructed on a different scale and with an entirely different pattern of organization, taking this trend towards display and symbolism to a new level. The House of Dionysos occupied more than 3000 m² in ground area, with the interior space arranged around two separate open courtyard spaces (Figure 6.5). Why did the residents of this house require ten times more space than the families whose houses we have seen at Olynthos, and how was that space used? Aspects of the architecture provide some clues. Both of the courtyards are colonnaded peristyles, but the rooms surrounding each court are different in character. Most of those around the larger peristyle to the south are relatively large and square in shape and several clearly had mosaic floors. In contrast, the rooms to the north tend to be smaller and some are organized in clusters, with an antechamber leading to several spaces behind. Remains of a staircase in the northeast corner of the house suggest that there was an upper storey, at least in this area.

On analogy with the houses at Olynthos it seems likely that at least some of the rooms in the southern court represent comfortable areas for living and entertaining. The reason why a variety of different rooms were needed for this purpose is less clear: were they occupied simultaneously by different groups? Or were different rooms used for different social occasions, or at different stages during a single occasion? Alternatively, perhaps owning a number of decorated rooms was

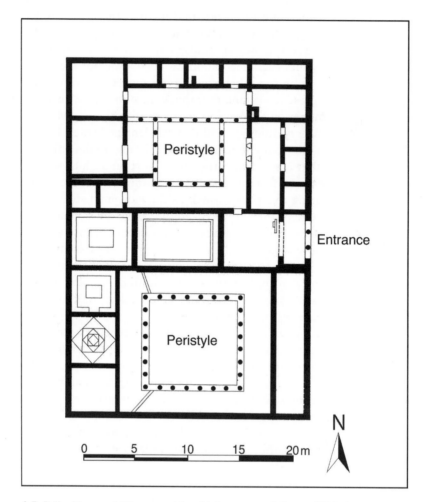

Figure 6.5 Pella, House of Dionysos. After Makaronas and Giouri 1989: figure 142

more a matter of making an impression on visitors than it was a practical necessity. By organizing their living space around two separate courtyards, the inhabitants of the Pella house ensured that some light and air reached all of the interior
rooms and that patterns of access did not become too labyrinthine. But this same
division would also have meant that the entertainment of guests and domestic
activities were now spatially separated. The two pursuits could take place independently and the participants would not have been within sight or earshot of
each other. Furthermore, the arrangement of the rooms of the northern court into
suites would probably have meant that, within an individual suite, the inhabitants
would have been able to pass from room to room without being observed from
the court or from other suites. The fact that this northern peristyle occupied a
relatively large amount of space suggests that the domestic activities which it
probably accommodated were an important aspect of the overall function of the

house. A similar balance between these two priorities is seen in a handful of smaller, fourth- and third-century houses which have a comparable double court-yard layout (for example, the House of the Mosaics at Eretria or the excavated house at Maroneia).

If the size and layout of the Olynthos houses make them suitable for occupation by a single family, then the scale, lavish decoration, and pattern of organization of the Pella house may suggest something else. Here the separate courtyards and discrete suites of rooms would have provided a variety of self-contained areas of different scales where groups of people could move about unobserved from other parts of the building. The implication is perhaps that the house was occupied, or at least frequented, by larger numbers of people who were less closely connected with each other, and who therefore required greater privacy from each other. In particular, the various elaborate rooms around the southern peristyle suggest the possibility that many guests were entertained here. The entrance to this house is at the center of the eastern side and leads into a lobby and only indirectly into either of the courts. This layout may have enabled guests to enter and leave without passing through, or even catching sight of, the domestic quarters, while at the same time members of the household could still enter and leave the domestic areas without being observed themselves. Thus whereas the Olynthos houses are essentially still intimate spaces, the Pella house seems designed to support a more "public" function, with larger numbers of people operating more independently of each other.

Both the scale and opulence of this house, and the fact that Pella is known to have been home to the Macedonian royal family, have been taken as evidence that this and other comparable houses at the site were once occupied by companions of the Macedonian monarch. Whether or not this is the case, it is clear that the owner was able to mobilize considerable wealth, which also implies that he had a certain amount of power. Providing a place to receive and entertain visitors in appropriate surroundings therefore seems to have been an important aspect of the house's function. This is a pronounced trend in housing of this period and may point to some degree of withdrawal from public life by wealthy individuals (Walter-Karydi 1998).

The Second and First Centuries B.C.: Housing and Cultural Identity

The House of Dionysos at Pella, with its separate domestic and recreational courtyards, may seem to follow a significantly different pattern of organization from the smaller, single-courtyard houses. Nevertheless, if we set aside the double courtyard layout, in some ways the house exhibits similar priorities to those seen at Olynthos, balancing the need for display against the provision of a comfortable working environment in the domestic quarters. This shows that in order to under-stand a house fully, it is necessary to think about the way in which it functioned as a living space, as well as simply looking at its architecture and layout. Housing from one final settlement, on the Cycladic island of Delos, will reinforce this point, and also add an extra dimension to the discussion, providing a link with the topic of Roman housing, the subject of the second part of this chapter. On Delos we see houses which look superficially similar to the courtyard house from Olynthos. Upon closer inspection, however, a number of features emerge which may have something to say about a new aspect of the families who once lived here: namely, their cultural identity.

Although the island has a long history of occupation, the surviving houses date from a relatively late period, the second century B.C. and later. Stone is used for many of the walls, and the individual structures retain a number of architectural features which are often lost elsewhere. One house, the House of the Dolphins, will serve as an example (Figure 6.6). The principal entrance is through a narrow corridor to the south. The domestic quarters are formed by a series of small rooms (B, B^I, B^{II} and B^{III}) in the southeast corner, and could be reached from the entrance corridor without the need to pass through the court. But the majority of the interior space is organized around a single large, decorated peristyle, featuring a mosaic pool at the center with images of the dolphins which give the house its name. Like the Pella house, there seem to have been a variety of different decorated apartments, including a large living room to the north (H) and smaller one on the east side (F), and there were further comparable spaces in an upper storey, detectable only from fallen mosaic fragments which once adorned the floors of the upstairs rooms. Although any of these areas might possibly have served for entertaining visitors, none of the ground floor rooms is configured like a typical andron: room H features a series of three doors on its south side, while F has a single broad opening on the west. In both cases the aim seems to have been to maximize the amount of light entering and to create a pleasing vista out into the peristyle. Furthermore, both of these rooms feature doorways leading directly into neighboring rooms, as well as into the courtyard. The number and width of the doorways in these rooms appear unsuited to the traditional square arrangement of couches, while their close connection with the rest of the house must have given a very different feel from the isolated and enclosed andron seen at Olynthos. Both these features suggest that the rooms in this house were designed to host a rather different kind of social occasion.

In the organization of the house as a whole, different priorities also seem to be followed from those we have seen previously. Here, the majority of space is devoted to comfortable rooms for living and entertaining, which clearly take precedence over other functions. What does this apparent imbalance tell us about the family who once lived here? It seems that the daily chores such as food preparation and cooking were being done in small side rooms, and that the comfort of the members of the household who were carrying out these tasks was not important. Such a pattern of organization suggests a different kind of social life from what we have seen before. We know from inscriptions that during this period the island of Delos was occupied by a range of merchants from different parts of the Mediterranean, including Italy and the eastern Mediterranean. Indeed, the influence of both of these areas can be seen in the decoration of the House of the Dolphins. At the time of excavation the south façade of the house featured paintings of religious

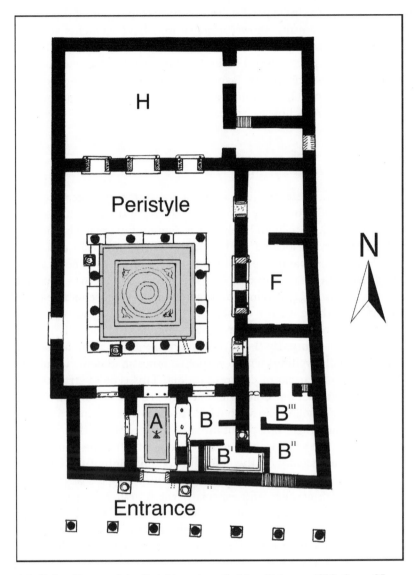

Figure 6.6 Delos, House of the Dolphins, phase 2. After Trümper 1998: figure 35

rituals of a kind traditionally associated with the Roman festival of the *compitalia*, while the mosaic pavement of the entrance hall (A) featured an image of Tanit, another religious symbol, this time originating in the eastern Mediterranean.

It seems possible, then, that the pattern of spatial organization we are seeing in this house is an indication of influences from new, non-Greek patterns of domestic life which introduced different priorities and social practices. Whether we can associate specific motifs, such as the Tanit mosaic, with individual house owners is less clear. Such features could have a relatively long life—longer, perhaps, than the ownership of a single person; and as the juxtaposition of the Tanit symbol with the compitalia painting shows, a house may have elements suggesting the influence of more than one culture. It therefore may be that what we are seeing at Delos is the process of "cultural fusion"—the creation of a new culture, which brought with it a fresh conception of what a house should be and how its occupants should live, and one which was only partly influenced by the conventions developed in the earlier Greek houses discussed above.

Conclusion

The houses discussed here are just a few of the numerous excavated examples from different periods, but they show how closely individual households were involved in the broader social and political changes taking place in the communities in which they were located. Between the Early Iron Age and the second century B.C., it is possible to see profound shifts, not only in the kinds of structures being built, but also in the ways in which domestic life was conceptualized and in the social priorities driving the organization of household space. During the ninth and eighth centuries we see the beginning of a transformation of a single, multifunctional space into physically separate, functionally specific areas used for storage and living. By the fifth century, although some households were still occupying small dwellings with few rooms, others had come to inhabit larger houses divided into a variety of different rooms. This type of structure seems to express a new requirement of domestic space: to provide visual and aural separation, both for the household as a whole from the wider community, and for its occupants from each other. The possibility for social control offered by the dominance of the courtyard as a circulation space suggests that the emergence of this form of house is connected with the gradual crystallization of the concept of citizenship, and thereby, perhaps, with the formation of the *polis* or city-state itself.

From the late fifth century and especially the fourth century, the increasing use of architectural decoration points to another trend, namely towards more explicit manipulation of private houses as symbols of the wealth and status of their occupants. This becomes particularly pronounced in the mid-fourth century when it is expressed in a proliferation of decorated reception and living-rooms. The growing number and lavishness of these facilities may correspond to the loss of political independence of individual poleis, expressing a decline in the importance of public life and civic institutions and an increase in the use of the house as a location for conducting business. At first, such structures seem to maintain the ideal of providing a comfortable environment for domestic activities, by arranging reception rooms and service quarters in separate suites, sometimes with their own courtyards. With some of the elite residences at Delos, however, we see a marked change: decorated display rooms and living-rooms take priority, while the domestic areas are relegated to small, cramped rooms, often close to the entrance or with separate access. This change suggests the introduction of new cultural norms and social practices accompanying the influx of merchants from the western and eastern Mediterranean during the second century B.C. It is less clear whether we can identify the influences of specific cultural groups from these new patterns of domestic spatial organization, or whether we can interpret the use of particular motifs used in wall and floor decorations as expressions of cultural affiliations, religious identity, or other personal statements being made by individual house owners. Such issues can best be addressed by viewing the organization and decoration of the houses at Delos in a wider Mediterranean context and looking at how housing generally was being manipulated by the elites of the expanding Roman empire. These themes are taken up in the next section of this chapter.

NOTE

The references for this chapter are on pp. 241–243.

6 (b)

Housing and Households

The Roman World

Bettina Bergmann

To the Romans, the house was a powerful symbol, a sign of man's social rank and a tool for learning. Educated Romans trained their memories by mentally constructing domestic interiors and placing cues at certain points to serve as visual triggers upon subsequent returns. No wonder that ancient writers portray the house as an extension of the self, signaling piety to divine protectors and social and genealogical status to the outside world. For this reason, when an important man suffered a *damnatio memoriae*, his house, along with his portraits and inscriptions, was wiped out of existence as a systematic eradication of his memory (*Ad C. Herennium* 3.16–24; Cicero, *De Oratore* 2.86.351–354; Quintilian, *Institutio oratoria* 11.2.17–22; Bodel 1997).

The metaphorical meanings of the Roman house distinguish it fundamentally from the Greek house. But we must remember that there was no single Roman house. The notion of "the" Roman house is a construct, based upon passages from elite Latin authors together with a few buildings in Republican Italy. Textbooks often illustrate a static ground plan with a canonical arrangement that, along with Roman law, language, and other social forms, conveys a view of cultural uniformity. In other accounts, the Italic house evolves along with Rome's territorial expansion in the Mediterranean: the small, introspective square building gradually spreads wings and opens out into light, air, and nature to include a spacious, colonnaded courtyard at the back. A microcosm of this evolution resides at the very place of Rome's origins on the Palatine Hill, where the post-holes of Romulus's Iron Age hut survive beside aristocratic, multilevel mansions and the massive terraces of later imperial palaces.

While this picture may hold truth for some parts of central Italy during the Republic, the story of Roman housing is far more complex. During the empire, between the first and fourth centuries A.D., peoples under Roman rule occupied areas extending from Scotland to Africa to Syria, and factors like climate, terrain, and local customs greatly influenced how they lived. So too did social class. While the elite could own several townhouses and country villas and fashion them as they wished, the majority inhabited cramped quarters in cities or rustic wooden shacks in the countryside. By the first century A.D., Roman cities featured row houses and high-rise apartment buildings (*insulae*), forerunners of the apartment blocks seen in many western cities today.

This chapter takes up a few contemporary issues concerning the Roman house. In contrast to the scarce evidence for Greek houses, information abounds about Roman dwellings. There survive ancient descriptions and relatively well-preserved buildings, replete with decorations, furniture, and, on the Bay of Naples, even the actual bodies of inhabitants and their pets (Guzzo 2005). Yet despite this abundance, the same basic questions raised for early Greek houses pertain to the Roman: how many people lived in a dwelling? What was their relationship to each other? And what was the full range of activities carried out there? In short, how similar was the role of this structure to what we think of as a "house" today? It is a curious fact that we still know very little about the actual goings-on in Roman homes, and recent research has thrown into doubt that which we thought we knew. Even structures that archaeologists have identified as dwellings in Pompeii were not exclusively residential, but incorporated shops, rental units, bakeries, fulleries, clubhouses, and restaurants. Indeed, the Latin word for house, *domus*, signifies not just the dwelling but the household or family unit, and that unit was not the nuclear family we know; it comprised a wide network of relationships including in-laws, distant relatives, slaves, and ex-slaves (Gardner and Wiedemann 1991; Nevett 1997).

This discussion thus addresses questions similar to those aimed at Greek houses, but it follows a typological and thematic order rather than a chronological one. The goal is for the reader to get a sense of the range of evidence for Roman housing at various times and places, and within that range to discern certain features and patterns in the ways space was constructed, not just for the universal requisites of shelter, water, and light, but also to meet individual needs and desires. A word should be said about the evidence for Roman housing, because the accidents of survival produce an unbalanced picture. In many provincial areas, such as Roman Britain, the scattered archaeological remains are difficult to identify, and, without ancillary texts, invite speculation and inevitable comparison with the small town of Pompeii, so well preserved from the volcanic eruption of Vesuvius in A.D. 79. What, then, makes houses across the Roman domain alike, and how do they differ? We shall see that Roman domestic architecture is characterized above all by variety, but often shares a few basic elements in plan and décor. Especially in wealthier homes across the empire, one finds the same prestigious, architectural elements and costly materials, especially marble. Indeed, great expense was taken to import marble into the densely-forested northern provinces, where its presence as columns and inlay conveyed an owner's wealth and status, just as did splashing jet fountains in domestic gardens planted in the dry terrain of North Africa.

The Atrium House

We begin with the atrium house, the perceived norm of Roman housing. Here one point must be stressed. The basic design of a central space with a partly-open roof surrounded by small rooms had been a hallmark of domestic space in the Mediterranean since the Bronze Age. Roman atrium houses can be seen as variations on this form, which was widespread in the ancient world long before Romulus's hut arose on the Palatine hill in the eighth century B.C. In Italy, the earliest remains of the atrium were discovered in Rome and at Roselle and date to the sixth century B.C.; painted Etruscan chamber tombs of the same date simulate an analogous layout (Gros 2001:35–37). By this time, Greek influence was pervasive in Italy and may well account for the adoption of a central open hearth ringed by small rooms. Whatever its origins in Italy, the atrium house reached its apogee in Republican Rome as the model residence for aristocrats, many of whom lived near the Forum Romanum. Two large, sixth-century B.C. dwellings found on the slopes of the Palatine, each with shops opening onto the street and an interior courtyard, remained relatively unchanged for 400 years, after which they were subdivided into multiple dwellings. One, perhaps the sumptuous residence of Aemilius Scaurus, contained a basement with baths and small cells (for slaves?) (Claridge 1998:111–112). By the first century B.C., as Cicero relates, homeowners in Rome had become highly competitive (*De domo sua*). Properties were bought and sold at a quick pace, and status accrued through a house's grand scale, imported materials, and unobstructed views; façades bore the spoils of battle and atria displayed extensive family genealogies (Wiseman 1987).

In his treatise on architecture dedicated in the late first century B.C. to the first Roman emperor Augustus, Vitruvius codifies the basic elements of a Roman house in distinction to the Greek. The heart of the house, he claims, is the atrium with its open roof (*compluvium*) and square basin below it (*impluvium*). As the main source of light, air, and water, the atrium functioned as the primary circulation space for the inhabitants and for the reception of visitors and clients, who entered from the street through the *fauces* (throat), the numinous boundary between home and the outside world. The atrium was a vital site of memory, the *focus* of the ancestors, and contained familial busts and epitaphs as well as active shrines to the indwelling spirits, the *Lares* and the *Penates*. The *tablinum*, directly across from the entrance, had traditionally housed the marriage bed that had produced the *familia*, and here sat the prosperous *paterfamilias* to receive his morning clients in the daily greeting of clients, *salutatio*.

With Rome's spreading influence in the third century B.C., atrium houses begin to appear elsewhere in central Italy. Archaeological remains in Pompeii suggest that the representational and performative functions of the axially-aligned reception spaces—the fauces, atrium, tablinum—encouraged the creation of carefully composed vistas into the house from the street. By the second century B.C., that view penetrated yet further to glimpse a new, secondary focus of the house, the peristyle, a colonnaded courtyard at the back of the house filled with plants and fountains, onto which opened *cubicula* and *triclinia* for intimate dining, leisure, and entertainment. But while such inviting prospects may have allowed ocular access to the interior, only a privileged few could actually enter and move along that axis, and much of domestic design catered to those high within the immediate social hierarchy. This is evident in the placement of more elaborate, figural frescoes and mosaics in particular rooms, as it is in the sculptural arrangements and gardens that tend to align with certain positions of reclining viewers in a room (Wallace-Hadrill 1994; Zanker 1998). Scholars have emphasized these views, shaped by geometric forms and planar recession, as paradigmatic of Roman vision, yet such a paradigm obviously excludes the multiple sightlines of those who were *not* standing at the front door or lying in a place of honor on a dining couch. In illustrating the house, we must allow for a variety of spatial arrangements that in turn complicate standard assumptions about Roman experience and house design.

Vitruvius's atrium house finds a few close parallels in first-century B.C. Italy; most townhouses, however, are rather loose variations on his plan. What is more, recent studies of texts and excavated contexts demonstrate that the uses of rooms are more ambiguous than Vitruvius infers. Rooms were multifunctional, as people and furniture moved around the house depending upon the season or the time of day. The atrium was used for mundane purposes like storage, cooking, and weaving by people of varying ranks, much like the central courtyard in classical Greek homes (Allison 2004). *Triclinium* and *cubiculum*, routinely translated as dining room and bedroom, in fact rarely connote a specific function in ancient usage (Leach 1997; Riggsby 1997). Romans did not reserve spaces for sleeping or eating. Even those triclinia and cubicula in which interior decoration demarcates the placement for a bed or couches could be used for any number of activities, and some formed parts of larger suites designed for entertainment (Wallace-Hadrill 1994:52–57). It also appears that most Romans did not retreat for solitude, except for the amorous couple or the wealthy villa owner who might construct a special space for his own personal reflection (Pliny *Epistulae* 2.17.24; Riggsby 1997). Still, even if the kind of privacy so cherished in the current Western home was not desirable, we must remember that "privacy" simply means not being seen, and missing from the excavated shells of houses are not only upper stories but the wooden doors and curtains that once divided spaces of the interior, as did slaves, the "talking equipment" of the home. It is here that the newer investigations of human, animal, and plant remains, long overlooked by archaeologists, can add much to the picture of life in the household (Jashemski 1979; 1993; 2002; Guzzo 2005).

In order to understand the Roman house, then, we must abandon modern notions of domestic space as segregated by activity, gender, age, or status. In this regard, Roman houses do, in fact, differ from those of classical Greece, where the *andron* served as a space for male gatherings and separate quarters may have existed for women (on this problem: Nevett 1999:154–155). Even in the atrium, where the *paterfamilias* received honors from the outside world, the *materfamilias* also held court, and household slaves would have been everywhere in the house, at night sleeping on the atrium floor or in a side room near the master or mistress.

The complexity of the Roman household with its diverse inhabitants, the mobility of furniture and objects, and the flexible uses of parts of buildings like upstairs quarters (which could serve short-term tenants and slaves alongside wealthy owners) can frustrate even the identification of "domestic space." It is clear that the presence of artisanal or commercial labor does not imply a lesser dwelling. What is more, the townhouse must be considered within its larger urban context, for its orientation, dimensions, and plan often arose from a preexistent street grid. The messier picture emerging from new research and excavations results from an oft overlooked dimension of Roman housing: change over time. While some homes remained within a family for several generations, others were frequently bought and sold or rented. Again, the houses in Pompeii are especially revealing, for some evolved over a span of four centuries, changed ownership, suffered fires and earthquakes, and in some cases were abandoned, subdivided, and transformed into something entirely new.

A current project sheds light on the development of one house together with its city block. The House of the Vestals (VI.1,7) a small masonry house built in the late third century B.C., underwent a series of expansions over two-and-a-half centuries, incorporating adjacent houses and shops and adding amenities like separate service quarters, a latrine, a cooking area, a bath with hypocaust heating, gardens with waterworks, and reception rooms with elaborate frescoes and floor mosaics. When Vesuvius erupted in A.D. 79, the House of the Vestals was again being refurbished but, unlike other houses damaged by earthquakes in the early 60s, showed no signs of decline. One significant change was that the house had become self-sufficient for its water; no longer dependent upon the town aqueduct, its splashing fountains and baths ceased to exist. This change reminds us of another critical factor in the appearance of a house, that of personal *choice*. For wealthy Romans, technology could be replaced by slave labor, in this case for lugging buckets of water (Jones and Robinson 2004).

Despite the numerous variations in layout, the atrium appears to have been standard in central Italy during the Republic and Early Empire, and a few atrium houses have been found in northern Italy and in Spain and southern France (George 1997; Gros 2001:144–145, 157–159). No atrium plan, in contrast, survives in North Africa. In Italy, the atrium began to go out of favor along with changes in land ownership in the Early Empire. In Rome, especially after the fire of 64 A.D. and Nero's vast appropriation of property for his Domus Aurea (Golden House), elite homeowners moved from the Palatine to other hills, where they resided among modest residences and shops. Apparently no new atrium houses were built after the first century A.D., but older atrium houses still survived in the capital city; as late as the third century A.D., the Severan Marble Plan records three on the Viminal Hill (Steinby 1995). By the fourth century, the atrium seems to have been replaced by the audience hall as the main room of a wealthy house (Patterson 2000).

The Peristyle House

If we must identify a typical dwelling within the Roman world as a whole, it would have to be the peristyle, or courtyard, house. Thousands of peristyle houses survive throughout the empire; here a few general observations and examples must suffice.

Important evidence exists on the small island of Delos for the transition from the Greek to the Roman plan in the late Hellenistic period. Dwellings built during the second century B.C. to house foreign merchants correspond in form to other peristyle houses in Greece, but manifest a new emphasis on reception rooms, whose embellishment with floor mosaics, colorful murals, and fountains resemble wealthy Pompeian homes like the House of the Faun, itself apparently inspired by Hellenistic precedents. This cross-cultural development engendered a cosmopolitan vocabulary in which architectural features like columns and pediments served semiotic, non-structural functions, and frescoes and figural mosaics evoked earlier masterworks of Greek art. At the same time that the houses on Delos were being built, in Italy peristyles began to appear at the back of atrium houses, evidently as a direct borrowing from Hellenistic Greek houses, palaces or, as Latin writers tell us, public buildings like the *gymnasium*. The resulting atrium-peristyle plan finds close parallels in Sicily and in other areas that came under Roman sway in Greece and the eastern Mediterranean (Nevett 2002:91–94).

Most houses and villas in Roman territories, however, omitted the atrium altogether and instead focused rooms around one or more peristyles, thereby following early precursors in Greece and Turkey. In northern Italy and the northwestern provinces, the peristyle house was a new phenomenon that needed to be adapted to local conditions. Radiant heating, for example, was provided through the hypocaust system: floors were supported on stacks of tiles (*pilae*) and hot air circulated under the floor from a furnace, passing along channels and up through vents in the walls. Other traits of the new, Romanized houses were roofs made of terracotta tiles, lead pipes to carry water into interiors, and, in wealthier homes, glass windows for light and solar heat in large rooms and baths (Perring 2002). In general, it seems that even when an atrium was included, more important than any canonical layout of rooms was the sheer size of a house (Wallace-Hadrill 1994:91–103; Gros 2001:136–230).

By the second century A.D., the peristyle had become the primary hallmark of an affluent Roman's home throughout the provinces, both east and west. Of the myriad variations found across the empire, two can be discussed here. Both conform to the larger urban fabric of gridded streets, which limits their size and shape; in both, columns, frescoes, and mosaics follow fashions seen in other Roman provinces. But each complex uniquely adapts such standard features to the local climate and terrain. At Ephesus in modern Turkey, two blocks of wealthy houses, built in the Augustan period and renovated over several centuries, rose on ascending terraces up a hillside in the center of the city (Figure 6.7 [a], [b]). Located between two main streets, inhabitants of the terraced complex looked

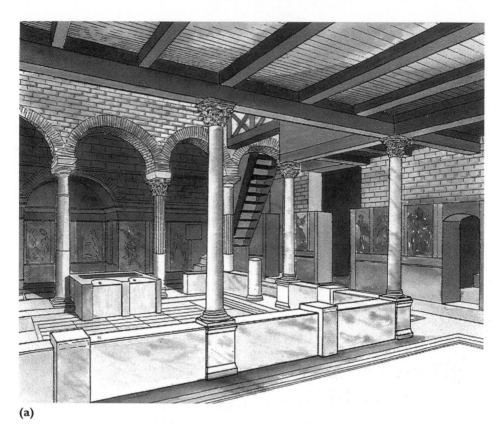

(a)

Figure 6.7 Terrace Houses, Ephesus. (a) View of peristyle of House II. After Özeren 1993:61; (b) Ground plan of terrace houses. After Özeren 1993:60. Reproduced with permission of Keskin Color

onto the bustling city with its baths, temples, and agora (Gros 2001:218–223). Individually, the houses follow the local Hellenistic plan, with rooms grouped around a 25–50 square meter, light-filled peristyle with an impluvium. Together, they comprised an ingenious arrangement whereby the roof of one story formed the terrace of the next above it; apartments shared baths, hypocaust heating, and water cisterns. A visitor reached a house's entry by ascending a narrow, stepped street. There, in contrast to Italian houses, the caller encountered no axial vista through the dwelling, but entered and approached the central peristyle from an angle. Nevertheless, shifting circulation patterns and new rooms added in the course of renovations do show Roman influence. For instance, the presence of a triclinium signals a shift in focus to the social ritual of the meal and its entertainments.

The condominium-like complex in Ephesus contained richly embellished interiors with precious marble inlay, fine floor mosaics, and wall frescoes very similar to domestic spaces in the Western provinces. The largest, Terrace House II, boasted two peristyles with Corinthian columns, a long corridor covered

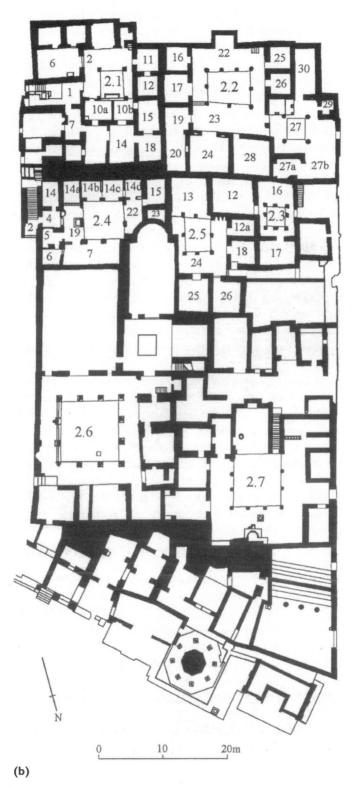

0   10   20m

(b)

Figure 6.7 *Continued*

end-to-end with black-and-white geometric mosaics, and another with vibrant marine mosaics depicting Triton and a Nereid riding a sea horse, recalling floor mosaics found in North African peristyle houses. The wall paintings, the best preserved in the Roman east, exhibit pictorial modes including *faux marbre*, painted gardens, and mythological battles that belong to a *koine* of patterns and motifs with the rest of the empire. Thus, while local topography inspired an original architectural arrangement, room use and interior decor express tastes and values of Roman life that were disseminated far and wide. The recent finds of houses at Zeugma bear close affinities to Ephesus (Early et al. 2003).

Another unique variation on the courtyard house is seen at Bulla Regia in North Africa, where several dwellings within a city block evolved over time (Thébert 1987:334–339; Gros 2001:177–180). Because outward expansion was limited, in the early third century A.D. owners dug 6 meters down into the earth to create a new underground level, replicating the axial layout upstairs (Figure 6.8). Descending a deep flight of steps into the subterranean suite in the House of the Hunt, residents could find respite from the grueling heat of summer in rooms that were insulated by the surrounding soil and cooled by a remarkable system of air conditioning that directed air through vents in the earth. Light and air entered through the above-ground windows, skylights, and open peristyle, which, although underground, otherwise resembles other Roman peristyles, with tall columns, vaults and arches, water pools and fountains, painted walls, and glittering mosaics.

The houses at Ephesus and Bulla Regia exemplify the immense adaptability of the peristyle scheme and the creative solutions made to suit local environmental conditions. A survey of the thousands of Roman houses in the provinces would show that in form, living spaces continued the tradition of the Hellenistic peristyle house, but that—within that framework—the objects and surfaces it contained, and most likely the social activities that took place, constituted something new, a dynamic mix of indigenous and imported, Roman elements. In the past, scholars have assumed that Rome set the patterns for the elite living in provincial towns, but factors of topography and climate were just as formative in shaping individual dwellings, as well as regional identity, during the empire.

Insulae and Multiple Dwellings

Despite the predominance of the individual domus in discussions of Roman life, most people did not reside in a single home but rather in rental units alongside many neighbors. New studies reveal that the city blocks in Pompeii and Herculaneum were far more than a simple collection of independent houses; even within a single house, exterior stairs, separate entries, and self-contained suites suggest rental units, especially in upper floors (Ling 1997; De Kind 1998; Jones and Robinson 2004). In fact, almost half the inhabitants in Pompeii did not own, but rented, their homes. When Vesuvius erupted, proprietors of larger houses were

Figure 6.8 House of the Hunt, Bulla Regia, Tunisia, fourth century A.D. Photo: Rebecca Molholt

seeking tenants to rent living quarters (known as *cenacula* or *pergulae*) and had advertisements painted on exterior walls; one announcement in the Praedia of Julia Felix (II.4) reads: "FOR RENT/ from August 13, with a 5-year lease/ on the property of Julia Felix, daughter of Spurius/ the elegant Venus Baths/ street-front shops and booths/and second-story apartments" (*Corpus Inscriptionum Latinarum* 4.1136).

But by far the biggest demand for multi-dwelling housing was in the city of Rome, where roughly a million people lived by the Early Empire. While the

Figure 6.9 Watercolor reconstruction of apartment block at the foot of the Capitoline Hill, Rome. After Connolly (1998:142). Photo: akg-images London

poorest slept in the streets or wherever they could find shelter, as in theaters or tombs, a large cross-section of society occupied spaces in high-rise complexes (Hermansen 1981). Called *insula*, or island, because it was surrounded on all sides by streets or alleys, an apartment block was usually owned by a prosperous individual who rented to long-term tenants and to the less wealthy on short-term leases. Regionary catalogues state that in the fourth century A.D. Rome had 44,300 insulae compared with 1,790 domus! Of these, only a few remain. An apartment complex of five or more stories survives at the base of the Capitoline Hill in Rome (Figure 6.9). Constructed in brick-faced concrete in the early second century A.D., the multi-use building had single-shop units in the first three stories, cell-like rooms on the fourth story (possibly for slaves), and a large apartment on the fifth story (Claridge 1998:232–234).

Multi-unit housing structures followed two main spatial principles: adjacency and containment. As was the case in city blocks of Pompeii and the terraced complex at Ephesus, adjacent living quarters of insulae shared walls, and the ceiling of a lower dwelling served as the floor for the one above. The principle of containment can be seen in the enclosure of separate living units within a single city block, with each unit turned in toward a common courtyard or light well for illumination, air, water, and, possibly, for communal cooking pits. While house owners of Bulla Regia expanded down into the earth, in most cities, planners exploited the vertical dimension and built skyscrapers. From early on, the height of Roman insulae was a problem, and Augustus limited their street fronts to 70 Roman feet (21 meters), allowing for five to seven stories, and possibly more at the back if the building was terraced against a slope. While ground floors of most insulae featured shops (*tabernae*) with a room at the back for boarding, upper stories show a variety of arrangements, usually of three-to-five rooms. Some apartments, reached by external staircases, had no central circulation space; instead, rooms opened onto each other, so that people would have to pass through one room to arrive at another, and light and air entered through windows and balconies. Although one would expect that a higher living unit would be less desirable due to the challenge of hauling goods and water, some luxury suites are located on the topmost floors, no doubt because of the benefits of exposure to daylight and views.

Similar patterns appear in apartment dwellings in other Roman cities: they take up entire city blocks, share walls and interior courtyards, and leave the lower floor for commercial and artisanal purposes. There are, of course, exceptions to these patterns. In Rome itself, old houses were converted, like a domus depicted on the *Forma Urbis* plan (Fragment 543; Najbjerg; n.d.). An important and rare survival of a multi-dwelling complex consisting of second-century houses and baths with their mosaics, murals, statues, and small objects *in situ* was found near Rome's Termini train station; called the Villa Negroni, the complex must be one of many creative solutions to housing in the congested capital city.

The best evidence for alternative apartment housing survives at Ostia, Rome's nearby port city. There, several blocks of insulae, called garden apartments, were grouped into a single complex and surrounded by green areas. Another complex, called *medianum* apartments, was more spacious and must have housed affluent renters; rooms grouped around three sides of a wide corridor (the *medianum*) that was lit through large external windows opened onto a court or the street (DeLaine 2004). A third type of multi-unit complex that became especially common in the northern and western provinces was the strip or row house; a long side faced the street, from which one or more wings extended behind, or, where frontage was expensive, the narrow end faced the street. Unlike the enclosed insula, this plan looked outward for light and air rather than onto an inner central court (Perring 2002).

In insulae, as in townhouses, wealthy and poor were close neighbors (Patterson 2000). Seneca lived above a bath complex in Rome and complained about the grunts of exercising bathers, the cries of hawkers, and splashes in the pools

(*Epistulae* 56). With more people living in close proximity came more disease and crime, and other city-dwellers relate the dangers and squalor of apartment living. Fire was a constant threat in apartments built with timber because tenants cooked on open fires and used oil lamps for illumination, and some landlords invested in fire insurance, but it seems that conditions improved when the use of brick-faced concrete became the norm in the Early Empire (Juvenal, *Satires* 3.193–202; Martial, *Epigrams* 3.52; Gardner and Wiedemann 1991). At present, the extent of rental housing throughout the empire is still unknown, but it seems to have been much greater than was formerly thought. The atrium house was, indeed, far from the norm. This fact implies more dynamic social relations between landlords and tenants and among neighbors, as well as a more fluid use of space.

Villas

Romans in the countryside lived a dramatically different existence than those in the city. The term *villa* conveys the range of dwellings on the land, from a modest farmhouse to a sprawling estate with fantasy architecture and pleasure parks (Gros 2001:265–379). During the Republic most of the land in Italy was owned by a few wealthy families, whose estates were managed and worked by tenant freedmen or slaves living in shacks; at least from the fifth century B.C., a villa, together with its land (*ager*), was known as a farm (*fundus*). During the Middle to Late Republic, *villa rustica* could designate such a farmstead, complete with accommodation for the owner; by the second century B.C., the term also connoted large country homes and retreats with *atria*, peristyles, and unprecedented amenities. Thousands of farms and villas existed in Italy in the late Republic, and tens of thousands more in the provinces by mid-empire.

Just as houses and insulae must be considered within their larger urban entity, productive villas belonged to a spatial and economic network, created by the Roman system of land-allotment (centuriation), combining town, suburb, and agricultural land. Such a landscape survives in the vicinity of Pompeii, where from the early first century B.C. land division linked villas with towns and main roads. The remains at Boscoreale give a good idea of the functioning villa rustica, with spaces for storage, wine- and olive-pressing, livestock, cooking, bathing, and a residential wing for the manager or landowner (Figure 6.10). Despite earlier divisions between rustic and urban villas, there was no strict separation between city and country. The central courtyard of the villa rustica, with its huge clay vessels boasting yields of wine and oil, seems to have been as aesthetically pleasing as the bright mosaics and frescoes of villa interiors (Purcell 1995; Bergmann 2002). Today the best preserved villa rustica, the Villa Regina, discovered at Boscoreale in 1988, stands reconstructed and surrounded by vines and fruit trees, planted just as they were in antiquity, thanks to advances in landscape archaeology (Jashemski 1993:288–291; 2002:24–26).

Beginning in the first century B.C., the basic Italian peristyle villa spread to the provinces, where remains show similar combinations of working and residen-

Figure 6.10 Model of Villa Pisanella, Boscoreale, Museo della Civiltà Romana, 1930s, inv. M.C.R. no. 3507. After Ciarallo and De Carolis 1999: 138, figure 116. Reproduced with permission of Photoservice Electa

tial units, but in a range of architectural forms. A late development in the northern villas of the Netherlands and Britain is the rectangular, aisled building with two rows of posts dividing the inside into a nave and two aisles. As in Italy, these buildings housed productive agricultural or industrial operations alongside the amenities of hypocaust heating, baths, mosaics, and frescoes.

Rus in urbe, the country in the city, indeed was a popular slogan among Romans, and wealthier villas exemplify the artful synthesis of both worlds in their gardens and interior décor (Bergmann 2002). From the Republic onwards, prosperous men owned several villas throughout Italy, complete with residential suites similar to townhouses, game and fish preserves, and elaborate aviaries. Some lived in their *horti*, extensive park-like estates in the suburbium of Rome with impressive sculpture parks that, like Nero's Domus Aurea, were urban versions of wealthy country estates, which in turn incorporated urban elements. Others enjoyed owning *villae maritimae*, which arose along coastlines with the open seas of empire. In Italy, maritime villas feature extensive porticoes for strolling, spacious reception rooms with picture windows, Greek and Latin libraries, salt and sweet water baths, even isolated belvederes on artificial islands built of hydraulic concrete. The mid-second-century B.C. Villa Prato at Sperlonga rose up on a huge platform (*basis villae*); by the first century A.D. its famous sculptural ensemble, displayed in a natural grotto before an artificial dining island, offered diners one example of a recurring *topos* in villa design, the so-called cave of the Cyclops. A visitor could re-enact Ulysses's deeds by confronting Scylla on a small boat or approaching the sleeping giant Polyphemus on foot. Three centuries later, a guest to the inland, wooded estate at Piazza Armerina in central Sicily encountered the same scene of Ulysses and the inhospitable Polyphemus in the form of an apsidal mosaic (Wilson 1983).

Such luxury villas displayed eclectic sculpture collections, best preserved from the Villa of the Papyri outside Herculaneum (late first century B.C.), the Villa of El Ruedo at Cordoba in Spain, and at Chiragon in southern France. Others boasted continuous figural mosaics (Piazza Armerina), formal gardens (Fishbourne), private harbors and detached pavilions in man-made landscapes (Sorrento). Imperial estates demonstrate the extent to which a patron could fashion his villa as another world. Hadrian's extravaganza at Tivoli invoked famous places the emperor had visited; of these, two have been identified: the legendary Vale of Tempe and the symbolic Underworld, where Hadrian could reenact his nocturnal initiation at Eleusis (*Historia Augusta* 26.5–6; MacDonald and Pinto 1985:58–59). The imaginary transportation to another place, most often into mythical and legendary Greece, was incited by visual stimuli in paintings, mosaics, statues, and architectural and landscape fantasies. From the modest farm to the lavish theme parks of emperors, the villa was a site where Romans engaged with the natural environment in ever novel ways.

Interior Décor

The Roman domestic interior was often a colorful, vibrant space, and it is here that we most easily recognize a common visual language in Roman housing (Gazda 1991; Zanker 1998). Poorer dwellings, of course, contained only the bare necessities: a lamp, a bed, a table. Whenever possible, however, a homeowner invested in the interior and in greenery, waterworks, and pleasurable views. Furniture was minimal, with niches, shelves, and cupboards built into the walls, and sometimes even beds and tables cut in masonry. Wooden, marble, and bronze furniture was portable, consisting of small tables, couches, chairs, lamp-stands, and strongboxes (McKay 1975:136–155; Allison 1999). Tapestries and curtains divided spaces and regulated light and ventilation. Sculpture, as a rule, animated outdoor garden settings, except for the portraits and religious statuettes displayed inside.

Best preserved are the built surfaces of Roman dwellings, and these suggest that when designing their homes, Romans desired to alter the boundaries and segments of their daily experience. Indoors, all sides of a room–ceiling, floor, and four walls–presented lively designs. Floors were covered with slabs of marble (*opus sectile*) or mosaics composed of small cubes set in mortar (*tesserae*). Muralists painted pigments onto fresh plaster (*fresco*) or molded plaster into decorative relief (*stucco*); certain pigments, like cinnabar red and cobalt blue, signaled high investment (Taylor 2003). Through certain arrangements of colors, themes, and motifs, craftsmen expanded small rooms and reproduced the rhythms of corridors and colonnades. A striking aspect is the ambivalent treatment of solid walls and floors in a play with depth of field, whereby frescoes and mosaics blurred actual and illusionary spaces, "opening" walls and floors onto exotic worlds for different spectator positions within the room.

In the late nineteenth century, August Mau introduced the Four Styles of Pompeian painting as a chronological classification that developed sequentially between the third century B.C. and A.D. 79, when Vesuvius erupted. The First Style (ca. 200–80 B.C.) imitates in painted stucco relief the wall veneering of marble and other precious materials of wealthy palaces and public buildings; it remained popular throughout the empire for centuries. The Second, Architectural, Style (ca. 90–10 B.C.) offers spectacular *trompe l'œil* illusions of projecting architecture, extensive gardens, even of life-size human figures; this mode, too, continues outside of Italy through the fourth century A.D., especially in the east. The Third Style (ca. 10 B.C.–40 A.D.) has been related to the onset of empire; more subdued in tone, it consists of large surfaces of red, yellow, and black, with pictures of myths, portraits, and landscapes in the center of each wall. The Fourth Style overlaps with the Third and draws upon the Second Style, producing infinite variations, with a primary focus on a central panel and fantastic architectural forms in the upper zone. Of late, Mau's chronology has proven problematic, even for Pompeii, and the situation is more difficult for paintings in the provinces or in contexts dating to the Middle and Late Empire. Yet despite changing fashions and uncertain dates, the ceilings, walls, and floors of Roman dwellings do adhere to the basic geometric grid derived from built architecture, with horizontal lines following dadoes, cornices and entablatures, and vertical columns or ornamental borders creating neat divisions for marble inlay, wall mosaic, stucco, or painted plaster (Clarke 1991; 2003; Ling 1991; Leach 2004).

The main development in the decor of Early to Late Imperial interiors is the shift of figural scenes from painted walls to the mosaic floor (Thébert 1987:392–405; Dunbabin 1999). Miles of floor mosaics survive in houses of North Africa, Sicily, Spain, and Turkey; many introduce new spatial dimensions and themes (marine scenes, muses, the hunt, and amphitheater), while others revive compositions of earlier, painted walls, at times in a veritable "painting in stone" as the central panel of a mosaic floor (*emblema*). We should remember that Romans often lay on their sides for business, repose, and entertaining, and it would have been natural for them to look down at such a picture or to lean back and gaze up at an intricately painted ceiling. The most frequent arrangement is of three to four framed scenes, one on each wall of a small room, in contrapuntal relationships that invite prolonged comparisons. Few scholars have considered the effects of different media, and multiple compositions, on six surfaces of a room, a complexity that increased with the constant shifting of the viewer's own position. Such interiors highlight a desire for optical and intellectual stimulation.

The most significant advance in scholarship on Roman housing and its decoration in the past 30 years has been the application of methods from the social sciences, specifically of spatial analysis (Wallace-Hadrill 1994; Bon and Jones 1997; Laurence and Wallace-Hadrill 1997; Allison 2001; Laurence 2004; Perring 2004). These studies examine space itself as an expressive entity, whereby its shape and contents constitute a system of signs within a social hierarchy. It is, of course, dangerous to impose rigid patterns upon archaeological remains. The vicissitudes of homes make it extremely difficult to determine the intention or agency behind building and décor, and whether these are due to individual, societal, or environmental factors. Who, for instance, was responsible for the appearance of a renovated interior—the patron, a beneficiary, an architect, a builder, the master of a fresco or mosaic workshop, a temporary renter? Nevertheless, the recent, holistic approach to the Roman house reveals new inter-relationships among structure, décor, and movement in certain sequences of spaces, circulation patterns, and charted sight-lines. From these, one can begin to understand more than one can from a static layout of rooms, namely, the experience of being in a Roman dwelling.

Conclusion

A few conclusions may be drawn. Considered within the larger picture of Roman housing, the atrium house emerges as one regional variation on the basic scheme of the courtyard house and appears primarily in central Italy between the second century B.C. and late first century A.D. More typical of single dwellings in the Roman world is the peristyle house. However, individual ownership of a home was not as prevalent as has been thought. Most people lived in small quarters, either in multi-unit housing or in modest houses in the countryside. The prevalence of rental housing implies a different kind of power structure and set of social relations, and it has implications for the choices behind, and meaning of, the physical appearance of a dwelling.

Patterns and features do emerge as distinctive of Roman housing. With the exception of the country villa, most dwellings responded to a rational urban design, maximized the potential of a built structure by sharing walls and floors, and took advantage of space, light, and air by grouping rooms or separate dwellings around a communal open court. City blocks, buildings, and single rooms were multi-functional, and new finds affirm that mercantile and living areas, lavish and modest homes, often resided cheek by jowl. Visual experience played a paramount role in planning, so that architecture, views, and decoration were coordinated to enhance activities and engage inhabitants.

Today, the major constraints on research into Roman housing across the empire lie in the modern boundaries of nations and of disciplines. There are advances in both areas. With Romanization no longer discussed as a monolithic process, new attention is being given to the interactions among local and imported habits, styles, and materials. As a result, we can begin to detect the variety and complexity of living situations during Roman rule. At the same time that new analytical models are applied to ancient housing, traditional criteria come into question, placing us at a healthy turning point in our quest for a clearer picture of the ways that Romans, and those individuals inhabiting Roman territory, actually lived.

REFERENCES

Allison, Penelope M., ed. 1999 The Archaeology of Household Activities. London and New York: Routledge.

——2001 Using the Material and Written Sources: Turn of the Millennium Approaches to Roman Domestic Space. American Journal of Archaeology 105:181–208.

——2004 Pompeian Households: An Analysis of the Material Culture. Cotsen Institute of Archaeology, UCLA, Monograph 42. Los Angeles: The Cotsen Institute of Archaeology, University of California.

Bergmann, Bettina 2002 Art and Nature in the Villa at Oplontis. In T. McGinn et al., Pompeian Brothels, Pompeii's Ancient History, Mirrors and Mysteries, Art and Nature at Oplontis, and the Herculaneum "Basilica." Journal of Roman Archaeology Supplementary Series 47. Pp. 87–120. Portsmouth, R.I.: Journal of Roman Archaeology.

Bodel, John 1997 Monumental Villas and Villa Monuments. Journal of Roman Archaeology 10:1–35.

Bon, Sara, and Rick Jones, eds. 1997 Sequence and Space in Pompeii. Oxford: Oxbow.

Cahill, Nicholas D. 2002 Household and City Organization at Olynthus. New Haven: Yale University Press.

Cambitoglou, Alexander, Ann Birchall, J. James Coulton, and J. Richard Green 1988 Zagora 2: Excavation of a Geometric Town. Athens: Archaologikis Hetairias.

——, J. James Coulton, Judith Birmingham, and J. Richard Green 1971 Zagora 1: Excavation Season 1967, Study Season 1968–69. Sydney: Sydney University Press.

Ciarallo, Anna, and Ernesto De Carolis, eds. 1999 Pompeii: Life in a Roman Town. Milan: Electa.

Claridge, Amanda 1998 Rome: An Oxford Archaeological Guide. Oxford: Oxford University Press.

Clarke, John R. 1991 The Houses of Roman Italy, 100 B.C.–A.D. 250: Ritual, Space, and Decoration. Berkeley: University of California Press.

——2003 Art in the Lives of Ordinary Romans: Visual Representation and Non-Elite Viewers in Italy, 100 B.C.–A.D. 315. Berkeley: University of California Press.

Connolly, Peter 1998 The Ancient City: Life in Classical Athens and Rome. Oxford: Oxford University Press.

Coulson, William 1983 The Architecture: Area IV. In Excavations at Nichoria in Southwest Greece III. William Coulson and John Rosser, eds. Pp. 18–56. Minneapolis: University of Minnesota Press.

——, and John Rosser, eds. 1983 Excavations at Nichoria in Southwest Greece III. Minneapolis: University of Minnesota Press.

De Kind, Richard 1998 Houses in Herculaneum: A New View on the Town Planning and the Building of Insulae III and IV. Amsterdam: Gieben.

DeLaine, Janet 2004 Designing for a Market: "Medianum" Apartments at Ostia. Journal of Roman Archaeology 20:146–176.

Dunbabin, Katherine M. D. 1999 Mosaics of the Greek and Roman World. Cambridge and New York: Cambridge University Press.

Gardner, Jane F., and Thomas Wiedemann, eds. 1991 The Roman Household. London: Routledge.

Gazda, Elaine K., ed. 1991 Roman Art in the Private Sphere: New Perspectives on the Architecture and Décor of the Domus, Villa, and Insula. Ann Arbor: University of Michigan Press.

George, Michele 1997 The Roman Domestic Architecture of Northern Italy. Oxford: British Archaeological Reports.

Gros, Pierre 2001 L'Architecture romaine 2: maisons, villas, palais et tombeaux. Paris: Picard.

Guzzo, Pier Giovanni 2005 Pompeii: Stories from an Eruption. Milan: Electa.

Hermansen, Gustav 1981 Ostia: Aspects of Roman Civic Life. Edmonton: University of Alberta Press.

Early, R. et al., ed. 2003 Zeugma: Interim Reports, Rescue Excavations. Journal of Roman Archaeology Supplementary Series 51. Portsmouth, R.I.: Journal of Roman Archaeology.

Jashemski, Wilhelmina 1979 The Gardens of Pompeii: Herculaneum and the Villas Destroyed by Vesuvius, vol. 1. New Rochelle, N.Y.: Caratzas Bros.

——1993 The Gardens of Pompeii: Herculaneum and the Villas Destroyed by Vesuvius, vol. 2, Appendices. New Rochelle, N.Y.: Caratzas Bros.

——2002 The Natural History of Pompeii. Cambridge: Cambridge University Press.

Jones, Rick, with Damian Robinson 2004 The Making of an Elite House: The House of the Vestals at Pompeii. Journal of Roman Archaeology 17:105–130.

Laurence, Ray 2004 The Uneasy Divide Between Ancient History and Archaeology. In Archaeology and Ancient History: Breaking Down the Boundaries. E. W. Sauer, ed. Pp. 99–113. London and New York: Routledge.

——, and Andrew Wallace-Hadrill, eds. 1997 Domestic Space in the Roman World: Pompeii and Beyond. Journal of Roman Archaeology Supplementary Series 22. Portsmouth, R.I.: Journal of Roman Archaeology.

Leach, Eleanor W. 1997 Oecus on Ibycus: Investigating the Vocabulary of the Roman House. In Sequence and Space in Pompeii. Sara Bon and Rick Jones, eds. Pp. 50–71. Oxford: Oxbow.

——2004 The Social Life of Painting in Ancient Rome and on the Bay of Naples. Cambridge: Cambridge University Press.

Ling, Roger 1991 Roman Painting. Cambridge and New York: Cambridge University Press.

——1997 The Insula of the Menander at Pompeii, I. The Structures. Oxford: Oxford University Press.

MacDonald, William, and John Pinto. 1985. Hadrian's Villa and its Legacy. New Haven and London: Yale University Press.

Makaronas, C. and Gionri, E. 1989. Oi oikies arpagis Elenis kai Dionysion. Athens: Archaeological Service.

Mazarakis Ainian, Alexander 1992 Nichoria in the Southwestern Peloponnese: Units IV-1 and IV-5 Reconsidered. Opuscula Atheniensa 19:75–84.

——1997 From Rulers' Dwellings to Temples: Architecture, Religion and Society in Early Iron Age Greece (1100–700 B.C.). Jonsered: Paul Åströms Förlag.

——2002 Les fouilles d'Oropos et la fonction des périboles dans les agglomerations du début de l'Age du Fer. Pallas 58:183–227.

McKay, Alexander 1975 Houses, Villas, and Palaces in the Roman World. Baltimore: Johns Hopkins University Press.

Morris, Ian 2000 Archaeology as Cultural History: Words and Things in Iron Age Greece. Oxford: Blackwell.

Najbjerg. N., n.d. "Domus", Stanford Digital Forma Urbis Romae Project. Electronic document, http://formaurbis.stanford.edu/index.php

Nevett, Lisa 1997 Perceptions of Domestic Space in Italy. In The Roman Family in Italy: Status, Sentiment, Space. Beryl Rawson and P. Weaver, eds. Pp. 281–298. Oxford: Clarendon Press.

——1999 House and Society in the Ancient Greek World. Cambridge: Cambridge University Press.

——2002 Continuity and Change in Greek Households under Roman Rule. *In* Greek Romans and Roman Greeks. E. Ostenfeld, ed. Pp. 81–97. Aarhus: Aarhus University Press.

Özeren, Ocal 1993 Ephesus. Istanbul: Keskin Color Kartpostalcilik

Patterson, John R. 2000 Living and Dying in the City of Rome: Houses and Tombs. *In* Ancient Rome: The Archaeology of the Eternal City. Jon Coulston and Hazel Dodge, eds. Pp. 259–289. Oxford: Oxford University School of Archaeology.

Perring, Dominic 2002 The Roman House in Britain. London: Routledge.

——2004 Concept, Design and Build: Romans beyond Pompeii. Antiquity 78:204–209.

Popham, Mervyn, and Hugh Sackett, eds. 1993 Lefkandi: The Protogeometric Building at Toumba II: The Excavation, Architecture and Finds. London: British School at Athens.

Purcell, Nicholas 1995 The Roman Villa and the Landscape of Production. *In* Urban Society in Roman Italy. Tim Cornell and Kathryn Lomas, eds. Pp. 151–179. New York: St. Martin's Press.

Riggsby, Andrew 1997 "Public" and "Private" in Roman Culture: The Case of the Cubiculum. Journal of Roman Archaeology 10:36–56.

Robinson David M. and V. W. Graham 1938 Excavations at Olynthus VIII: the hellenic house. Baltimore: Johns Hopkins University Press.

Steinby, Eva Margareta, ed. 1995 Lexicon Topographicum Urbis Romae. Vol. II: D-G. Rome: Quasar.

Taylor, Rabun 2003. Roman Builders: A Study in Architectural Process. Cambridge: Cambridge University Press.

Thébert, Yves 1987 Private Life and Domestic Architecture in Roman Africa. *In* A History of Private Life, Vol. I. Paul Veyne, ed. Pp. 313–409. Cambridge, MA: Harvard University Press.

Thompson, Homer A. and R. E. Wycherley 1972 Excavations in the Athenian Agora XIV: the history, shape and uses of an ancient city center. Princeton: American School of Classical Studies.

Trümper, Monika 1998 Wohnen in Delos: eine Baugeschichtliche Untersuchung zum Wandel der Wohnkultur in hellenistischer Zeit. Internationale Archäologie 46.

von Heintze, Helga 1971 Roman Art. New York: Universe Books.

Walker, Susan 1983 Women and Housing in Classical Greece. *In* Images of Women in Antiquity. Averil Cameron and Amélie Kuhrt, eds. Pp. 81–91. London: Croom Helm.

Wallace-Hadrill, Andrew 1994 Houses and Society in Pompeii and Herculaneum. Princeton: Princeton University Press.

Walter-Karydi, Elena 1998 The Greek House: The Rise of Noble Houses in Late Classical Times. Athens: Athens Archaeological Society.

Wilson, Roger 1983 Piazza Armerina. Austin: University of Texas Press.

Wiseman, T. P. 1987 Conspicui Postes Tectaque Digna Deo: The Public Image of Aristocratic and Imperial Houses in the Late Republic and Early Empire. *In* L'Urbs: Espace urbain et histoire (1er siècle av. J.C–IIIe siècle ap. J.C.). Collection de l'Ecole Française de Rome 98. Pp. 393–413. Rome: L'Ecole française de Rome.

Zanker, Paul 1998 Pompeii: Public and Private Life. Cambridge, MA: Harvard University Press.

7

Cult and Ritual

Introduction

Greek and Roman temples, like medieval Christian cathedrals, attracted the most innovative architecture and the largest concentration of investment, whether of labor or of money. The deities to whom super-human powers were ascribed were considered to deserve the best that human endeavors could achieve. And the size and elaboration of the buildings were rivaled by the length and elaboration of the ceremonial, as festivals extended over several days and processions paraded through the whole town or even across the whole city-state. As paintings of Christ and the saints became the icons of the medieval world, not only attracting worship and displaying miraculous powers but becoming its most widely disseminated images, so too statues of gods were the prime icons of the Greek and Roman worlds, held to display supernatural power and becoming widely known symbols of the place where they were set up—often through their representation on coins.

But if pomp of ritual and magnificence of cult buildings and cult images link the worship of the pagan gods of Greek and Roman antiquity to late antique, medieval and indeed some modern manifestations of Christian worship, they cover profound differences. Take the fact that the most widely disseminated icon of a god in the early Roman empire was the image of the deified emperor. Or take the fact that the central cult act to the Olympian gods was the killing of an animal (or at major festivals of a hundred or more animals) and that it was the meat of sacrificed animals which provided most people with their only regular meat meals. Or consider that the sacrifice took place outside the temple, and that worshippers had little occasion to go inside a temple except to admire the sculpted image of the god.

These salient differences between Greek and Roman religious practices and the ways in which Christians worship indicate nicely the different ways in which cult and ritual in Classical antiquity related to other aspects of life. As the worship of Hellenistic rulers and Roman emperors shows, and as the presence of temples within the agoras and fora of Greek and Roman cities has already revealed, religion could not be separated from politics. As the prominence of animal sacrifice indicates, civic ritual continued to center upon the products of agriculture and to keep in the foreground the precarious provision of subsistence. As the way temples were showcases for the gods, not meeting places for humans, betrays, there were no privileged interpreters of gods to men, no religious teachers explaining the ways of god to assembled men, and worship was a matter of awe and wonder at the manifestation of the divine, not a preparation for the presentation of man to god.

This chapter looks at the ways in which the material remains of religious activity—sanctuaries, temples, votive offerings, the bones of sacrificial beasts—draw our attention not merely to the conspicuous display of material wealth in religious cult, but to the ways in which cult activity was inseparable from wider civic life, and offer us a vivid picture of civic priorities, secular as well as sacred.

7 (a)

Cult and Ritual

The Greek World

Robin Osborne

Introduction

The gods were so much of a presence for the Greeks that some people found it hard to do anything without making explicit allowance for them. Theophrastos sketches the life of the superstitious man in his *Characters*: he is a man forever washing his hands, conducting purifications, interpreting the movements of animals and birds as portents, and consulting specialists about the interpretation of his dreams. Theophrastos' ridicule indicates the degree to which over-sensitivity to the gods could seem excessive, but individually all the actions that the superstitious man undertakes were actions which, on their own and in the right context, an individual or city might reasonably adopt. Just as potential divine intervention pervades the superstitious man's life, so the material contents of and context for acts of religious cult pervade the archaeological record.

All communities in the Greek world were also religious communities. Worshipping the gods was something that any group did together. Households carried out various religious rituals together; extended families and other self-proclaimed descent groups engaged in cult activities when they met together; local village communities had their own calendars of sacrifice. Soldiers poured drink offerings to the gods before leaving home for military service, they sacrificed before setting out for campaigns and before battle, and they might return from battle with stories of a hero manifesting himself for or against them in the battle line. Meetings of citizens in a political assembly were prefaced by purificatory and other rituals. The whole body of citizens in a state, or sometimes the whole body of residents in a city, even (representatives from) all cities of the Greek world, met together for religious festivals. There were, to be sure, some elective cults, which individuals decided to join, but such cult membership was additional to, not in competition with, the worship of the gods that went with belonging to a family or a local group as a result of being born in a particular place. Even in the case of elective cults, the political assembly of citizens might reckon to regulate fees and activities. All ideas of a separation of "church" and "state," and of competing exclusive mono- theistic religions, need to be banished if religion in the polytheistic Greek (or Roman) city is to be understood. The city took responsibility for relations with the gods, and if actions that could be construed as mocking or opposing the gods took place—for instance, vandalism to statues of the gods or mock religious rituals—then the state itself would take serious action to find the culprits and so protect itself from divine anger.

Since the divine does not manifest itself to humans directly, all religions have to represent the divine to themselves. Unlike contemporary Judaism, the Greeks had qualms neither about naming the divine nor about representing the divine to themselves in images. Not all religious activities in the Greek world have left material residues—acts of prayer required no physical assistance, although they might be represented in images. But much cult activity has left material traces, either because the place in which it happened was specially equipped as a sacred place with structures (altars) and buildings (temples, theaters, stoas), or because the objects given to the gods (sacrifices, dedications), or traces of them, survive. In addition, objects associated with cult activity, or with occasions on which the gods might be reckoned to be especially present, as Dionysos might be reckoned especially present when wine was consumed, might themselves be decorated with images of the gods or of cult.

Literary evidence for religious activities is relatively thin. Cult activities were so regular as to excite little notice. Ordinary religious rituals are described, some- what selectively, in comic dramas when they are portraying return to normality from the extraordinary worlds they have been imagining, but in tragedy and other literary texts it is abnormal cultic activity that is more likely to attract attention than everyday activity. Similarly, although a large body of inscriptions survives that prescribes and proscribes particular activities in sanctuaries (the so-called "Sacred Laws"), the prescriptions are often over and above the expected norm rather than descriptions of that norm. It is against this tendency of texts to empha- size the odd, that the archaeological evidence for routine cult actions, and for cult actions in communities which have left no mark at all on the written record, is particularly valuable.

Cult Acts

When Socrates was accused of not recognizing the gods recognized by the city, his defenders retorted that "He was to be seen frequently sacrificing at home and frequently also at the public altars of the state" (Xenophon, *Memorabilia* 1.1.2). Sacrifice was the central ritual of Greek religion, fundamental to every religious festival and accompanying any attempt to attract the attention of the gods to secure a major end (Figure 7.1). As with many rituals, the explanation for why this particular act was undertaken was not apparent to the worshippers. Some of

Figure 7.1 Athenian red-figure bell krater of mid-fifth-century date showing sacrificial ritual just before the animal is killed. Photo ©Museum of Fine Arts, Boston

the earliest Greek poetry surviving gives a story to explain why Greeks sacrificed in the way that they did, offering the bones and fat to the gods and themselves consuming the meat (Hesiod, *Theogony* 535–557). Later writers speculated that animal offerings had replaced earlier offerings that were purely vegetable. But these discussions only confirm that sacrifice came without mythical or other explanatory exegesis.

Although the ritual of sacrifice might be more or less elaborated, it generally involved an animal being led to an altar, making a movement of the head that could be taken as assent, and then having its throat slit. This was regularly followed by the butchering of the animal, and the cooking and eating of the meat, although on some occasions it was prescribed that the animal be burnt whole. The number of animals involved on any one occasion, their species, size, and gender depended partly on cultic considerations—some animals were characteristically sacrificed to one deity, some to another (so pigs to Demeter)—but partly also on the wealth of the person or body providing the sacrificial victim and the number of persons involved. At the major festivals of large cities a hundred cows might be slaughtered; at a sacrifice made by an individual or family only a sucking-pig or a chicken, a favorite offering to the healing god, Asklepios, might be involved.

Sacrifice leaves various sorts of archaeological evidence. The bones of the sacrificed animals may be deposited in the sanctuary and recovered by excavation. Identification of the species of sacrificial animal can help indicate the deity worshipped, in cases where this is not otherwise known. Representations of the sacrificial beast may be offered as dedications, either to commemorate sacrifices or as substitutes for real sacrifices: a particularly lavish example of the former is a dedication made by one Hermesandros at Cyrene to commemorate having financed the sacrifice of 120 cows to Artemis (Osborne 1987:186); more modestly, terracotta cocks have been found dedicated at sanctuaries of Asklepios at both Athens and Corinth (van Straten 1995). Votive reliefs set up in sanctuaries often show families bringing a sacrificial beast to the deity worshipped in that sanctuary. All the stages of sacrifice, from the bringing of the animal to the altar to the jointing of the animal and the roasting of the meat are shown on painted pottery, though the actual kill is rather rarely depicted.

Sacrifice demanded various items of equipment. Carrying a knife became a symbol by which a man might be identified as a priest on his grave stone, and knives in graves have been thought to have a similar role. Certain ritual vessels were standardly employed: a basket of particular shape (the *kanoun*) in which the knife and the barley grains sprinkled upon the victim were placed, an open bowl to catch the blood. But above all sacrifice demanded the provision of an altar (Aktseli 1996). Portable altars are widely found in houses; sanctuaries had permanent altars of various kinds, which might be very large indeed. A place to sacrifice was all that was required to make a place a sanctuary, and there was no particular relation between the place of sacrifice and any temple building, although frequently the altar is found east of a temple—in the sight, as it were, of the cult statue within the temple.

Sacrifices were often accompanied by drink offerings or libations, usually of wine but on some occasions required to be "wineless," but libations were also made on many occasions when no animal was killed. Libations were not thought of simply as lesser forms of sacrifice, but as different in kind from sacrifice: on painted pottery gods receive but do not make sacrifices, but they are quite frequently shown making libations (Lissarrague 1995). A sacrifice is an offering to the gods, and gods do not make offerings to themselves. A libation is different, less an offering than a gesture that indicates a recognition of the sacredness of the place or moment. Images of libations are very common indeed on Athenian red-figure pottery, but little archaeological trace is left of the act itself. However, although libations might be made from drinking vessels of all sorts, they are particularly associated with the footless bowl known as the phiale. Some ceramic examples of this shape exist, but it was primarily a metal shape and metal phialai are found in temple deposits. Particularly notable is a deposit of a large number of bronze phialai found in a pool at Perachora (Tomlinson 1997). It is phialai that the Caryatids of the Erechtheum carry in their left hands.

The particular rituals associated with individual festivals might also generate material residues. Festivals frequently included competitions, whether in athletic, dramatic, or musical prowess, and the prizes awarded ranged from wreaths of olive, which were of little intrinsic and no lasting value, through decorated clay amphoras full of oil, to animals (for sacrifice) and sums of money. Those prizes frequently ended up themselves being dedicated, in whole or part, to the deity whose festival it was.

In a number of instances, and most clearly in the case of pots that were dedicated in the sanctuary where the festival in question was held, the scenes on painted pottery seem to relate directly to festival activity. So, the Brauronia festival, named after the sanctuary of Artemis at Brauron in eastern Attica in which it was held, seems to have featured rituals associated with the end of childhood and the arrival of maturity in girls. That sanctuary has yielded to the archaeologist not only inscribed records of the dedication of garments, including garments specifically noted as small versions of adult clothing, but also pots of a peculiar shape and decoration. The shape is one found almost exclusively in sanctuaries connected with Artemis, and the decoration takes the form of images of young girls, clothed in short garments or naked, running, in one case apparently in the vicinity of a bear. These plausibly commemorate the ritual of the *arkteia*, the "bear ritual," which is mentioned in textual sources as taking place at the sanctuary (Kahil 1977; Sourvinou-Inwood 1988).

More or less equally straightforward are the amphoras, of distinct shape and decoration, that were given in large numbers as prizes in some events at the Panathenaic games. These amphoras, which go back to the reorganization of the Panathenaea in the 560s and continued to be decorated in the black-figure technique even after red-figure had been adopted for other pottery, showed on one side a standing martial Athena and on the other side a scene of athletics (Bentz 1998). A variety of athletic scenes were shown, but on the basis of preserved examples it seems that the particular scene did not necessarily correspond to the event for which the amphora was given as a prize, so that even these scenes which appear to represent the competitions at which they were awarded turn out to contain an element of imagination.

A more problematic case concerns the Choes ("Jugs") festival, which was part of the three-day festival at Athens known as the Anthesteria. Miniature clay jugs were produced to mark this festival, and surviving jugs (generally found in tombs and in settlement contexts, not as dedications) carry images of toddlers engaged in a variety of childish and not so childish activities—they are shown both pushing wheeled toys and also brandishing wine jugs. There is some evidence that the

Figure 7.2 Athenian red-figure stamnos from the second quarter of the fifth century showing women engaged in ritual activity around a mask of the god Dionysos. Photo ©Museum of Fine Arts, Boston

festival of the Choes was indeed a festival in which small children had a special part, but scholars dispute whether the miniature jugs give us snapshots of the sorts of activities in which toddlers were actually involved at this festival, or whether the miniature size of the jugs has encouraged the miniaturization of what were in fact purely adult activities (van Hoorn 1951; Hamilton 1992).

More difficult still are the so-called "Lenaian" vases. Two distinct groups of Athenian vases, one a group of black-figure *lekythoi* (oil flasks) from the very beginning of the fifth century, the other a group of red-figure *stamnoi* (round closed vessels) from the second quarter of the fifth century, show women dancing round or performing other apparently ritual acts around a mask of Dionysos on a pole (Figure 7.2). The imagery on the lekythoi includes scenes of the women handling wild animals and, in one case, a satyr; the presence of the satyr guarantees that what is shown is, in some senses at least, imaginary. The images on the stamnoi show the women ladling something, presumably wine, out of stamnoi that stand on a table by the mask of Dionysos and into deep cups. The self-reference here to a ritual use of the vessel which is decorated with the images encourages the idea that these pots were made for use in the ritual that they show. However, since women are thought to have usually been kept away from wine, and since these stamnoi have all been found in Italy, questions arise as to whether we should interpret the scenes as showing an Athenian ritual, a generic and purely imaginary ritual, or practices in Etruria (Osborne 1997).

Similar questions about the relationship of imagery to ritual arise also on pots made outside Athens. In Boiotia, a particular distinctive shape of deep cup was manufactured in connection with the Kabirion sanctuary just west of Thebes. These cups are variously decorated. Some of the scenes certainly relate to the cult, in as far as they show a figure named "Kabiros." Other scenes show symposia, athletics or hunting, or explicitly relate to well-known myths (Odysseus and Circe, the battle of the Pygmies and Cranes). Very frequently the figures in these scenes are grotesque caricatures, and this has encouraged speculation that performances of mythical parodies may have taken place as part of the ritual in the theater that is part of the Kabirion sanctuary (Schachter 2003).

Just as images of rituals may occur on pots which were not dedicated in connection with the ritual, so also the form of many dedications in sanctuaries seems to have no direct connection with the rituals held there. Objects of all sorts are dedicated, from pins (including outsize examples) and everyday pottery vessels, through bronze figurines of animals and birds, both wild and domestic, to house or temple models, relief sculptures, and life-sized stone or bronze statues of men and women or even of equestrian groups. Most of these objects were made specially for dedication in the sanctuary; this is particularly clear in the case of the practice of dedicating miniature versions of objects used in everyday life—whether miniature armor, as in the votive shields found, for example, at the temple of Apollo at Bassai in Arkadia, or miniature pottery vessels, such as the 6,000 miniature water-jugs (*hydriai*) found at the sanctuary of Demeter at Abdera (Cole 1994:211). Patterns of dedication vary markedly from sanctuary to sanctuary, and although the pattern of dedications at any given sanctuary may stay stable over a relatively long period, in the course of two or three centuries, both the quantity and the nature of dedications often change significantly.

One example of such a change is to be found in the eighth century B.C. when there was an enormous rise in the number of dedications, particularly of small metal objects, made in sanctuaries. This increase in numbers has often been associated with the contemporaneous decline in the number of objects deposited in graves (Snodgrass 1980). But although the rise in numbers is found all over Greece, what exactly the objects are varies from sanctuary to sanctuary. Some sanctuaries, such as the sanctuaries of Zeus at Olympia, Hera at Perachora near Corinth, and Hera on Samos, attracted particular exotic goods, statuettes, seals, and so on from both the eastern Mediterranean and from Italy. Other sanctuaries, such as the sanctuary at Pherae in Thessaly, are dominated by locally made goods (Kilian-Dirlmeier 1985). Even sanctuaries that are close together might attract quite different ranges of goods. In the eighth century the contrast between the two Corinthian sanctuaries at Perachora and at Isthmia is particularly marked. But the contrasts could occur between sanctuaries that were even closer together: at a slightly later date this can be observed in the contrast between the acropolis sanctuary at Emborio on Chios, with its dedications that seem to point to the martial service of men and the domestic activity of women, and the harbor sanctuary whose fish-hooks and exotic bronze belts point in a different direction (Morgan 1990:230–232). In part, differences in patterns of dedication may be linked to the different cultic personalities of the deities involved, for although a particular god might be invoked in a wide range of circumstances, the range of concerns attributed to one god was distinct from the range of concerns attributed to another. But above all the variety in the dedicatory assemblages seems to relate to the different social place of the sanctuaries—a social place partly linked to the physical location of the sanctuary.

In the late seventh century, life-sized or larger than life-sized stone statues appeared in sanctuaries for the first time. Although these take a variety of forms, sometimes, for example, figuring a man carrying a sheep or calf, the dominant forms are the naked beardless male figure with hands firmly by his sides (the *kouros*), and the more or less elaborately clothed standing female figure with one hand held out carrying an offering (the *kore*) (Richter 1968; 1970). The figures carrying sacrificial animals must stand for mortals, but whether the other figures stand for mortals (they do not straightforwardly stand for the dedicant since men dedicate female figures) or gods (but male as well as female figures were dedicated on Athena's Acropolis at Athens) is still disputed (Keesling 2003, on the Athenian Acropolis *korai*). Sanctuaries of Apollo may have particularly attracted *kouroi*: certainly the Boiotian sanctuary of Apollo Ptoios seems to have received more than a hundred kouros dedications in less than a century (Ducat 1971). But any interpretation of these figures has to recognize that statues of identical form also, in Attica at least, stood as grave markers.

From the late sixth century onwards, the variety of sculpted figures set up in sanctuaries seems to have increased, partly in association with the development of the "lost wax" bronze-casting technique which enabled bronze more easily to become a medium for large-scale sculpture. Sculptures of gods generally showed them in action, sometimes as part of a mythological narrative. Men too, at this period, had themselves represented in action: victors at the great athletic festival at Olympia seem regularly to have commemorated themselves in competition. Unfortunately bronze could be melted down and re-used, and so the survival rate for bronze sculptures is low (many classical bronzes that survive do so because they were lost at sea at some stage when they were being taken away by Romans to adorn their villas). The loss of the original statues makes it hard to trace patterns of dedication, but frequently statue bases survive even if the statue is lost, and it does appear that in many sanctuaries the total number of free-standing sculptural dedications may have decreased in the fifth century along with the total number of dedications (Whitley 2002:311–313).

Sanctuaries were places of publicity for communities as well as for individuals. What is perhaps the earliest attested law was found in a sanctuary at Dreros in Crete, though it relates entirely to a political, not a cultic, office. During the sixth century, many different cities erected treasuries, small temple-like buildings in which they could display their offerings to the god, at the so-called Panhellenic sanctuaries at Olympia and Delphi. These two sanctuaries were not in the territory of any powerful city and people came from all over the Greek world to their festivals (and, in the case of Delphi, oracle). Cities dedicated the spoils of war against other Greek cities both at their own sanctuaries and at Delphi and Olympia; equally they put their treaties with one another on display at Olympia. A visitor to Olympia could read in the inscriptions placed upon or accompanying the various dedications the story of most of the major events in the military history of the Greek world (Pausanias *Periegesis* books 5–6 do pretty well that). Archaeologists have also recovered from Olympia sufficient examples of armor to enable them to tell the story of the changing technologies of those wars.

Placing Cult

Cult acts were not restricted to sanctuaries or other sites which the placing of altars had marked out as places of cult. But the placing of cult was nevertheless significant. Sacrifice before battle happened on the selected battlefield (Jameson 1991). Oath sacrifices were made at the place where the oaths were exchanged. Offerings to heroes that did not occur at shrines occurred at old tombs (Whitley 2002:150–156).

Stories associated with the foundation of sanctuaries sometimes explained their location with reference to some specific act. So Pausanias reports a statue of Shame 4 miles from Sparta because it was at that point that Penelope hid her face to indicate that she wished to go to be the bride of Odysseus rather than stay with her father Ikarios (Pausanias 3.20.10–11). But sanctuaries were also placed in relation to both natural and political geography. The sanctuary of Zeus at Olympia lies at the confluence of the rivers Alpheios and Kladeos. The sanctuary at Delphi lies on a natural mountain terrace commanding a tremendous view and equipped with an abundant spring, and the association between springs and sanctuaries is widespread (cf. for the territory of Metaponto, the sanctuaries of San Biagio and Pantanello: Carter 1994). The sanctuaries of Poseidon at Tainaron and Sounion lie at the end of major promontories and are visible from far out to sea. Numerous sanctuaries lie on the top of hills or mountains, whether hills that form the acropoleis of towns, as with the Athenian Acropolis, the Kadmeia at Thebes, and so on, or at the top of relatively isolated mountains (Scully 1979).

Town acropoleis are over-determined as cult sites by both natural and political geography, but for other sites political factors seem to be the main determinant, if not in the original siting of a sanctuary then at least in its development. One striking phenomenon of the Greek mainland in the eighth century has received particular attention (de Polignac 1995). This is that in the eighth century major sanctuaries are built up in locations far from centers of population, and often on what is very likely to have been the edge of a territory. Such sanctuaries often turn out later to be linked to the population centre by festal processions. The classic example of this is the Argive Heraion, a sanctuary already in use in the Bronze Age but in which enormous investments were made in the eighth and seventh centuries to construct the temple terrace and dedicate tripod cauldrons and a great array of metal objects including outsize pins 0.8 meters long and bundles of spits. But the pattern is many times repeated and the intimate links between the city and outlying sanctuary are expressed in various archaeologically visible ways. At Samos, for instance, where the great sanctuary of Hera lies at the west end of the plain, at the east end of which was the harbor town of Samos itself, a monumental sacred way was constructed along which, as it entered the sanctuary, dedicatory statues were lined up. It is tempting also to connect the dedication of two massive larger than life-sized *kouroi* in the Samian sanctuary with the challenge to be visible to worshippers coming from afar, just as the similarly monumental *kouroi* at Sounion are plausibly linked to its headland position. In the case of Athens, the phenomenon of the outlying sanctuary is arguably multiple, with the development in the eighth and seventh centuries of a number of different sanctuaries on or towards the borders of the city's vast territory. In the classical period city-center duplicates of the outlying sanctuaries were developed in the city center (in the case of the Brauronion on the Acropolis) displaying duplicates of the inscribed lists of dedications at the outlying sanctuary. A similar pattern of duplicating rural cults is found in the city of Megalopolis, founded in the fourth century, which used such doublets to link itself to an existing cultic landscape (Jost 1994).

Archaeological survey has yet to reveal much in the way of rural settlement in the eighth century anywhere in Greece, but it seems quite likely that the development of outlying sanctuaries on the Greek mainland and the Aegean islands marked the formulation of political claims to an already populated and exploited countryside. However, in areas of Italy and Sicily settled by Greeks, the spread of sanctuaries seems sometimes to mark a secondary move into the countryside by a community which initially looked rather towards the sea. Such is arguably the case in the territory of Metapontum, where large-scale religious investment in the territory appears to go with a massive exercise in regular land division that comes more than a century after the initial foundation of the city (Carter 1994).

One of the ways in which sanctuaries developed in the eighth century was in the building of temples. Although there are buildings in sanctuaries earlier (in the tenth century at Mende-Poseidi in the Chalkidike), and some signs of cult activity in buildings elsewhere during the dark ages, it is from the eighth century on that it becomes possible to talk with confidence about temples (Mazarakis Ainian 1997). Yet the purpose of the Greek temple is not entirely clear (Morgan

2003:142–148). Temples frequently housed cult statues, and their architecture might be very much determined by the need to provide an effective backdrop for that statue, but it was possible for a cult statue to be in the open air, or for a temple to have no statue. It may be that early temples had no single purpose and that in different places they provided a space for different rituals, but that the existence of temple buildings itself encouraged the making of offerings of more precious and delicate materials.

Some eighth-century temples marked themselves out from ordinary dwellings not simply through being built in sanctuaries, where houses might in any case be found, but by their size. Eighth-century temples one hundred feet long are known from the sanctuary of Hera on Samos (rectangular) and from the sanctuary of Apollo at Eretria (apsidal ended). During the seventh century, a still more distinctive architectural style was developed for temples. In quick succession temple buildings acquired colonnades (first found in the eighth-century temple of Artemis at Ephesus), tiled roofs and stone walls (first found in the temple of Poseidon at Isthmia in the second quarter of the seventh century), and between 625 and 575 B.C. coherent systems of architectural detailing emerge that come to be known as "Doric" and "Ionic" (Barletta 2001).

The systems of Doric and Ionic temple architecture are remarkable because they cannot be accounted for functionally. In Doric architecture neither the three steps of the temple base (the top step known as the stylobate), nor the fluting of columns, nor the two-part capital to the column (the swelling echinus and square abacus), nor the surmounting of the plain beams of the entablature with alternating metopes and triglyphs, are structurally necessary, and the same applies still more forcibly to the regulae and guttae, the mutules and the hawksbeak moldings. Similar reservations must be expressed about the structural role of the Ionic architecture, with its separate column bases, its three-part architrave, and its rich repertoire of moldings. The explanation for all these features must be in large part aesthetic, but, that being the case, it is all the more remarkable that Doric and Ionic schemes were so rapidly and widely adopted, with remarkably little variation and even less contamination between the two systems.

Emulation, or what has been called "peer-polity interaction" seems the most likely explanation for the rapid adoption of Doric and Ionic temple architecture. Temples in fact provide some of the best evidence for competition between cities (Snodgrass 1986): it is hard to believe that it is mere coincidence that the fourth temple of Hera at Samos just surpasses the first temple of Artemis at Ephesus in ground area (6,038 square meters compared to 6,017) or that the Parthenon has columns that are a quarter of an inch higher than those of the temple of Zeus at Olympia. The impression made by the earliest Doric and Ionic temples, on this view, encouraged other communities to demand their own sanctuary buildings that were comparable. Indeed, the period from 575 to 475 saw a massive program of building across the whole Greek world in which many communities erected not one but often several temples, many of them on a quite colossal scale. A count of simply those temples which are best attested archaeologically gives a total of more than 50 temples, of which half have stylobates over 20 meters wide (Osborne

1996:263–264). No fewer than nine of these temples, including one over 40 meters wide, were built by the Sicilian city of Selinus (whose neighbor, Akragas, responded with a temple just bigger than Selinus' largest).

Within the broad uniformity of the Doric and Ionic traditions there was also scope for variation. Sculptural decoration was one feature that differed markedly from temple to temple. Already in the seventh century the Aitolian city of Thermon seems to have decorated its temple with painted plaques. The early sixth-century temple of Artemis on Corcyra sported massive pedimental sculptures, and pedimental sculptures seem to have become a regular feature of the sixth-century temples on the Athenian acropolis. The earliest pedimental sculptures seem more concerned with presenting an aspect of divine power (the gorgon Medusa, other monstrous figures, Apollo in his chariot) than with alluding to a particularly mythological episode, but towards the end of the century some narrative element appears (the rape of Antiope by Theseus at Eretria, for example). Sculpted metopes also appear for the first time in the sixth century, initially on small buildings ("Treasury I" at Foce del Sele, the Sicyonian treasury at Delphi), and catch on particularly in Sicily and South Italy. Most of the surviving metopes seem to allude to mythological stories, usually with only a single metope devoted to a particular story, although in the Sicyonian Treasury even a single scene is split between two metopes. Ionic architecture allowed the possibility of a continuous frieze where the Doric had metopes and triglyphs. A stunning example of the possibilities this offered is provided by the frieze of the Siphnian treasury at Delphi, from the last quarter of the sixth century. In Asia Minor, examples of such friezes are few, although the earliest, from Myous, dates to before the middle of the century. Large Ionic temples in Asia Minor, as at Didyma, seem to have preferred the lower drums of columns as their chief space for relief sculpture. Whatever the order or form of the temple, the cult statue it housed might be anything from a more or less featureless wooden plank, venerable because of its age, to a showy construction of gold and ivory (Lapatin 2001; Figure 7.3).

There was also considerable variation in temple plan. Even within the model of the peripteral Doric temple, with roughly twice as many columns on the flanks as on the façades, there was scope for various internal arrangements (in particular whether there were one or two rooms in the central naos). But in the Cyclades the Doric architectural system was used for buildings that were not peripteral, were wider than they were long, and might consist of two rooms side by side fronted by a colonnade. The terracotta facings with brightly colored surface decoration excavated from the treasury erected at Olympia by the Sicilian city of Gela also serve to show that, even when the plan and architectural elements might be more or less standard, the way in which they were executed might radically change the visual impression.

Even the largest of fifth-century temples was smaller than the monstrous buildings erected in the sixth century. This may in part have been due to technical factors: the introduction of the block and tackle at the end of the sixth century reduced the size of the blocks that could be used, although it enabled the buildings to be erected with far less manpower (Coulton 1974). But it seems also to

Figure 7.3 Gold and ivory statue identified as Apollo, from the Halos deposit, Delphi. Courtesy of the École Française d'Athènes; photo: P. Collet

have been a product of a change in emphasis. The notable feature of the two largest fifth-century temples erected on the mainland, the temple of Zeus at Olympia and the Parthenon, is their wealth of sculptural decoration (Ashmole 1972; Lapatin 2001). The temple of Zeus had an east pediment—looking towards the race track—showing the line-up for the race between Pelops and Oinomaos in which Pelops won the hand of Oinomaos' daughter at the cost of Oinomaos death by foul play. The west pediment showed the struggle between lapiths and centaurs at the wedding of Peirithoos. Inside the peristyle, above the front and rear porches, 12 sculpted metopes showed the labors of Heracles. To these architectural sculptures was added a massive gold and ivory cult statue of a seated Zeus. But the decision to add this was taken two decades after the rest of the temple was complete, and was provoked by the Athenian decision to create a gold and ivory standing Athena, carrying Victory in her hand, for their new temple of Athena, the Parthenon. The Parthenon was even more richly decorated than the temple of Zeus. It had pedimental sculptures, showing the birth of Athene and her struggle with Poseidon over who was to be patron goddess of Athens; it had all 92 metopes carved with scenes of mythological combats—lapiths against centaurs, gods against giants, Greeks against Amazons and Greeks against Trojans; and it also had a continuous frieze, as in the Siphnian treasury at Delphi, around the central naos, inside the peristyle.

The temple of Zeus and the Parthenon set the standard for sculptural decoration that could not be emulated by others, although even humble places, like Skillous near Olympia, did add sculpture to their new temples in the later part of the fifth and in the fourth century. Although the architecture of many of these temples was externally conservative, internally they are far more varied. Round buildings were developed for sanctuary use, and with them a new order, the Corinthian, modeled on Ionic but with capitals that were both more ornate and had the advantage of being basically round rather than rectangular.

Temples had never been the only buildings in sanctuaries. Just as the variety of cult practice is reflected in the variety of dedications found in sanctuaries, so it is also reflected in the nature of the cult buildings (Tomlinson 1976). Many sanctuaries acquired stoas, all-purpose structures which could shelter worshippers or offerings, serve as places in which to feast (although purpose-built dining rooms were widely constructed in the classical period) or as places in which to sleep while awaiting a visit of the god to provide healing (Coulton 1976). But other cult activities required more specialist facilities. As drama developed as part of religious festivals, in particular to Dionysos, from the late sixth century on, theaters were constructed as part of some sanctuaries. Often, as in the theater of Dionysos at Athens, these exploited a natural hillside, but the magnificent and magnificently preserved fourth-century theater at Epidauros was a partly freestanding structure and in a sanctuary of the healing god Asclepios, not of Dionysos. But some distinctive cult activities left no material trace: were it not for literary and epigraphic sources, it is unlikely that any archaeologist would have guessed from remains at Delphi that it was oracular consultation that brought most visitors to Apollo's sanctuary. Nor did the introduction of cults from abroad lead to much that was archaeologically distinctive: it is notable that the festival of the Thracian goddess Bendis, introduced to Athens in the fifth century, was made up of elements that could also be found in existing Athenian festivals.

The number and range of structures in sanctuaries increased over time, and the space of the sanctuary became more obviously planned (Bergquist 1967). In some part, this may be linked with the need to manage greater numbers of worshippers. In the sixth century, major pan-hellenic games had been founded in association with festivals at Delphi, Isthmia, and Nemea, and during the fifth and fourth centuries it seems to have become more regular for cities to send out invitations to the cities of Greece for them to send sacred embassies to festivals. Surviving epigraphic evidence for invitations from one city to others to attend its festivals stem largely from the fourth century or later, and although this does not mean the phenomenon did not occur earlier it is probably an indication that it increased in these years. To understand the placing of cult in the later classical period we need to put it into a wider framework than simply the context of the individual city.

Much cult activity, however, remained very local. Excavation of villages in Attica has revealed tiny shrines in among the houses, and in Athens itself the hero shrines that have been discovered scattered across the city are likely to have received primarily local worship. Divisions between gods and heroes were not always straightforward, and a figure might become a god by being treated as a god locally: Pausanias (1.34.2) records that "it was the Oropians who first honored Amphiaraus as a god. Subsequently the rest of the Greeks have come to consider him so too." This was perhaps something particularly inclined to happen to a figure renowned for healing powers (something similar happened in the case of Asklepios). Divisions between heroes and the ordinary dead were also not clear: the figures worshipped by depositing votives at old tombs might or might not be identified with named heroes. Some Bronze Age tombs, such as the tholos at Menidhi in Attica, received high-quality offerings over a long period, suggesting an organized cult group devoted to whoever they considered the occupant of that tomb to be. Other tombs received offerings only briefly, and are distinguished from the offerings made routinely at the graves of the recently dead only by the fact that the tomb in question is not recent. Whether or not we should read a particular political claim into tomb cult, those who made offerings to heroes and at tombs were thereby ascribing power of some sort to these figures from the past, and trying to embrace that power to their own advantage.

The Margins of Religion

Attempts to embrace supernatural power not only took the form of making libations, sacrifices, prayers, and offerings, whether in sanctuaries or at tombs. People attempted to influence supernatural powers in very specific ways. Archaeologically the best attested of these are curse tablets. From the classical period on, large numbers of curse tablets, pieces of lead written on and then deposited, have been recovered, in particular from graves though also from wells (underground water being thought to link to the underworld) and from sanctuaries, especially of Demeter (Ogden 1999:15–25). Just as some individuals who had been initiated into Dionysiac mystery cults chose to be buried with gold leaves inscribed with instructions as to how they were to negotiate the underworld, so by giving messages to the newly dead, particularly to those who had died untimely or by violence, those writing the curses hoped that the dead person would ensure that the fate they described was visited upon the persons they named or otherwise referred

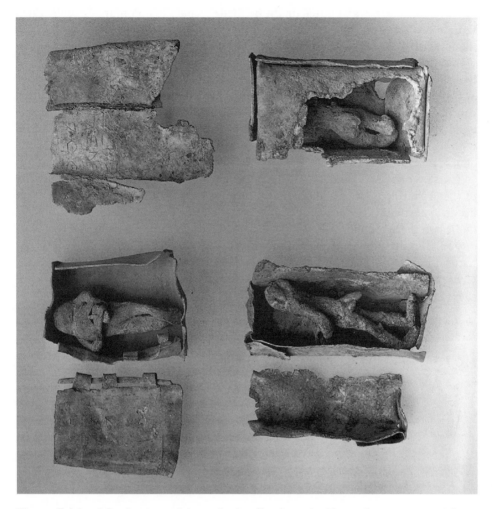

Figure 7.4 Lead figurine in a miniature lead coffin, from the Kerameikos cemetery, Athens. Photo: German Archaeological Institute, Athens. Neg. no. Ker 8805

to. Smaller numbers of what have been termed "voodoo dolls" have also been found (Figure 7.4). Texts make it clear that wax dolls were often made, but surviving examples from Greece are of lead, bronze or clay. The doll represents the figure against whom supernatural powers are being invoked, and is treated in the way that it is desired that that figure be treated—twisted up, deprived of parts of the body, with pins stuck in, bound up, or, in the case of wax, melted down. Sometimes they are themselves wrapped in a lead "coffin," or even in an inscribed lead curse tablet.

It is hard to tell how far cursing and the production of voodoo dolls were socially acceptable. Cities themselves might lay curses upon classes of potential enemies (for an example from fifth-century B.C. Teos, see Meiggs and Lewis 1969:

no. 30). Similarly, wax figures might be made as part of communal rituals. Such figures are referred to in the oath which fourth century Therans claimed was made in the seventh century by their ancestors when settlers were sent out to Cyrene (Meiggs and Lewis 1969: no. 5). In a fourth-century Cyrenean sacred law, figures are part of the ritual employed to deal with (spirit) "visitants" (Rhodes and Osborne 2003: no. 97). But seeking to harm others by supernatural means can have been no more acceptable than seeking to harm them by poison, and it is notable that a number of curse tablets themselves target individuals involved with legal trials, presumably seeking by supernatural intervention to pervert the course of justice.

Curse tablets and voodoo dolls form an appropriate conclusion to a discussion of the archaeology of cult and ritual in the Greek world, for they remind us that however aesthetically pleasing Greek temples and the sculpture and other objects dedicated there might be, they were not created to give idle pleasure to either man or god. Temples, dedications, and sacrifices were part of an exchange with super-natural powers, part of an attempt to influence them and produce divine favor. Curse tablets remind us not to forget that the objects archaeologists describe were there not primarily to be looked at, but to do things.

NOTE

The references for this chapter are on pp. 280–285.

7 (b)

Cult and Ritual

The Roman World

Christopher Smith

Introduction: Evidence and Theory

The ancient world was full of gods (Hopkins 1999) and religion bulks large in the archaeological record, both in terms of monumentality and of individual deposits. Although we also have abundant evidence of houses, palaces, roads, and aqueducts, shops and so forth, many of the most prominent surviving buildings from antiquity are temples (MacDonald 1986:129); they were often built in durable brick and marble, often dominant in size, and sometimes reused as Christian churches and/or mosques, which assisted their survival—the Pantheon in Rome is a good example. Moreover, the fact that religion was pervasive, and not readily divisible from a secular sphere, means that many archaeological remains which are not overtly sacral are nevertheless features of ritual. Burial is a clear example.

The material traces that ritual leaves are often the indirect representation of original actions, since a great deal of religious behavior leaves no physical record. Processions and feasts, for example, have left no physical evidence. The *lectisternia* at Rome, feasts held for gods whose images were present, are archaeologically invisible. At the same time we know that early theatrical performances which were part of religious games took place in the vicinity of temples. The temple of Magna Mater (a deity brought to Rome from the east in 205/204 B.C.) was on the Palatine, and the Ludi Megalenses took place on the large plaza in front. It has been argued that spectators sat on the steps leading to the temple to watch early Roman comedy; the lower part of these steps were preserved by later vaulting (Goldberg 1998). Some major votive deposits represent the closure of ritual activity, and have to stand for all that has gone before. Quite ordinary food and drink vessels can be the clue to communal ritual activity. Context is always vital (see Insoll 2004, for the theoretical problems).

The rich legacy of inscriptions also reflects a part of the material remains of religious activity (MacMullen 1981). From the study of these inscriptions (epigraphy) on buildings or attached to statues or other objects, we can identify the nature of the temple, dedicators, their status and roles, and on rare occasions, their intentions (particularly related to things like curse tablets, a feature of the Roman as well as the Greek world). While not all worshippers were literate, paganism and writing are intertwined (Beard 1991).

The challenge therefore is to identify the extent to which archaeology can contribute to an understanding of one of the deepest human drives, while at the same time reflecting its infinite diversity. This is especially difficult given that the phenomenon of *Romanitas* encompasses at the one end the near-prehistoric, and at the other the sophisticated interplay between pagan and Christian, and remained focused on the city of Rome, while being replicated and reinvented from Bath to Dura Europos. It is arguable that it makes more sense to speak of "religions of Rome" than Roman religion (see Beard et al. 1998), given that one is considering a phenomenon which has a chronological range of about 1,500 years (rather longer than the history of Islam), and which also has to embrace both the traditional Roman pantheon, its murky predecessors, and manifold alternatives. Archaeology has a vital role in helping us trace change and conservatism, similarity and difference, as well as offering different perspectives to deepen our comprehension of religion in action.

It is worth indicating in brief outline the recent transformation of the study of Roman religion. Older studies traced a trajectory from primordial early cult, deeply rooted in agriculture yet also at the service of the state, steadily declining in the face of the influence of new cults which appealed more to individuals, then revived by Augustus as a formalized system dependent on strict adherence to prescribed forms, and devoid of emotional content (Warde Fowler 1911). Few resisted the excitements of the new cults, and few paid more than lip service to the old state cults. Recent scholarship questions much of this, finding external influence from the earliest period, denying decline, emphasizing the importance and innovation of public cult, and worrying about the opposition between the formalism of Roman state cult and the emotional impact of new foreign beliefs (Feeney 1988:2–6).

This change in the way that Roman religion is described and understood has an impact on the way we consider the archaeology of religion. We cannot assume that any deposition merely reflects the contractual obligations of human agents, caught in a fossilized system. Nor can we easily divide private and public religion. The Roman antiquarian and legal scholars seem to have had a fairly clear-cut distinction between public and private cult, in which the former took place in specified places and in relation to some aspect of the state, but in practice the lines may have been slightly more difficult to identify (Beard et al. 1998:1.48–53). The private appropriation of public cult needs attention, as well as the continuity and vitality of private cult (Woolf 2003).

We may begin with an example which demonstrates some of these themes. The centrality of sacrifice within the Roman religious context is demonstrable, and early modern presentations of Roman religion spent much time reconstructing the ideal sacrifice (Graevius 1694–1699 collects several early accounts). These were aided by the prominence of representation of various stages of the process on, for example, Roman reliefs (Ryberg 1955). From this they were able to present detailed information on aspects such as dress, implements, musical instruments; from the literary sources evidence that could be gathered about the purity of the sacrificial animal suggest a very formalized and rigid ritual. Modern presentations have little additional evidence to bring to bear although the archaeological discovery of the inscribed Acts of the Arval Brethren (an elite Roman priesthood) in a grove 5 miles outside Rome allows us to reconstruct their structure, actions, their sacred hymn, and we now also know that there was a dining-room, bath building, circus and a shrine to the imperial cult all in the same complex (Scheid 1990; 2003:86–89).

We can derive from this information the major stages of a sacrifice, at least at Rome; the rites began at daybreak, the celebrants washed themselves, and wore special ceremonial robes, and covered their heads; the nature of the victims was determined in advance by the nature of the deity to whom the sacrifice was made, and they were made ready by washing and decking out with ribbons. A fire was lit at the altar, the offering was consecrated by prayer, scattering of salted flour, and the touch of a knife, and after various other actions, the animal would be struck down, or have its throat cut. It would then be opened up, the entrails inspected for omens, part of the body would be offered to the gods, and the rest divided (Scheid 2003:79–93). It is highly probable that sacrifices differed though, not only from one ritual to another but also from one iteration to another. A huge number of things could go wrong—was the animal cleanly killed?; were there bad omens that required expiation?; was there a problem (*vitium*) which demanded a repeat of the sacrifice? Smaller offerings, more private dedications, and regular libations are also attested.

Some additional focus has been given to wider historical interpretations, for instance, the prominence of images of Augustus in sacrificial mode through the empire (Fishwick 1987–1991; Gradel 2002). This image is widespread through Italy and the West in particular, and one may therefore make arguments about the significance of a depiction of the emperor in the act of sacrifice in the context of local sacrificial acts (Gordon 1990a). In general, the deposit of an image of the sacrificial act may itself have been an act of worship, and the votive altar may perpetuate the fulfillment of a vow (Derks 1998). Here we see, perhaps, a private act within the context of public or state cult.

What is much harder to recover is the atmosphere and significance of sacrifice, despite its absolute centrality, for it requires an archaeology of *mentalités* which is much harder to recover. The fact of sacrifice, and the archaeological representations of it, indicate some commonality of experience that united, over long periods, people from the Roman cities of Spain, to the still heavily Hellenized cities of the eastern empire. There was a ritual and an architectural grammar of Roman religion which, although deeply varied, was also comprehensible. This makes it legitimate to ask if there was anything specifically Roman about Roman religion, which might help us to understand the way in which sacrifice could be perceived.

What Was Roman about Roman Religion?

In seeking a definition of Roman religion it might be tempting to look at origins, but in fact there is little specifically Roman about the beginning of Roman religion. The evidence we have for the earliest forms of religious behavior is found in burials and in votive deposits that date from towards the end of the tenth century onwards. The burials indicate various kinds of ritual behavior, and there are indications of status and gender in the differentiated grave goods, but the patterns of deposition are more or less common to a wide swathe of central Italy in terms of the nature and quantity of the goods, and a general shift from cremation to inhumation (Bietti-Sestieri 1992). Within the general practices of depositions with burials and in votives, there is a distinct set of artistic preferences which mark out a culture within Latium (formally called Latial) with important centers in the Alban Hills, on the coast and at Rome itself, which can be demonstrated to be in close contact with Etruria to the north and Campania to the south (Smith 1996). Among the objects found are occasional miniature clay figures of undifferentiated individuals with an arm extended in offering, and models of cakes, which presumably replicate the actual food offerings. Vessels for food and liquid are common in dedications (Smith 1996).

In addition, we find votive deposits scattered through Rome, and these are of immense importance (Bartoloni 1989–90). Typically they reveal long continuity of ritual significance, as at S. Omobono near the banks of the Tiber at Rome, where a votive deposit precedes a temple of late sixth century date, which was followed by a double temple of mid-Republican date, and subsequent rebuilding, or at the temple site of Satricum (Borgo le Ferriere) 20 kilometers or so outside Rome (Smith 1999). Other places of ritual deposition include the Tiber itself, from which substantial quantities of votive material have been recovered from the fourth to the first centuries B.C. (Pensabene et al. 1980) and the wall on the Palatine hill was inaugurated in the eighth century by a votive deposit (Carandini 2000:280).

We first see Roman religion in monumental form in terms of temples in Rome in the sixth century B.C., and in the accompanying statuary and architectural decoration which already shows the influence of eastern models, from Greece and further afield. In the rather complex set of chronological descriptors for this area, the seventh and sixth centuries constitute the archaic period; the Republican period begins with the expulsion of the last king in 509 B.C., and lasts until Augustus' victory at Actium in 31 B.C. The temple form is usually described as Etrusco-Italic, and its characteristics are a podium on which a walled and roofed space sits behind a row or more of columns (colonnaded *pronaos*). The Roman word *templum* refers to the plot of land on which the building (or *aedes*) is situated. Roofs are typically pitched and project beyond the temple. The closed space often contains more than one *cella* or room, and is accessible only from the front. In the *cellae* were kept cult statues and dedications. The altar is outside the temple, and in front. Crucially, the temple was not intended to be entered; sacrifices took place outside, and the area around the building was therefore of great significance; there is no attempt to house or cater for a congregation. There are manifold variations on this architectural theme which should not be overlooked, but the basic form is clear and distinctive. It is in the decoration (statues on the ridge-pole, reliefs on the pediment) that the debt of central Italy to eastern influences becomes clear; there are fine examples at Veii and Satricum (Boëthius 1978:35–64).

One consequence of the architectural form of the ancient temple, and its externality, may have been the significance of its relationship with other temples and with the urban layout. Many of the great central Italian temples have to be understood in the context of a processional way, and it is interesting that some of these ways were constructed using spoil from earlier temple buildings (Glinister 2000). At Rome, temples were often constructed as the result of a vow, especially by a general in battle, and it is therefore unsurprising that so many are clustered along the triumphal processional route for victorious armies (Orlin 1997). Within the context of the Republican city, the temple is a core part of the urban fabric of the city, as well as being intimately connected with military and political success; it is no accident that the Roman senate could only meet in spaces designated as *templa*. As for the visibility and density of temples, it is indicative that there were some thirty temples in the roughly square kilometer that Ostia covered in the imperial period, and dozens of Mithraea (shrines to Mithras; see Meiggs 1973).

The earliest Roman religion was said by the great first-century B.C. scholar Varro to have been aniconic, that is, the gods were not represented. This is unlikely ever to have been true, but it is certainly no longer the case by the sixth century B.C. The traditional Roman deities were evolving, by then, along the same kinds of lines as Etruscan deities as far as we can tell, into passable likenesses (mythically as well as artistically) of the Greek pantheon, and being no doubt influenced by Greek tales (Wiseman 2004:13–26). So Jupiter is the central male deity, and the standard Capitoline triad of Jupiter, Juno and Minerva had taken shape at Rome by the time of the dedication in 509 B.C. of the great temple on the Capitoline hill, usually referred to simply as the temple of Jupiter Optimus Maximus (see chapter 5 [b]). It is worth noting that the podium of this temple (204 by 175 feet) was the largest in Italy at the time, and ranked with the largest Greek temples, which tells us something about Rome's self-perception, or the perception it wanted others to have. Not all the Greek deities arrived at once; the first temple of Apollo was only vowed in 433 B.C. in response to a plague. This is a good illustration of a key general fact about Roman religion, which is its receptiveness to new cults. One of the more remarkable Roman rituals is that of *evocatio* in which the tutelary deity of a conquered city is invited into Rome (Beard et al. 1998:1.132–134), and this generally entailed the building of a temple, re-housing the deity. So the Roman temple, Italian in form but Hellenized in decoration, stands as a good material correlate for a religion which had indigenous roots but was receptive to innovation.

Throughout the Republic, the characteristic dynamic of Roman religion was to incorporate the cults of others. On the whole this was not particularly challenging; Italic cultures were often similar enough, or simply subdued, and Greek culture had anyway heavily influenced the early development of the Roman forms. The exception to this is usually thought to be the second-century B.C. suppression of the so-called Bacchanalian conspiracy, where a cult, which was not readily localized within a temple and was allegedly associated with orgiastic celebrations, was exposed and regulated. Not only does this remain an unusual event, however, it is also evident from inscriptions and archaeology that this particular cult continued beyond the second century B.C., and that it was joined by several others of a similar nature (Pailler 1988). It is perhaps better to see this event as the forerunner of the successful subsequent assimilation of Syrian, Egyptian, and Iranian cults.

At the same time as Rome was assimilating foreign cult and new religious practice, it is clear from the archaeological record that characteristically Roman expressions of religion were being exported. As Rome expanded, she founded *coloniae*, settlements of Roman citizens in Italian territory. These were built around a central urban complex of forum and Capitolium. Cosa, Ostia and Pompeii are good examples of the type (MacDonald 1986:129). The export of the Capitolium would come to be one of the most visible signatures of Roman imperialism (Barton 1989), though indigenous architectural development is also evident; Rome did not have a permanent stone theater until 55 B.C., long after many of its neighbors in Italy, and the orthogonality of many of the coloniae is in striking contrast to Rome's own haphazard urban development, and arose from a combination of Greek models and military exigency.

The sources make clear the continuity of forms of religious behavior which could be characterized as specifically Roman, and they often cluster around definitions of the city itself, and the origins of the Romans—hence the importance of festivals like the Lupercalia which purport to be recreations of early Rome. The religion of Rome is inseparable from its history. We know that an Iron Age hut was preserved on the Palatine into the imperial period, and said to be the original hut of Romulus. The Regia in the Forum, traditionally the house of the king, *rex*, and subsequently of an obscure official called the *rex sacrorum*, was preserved in the shape it had reached by the end of the sixth century and the downfall of the monarchy. Rome was divinely ordained, and its expansion foretold and sanctioned. There is much debate about the processes by which these ideas, and this historical consciousness, were formed, but there is no doubt that when Augustus came to power after a century of infighting among the Roman elite, he was able to harness Rome's historical and religious traditions to his own purposes, and to bring them to greater definition (Zanker 1988).

Augustus presented himself as a conservative, restoring temples and reviving forgotten behaviors, but it is better to see him as at the center of a period of radical innovation. The Augustan style of architecture became the benchmark and was widely imitated, nowhere more so than in religious architecture and iconography. The city of Rome bears Augustus' mark everywhere; his forum, for example, dominated by the huge temple of Mars Ultor, together with his completion of Julius Caesar's more modest forum, set the precedent for later developments of urban space combined with religious imagery (Zanker 1988). But for our purposes Augustus' key innovation was the development of an imperial cult. Worshipped as a god after his death, like Julius Caesar and many subsequent emperors, Augustus also encouraged worship of his Genius, or guardian deity, in the western empire, and of his living person in the east, where the tradition of offering Hellenistic kings divine honors was deeply rooted. It is the imperial cult, ultimately, which may have become what was most distinctively Roman about Roman religion, but even this was not a single phenomenon, or one which could be isolated from other religious practices, beliefs or material correlates (Beard et al. 1998:2.348–363).

What Was Material about Roman Religious Culture?

The problem to be addressed here is the extent to which religious behavior was inscribed in material culture. Some artifacts are exclusively religious in nature; examples include miniaturized pottery used in burials and votive deposits, or Sabazius votive hands with a multitude of images clustered around a model hand (Figure 7.5; Turcan 1996:332), or altars, of which standard forms are found widely across the area in which Roman culture dominated. One of the aspects of the dissemination of the Augustan style was the replication of the central images of the emperor and sacrifice, and these show that the core sacrificial rites were performed in very much the same way and with very much the same kind of implements (Siebert 1999). Although there are local trends, one can see a common pattern of dedicating models of parts of the body in the hope of healing, which one sees in Italy and is picked up across the empire (Blagg 1986). Above all, the empire created a kind of unity over a vast geographical spread, facilitated trade and enforced movement of soldiers, and brought different cultures into contact with each other. Egyptian imagery and Egyptianizing objects, all related in some way to religion, can be found in Britain, and are just one aspect of the wide range of deities worshipped in the province; and red slip ware, originally developed in Italy, is picked up by manufacturers in the east, and finds its way into dedications everywhere (Harris and Harris 1965; King 1983:186–189).

Much of our evidence for religion comes from the depictions of ritual activity. The ubiquity of images of the divine in one form or another, coupled with the now rather outdated view of Roman religion as essentially contractual, means that art has not always been sufficiently considered as part of the religious framework of an individual's life. If we take a house in Pompeii, for instance, we might find: depictions of mythical scenes painted on the walls, or in relief; a *lararium*, or shrine to the household gods, the Lares, who might be present as small statues; a priapic figure or representation of a phallus as an invocation of fertility and prosperity; a bronze rattle and cymbals for worship of Isis; lamps and vessels for use in household rituals, perhaps decorated with motifs reminiscent of those found

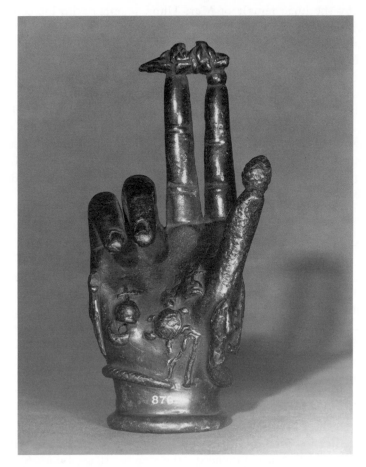

Figure 7.5 Sabazius hand: a hand which comprises various religious symbols. ©Copyright the Trustees of The British Museum

on architectural decoration in temples; high quality silverware and jewelry with religious iconography; coins depicting temples or deities as well as emperors, some of whom may be dead and now worshipped as gods in their own right (Ward-Perkins and Claridge 1976).

Such a pattern is not unique to Italy, similar material expressions of religious conceptions are found across the empire; consider, for instance, the pervasiveness of well-known mythical scenes and figures in floor mosaics from Cordoba to Palmyra (Dunbabin 1999). Some cults which are immediately identifiable by their iconography—the image of the slaying of a bull is stereotypical of Mithraism—and were not simple decoration. Cult statues were worshipped, clothed, bathed, processed, and so forth, but this does not reduce the significance of the individual image; rather it reinforces collective interpretations and experiences. So, statuettes and reliefs of Ephesian Artemis, copying the many-breasted original at

Figure 7.6 Inscribed tablet from Bath. The text is not a curse but a sanction against perjury, with an oath taken at the spring and invoking the goddess' action. See Cunliffe 1988:226–227. Copyright: Oxford University Committee for Archaeology/Prof B. W. Cunliffe

Ephesus itself, are found in many places (Turcan 1996:255–256), but that does not mean that her image and significance were blurred or reduced for the individual possessing or observing it (Elsner 1997). If we accept that ancient viewers regarded religious art as imbued with divine attributes, or in more modern terms that material culture stabilizes and reproduces religious views (Gordon 1979), then the richness of the visual environment of individuals within the Roman empire, which archaeology is uniquely able to recover, becomes truly remarkable.

Magic is another area where material culture reveals a world which is only occasionally hinted at by literature (Ogden 1999). It takes little to turn an action which is religious into one which is disturbing. The quantities of curse tablets are striking; there are over a hundred at Bath, for instance (Cunliffe 1988:59–277; Figure 7.6). Divination kits survive from Pergamum and elsewhere (Gordon 2002), and the model liver from Piacenza is our best, yet still enigmatic, evidence for the vitally important skill of extispicy (the examination of the entrails of sacrificed animals; Beard et al. 1998:2.176–177). This is an area where the difference between rightful and wrongful use of religion is particularly sharp, since a sacrifice at night was automatically perceived as dangerous, and extispicy clearly took place in private sacrifice as well as public. We know from literary sources of the importance of astrology (Barton 1994), but one might not have expected to find an Egyptian astrological chart, used for predictive purposes, in the healing sanctuary of Apollo at Grand (in Vosges, France; Beard et al. 1998:1.232–233).

Moreover, many objects which were originally functional became religious artifacts. A good example here would be armor or weaponry which was used in a votive deposit. A Roman soldier even dedicated a miniature *ballista* (catapult) at Bath (Henig 1984:149). Context is often the key element in revealing the ritualization of objects, and can change one's understanding, as with recent work on the major votive deposits sometimes called *favissae* (Haynes 2006).

Roman religion was never confined to the city. Religion was a marker of control in the same way, and sometimes coterminously, with frontiers. We have mentioned the distribution of the classic forum and Capitolium combination in Republican Italy as the *coloniae* marked the expansion of Roman control. Another example would be the development of the imperial cult in the provinces, for example, at Lyon (King 1990:66) or Colchester (Wilson 2002:210–228), associated in both instances with affirmations of Roman authority. In the east, the development of Philippopolis at Shahba in Syria, where the emperor Philip (A.D. 244–249) transported a more or less Greco-Italic city into his birthplace, together with a statue honoring his family and his "divine" father, could be seen as a mark of piety, but it was also a sign of resistance, since Philip inherited a military situation in the east where this frontier was in jeopardy. Less grand but no less telling are the rural shrines of the western empire, with Latin inscriptions replacing indigenous dedications in the record (Henig and King 1986).

Religion is therefore unavoidable in the archaeology of the Roman world. From the domestic interiors of Pompeii to the grandest temples from Nîmes in southern Gaul to Aizanoi in Asia Minor, to the urban fabric of Rome itself, one cannot escape the gods. Christians, and to a lesser extent the Jews, turned their faces against the beneficent world of Roman religion, yet when Christianity became sanctioned by the state, it rapidly assimilated many of the artistic skills of the pagan period for its own benefit (Elsner 1995).

That said, there is also much about Roman religion which does not survive in material form. Texts reveal the ephemeral and temporary nature of Roman religious action. But evidence for public dominates over evidence for private religion (Woolf 2003), and archaeology has a role in revealing what texts overlook. One of the most exciting areas for future development lies in harnessing the sophistication of discussion about ritual and belief which characterizes the archaeology of the archaic period to the complex issues surrounding the individual understanding of public religion in the classical period; in other words, how and where do we find the individual in Roman religion?

The Diffusion of Roman Religion

While it would be unreasonable simply to characterize Roman religion as a tool of state imperialism, it would be equally false to deny its role in the expansion and unification of the Roman empire. The export of the state cult holds a key role

Figure 7.7 Reconstruction drawing of the Temple of Mars Lenus complex at Irminenwingert in Trier, second century A.D. Copyright: Rheinisches Landesmuseum Trier

in the creation of miniature imitations of Rome in the colonies of Italy, as we have seen, and further afield.

Major temples to Roman deities are a key part of the visible diffusion of Roman religion. At Pompeii, in the mid-second century B.C., a forum and Capitolium, with a temple (probably) to Jupiter was built, in what has been called self-Romanization, and the Sullan colonists built a temple to Venus in the early first century, both additions to the old temple of Apollo. The Augustan period saw renovation of both temples as well as the addition of imperial cult. The cult of the emperor is included in the major state cults (Zanker 1998:78–102). A syncretistic cult to Mars Lenus in the territory of Trier in Germany received a temple in the second century A.D. (Figure 7.7), but nearby were altars for the *pagi* or subdivisions of the state, and pagi are often involved in imperial cult (Woolf 1998:224). The diffusion of the state religion, and its acceptance in local communities, provides the basis and often even the location within which imperial cult also takes place.

We can identify the importance of the imperial cult without necessarily assuming an organized dissemination. Worship of kings was commonplace in the East; somewhat different forms develop in the West, and throughout we have to be alive to the syncretizing and self-aggrandizing use of Roman religion by local elites. By identifying aspects of local religion with Roman gods and beliefs, and controlling access to and knowledge about both, religion could become part of the way in which local elites maintained and legitimized their position. Thus within the standardized repertoire of the Roman Capitolium and temple complexes, such as those we find in Spain, we have more disparate and varied phenomena, such as the Jupiter columns in Germany (King 1990:140–141), Romano-Celtic temples (Horne 1986), the development of Bath in Britain (Cunliffe 2000), or Sabratha in Tripolitania (Mattingly 1995:167–168), the continuing local features and practices found at Palmyra (Colledge 1976:24–57), and so forth. What can we say about individual responses to this cultic framework?

We should begin at Rome itself. The early emperors participated in a general caution regarding overt celebrations of the emperor while alive, but there was no mistaking the impact that Augustus had on the landscape. His Mausoleum, begun in 28 B.C., almost at the beginning of the principate, towered over the Campus Martius; the Ara Pacis, vowed in 13 B.C. and erected in 9 B.C., was decorated by reliefs of astonishing quality, on which the emperor and his family are prominently displayed; the Forum of Augustus had a series of sculptures of famous predecessors, in particular members of the *gens Julia*. Those are the well-known and visible monuments, but there is a whole structure of cultic activity which underpin them; the celebration of Augustus' Genius in the *vici* and *compita*, the districts of the city, is crucial here, and surviving compital altars show scenes of sacrifice, using iconography which then transfers to the ubiquitous *lararia* found in Pompeii, where shrines also mark out the intersections of the city (Gradel 2002).

One of the most striking aspects of the imperial cult is its social diffusion. The great state cults and the religious activities and laws of Rome were still administered by priests who came from the highest ranks of Roman society. The imperial cult, however, is repeatedly accessed and administered by members of lower social strata. The magistrates of the vici in Rome were usually freedmen and assisted by slaves. There are abundant instances of elite display in the provinces connected with the imperial cult; for example, one might cite the early first-century A.D. monumental arch at Saintes (Mediolanum Santonum) dedicated by one Gaius Julius Rufus, son of Gaius Julius Otuaneunos, grandson of Gaius Julius Gedomo, great-grandson of Epotsorovidos. Gedomo received citizenship from Julius Caesar; Rufus, with a completely Roman name, was priest of the cult of Rome and Augustus at Lyon, and *praefectus fabrorum* in the Roman army (King 1990:66; Corpus Inscriptionum Latinarum 10.1036). Rufus may have been Romanized but he was also perhaps using the arch and the association with the imperial family to assert his own family's dynastic power (Woolf 2000). At the same time, as at Rome, lower social orders worshipped the imperial cult. At Carthage, there was an enormous amount of building in the Julio-Claudian period, and abundant epigraphic evidence for *flamines* (priests) of the imperial cult, and of individual emperors. There is also a small altar, about a meter wide and high, which depicts what has been called by Rives "virtually a textbook summary of Roman official iconography," with a scene of sacrifice, the flight of Aeneas from Troy, and Apollo and Rome with a figure of Victoria (Figure 7.8). This altar has been connected with an inscription from P. Perelius Hedulus, who has been described as "an enterprising

Figure 7.8 Altar from Tunis (Bardo Museum) showing Aeneas fleeing Troy with father and son. Deutsches Archäologisches Institut Rom, Koppermann, 63.387

freedman," who emigrated to Carthage in the reign of Augustus and there acquired a brick and tile workshop: from which he prospered, in part due to the booming building market in Carthage, itself a result of imperial patronage (Rives 1995:55–57; Beard et al. 1998:1.335 for further photographs).

This is a tiny case study of a much wider phenomenon. The imperial cult is one element of public cult, and one which was widely disseminated, and if one looks for any aspect of the religious experience of the Roman empire which is a uniting factor, it is this. There is much more to say, however. In 104 A.D., C. Vibius Salutaris bequeathed to the city of Ephesus a very substantial sum of money and a set of instructions in relation to the goddess Artemis and the imperial family. On the face of it, this might appear a fairly straightforward case of the shackling of local religious practice to the imperial cult, but a detailed analysis demonstrates that the bequest actually reaffirms the specifically Ephesian character of the worship of Artemis, after a century of intense Roman intervention. Ephesus can be said to have used the imperial cult in conjunction with its own very special relationship with Artemis to find a new identity (Rogers 1991; Koester 1995). At the same time, there is a host of alternative religions, like Mithraism, or Christianity, or other cults (typically eastern) which challenge the influence of what has been called the "civic compromise" (Gordon 1990b; Woolf 2003) that religion bolstered the power of an elite, and that elite then maintained dominance over the organization of religion. In a sense, the paradox of the imperial cult is that while it is the state cult par excellence, the evidence of its penetration of the home and of its dissemination across the social barriers which are so prominent in other areas of contemporary Roman life suggests that it was available to the kinds of individual choices that we associate with the mystery cults. This problem will become even sharper if we look at what happens to other aspects of Roman religion as it meets long-standing indigenous tradition.

The Adaptability of Roman Religions

Continuity of local religious practice or belief across the empire is remarkably evident. Even if one leaves aside the mystery religions like Mithraism, what one finds throughout the empire are instances of syncretism. As an example, consider the temple complex at Baalbek in Lebanon (Heliopolis). This lay in the territory of the Roman colony at Berytus, which was founded in 16 B.C., and it became a free city under Septimius Severus. The huge temple of Jupiter (Figure 7.9) sits within a massive courtyard with a tower-like altar, both fundamentally eastern architectural forms. (There are other temples within the complex as a whole— one, often attributed to Venus, is unique in its construction.) Dozens of pink Egyptian granite columns were imported from Aswan; the monoliths to construct the podium were huge. The temple, dedicated to Jupiter Optimus Maximus Heliopolitanus, stood on a tell and was built over previous temples, perhaps to Ba'al. The cult of Jupiter Heliopolitanus spread far beyond Baalbek, possibly spread by the army; votives are found in Syene in Egypt, Nîmes in Gaul, Stockstadt in Germany, and so forth, and on the Janiculum at Rome (Beard et al. 1998:1.384–386).

At the other end of the empire the Pillar of the Nautae (or Shippers) in Paris was dedicated in Tiberius' reign to Jupiter Optimus Maximus, the gods on the column ranged from Venus, Fortuna, Vulcan, Castor and Pollux, and Mars, through to local deities Boudana, Cernunnos (with horns and a torc), Smertrios attacking a temple, Tarvos Trigaranus, Esus cutting down a tree, and so forth (Woolf 1998:233). Even the typical temple form was a composite of Roman and Celtic (Ward-Perkins 1981:227; Horne 1986).

Syncretism reveals the permeability of the religions of Rome. That includes the level of public or state cult. Just as Roman imperialism adapted to complex local situations, so the specific nature of the engagement of Roman religion and indigenous cult proves to be dependent on local circumstances. Every sanctuary, every religious area, while it may contain a whole sequence of objects that are common to every other comparable site in the empire, will nonetheless have its own peculiar taxonomy, and the more detailed the archaeology, the more idiosyncratic the outcome is likely to be.

The vehicles of this process include the army. The soldiers of imperial Rome's standing army often found themselves serving away from their homeland, which

Figure 7.9 Temple of Jupiter at Baalbek, with Temple of Bacchus in the background. Photo: R. M. Cook. Copyright: Museum of Classical Archaeology, Cambridge

perhaps created a sense of alienation that both encouraged the preservation of local identities and also the adherence to cults with strong martial connections, like Mithraism (Clauss 2000). The worship of Mithras is as far from Roman state cult as one can get, with its strange sequence of initiations, its astronomical and cosmological overtones, its ubiquitous bull-slaying scenes, its secrecy, but the spread of Mithraism is itself a good trace element of Romanization (Clauss 2000:26–27, for a map).

Once regarded as a rigid fossilized system, incapable of change or adaptation, and therefore doomed once the more radical and inspirational religions, including Christianity, entered the scene, Roman religion now appears an ever-changing network of ideas and associations, capable of great innovation and tolerant of huge diversity. Such is the merit of this approach that it is being extended to religious systems like Judaism and Christianity, whose art has sometimes been treated entirely separately from its cultural context, and labeled in ways which fail to fit a world in which "every cult reflected a range of views and practices, some of which will have been mutually exclusive and some syncretistic with other cults" (Elsner 2003:127).

Nevertheless there continued to be a strong view from the center about what was acceptable public cult, and what was not. Mithraism was never admitted to the core of Roman religion; Jews and Christians were sporadically persecuted (Beard et al. 1998:1.211–244). The third century A.D. saw a much more rigorous patrolling of the boundaries of what was acceptable, perhaps most particularly in the city of Rome itself. A key area of conflict was sacrifice, an indispensable core of the expanded notion of imperial cult, an absolute anathema to Christians. Literary sources' discussion of the undesirable, transgressive, and proscribed are paralleled in the material record by such things as a third-century A.D. graffito from the Palatine palace showing a man worshipping a figure with an ass' head on a cross, a common pagan slur against Christianity, and by gaps: in the first and second centuries A.D. there were "no blatant, unofficial 'foreign' sanctuaries in the monumental centre of Rome" (Beard et al. 1998:2.57–58; 1.269–270).

The Ends of Roman Religion

What happened to Roman religion? Late paganism deserves more space than can be given here, and is an important area for future study. Grand architectural projects, notably but not exclusively in Rome (Curran 2000), and a vigorous philosophical and literary culture are evident, but we can also see other forerunners of Christian and Islamic practices such as pilgrimage (Elsner and Rutherford 2005). The story of how one cult, Christianity, rose from origins less prepossessing in some ways than many of the alternatives is one which still requires an effort to understand, but the context and continuities with late paganism must also be part of the picture.

Archaeology can make an important contribution to the progress of Christianity. We find cemeteries where the orientation of burials changes from typically

Roman north–south to the Christian east–west (King 1990:203). From Rome we have the abundant evidence of the catacombs: much more comprehensible now that we have largely dissociated them from myths of Christians hiding from interminable persecution (Beard et al. 1998:1.270–271). Buildings are themselves narratives of the emergence of Christianity. S. Clemente, in Rome, for instance, has a sequence of house, Mithraeum, and then basilica. The development of late Roman art into early Christian art in various ways across the empire is another area where archaeology is vital (Reece 1983:234–248; Strong 1988:298–327).

There are some telling moments in this story of transition. At Ostia, Mithraic shrines were deliberately destroyed, and pagan cult objects walled up in buildings, perhaps in the hope of saving them (Meiggs 1973:397–401). The magnificent silver hoards of late Roman Britain may show similar signs of pagan anxiety (Johns 1986). Some of these silver items combine pagan and Christian iconography, which reminds us once again that the process of Christianization, like Romanization, is bound to have been complicated in ways we can no longer recover; so the great Mildenhall silver dish with its pagan iconography was found alongside spoons bearing the Christian chi-rho sign (Wilson 2002:651). Elsewhere, in the so-called Dead Cities between Aleppo, Antioch, and Apamea, for instance, 1,200 churches have been found (approximately one for every 4.5 square kilometers) in areas of relatively sparse population; the greatest was the church of St Simeon Stylites, built towards the end of the fifth century, and capable of holding a congregation greater than that of Notre Dame in Paris (Ball 2000:221–229). Christianity was capable of developments as different as desert monasticism and Celtic Christianity.

Also the interplay of pagan and Christian artistic developments in Italy and the east is complex, parallel to the difficult accommodations of a pagan elite with the new Christian powerbrokers evident in fourth- and fifth-century literature (Elsner 2003). The increasingly centralized approach of the later third-century pagan emperors may have assisted the shift to centralized Christian imperial policy in the fourth century, but we must also acknowledge that Christianity, and subsequently Islam, had powerful attractions. If we can only genuinely understand the popularity of the imperial cult by acknowledging that it was not simply an imposed system of beliefs to which no-one really had any affinity, then one must also give full credit to the power of conversion, and the seductive sense of community and belonging, in the spread of these two great religions of late antiquity (Hopkins 1999:167–168; 335).

Conclusion

Archaeology has sometimes struggled with Roman religion in the periods where our textual evidence is at its most illuminating (from the second century B.C. to fourth century A.D.) because, paradoxically, the wealth of material channeled interpretation into rather well-defined areas. We are far better informed about the development of the Roman temple than about the development of Roman religious mentalities, and where the latter has been sought, it has been derived from the great classical authorities like Cicero and Virgil. Yet the actual diversity of physical expressions of religion in the period we call Roman, over the geographical extent of Roman power, ought to have discouraged the conclusion that there was any degree of fixity within the concept of the religious, and to have cautioned against generalizing from elite and state-centered experience. The archaeology of cult in the Roman period reveals a much more interesting if challenging agenda, and requires some of the creativity of interpretation pioneered in the archaeology of less well-known periods to interpret the complexity of classical times.

REFERENCES

Aktseli, Dimitra 1996 Altäre in der archaischen und klassischen Kunst: Untersuchungen zu Typologie und Ikonographie. Espelkamp: Leidorf.

Ando, Clifford, ed. 2003 Roman Religion. Edinburgh: Edinburgh University Press.

Ashmole, Bernard 1972 Architect and Sculptor in Classical Greece. London: Phaidon.

Ball, Warwick 2000 Rome in the East: The Transformation of an Empire. London: Routledge.

Barletta, Barbara 2001 The Origins of the Greek Architectural Orders. Cambridge: Cambridge University Press.

Bartoloni, Gilda 1989–90 I depositi votive di Roma arcaica: Alcune considerazioni. Scienze dell' antichità 3–4:747–759.

Barton, Ian M. 1989 Religious Buildings. In Roman Public Buildings. I. M. Barton ed. Pp. 67–96. Exeter: University of Exeter Press.

Barton, Tamsyn S. 1994 Ancient Astrology. London: Routledge.

Beard, Mary 1991 Ancient Literacy and the Function of the Written Word in Roman Religion. In Literacy in the Roman World. Mary Beard et al., eds. Pp. 35–58. Journal of Roman Archaeology Supplementary Series 3. Ann Arbor: Journal of Roman Archaeology.

——, and John North eds. 1990 Pagan Priests. London: Duckworth.

——, John North, and Simon Price 1998 Religions of Rome. Cambridge: Cambridge University Press.

Bentz, Martin 1998 Panathenäische Preisamphoren: eine athenische Vasengattung und ihre Funktion vom 6.–4. Jahrhundert v.Chr. Basel: Vereinigung der Freunde antiker Kunst.

Bérard, Claude et al. 1989 A City of Images: Iconography and Society in Ancient Greece. Princeton: Princeton University Press.

Bergquist, B. 1967 The Archaic Greek Temenos: A Study of Structure and Function. Skrifter Utgivna av Svenska Institutet i Athen 4.13. Lund: C. W. K. Gleerup.

Bietti-Sestieri, Anna Maria 1992 The Iron Age Community of Osteria dell'Osa. Cambridge: Cambridge University Press.

Blagg, Thomas F. C. 1986 The Cult and Sanctuary of Diana Nemorensis. In Pagan Gods and Shrines of the Roman Empire. Martin Henig and Anthony King, eds. Pp. 211–220. Oxford: Oxford University Press.

Boëthius, Axel 1978 Etruscan and Early Roman Architecture. Harmondsworth: Penguin.

Carandini, Andrea, ed. 2000 Roma: Romulo, Remo e la fondazione della città. Milan: Electa.

Carter, Joseph Coleman 1994 Sanctuaries in the Chora of Metaponto. *In* Placing the Gods: Sanctuaries and Sacred Space in Ancient Greece. Susan E. Alcock and Robin Osborne, eds. Pp. 161–198. Oxford: Clarendon Press.

Clauss, Manfred 2000 The Roman Cult of Mithras: The God and his Mysteries. Edinburgh: Edinburgh University Press.

Cole, Susan Guettel 1994 Demeter in the Ancient Greek City and its Countryside. *In* Placing the Gods: Sanctuaries and Sacred Space in Ancient Greece. Susan E. Alcock and Robin Osborne, eds. Pp. 199–216. Oxford: Clarendon Press.

Colledge, Malcolm R. A. 1976 The Art of Palmyra. London: Thames and Hudson.

Coulton, J. J. 1974 Lifting in Early Greek Architecture. Journal of Hellenic Studies 94: 1–19.

——1976 The Architectural Development of the Greek Stoa. Oxford: Clarendon Press.

Crawford, Michael H., ed. 1996 Roman Statutes. Bulletin of the Institute of Classical Studies Supplement 64. London: Institute of Classical Studies.

Cunliffe, Barry, ed. 1988 The Temple of Sulis Minerva at Bath, vol. 2: The Finds from the Sacred Spring. Oxford: Oxford University Press.

——2000 Roman Bath Discovered. 4th edition. Stroud: Tempus.

Curran, John R. 2000 Pagan City and Christian Capital: Rome in the Fourth Century. Oxford: Oxford University Press.

Derks, Ton 1998 Gods, Temples and Ritual Practices: The Transformation of Religious Ideas and Values in Roman Gaul. Amsterdam Archaeological Series 2. Amsterdam: Amsterdam University Press.

Ducat, Jean 1971 Les kouroi du Ptoion. Paris: E. de Boccard.

Dunbabin, Katherine 1999 Mosaics of the Greek and Roman World. Cambridge: Cambridge University Press.

Elsner, Jaś 1995 Art and the Roman Viewer: The Transformation of Art from the Pagan World to Christianity. Cambridge: Cambridge University Press.

——1997 The Origins of the Icon: Pilgrimage, Religion and Visual Culture in the Roman East as "Resistance" to the Centre. *In* The Early Roman Empire in the East. Susan E. Alcock, ed. Pp.178–199. Oxford: Oxbow Books.

——2003 Archaeologies and Agendas: Reflections on Late Jewish Art and Early Christian Art. Journal of Roman Studies 93:114–128.

——, and Ian Rutherford, eds. 2005 Pilgrimage in Graeco-Roman and Early Christian Antiquity: Seeing the Gods. Oxford: Oxford University Press.

Favro, Diane 1996 The Urban Image of Augustan Rome. Cambridge: Cambridge University Press.

Feeney, Denis 1988 Literature and Religion at Rome: Cultures, Contexts, Beliefs. Cambridge: Cambridge University Press.

Fishwick, Duncan 1987–91 The Imperial Cult in the Latin West, vols. i.1–3, ii.1. Leiden: Brill.

Glinister, Fay 2000 Sacred Rubbish. *In* Religion in Archaic and Republican Rome and Italy. Ed Bispham and Christopher J. Smith, eds. Pp. 54–70. Edinburgh: Edinburgh University Press.

Goldberg, Sander 1998 Plautus on the Palatine. Journal of Roman Studies 88:1–20.

Goodman, Martin 1997 The Roman World, 44 BC–AD 180. London: Routledge.

Gordon, Richard 1979 The Real and the Imaginary: Production and Religion in the Graeco-Roman World. Art History 2:5–34.

——1990a The Veil of Power: Emperors, Sacrificers and Benefactors. In Pagan Priests. Mary Beard and John North, eds. Pp. 199–232. London: Duckworth.

——1990b Religion in the Roman Empire: The Civic Compromise and its Limits. In Pagan Priests. Mary Beard and John North, eds. Pp. 233–255. London: Duckworth.

——2002 Another View of the Pergamon Divination Kit. Journal of Roman Archaeology 15:188–198.

Gradel, Ittai 2002 Emperor Worship and Roman Religion. Oxford: Oxford University Press.

Graevius, Johann G. 1694–1699 Thesaurus Antiquitatum Romanarum (12 vols). Utrecht and Leiden.

Hamilton, Richard 1992 Choes and Anthesteria: Athenian Iconography and Ritual. Ann Arbor: University of Michigan Press.

Harris, Eve, and John R. Harris 1965 The Oriental Cults in Roman Britain. Leiden: Brill.

Haynes, Ian 2006 The Favissae Project Homepage. Electronic document, http://www.bbk.ac.uk/hca/staff/haynes/favissae.htm

Henig, Martin, ed. 1983 A Handbook of Roman Art: A Survey of the Visual Arts of the Roman World. London: Phaidon Press.

——1984 Religion in Roman Britain. London: Batsford.

——, and Anthony King, eds. 1986 Pagan Gods and Shrines of the Roman Empire. Oxford: Oxford University Press.

Hopkins, Keith 1999 A World Full of Gods: Pagans, Jews and Christians in the Roman Empire. London: Weidenfeld & Nicolson.

Horne, Peter D. 1986 Roman or Celtic Temples: A Case-study. In Pagan Gods and Shrines of the Roman Empire. Martin Henig and Anthony King, eds. Pp. 15–24. Oxford: Oxford University Press.

Insoll, Timothy 2004 Archaeology, Ritual, Religion. London: Routledge.

Jameson, Michael H. 1991 Sacrifice Before Battle. In Hoplites: The Classical Greek Battle Experience. Victor D. Hanson, ed. Pp. 197–227. London: Routledge.

Johns, Catherine 1986 Faunus at Thetford: An Early Latin Deity in Late Roman Britain. In Pagan Gods and Shrines of the Roman Empire. Martin Henig and Anthony King, eds. Pp. 93–104. Oxford: Oxford University Press.

Jost, Madeleine 1994 The Distribution of Sanctuaries in Civic Space in Arkadia. In Placing the Gods: Sanctuaries and Sacred Space in Ancient Greece. Susan E. Alcock and Robin Osborne, eds. Pp. 217–230. Oxford: Clarendon Press.

Kahil, Lily 1977 L'Artémis de Brauron: rites et mystères. Antike Kunst 20:86–98.

Keay, Simon, and Nicola Terrenato, eds. 2001 Italy and the West: Comparative Issues in Romanization. Oxford: Oxbow Books.

Keesling, Catherine M. 2003 The Votive Statues of the Athenian Acropolis. Cambridge: Cambridge University Press.

Kilian-Dirlmeier, Imma 1985 Fremde Weihungen in griechische Heiligtümern vom 8. bis zum Beginn des 7. Jahrhunderts v. Chr. Jahrbuch des Römisch-Germanischen Zentralmuseums Mainz 32:215–254.

King, Anthony 1983 Pottery. In A Handbook of Roman Art: A Survey of the Visual Arts of the Roman World. Martin Henig, ed. Pp. 179–190. London: Phaidon Press.

——1990 Roman Gaul and Germany. London: British Museum Press.

Koester, Helmut 1995 Ephesos, Metropolis of Asia: An Interdisciplinary Approach to its Archaeology, Religion and Culture. Harvard Theological Studies 41. Pennsylvania: Trinity Press International.

Lapatin, Kenneth D. S. 2001 Chryselephantine Statuary in the Ancient Mediterranean World. Oxford: Oxford University Press.

Lissarrague, François 1995 Un rituel du vin: la libation. *In* In Vino Veritas. O. Murray and M. Tecusan, eds. Pp. 126–144. London: British School at Rome.

MacDonald, William L. 1986 The Architecture of the Roman Empire. Volume 2: An Urban Appraisal. New Haven and London: Yale University Press.

MacMullen, Ramsey 1981 Paganism in the Roman Empire. New Haven and London: Yale University Press.

Mattingly, David J. 1995 Tripolitania. London: Batsford.

Mazarakis Ainian, Alexander 1997 From Rulers' Dwellings to Temples. Architecture, Religion and Society in Early Iron Age Greece (1100–700 B.C.) Jonsered: Paul Åströms Förlag.

Meiggs, Russell 1973 Roman Ostia. 2nd edition. Oxford: Oxford University Press.

Meiggs, Russell, and David M. Lewis 1969 A Selection of Greek Historical Inscriptions to the End of the Fifth Century B.C. Oxford: Clarendon Press.

Morgan, Catherine 1990 Athletes and Oracles: The Transformation of Olympia and Delphi in the Eighth Century B.C. Cambridge: Cambridge University Press.

——2003 Early Greek States Beyond the Polis. London: Routledge.

North, John 2000 Roman Religion. Greece and Rome. New Surveys in the Classics 30. Oxford: Oxford University Press.

Ogden, Daniel 1999 Binding Spells: Curse Tablets and Voodoo Dolls in the Greek and Roman Worlds. *In* Witchcraft and Magic in Europe: Ancient Greece and Rome. Bengt Ankarloo and Stuart Clark, eds. Pp. 1–90. Philadelphia: University of Pennsylvania Press.

Orlin, Eric M. 1997 Temples, Religion and Politics in the Roman Republic. Leiden: Brill.

Orr, David G. 1978 Roman Domestic Religion: The Evidence of the Household Shrines. Aufstieg und Niedergang der römischen Welt II.16.2:1557–1591.

Osborne, Robin 1987 Classical Landscape with Figures: The Ancient Greek City and Its Countryside. London: George Philip.

——1996 Greece in the Making, 1200–479 B.C. London: Routledge.

——1997 The Ecstasy and the Tragedy: Varieties of Religious Experience in Art, Drama and Society. *In* Greek Tragedy and the Historian. Christopher B. R. Pelling, ed. Pp. 187–211. Oxford: Clarendon Press.

Pailler, Jean-Marie 1988 Bacchanalia: La repression de 186 av. J.-C. à Rome et en Italie. Rome: L'Ecole Française de Rome.

Painter, Kenneth, ed. 1994 "Churches Built in Ancient Times": Recent Studies in Early Christian Archaeology. London: Society of Antiquaries and Accordia Research Centre.

Pensabene, Patrizio, Maria A. Rizzo, Maria Roghi, and Emilia Talamo 1980 Terracotte Votive dal Tevere. Studi Miscellanei 25. Rome: "L'Erma" di Bretschneider.

Polignac, François de 1995 Cults, Territory, and the Origins of the Greek City-State. Chicago: University of Chicago Press.

Price, Simon R. F. 1984 Rituals and Power: The Roman Imperial Cult in Asia Minor. Cambridge: Cambridge University Press.

Reece, Richard 1983 Late Antiquity. *In* A Handbook of Roman Art: A Survey of the Visual Arts of the Roman World. Martin Henig, ed. Pp. 234–248. London: Phaidon Press.

Rhodes, Peter J., and Robin Osborne 2003 Greek Historical Inscriptions 404–323 B.C. Oxford: Oxford University Press.

Richter, Gisela 1968 Korai: Archaic Greek Maidens. London: Phaidon.

——1970 Kouroi: Archaic Greek Youths. 3rd edition. London: Phaidon.

Rives, John B. 1995 Religion and Authority in Roman Carthage from Augustus to Constantine. Oxford: Oxford University Press.

Rogers, Guy 1991 The Sacred Identity of Ephesos: Foundation Myths of a Roman City. London: Routledge.

Ryberg, I. Scott 1955 Rites of the State Religion in Roman Art. Rome: Memoirs of the American Academy at Rome.

Schachter, Albert 2003 Evolutions of a Mystery Cult: The Theban Kabiroi. In Greek Mysteries. The Archaeology and Ritual of Ancient Greek Secret Cults. Michael B. Cosmopoulos, ed. Pp. 112–142. London: Routledge.

Scheid, John 1990 Romulus et ses frères. Le collège des frères Arvales, modèle du culte public romain dans la Rome des empereurs. Rome: L'Ecole Française de Rome.

——2003 An Introduction to Roman Religion. Edinburgh: Edinburgh University Press.

Scully, Vincent 1979 The Earth, the Temple and the Gods: Greek Sacred Architecture. Rev. edition. New Haven: Yale University Press.

Siebert, Anne V. 1999 Instrumenta sacra: Untersuchungen zu römischen Opfer-, Kult- und Priestergeräten. Berlin: Walter de Gruyter.

Smith, Christopher J. 1996 Early Rome and Latium: Economy and Society c. 1000 to 500 BC. Oxford: Oxford University Press.

——1999 Reviewing Archaic Latium: Settlement, Burials and Religion at Satricum. Journal of Roman Archaeology 12:453–475.

Snodgrass, Anthony M. 1980 Archaic Greece: The Age of Experiment. London: Dent.

——1986 Interaction by Design: The Greek City State. In Peer Polity Interaction and Socio-Political Change. Colin Renfrew and John F. Cherry, eds. Pp. 47–58. Cambridge: Cambridge University Press.

Sourvinou-Inwood, Christiane 1988 Studies in Girls' Transitions. Athens: Kardanitsa.

Strong, Donald 1988 Roman Art. Harmondsworth: Penguin.

Tomlinson, Richard A. 1976 Greek Sanctuaries. London: Elek.

——1997 The Upper Terraces at Perachora. Annual of the British School at Athens 72:197–202.

Turcan, Robert 1996 The Cults of the Roman Empire. Oxford: Blackwell.

van Hoorn, Gerard 1951 Choes and Anthesteria. Leiden: Brill.

van Straten, Folkert T. 1995 Hiera Kala: Images of Animal Sacrifice in Archaic and Classical Greece. Leiden: Brill.

Warde Fowler, William 1911 The Religious Experience of the Roman People. London: Macmillan.

Ward-Perkins, John B. 1981 Roman Imperial Architecture. Harmondsworth: Penguin.

——, and Amanda Claridge 1976 Pompeii, AD 79. London: Imperial Tobacco Limited.

Weinstock, Stefan 1970 Divus Julius. Oxford: Oxford University Press.

Whitley, James 2002 The Archaeology of Ancient Greece. Cambridge: Cambridge University Press.

Wilson, Roger J. A. 2002 A Guide to the Roman Remains in Britain. 4th edition. London: Constable.

Wiseman, T. Peter 2004 The Myths of Rome. Exeter: University of Exeter Press.

Woolf, Greg 1998 Becoming Roman: The Origins of Provincial Civilization in Gaul. Cambridge: Cambridge University Press.

——2000 Urbanization and its Discontents in Early Roman Gaul. *In* Romanization and the City: Creation, Transformations, and Failures. Journal of Roman Archaeology Supplementary Series 38. Elizabeth Fentress, ed. Pp. 115–131. Portsmouth: Journal of Roman Archaeology.

——2003 Polis-Religion and its Alternatives in the Roman Provinces. *In* Roman Religion. Clifford Ando, ed. Pp. 39–54. Edinburgh: Edinburgh University Press.

Zanker, Paul 1988 The Power of Images in the Age of Augustus. Ann Arbor: University of Michigan Press.

——1998 Pompeii: Public and Private Life. Cambridge, MA: Harvard University Press.

8

The Personal and the Political

Introduction

Reading the chapters of this volume so far, one might be struck by the relative lack of personal names, or of individual biographies. This does not reflect our ignorance of "great men" in the ancient world—Plutarch's *Parallel Lives* (written in the decades around A.D. 100) alone provides a remarkable cast of characters—although admittedly women, children and barbarians do, by and large, remain obscured in our extant literary texts.

Why the relative lack of the "personal" therefore? To a great extent, this mirrors a dominant archaeological concern with tracing and analyzing structures of human organization and self-representation, rather than the vicissitudes of any single life story. That emphasis is today being reconsidered and modified, with the rise of post-processual approaches in archaeology, approaches that encourage material exploration of the individual, individual experience, memories, and emotions. Classical archaeology, with its rich mixed data set of text and material culture, emerges as a potentially productive arena for such investigations.

"Finding individuals" in the archaeological record, however, is no straightforward task. It is exceedingly difficult to connect an individual life history with a specific constellation of material remains: a landscape, a house, a city, a sanctuary. Tombs and their associated acts of individual commemoration appear a better way forward, though caution is required even there. The persona remembered in death, it is now realized, rarely echoes the full complexity of a life experience; moreover, the interventions of those surviving (and organizing the funeral and grave monuments) often mask or modify commemoration to their own purposes. Finally, certain social and political configurations, such as the Athenian democracy, outright discouraged the public expression of individual achievement and family emotion.

The difficulty of the endeavor does not justify its neglect, however, and it is vital to consider, as far as possible, the ways and means through which people made their mark upon the worlds in which they lived. This chapter explores this problem through a variety of strategies: not least by choosing to examine how men of power (Alexander the Great, Roman emperors) crafted their personal image—the public self they wished to promulgate—through gesture, portraiture, and architecture. The extent to which this reflects an actual individual conscious-ness, versus the desire to represent accepted values and virtues, will remain a debated point. The force and significance of these decisions, however, are clear in their visible consequences, traceable in the success or failure of political regimes and in the daily lives of subjects or enemies. In this analysis, the "archaeology of the individual" in classical antiquity emerges as a complicated intersection of the personal and the political.

8 (a)

The Personal and the Political

The Greek World

John F. Cherry

The Problem of the Individual in Archaeology

Without question, it is when archaeology is able to engage not just with "people in the past," but also with the lives or deaths of single individuals that it most comes alive and often has the greatest popular appeal. One thinks of such examples as the unfortunate souls whose bodies were buried in the volcanic ash of the eruption of Vesuvius in A.D. 79, preserving the circumstances and the agonies of their very last moments; or the details (as revealed by examination of his stomach contents) of the last meal eaten by the "Ice Man," who expired some 5,300 years ago atop a 10,000-foot Alpine pass; or the letters on wooden tablets, written and received by lonely soldiers stationed at Vindolanda on Hadrian's Wall, at the very limits of the Roman empire, discussing their need for fresh pairs of socks and underwear. Such cases, because they are so vivid in "making the past come alive," rightly receive a great deal of attention in the popular press and on television.

Yet these are quite atypical instances. Classical archaeology, for most of its existence as a discipline, has been focused not on named, known individuals, but on structures, whether material or socio-political. Traditionally, classical archaeologists have been drawn to the excavation of temples, sanctuaries, theaters, civic buildings, houses, and the like; but it is extraordinarily difficult to connect the evidence unearthed by such endeavors with individual life histories. Even research that concentrates on *Classical Landscapes with Figures* (Osborne 1987) finds it problematic, as chapter 4 also makes clear, to populate the villages, hamlets, and farmsteads discovered by survey with anything other than "faceless blobs." For those seeking to understand, say, the role of slavery or patterns of trade and exchange in the ancient world, the unit of analysis is largely at the level of the group, and involves study of anonymous agents or collectivities. There is, in short, a disconnect between the rich prosopography (i.e., descriptions of individuals' careers, family connections, etc.) available from the Classical written record and the ability of archaeology to produce data about identifiable people.

Burial evidence, one might suggest, offers a more direct route to the individual. The excavation of an unrobbed grave, after all, surely provides invaluable evidence. This includes not only all that physical anthropology can deduce from the remains of the dead person (age, sex, stature, facial reconstruction, health, pathology, trauma, and now, with the help of DNA evidence, even family relationships: see Carter 2006:39–46, for an impressive case study in the territory of Metapontum in southern Italy). The burial can also tell us much about his or her status, beliefs, and treatment in death, as reflected in the form and monumentality of the grave, in the objects interred with the deceased, in above-ground markers of the burial, etc. A remarkable example discovered not many years ago is the so-called "Heroön" at Lefkandi on Euboea, a massive stone and mud-brick structure measuring almost 50 × 10 meters, thought to represent the residence or tomb (or both) of a local early tenth-century B.C. chieftain and his wife (Popham et al. 1993). The site is striking both in its scale and in the exoticism of the associated artifacts. But in reality this tells us little about these two people, no matter how important they may have been within their own society: we cannot identify their names (this was not a literate age in Greece), and we know nothing of their life histories, how they achieved the prominence reflected in their treatment at burial, or how they were regarded by their contemporaries. In any case, it is abundantly clear that the funerary "persona" does not necessarily reflect the living individual and his/her life experience directly: status in life may be deliberately downplayed in death (Morris 1987), and survivors may intervene to mask reality, by creating what one scholar (Fleming 1973) engagingly termed "tombs for the living," rather than for the dead.

Ironically, the majority of recent discussions about how to recognize individuals in the archaeological record have been by prehistorians (beginning, arguably, with Hill and Gunn 1977), despite what seems the obvious fact that accessing individuals, persons, and identities should be easier in a historical context than in prehistory. This development has been fostered in large part by the post-processual theoretical turn away from sociopolitical and technological styles of explanation at the systems level, towards an acknowledgement of the importance of individual actors and agency (Dobres and Robb 2000). Meskell (1999:34–36), writing about Egypt in a literate era, usefully discusses a number of dimensions of the individual that archaeologists might hope to recognize, whether or not they have written records available:

1. The cultural concept of what constitutes a person: for instance, how did Classical Greeks perceive themselves?
2. The anonymous individual person or individual bodies (as reflected, e.g., in mortuary remains or figurines).
3. Individuals distinguished by their actions (in Classical archaeology, good examples concern attempts to identify individual craftsmen or artists' hands).

4. The mention or representation of individuals in texts, iconography, or archi-
    tecture (examples would include an inscribed bust of a ruler, or personal
    names on the Greek Linear B tablets).
5. Historically known individuals (whether Egyptian pharaohs or Roman
    emperors).

This is a promising-sounding list, but in practice there are many complexities that
surround study of this concept (see Hodder and Hutson 2003:121–124). To take
just one example (item 3 on the list), the study of works of art has long been considered an arena in which Classical archaeologists can "see" the hand of the
individual artist at work. After all, our best surviving source on ancient painting
and sculpture—the Elder Pliny (Jex-Blake and Sellers 1896)—casts his entire
discussion not in terms of trends and traditions, but of named artists, many of
whose works modern scholars have sought to identify in either original works or
recognizable later copies. Sir John Beazley extended such efforts into the field of
figured vase-painting: despite the fact that ancient writers barely mention this art
form, and extremely few vases are signed, his application of the methods of connoisseurship first developed by Giovanni Morelli for the study of Renaissance
painting led to Beazley's recognition of many hundreds of black- and red-figure
vase-painters with distinctive, individualized styles (cf. chapter 1 [a]). His work,
notwithstanding some criticism and refinement, still serves as an essential underpinning of dating and classification in the Archaic and Classical periods. (Aegean
prehistorians, indeed, have been emboldened by the apparent success of Beazley's
methods to apply them, sometimes unwisely [Cherry 1992], in the search for
individuals in the altogether murkier artistic environment of the Bronze Age.) Yet
the reality is that, although flesh-and-blood people of course produced these
works, the names Classical archaeologists have given them merely reflect analytical classifications; fictional elaborations of the life histories of largely hypothetical
ancient artists (e.g., Boardman 1975:91–94) can provide no reliable insights into
the lived experience of these people as individuals (Beard 1991).

Even so (the reader may insist), it must surely be the case that individual
persons, their identities, their embodied selves—what a recent book calls "the
archaeology of personhood" (Fowler 2004)—are more fully accessible in historical settings, with their rich and varied material culture and, especially, written
records, which are hardly just "one more piece of evidence" (Shennan 1989:14).
And would this not be especially so in Classical Greece, from which we have such
abundant literary evidence, as well as the benefits of an almost obsessive drive in
certain cities to erect inscriptions on stone?

Classical Athens is the city-state that has yielded by far the richest body of
evidence—archaeological, epigraphic, and literary—and not only because it is also
the most thoroughly explored. Even in this case, however, it remains surprisingly
difficult to connect material remains directly with distinct individuals about
whom we know more than simply a name. While this is a challenge for archaeology in every time and place, in Athens an additional factor intervenes. The very
ideology of democracy, for which this city above all others is rightly celebrated,

was also a confining one, and it militated strongly against the celebration of individual merit. Indeed, political practices such as ostracism—a procedure whereby a citizen could, by popular vote, be expelled from the state for ten years—developed precisely to neutralize the political power of individuals whose prominence was felt to constitute a threat to the democratic body-politic (Forsdyke 2005). Unlike in the modern world, where university buildings, hospital wings, and sports stadiums are routinely named in honor of a benefactor or even as acts of unashamed self-promotion, Athenian temples, sanctuaries, and many types of public building were invariably dedicated in the names not of individuals, but of gods or the *demos* (the people), for these were seen as spaces that belonged to a civic community and in which there could be little or no scope for personal aggrandizement.

These attitudes spilled over into artistic production. In the earlier decades of the fifth century B.C. we can see from a number of examples (e.g., the so-called Riace bronzes, representing two warriors) a growing interest in particularity and the representation of "real people" (albeit unknown to us); but from mid-century, around the time of the great sculptor Polyclitus, and throughout the High Classical era, sculptures become more generalized constructs, and it it is scarcely possible to find anything that could plausibly be described as a portrait, in the sense of a recognizable likeness of a specific living (or dead) individual (Brilliant 1991). Even those that we know, from an accompanying inscription, were intended to represent a particular person appear to us as generalized abstract "types" (the heroic soldier, the victorious athlete); well known among these is the bust of the helmeted Pericles, depicted as a weary but wise soldier-statesman (Stewart 1993:figure 2) The very epitome of this tradition, of course, is the sculptural program of the Parthenon, and especially its great frieze: intended as a self-representation of democratic Athenians in action, in reality it homogenizes them and strips from them any trace of true individuality, all the more so by depicting anthropomorphized gods and heroes in the same style (see Figure 9.4). In this context, it is no wonder that the sculptor Pheidias, by (allegedly) portraying himself among the figures on the shield of the cult statue of Athena Parthenos that stood inside the Parthenon, came to feel the opprobrium of his fellow-citizens: he had inserted the personal into the work of the body-politic.

Orthodox opinion is that it was only in the late Hellenistic period, and under Roman influence, that Greek portraits exhibited a wide range of styles, including descriptive realism. New research (Dillon 2006) is suggesting that the proliferation of portrait styles takes place rather earlier, in the late Classical period (fourth century B.C.), and that the identity encoded in these largely nameless, anonymous portraits is much more complex and layered than has previously been realized. That may be so, but this was also a time during which sweeping and dramatic changes occurred in the political configuration of the Mediterranean. As Osborne (1998:218) puts it, "In the fourth century, and particularly on the fringes of the Greek world, the big man came to impress himself upon the Greek state in a monumental way." The rise of non-democratic political systems allowed, even demanded, representations of rulers and the celebration of dynasties in ways that would have been unthinkable earlier—even in the Archaic period, when certain individuals ("tyrants") ran rough-shod over established constitutions to grab absolute political power. In this new convergence of the political and the personal in the fourth century B.C., some of the same artists who had created great public art for the democratic city were co-opted to very different political situations, and a quite different sort of art resulted. The most celebrated "big man" monument is one of the seven wonders of the ancient world, the Mausoleion at Halikarnassos in Turkey (352–351 B.C.)—a tomb, but also a sort of hero-shrine, for the local dynast Mausolus, begun during his own lifetime, involving massive amounts of sculpture (including portrait-statues), and created by most of the best-known fourth-century sculptors, if ancient accounts are to be believed.

Men such as Mausolus clearly aspired to place their personal stamp on their own world, and on posterity too; Mausolus of course succeeded in one respect, since his is the name that all subsequent mausolea bear. Yet the reach of his political power and influence was in reality quite limited, indeed utterly insignificant when compared with the vast eastern empire carved out only a quarter-century later by a man born some four years before the Mausoleum's construction. Alexander of Macedon—a small and hitherto obscure state in Mediterranean terms—transformed a traditional monarchy into a charismatic autocracy dominated by an individual whose sheer force of personality made possible a campaign of eastward military expansion that not only abruptly demolished the ageing Persian Empire, but rewrote the political map and cultural landscapes from Greece to the Indus. Of all "big men" in later Greek history, Alexander must be adjudged the biggest, as his by-line "the Great" itself attests (this epithet, however, was not used by Alexander himself, nor by his contemporaries and immediate successors, and is first mentioned in the Roman playwright Plautus's *Mostellaria* in the early second century B.C.). Here is an extreme example of the linkage of the personal and the political: a spectacular individualist, much concerned with image, who made his mark upon the world(s) in which he lived to an extent wholly unimaginable at the time of his birth. In what follows, then, we focus on some aspects of how this one man's life, and his choices of self-representation, can be observed in the material record, and how this relates to our written sources.

A Little History

"Alexander's tale is so well known a tune/ That everyone who is not simple grown/ Has heard somewhat, or all, of his fortune," wrote Chaucer in "The Monk's Tale"; "Some talk of Alexander," begins the 18th-century British song "The British Grenadiers." Indeed, talk of Alexander has never ceased since his death in 323 B.C., an event of such significance as to have become the conventional pivot between the Classical and Hellenistic eras. Alexander was of immense cultural significance to Rome (Spencer 2002), a topic of endless fascination and story-spinning throughout the medieval world (Cary 1956; Ross 1988), and a favored subject for post-Renaissance artists (Hadjinicolaou 1997); lately, he has become a flashpoint in Balkan ethnic politics (Darnforth 1995), and even an exemplar of strategic planning which business corporations might emulate (Bose 2003). Scores of historical novels have retold and reformulated Alexander's story from the perspectives of various of the *dramatis personae*, both great and small. Traveling blockbuster museum shows centered around the person of Alexander (e.g., Yalouris et al. 1980) have been put on display worldwide in an almost unbroken sequence, beginning shortly after the 1977 discovery at Vergina in Greek Macedonia of a spectacular royal tomb held by many to be that of Alexander's father Philip II (Andronikos 1994). Michael Wood, with an intrepid camera crew, trod in Alexander's supposed footsteps to create a widely watched and colorful BBC-TV series, with accompanying book (Wood 1997). Most recent of all is the long-anticipated (but in the event disappointing) Oliver Stone movie *Alexander* (Lane Fox 2005), which itself triggered the publication of a spate of new historical studies of Alexander, and the reprinting of many old ones too.

So Alexander's career scarcely needs a re-telling. Simply to provide some background for the discussion that follows, here is the briefest outline account of the facts—although, as we will see, disentangling truth from rumor and even fiction is surprisingly tricky, even in the case of so famous a man.

Alexander was born in 356 B.C. at Pella in Macedonia, the son of King Philip II of Macedon (383–336 B.C.) and the Epirote princess Olympias, just one among several wives the very able ruler Philip took to cement alliances with neighboring tribes in order to expand the power and territory of Macedon (according to words put into Alexander's mouth by the much later biographer Plutarch, Philip persuaded his tribal highland subjects to stop wearing sheepskins and settle in cities). Alexander's early years, replete with oft-told stories such as the taming of the horse Bucephalas, famously included the philosopher Aristotle as one of his teachers, spawning both chatter about Alexander as a "philosopher-king" and a late tradition of fictitious letters between teacher and pupil (Stoneman 1994). It was during these years that Philip, by dint of virtually non-stop military campaigning against surrounding tribes and using the resources of the rich gold mines of Mount Pangaion, greatly enlarged his domain and made Macedon a force to be reckoned with in the power politics of the fourth century B.C., including those of the Greek states. Alexander, age 18, led the cavalry wing at the decisive battle of Chaeronea in 338 B.C., in which Philip's forces defeated a coalition of Greek cities including Athens and Thebes, thus effectively ending true Greek freedom.

Philip's plans to expand to the east into Asia against Persia were cut short just two years later by his assassination at Pella during the wedding of his daughter Cleopatra, Alexander's full sister. (Whether or not one of the lavishly appointed tombs excavated in the royal cemetery at Vergina is indeed the burial place of Philip II, as several lines of evidence strongly suggest, remains debated, again serving to illustrate the difficulty—absent explicit epigraphic evidence—of associating individuals with mortuary remains.) Alexander seized the throne, eliminating potential rivals and gaining official recognition as king by the army. He then took rapid action to consolidate his power, quelling dissidence among Thracian, Illyrian, and other tribes to the north, and crushing a Greek revolt led by Thebes with the ruthless annihilation of the city. Elected commander of the panhellenic anti-Persian forces, he set out for Asia against the Persian Great King, Darius III, in spring 334—the start of what would prove to be a relentless march of more than 20,000 miles over the following decade, taking him all the way to India. The events of these years radically transformed the worlds of the eastern Mediterranean and the Near East, bringing them into ever closer contact within what we now refer to as the Hellenistic world and, indirectly, paving the way for the Roman empire and the spread of Islam.

In the first of many brilliant tactical moves, Alexander, with Greece secure in the control of Regent Antipater, proceeded to neutralize the Mediterranean-based Persian navy not by direct encounter, but by capturing its bases one by one; key among these was the Phoenician port-city of Tyre, taken in 332 only after a protracted and ruthless seige. These actions left Alexander free to focus on moving his army steadily east and south through Anatolia, the Levant, and Egypt. Major battles resulted in victories at the Granicus River in northwestern Turkey in 334 and at Issus in southeastern Turkey in 333, the latter decisive in that it marked the beginning of the end of Persian power: it was the first time the Persian army had been defeated in the presence of Darius, who fled the field of battle, leaving his mother, wife, and children, as well as rich spoils, to be captured. Terminal defeat for Darius, and Alexander's mastery of the Persian Empire, came two years later at the battle of Gaugamela near Irbil in modern-day Iraq. It allowed Alexander's men to sweep on through Mesopotamia, taking key cities such as Babylon, and on to Persepolis—the symbolic and ritual center of the Empire—which in 330, after a stay of several months, he put to the torch, perhaps to remind the Greeks back home that he had not forgotten the ostensible purpose of his eastern mission, panhellenic revenge against the Persians.

The Persian king's treasure at Persepolis (requiring 7,000 pack animals to cart away) provided Alexander the means to reward his troops for their victories, but it also bankrolled ongoing war across the entire landmass of Asia and the annexation of domains as far afield as Afghanistan and Pakistan. Arguably, with all of the old Persian heartland of Iran firmly under control by 327, more conquest was unnecessary: why cross the Hindu Kush to retake territory in Pakistan that the Persian Empire itself had long since lost? Yet, for Alexander, pressing on ever further eastwards to "Ocean" (the very edge of the world, as then conceived) itself became an almost existential quest, one requiring great determination and sheer force of personality to inspire or drive his men. The fighting was very hard in this phase of the expedition, being not set-piece battles, but something more akin to irregular guerilla warfare against fierce tribal bands; Alexander himself suffered serious wounds and found it expedient to contract a political marriage alliance with the Sogdian princess Roxane in an attempt to maintain his authority. A remarkable victory in a fierce battle, involving elephants, against King Porus at the River Hydaspes in 326 was to be his last, for not long thereafter at the River Hyphasis his own men mutinied, forcing a savage retreat down the Indus and a grueling forced march, with much loss of life, back to Iran through the Makran desert of Baluchistan.

Alexander never returned home to Macedon: he died just short of his 33rd birthday, probably of fever, and after heavy drinking, at Babylon in 323 B.C. His last couple of years show him wrestling with the problems of administering the empire he had forged, but weakened by the defection (along with a vast amount of treasure) of his High Chancellor Harpalus, and distraught with grief over the death of his closest friend and partner Hephaestion. Alexander's son, born post-humously, did not survive long, and his empire was quickly broken up by his generals and *de facto* heirs. From a period of conflict and bloody political killings, there emerged three chief successor states, each legitimized by their rulers through their connections to Alexander: the Ptolemaic kingdom of Egypt, the Seleucid empire embracing much of Syria and the Near East, and the Antigonid kingdom based in Macedonia. These became the key political blocs of the Hellenistic world.

Sources, Written and Material

How do we know even these bare facts about Alexander? Concerning a man who so dominated his age one would suppose, rightly, that a great deal was written, both during and after his lifetime. But as a very recent discussion of the extant source materials puts it, "although the surviving evidence is quite ample in quan-tity, it is poor in quality, being contradictory, tendentious and mainly non-contemporary" (Cartledge 2004:269). Source criticism of the spate of historical writings prompted by Alexander's career is a major headache for ancient histori-ans, and the lack of agreement among them one reason why there can really be no such thing as "the historical Alexander."

Briefly, there are five extant continuous narrative accounts. The earliest of these, the incomplete Book 17 of Diodorus' *Library of History*, was published fully three centuries after Alexander's death, while a history by the Romanized Gaul Trogus, writing perhaps just slightly later than Diodorus, exists only in an abridge-ment by Justin in the third century A.D., and Curtius's *History of Alexander the Great*, probably composed during the reign of Claudius, is missing its first two books. From later still, in the second century AD, we have two works in Greek: Plutarch's *Life of Alexander*, which (as he himself reminded his readers) was not history, but biography with moralizing purposes, and Arrian's detailed *Anabasis Alexandrou*, widely regarded today as the best surviving account. All these later authors—the last two especially—rely upon and quote passages from a wide range of earlier works about Alexander, none of which have otherwise survived. Known only in highly fragmentary form, these are nevertheless significant because they include a number of eyewitnesses (which, of course, does not mean that all they say is reliable, and they each have axes to grind or angles to push): Callis-thenes (Alexander's official historian, until his execution in 327 B.C.), Ptolemy (a member of his military staff), Onesicritus and Nearchus (chief helmsman and admiral of his fleet), and Chares (his chamberlain). A key contemporary who was not himself a participant in the events was the historian Cleitarchus, popular in

Antiquity because his writings had a sensational flavor, and important as one of the chief works on which Diodorus, Trogus, and Curtius relied. The surviving sources claim to draw information from other types of documentation as well, including royal diaries, personal notebooks, and letters, but there are grave doubts about how authentic most of these are.

In short, this is information of uncertain veracity, probably subjected to a good deal of political "spin," passed on at second or third hand by authors writing centuries later in pursuit of their own agendas. It is precisely because of the unsatisfactory character of so many of the literary sources that other forms of archaeological material evidence, both contemporary and non-contemporary, and from places throughout the vast expanse of Alexander's empire, assume real importance in attempts to understand Alexander as a person, and the impact of his actions.

For example, coins survive in huge quantities from throughout his realm. They provide direct evidence not only about economic history and monetary policy, but also about ideology, propaganda, and political history. Infinitely more of his subjects would have held a coin of Alexander in their hands than could read accounts in Greek, official or otherwise, of his doings—so what they saw mattered. He certainly showed interest not only in controlling what was written about him, but in authorizing his official images too; thus the repertoire of allusions, symbolic attributes, and metaphors that appear on his coinage speak very directly to the image- and myth-making that went on throughout his reign, while those appearing on coins issued by the successor kingdoms speak volumes about how they drew on his reputation and status. We will not treat this body of evidence further here; excellent studies of it are available elsewhere (Davis and Kraay 1973; Oikonomides 1981; Price 1991). Instead, we turn first to the many hundreds of images of Alexander in portrait busts, sculptures, painting, and mosaic, in order to evaluate how such intensely personal expressions shed light on larger political and institutional concerns. We then examine Alexander's city-foundations, in light of both textual and archaeological data, and consider their role as catalysts for sweeping cultural changes throughout the Middle East during the Hellenistic era.

The Image of Alexander

With the rise of the Greek and Asiatic monarchs, dynasts, and other sorts of "big men" in the fourth century B.C. came the need for ruler portraiture, the promotion of self-image, and thus of court artists. Alexander's father was no exception: the Philippeion he had erected within the sanctuary at Olympia made a bold break with longstanding Greek tradition by displaying sculpted representations of Philip and various family members, and we are also told that statues of the Macedonian royal family were being carried into the theater at Aegae on the occasion of his assassination. One of the reasons many archaeologists regard Tomb II at Vergina as that of Philip is that it contained a couch sumptuously decorated with 14 ivory heads, including three that the excavator, Manolis Andronikos, was convinced could only be representations of Philip, his wife Olympias, and their son

Figure 8.1 Marble head of the youthful Alexander the Great from Yannitsa near Pella, ca. 300–270 B.C.

Alexander (Osborne 1998: figure 131). If so, this would be among the earliest portraits of the youthful Alexander, shown at an age roughly the same as that of an early Hellenistic stone head from Yannitsa near Pella (Figure 8.1).

Yet how can we be sure that either of these creations, or indeed hundreds of others claimed to portray Alexander, is in fact a portrait of him? As the art historian Andrew Stewart shows in his definitive study of Alexander images, *Faces of Power* (1993), there exist only three wholly indisputable examples: the inscribed "Azara herm" (a Roman-period work); the so-called "Alexander mosaic" in the House of the Faun at Pompeii, depicting the battlefield encounter of Alexander and Darius (presumed to be a copy of an early Hellenistic painting: Cohen 1997); and the images on coins issued by his immediate successors, especially

Ptolemy I and Lysimachos. Happily, these bits of evidence can be supplemented by a wide array of literary sources that provide descriptions of Alexander himself and of some of his portraits. Plutarch, for instance, refers to distinctive peculiarities such as "the poise of his neck, which was tilted slightly to the left, and the melting glance of his eyes" (*Alexander* 4.1), and remarks that most sculptors "in their eagerness to represent his crooked neck and melting and limpid eyes, were unable to preserve his virile and leonine demeanor" (*On the Fortune or Virtue of Alexander* 2.2). Most images of Alexander (and nearly all of them are later Hellenistic or Roman "copies," which further complicates matters) are so identified by their wavy, "lion-like" hair with a parted quiff at the front, the turn of the head, and a thoughtful, dreamy facial expression with uplifted eyes. Of course, there are other artistic representations that can only be of Alexander—of whom else would the viewer think when seeing a small, Hellenistic bronze statuette of a youth subduing a huge horse (Cartledge 2004:83)?—but these come close to being merely souvenirs, and can tell us little about the *political* imagery of Alexander.

The importance of his own image to Alexander is clear. Just as he appointed an official historian (Callisthenes) to the retinue of his expedition to record its successes, he chose the very best Greek artists of the day and, seemingly, allowed only them to portray him: the sculptor Lysippus, the painter Apelles, and the gem-cutter (important also for portraits on coinage) Pyrgoteles. This gave Alexander tight control over the kinds of essential questions to which, according to Brilliant (1991:14–15), any portrait is a response—What do I look like? What am I like? Who am I? In the absence of mass media in the ancient world, an emphasis on a close degree of resemblance between the portrait image and Alexander's actual appearance may not have been important, or at least was readily elided. But the other questions invoke character, aspects of personal behavior, and sociopolitical status and power, and we see these played out in images that must relate to different roles he wished to emphasize at different stages of his career: the young Macedonian king, the daring hunter (a key element in Macedonian culture, and one with royal oriental associations), the victor in the battles with Darius, as an Asian king, as conqueror of the east, as a quasi-divine absolute monarch, and so on (Stewart 1993).

A more subtle, but quite pervasive, element of image-creation was the working in of details which implied connections with, or referenced Alexander's emulation of, various heroic models. For example, the Macedonian royal family claimed direct lineal descent from the hero-god Herakles, among whose celebrated labors was the killing of the Nemean lion. Thus busts and coin-portraits showing Alexander wearing a lion-skin carry a complex semantic load: they reminded the viewer at once that Alexander was a legitimate king and scion of a noble line, that he shared Heracles' boldness in the pursuit of fierce wild animals, that his own expeditionary conquests were akin to Herculean labors, that he too was a universal hero made god-like through his own efforts, and other overtones besides. Similar allusions are to be found to Achilles the heroic hero (Alexander's first act on crossing into Asia was to sacrifice at Achilles' tomb at Troy, and he is said to have traveled with Homer's *Iliad* beneath his pillow). Once Alexander passed beyond

Figure 8.2 Silver tetradrachm of Ptolemy I, 322 B.C., showing the head of Alexander wearing an elephant headdress, with horns of Ammon beneath it. Reproduced with permission of the American Numismatic Society

the frontiers of the Persian Empire and into India, rivalry with Dionysus came into play (and found artistic reflection), since this god too had famously journeyed to the east, bringing back wine and the arts of civilization. This sort of conflation of imagery, naturally, very much suited Alexander's own purposes; it created a subtly ambiguous and immensely influential representational tradition that lasted throughout the rest of Antiquity.

It was also hugely important to Alexander's successor dynasties and to many later rulers too, as a device of political legitimization whereby adoption of Alexander's image and symbolism, they hoped, would arrogate to themselves some of his power and charisma. In this, coinage, the most effective propaganda tool of the ancient world, played a key role. A good example is the silver coin issued by Ptolemy I of Egypt, depicting Alexander wearing an elephant-scalp headdress (Figure 8.2)—a reference to his mighty victory over Porus in India, but also a reminder that Ptolemy too had participated in these battles as one of Alexander's generals, and was now, thus, rightfully ruling as a successor. Peeping out from under the scalp, however, are the horns of the Egyptian god Ammon (syncretized by the Greeks with Zeus), whose oracular shrine in the Libyan desert Alexander had visited in 332/1 with results obscure to almost all present, although he thereafter acted as though he had a special relationship (perhaps even filiation) with the god. Alexander, who became Pharaoh and is depicted as such in a bas-relief from the Temple at Luxor (Briant 1996:59), himself capitalized on this association by issuing his own coinage on which he is shown wearing Ammon's horns, and this politically powerful image remained useful for later rulers, such as the Seleucid Lysimachos.

The Romans were fascinated, almost obsessed, with Alexander and his image (Green 1989; Spencer 2002), and *imitatio Alexandri* played a vital role in the political style of many leading figures. Rome's was the first empire of comparable scale to Alexander's, and comparison was thus inevitable; moreover, the fact that Alexander did not live to take on Rome led to endless speculation, both by reputable historians (e.g., Livy 9.17.17–18.5) and in schoolroom rhetorical exercises, about the counterfactual historical question of who would have won, had he done so. Romans were in drop-jaw admiration of Alexander's military successes (although they also argued the toss about whether this was due to sheer luck or capability), while also deploring Alexander's personal excesses and regarding him as a symbol of the *luxuria* which in Roman literature symbolizes the depraved living of the Greek east which he had both conquered and created. In short, Alexander's personal legacy could be a political hot potato.

Yet Pompey co-opted his tag "the Great," and had himself depicted "as" Alexander in one of the most ridiculous and unconvincing portraits from antiquity (Beard and Henderson 2001: figure 155): a simple peasant's face with a smug grin done up with the standard hairstyle formula that "says" Alexander (producing, according to Plutarch, "a resemblance more talked about than actually apparent"). Julius Caesar famously lamented his own lack of achievements when the same age as Alexander, and Plutarch found it natural to pair his Life of Alexander with that of Caesar. Augustus used a signet-ring bearing a representation of Alexander, and he made a trip to Alexandria to view Alexander's burial and body (remarking, allegedly, "I came to see a king, not a corpse"). Nero, too, adopted the hairstyle, enrolled legionary recruits under the name "the phalanx of Alexander the Great" in preparation for an imagined expedition to the Caspian Sea, and at the entrance of his Golden House between two of Rome's seven hills set up the colossal statue of himself as Helios-Sol, whose visage bore a striking resemblance to Alexander's. Later still, in the early third century A.D., the entire Severan dynasty (especially Caracalla and Severus Alexander) wrapped themselves around the cult and image of Alexander—as seen most notably in the series of large, gold Aboukir medallions that contain a complexly interrelated series of mythological, historical, and artistic allusionary references linking the Severan dynastic family, Alexander's family, and his heroic models. Evidently, Alexander's image remained politically potent half a millennium later.

Oddly enough, what is missing from all of this is a body, from which we might determine Alexander's actual appearance. Cremated bones from the "Tomb of Philip" at Vergina have been subjected to techniques of facial reconstruction, resulting in a recognizable facsimile of Philip's physiognomy, blind eye and all, and adding plausibility to the idea that this is indeed Philip's body (Musgrave 1991; Prag and Neave 1997). Alexander's corpse, however, was at first embalmed in Babylon, and a huge, ornate funeral bier was prepared to transport it to Vergina for burial (the description of it by Diodorus Siculus is sufficiently detailed to allow its reconstruction on paper—Briant 1996:126–127). But en route to Macedonia two years later, it was hijacked to Memphis in Egypt in a swift tactical move by the satrap Ptolemy, who after he became king transferred it to his capital, Alexandria—the first city that Alexander founded thus ironically also serving as his final resting-place. The lavish mausoleum-tomb came to be treated almost as a pilgrimage shrine (see the case of Augustus, mentioned above), but its where-abouts were lost at some point in late Antiquity and remain missing today, despite more than one hundred unsuccessful attempts over the past century to relocate it (Saunders 2006). Nothing could better demonstrate the impact of the personal on the political than this dead man's tale: even in death, Alexander remained so powerful as to provoke extraordinary action to ensure control of access to his body and the mantle of legitimacy it conferred.

City Foundations and the Spread of Hellenism

Alexander's expedition, undertaken as a pan-hellenic war of vengeance, led to regime change—the unseating and death of the Great King—and the take-over and transformation of the old Persian empire. Without Alexander this very prob-ably would not have occurred. Yet there is the danger of attributing to him per-sonally the credit and responsibility for all of the sweeping institutional and cultural changes that took place in the course of the following two or three cen-turies. Thus, it was ultimately thanks to Alexander's expedition, and especially the settling of Greek-speaking veteran soldiers throughout the east, that the Greek *koine* language came to be spread so widely, leading, for instance, to the trans-lation into Greek of the Hebrew Bible; but this was obviously not something Alexander consciously planned. In much the same way, it was the election of George W. Bush and the implementation of his policies that resulted in the over-throw of Saddam Hussein, even though many subsequent developments now roiling the Middle East were neither foreseen nor intended.

In this regard, one aspect of Alexander's activities to which Classical archaeol-ogy can make useful contributions and provide clarifications of confused written sources is his foundation of cities, and their cultural consequences—an essential part of his overall achievement, both directly and indirectly. The idea of city-foundations was a well-established tradition, which in its seventh- and sixth-century B.C. heyday saw Greeks implanted on the Aegean coast of Asia Minor, in the northern Aegean, around the Black Sea, and above all in Sicily and southern Italy. Even in Alexander's day, the idea was alive and well: Phillip II founded Philippi and Philippopolis after his conquest of Thrace, and Alexander himself apparently founded an Alexandroupolis there, well before he conquered the Persian Empire and became a colonizer and city-founder on a grand scale.

In an early rhetorical essay (*On the Fortune or Virtue of Alexander* 1, 328e), Plutarch flatly states: "Alexander established more than 70 *poleis* among barbarian peoples, and planted all Asia with Greek magistrates, and thus overcame its uncivilized and brutish mode of life." Certainly, this figure is greatly exaggerated, and no modern scholar claims more than about two dozen; the most skeptical recent study puts it as substantially less than that (Fraser 1996). There are a number of possible reasons for the discrepancy. After his death, there was a growing tendency to ascribe to him actions he never performed. Places Alexander did visit, and where he established something, may have been included in such lists, irrespective of what they were (small military garrison posts, for example). Alexander's pedigree became so prized that his name may have been adopted later by cities in whose foundation he played no role at all, either as an act of homage or to co-opt the legitimacy conferred by an alleged connection. Of course, some places that may have begun life in a modest way in Alexander's time were referred to as *poleis* by later writers, because they had actually grown to be significant settlements by their time.

Whatever the case in individual instances, these new foundations differed in significant ways from "traditional" Greek colonial cities. The latter were generally on or close to the sea, drew on mainly Greek settlers, maintained strong links (at least initially) with the founding city via trade and religious practice, and were independent and legally autonomous (Tsetskhladze and De Angelis 1994). Alexander's cities, in contrast, were founded and usually also named after a single individual, to whom they remained subject, and they were populated, in some cases forcibly, by mixed populations of Greek mercenaries and veteran or disabled Macedonians, together with large numbers of natives, especially women. Distributed from Egypt to central Asia, the majority of the Alexandrias we know lie in or beyond eastern Iran, far from any sea: some still-surviving cities in Afghanistan, Tajikistan, and Uzbekistan (Herat, Merv, Termez, and Khodjend, for example) are certainly ancient Alexandrias, which limited excavations have shown flourished mainly in the third and second centuries B.C. (Romey 2004; Holt 2005).

Some of these places were pre-existing forts or posts, military installations that had been a part of the Persian system of imperial control and now played a similar role in Alexander's far-flung empire, both for administration and for the communications and supply network it required. Especially in under-developed areas of the east, these cities—if we should even call them as such—came to serve as stations on the trade routes to India, where caravans could assemble in security and conduct exchange. Economic motives lie behind other foundations too: Charax-Alexandria at the head of the Tigris, for example, and the queen of them all, Alexandria-by-Egypt on the Nile delta, in whose foundation Alexander took an active personal role and whose location was a vital factor in its rapid growth to become the richest, most populous, and most powerful city of the entire Hellenistic world. Despite the difficulties posed by its long and complex later history, destructive rebuilding in the 19th and 20th centuries, and the fact that it has sunk more than 20 feet since antiquity so that many remains are now underwater, archaeologically this is the best-explored of all Alexander's cities (even if little has yet been found that dates to his own age) (Fraser 1972; La Riche 1997; Empereur 2002). It was also the closest to a true *polis*-foundation, with many architecturally Greek buildings such as an agora and a gymnasium, but also Greek-style magistrates, law courts, and other civic structures modeled on Athens.

Although few Alexandrias have received much archaeological exploration, one notable and fascinating exception that lies at the other pole of the empire is Aï Khanoum (very likely, Alexandria in Oxiana) on the northern border of Afghanistan (see also chapter 4 (a)). What this site reveals are the unique, hybrid

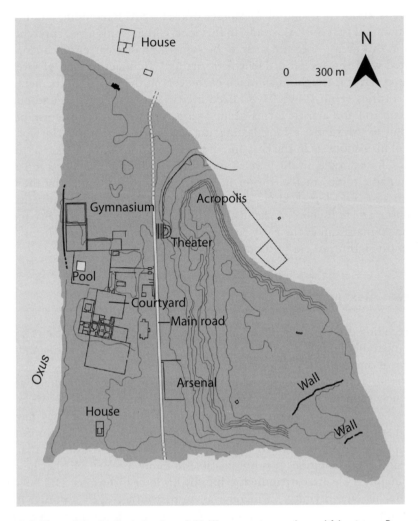

Figure 8.3 Plan of the Hellenistic city of Aï Khanoum in northern Afghanistan. Reproduced with permission of Thames & Hudson Ltd

forms of material culture that emerged in central Asia as a consequence of Alexander's conquests. Much struck by the presence of such obviously Greek features as an acropolis, theater, gymnasium, temples, and naturalistic sculptures in Hellenized styles, and even quotations in Greek from the oracle at Delphi, the French archaeologists who worked there in the 1960s and 1970s took it for a "purely Greek" city-site (Green 1990:332–335) (Figure 8.3). This verdict now seems overblown, since there are many significant aspects of the site that are either antecedent to the Greek presence or are not recognizably Greek at all. Regrettably, it may not now be feasible to follow up on these explorations of a generation ago, since the site has subsequently been massively looted and also much damaged by bulldozing during the Taliban régime.

There is, in fact, no sign of Alexander himself at Aï Khanoum, and it may be fair to maintain that the "Alexandrian incident"—that is, his actual presence, very briefly, in this area—does not seem to be something of great significance, at least compared with the spread of Hellenistic art and architecture and of Greek language and script throughout so much of the east in the course of the next two or three centuries (Holt 1999). Hybridized mixtures of native Asian and borrowed Greek cultural and artistic forms occur over a very wide area and form powerful testimony to Alexander's long-lasting impact, notwithstanding the ephemeral nature of his conquests in the east and of the institutions he established there. We see them, for example, in the jewelry and weaponry found in late first millennium B.C. nomadic tombs in Bactria; or in the unique coinage issued by the Greco-Bactrian and Indo-Greek kings such as Menander I; and, most influentially, in Gandharan art, the school of classically influenced sculpture that thrived in Pakistan and Afghanistan in the early centuries of our era and that gave form to some of the most significant early Buddhist art.

Epilogue: Alexander "the Great"?

The preceding discussion is intended to suggest that even in the case of someone so incomparably famous as Alexander III of Macedon, and notwithstanding the plethora of surviving textual, artistic, and archaeological evidence about him, many details at the purely personal level must remain largely invisible. They have been much spun through texts, penned centuries later by authors drawing on earlier accounts written either with animus or to eulogize; and they have been recast in art, especially by the successor dynasties as a device of legitimization, to the extent that we know more about the changing *concept* of Alexander than about his physical representation. It is not possible to know for sure whether he said, or even thought, the words attributed to him by his later historians. Did he actually believe in his own divinity, or merely fail to discourage such a notion in those around him, for opportunistic reasons? Were attempts to integrate Persians and other Orientals into his Macedonian and Greek army and administration really signs of an explicit policy of racial fusion to promote a "unity of mankind"? Was his sexual life one of near-impotency or of gross excess (ancient writers cannot agree) and did it also involve homosexual relationships (they do not explicitly say)? What motivated his relentless quest for empire—some Oedipal desire to please his mother and outdo his father? A desire to live a life worthy of his favored hero Achilles or of the "son of Zeus" (which he certainly considered himself to be)? A passionate yearning (the word occurs frequently in the sources, especially Arrian) to seek constantly after superhuman achievement?

Such speculations may appear to be rather far from archaeology. On the other hand, it seems perverse not to take them on board, if we are serious about individual agency, considering the personal alongside the societal, as crucial elements in attempts to recreate and understand the human past—all the more so in the Classical world where knowledge of individual actors is so very much better than for many another era. Yet while many aspects of Alexander as a person remain obscure (or, at least, judgments about them remain moot), what is more clearly visible, and where archaeology plays a key role, is the impact of his decisions and actions, for these had tangible, material consequences we can explore. Some have argued that Alexander's legacy was nothing less than the creation of the Hellenistic world (Hammond 1993); his actions were responsible for the physical formation of the Hellenistic kingdoms, and his career resulted in a marked caesura in political and cultural traditions in countries throughout the entire eastern Mediterranean and the Near East. Bringing Mediterranean Classical peoples and institutions into direct contact with those of western and central Asia resulted in manifold changes: the opening up of possibilities for long-distance trade and the mutual exchange of hitherto exotic commodities; the implantation of cities planned on Classical principles and the spread of Greek building-types, architectural forms, and artistic styles; a general dissemination of Greek language, culture, and education, repaid by the wealth of geographical, anthropological, and biological knowledge that flowed back to the west, prompting the systematization of knowledge in libraries such as that at Alexandria itself; and so on.

The unparalleled influence Alexander has exerted on cultures and history from his death until today, combined with his military brilliance, the speed and boldness of his expedition, the scale of the empire it created, and of course his early death, are all reasons why he is styled "the Great." Unfettered admiration has resulted in some odd 20th-century conceptions of him as a rational, almost gentlemanly genius, a man entirely beyond reproach (Tarn 1948; Hammond 1997). Modern scholarship shades to the darker side, or at least takes a more "realist" approach (Bosworth 1988). If not quite regarding him as a megalomaniacal mass murderer who believed himself divine, then it at least cites him as a man who evidently preferred constant warfare to settled normalcy, whose campaigns resulted in slaughter on a vast scale, who can be charged with not-infrequent reckless endangerment of his own and his men's lives, whose army mutinied, whose violent temper and drunkenness led him to murder some of his own friends, and whose failure to name an heir led directly to the chaos and melt-down of his empire upon his death. Debate over these conflicting visions of Alexander is one that will run and run (see, e.g., Worthington 2003:296–325).

It is also a debate, however, that intersects with the very question implied by the inclusion in this volume of a chapter on "the personal and the political": what is the relationship between individual history and wider social forces, or, in the case of Alexander, between the agency of "Great Men" and that of collective entities? Thucydides' account of the Peloponnesian War, for instance, a foundational work for western conceptions of history, presents an alternation between individual (e.g., Pericles, Themistocles) and collective (e.g., Athenians, Spartans) actors in the making of history. In contrast, the cultural anthropologist Leslie White, in a study of the 18th-dynasty Egyptian ruler Ikhnaton, renowned for a terror-filled reign dominated by his fanatical abandonment of polytheism in favor of monotheistic sun-worship, suggested that the cataclysmic occurrences of Ikhnaton's rulership were merely links in a cultural chain extending centuries before and after his lifetime, and he concluded provocatively that "the *general trend of events* would have been the same had Ikhnaton been but a sack of sawdust" (White 1948:113). Even at the time, nearly 60 years ago, this must have seemed an extreme position. Archaeology certainly needs to take account of social institutions and cultural forces, and even in the Classical world is perhaps best positioned as a discipline to study the material outcomes of behavior by individuals acting in the context of many different types of groupings. But faced with a man such as Alexander, surely we cannot afford to ignore the role of an individual's personal power? And while archaeological evidence can only rarely give us direct access to Alexander's dominating charisma, of which the written records speak so often, it nonetheless is remarkably effective (arguably, better than the texts) in allowing us to see how and why his successors found it so important to plug into the "memory" of that charisma.

NOTE

The references for this chapter are on pp. 329–334.

8 (b)
The Personal and the Political

The Roman World

Penelope J. E. Davies

The intersection between the personal, the political and material culture in ancient Rome was not a straightforward one. On the one hand, artists and architects were plentiful and highly skilled. The general populace, as far as we can tell, was also unusually astute in terms of visual literacy, and recognized the extraordinary power of images. The temptation, then, was for the politically minded to exploit visual culture to its fullest potential. Indeed, the archaeological evidence that survives is remarkable for its sheer bulk and ubiquity, much of it of high quality and executed in durable materials, and this suggests a concern for permanence more usually associated with cultures such as dynastic Egypt. Yet, on the other hand, Romans had a deep-seated sense of what was and what was not appropriate in terms of self-promotion, forcing public figures to operate in nebulous shades of gray, where even a politician as seasoned as Julius Caesar could go calamitously wrong.

This section of the chapter first traces the development of this difficult game of visual diplomacy. It then offers some strategies for finding individuals in the archaeological record, beginning with a discussion of portraits to distinguish between psychological profiles—which remain elusive—and political personalities, which are richly preserved, and moves on to discuss a wider range of monuments. Strategies include: analyzing the subjects chosen, as well as the location of and relationships between monuments; considering materials selected for use, as well as style and design; and, finally, assessing the dynamic qualities of architecture. Discussion focuses on portraits and tombs—privately funded works that Romans exploited to suggest individuality—and on temples, public monuments that feature as large in the Republic as in the empire. Though commissioning patrons and their audiences were drawn from an extraordinarily wide range of social backgrounds, from emperor to slave, the examples illustrated in these pages are drawn mainly from works of the ruling elite within the city of Rome, who are predominantly male. On the whole, their commissions were intended to support their legitimacy in political circles, where legitimacy is the outcome of continuous negotiation between ruler and ruled (Cullhed 1994:13). All the same, similar investigative strategies could be applied to the commissions of the working classes (see, for instance, Kleiner 1977; Kampen 1981; Kleiner and Matheson 1996; D'Ambra 1998).

General Patterns

During the Roman empire, the most prominent individuals in the archaeological record are emperors (see, in general, Anderson 1997:88–95). Their portraits, executed by the most skilled artists of the day, were distributed far and wide and often set the fashion for patrons of lesser status (Bonacasa and Rizza 1988; Gazda and Haeckl 1993:294–295). It was their tombs that loomed most dramatically in the cityscape, like the vast Mausoleum of Augustus on the Campus Martius (Figure 8.4), or the Column of Trajan, with its famed sculptural narrative (Settis et al. 1988; von Hesberg and Panciera 1994); and it was they, for the most part, who commissioned and restored public buildings—temples, basilicas, baths—in conspicuous places and who inscribed their names upon them. The emperor usually sought the Senate's stamp of approval for his buildings, but scholars presume that this was more or less a formality, and he could in effect build somewhat as he pleased. There are several reasons for the emperor's prominence in the

Figure 8.4 Mausoleum of Augustus, Rome, ca. 28 B.C., actual state. Photo: author

archaeological record: he controlled the state's purse strings, for one; for another, members of the elite were careful not to appear to compete with the monarchy for public visibility. Such individuals tended to finance public buildings outside Rome, to construct tombs (often in the privacy of their own estates) that came nowhere close to imperial standards of magnitude, and to display their portraits in their homes and tombs but not in Rome's public spaces. Moreover, since all magistrates were now subordinate to a higher authority, the institution of monarchy had removed much of the competition between peers, one of the greatest motivations for individual display in the political sphere. The result is that we believe we know more about the personalities of emperors than about any other class of people in the empire.

If the emperor was free to craft a public persona as he wished, for the most part, he seems to have been all too aware of a certain line that he could not cross in his exploitation of things material. Beyond that line were buildings and works of art that shone too bright a light upon his claim to absolute power, or positioned him too blatantly as a god. That this was forbidden territory sets the Roman emperor apart from kings in other cultures: ancient Egyptians make a good comparison again, since their kings were acknowledged divinities on earth and could commission works of art that reflected their divine status. The need for restraint in Rome appears to be a residue from times when Romans first learnt to manipulate images for political ends, in the aftermath of Rome's first monarchy (see, in general, Holliday 2002; Kuttner 2004).

During the Republic, politicians were faced with a dilemma. On the one hand, they had vowed, in the backlash of the expulsion of Rome's last king, Tarquinius Superbus, to denounce aspirations to supreme power (Livy 2.1). Government of the growing state was conducted instead through a successive series of elective magistracies with relatively specific mandates advised by a senate; the positions of greatest responsibility went to two consuls (Lintott 1999). On the other, the very nature of the Republican system, with magistracies diminishing in number the higher one climbed the ladder of power, and with public service valued above all else, yielded a society that was ferociously competitive, and that grew more so with the passing years (Beard and Crawford 1999:14). Several factors therefore made it sorely tempting to use material culture for self-advancement. For one thing, through such structures as the vast Capitoline Temple of Jupiter and the innovative, monumental drainage system, the Cloaca Maxima, the sixth-century kings had bequeathed a powerful lesson in how to exploit architecture for promotion of self and state (Sommella 2000; Hopkins 2004; Davies 2006). For another, all around the Mediterranean these were years of rapid urban development, something perceived to be the responsibility of the ruling elite.

In the early Republic, individual promotion could be masked as a by-product of religious piety. In moments of crisis—a battle, for instance, or a famine or plague—members of the governing elite would vow temples to chosen gods, in exchange or in gratitude for assistance (Ziolkowski 1992; Orlin 1997). Necessarily, the individual's identity was subordinated to the temple's god, whose help was acknowledged in an hour of need; all the same, the act bestowed glory on the magistrate who vowed the temple and aligned him with the gods and the interests of Senate and state. Literary sources indicate that the state generally financed these projects, so that wealth was not a direct prerequisite; yet since the chance to vow a temple was effectively reserved for generals and the highest-ranking magistrates, and since only the wealthy could lead the army and enter the Senate, this form of display effectively served to perpetuate a select elite. All the same, checks were in place to prevent the practice from being excessively useful to the ambitions of any single individual within that elite. For one, the Senate had to ratify the vow (Orlin 1997:48–50). Second, an individual did not automatically get sole billing alongside his god of choice. Since magistracies were elected positions of limited duration (one year for a consul; five years, later reduced to 18 months, for a censor), an individual who vowed a temple was not necessarily in a position to dedicate it. In theory at least, the system controlled individual display tightly enough to prevent individual ambitions from threatening the system.

Despite constitutional ideals, ambitious individuals looked for additional ways to work within the state's stringent controls, just as they maneuvered around the constitution's regulation of individual power by holding repeated magistracies. This was especially true as unprecedented wealth began to flow into the city from military expansion, bringing with it, perhaps, new standards for acceptable modes of self-promotion (Gruen 1992). One course was to exploit the privileges inherent in their honors, and the responsibilities inherent in their offices, to further their personal ambitions. For instance, victorious generals could be voted the right to mount a triumph by the Senate (Versnel 1970). This brought unsurpassed prestige in real time, and the generals learnt to translate the fame of the moment into lasting renown by dedicating works of art captured abroad and publicly displayed in the triumph (Hölscher 2006), and by commissioning appropriate venues for them. The charge of maintaining buildings with public funds usually fell to aediles, and they could record their interventions publicly in inscriptions (Pobjoy 2000), as well as commemorating entertainments they put on, such as gladiatorial shows and circuses, on coins and in reliefs (Holliday 2002: figure 103). One of the censor's mandates was to let out contracts for the expenditure of public money on works and management of public property (Anderson 1997:79–88; Lintott 1999:119); Appius Claudius Caecus was merely exploiting his charge when, as censor in 312 B.C., he bestowed his own name on a new road to Capua, the Via Appia, and on the first aqueduct of Rome, the Aqua Appia. All the same, Romans recognized that the road would commemorate him in perpetuity (Diodorus Siculus 20.36.2), and these acts also served his political career well by enhancing his prestige in Rome's territories (MacBain 1980).

If working within the system was one way to stand out in politics, another was to work around it, developing types of monument, such as columns and arches, that could be raised without Senatorial control, either financial or by right of veto (De Maria 1988; Wallace-Hadrill 1990; Richardson 1992; Steinby 1993–). Remarkably enough, these could be built on public land, and offered highly visible opportunities for self-promotion. Where individuals were even less constrained was in the construction of their tombs. Early Republican burials were simple earthen mounds or subterranean chambers carved out of the living tufa, but by the mid-Republic they could take grander shape and, by the first century B.C., they were built in any size or form, so long as the monument would appeal to casual passersby (von Hesberg 1992). Evoking the memory of deceased family members, a tomb provided a historical setting for the living, in a world where an illustrious pedigree was still the most dependable stepping-stone to a successful career in public service (Walker 1985).

The surge in tomb building went hand in hand with a lessening of property requirements for military service and the opening up of political office to munici-pal Italians. As wealth spread down the social pyramid, so rivalry for offices grew more heated, and the language of political competition was co-opted by those seeking social recognition outside of politics. Though sculpted portraits had been made throughout the Republic, it was at about this time that they became wide-spread (see Kleiner 1992; Sehlmeyer 1999; and Tanner 2000, for the extensive bibliography); the sheer number of surviving male portraits suggests that most were commissioned by the sitter for his own purposes, rather than by others to bestow honor.

The dramatic change in patronage patterns from Republic to Empire took root in the last century B.C., when, in swift succession, Sulla, Pompey, and Julius Caesar turned the system to their own advantage, holding supreme power for long enough to initiate large-scale interventions in the urban landscape. By taking on Rome's road systems and building massive arenas—Pompey's Theater complex, Caesar's Forum—as backdrops for their own public "performances," they effec-tively overruled the state's control on visual propaganda. Just as their extended authority afforded them grander plans than earlier Republicans, so these very works helped legitimize that rule. It comes as little surprise, then, that Cassius Dio (44.3–7) mentions visual honors among the causes leading to Caesar's assas-sination, carried out to safeguard the Republic.

Even a cursory analysis of the material record suggests that Romans used visual works to serve two ends: to improve and/or maintain public status, and to com-memorate. These goals were intertwined: a monument named and designed to last through the ages in commemoration brought visibility to the patron during his lifetime, and social status to his heir after death.

Where Personalities Emerge

The general pattern outlined above offers a sense of who, among the elite, were patrons at different times in Roman history, and the types of monument they exploited to make their mark. The remainder of this chapter focuses on a select group of works in order to distinguish what kinds of personality we might expect to see emerge from the archaeological record, and to explore specific strategies for exposing them.

Personalities and portraits

Susceptible as we are to looking for signs of personality in faces, we might turn
to portraiture when searching for individuals. Yet the instinct to paint a psychological profile on the basis of archaeological evidence can be misleading. Some of
the greatest pitfalls in dealing with Roman portraits are generated, paradoxically,
by the very familiarity they appear to present. Portraits in museums and private
collections around the world number in the thousands; moreover western society
has largely constructed itself in Rome's image, and this includes fashioning bust-
length sculptural portraits of Roman type (Beard and Henderson 2001:205–209).
Because we have made our forms so much like those of the Romans, it is hard
not to believe that they were very much like us. In some ways, they may have
been; yet in just as many important ways, they were not (Clarke 1996). We need
only consider how few people commission sculpted portraits for tombs today, and
what such a commission might say about income, taste, and social milieu, to
realize how differently we use and perceive the forms we have borrowed. In contrast to psychological profiles, political personalities can be extracted in a variety
of ways, and the distinction between the two is readily discernible in what can—
and what cannot—be learnt from Roman portraits.

In general, it is hard for archaeologists to identify the specific figure portrayed
in a Republican portrait, whereas members of the imperial household can often
be recognized. This is because inscriptions identifying the sitter are rare, and the
practice of depicting Roman individuals on coins, with accompanying legends,
is relatively late; comparison with coin and gem portraits is the archaeologist's
primary tool for establishing identity. This approach is more fruitful than using
literary descriptions but still fraught with complications (Beard and Henderson
2001:209–213). Work of extremely high quality may signal that a portrait depicts
a public figure; more telling are multiple versions and copies of a portrait: members
of the imperial family, for example, would commission a new portrait to mark an
occasion—a victory, accession to the throne, the birth of an heir—and that portrait would be copied for dissemination around the empire (Swift 1923; Stuart
1939). If archaeologists can determine the event that occasioned the new portrait,
they can also gain insight into the sitter's values (for instance, Fittschen 1982).

Once a portrait is associated with a known individual, the temptation arises to
read its expression and demeanor for insights into his or her personality. Early
studies of Roman portraits were often explicitly psychological, especially in the
wake of Freud's theories of analysis; implicit psychological readings still abound,
often presenting portraits as simple illustrations of what literary sources describe.
Adult portraits of the emperor Caracalla illustrate both tendencies (Figure 8.5).
These images feature a distinct "X" forged across the face by diagonal creases
rising from the center of his eyebrows and deep lines running from his nose to
the edges of his mouth, as well as a twist of the head on the neck, which appears
to capture the tense energy of a tightly-coiled spring (Wood 1986:28–30). The
portraits are so distinctive, and the originals of such high quality, that scholars

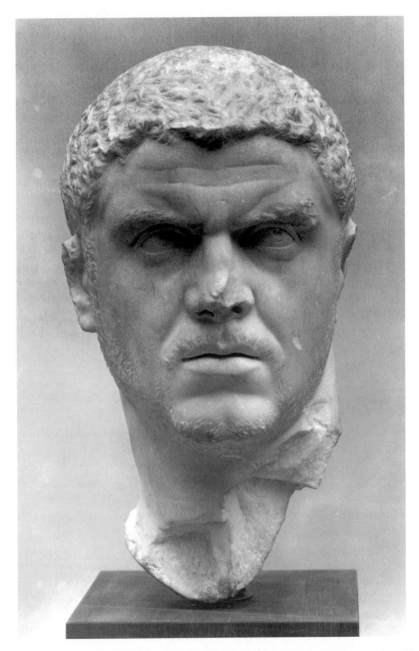

Figure 8.5 Portrait head of the emperor Caracalla, A.D. 211–217. The Metropolitan Museum of Art, New York. Photo: The Metropolitan Museum of Art, Samuel D. Lee Fund, 1940 [40.11.1A]

attribute them to a single sculptor, dubbed the Caracalla Master. To modern eyes, they seem to scowl, representing displeasure or ferocity. In doing so, they neatly complement and visually illustrate literary depictions of an unusually cruel man: co-emperor from A.D. 198 with his father, Septimius Severus, and then with his brother, Geta, he achieved sole authority in 212 by having Geta executed and condemning his memory—a fate he had already meted out to his own wife, Plautilla, and his father-in-law, Plautianus (*Scriptores Historiae Augustae*, Marcus Antoninus). The psychological interpretation of his portraiture aims to read the sculpture for insight into the sitter's character, while at the same time imposing on the visual evidence personality traits described by ancient writers.

Yet when read in the context of other Greek and Roman sculptures, Caracalla's images tell a different story. In his sculpted portraits of Alexander the Great, Lysippus turned the general's head on his neck, and this pose, like Alexander's famous cowlick, was imitated by Roman leaders who identified themselves with him (Wood 1986:29). Moreover, in Roman relief sculptures like the Great Trajanic Frieze, an expression that appears today to be a snarl, and a suggestion of pent-up energy, are traits that characterize Roman soldiers, expressing qualities valued in men of action: they amount to a military "style" (loosely defined as the treatment of surface and decorative detail). What the portraits of Caracalla actually reveal is the emperor's *political* personality: they align him with the soldiery, whose loyalty had raised his father to the throne. If any consonance exists with literary sources, it lies in Cassius Dio's record (75.2.2–3) of Severus' death-bed exhortation to his sons: enrich the soldiers and despise the rest of the world. These portraits belong squarely within a Roman visual language which, like Latin literary genres, operated with distinct conventions. To an untrained eye, Roman conventions may not be as apparent as, for instance, the half-profile, half-frontal stance of an Egyptian figure. Yet recognizing them is critical to understanding what Roman individuals hoped to express in their images. During the empire, the kind of stylistic "quotation" identified in the portrait of Caracalla is commonplace; so for the early Julio-Claudians, or Trajan, we might suspect that any quotation from Augustus' portraiture—characterized by a smoothness of features that deliberately evoked Classical Greek sculptures, a particular arrangement of locks in a full head of hair (evocative of Alexander the Great's cowlick)—should be treated with suspicion (although Tiberius or Caligula might have chosen to cultivate the looks of Augustan portraits in life). Quotations in architectural style, and not just portraiture, could add a layer of meaning as well. Scholars interpret Augustus' sustained and widespread use of Classical and Hellenistic styles (Corinthian column capitals, for instance) as an attempt to suggest that Augustan Rome was both the cultural heir to, and the conqueror of, Classical Athens and the great Hellenistic cities (Zanker 1988; Favro 1996).

If literary sources can be misleading as one attempts to read visual culture, they are doubly hazardous when they have influenced restorations. Emperor from A.D. 54 to 58, Nero is best known today from ancient historians' accounts of the later, tumultuous years of his reign, which portray a tyrannical, self-indulgent *artiste*, at violent odds with the people he ruled (Suetonius, *Nero*; Tacitus, *Annales*

13–15). Revisionist histories now recognize these accounts to have been penned by a hostile elite (Griffin 1985; Elsner and Masters 1994; Champlin 2003); yet their effect lingers on in a portrait in Rome's Capitoline Museum, which depicts a heavy-set, double-chinned man, with a full-lipped mouth and side-burns meeting under the chin as a weak beard—the imagined visual equivalent of Suetonius' decadent despot. In fact, that is exactly what it is: only a small fragment—the foremost locks of hair, the forehead, the eyes and most of the nose—is ancient, and derives not from a portrait of Nero, but from a portrait of Domitian; the rest is a baroque restoration (Fittschen and Zanker 1985:1.35, no. 31, pls. 32–33).

The fact that visual ideals and notions of beauty, like facial expressions, are culturally determined contributes further to the complexities inherent in finding an individual in a portrait. These ideals influence the style in which a sitter is represented, as is easily illustrated in Republican male portraits (Figure 8.6). Their faces are seared with deep lines, and marked with warts and crooked features; sagging jowls and balding pates capture the ravages of age (Kleiner 1992:31–40; Kuttner 2004:318). As a group, in fact, they seem distinctive precisely for being individual; the modern term applied to them, veristic (from Latin *verus*, true), exacerbates this impression. Because of the preferences of such influential early art historians as J. J. Winckelmann, today's dominant western ideal is deeply influenced by the smooth planes of classical Greek sculpture (Potts 1994), and as a result these Republican images do little to appeal to a modern sensibility. Yet, like the Greek images, they represent an ideal, which lay deep at the heart of the Republic: the governmental system was built upon the premise that with age and experience came the requisite wisdom to govern at the highest levels, with their minimum age requirements. A youthful image in the Greek mold, while befitting a youthful Augustus whose authority lay outside the terms of the Republican constitution, would not have furthered an aspiring praetor or consul in the Republican period (Kleiner 1992:31–38).

Reading Republican examples of portraiture for physical individuality is something of an act of faith. The possibility exists that the sitter yielded entirely to contemporary idealization, and may not have remotely resembled his own portrait. Conversely, he may have looked very much like his image. In between are all kinds of other possibilities: for instance that, in life, he contrived to look exactly as his portrait suggests, in response to society's ideals. Taking a middle road, one might conclude that the language of verism was one of exaggeration; a strategy for finding the man, then, would be to remove the idealization, leaving a sitter who looked somewhat like his portrait, but less so.

In portraits produced by the Tetrarchs at the end of the third century A.D. and the beginning of the fourth, one can no longer even identify a political individual. Four porphyry statues now immured in the southwest corner of the Basilica of San Marco in Venice depict the two Augusti and two Caesars who shared rule of the empire (Figure 8.7). The men are arranged in two pairs, and each pair is engaged in a close embrace. Clad in nearly-identical military gear, with Pannonian caps and ornate bird's-head handled swords, the figures are all

Figure 8.6 Veristic portrait of veiled man, mid-first century B.C., Vatican Museums. Photo: author

Figure 8.7 Portrait group of Tetrarchs, ca. A.D. 300, Venice. Photo: author

but indistinguishable from one another; in fact, the only notable difference between them is that two are bearded and two close-shaven (Kleiner 1992:401–404). The omission of personal traits, the relatively smooth planes of the faces, along with the squat, unnaturalistic proportions, render the statues abstract in style—a style that, along with the close grouping of the figures, suitably expresses Diocletian's aim to subordinate individual rulers to the office they occupied (L'Orange 1965).

What to commission?

Buildings may appear to yield fewer clues about political personalities and their ideologies than portraits. Yet information emerges from architecture and sculpture in a multitude of similar ways. For instance, the simple evidence of what individuals chose to commission is telling. As we have seen, tombs formed an especially versatile type of commission, and by the late first century B.C. it was not unusual for powerful Roman families to build conspicuous ones. Augustus appears to have been especially anxious to do so: his Mausoleum was one of the first buildings of his long reign, begun immediately upon his delayed return to Rome after defeating Mark Antony at Actium (Figure 8.4). In many ways, this was the most challenging period of his career: he had killed a fellow-Roman, and a man with strong support in Rome, in civil war; and he had returned in power but with no constitutional place in a Republic (Galinsky 1996). Many Romans seemed inclined to accept his authority, and the Senate had made a god of the last man to hold a quasi-monarchic position—but not without first assassinating him (Weinstock 1971; Meier 1982). Archaeologists have puzzled over the priority the relatively young general made of constructing a tomb at this juncture. Until recently, a popular (and highly improbable) explanation drew heavily upon literary accounts of his poor health, and proposed that he anticipated an early death (Gardthausen 1891:980).

A more likely possibility is that Augustus wanted a permanent marker to position him in the Roman landscape, and, like a column or an arch, a tomb—though implicitly public—was a privately funded monument with no need for the Senatorial sanction that might have begged too many awkward questions. As a tomb, moreover, none would dare desecrate it, as Sulla had desecrated Marius' trophy on the Capitoline (MacKay 2000). In the context of recent events, it was also a politically charged monument, through which he might have hoped to frame his own ideals and gain public support by confirming his victory and justifying civil war. Literary sources (Suetonius, *Divus Augustus* 17; Plutarch, *Antonius* 58.3–8) indicate that, before Actium, Augustus had illegally procured his rival's will from the Vestal Virgins. When he read its contents to the Senate, Romans learnt of Mark Antony's instructions for his burial in Alexandria, which they saw as a breach of loyalty and a readiness to marginalize Rome in favor of Egypt. The contrast with Mark Antony's intentions for burial bolstered Augustus' image as the city's savior, and further cast his enemy as a foreign, rather than a civil, foe

(Kraft 1967:195–196; Davies 2000: 50–67). There may even have been an ironic twist: Mark Antony's death, an ignominious suicide in the arms of Cleopatra, had occurred within the walls of her unfinished tomb, a fact that paintings displayed in Augustus' triumph may well have depicted.

Like Republican statesmen, Augustus aligned his political agendas with piety, boasting, in his *Res Gestae* (*RG*), that he constructed 12 temples and restored 82 (*RG* 19–20). He turned down the recommendation of a temple in his own honor (Suetonius, *Divus Augustus* 52). Instead he claimed credit for the temple to the deified Julius Caesar in the forum (*RG* 19), which unambiguously proclaimed his adoptive father the first divinized Roman since Romulus; the first temple he built after Actium (at about the same time as the Mausoleum) was the Pantheon, with Marcus Agrippa as overseer (De Fine Licht 1968; MacDonald 1976, Heene 2003). The choice speaks volumes about his intentions: celebrating all the gods together, it placed his authority under the expansive aegis of the whole pantheon. The display of a statue of Julius Caesar in the cella, and statues of Augustus and Agrippa in the porch, shows that the building stayed close to the Hellenistic origins of the concept of a pantheon, which included living and deceased members of the ruling family among the gods (Cassius Dio 53.27.2–4; Loerke 1982). The inclusive nature of a pantheon, and the range of statues placed in this structure, spelt out the implications of Augustus' close tie to Caesar's divinity.

What an emperor chose to restore or rebuild can speak as eloquently as what he built from the ground up. Agrippa's Pantheon perished in a fire that coursed through the Campus Martius in A.D. 80, and Domitian's restoration of it was destroyed by lightning. As it now stands, the Pantheon is a Hadrianic (or possibly Trajanic) structure, dated on the basis of brickstamps. The later emperor's debt is made clear by the inscription, M·AGRIPPA L·F· COS·TERTIUM FECIT (Marcus Agrippa, son of Lucius, three times consul, made this). The restoration placed its patron in a selectively edited historical context, visibly tying Hadrian to the empire's founding father (and emphatically *not* to the discredited Domitian, whose restoration is nowhere mentioned); and the very nature of the building stressed the divine status of those who had successfully occupied Hadrian's position.

The significance of the site

A great deal can also be revealed about an individual both by the site he selects for a work of art or architecture, and by its spatial relationship to other works. Regrettably few portraits were found in their original context, but scholars believe that they were displayed in public rooms of homes, in tombs, and, in some cases, in public spaces like the forum (Anderson and Nista 1988; Gazda and Haeckl 1993; D'Ambra 1998). In each case, the audience differed, as did, presumably, the intended message. A portrait within a home primarily addressed visiting clients and peers. Taking its place among images of ancestors in the atrium, it established the patron's social place, in order to express authority or a competitive edge (Flower 1996). Portraits in public spaces, with their huge and diverse crowds,

Figure 8.8 Funerary relief of freedpersons, early Augustan period. Rome, Museo Nazionale delle Terme, Inv. 80728. Photo: author

gave an individual a political presence. It was mostly family members who viewed portraits within tombs, while any passerby on the way to or from the city, or milling around during festivals for the dead, might see a portrait on the tomb's exterior. This made decoration of the tomb façade an attractive option for freed-persons, who did not run for office, and who, during enslavement, had no legal status or family relationships. Toward the end of the Republic and in the early Empire, they would place rectangular reliefs depicting groups of (usually) frontal bust-length portraits on tomb façades lining roads outside the city (Kleiner 1977) (Figure 8.8). Accompanying inscriptions would indicate their freed status, as would rings carved or painted on their fingers. The use of a sculptural style that was dominant in elite circles—in this case Augustan classicism—may likewise indicate the individuals' desire to stress their integration into free society. The group panel format enables the freedpersons to stress familial relationships (some-times emphasized by linked right hands, indicating marriage), now legally acknowledged. Similarly, archaeologists occasionally discover free-standing sculptures (or their inscriptions) in groups, and the spatial relationships between figures can be read for meaning—to suggest dynastic succession, for instance, or relative hierarchy (Rose 1997).

What little we know about the constraints put upon public figures when choos-ing a location for a building suggests that they were remarkably free to build certain types of monument upon public land; naturally they had an even freer hand in placing buildings on land they owned, which in the emperor's case meant an increasingly large portion of the city. Some choices were made simply to emphasize visibility. For example, changes in tomb placement during the course of the Republic bear witness to a growing awareness of the value of a conspicuous site: in the early years, tombs were arranged in loosely scattered cemeteries outside the city gates, and only vaguely oriented toward nearby roads. By at least the second century B.C., patrons began to align tomb façades with the road's edge, so that the monument would not just be seen by family members visiting for funerary rituals on anniversaries and cult days, but would also address passers-by head-on (von Hesberg 1992). Moreover, literary evidence suggests that Romans were even more conscious of topographical associations than we tend to be (Edwards 1996; Davies 2001:29–31). Setting was integral to stories of history and legend that were passed down the generations, establishing a connection between past and present, and creating a sense of history's relevance to the present and the future. As a result, buildings and landmarks were impassive but powerful stimuli for memories of events and people. Conscious of this, Romans exploited the emotive and evocative qualities of places, learning to harness topographical associations, as well as juxtapositions and alignments with other structures or landmarks, for ideological objectives. Understanding a patron's choices generally requires developing a deep familiarity with the city, its image, and civic associations (Favro 1996).

Two particularly monumental tombs reveal different ways in which a site could reinforce a political agenda. In the early third century B.C., L. Cornelius Scipio Scapula "Barbatus," consul in 298 B.C. (or his son, L. Cornelius Scipio, consul in 259) built a large sepulcher for his family, known from literary sources to be outside the Porta Capena (Cicero, *Tusculanae Disputationes* 1.7.13; Livy 38.56). The discovery in 1614 of an inscription commemorating L. Cornelius Scipio went largely unnoticed; but on finding two sarcophagi naming members of the Scipio family in 1780, the Sassi brothers, then owners of the land, recognized that they had come across the famous tomb, between the Via Latina and the Via Appia. Subsequent excavations proved that access to it was from the Via Appia (Coarelli 1988:8–9). Since this new road led toward Greece, some archaeologists believe that Scipio selected a location close to it to promote his philhellenic political ideas (Coarelli 1988:26–27).

As for Augustus' Mausoleum, logistical reasons might go a long way in explaining its placement on the northern Campus Martius: the broad plain beside the Tiber afforded easy access for building materials arriving by boat, as well as an unobstructed view from afar for the multitude of people who frequented the area. Yet, for a Roman, the Campus was also rich in associations and civic memories (Favro 1996; Coarelli 1997). The region was one of Rome's most sacred, and burial there implied privilege: Sulla, Hirtius and Vibius Pansa (consuls who died at Mutina opposing Mark Antony), as well as Julius Caesar and his daughter Julia, were all interred there by the Senate's special dispensation after their deaths. Implicit in building a tomb in such a place was the promise of a life spent in honorable service to the state. For most Romans, the Campus Martius also evoked a dramatic moment in the career of Rome's first founder, Romulus: it was there, according to tradition, that Romulus was last seen, before his ascension to the heavens (enveloped in a cloud) and the unanimous recognition that he had become an immortal (Livy 1.16.1). Although Augustus would be advised that adopting the title "Romulus" was too bold a move for Roman palates, the topographical association nevertheless alluded to the first king; and although Augustus could not presume present or future divinity, the site hinted at what he could not claim outright (Coarelli 1983; Davies 2000:137–142).

With the benefit of advanced surveying and planimetry available to the ancient Romans, individuals could move beyond juxtaposition and general association to contrive significant alignments between buildings and other topographical features (Dilke 1985). The broad implications of the site of Augustus' Mausoleum drew additional strength from its calculated planimetrical relationship with Agrippa's Pantheon. Scholars debate the Agrippan Pantheon's form and orientation; yet drawings executed by Georges Chédanne after excavations beneath the existing Pantheon in 1892 offer evidence that it may have consisted of a circular unroofed cella, surrounded by a barrel-vaulted ring-colonnade, and entered through a rectangular porch on the north side (Loerke 1982; Dumser 2002). If this is the correct reconstruction, then the Pantheon and the Mausoleum of Augustus, under construction contemporaneously, shared a common circular form (Broucke 2000; Davies 2000:137–142). The axis through the center of the Pantheon was 5° west of north, and—if projected northward—it ran into the Mausoleum: thus a visitor standing in the temple's porch had a direct sight-line to the tomb. The alignment expressed visually a progression from mortal (deceased, cremated and buried within the tomb) to immortal (honored amongst fellow-deities in the Pantheon; Castagnoli 1947). This change of status was precisely what the Senate would agree upon in A.D. 14, symbolized at the late emperor's cremation by the release of an eagle from the pyre to carry Augustus' spirit through the flames to the heavens (Cassius Dio 56.41–42; also Suetonius, *Divus Augustus* 100).

Meanings in materials

Just as we tend to be less conscious of the power of place than the Romans were, so, in many ways, we have become de-sensitized to materials, other than to recognize that opulent materials—colored marbles, precious metals—signify wealth and luxury. This is due in large part to the present-day wide availability of these materials, and also to the easy mastery of the technologies that make them available. Today, for instance, a portrait in bronze is just an expensive commission; yet for many early societies it marked formidable power, showing that the patron could control the technology that was necessary to craft weaponry. Similarly, the use of porphyry for the tetrarchic portraits described above clearly marked the figures as imperial, since the deep purple stone, quarried in Egypt, was reserved for royal use (Delbrück 1932).

In early Rome, the chief construction materials were wood, tufa, mud-brick, and terracotta (Adam 1994; Claridge 1998:37–43; in general, Taylor 2003). As Roman armies faced Greek cities in south Italy and Sicily, marble began to trickle into the city, and the flow grew steady with the conquest of Greece. The reaction of many Romans was positive: just as Scipio Barbatus demonstrated an expansive worldview in locating his tomb, so, around 146 B.C., Q. Metellus Macedonicus could commemorate his Macedonian triumph by commissioning, from the Greek architect Hermodorus, Rome's first marble temple (Gruen 1992:116). The translucent stone publicized the wide implications of Metellus' valor, and promised to transform Rome into the visual rival of any Mediterranean metropolis. Yet some conservatives, like Cato, built political careers on denouncing marble as a symptom of eastern luxury, representing a dangerous hubris. In a speech crafted for him by Livy, Cato nostalgically celebrated the humbler building materials that had kept Rome's gods favorable (Livy 34.4.4; Pollitt 1986:159).

The emperors used materials most effectively to disseminate ideology. To reduce the cost of importing Greek stone, Augustus initiated full-scale exploitation of marble quarries Caesar had opened in Carrara, and marble became the signature material of his urban renewal program (Suetonius, *Augustus* 28.3). This stone, with its bright whiteness and luminosity, was the material of choice for his own buildings (sections of the drum of his Mausoleum, for instance), and, presumably with his encouragement, for construction by others during his reign (such as Tiberius' restoration of the Temple of Castor; Favro 1996). It must have buttressed his claim of ushering in a brand new age, at the same time as drawing inevitable parallels with other leading cities of the Mediterranean. Archaeologists are divided on how rigidly emperors subsequently controlled the marble trade (for instance, Fant 2001), and with it the message-bearing potential of rich stone. It is clear that they had a monopoly on the use of porphyry, as discussed; and it is also certain that by the second century a wide array of colored marbles was available for imperial exploitation in Rome (see Claridge 1998:37–43). Their use offered more than a coloristic effect: it emphasized the far reach of imperial authority. The decoration of Hadrian's Pantheon alone, for instance, presupposed trade with or control over Egypt (gray and rose-pink granite, porphyry), Phrygia (Phrygian purple and white), Chemtou, Tunisia (Numidian yellow stone), and Teos (Lucullan red and black stone) (Figure 8.9). In a sense, these stones were symbolic of the ecumenical reach of empire that was at the heart of Hadrian's political persona.

Decoding design

Just as style was open to manipulation to serve a political ideology in portraiture and architecture, so was architectural design (ground-plan and tectonic qualities; see, in general, Wilson Jones 2000). For the most part, for instance, Republican temples in Rome are startlingly similar in design, even when concrete technology had been adequately mastered to free architects from post-and-lintel construction (Boëthius 1978). Where their designs are known, the vast majority appear to have been raised on a high platform, with a frontal staircase, a deep columned porch and a single or triple cella. Where variation occurs—the transverse cellas of the Temples of Veiovis and Castor and Pollux *in circo* (Coarelli 1993; Albertoni 1999), for example— archaeologists have tended to ascribe the choices to topographical restrictions.

Figure 8.9 Pantheon, Rome, interior view, A.D. 117–125. Photo: Art Resource

This overwhelming conservatism in design may be due in part to the relative speed with which the temples were often constructed. It also suggests that those who commissioned them were conscious of working for the well-being of the state within a collaborative system, one which valued a standard—egalitarian—vocabulary over blatant innovation and singularity. Thus, the commissioning magistrate drew individual prestige from the *commission* itself, but subordinated individuality to common state interests in the *design*. A greater diversity in forms by the mid-first century B.C. mirrors the degeneration of such a collaborative spirit.

The circular Mausoleum of Santa Costanza on Rome's Via Nomentana, usually assigned to the mid-fourth century A.D. and a daughter of Constantine the Great, offers a good illustration of how an architect could draw on earlier designs to

Figure 8.10 Mausoleum of Santa Costanza, Rome, interior view, ca. A.D. 340. Photo: Art Resource

make his building speak (Figure 8.10) (Mackie 1997). Inside the Mausoleum, an annular ambulatory, covered with lavish decorative and figural mosaics, recalls the annular corridors of Augustus' Mausoleum, discussed above, and, with its low ceiling level, contributes to the creation of an intimate, shadowy terrestrial space. Meanwhile, the tomb's soaring dome, pierced with windows, calls to mind the Pantheon's celestial dome with light entering from on high (a point to be returned to below). As suggested earlier, Augustus implied a progression from mortal to immortal status through the choice of a Mausoleum and a Pantheon, through their shared circular form and their topographical alignment. Through allusive design, the Mausoleum of Santa Costanza powerfully condenses the same message into a single building.

While archaeologists readily acknowledge that a patron's adherence to a design or style might suggest allegiance to a shared ideological stance, and that, conversely, a departure from norms might indicate ideological difference, isolating intended style and design is not always straightforward. Augustus' Mausoleum illustrates just how elusive an individual's public persona can be for archaeologists (Figure 8.4). Ravages inflicted on the tomb over time have left much of its design and decoration unclear, and while scholars agree that Augustus' ideology is reflected in references to earlier design prototypes, there is little consensus on what those prototypes might have been. Etruscan tumulus tombs are a possibility, as is the ancient site of Troy, where huge mounds covering prehistoric villages resembled magnificent royal graves. The Mausoleum's architectural qualities, as well as its name and sheer size, recall dynastic tombs of Asia Minor such as the Mausoleum at Halicarnassos, while a number of scholars see Egyptian qualities in the tomb which may have brought to mind the mausoleum Ptolemy IV Philopator built for Alexander the Great in Alexandria (see bibliography in Davies 2000). Given the complexity of the political climate in which Augustus maneuvered, and the necessary nuances of his public persona, the possibility exists that all or some of these prototypes played a controlled part in some measure. Just as predetermined assumptions about Nero led to the faulty reconstruction of Domitian's portrait, so scholars' convictions about a political personality can become inseparable from their interpretations and reconstructions of architectural evidence. Thus, it is unclear which came first, Giglioli's conviction that the grass-covered earthen tumuli of Etruria would—with their archaic simplicity and evocation of the *mos maiorum* of the Republic that Augustus claimed to restore—make ideologically appropriate prototypes for Augustus' Mausoleum, or his conclusion that a simple earthen mound was the best way to make sense of the surviving archaeological evidence.

Experiencing the dynamics of design

For all that a building could project about an individual through location, material, style and design, it was perhaps at its most powerful when it presented and framed the individual through the dynamic qualities of its design (Arnheim 1977). At the simplest level, a building's design could draw public attention, and this is presumably the motivation behind the increasing eclecticism of tomb design in the late Republic. Adjustments to the Tomb of the Scipios, already mentioned, constitute a particularly early and sophisticated solution to the problem of how to draw attention to the message an individual hoped to express. As initially designed by Scipio Barbatus, the tomb had four subterranean galleries in a quadrangular plan, with two intersecting corridors in the center. In ca. 150–135 B.C., Scipio Aemilianus raised a monumental columned tufa façade above this, matching attention to old interior details with an impressive new exterior which signaled the family's political prominence and wealth from afar. Statues stood in niches in the façade and beckoned visitors to approach; like the masked actors who played the parts of deceased ancestors in funerary rituals (Polybius 6.54.2), the statues would remind them as they drew near of the exploits of two particularly illustrious ancestors, Scipio Africanus, conqueror of Hannibal in 202, and Scipio Asiaticus. A third, depicting the poet Ennius, represented the Scipios' intellectual pursuits. Scenes of warfare painted on the podium inserted the static figures into a visual narrative that activated and controlled a viewer's memories (Coarelli 1988: 26–32). As an entirety, the façade both commemorated ancestors and celebrated their living descendants; equally importantly, by displaying them as *exempla* for the living, it projected the family into the future.

On the interior of the family tomb, Scipio Aemilianus added subsidiary galleries, enlarging the underground complex, where sarcophagi and urns were displayed for a visitor as if in a museum. The notion that a visitor's physical response to a building could be controlled and manipulated through design appears to have gained force here and elsewhere. At the Tomb of Caecilia Metella, a masonry circular tomb surmounted by a grass mound built beside the Via Appia in the late first century B.C., there appears to have been a special passageway into the burial chamber for visitors, designed as an elevated "viewing gallery" (Paris 2001). And in Augustus' Mausoleum, a series of concentric walls surrounding the burial chamber encouraged a visitor to walk around the burials at the center, re-enacting a characteristic Roman funerary ritual of circumambulation which served both to protect the dead and to honor them in perpetuity (von Hesberg and Panciera 1994; Davies 1997). Even in death, the Mausoleum framed and preserved the emperor's image.

Just how effectively an architect could exploit a building's dynamic qualities to control a visitor's experience and to frame and promote a living being is clear in one of the best preserved temples of antiquity, the Pantheon. As observed already, the concept of a pantheon, the rebuilding of an Agrippan structure, the location, and the very materials used in the temple: all provided perspectives on the emperor as a public figure. The building's design offered the *coup de grâce*, the stage upon which he appeared in relation to others, as if in a climactic revelation.

In antiquity, the Pantheon stood at the south end of a large rectangular court. On the three remaining sides were porticoes, which also extended on the south up to the sides of the temple's magnificent pedimented porch, obscuring the view of the temple's drum (see MacDonald 1982:96). Stepping up to the temple's octastyle façade, a visitor would have been struck by the forest of massive monolithic columns in gray and pink granite, soaring upward. In other respects, however, the form would have been familiar, evoking the usual expectation of a rectilinear cella beyond the great bronze doors, with a vast cult statue inside. Yet on crossing the threshold, nothing was perceptible but a brilliant shaft of light, piercing a pervasive darkness from high above. As eyes grew accustomed to the shadows, a huge circular hall was revealed, pierced at ground level by seven niches; an attic level was decorated with engaged pilasters and bronze grilles, and high overhead soared a vast dome, pierced at its apex with a 27-foot *oculus* opening onto the sky (Figure 8.9). For many an ancient viewer, the cella's spherical form would probably have evoked thoughts of perfection and eternity, both symbolized by circles; and the dome's coffered surface, emblazoned with bronze rosettes, must have conjured up the night sky (MacDonald 1976:76–92).

For all its suggestive symbolism, the cella's circular plan offered no clear sense of where to progress from the door, except that with its vision of the heavens the oculus seemed to beckon—an effect exacerbated by the calculated perspective of the dome's coffers, which makes sense only from the center of the hall. The effect on a visitor when he reached the center was startling because of the dramatic synergy of molded space and applied decoration. For centuries, applying the standards of architectural design in the Renaissance and later, scholars have faulted the Pantheon's architect for failing to align the ribs of the dome coffers with the pilasters in the attic zone and with the columns in the ground-level niches, and to be sure, he did not achieve a static linear perfection (MacDonald 1976:72–74). Yet, by avoiding continuous lines from the top of the interior to the bottom, he deprived the dome of "anchors," creating instead the visual effect that it hovers at an indeterminable height above a visitor, neither close nor far; the visitor thus stands, paradoxically, both sheltered and exposed. Moreover, without anchors the dome appears cast into perpetual motion; for a visitor standing at the cella's center with head tilted to the sky, it seems to spin overhead like the heavens it evokes (Loerke 1990). Exacerbated by an all-but-imperceptible rise in the floor at the center, this phenomenon produces a sensation so close to vertigo that one's instinct is to return to the safe embrace of the curved wall. This was the building, so Cassius Dio declares (69.7.1), in which Hadrian liked to hold court, greeting embassies from other nations and resolving disputes, with the emperor cast by the building's form into controller of this revolving universe, at one with the forces of his cosmos. Illuminated, one might presume, by the oculus, the emperor appeared as a divine revelation to a guest already overawed and entirely manipulated by the building enclosing him.

Conclusion

These pages have offered a number of strategies for reaching into the archaeological record in search of individual personalities. These include exploring the significance of an object's style, design and location, as well as considering why the patron commissioned one type of object rather than another. Inevitably, the richest picture emerges from deploying as many different tactics as possible. Still, in the end, what classical archaeology yields is a masterfully crafted public image. What it does not yield so easily with these methods—if at all—is the individual behind the image, either subject or artist. It does not divulge, for instance, the extent to which a finished work reflects a patron's wishes, versus an artist's or architect's intervention. While archaeology reveals some evidence for workshop practice (e.g., Conlin 1997), the relative roles of patron and artist or architect remain poorly understood, leaving scholars to conjecture that on the whole, the artist, while never completely absent, aimed to fulfill his patron's goals rather than express his own personality or concerns. Conversely, though ancient authors and modern archaeologists speak of a statesman or an emperor building monuments, and inscriptions such as that of Pantheon seem to agree, archaeology does not tell us how involved he was in the details and decisions involved in his visual programs. The answer is probably that each case was different, and it is not unlikely that politicians relied on advisors to craft a public image to legitimate their power. What the crafted image yields in turn, in some abundance, is insight into the values of Roman society that these individuals were anxious to embody.

REFERENCES

Adam, J.-P. 1994 Roman Building: Materials and Techniques. Trans. A. Mathews. Bloomington and Indianapolis: Indiana University Press.

Albertoni, M. 1999 Veiovis, Aedes (in Capitolio). *In* Lexicon Topographicum Urbis Romae, vol. 5. Eva Margareta Steinby, ed. Pp. 99–100. Rome: Edizioni Quasar.

Anderson, James C., Jr. 1997 Roman Architecture and Society. Baltimore: Johns Hopkins University Press.

Anderson, Max, and L. Nista 1988 Roman Portraits in Context: Imperial and Private Likenesses from the Museo Nazionale Romano. Rome: De Luca Edizioni d'Arte.

Andronikos, Manolis 1994 Vergina: The Royal Tombs and the Ancient City. Athens: Ekdotike Athenon.

Arnheim, Rudolph 1977 The Dynamics of Architectural Form. Berkeley: University of California Press.

Beard, Mary 1991 Adopting an Approach, II. *In* Looking at Greek Vases. Tom Rasmussen and Nigel Spivey, eds. Pp. 12–35. Cambridge: Cambridge University Press.

——, and Michael Crawford 1999 Rome in the Late Republic. 2nd edition. London: Duckworth Press.

——, and John Henderson 2001 Classical Art: From Greece to Rome. Oxford: Oxford University Press.

Boardman, John 1975 Athenian Red Figure Vases: The Archaic Period. London: Thames and Hudson.

Boëthius, Axel 1978 Etruscan and Early Roman Architecture. New Haven: Yale University Press.

Bonacasa N., and G. Rizza, eds. 1988 Ritratto ufficiale e ritratto privato: Atti del II Conferenza internazionale sul ritratto romano. Rome: Consiglio nazionale delle ricerche.

Bose, Partha 2003 Alexander the Great's Art of Strategy: The Timeless Leadership Lessons of History's Greatest Empire Builder. New York: Gotham.

Bosworth, A. B. 1988 Conquest and Empire: The Reign of Alexander the Great. Cambridge: Cambridge University Press.

Briant, Pierre 1996 Alexander the Great: Man of Action, Man of Spirit. New York: Abrams.

Brilliant, Richard 1991 Portraiture. Cambridge, MA: Harvard University Press.

Broucke, Pieter B. F. J. 2000 The Mausoleum of Augustus and the Pantheon of Agrippa. American Journal of Archaeology 104:366.

Carter, Joseph Coleman 2006 Discovering the Greek Countryside at Metaponto. Ann Arbor: University of Michigan Press.

Cartledge, Paul 2004 Alexander the Great: The Hunt for a New Past. New York: The Overlook Press.

Cary, George 1956 The Medieval Alexander. Cambridge: Cambridge University Press.

Castagnoli, F. 1947 Il Campo Marzio nell'antichità. Memorie. Atti della Accademia nazionale dei Lincei, Classe di scienze morali, storiche e filologiche 8.1:93–193.

Champlin, Edward 2003 Nero. Cambridge and London: Harvard University Press.

Cherry, John F. 1992 Beazley in the Bronze Age? Reflections on Attribution Studies in Aegean Prehistory. *In* EIKON: Aegean Bronze Age Iconography: Shaping a Methodology. Robert Laffineur and Janice L. Crowley, eds. Pp. 123–144. Aegaeum, Annales d'archéologie égéenne de l'Université de Liège 8. Liège: Université de Liège.

Claridge, Amanda 1998 Rome: An Oxford Archaeological Guide. Oxford: Oxford University Press.

Clarke, John R. 1996 "Just Like Us": Cultural Constructions of Sexuality and Race in Roman Art. The Art Bulletin 78:599–603.

Coarelli, Filippo 1983 L'apoteosi di Augusto e l'apoteosi di Romolo. Analecta Romana Instituti Danici Supplementum. 10:41–46.

——1988 Il Sepolcro degli Scipioni a Roma. Rome: Fratelli Palombi Editori.

——1993 Castor et Pollux in Circo (fasti): Aedes Castoris in Circo Flaminio (Vitr.). In Lexicon Topographicum Vrbis Romae I. Eva Margarete Steinby ed. Pp. 245–46. Rome: Edizioni Quasar.

——1997 Il Campo Marzio dalle origini alla fine della repubblica. Rome: Quasar.

Cohen, Ada 1997 The Alexander Mosaic: Stories of Victory and Defeat. Cambridge: Cambridge University Press.

Conlin, Diane A. 1997 The Artists of the Ara Pacis: The Process of Hellenization in Roman Relief Sculpture. Chapel Hill and London: University of North Carolina Press.

Cullhed, Mats 1994 Conservator Urbis Suae: Studies in the Politics and Propaganda of the Emperor Maxentius. Stockholm: Acta Instituti Romani Regni Sueciae.

D'Ambra, Eve 1998 Art and Identity in the Roman World. London: The Everyman Art Library.

Danforth, Loring 1995 The Macedonian Conflict: Ethnic Nationalism in a Transnational World. Princeton: Princeton University Press.

Davies, Penelope J. E. 1997 The Politics of Perpetuation: Trajan's Column and the Art of Commemoration. American Journal of Archaeology 101:41–65.

——2000 Death and the Emperor: Roman Imperial Funerary Monuments from Augustus to Marcus Aurelius. Cambridge: Cambridge University Press.

——2001 "What Worse Than Nero, What Better Than His Baths?" Damnatio Memoriae and Roman Architecture. In From Caligula to Constantine: Tyranny and Transformation in Roman Portraiture. Eric R. Varner, ed. Pp. 27–44. Atlanta: Michael C. Carlos Museum.

——in press Exploring the International Arena: The Tarquins' Aspirations for the Temple of Jupiter Optimus Maximus. In The Proceedings of the XVIth International Congress of Classical Archaeology. Carol Mattusch and Alice Donohue, eds. Boston 2003.

Davis, Norman, and Colin M. Kraay 1973 The Hellenistic Kingdoms: Portrait Coins and History. London: Thames and Hudson.

De Fine Licht, Kjeld 1968 The Rotunda in Rome: A Study of Hadrian's Pantheon. Copenhagen: Jutland Archaeological Society Publications 8.

De Maria, Sandro 1988 Gli archi onorari di Roma e dell'Italia romana. Rome: "L'Erma" di Bretschneider.

Delbrück, R. 1932 Antike Porphyrwerke. Berlin: W. de Gruyter & Co.

Dilke, O. A. W. 1985 Greek and Roman Maps. Baltimore: Johns Hopkins Press.

Dillon, Sheila 2006 Ancient Greek Portrait Sculpture: Contexts, Subjects, and Styles. New York: Cambridge University Press.

Dobres, Marcia-Anne, and John E. Robb, eds. 2000 Agency in Archaeology. London: Routledge.

Dumser, Elisha A. 2002 Pantheum. In Mapping Augustan Rome. Lothar Haselberger, David G. Romano, and Elisha A. Dumser, eds. Pp. 188–189. Journal of Roman Archaeology Supplement 50. Portsmouth, R.I.: Journal of Roman Archaeology.

Edwards, Catharine 1996 Writing Rome: Textual Approaches to the City. Cambridge: Cambridge University Press.

Elsner, Jaś, and Jamie Masters, eds. 1994 Reflections of Nero: Culture, History and Representation. London: Duckworth Press.

Empereur, Jean-Yves 2002 Alexandria: Jewel of Egypt. New York: Harry Abrams.

Fant, J. Clayton 2001 Rome's Marble Yards. Journal of Roman Archaeology 14.1: 167–198.

Favro, Diana 1996 The Urban Image of Augustan Rome. Cambridge: Cambridge University Press.

Fittschen, Klaus 1982 Die Bildnistypen der Faustina minor und die Fecunditas Augustae. Göttingen: Vandenhoeck and Ruprecht.

——, and Paul Zanker 1985 Katalog der römischen Porträts in den Capitolinischen Museen und den anderen kommunalen Sammlungen der Stadt Rom. Mainz am Rhein: Verlag Philipp von Zabern.

Fleming, Andrew 1973 Tombs for the Living. Man 8(2):177–193.

Flower, Harriet 1996 Ancestor Masks and Aristocratic Power in Roman Culture. Oxford: Clarendon Press.

Forsdyke, Sara 2005 Exile, Ostracism, and Democracy: The Politics of Expulsion in Ancient Greece. Princeton: Princeton University Press.

Fowler, Chris 2004 The Archaeology of Personhood: An Anthropological Approach. London: Routledge.

Fraser, Peter M. 1972 Ptolemaic Alexandria. Oxford: Clarendon Press.

——1996 Cities of Alexander the Great. Oxford: Clarendon Press.

Galinsky, Karl 1996 Augustan Culture. Princeton, NJ: Princeton University Press.

Gardthausen, V. 1891 Augustus und seine Zeit 1. Leipzig: B. G. Teubner.

Gazda, E. K. and A. E. Haeckl 1993 Roman Portraiture: Reflections on the Question of Context. Journal of Roman Archaeology 6:289–302.

Green, Peter 1989 Caesar and Alexander: Aemulatio, Imitatio, Comparatio. In Classical Bearings: Interpreting Ancient History and Culture. Peter Green, ed., Pp. 193–209. London: Thames and Hudson.

——1990 Alexander to Actium: The Hellenistic Age. London: Thames and Hudson.

Griffin, Miriam T. 1985 Nero, the End of a Dynasty. New Haven: Yale University Press.

Gruen, Erich S. 1992 Culture and National Identity in Republican Rome. Ithaca, NY: Cornell University Press.

Hadjinicolaou, Nicos, ed. 1997 Alexander the Great in European Art. Thessaloniki: Institute for Mediterranean Studies, Foundation for Research and Technology—Hellas.

Hammond, Nicholas G. L. 1993 The Macedonian Imprint on the Hellenistic World. In Hellenistic History and Culture. Peter Green, ed. Pp. 12–23. Berkeley: University of California Press.

——1997 The Genius of Alexander. London: Duckworth.

Heene, Gerd 2003 Baustelle Pantheon-Planung. Konstruktion, Logistik. Dusseldorf: Verlag Bau und Technik.

Hill, James N., and Joel Gunn, eds. 1977 The Individual in Prehistory: Studies of Variability in Style in Prehistoric Technologies. London: Academic Press.

Hodder, Ian, and Scott Hutson 2003 Reading the Past: Current Approaches to Interpretation in Archaeology. 3rd edn. Cambridge: Cambridge University Press.

Holliday, Peter J. 2002 The Origins of Roman Historical Commemoration in the Visual Arts. Cambridge: Cambridge University Press.

Hölscher, Tonio 2006 The Transformation of Victory into Power: From Event to Structure. *In* Representations of War in Ancient Rome. Sheila Dillon and Katherine Welch, eds. Pp. 27–48. Cambridge: Cambridge University Press.

Holt, Frank L. 1999 Thundering Zeus: The Making of Hellenistic Bactria. Berkeley: University of California Press.

——2005 Into the Land of Bones: Alexander the Great in Afghanistan. Berkeley: University of California Press.

Hopkins, John 2004 Reflections of Expansion: The Cloaca Maxima and Urban Image in Tarquin Rome. MA thesis, University of Texas at Austin.

Jex-Blake, K., and Eugénie Sellers, 1896 The Elder Pliny's Chapters on the History of Art, Trans. K. Jex-Blake, with Commentary and Historical Introduction by E. Sellers. London: Macmillan. (Reprint 1986, Chicago: Argonaut.)

Kampen, Natalie B. 1981 Image and Status: Roman Working Women in Ostia. Berlin: Gebr. Mann Verlag.

Kleiner, Diana E. E. 1977 Roman Group Portraiture: The Funerary Reliefs of the Late Republic and the Early Empire. New York: Garland Press.

——1992 Roman Sculpture. New Haven: Yale University Press.

——, and Susan B. Matheson, eds. 1996 I Claudia: Women in Ancient Rome. New Haven: Yale University Press.

Kraft, Konrad 1967 Der Sinn des Mausoleums des Augustus. Historia 16:189–206.

Kuttner, Ann L. 2004 Roman Art During the Republic. *In* The Cambridge Companion to the Roman Republic. Harriet Flower, ed. Pp. 294–321. Cambridge: Cambridge University Press.

Lane Fox, Robin 2005 The Making of *Alexander*: The Official Guide to the Epic Film Alexander. Oxford and London: R & I.

La Riche, William 1997 Alexandria: The Sunken City. London: Weidenfeld & Nicolson.

Lintott, Andrew 1999 The Constitution of the Roman Republic. Oxford: Clarendon Press.

Loerke, William C. 1982 Georges Chédanne and the Pantheon: A Beaux Arts Contribution to the History of Roman Architecture. Modulus: The University of Virginia School of Architecture Review: 40–55.

——1990 A Rereading of the Interior Elevation of Hadrian's Rotunda. Journal of the Society of Architectural Historians 49:22–43.

L'Orange, Hans Peter 1965 Art Forms and Civic Life in the Late Roman Empire. Princeton: Princeton University Press.

MacBain, Bruce 1980 Appius Claudius Caecus and the Via Appia. The Classical Quarterly 30:356–372.

MacDonald, William L. 1976 The Pantheon: Design, Meaning and Progeny. Cambridge, MA: Harvard University Press.

——1982 The Architecture of the Roman Empire, I: An Introductory Study. 2nd edition. New Haven: Yale University Press.

MacKay, Christopher S. 2000 Sulla and the Monuments: Studies in his Public Persona. Historia 49:161–210.

Mackie, G. 1997 A New Look at the Patronage of Santa Costanza, Rome. Byzantion 67:383–406.

Meier, Christian 1982 Caesar: A Biography. New York: Basic Books.

Meskell, Lynn 1999 Archaeologies of Social Life: Age, Sex, Class *et cetera* in Ancient Egypt. Oxford: Blackwell.

Morris, Ian 1987 Burial and Ancient Society: The Rise of the Greek City-State. Cambridge: Cambridge University Press.

Musgrave, Jonathan H. 1991 The Human Remains from Vergina Tombs I, II, and III: An Overview. The Ancient World 22.2:3–9.

Oikonomides, A. N. 1981 The Coins of Alexander the Great. Chicago: Ares.

Orlin, Eric M. 1997 Temples, Religion and Politics in the Roman Republic. Leiden: E. J. Brill.

Osborne, Robin 1987 Classical Landscape with Figures: The Ancient Greek City and its Countryside. London: George Philip.

——1998 Archaic and Classical Greek Art. Oxford: Oxford University Press.

Paris, Rita 2001 Mausoleo di Cecilia Metella e Castrum Caetani. In Archaeologia e Giubileo. Gli interventi a Roma e nel Lazio nel Piano per il Grande Giubileo del 2000. Fedora Filippi, ed. Pp. 316–321. Naples: Electa Napoli.

Pobjoy, Mark 2000 Building Inscriptions in Republican Italy: Euergetism, Responsibility and Civic Virtue. In The Epigraphic Landscape of Roman Italy. Alison E. Cooley, ed. Pp. 77–92. London: Institute of Classical Studies.

Pollitt, Jerome J. 1986 Art in the Hellenistic Age. Cambridge: Cambridge University Press.

Popham, M. R., P. G. Calligas, and L. H. Sackett, eds. 1993 Lefkandi II. The Protogeometric Building at Toumba, Part 2: The Excavation of the Building, its Architecture and Finds. British School at Athens Supplementary Vol. 23. London: British School at Athens.

Potts, Alex 1994 Flesh and the Ideal: Winckelmann and the Origins of Art History. New Haven: Yale University Press.

Prag, A. W., and R. Neave 1997 Making Faces: Using Forensic and Archaeological Evidence. London: British Museum Press.

Price, Martin J. 1991 The Coinage in the Name of Alexander the Great and Philip Arrhidaeus. London: British Museum Press.

Richardson, L., Jr. 1992 A New Topographical Dictionary of Ancient Rome. Baltimore: Johns Hopkins University Press.

Romey, Kristin 2004 The Forgotten Realm of Alexander. Archaeology 57(6):18–25.

Rose, C. Brian 1997 Dynastic Commemoration and Imperial Portraiture in the Julio-Claudian Period. Cambridge: Cambridge University Press.

Ross, David J. A. 1988 Alexander Historiatus: A Guide to Medieval Illustrated Alexander Literature. 2nd edition. Frankfurt: Athenäum.

Saunders, Nicholas 2006 Alexander's Tomb: The Two-thousand Year Obsession to Find the Lost Conqueror. London: Perseus Books Group.

Sehlmeyer, Markus 1999 Stadtrömische Ehrenstatuen der republikanischen Zeit. Stuttgart: Franz Steiner Verlag.

Settis, Salvatore, A. La Regina, G. Agosti and V. Farinella 1988 La Colonna Traiana. Turin: G. Einaudi.

Shennan, Stephen 1989 Archaeological Approaches to Cultural Identity. London: Unwin Hyman.

Sommella, Anna Mura 2000 La grande Roma dei Tarquini, alterne vicende di una felice intuizione. Bullettino della Commissione archeologica del Governatorato di Roma 101:7–26.

Spencer, Diana 2002 The Roman Alexander: Reading a Cultural Myth. Exeter: University of Exeter Press.

Steinby, Eva Margareta, ed. 1993 Lexicon Topographicum Urbis Romae. Rome: Edizioni Quasar.

Stewart, Andrew 1993 Faces of Power: Alexander's Image and Hellenistic Politics. Berkeley: University of California Press.

Stoneman, Richard 1994 Legends of Alexander the Great. London: Dent.

Stuart, M. 1939 How were Imperial Portraits Distributed throughout the Empire? American Journal of Archaeology 43:601–617.

Swift, E. 1923 Imagines in Imperial Portraiture. American Journal of Archaeology 27:286–301.

Tanner, Jeremy 2000 Portraits, Power, and Patronage in the Late Roman Republic. Journal of Roman Studies 90:18–50.

Tarn, William W. 1948 Alexander the Great. 2 vols. Cambridge: Cambridge University Press.

Taylor, Rabun 2003 Roman Builders: A Study in Architectural Process. Cambridge: Cambridge University Press.

Tsetskhladze, Gocha R., and Franco De Angelis, eds. 1994 The Archaeology of Greek Colonization. Oxford Committee for Archaeology Monograph 40. Oxford: Oxford University School of Archaeology.

Versnel, H. S. 1970 Triumphus: An Inquiry into the Origin, Development and Nature of the Roman Triumph. Leiden: E. J. Brill.

von Hesberg, Henner 1992 Römische Grabbauten. Darmstadt: Wissenschaftliche Buchgesellschaft.

——, and Panciera, S. 1994 Das Mausoleum des Augustus. Der Bau und seine Inschriften. Munich: Verlag der Bayerischen Akademie der Wissenschaften.

Walker, Susan 1985 Memorials to the Roman Dead. London: British Museum Publications.

Wallace-Hadrill, Andrew 1990 Roman Arches and Greek Honours: The Language of Power at Rome. Proceedings of the Cambridge Philological Society 36:143–181.

Weinstock, Stefan 1971 Divus Julius. Oxford: Clarendon Press.

White, Leslie A. 1948 Ikhnaton: The Great Man vs. The Culture Process. Journal of the American Oriental Society 68:91–114.

Wilson Jones, Mark 2000 Principles of Roman Architecture. New Haven: Yale University Press.

Wood, Michael 1997 In the Footsteps of Alexander the Great: A Journey from Greece to Asia. Berkeley: University of California Press.

Wood, Susan 1986 Roman Portrait Sculpture 217–260 A.D.: The Transformation of an Artistic Tradition. Leiden: E. J. Brill.

Worthington, Ian, ed. 2003 Alexander the Great: A Reader. London: Routledge.

Yalouris, Nicholas, Katerina Rhomiopoulou, and Manolis Andronikos 1980 The Search for Alexander: An Exhibition. Boston: New York Graphic Society.

Zanker, Paul 1988 The Power of Images in the Age of Augustus. Trans. A. Shapiro. Ann Arbor: University of Michigan Press.

Ziolkowski, Adam 1992 The Temples of Mid-Republican Rome and their Historical and Topographical Context. Rome: Bretschneider.

9

The Creation and Expression of Identity

Introduction

For much of this book we have emphasized what is common to communities across the Greek and Roman worlds, discussing features which are typical and replicated from one community to another. In the last chapter we emphasized the archaeological evidence for the particular role played by individuals in these communities, and looked at the mark which the individual made upon the fabric of the world they set out to impress. In this chapter we look at the ways in which the material record reveals cities and communities within cities to have lined themselves up against one another and to have variously courted and resisted signaling in their material expression changes to their social and political status.

Faced with the question "Who are you?," most people in the western world expect to answer by identifying themselves by their individual name. But when pressed to identify themselves as part of a group, they are likely, depending on the circumstances, to identify themselves by gender ("I'm a woman") or sexual orientation ("I'm gay"), by religion ("I'm a Buddhist"), by nationality (normally by citizenship) ("Actually, I'm Canadian"), by ethnic group ("I'm Hispanic"), or by class ("I'm working class"). In the last chapter we saw that some women impressed themselves on their communities as individuals, but there is little evidence of gender-consciousness in classical antiquity beyond the context of religious festivals exclusive to men or to women. Homoeroticism is well attested within the Greek city and well displayed on Greek painted pottery, but there is little indication in antiquity of homosexuals considering themselves, or being considered, a distinct class. Polytheism was non-exclusive, and until Greek and Roman culture came into contact with Judaism and then Christianity, religious identification would be found only in specialized contexts in which a person might admit to having been initiated into a particular cult not open to all, such as the Dionysiac mysteries. By contrast, both men and women, despite women's lack of political rights, regularly identified themselves to those outside their city by declaring themselves to be, or being identified by others as, Athenians or

Corinthians or from Padua. In certain circumstances within the Greek world that same Athenian might identify himself as Ionian and that same Corinthian as Dorian, but to a wider world they would both identify themselves as Hellenes— Greeks. Such identification by city, ethnic group, or nation extended beyond men and women to things, as the products of particular cities were singled out (Arretine pottery), or particular styles were identified with particular groups (Ionic architecture).

Particularly interesting is the question of identification by class. In response to a question, the closest equivalent answer in antiquity would be an answer in terms of legal status ("I'm a slave") or precisely defined status group ("I'm an *eques*"— the equivalent of "I'm a Knight of the Realm"). But in terms of material culture it is possible to see a broader class grouping being expressed, as people seek to distinguish themselves as, or distinguish themselves from, the wealthy elite. The demonstration here of the way in which material culture suggests social divisions not explicitly manifested in our textual record provides an object lesson in the importance of allowing that objects may not only speak louder than texts, they may actually say something different.

9 (a)

The Creation and Expression of Identity

The Greek World

Jonathan M. Hall

The Archaeology of Identity

People conduct their lives in different ways from place to place and it is not, therefore, unreasonable to expect that the material residue of their actions will display spatial variations. Such distinct, bounded patterns of spatial variation, embracing what Gordon Childe (1956:123) defined as "a plurality of well-defined diagnostic types that are repeatedly and exclusively associated with one another," are termed "culture areas" or simply "archaeological cultures" and feature prominently in treatments of the classical world. Anthony Snodgrass (2000), for example, has identified regional variations in pottery styles, burial practices, and iron artifacts for Dark Age Greece (ca. 1100–700 B.C.) and Ian Morris (1998) has examined the evidence of burials, sanctuaries, and houses to divide the Archaic Greek world (ca. 750–480 B.C.) into four culture areas: Central Greece, Northern Greece, Western Greece, and Crete. Others, however, have gone further and assumed that archaeologically observable patterns of material behavior should correspond directly with the self-conscious ethnic groups whose existence is attested in literary texts. Thus, on Sicily, as we shall see later, archaeologists have sought to identify the Greek, Sicel, Sican, and Elymian populations enumerated by Thucydides (6.1–5) on the basis of variations in artifact type, architectural plans, and burial practices (Bernabò Brea 1957).

The "culture-historical method," as it has come to be called, has met with sustained critique in recent decades. It has long been noted that material divisions do not always coincide with ethnic boundaries but cultural anthropologists have even questioned the very existence of essentialized entities such as "societies" or "populations," arguing that "society" is as much a symbolic construct as any other aspect of culture. Archaeological theorists, on the other hand, note that while archaeological cultures should ideally be identified polythetically (e.g. on the basis of a wide range of components where no single component is either necessary or sufficient for defining the group), they are in practice often distinguished according to a limited number of features and are consequently dependent upon the subjective interpretation of the analyst. Both objections are probably overstated. One may legitimately dispute the *a priori* existence of essential, discretely bounded social units but the perception, on the part of the individual subject, of belonging to at least one, and normally several, social groups would appear to be a basic human need. And while any analysis of material culture variation should ideally be multivariate, the blunt reality is that we are hostages to what has survived, been retrieved, and published from the archaeological record. Fortunately, recent theories of social identity and the manner in which it may be communicated through material culture circumvent some of the criticisms that have been made against the culture-historical method.

Identity is normally taken today to denote a self-conceptualization, predicated on perceptions of similarity and difference, that conveys a distinctive sense of being to the subject. It is often—though not universally and not always in the same ways—recognized by others and in some cases it may even be an internalization of the perceptions of outsiders. Social identity, distinct from the expression of individuality, refers to the internalization within the individual of the knowledge that she or he belongs to a broader social group, along with the value and significance that are attached to such an affiliation. It is important to emphasize that the study of social identity is not the same as the study of social groups. Any one individual typically belongs to a broad range of overlapping social networks, be they related to political membership, locality, gender, sexuality, class, ethnicity or occupation. Not all of these affiliations are equally important to any individual or group at all times and tend to assume varying degrees of significance according to different circumstances. The ethnicity of an Ulsterman, for example, will probably be less significant at family meals, at a trade fair, or on the beach at Benidorm than when marching through a predominantly Catholic area of Belfast.

The crucial characteristic of identity, then, is its profoundly subjective, active, and often transitory qualities. Furthermore—and fortunately in light of the fragmentary nature of the archaeological record—it is normally only a restricted range of artifacts that is "selected to carry social or political meaning under particular circumstances, rather than the totality of a society's material culture" (Morgan 1991:134). While the identification of an archaeological culture area may not in itself reveal much concerning the creation and expression of identity, it does at least generate an indispensable context or repertoire of normative behavior against which one is more likely to recognize the mobilization by individuals or groups of certain symbols, objects, and practices within active strategies of self-proclamation (Hall 1997:136).

The issues involved with the archaeological expression of identity are paralleled by recent debates concerning style in material culture. Traditionally, style was regarded as the residual, information-bearing element of an artifact, distinct from its practical function, which—aside from its diagnostic utility in terms of date and provenance—could serve as an index of the degree of interaction between different groups. However, with specific regard to ceramic style, James Sackett (1977) has argued that it is fallacious to distinguish style from function since there exists a spectrum of equally viable alternatives ("isochrestic options") in the manufacture and use of material culture; decisions have to be made, for example, regarding the type of clay or tempers to use, the specific form of the vessel, or the correct firing-temperature in addition to which decorative motifs to adopt. In Sackett's view, isochrestic options are embedded in the technological traditions in which their producers have been enculturated and their unique conjuncture can be employed to identify specific social groups. Other archaeologists, on the other hand, prefer a more active, or "iconological," role for material culture. Polly Wiessner (1983; 1989), for example, distinguishes between "assertive style," where the personal identity of the producer is—consciously or unconsciously—projected, and "emblemic style," which serves to convey information concerning group identity. Taking the example of the Eipo of eastern Irian Jaya, she notes that the diversity of dress styles observable in local village dances is far less noticeable when it comes to competitions between villages since these are situations in which group identity becomes more important than individual expression.

In what follows, three case studies are presented, drawn from different periods and regions of the Greek world, that illustrate some of the theoretical issues at stake in the archaeology of identity. The first concerns attempts to identify an ancient ethnic group, the Dorians, in the material record. The second outlines how non-elites at Athens in the early fifth century usurped and adapted formerly elite symbols to carve out a new identity for themselves. Finally, I consider how contact between Greek settlers and indigenous populations on Sicily created a new "hybrid" identity that was predominantly communicated through material culture.

The Elusive Dorians: Archaeology and Ethnicity

By the fifth century B.C., the populations of numerous cities throughout the Mediterranean professed their affiliation to the Dorian branch of the Greek family. According to ancient authors, their ancestors had originally lived in northern-central Greece, but had banded together to migrate southwards, conquering the Peloponnese and ousting the dynasties of the Heroic Age (generally associated today with the world of the Mycenaean palaces). From there, secondary foundations were sent out to the islands of the southern and southeastern Aegean, southwest Asia Minor, southern Italy and Sicily, and Libya.

Various attempts have been made to identify the arrival and presence of these Dorians in the material record of Early Iron Age Greece. Types of pottery, items of jewelry and weaponry, modes of burial, and even ironworking, have all been cited as new, intrusive elements of northern provenance following the collapse of the Mycenaean palaces ca. 1200 B.C., yet all have been challenged on at least one of two grounds. First, many of these items were already present in the Mycenaean world, in which case they cannot be associated exclusively with a new, post-Mycenaean population. Second, many of these apparent novelties are attested first, and most prolifically, in regions such as Attica and Euboea which were never home to Dorian populations. The cist grave is a case in point. Designed for single inhumation—though they were sometimes reused for subsequent interments—the cist grave was considered to reflect a new mode of mortuary disposal, radically different from the preference for multiple inhumation in chamber tombs that had existed during the Mycenaean period, and its seemingly early attestation in Epirus, Macedonia, and Thessaly hinted at a northern origin. But if the cist grave was not a popular form of burial in the Mycenaean period, it was certainly not unknown, and in the preceding Middle Helladic period (ca. 1900–1550 B.C.) it had been common throughout Greece. Furthermore, its most visible appearance in the post-Mycenaean world is in the Pompeion cemetery at Athens and in the Arsenal cemetery on the offshore island of Salamis—both non-Dorian areas.

A non-classical archaeologist would probably circumvent the problem by dismissing the authenticity of the literary traditions concerning the Dorian migration, but denying the historical substance of the traditions does not negate their historical function. Even if we accept that these myths of ethnic origin were not the hazy recollection of genuine prehistoric migrations but were inventions of a later period, the reason they were invented was to serve as a charter for an ethnic consciousness that—by the sixth century, if not earlier—was real enough. Put another way, the traditions are an expression, if not the origin, of an ethnic identity that it is reasonable to expect was also communicated through material culture, though perhaps at a date somewhat later than the transition from the Bronze to Iron Age. If the Dorians are at all archaeologically traceable, it is less likely to be in the appearance of a bounded set of exclusive and recurrent types at the end of the Mycenaean age as it is through the mobilization of certain distinctive symbols in subsequent centuries. Like other expressions of social and cultural identity, ethnicity is

> a statement of consciousness and a strategy of self-perception that can be identified and analyzed only in terms of contingent circumstances . . . It is highly probable that well-established cultural referents will be assigned new or enhanced meanings in the process; the innovation lies in their politicization, not their existence. (Morgan 2001:76–77)

A reorientation along these lines would concede that there is no direct or universal association between cist burial and the Dorians but it would also leave open the possibility that interment in a cist grave might be adopted by the Dorian populations of certain cities in order to communicate their ethnic distinctiveness. The Peloponnesian city of Argos was, according to tradition, captured by Dorians in the third generation after the Trojan War—the Sicilian historian Diodorus (7.8.1) dated this "event" to 1104 B.C. The ancient authors appear to believe that the Dorian newcomers dominated pre-existing populations, although tradition also held that many "Achaeans" fled Argos to establish a new home for themselves on

the southern shores of the Corinthian Gulf. From around the start of the Sub-
mycenaean period (ca. 1100 B.C.), individual inhumation in cist graves replaced
multiple inhumation in chamber tombs as the dominant mode of burial at Argos.
Interments were also made in simpler pits and, in the case of infants, in vases,
while from the ninth century adults were often buried in large clay ovoid containers or *pithoi*. Yet cists outnumber pithoi by about 2:1 and pits by around 4.5:1;
they are, on average, wealthier in terms of grave goods; and, according to Anne
Foley (1998), they appear in more central locations while pithoi tend to be situated in more peripheral cemeteries. On the assumption that the Dorians constituted the dominant and wealthiest class in Dark Age Argos, Foley argues that it
is they who adopted inhumation in cist graves as one way of distinguishing themselves from their sociopolitical inferiors.

Unfortunately, there are a number of objections to this inference. First, cists
are, by their nature, more suited to the deposition of grave goods than are pithoi,
but in reality the differential between the two modes of burial is not so extreme:
in burials which contained offerings, a pithos is, on average, likely to hold one
ceramic artifact while cists will have three ceramic and two metal objects, but
some pithoi could contain as many as 14 vases while a large number of cists had
no gifts at all. Furthermore, while some cists were of more monumental dimensions and lined with dressed masonry, most were of simple construction from
sundry pieces of stone and, as such, probably represented a cheaper facility for
disposal than the large clay pithoi. Second, it is not, in fact, the case that cists are
more centrally located than pithoi (Figure 9.1). Rather, the various modes of
burial are found alongside one another, with uniform orientation, in the same
cemeteries. If a particular burial practice had been adopted for the purposes of
social or ethnic exclusivity, it is difficult to believe that the self-distinguishing
group would have been content to share its necropolis with those it sought to
exclude. Third, cist burial ceases to be practiced at the end of the eighth century,
being replaced by inhumation in cylindrical pithoi. A "trickle-down" effect,
whereby high-status burial practices might become more widely diffused among
the population, would probably not cause too much surprise; the converse, on the
other hand, is less likely. We should probably conclude either that Dorian identity
at Argos in the eighth century was barely salient enough to receive material
expression or that it was expressed through channels other than those of burial
practices.

A possible instance where there may be a correlation between ethnicity and
burial practices comes from Asine, some 12 miles to the southeast of Argos. At
first sight, the burial customs at Asine do not seem to differ significantly from
those of other communities in the Argive plain. Like the Argives, the population
of Asine interred its dead in cists and pits. However, inhumation in pithoi was
studiously avoided, and there are one or two instances of possible cremation
burials. Furthermore, corpses at Asine were typically laid out in a supine, out-
stretched position, unlike the "contracted" position adopted at other Argolic sites,
necessitating cists that were generally longer and narrower. And while westerly
orientations for graves were generally preferred at sites in the Argive plain, the

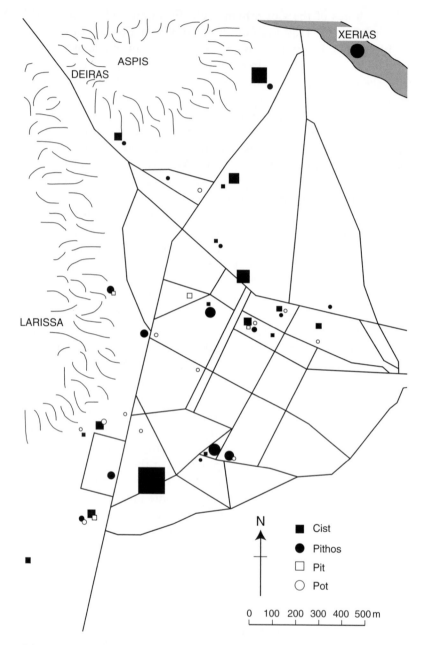

Figure 9.1 Distribution of Late Geometric graves at Argos. After Hall 1997:127

graves at Asine tend to favor east or northeasterly orientations (Hägg 1998). These "variations on a theme" are also evident in the ceramic assemblages of Asine. In terms of painted decoration, the pottery of Asine is remarkably similar to that of Argos, especially in the course of the eighth century, but the city was also receptive to imports from Attica, the Cyclades, and Crete to an extent that is unmatched at other Argolic settlements (Morgan and Whitelaw 1991).

These instances could all represent the material expression of a civic identity that became especially relevant in the decades prior to the destruction of Asine by Argos ca. 710 B.C. But ancient authors are insistent that the population of Asine was ethnically different from that of Argos, being Dryopean rather than Dorian. Interestingly enough, the ethnic myths of the Dryopes present several points of contact with those of the Dorians. Like the Dorians, the Dryopes were believed to have originated in central Greece. Herodotus (8.31, 43) actually maintains that the Dorians had once inhabited Dryopis and the Dryopes Doris, the small land-locked region at the foot of Mount Parnassus which—by the fifth century at any rate—was often regarded as the original homeland of the Dorians. But tradition told how the Dryopes had been expelled from their homeland by Heracles, whose descendants were later to lead the Dorians into the Peloponnese, and also how they were subsequently established in the Argolid by Heracles' arch-enemy, Eurystheus (Hall 1997:74–77). This focus on analogous distinctiveness is precisely what we find in the material record of Asine, whose population expressed its identity not through a unique or distinct repertoire of material items and practices but rather through a more subtle modulation of a common regional inheritance whereby a limited range of symbols was endowed with an ethnic efficacy.

Taming the Elite: The Material Expression of Athenian Democracy

In the history of Greek sculpture, few stylistic changes are as abrupt or as pervasive as the adoption of a new female dress in the early decades of the fifth century B.C. (Figure 9.2). From this moment, the standard garment for women becomes the *peplos*—a simple, sleeveless woolen tunic which was often termed "Dorian" by ancient authors, though Herodotus' observation (5.87) that Athenian women had once worn the Dorian dress would appear to preclude any exclusive ethnic association. The sober and severe austerity of the peplos projects an ideology of simplicity and moderation that signals a stark departure from the luxuriant and sumptuous fashions worn by the series of *korai*, or draped female statues, dedicated on the Athenian acropolis in the last third of the sixth century (Figure 9.3). Bedecked with expensive jewelry and sporting elaborate coiffures and head dresses, the acropolis korai, influenced by the styles of East Greece, wear variations of the "Ionic" *chiton*—a linen garment, normally with sleeves—and the *himation* or mantle. Together, the two items of dress were detailed with complex patterns of folds and pleats and decorated with brightly colored geometric motifs. There is good reason to believe that the stylistic change reflected a genuine shift in fashion preferences—at least at Athens—rather than a mere artistic convention and that it affected men as much as women. Thucydides (1.6.3), for example, claims that it was "only very recently" that the more elderly male members of Athenian elite families gave up wearing Ionian linen chitons and hair-clasps in the form of golden grasshoppers. To understand the shift, it is first necessary to

Figure 9.2 Female figure (Sterope?) from the east pediment of the Temple of Zeus at Olympia, ca. 470–460 B.C. Photo: Hege 642, courtesy of the Deutsches Archäologisches Institut, Athens

consider the symbolism of easternizing fashions for earlier generations of Athenians.

The Mycenaean elites of the Late Bronze Age had advertised their status by displaying "exotic" luxury items from the east. After the collapse of the Mycenaean palaces, the practice resumed in the tenth century, when objects of predominantly North Syrian origin came to be interred in graves in Attica, Euboea,

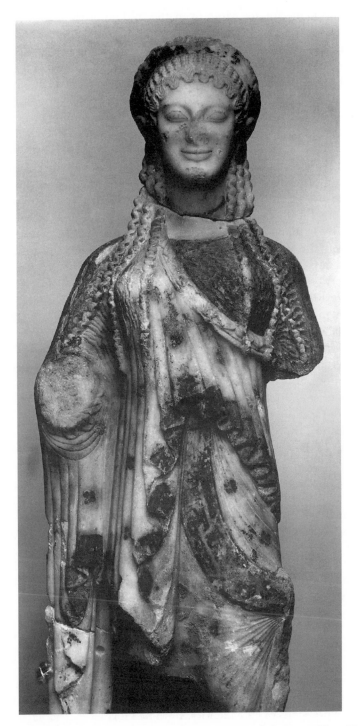

Figure 9.3 Kore 675 from the Athenian acropolis, ca. 520–510 B.C. Photo: Hege 795; courtesy of the Deutsches Archäologisches Institut, Athens

Crete, and the Dodecanese, while from the middle of the eighth century such items came to be dedicated in the more public space of sanctuaries. Around one quarter of the late eighth-century and early seventh-century metal dedications at Olympia, for example, were of non-Greek manufacture, and while the jewelry and weapons of Italian provenance may represent the personal dedications of occidental pilgrims, the North Syrian and Phrygian bronze vessels are almost certainly prestige items acquired through gift exchange and trade among the aristocracies from both sides of the Aegean.

The difficulty of acquisition of such goods guaranteed their prestige value and marked their dedicators out as members of a transregional elite: the more exotic the item, the more extensive the social network, and the higher the status of its owner. In the late seventh century, the poetry of Sappho and Alcaeus offers eloquent testimony for the fascination that East Greek elites had for Near Eastern— and specifically Lydian—fashions and accessories and, in the course of the sixth century, it was the turn of Athenian elites to come under the influence of the cultured and cosmopolitan world of the Orient, as witnessed by the adoption of East Greek styles and fashions for Attic korai from ca. 530 B.C. Paradoxically, then, membership of the Greek elite in the Archaic period was defined and communicated by means of a symbolic currency in non-Greek objects. This provides yet another salutary reminder that identities frequently overlap rather than cluster within more inclusive categories and further highlights the poverty of the culture-historical method which assumes patterns of normative behavior determined by ethnic affiliation.

Given the aristocratic connotations of eastern fashions in the Archaic period, the adoption of a more "severe" or "international" canon of female dress in the early fifth century must represent more than a simple reaction against the "barbarian" tastes of the Orient in the wake of the Persian invasions of 490 and 480–479 B.C.—as suggested by, among others, Jerome Pollitt (1972:43). At Athens in particular there was probably a more internal political resonance. The decimation of the Persian fleet in the straits of Salamis in the autumn of 480 B.C. was largely the achievement of an Athenian fleet crewed by the poorer citizens, and in the years immediately following the expulsion of the occupying forces these newly-empowered citizens grew ever more self-conscious of their political power. Democracy involved notions of equality (*isonomia*) and freedom of speech (*isegoria*), but the term itself signified the power, or rule (*kratos*) of the *demos*—a word that had, in the Archaic period, denoted the non-elite population of a city. The emergence of democracy at Athens, then, represented not so much the extension of political privileges and obligations to a wider section of society but rather a revolution, whereby the less wealthy citizens secured a political victory at the expense of the Athenian elite. One effect of this was the suppression of elite symbols.

Indeed, it is not just that a new female dress appears in sculptural representations but that korai and *kouroi*, their male counterparts, were no longer considered appropriate expressions of elite identity. Both had formerly articulated ideas about gender that were specifically aristocratic. True kouroi are completely nude, lacking any specific attributes or explicit functions, yet it is this very liberation from the distraction of everyday trappings that compels the viewer to search deeper for some innate quality and inner beauty—in short, the natural *arete*, or "excellence," that epic and lyric poets regarded as a distinguishing criterion of aristocratic males. Instead, the iconography of the draped and bejeweled korai symbolizes the role that aristocratic daughters played as transmitters of moveable property and as commodities of exchange within networks of reciprocity that linked elite families from different areas of Greece and even beyond. This role is made explicit on the inscribed base of a funerary *kore*, found at Merenda (ancient Myrrhinous) to the southeast of Athens and dating to ca. 550–540 B.C., which commemorates a girl named Phrasikleia and bewails the fact that she will "always be called 'maiden' (kore), having been allotted this name by the gods instead of marriage." But funerary korai are vastly outnumbered by dedicatory korai and the connotations that they convey of aristocratic women as commodified items of exchange are accentuated by the fact that several of the acropolis korai were actually dedicated by men.

It is, then, little surprise that both kouroi and korai disappear from votive and funerary contexts in Attica in the early fifth century. In contrast to the elaborate grave monuments of the sixth century, Attic gravestones under the early democracy were simple and uncarved. It is only in the last third of the fifth century, during the Peloponnesian War, that carved reliefs reappear, but the iconography is now more focused on non-heroic, domestic contexts. Women in particular are portrayed less as mobile commodities cementing alliances between distant elites and more as protectresses of the *oikos* or household, the fundamental and irreducible building block of democratic Athens (Osborne 1997). Carved gravestones were, of course, still a luxury that few but the wealthiest could afford, and it is interesting that this tension or contradiction between the ability to commission a grave relief, on the one hand, and the iconographical emphasis on the unexceptional and regular life of the deceased, on the other, mirrors very closely the delicate balance that Athenian elites attempted to strike in law court speeches between extolling their generosity and services to the city and seeking to represent themselves before less affluent jurymen as average, run-of-the-mill fellow-citizens (Ober 1989).

The fledgling Athenian democracy, then, celebrated its victory by suppressing practices—and especially orientalizing fashions—that had previously served as a badge of elite identity. A particularly early manifestation of this attitude is perhaps represented by Cleisthenes' substitution in 508 B.C. of ten new tribes, named after native Athenian heroes, for the old four Ionian tribes. Likewise, the aristocrats, "ostracized" or exiled in the 480s and 470s by the Athenian populace, were frequently named, and sometimes even graphically depicted, on the voting ballots as "Medes" or Persians. The ethnic characterization drew attention to the relationships that Athenian elites had contracted, through intermarriage and guest friendship, with high-ranking Persian families but it also served to proscribe the easternizing habits through which they identified themselves. This rejection of orientalizing practices and commodities was, however, only half the story. Another possible strategy was to appropriate formerly elite symbols for democratic ends.

In 477/6 B.C., for example, the sculptors Critius and Nesiotes usurped the form and value-associations of the nude male for their replacement of what can be considered one of the founding monuments of the Athenian democracy. The original statue group of Harmodius and Aristogeiton, realized by Antenor but carried off by the Persians in 480 B.C., commemorated the assassination, in 514 B.C., of Hipparchus, the younger son of the Athenian tyrant Pisistratus. In popular thought, if not necessarily in fact, the two were credited not only with the overthrow of the tyranny but also with the establishment of the democracy.

Such appropriations extended also to *orientalia*. As Margaret Miller (1997) has demonstrated, from the late sixth century Attic black-gloss wares began to imitate the shapes of Achaemenid Persian vessels and then to adapt them through the addition of handles or feet—a process that intensified markedly in the decades immediately after the Persian wars. The fact that it was a restricted range of mainly drinking vessels that was imitated suggests that the models for the ceramic copies were the metal cups that Athenian elites acquired from the Persian world, but their adaptation to more Athenian ceramic conventions served further to strip them of their elite status and, in a sense, to "democratize" them. By the middle of the fifth century these innovations had become so engrained within traditions of manufacture that they were almost unconsciously replicated as expressions of democratic Athenian material culture. Miller sees a similar process operating in the adoption of dress items such as the *kandys*, which in Achaemenid art is a leather sleeved cloak for males but is described in an inscription from Brauron as being a linen coat for women. Indeed, vase paintings of the early fifth century represent figures such as musicians and dancers, dressed in Persian apparel and participating in highly public contexts such as religious festivals. The phenomenon may also be registered in the architectural program of democratic Athens, where the circular *tholos*, which housed the executive council of the Athenian democracy, was perhaps modeled on a Persian tent while the great continuous frieze that adorns the Parthenon may have been designed to evoke the ceremonial processions depicted on the Apadana of Persepolis.

This strategy of retaining but neutralizing—rather than suppressing—orientalia has also been highlighted by Beth Cohen (2001) in a study of Athenian democratic art. On vases of the later sixth century symposiasts are sometimes represented sporting oriental accessories such as turbans (*mitrai*), loose-boots (*kothornoi*), and earrings, while horsemen in particular are depicted with articles of Thracian dress such as a fox-skin cap (*alopekis*), a patterned woolen cloak (*zeira*), and fawn-skin boots (*embades*), alongside items of Athenian dress. Once considered evidence of the presence of foreign mercenaries at Athens, the Athenian identity of those depicted is relatively secure thanks to the fact that typically Athenian names are inscribed alongside such figures on a wine-cooler painted by Smikros ca. 515 B.C. Furthermore, the fact that the horsemen typically sport a non-standardized pastiche of Thracian and Athenian dress strengthens the suspicion that the representations are intended to reflect real fashions rather than conform to any particular iconographical convention. Unlike the Ionian-influenced female fashions, these items of male Thracian dress did not disappear

Figure 9.4 Mounted procession from the west frieze of the Parthenon, ca. 440–430 B.C. Photo: Hege 1998; courtesy of the Deutsches Archäologisches Institut, Athens

with the growth of the Athenian democracy in the early fifth century but were instead co-opted alongside more indigenous garments and even nudity within a democratic visual vocabulary. Thus, on the Parthenon frieze (Figure 9.4), while some of the horsemen are depicted naked, others wear tunics or corselets, capes or animal-skin cloaks; some are bare-headed, while others wear helmets, broad-brimmed hats, or *alopekeis*; and some are bare-footed, while others have sandals or *embades*. The formerly elite connotations of such exotic dress items have been blunted and neutralized by their juxtaposition alongside varying styles—and states—of dress.

The democratization of luxury items was in many senses a more efficacious strategy than their proscription, but it also served to express another key component of Athenian democratic identity—namely, the cosmopolitanism that resulted from Athens' imperial domination of her former allies. In his *epitaphios* or funeral oration for the war dead of 430 B.C., Pericles boasts that the greatness of Athens' empire allows its citizens not only to enjoy, but also to become accustomed to, imported products as much as local ones (Thucydides 2.38.2). Those material items that had formerly signaled an elite identity had by now been usurped by the entire Athenian populace: the attempt to democratize elite expressions of status had thus also served to aristocratize the Athenian demos.

Colonialism and Hybridity

The intensive contacts that had existed, during the Mycenaean period, between the Aegean basin and the central Mediterranean began to be resumed towards the end of the ninth century; from the last third of the eighth century onwards, permanent communities were founded on the coasts of southern Italy and Sicily by settlers from the Greek mainland and islands such as Euboea, Crete, and Rhodes. Save for the attempts of Italian nationalist scholars such as Emanuele Ciaceri and Biagio Pace to emphasize the indigenous contribution to the development of Italian and Sicilian culture, the history of these encounters between Greek-speakers and Italic populations has often been analyzed from a profoundly Hellenocentric perspective. The settlers, or "colonists," are judged to have exerted a political and military dominance over the previous inhabitants of the interior and to have fundamentally "Hellenized" indigenous cultural traditions to the extent that, when the Romans extended their dominion over southern Italy and Sicily in the third century, it was largely Greek beliefs and practices that they encountered and eventually incorporated within their own cultural repertoire.

The mechanics and consequences of the cultural confrontation between Greeks and Romans will be considered in the second part of this chapter. Here, I shall give some consideration to the encounter between Greek-speakers and the indigenous populations of Sicily. It is certainly undeniable that artifacts manufactured in the Aegean basin were imported into Sicily from the time of the earliest contacts and that Greek decorative styles and techniques of manufacture in ceramics, metalwork, and architecture were imitated and incorporated within indigenous cultural traditions—especially with regard to the eighth- and seventh-century "Finocchito" and "Licodia Eubea" cultures of eastern Sicily, where the earliest and densest concentration of Greek settlement was to be found. By contrast, the "Sant' Angelo Muxaro" culture of central and western Sicily perpetuated to some degree traditions with roots in the Late Bronze Age and was therefore a little more resistant to innovations, though it too displays Greek influences by the second half of the sixth century. Yet when some attempt is made to reconstruct the total social and cultural context within which such objects and practices functioned, a far more complicated picture results.

The standard account of Hellenization conforms to a "colonialist" model of cultural contact, whereby it is assumed that indigenous populations would be so immediately struck by the inherently superior cultural and technological level of the new settlers that they would prove to be ready passive consumers of whatever was offered to them. Already, in the 1930s, this patronizing outlook had been challenged by Robert Redfield and his associates, who preferred a theory of acculturation in which "groups of individuals having different cultures come into continuous first hand contact with subsequent changes in the original cultural patterns of either or both groups" (Redfield et al. 1936:148). In reality, however, much of the research conducted in the United States at the time was sponsored by government agencies whose primary concern was the effect that contact with dominant western states had on small-scale societies—an understanding not so different from that which informed the colonialist model (see Dietler 1999). More recently, postcolonial theorists such as Homi Bhabha (1994) have championed the notion of hybridity. Questioning the monolithic boundedness of cultural groups and emphasizing the active role that individual agency plays in intergroup relations, Bhabha argues that culture contact in colonial situations creates new, hybrid or creole cultures, distinct from the cultural traditions and initial power structures of the original parties to the encounter. The theory has been applied with good effect to the Greek settlement of Sicily (Antonaccio 2003).

In material terms, it is once again not so much a question of identifying a unique and exclusive set of recurrent types that might serve as an archaeological "footprint" for a new hybrid culture but rather of being attentive to the distinctive conjunction and specific application of cultural elements that need not in themselves be innovative. For example, it was common practice throughout the Greek world to decorate public buildings, and especially temples, with painted terracottas, though the brightly painted terracotta revetment with its intricate interlaced patterns that adorns the pediment of the mid-sixth-century treasury of Gela at Olympia is eloquent testimony to a particularly Sicilian expertise in the design and manufacture of polychrome architectural terracottas. Similarly, Sicilian temples of the sixth century tend to favor the Doric order of architecture, pioneered in the Peloponnese, but their distinctiveness arises from the adoption of somewhat unusual floor plans and the co-option of elements that more properly belong to the Ionic order of architecture—an innovation that predates by about a century similar experimentation at Athens. But the situation is complicated yet further by the fact that, in the Greek case, there were multiple foci of interaction between Greek settlers and the indigenous populations of Sicily: according to Thucydides (6.3–5), no fewer than 13 Greek cities were founded on the island before the beginning of the sixth century. The inevitable rivalry that characterized relations between Greek communities on Sicily as much as between their Aegean metropoleis provides an additional dimension to the forging of new identities in the west.

Nowhere, perhaps, is this illustrated better than in the burial practices employed by Greek settlers on Sicily, where our normative expectations that such rites would replicate those of the Greek mainland are thoroughly confounded. As Gillian Shepherd (1995) notes, the preference for cremation and inhumation in vases at Megara Hyblaea is not attested at Greek Megara, its supposed metropolis, while the rite of cremation, favored for adults on Rhodes and Crete, is less popular than inhumation at their joint foundation at Gela. At Syracuse, the prevalence of rock-cut *fossae* or trenches does not reflect the preference for monolithic sarcophagi at Corinth, the city which was traditionally credited with founding the Sicilian city, and the practice of multiple inhumation that accounts for around 14 percent of Syracusan burials is not attested at Corinth, though it is a common enough custom in the indigenous chamber-tomb cemeteries of eastern Sicily. This usurpation of indigenous burial practices is also documented for the Greek city of Leontini, where interments prior to the sixth century were made in chamber-tombs and accompanied by grave assemblages in which local, indigenous interpretations of Greek pottery outnumber genuine imports (Leighton 1999:241). The material culture of Greek Sicily, then, derived its individuality from multiple sources. On the one hand, it was a highly eclectic expression of a complex series of engagements, forged both in conjunction and in confrontation with indigenous practices. On the other, it evolved within a context of competition and emulation between the Greek communities on the island with the aim of creating a deliberate distinction from the Greek homeland. And the political and cultural autonomy that these communities enjoyed was given visible form in the costly treasuries that Syracuse, Selinus, Gela, and perhaps Megara Hyblaea dedicated in the heart of Old Greece at Olympia.

The culture of the Greek settlers of Sicily was not, then, unaffected by the act of settlement, but nor was the culture of the indigenous populations necessarily effaced by the encounter with the newcomers. In fact, the same type of hybridity, albeit articulated in different ways, is to be found in the settlements of the interior. The site of Morgantina, situated on the Serra Orlando ridge 9 miles northeast of Piazza Armerina, was inhabited since at least the tenth century B.C., but in the early sixth century a new settlement of mud brick structures replaced the earlier community of scattered longhouses. The material associated with this settlement includes imported Greek ceramics alongside a large variety of locally produced wares; in terms of both shape and decoration, the local wares are indebted to both Greek and earlier Sicilian and South Italian ceramic traditions. Similarly, although the indigenous practice of multiple inhumation in chamber tombs was retained, the sixth century sees the adoption of a wide diversity of Greek burial practices, including both cremation and inhumation in fossae, sarcophagi, and vases. Even after the destruction and refoundation of Morgantina towards the middle of the fifth century, the hybrid character—neither wholly Greek nor entirely indigenous—of the material culture of the settlement persists (Antonaccio 2001).

Further west, at Sabucina, imports and local imitations of Protocorinthian, Rhodian, and Cretan wares indicate the existence of contacts with the Greek city of Gela to the south. In the course of the seventh century, three small circular structures were built which perpetuate indigenous architectural traditions but to two of them was added a trapezoidal portico with decidedly Greek features, while inside one was found a terracotta model of a temple whose form and decoration evoke Greek prototypes. In the middle of the sixth century, one of the hut-shrines was enclosed within a Greek-style rectilinear structure, to which, in the fifth century, a thoroughly indigenous offering bench was added. It was not, however, only Greek models that might be selected and incorporated within indigenous Sicilian cultural traditions. In the far northwest of the island a new style of ceramic emerges in the seventh century which distinguishes itself from the earlier wares of central and western Sicily through the addition of painted decoration and handles in the shape of human and animal faces. Conventionally named "Elymian ware" because it appears in areas such as Eryx and Segesta that were, according to fifth-century historians, inhabited by Elymian populations, parallels have been suggested with the pottery of Italian Puglia. Whatever the influence, it is difficult not to recognize in this active and conscious manipulation of material culture the real political, social, and economic restructuring that resulted from Greek—and Phoenician—exploitation of the region.

The issue of identity had evidently become especially salient in the Elymian city of Eryx shortly after the middle of the fifth century when coins were issued with legends in "Elymian"—a language, probably Italic in derivation, that is known from hundreds of short inscriptions dating from the later sixth and fifth centuries. That a city should employ its own language on its coinage would hardly warrant mention were it not for the fact that Eryx's earliest issue of coinage, dated a decade or so earlier, carried legends in the Greek language. By contrast, material distinctiveness is less readily apparent among the indigenous "Sicel" settlements of eastern Sicily in this period: the first issues of silver coinage here were modeled on Greek prototypes in terms of appearance, types, and legends (Rutter 1997: 140–141). Yet, surprisingly perhaps, it was precisely at this time that the Sicel leader Ducetius was attempting to establish an autonomous Sicel federation against the wishes of the Greek city-states.

The Sicel rebellion may have galvanized a certain spirit of unity among the Greek cities that had hitherto not been entirely evident but it is not until later in the fifth century that hints of a common Greek-Sicilian identity are attested in the creation of the ethnonym *Sikeliotai* (Antonaccio 2001). The name originally denoted only the Greek residents of Sicily, but, if we are to believe Thucydides (4.61.3), it was introduced to foster a sense of collective consciousness in the face of aggression from the Athenians, who launched their disastrous invasion of the island in 415 B.C., rather than as a result of indigenous dissent. Ultimately, in its attempt to give a geographical basis to a specifically Sicilian identity, distinct from the Greek homeland, it could hardly exclude the non-Greek peoples of Sicily indefinitely. With the influx of fresh Greek colonists as a result of the Corinthian general Timoleon's settlement of the island in the third quarter of the fourth century, a distinct indigenous Sicel identity dissipated. By the Roman period, all the indigenous inhabitants of Sicily had apparently become so enculturated in Greek ways of education that they abandoned their own languages and even their names, calling themselves instead Sikeliotai (Diodorus 5.6.5). What is interesting is that while an examination of Sicilian material culture reveals a pattern of hybridity and eventually assimilation that is broadly analogous to the process described by literary sources, its developmental trajectory appears—if anything— to run a little ahead of the stages that are outlined in our texts. One is tempted to wonder whether the discursive construction of Sicilian identity was so successful precisely because it could be accommodated within a symbolic structure whose framework had already been outlined through material cultural strategies.

Conclusion

All three of the examples considered here have involved some consideration of textual evidence alongside the material record. Indeed, the existence of a rich, literary context is one of the principal distinguishing features of classical archaeology as opposed to other archaeologies. Yet, strangely enough, one sometimes gains the impression from reading recent studies in classical archaeology that the existence of the textual record constitutes something of a cause for embarrassment, as if the "scientific" credentials of archaeology might somehow be tainted by its association with more literary materials. I should like to suggest instead that this is a cause for celebration rather than apology. Naturally, there are innumerable aspects of the ancient Mediterranean world about which our literary sources are silent and for which archaeology provides our only information. Of course, ancient authors—no less than modern scholars—had their own agendas and often, though not always, presented a somewhat elitist view of the world around them. On the other hand, the notion that archaeology can always rectify this bias may be overstated: Morris (1987), for example, has argued that from the eleventh through to the second quarter of the eighth century and again from the beginning of the seventh through to the end of the sixth century, non-elites are practically absent from the burial record of Attica.

Ancient historians are finally—if a little belatedly—coming to the realization that the role of classical archaeology in illuminating the past is not simply to illustrate literary texts. Indeed, as the examples above show, literary texts are seldom entirely congruent with the picture that we generate from a study of material culture. Each represents a different discourse and mode of expression, and the richer and more nuanced representation of social life that results from the incompatibilities and contradictions between the two offers paradigms that are invaluable for the development of models and hypotheses with a wider applicability. Some of the more significant developments in classical archaeology in recent decades have arisen from the readiness scholars have shown in borrowing theories and methods from other disciplines—especially anthropology. But a new self-critical synthesis between literary and material evidence offers its own insights into the relationship between ideas, actions, and the material record that is of potential interest well beyond the confines of the ancient Mediterranean World. Now is perhaps the time for classical archaeologists to consider assuming the role of donors rather than recipients.

NOTE

The references for this chapter are on pp. 376–380.

9 (b)
The Creation and Expression of Identity

The Roman World

Andrew Wallace-Hadrill

This chapter follows on from the concerns of the previous part by turning its attention to the forging not of individual but of social identities. It is concerned with issues of ethnicity and political identity and with the material ways in which these were signalled, for example, by choosing clothes (or nudity), by constructing or frequenting the *gymnasium*, the military camp, the necropolis, or the sanctuary, and so on.

The epic poet Ennius, whose *Annales* of the early second century B.C.E. did so much to give expression to a national Roman identity, defined himself as having *tria corda*, "three hearts": for he spoke Greek, Oscan, and Latin. Born in the heel of Italy at Rudiae (near Lecce), he belonged to the Hellenized Magna Graecia, and thus was "Greek." The native tongue of the area was Messapic, though his family defined itself as belonging to the broader group of dialects, stretching southwards from "Samnite" central Italy, known to the Greeks generically as "Oscan" (Skutsch 1985:749). But he spent the larger part of his career in the company of the leading Roman generals of the day, including Cato (who brought him to Rome), Fulvius Nobilior, whose Aetolian campaigns he followed and described in his epic, and the Scipios, on whose sepulchral monument he was commemorated. What made this Greek/Oscan "Roman"? Later generations attributed to him a prophetic status in defining Roman character. Cicero, and later St Augustine, were to quote as emblematic his line:

> moribus antiquis res stat Romana virisque
> (by ancient customs and by men stands the Roman state). (*Annales* 5.156)

Ennius put these words in the mouth of Manlius Torquatus Imperiosus, that model of ancient Roman severity, discipline, and paternal authority, who executed his own son on the battlefield for stepping out of line (Skutsch 1985:317). Adherence to traditional ways, however grim and uncouth, was one potent way of defining Roman identity. But of course what made Ennius undeniably Roman was neither his friendship with the elite, nor his articulation of their morality, but the legal fact that he was a Roman citizen.

The attempts by Gordon Childe and his generation of archaeologists to use patterns of assemblages of material culture to pin down boundaries of cultural groups with some ethnic (let alone linguistic) identity relied on a concept of identity that was unitary: if a people had only one identity, it must reveal or express that identity in its distinctive ways and hence its distinctive pattern of material culture (Shennan 1989; Graves-Brown et al. 1996; Hall 1997). Such assumptions to some extent underlie the old model of "Romanization" which has recently undergone radical questioning (Metzler et al. 1995; Webster and Cooper 1996; Mattingly 1997; 2002; Keay and Terrenato 2001). That Roman conquest spread Roman ways is obvious. But to read into the progressive adoption of Latin language, Roman dress, Roman law and customs, and hence Roman material culture an expression of the abandonment of one identity and the adoption of another, is to assume that only one identity is possible. Just as post-colonial approaches question the "Hellenization" of the native peoples of Sicily, substituting the idea of "hybrid" or "creole" identities (Antonaccio 2003), so they deconstruct the "Romanization" of the Roman world, and expose its complexities and "creole" mixes (Webster 2001 2003). We must leave room for Ennius to be a model Roman without excising either his Greek or his Oscan hearts.

This brief chapter traverses a vast territory, and can do so only by exemplification. In looking at the apparently contradictory phenomena of the "Hellenization" of the Roman, and the "Romanization" of the empire, it aims not to offer a theory of cultural transformation, but an exploration of multiple identities. In examining how the "Roman" positioned itself in relation to the "Greek," the local Italian, the provincial and the barbarian, it will question the view that the outcome of Roman empire was a progressive homogenization of material (or other) culture.

Clothes and Language: What Is "Hellenization"?

In recounting the final days of Augustus' life, the biographer Suetonius gives an anecdote set on the Bay of Naples, that mixing bowl of Greek and Roman. He distributed new clothes to his companions, the Roman *toga* to the Greeks, the Greek *pallium* to the Romans, on the condition that the Romans speak Greek and the Greeks Latin (Suetonius, *Augustus* 98). Clothes are the material correlate to language, an expression of identity that depends on choice: you speak Latin or Greek, you wear the toga or the pallium (Figure 9.5 [a, b]). Augustus' game underlines distinction and difference. But it also reveals the possibility of interchangeability. Identities can be swapped, put on and off as easily as a set of clothes (Wallace-Hadrill 1998a; 1998b). Speaking one language does not imply incapacity in another: the codes, as the linguists put it, can be switched (Adams et al. 2002;

Adams 2003). What we call "identity," in a language redolent of 20th-century psychology and politics (Gleason 1983; Niethammer 2000), was for a Roman something more like a theatrical mask, a *persona* to be put on and off as circumstances demanded (Hölscher forthcoming). The skill lay in understanding which *persona* was suitable to the occasion.

There were dangers in getting it wrong. Cicero defended Rabirius Postumus, among other charges, on the count that when working at the royal court at Alexandria, he was frequently seen in Greek dress, the pallium. Cicero can cite precedent for appropriate behavior (wearing the pallium in Alexandria, the toga at Rome): the dictator Sulla wore the *chlamys* in Naples, and Scipio Asiaticus was actually represented in Greek chlamys and boots in a statue on the Capitoline (Cicero, *pro Rabirio Postumo* 25–27). Not wearing "proper" Roman clothing was a relative, not absolute, charge: Roman dress could vary according to occasion, at home or outside, morning or evening, relaxed or formal. In the end, Augustus himself reinforced the definition of the toga as the required formal wear of the Roman citizen for appearance on business in the Forum, lamenting that the Forum was full of people in lower-class working dress, *pullati*, at variance with Vergil's definition of the imperial people:

> Romanos, rerum dominos, gentemque togatam
> (Romans, lords of the world, and people of the toga). (ap. Suetonius, *Augustus* 40)

With this sort of emotive charge, the toga could be taken to symbolize the core of Roman identity, the possession of citizenship, and as such is represented in thousands of portrait statues of Romans (Zanker 1975 1983; Kleiner 1977). The potency of the material object in constructing identity lay in its relationship to the alternatives: in opposition to the military garb donned on service (so indicating civil activity in the forum), to the *pulli* of the poor and slaves, to the *stola* of the matron, to the pallium of the Greeks, to the *bracae* of the barbarian Gauls. That did not mean that to put on a pallium was to cease to be Roman. But to put on a toga, if not a Roman citizen, could be construed as passing yourself falsely as a citizen. The emperor Claudius made a defendant on the charge of false claim to citizenship wear his toga when speaking in his own defense, but change it for the pallium when being accused (Suetonius, *Claudius* 15).

Ironically, there is little sign that the Greeks themselves regarded the pallium as a critical sign of Hellenic identity. Even the word is purely Latin (for the Greek *himation*), as alien as the Roman naming of Hellenes as *Graeci*. It is a Roman construction of Greekness, exemplified by the labeling of Latin comedies adapted from the Greek as *fabulae palliatae*. Stage dress for Greeks offered up an image of alterity, a difference to reassure Romans of their own sameness.

Choice of language too carried different charges for Greek and Roman. Latin was always a language the Romans shared with neighboring peoples, and its use could not define the Roman. Only possession of Roman citizenship could do that. Hellenes, by contrast, never had a national identity definable by citizenship (which was linked rather to individual *poleis*): their identity was from the first a cultural

(a)

Figure 9.5 (a) Augustus wearing a toga (Ny Carlsberg Glyptotek, Copenhagen); (b) Hadrian wearing the pallium, from the Temple of Apollo at Cyrene. © Copyright the Trustees of The British Museum

(b)

Figure 9.5 *Continued*

one, defined by common language, common usages, and common gods (Herodotus 8.144.2). Anyone might opt, culturally, to "become" a Hellene, by speaking Greek, following Greek ways. It is precisely in the colonial situation of the multiplication of Greek cities in the eastern kingdoms, Egypt and south Italy, that the need for clear signifiers of Hellenic identity grew: above all the gymnasium with its complex of athletic practices and education, *paideia*. Those Jews who spoke Greek and attended the gymnasium, exercising naked, and even imitating the tied foreskin of the Greek athlete, were "Hellenizing" in the way required by Hellenic culture (Hengel 1980:55–66; Wallace-Hadrill 1998b:941–945).

This leaves the relationship of Greek and Roman significantly lopsided. For a Roman to learn and speak Greek was already "Hellenizing" from the viewpoint of Greek culture. From a Roman viewpoint, it in no sense diminished Roman identity. Cicero defended Archias, a Greek poet born in Syrian Antioch, who through being granted the citizenship of south Italian Heraclea consequently acquired Roman citizenship after the Social War. He wrote poems in praise of Roman generals in Greek. Did the prosecution regard that as a problem? Latin was a language of limited usage, whereas Greek was understood throughout the world: it was surely a good thing for Romans to be celebrated in the world language (Cicero, *pro Archia* 23).

A principle of Roman citizenship under the Republic was that it was not compatible with that of any other city. Cornelius Balbus of Gades, so Cicero emphasizes, ceased to be a citizen of Gades at the moment of his grant of Roman citizenship by Pompey. He earned his citizenship by putting his life at risk in the cause of Roman arms: exercise of "virtue" on Rome's behalf was the crucial requirement of the citizen. He could at any point return to Gades and resume his local citizenship (so abandoning that of Rome); and by the principle of *postliminium*, a right of recovery of citizenship originally given to protect war captives, he could at any moment return to Rome and resume Roman citizenship (Cicero, *pro Balbo* 27–29, Sherwin-White 1973:301–303). Thus you could both become, and unbecome, a Roman: it was a legal status, unaffected by cultural choices. On the other hand, in learning Greek culture, you Hellenized forever.

These contrasts are essential to grasp if we are to interpret the innumerable examples, in material and non-material culture, of the spread of "Hellenic" styles and ways in Roman Italy, particularly in the last two centuries B.C.E. Roman literature, Roman art, and Roman architecture were profoundly, and gloriously, transformed in this period into direct, continuous, and open imitation of Greek models, and frequently through the agency of Greek writers and artists. There was, and could be, no sense of the progressive elimination of the Roman: on the contrary, each successful imitation conquered new territory for Rome, as Cicero and others boasted.

The relationship can be better illustrated by looking at some limiting cases and exceptions, rather than by listing the endless positive examples. In the third quarter of the first century B.C.E., Cornelius Nepos prefaces his lives of Greeks and Romans by saying that Roman readers must understand some deep contrasts between their ways and those of the Greeks. When they read that the Theban hero Epaminondas excelled in dancing and singing to the pipes, they must not be shocked: for musical skill was a fundamental accomplishment for a Greek gentleman, though to a Roman it might be disgraceful. In Roman eyes, singing and dancing were for professional entertainers, slaves, and prostitutes. At this point, perceived "ancestral customs" were seemingly antithetical and irreconcilable. This helps to explain the Roman failure to "conquer" the field of music. It also explains why the emperor Nero's performances in public as a *citharoedus* were held shocking by many (not all) Romans, especially those of old-fashioned ways from the provincial colonies. Nero was indeed "Hellenizing" enthusiastically. It might shock, but it might also set a fashion (the future emperor Titus was a skilled musician). Each experiment in Hellenization was a gamble, which might take or not. Roman *mores* were constantly subject to change, and that change was only represented as a loss of identity by the enemies of the innovator. The elite were simultaneously guardians of ancestral ways, and the most vigorous innovators.

A second example of a limiting case is the Roman construction of theaters. Stone-built theaters were among the most conspicuous elements of the self-presentation of the Greek city, the focus of ritual, shared culture, and communal self-definition. Republican Rome followed a tradition which was articulated in a particularly aggressive form in the last century of the Republic, of avoiding any form of permanent theater building. This "tradition" was advertised in the conspicuous demolition of such a theater in the 150s, and a century later in the special pleading attached to Pompey's construction of the first stone theater on the Campus Martius, presented as a "temple with steps." The reasons for this refusal may be analysed as "political": on the one hand, a desire to protect the competitive elite tradition of the erection of temporary wooden theaters (each bringing ephemeral credit to its builder), on the other, the fear of the theater as a place of popular sedition (literally, "sitting down"), illustrated by the uses of theaters in the east as places of riotous political assembly (Gruen 1992:205–210).

Whatever the reasons, the effect was to place a limitation on what was otherwise a wholesale example of "Hellenizing." Rome had a long tradition of drama, going back to the Archaic period (Wiseman 1998:17–19). When, in the second century, the process of Roman "conquest" of Greek literature begins, drama plays a central role: the *fabulae palliatae* of Plautus and others were vigorously promoted by the elite, for their own political benefit. The Republican theater was a key location for the definition of Roman social order: the equestrian upper class was defined by the reservation of the front 14 rows in the theater (Rawson 1991:508–545). There was no resistance to drama on the grounds of being Greek or alien. Permanent theaters were constructed in numerous cities of central Italy, including the sanctuary of Praeneste (Figure 9.6; Rawson 1991:468–487).

Moreover, a new architectural form was developed in the amphitheater, designed for the distinctively Roman practices of gladiatorial fights and beast hunts, but while examples were put up in Roman colonies like Pompeii or Capua in the early first century B.C.E., the same ban on permanent theaters meant that Rome was late in acquiring the archetypally "Roman" architectural form, which occurred only under Augustus (Welch 1994).

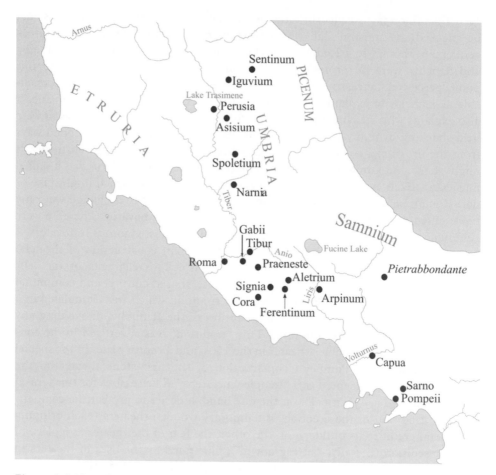

Figure 9.6 Map of central Italy. Drawing: Amy Richardson

The result is an extremely revealing misfit between the record of material culture and of the literary sources. The archaeological record of Roman theater building would suggest that it was a practice limited under the Republic to south Italian (i.e. Greek) cities and some central Italian cities under their influence, which only reaches Rome at the very end of the Republic, and subsequently flourishes there under the empire. The literary record enables us to say that this is because earlier Roman theaters were built in wood; and that the period of the greatest popularity of drama in its classic Hellenic forms of tragedy and comedy was under the Republic, and effectively died out under the empire. More stone theaters do not mean that Rome has become more Hellenized.

How to build a theater was set out in the late first century B.C.E. by Vitruvius (*de Architectura* 5.6–7). His account is eloquent of the constructed distances between Greek and Roman. In successive chapters, he provides alternative sets of rules for Greek and what he calls "Latin" theaters (acknowledging that in Rome they are only built of wood—5.5.7). He argues that the underlying mathematical logic is different: the Latin layout being based on four triangles, the Greek on three squares. He underlines different usage of space: the Greeks use the orchestra for performance (he leaves it to his readers to know that in Italy it was for elite seating). We can perhaps see this as a classic of cultural hybridization. The Latin theater may be a derivative of the Greek, but its variants guarantee its diverse identity.

The Romans themselves encouraged an image of the cultural development of Rome from the "uncouth," "rustic" autochthonous Latium to the newly won civilization (cultus) owed to the Greeks. Its most epigrammatic, and so most quoted, expression was by Horace:

> Graecia capta ferum cepit victorem, et artes/intulit agresti Latio
> (Captive Greece captured the wild victor, and brought the arts into rustic
>   Latium). (Horace, Epistles 2.1.156–157)

That was partly a myth serving their own ideological agenda, projecting a fantasy of the "real Roman" into a primitivized past, and maintaining an alibi, where it served, from the cultural forms so enthusiastically embraced. Cultural expressions of Roman identity were indeed very different by the end of the first century B.C.E. from two hundred years before, vastly richer and more complex. But rather than thinking of this as an effacement of Roman identity by the superior culture of the Greeks, we should surely regard it, as the Romans themselves did, as the acquisition of more ways of expressing, more forcefully and to a Mediterranean-wide audience, what being Roman was about. The more they learnt about being Greek, the more clearly they could explain why being Roman was different.

Romanizing Italy

It is scarcely surprising to conclude that in "Hellenizing," Romans suffered no loss of identity. On the normal model, culture spreads from the dominant power to the subject: for the Romans to take on Greek ways is no more a sign of subordination than for the British to eat chicken tikka massala, though they played ironically with the notion of the cultural subordination of the imperialist (Gallini 1973). Indeed, the adoption of a sort of dominant bilingualism of Latin and Greek was an essential device of the Roman control of the Mediterranean (Momigliano 1975; Adams 2003). The bilingualism was broadly cultural, not simply linguistic. The ambidextrous command of two traditions, kept notionally distinct from each other, produced a degree of interconnection between east and west Mediterranean that has never been paralleled since.

Similar arguments are much harder to apply to the relationship between Rome and the peoples of the Italian peninsula. The enormous variety of the area that only later was characterized as "Italy" is reflected in the extraordinary diversity of its languages: the "Italic" group alone comprised at least three distinct languages in the centre of Italy, Latin, Oscan, and Umbrian, which in turn had local subvariants, in addition to the Venetic of the north, the Illyrian-related Messapic of the south, the Greek of Magna Graecia, the Punic of Sardinia and western Sicily, and the non-Indo-European language of the Etruscans. The progressive elimination of the local variants, and the spread (or imposition) of Latin as *the* language of Italy, with Greek as its only permissible alternative, are widely taken as symbolic of the elimination of local identities and the spread of a central "Roman" model.

Conquest transforms cultures, and there is no point in pretending that Romans were not conquerors set upon the total subordination of Italy to their control. Without either a triumphalist celebration of the "success" of Roman imperialism, or a nostalgic sympathy for the loss of autonomous local cultures, we can observe in the longer term a substantial transformation in the archaeological record between the late fourth century, at the beginning of the process, and the end of the first B.C.E. which marks the moment, in a sense, of "unification" (David 1994). But the story is a great deal more complex than one of merciless and deliberate suppression of local identities; at the very least, it must allow room for a negotiation and dialogue between central and local, and an acknowledgment that the price paid for the "universalization" of the central identity is its own transformation.

Umbria is a test case that has provoked sharp debate (Bradley 2000; Sisani 2002). Roman conquest, between 310 and the battle of Sentinum in 295, was swift and decisive. Subjection was maintained by the classic instruments of Roman colonialism: the confiscation of territory, the founding of colonies at strategic points, Narnia and Spoletium, and the building of a trunk road, the via Flaminia, traversing the territory. These instruments decisively changed Umbria, as at the same time Etruria (Harris 1971).

But there are evident limits on the determination to "Romanize." In theory, Rome might have imposed from the start the solution which emerged two centuries later: to make all Umbrian towns "Roman," to make all Umbrians Roman citizens, imposing the use of Latin and of Roman law. Not only was that solution inconceivable in the early third century: it was one that could only be achieved after a bitter war which transformed the very concept of Roman citizenship. In 295, citizenship was still closely allied with active and exclusive participation in the affairs of the city of Rome. Even the Roman citizens given land in the new colonies of Narnia or Spoletium sacrificed their Roman citizenship for a new colonial identity, enjoying the privileges of the towns of Latium to exchange and intermarry with Romans.

Citizenship was (and always remained) a privilege, not a sign of subjection, except indeed for those whose lower status was marked by the lack of right to vote (*suffragium*). The subjection of the Umbrians lay in the fact that they did not become Romans, but were compelled as allies to supply troops to support Rome's campaigns. Rome at this stage had no interest in suppressing local identity or local language, only in ensuring the Umbrians loyally served the Roman cause, or in the standard language of their treaties, "gave friendly support to the majesty of the Roman people."

Significant cultural changes can be traced in Umbria over these two centuries. Urban centers develop, in size, sophistication, and monumental expression. But urbanism is not a Roman importation into Umbria, and it has its roots much earlier (Bradley 2000). Nor, as the development of the Sabine and the Samnite heartlands shows, did Romans impose urban development in all areas (Patterson 1991). It is much more plausible to argue that urban growth was a result of the requirement to supply troops on a regular basis, so promoting the sort of centralized institutions of taxation that were linked to urbanism.

We can speak convincingly of "self-Romanization." At Asisium, probably in the early second century, in close parallel to neighboring Perusia, the local magistrates built an imposing circuit of walls and gates, together with a system of terracing, that is the basis for the future urban layout of Assisi. This example of monumental planning, and the possibility of a conscious imitation of contemporary Rome with its colonnaded streets and circus, are read as pointing to a willing act of cultural borrowing (Coarelli 1996). The prestige and influence of the larger Roman colonial settlement of Spoletium, coupled with intimate knowledge of Roman ways and the Latin language through constant service in the army, provide a plausible context in which Roman ways might be voluntarily taken on by Umbrians, and specifically by local elites, whom the Romans typically encouraged as their local supporters.

That leaves room for a very considerable cultural bilingualism, which can be traced most clearly in the language of inscriptions. Because we are only dealing with a few dozen surviving examples, it is impossible to give reliable statistics or a definite chronology. What is evident is that Umbrian and Latin have a parallel existence in the course of the second century, with Latin coming to displace Umbrian, but gradually and seemingly voluntarily (Bradley 2000:203–217; Sisani 2002). The spectacular Iguvine tablets from Gubbio, the key text for the Umbrian language, are written in Umbrian language and Umbrian script at the beginning of that century, in Umbrian language but Latin script towards the end (Sisani 2001). Latin language as well as Latin script become quite common in Umbria, as in Etruria, before the Social War. That the languages sit for a while alongside each other is seen in the fact that the same Ner. Babrius, who as one of six local magistrates, *marones*, in Asisium celebrated the work on the wall circuit with an inscription in Latin, was also responsible for a boundary stone, probably on the border with Perusia, in Latin script but Umbrian language (Bradley 2000:210). At least for a period, scripts and languages are interchangeable. So too are institutions. *Maro* is the classic Umbrian title for a magistrate, but the Roman office of *quaestor* is met in this period, as the *cvestur* of the Iguvine tablets, or of the elegant late second-/early first-century sundial inscribed in Umbrian script and language by the *cvestur* (Bradley 2000:210).

We do not need to resort to the hypothesis of a deliberate imposition of Roman ways to explain this phenomenon. Where one language enjoys a position of dominance and wider diffusion, as was the case with the language in which Roman generals gave commands to Umbrian contingents, but also in which Umbrian officers and troops could communicate with their Oscan- or Messapic-speaking fellow soldiers, it is normal for its use to spread at the expense of the language of subordination. That does not mean that Latin-speaking Umbrians ceased to feel Umbrian, or indeed ceased to resent their subaltern status: it has been justly observed that in modern colonialist situations, rebellion often comes from the most "westernized" elements (Sherwin-White 1973:149).

The Social War of 91–89 B.C.E., led indeed by many of the most "Romanized" elements of the local elites of the allied states, produced radical changes in the cultural record. Public inscriptions in Umbrian (whether language or script), cease, as do inscriptions across Italy in virtually all non-Latin languages except Greek (Crawford 1996:425, 983–985). To judge by the epigraphic record alone, the Social War was a turning point in the story of local identities, though there are no clean breaks, and there is enormous variation from area to area (Benelli 2001). Does this mean that the war was to some extent about local identities, a reassertion of local autonomy and pride, followed by its final suppression? It is extraordinarily hard to read the archaeological record as supporting this argument. However, it is relevant to observe a phenomenon which is notably widespread in the cities of central Italy, the outbreak of major building schemes in the last part of the second century. In them we can certainly see some of the advantages of participation in Roman conquest, and probably see an assertion of local pride.

A particularly striking group is that of the allied cities with "Latin" status to the east and south of Rome, along the Sacco valley. The patchwork of statuses left by the history of Roman relations divided central Italy into areas fully incorporated into the Roman state, with *municipia* of Roman citizens (no issue of dual loyalty here, since the only citizenship was Roman, in that the *municipium* though self-governing was part of the Roman state), "Latin" (including Hernican) cities which were not part of the citizen body, but enjoyed certain privileges, "Latin" colonies, which like Latin cities were independent, and *socii* or allies which had neither Roman citizenship nor the privileges of the Latins, but the obligation to supply troops. It is impossible for us to tell whether it felt "better" to be from a Roman municipium, like Arpinum, the home of both Marius and Cicero, or from a Latin city like Tibur or Praeneste, which did not convey citizenship except possibly for magistrates (who often became part of the Roman elite), or to be an independent "ally," with all the obligations but none of the privileges of citizenship.

But in this context, it is interesting to see that the cities most active in major building schemes in the late second and early first centuries include a group of "Latin" cities not incorporated in the Roman state. At Tibur, both the magnificent sanctuary complex of Hercules Victor that straddled the approach road from Rome, and the smaller temples of the acropolis (Tiburnus and the Sibyl Albunea), belong to this period (Coarelli 1987; Giuliani 2004:87–89). At Praeneste, one of the most impressive sanctuary complexes of the Mediterranean world was constructed, in an architectural language steeped in Hellenistic models, by members of the same elite families that seem to have been virtually eliminated in the civil wars of the 80s (Coarelli 1992). To the south of the Alban hills, Latin Cora embellished its citadel with an elegant Doric temple, while the Latin colony of

Signia rebuilt its acropolis, on its high point commanding the Sacco valley, in the best Hellenistic style (Zevi 1994; Cifarelli 2003). Across the valley, the Hernican towns of Ferentinum and Aletrium monumentalized their own wall circuits and acropoleis; the fine inscription of Lucius Betilienus Vaarus, who endowed his town with walls, promenades, a sundial, a pool, cistern and siphon that raised the water supply 340 ft, verbally expresses the local pride implicit in the buildings (Zevi 1976).

What sort of statement of identity do they constitute? The architectural language employed belongs to a recognizable *koine* or common tongue with models in the east Mediterranean which we refer to as "Hellenistic." They were surely "Hellenizing" in the Greek sense of consciously adopting a Greek cultural language; and the fact that many elite families from these towns are recorded as having members active in the great market of Delos and in other eastern cities makes it likely that this "Hellenizing" was conscious and deliberate (Coarelli et al. 1982). Cicero twice claimed that in his boyhood, before the Social War, Greek literary studies flourished more in the Italian towns than at Rome (Cicero, *De oratore* 3.43, *Pro Archia* 5; cf. Rawson 1991:474). At the same time, there can be no sense of deletion of local identity. All these sites have circuits of "polygonal" or "Cyclopean" walling, which typically go back to the fourth century. They deliberately revived and emphasized this building technique, despite the availability and simultaneous use of construction techniques in *opus caementicium* ("concrete") which were pioneered by Roman architects. It is hard to escape the impression that their main concern was to compete with each other in investing the profits of campaigning in enhancing the pride of their own particular town.

Such efforts were by no means limited to Latin cities. We may look finally at two examples of Oscan allies. In Campania, Pompeii was already an impressive city with its ample later wall-circuit in the archaic period, under Etruscan influence. The period of Samnite domination, from the late fifth century to the end of the fourth, leaves hardly any archaeological trace, and it is almost certain that the city underwent significant decline (Guzzo 2000). Recovery and new building start in the third century, with Pompeii's new status as a Roman ally (and the obligation to supply troops). But it is only in the second century that a major boom starts. New housing rapidly spreads, and in the second half of the century there is a significant programme of public works: houses on the main streets are given new and grandiose façades in dressed stone ("Nocera tufo"), and the buildings round the Forum are transformed, a new basilica built, and the temple of Apollo rebuilt with a surrounding colonnade. A recently discovered inscription in that colonnade provides a clear historical context: a dedication in Oscan lettering to "Lucius Mummius son of Lucius, consul," the commander who sacked Corinth in 146 B.C.E. (Martelli 2002). It is not hard to imagine that a Pompeian contingent took part in the Achaean campaign, and that this and other service provided a major injection of capital invested in the "modernization" of the city.

Pompeians continued to use Oscan for their public inscriptions down to the Social War. Latin was a rarity, though the most magnificent house in town, that

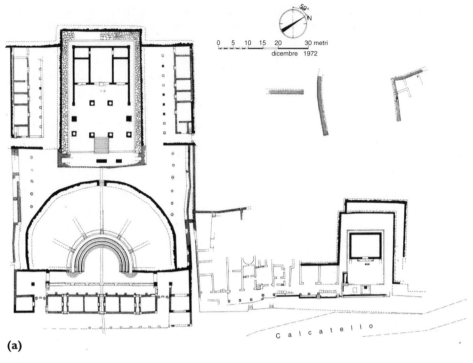

(a)

Figure 9.7 (a) Theater at Pietrabbondante. La Regina 1976; (b) Figure of Atlas at Pietrabbondante. Photo: author

of the Faun, built in the second half of the second century, perhaps by the local elite family of the Satrii (Pesando 1996), greeted its visitors with a Latin HAVE, before exposing them to the astonishing Greek masterpiece of the Alexander mosaic (Zevi 2000). Why not envisage a Satrius as trilingual like Ennius? But the Bay of Naples was exactly a point at which cultures met: where the Oscans came down to the sea, and met Greeks and Romans (D'Arms 1970). What of a site in the Samnite heartland like Pietrabbondante?

Few sites convey so strongly a sense of autonomy and difference: the physical location high in the mountains, the absence of the standard urban formulae of the coast cities, and the expressiveness of a sanctuary complex which served as periodic gathering point of a scattered rural population. In fact, the format of the sanctuary, combining temple and theater, is a widespread formula, met at Latin Gabii, Praeneste and Tibur (Figure 9.7 [a, b]). The architectural language of the theater is deeply Hellenistic, with specific features like the use of giant figures ("Telamones") as supports, and the elegant double curves of the bottom row of seats, that are close to the theaters of Pompeii and Sarno (Strazzulla and Di Marco 1972). Numerous dedications in Oscan by local magistrates create a more aggressively independent impression than the half-Latin Umbria (La Regina 1976; Tagliamonte 1996:221–234). Yet bilingualism is eloquently illustrated here

(b)

Figure 9.7 *Continued*

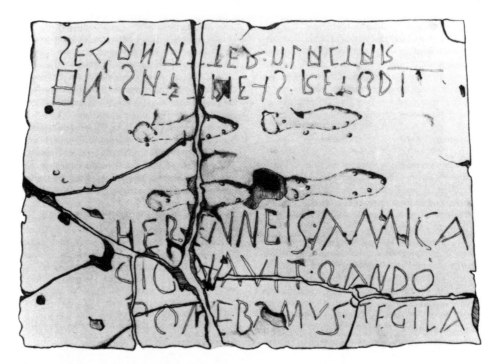

Figure 9.8 Tile from Pietrabbondante with inscribed names and footprints. *Studi Etruschi* 44 1976:285

too, by a roof-tile from the temple, upon which two female slave workers (unless it is just one playing games) had impressed their footprints, signing their names in mirror image, one in Oscan, the other in Latin (Figure 9.8; Adams 2003:124–126).

There are variations from site to site, but the impression of the century preceding the Social War is not of conflict or competition between cultures, but coexistence and interpenetration. The Italic cities are using both the profits and the knowledge that resulted from participation in conquest to innovate culturally, competitively taking on the architectural language of the Greek east (Zanker 1976). The handsome temple B at Pietrabbondante replaces an earlier shrine characterized by a specific shape associated with the oath of resistance to Rome taken during the Roman conquest of the fourth century B.C.E., and with ample dedications of captured armor (Coarelli and La Regina 1984:234–239). The rebuilt, modern temple is undoubtedly a Place of Memory of independence, but these Hellenized Samnites are not fastidious about sharing the profits and pleasures of empire.

From this perspective, the Social War cannot be about an unwillingness of the allies to be part of a Roman empire. The sources state with some clarity that their demand was full citizenship (Brunt 1988:93–143). It has been urged that this cannot have been the motive since Roman citizenship as conceived at the time up to the Social War would not have been beneficial or desirable (Mouritsen 1998).

Of course, the model of citizenship sought by the allies was that which was obtained *after*, not before, the war: its effect was to make the allies full and equal partners in the imperial enterprise, with their rights guaranteed by the vote.

It is surely at this point that the reciprocity of the historical compromise and the cultural deal lies. By becoming citizens, the allies sacrificed many signs of cultural diversity. By definition, all their public business must be conducted in Latin, under Roman law. The inscriptions documenting the collapse of local languages in public life reflect this, but do not prove that local languages died out (we hear of Oscan farces continuing, even in Rome, though then they were not necessarily in the Oscan language). What they take from Roman culture, they do by their own choice. If that can be described as a process of "bricolage," or "do it yourself," it is precisely because they are doing it themselves, and for themselves (Terrenato 1998; Keay and Terrenato 2001).

But if the allies have to give up something, so do the Romans. Against their will, they are constrained to redefine radically the one thing that most crucially constitutes their identity: Roman citizenship. Though they maintained the strict rule that Roman citizenship was incompatible with any other, the idea that you could belong to another municipium, though not another *civitas*, allowed the citizens of all Italic cities to be Roman. That vast extension of what "being Roman" means throws a new weight of definition on non-legal features. Ironically, the toga, which for Augustus defined the "Roman," had been standard wear before the Social War in the allied cities, which provided troops "according to the formula of the toga-wearers, *togati*." Standard Italic dress came to define the Roman, just as standard Italic ways of building theaters came to define the "Roman" as against "Greek" theater. The Italians became Roman on the condition that the Romans became Italian. Both sides found the point of cultural convergence in Hellenism, in relation to which Roman identity now defined itself, both by similarity and by difference.

Romanizing the Barbarian: Baths and Seduction

From this viewpoint, the "Romanization" of Italy is not a process by which the Romans deliberately turned the Italians into Romans. It is the process by which the Italians, resisting the Roman desire to hold them in subjection and in a culturally subaltern position, asserted their right to be taken as Romans too. Any loss of local identity is the sacrifice paid for a preferred and more potent identity. The loss of local languages is a familiar effect of centralization (Gaelic, Welsh, Cornish . . .), but it is not true that this results in the extinction of the sense of local identity. We may contrast Umbrian Plautus, born in Sarsina in the late third century, whose Latin plays betray nothing of his local origins, with Umbrian Propertius, born at Asisium in the mid first, who asserts with some vigor the local pride of the "Umbrian Callimachus," and remembered too well the bitter local wounds of the siege of Perusia. The sense of pride in local origins is typical of the Augustan age, and evidently encouraged by the emperor himself, who made play of his Italian credentials (Syme 1939).

What follows for the "Romanization" of the provinces? It could be argued that by the time of Augustus, the Roman-ness of Roman culture had been better defined (Vergil's epic provided an even better founding charter than Ennius', while Varro and other antiquarians had defined "the Roman way" and Vitruvius had defined Roman architecture). It was now an exportable culture in a way unthinkable even a century before. Augustan ideology and propaganda set models that diffuse spectacularly (Zanker 1988).

But to assume the Romans simply set about exporting their culture is to assume the Romans wished to make full Romans of all barbarians—which meant necessarily sharing with them citizenship, access to power, influence, office, and profit. That, to some extent, is what happened, and we watch in awe the ripples by which citizenship, membership of the Senate, access to imperial power, and domination of the lucrative Mediterranean-wide markets spread to Spain, North Africa, the Illyrian provinces, and the East (Syme 1958). But though the enlightened Claudius may have grasped that this was in a sense Rome's historic tradition and mission, the credit for extension of power must go as much to those who fought for it as to those who conceded it. "Romanization" is above all the *claim* by the provincials themselves to belong, the *demand* to participate, the *release* not the extinction of local energies. It is consequently forever a dialectic, by which central identity makes its necessary compromises with the latest claimants to participation (Millett 1990).

The starting point for those who see Romanization as a conscious instrument of a Roman *mission civilisatrice*, among whom Francis Haverfield nearly a century ago played a pioneering role, is Tacitus' description of Agricola's conduct as governor of Roman Britain (*Agricola* 21). He wishes to convert a people who are scattered (i.e. not city-based) and uncivilized and hence prone to fighting, and pacify them through "pleasures," and hence encourages in private, and supports in public, the building of temples, *fora*, and houses. The sons of the leading men are urged by the comparison with the Gauls to be educated, so not only mastering Latin, but acquiring the higher communication skills of eloquence. Roman ways spread, and the toga becomes common; so do the luxurious appurtenances of porticoes, baths and elegant dinners.

What has fed the idea of centre-driven Romanization is Tacitus' ironic coda: "The inexperienced called it 'humanity', when in truth it was a part of slavery" (Tacitus, *Agricola* 21.2). Here are the chains of cultural imperialism. Yet what is notable in his entire account is his emphasis on the voluntary participation of the natives. Agricola works by encouragement, specifically to members of the local elites: "by praising the keen, and castigating the sluggish, so that competition for prestige became a virtual necessity" (Tacitus, *Agricola* 21.1). There is no compulsion here, only incitement, and the entire point is that the process can only work if the elite itself actively plays the game. *Honoris aemulatio* is a key phrase: it is a competition for prestige between members of existing elites that is redefined in Roman terms. Agricola understands that if the elites compete for Roman, not native, status symbols, they enter the Roman stream. Hence the vital emphasis on pleasure and seduction. The natives need to be seduced by the pleasures of baths and dinners, and come to regard these typically Roman elite behavior patterns as natural.

All of this, it should be noted, is for Agricola only a sideshow: just one chapter covering the activities of his second winter, amidst so many chapters of campaigning. The active Roman contribution to Romanization is conquest: it is up to the locals to decide (or not) whether to turn themselves into Romans. Two hundred years after the Italian Social War, the Romans are fully alert to the processes which help to assimilate the conquered to themselves, and have a clearer (if somewhat ironical) grasp of what the Roman way is. But they also know that it only works so long as, and to the degree to which, the conquered actively wish to become Roman.

The success and limitations of the Romanization of Britain, it has been urged, are defined by the compatibility of the Roman model with the structures and needs of the old Iron-Age elites (Millett 1990). They do not wholeheartedly embrace the Mediterranean model of urban euergetism, the investment by elite families in conspicuous urban monuments. That observation surely forms the flip side of another observation, the relative failure of the British elites to penetrate the central Roman system, by supplying officers, senators, emperors to the center. It is those elites who want most actively to participate in the central Roman state (e.g. those of North Africa), who are also most vigorous in local euergetism. There is a loop: the elites which Romanize most vigorously, promoting urban growth and its capacity to convert agricultural surplus into cash, raise most resources to carry them to the center, and bring back from the center the greatest profits to reinvest locally. Britons seem half-hearted players in this game.

Nevertheless, the cultural impact on Britain was enormous. Sometimes such changes are seen best in small details. Agricola was right about the seduction of bathing (Fagan 1999). Not only did heated baths become common, in military camps, towns, and rural villas, but also the bodily regimes that go with bathing spread. We catch them archaeologically in the finds of toilet instruments, especially for depilation: tweezers, probes, razors, and nail-cleaners (Hill 1997). Hairiness was a key feature of the Roman depiction of the barbarian, while the bathed, groomed, and perfumed body spelled *cultus*, cultivation. Just as is suggested by the spread of such tell-tale signs of cultural choices in Gaul, it is hard to believe that the participants are not "internalizing" the values implicit in such practices, that make them feel akin to the conqueror, and distant from barbarians (Woolf 1998; 2001).

The same example of baths allows a link to Greece and the Eastern Mediterranean. The vocabulary of Romanization is not generally applied to discussion of this area, since Hellenization is felt to have functioned as an equally valid alternative. From the viewpoint of cultural identity here proposed, it is not enough to say that Rome did not feel the need to "Romanize" Greek areas; it should rather be the case that Hellenes felt no need to Romanize in order to secure such benefits and participation that they sought. But in fact the collusion between Greek elites and Roman rule was profound, and it made a significant impact on their landscape, concentrating settlements and wealth (Alcock 1993). The pleasures of bathing similarly seem to have exercised some seduction. The physical aspect of the *gymnasion*, long a key feature of a Greek city, changes significantly in the Roman period, in the direction of developing elaborate heated bath suites on the Roman model (Delorme 1960; Ginouvès 1962). A mark of this on the countryside is the construction of aqueducts to supply the water. Only part of the story is the "musealization" by which Greeks reclassicize their culture and parade its "superior" credentials (Bowie 1970; Swain 1996). Another part of the story is compromise and energetic participation in the perceived advantages of empire. Agricola's formula of "porticoes, baths and mansions" is no less applicable to the eastern cities.

The material culture of the Roman empire does, in conclusion, tell a story about changing and multiple identities. Whether in its large, distinctive structures, like baths or amphitheaters, or in the "small things forgotten" of everyday life, like tweezers for removing body hair, it tells of the advantages, in places widely separated in distance and cultural background, of presenting oneself as Roman. *Civis Romanus sum*. Greeks referred to those from a non-Hellenic background who learned the Greek language and embraced Hellenic culture as "Hellenizing." It is perhaps in this intransitive usage that "Romanization" can carry greatest conviction: to "Romanize" was not what the Romans did to others, but what those who wished to be taken as Romans did themselves. Even to speak of "self-Romanization" or "autoromanizzazione" is to imply that the normal and natural phenomenon is for cultural change to be wished on you from above. But not even Tacitus' *Agricola*, the only text which explicitly discusses the process, claims this.

From this perspective, "Hellenization" and "Romanization" cease to appear in conflict. Romans Hellenized with enthusiasm, above all to gain advantage over each other in a highly competitive system. Non-Roman Italians also "Hellenized" for the same motives. Neither experienced a "loss of identity" in so doing: enhancing and embellishing their cities boosted local pride rather than the opposite. At the same time, non-Roman Italians Romanized. In the course of the second century, they developed the desire to be Roman citizens, one which the existing citizen body long resisted. To Romanize was to lay claim to full participation in the Roman system of power.

That "the Romans" (that is, those already in power in the system) continued to allow ever wider circles of the conquered access to power at the centre remains a remarkable exception among imperial systems. There might be those like the emperor Claudius who thought that it had always been the Roman way to welcome in new blood: that was certainly not obvious to the majority of Romans in 91 B.C.E. And though it may appear that it was Roman generosity that spread power to the provinces, it is not clear in practice that those at the center welcomed the competition of newcomers. Only the emperors themselves can be said to have an interest in promoting "new men," precisely to destabilize the embedded interests of the existing elite (Hopkins 1983:171–175).

Figure 9.9 Portrait from Palmyra. Ny Carlsberg Glyptotek, Copenhagen

The possibilities of multiple identities were endless (Dench 2005). Those on the Syrian border of Roman control could express many identities in many languages (Millar 1993). A Palmyrene in his toga asserts his rights in the Roman system; his camel and the style of execution point to regional ties. Identity is not a zero-sum game, nor are its expressions in material culture (Figure 9.9). Across the empire, the record is eloquent of the complexity of what those who could call themselves "Roman" wished to claim for themselves.

REFERENCES

Adams, James N. 2003 Bilingualism and the Latin Language. Cambridge: Cambridge University Press.

——, Mark Janse, and Simon Swain, eds. 2002 Bilingualism in Ancient Society: Language Contact and the Written Text. Oxford: Oxford University Press.

Alcock, Susan E. 1993 Graecia Capta: The Landscapes of Roman Greece. Cambridge: Cambridge University Press.

Antonaccio, Carla M. 2001 Ethnicity and Colonization. In Ancient Perceptions of Greek Ethnicity. Irad Malkin, ed. Pp. 113–157. Washington, DC: Center for Hellenic Studies, Trustees for Harvard University.

——2003 Hybridity and the Cultures Within Greek Culture. In The Cultures Within Greek Culture: Contact, Conflict, Collaboration. Carol Dougherty and Leslie Kurke, eds. Pp. 57–74. Cambridge and New York: Cambridge University Press.

Benelli, Enrico 2001 The Romanization of Italy through the Epigraphic Record. In Italy and the West: Comparative Issues in Romanization. Simon Keay and Nicola Terrenato, eds. Pp. 7–16. Oxford: Oxbow.

Bernabò Brea, Luigi 1957 Sicily Before the Greeks. C. M. Preston and L. Guido, trans. London: Thames and Hudson.

Bhabha, Homi K. 1994 The Location of Culture. London and New York: Routledge.

Bowie, Ewen L. 1970 The Greeks and their Past in the Second Sophistic. Past and Present 46:3–41.

Bradley, Guy 2000 Ancient Umbria: State, Culture and Identity in Central Italy from the Iron Age to the Augustan Era. Oxford: Oxford University Press.

Brunt, Peter A. 1988 The Fall of the Roman Republic and Related Essays. Oxford: Clarendon Press.

Childe, V. Gordon 1956 Piecing Together the Past: The Interpretation of Archaeological Data. London: Routledge and Kegan Paul.

Cifarelli, Francesco Maria 2003 Il tempio di Giunone Moneta sull'acropoli di Segni: storia, topografia e decorazione architettonica. Rome: "L'Erma" di Bretschneider.

Coarelli, Filippo 1987 I santuari del Lazio in età repubblicana. Rome: La Nuova Italia Scientifica.

——1992 Praeneste in età repubblicana. Società e politica. La Necropoli di Praeneste "Periodo orientalizzante e medio repubblicano." Atti 2° convegno di studi archeologici, Palestrina 21/22 Aprile 1990. Pp. 253–268. Palestrina: Commune di Palestrina.

——1996 Da Assisi a Roma. Architettura pubblica e promozione sociale in una città dell'Umbria. In Assisi e gli Umbri nell'Antichità. Atti del Convegno Internazionale Assisi 18–21 dicembre 1991. G. Bonamente and Filippo Coarelli, eds. Pp. 245–263. Assisi: Soc. Editrice Minerva.

——, and Adriano La Regina 1984 Abruzzo, Molise. Guide archeologiche Laterza. Rome: Laterza.

——, Domenico Musti, and Heikki Solin, eds. 1982 Delo e l'Italia. Rome: Bardi.

Cohen, Beth 2001 Ethnic Identity in Democratic Athens and the Visual Vocabulary of Male Costume. In Ancient Perceptions of Greek Ethnicity. Irad Malkin, ed. Pp. 235–274. Washington, DC: Center for Hellenic Studies, Trustees for Harvard University.

Crawford, Michael H. 1996 Italy and Rome from Sulla to Augustus. In Cambridge Ancient History X²: The Augustan Empire, 43 B.C.–A.D. 69. Edward Champlin, Andrew

Lintott, and Alan Bowman, eds. Pp. 414–433, 939–989. Cambridge: Cambridge University Press.

D'Arms, John H. 1970 Romans on the Bay of Naples: A Social and Cultural Study of the Villas and their Owners from 150 B.C. to A.D. 400. Cambridge, MA: Harvard University Press.

David, Jean-Michel 1994. La Romanisation de l'Italie. Paris: Aubier.

Delorme, Jean 1960 Gymnasion: étude sur les monuments consacrés à l'éducation en Grèce (des origines à l'Empire romain). Paris: De Boccard.

Dench, Emma 2005 Romulus' Asylum: Roman Identities from the Age of Alexander to the Age of Hadrian. Oxford: Oxford University Press.

Dietler, Michael 1999 Consumption, Cultural Frontiers, and Identity: Anthropological Approaches to Greek Colonial Encounters. *In* Confini e frontiera nella Grecità d'Occidente. Atti del 37° Convegno di Studi sulla Magna Grecia. Pp. 475–501. Taranto: Istituto per la Storia e l'Archeologia della Magna Grecia.

Fagan, Garrett G. 1999 Bathing in Public in the Roman World. Ann Arbor: University of Michigan Press.

Foley, Anne 1998 Ethnicity and the Topography of Burial Practices in the Geometric Period. *In* Argos et l'Argolide: topographie et urbanisme. Actes de la table ronde internationale, Athènes-Argos 28.4.1990–1.5.1990. Anne Pariente and Gilles Touchais, eds. Pp. 137–144. Athens and Nafplio: L'Ecole Française d'Athènes and the 4th Ephoreia of Prehistoric and Classical Antiquities.

Gallini, Clara 1973 Che cosa intendere per ellenizzazione. Problemi di metodo. Dialoghi de Archeologia 7:175–191.

Ginouvès, René 1962 Balaneutike: recherches sur le bain dans l'antiquité grecque. Paris: De Boccard.

Giuliani, Cairoli Fulvio 2004 Tivoli: il santuario di Ercole Vincitore. Tivoli: Tiburis Artistica.

Gleason, Phillip 1983 Identifying Identity: A Semantic History. Journal of American History 69:910–931.

Graves-Brown, Paul, Sian Jones, and Clive Gamble, eds 1996 Cultural Identity and Archaeology: The Construction of European Communities. London and New York: Routledge.

Gruen, Erich 1992 Culture and National Identity in Republican Rome. Ithaca: Cornell University Press.

Guzzo, Pier Giovanni 2000 Alla ricerca della Pompei sannitica. *In* Studi sull'Italia dei Sanniti. Rosanna Capelli, ed. Pp. 107–117. Rome: Soprintendenza Archeologica di Roma.

Hägg, Robin 1998 Argos and its Neighbours: Regional Variations in the Burial Customs of the Protogeometric and Geometric Periods. *In* Argos et l'Argolide: topographie et urbanisme. Actes de la table ronde internationale, Athènes-Argos 28.4.1990–1.5.1990. Anne Pariente and Gilles Touchais, eds. Pp. 131–135. Athens and Nafplio: L'Ecole Française d'Athènes and the 4th Ephoreia of Prehistoric and Classical Antiquities.

Hall, Jonathan M. 1997 Ethnic Identity in Greek Antiquity. Cambridge and New York: Cambridge University Press.

Harris, William V. 1971 Rome in Etruria and Umbria. Oxford: Clarendon Press.

Hengel, Martin 1980 Jews, Greeks and Barbarians: Aspects of the Hellenization of Judaism in the Pre-Christian Period. London and Philadelphia: SCM Press.

Hill, J. D. 1997 The End of One Kind of Body and the Beginning of Another Kind of Body? Toilet Instruments and Romanization. *In* Reconstructing Iron Age Societies. A. Gwilt and Colin Haselgrove, eds. Pp. 96–107. Oxford: Oxbow.

Hölscher, Tonio, forthcoming The Concept of Roles and the Malaise of "Identity": Ancient Rome and the Modern World. *In* Role Models: Identity and Assimilation in the Roman World. S. Bell and I. L. Hansen, eds. Ann Arbor: University of Michigan Press.

Hopkins, Keith 1983 Death and Renewal. Sociological Studies in Roman History 2. Cambridge: Cambridge University Press.

Keay, Simon and Nicola Terrenato, eds. 2001 Italy and the West: Comparative Issues in Romanization. Oxford: Oxbow.

Kleiner, Diana E. E. 1977 Roman Group Portraiture: The Funerary Reliefs of the Late Republic and Early Empire. New York: Garland.

La Regina, Adriano 1976 Il Sannio. *In* Hellenismus in Mittelitalien: Kolloquium in Göttingen vom 5. bis 9. Juni 1974. Paul Zanker, ed. Pp. 219–254. Göttingen: Vandenhoeck und Ruprecht.

Leighton, Robert 1999 Sicily Before History: An Archaeological Survey from the Palaeolithic to the Iron Age. Ithaca: Cornell University Press.

Martelli, Andrea 2002 Per una nuova lettura dell'inscrizione Vetter 61 nel contesto del santuario di Apollo a Pompei. Eutopia, n.s. II, 2:71–81.

Mattingly, David J., ed. 1997 Dialogues in Roman Imperialism: Power, Discourse and Discrepant Experience in the Roman Empire. Journal of Roman Archaeology Supplementary Series No. 23. Ann Arbor: Journal of Roman Archaeology.

——2002 Vulgar and Weak "Romanization", or Time for a Paradigm Shift? Journal of Roman Archaeology 15:536–540.

Metzler, J., Martin Millett, Jan Slostra, and Nico Roymans, eds. 1995 Integration in the Early Roman West: The Role of Culture and Ideology. Luxembourg: Dossiers d'Archéologie du Musée National d'Histoire et d'Art IV.

Millar, Fergus 1993 The Roman Near East, 31 BC–AD 337. Cambridge, MA: Harvard University Press.

Miller, Margaret C. 1997 Athens and Persia in the Fifth Century: A Study in Cultural Receptivity. Cambridge and New York: Cambridge University Press.

Millett, Martin 1990 The Romanization of Britain: An Essay in Archaeological Interpretation. Cambridge: Cambridge University Press.

Momigliano, Arnaldo 1975 Alien Wisdom: The Limits of Hellenization. Cambridge: Cambridge University Press.

Morgan, Catherine 1991 Ethnicity and Early Greek States: Historical and Material Perspectives. Proceedings of the Cambridge Philological Society 37:131–163.

——2001 Ethne, Ethnicity, and Early Greek States, ca. 1200–480 B.C. *In* Ancient Perceptions of Greek Ethnicity. Irad Malkin, ed. Pp. 75–112. Washington, DC: Center for Hellenic Studies, Trustees for Harvard University.

——, and Todd Whitelaw 1991 Pots and Politics: Ceramic Evidence for the Rise of the Argive State. American Journal of Archaeology 95:79–108.

Morris, Ian 1987 Burial and Ancient Society: The Rise of the Greek City-State. Cambridge and New York: Cambridge University Press.

——1998 Archaeology and Archaic Greek History. *In* Archaic Greece: New Approaches and New Evidence. Nick Fisher and Hans van Wees, eds. Pp. 1–91. London: Duckworth.

Mouritsen, Henrik 1998 Italian Unification: A Study in Ancient and Modern Historiography. London: Institute of Classical Studies, University of London.

Niethammer, Lutz 2000 Kollektive Identität. Heimliche Quellen einer unheimlicher Konjunktur. Reinbeck bei Hamburg: Rowolht.

Ober, Josiah 1989 Mass and Elite in Democratic Athens: Rhetoric, Ideology, and the Power of the People. Princeton: Princeton University Press.

Osborne, Robin 1997 Law, the Democratic Citizen and the Representation of Women in Classical Athens. Past and Present 155:3–33.

Patterson, John R. 1991 Settlement, City and Elite in Samnium and Lycia. In City and Country in the Ancient World. John W. Rich and Andrew Wallace-Hadrill, eds. Pp. 147–168. London: Routledge.

Pesando, Fabrizio 1996 Autocelebrazione aristocratica e propaganda politica in ambiente privato: la casa del Fauno a Pompei. Cahiers du Centre Gustav-Glotz 7:189–228.

Pollitt, Jerome J. 1972 Art and Experience in Classical Greece. Cambridge: Cambridge University Press.

Rawson, Elizabeth 1991 Roman Culture and Society. Collected Papers. Oxford: Clarendon Press.

Redfield, Robert, Ralph Linton, and Melville J. Herskovits 1936 Memorandum for the Study of Acculturation. American Anthropologist 38:149–152.

Rutter, N. K. 1997 The Greek Coinages of Southern Italy and Sicily. London: Spink.

Sackett, James 1977 The Meaning of Style in Archaeology. American Antiquity 42:369–380.

Shennan, Stephen J., ed. 1989 Archaeological Approaches to Cultural Identity. London and New York: Routledge.

Shepherd, Gillian 1995 The Pride of Most Colonials: Burial and Religion in the Sicilian Colonies. In Ancient Sicily. Tobias Fischer-Hansen, ed. Pp. 51–82. Acta Hyperborea 6. Copenhagen: Museum Tusculanum Press.

Sherwin-White, A. N. 1973 The Roman Citizenship. 2nd edition. Oxford: Clarendon Press.

Sisani, Simone 2001 Tuta Ikuvina. Sviluppo e ideologia della forma urbana a Gubbio. Rome: Edizioni Quasar.

——2002 British Umbria (quasi una recensione ad uno studio recente). Eutopia II.1:123–139.

Skutsch, Otto 1985 The Annals of Quintus Ennius. Edited with Introduction and Commentary. Oxford and New York: Oxford University Press.

Snodgrass, Anthony 2000 The Dark Age of Greece. 2nd edition. New York: Routledge.

Strazzulla, Maria J., and Benito Di Marco 1972 Il Santuario sannitico di Pietrabbondante. Molise: Soprintendenza del Molise.

Swain, Simon 1996 Hellenism and Empire: Language, Classicism and Power in the Greek World, AD 50–250. Oxford: Clarendon Press.

Syme, Ronald 1939 The Roman Revolution. Oxford: Clarendon Press.

——1958 Tacitus. Oxford: Clarendon Press.

Tagliamonte, Gianluca 1996 I Sanniti. Caudini, Irpini, Pentri, Carricini, Frentani. Milan: Longanesi.

Terrenato, Nicola 1998 The Romanisation of Italy: Global Acculturation or Cultural Bricolage? In TRAC 97. C. Forcey, J. Hawthorne, and R. Witcher, eds. Pp. 20–27. Oxford: Oxbow.

Wallace-Hadrill, Andrew 1998a To Be Roman, Go Greek: Thoughts on Hellenization at Rome. *In* Modus Operandi: Essays in Honour of Geoffrey Rickman. M. Austin, J. Harries, and C. Smith, eds. Pp. 79–91. London: Institute of Classical Studies.

——1998b Vivere alla greca per essere Romani. In *I Greci. Storia Cultura Arte Società 2. Una storia greca. III Transformazioni.* Salvatore Settis, ed. Pp. 939–963. Turin: Einaudi.

Webster, Jane 2001 Creolizing the Roman Provinces. American Journal of Archaeology 105:59–180.

——2003 Art as Resistance and Negotiation. *In* Roman Imperialism and Provincial Art. Sarah Scott and Jane Webster, eds. Pp. 24–51. Cambridge: Cambridge University Press.

——, and Nick Cooper 1996 Roman Imperialism: Post-Colonial Perspectives. Leicester Archaeological Monographs 3. Leicester: University of Leicester.

Welch, Katherine 1994 The Roman Arena in Late-Republican Italy: A New Interpretation. Journal of Roman Archaeology 7:59–80.

Wiessner, Polly 1983 Style and Social Information in Kalahari San Projectile Points. American Antiquity 49:253–276.

——1989 Style and Changing Relations Between the Individual and Society. *In* The Meaning of Things: Material Culture and Symbolic Expression. Ian Hodder, ed. Pp. 56–63. London and New York: Routledge.

Wiseman, T. P. 1998 Roman Drama and Roman History. Exeter: University of Exeter Press.

Woolf, Greg 1998 Becoming Roman: The Origins of Provincial Civilization in Gaul. Cambridge: Cambridge University Press.

——2001 The Roman Cultural Revolution in Gaul. *In* Italy and the West: Comparative Issues in Romanization. Simon Keay and Nicola Terrenato, eds. Pp. 173–186. Oxford: Oxbow.

Zanker, Paul 1975 Grabreliefs römischer Freigelassener. Jahrbuch des Deutschen Archäologischen Instituts 90:267–315.

——, ed. 1976 Hellenismus in Mittelitalien: Kolloquium in Göttingen vom 5. bis 9. Juni 1974. 2 vols. Göttingen: Vandenhoeck und Ruprecht.

——1983 Zur Bildnisrepräsentation führender Männer in Mittelitalischen und campinischen Städten zur Zeit der späten Republik und der julisch-claudischen Kaiser. *In* Les "bourgeoisies" municipales italiennes aux IIe et Ier siècles av. J.-C. Pp. 251–266. Paris: Editions du Centre national de la recherche scientifique.

——1988 The Power of Images in the Age of Augustus. Ann Arbor: University of Michigan.

Zevi, Fausto 1976 Alatri. *In* Hellenismus in Mittelitalien: Kolloquium in Göttingen vom 5. bis 9. Juni 1974. Paul Zanker, ed. Pp. 84–96. Göttingen: Vandenhoeck und Ruprecht.

——1994 Considerazioni vecchie e nuove sul santuario della Fortuna Primigenia: l'organizzazione del santuario, i Mucii Scaevolae e l'architettura "mariana." Le Fortune dell'età arcaica nel Lazio ed in Italia e loro posterità. Atti 3° convegno di studi archaeologici, Palestrina. Pp. 137–183. Palestrina: Commune di Palestrina.

——2000 Pompei: Casa del Fauno. *In* Studi sull'Italia dei Sanniti. Rosanna Capelli, ed. Pp. 118–137. Rome: Soprintendenza Archeologica di Roma.

10

Linking with a Wider World

Introduction

Every book on the classical past in some fashion holds up a mirror to the age in which it was written. This volume is no exception: a fact perhaps seen most clearly in this chapter, with its emphasis on cultural interaction, human connectivity, and the consequences of global exchange.

Some of the sharpest criticisms applied to "old-fashioned" classical studies converge on its once serene assumption of the impermeability and innate superiority of the cultures of Greece and Rome. Archaeologists were complicit in such models, as they traced unidirectional, Hellenic influences on the colonial western Mediterranean or across the Hellenistic kingdoms to the east. Roman archaeologists, in turn, measured the spread of "Romanization" through the movement of artifacts such as wine amphoras and shiny red pottery. Greece and Rome, it seemed, could expand at will, but remained somehow unaffected.

The fallacy of such attitudes is clearly illustrated in the following chapter, which traces innumerable back-and-forth processes of contact, exchange, influence, emulation, and annexation across the ancient world. All manner of people, goods, skill-sets, and beliefs were mobilized around the Mediterranean and far beyond, with implications—direct or indirect—for all actors caught up within these networks, be they local or long-distance. While we do possess some travelers' accounts or ethnographies which can occasionally testify to these multiple forms of contact, archaeology stands in the strongest position to detect and make sense of them. Categories of data range widely, including stylistic influences in statuary or architecture, imported foodstuffs, shipwreck contents, new ritual practices, and the presence of exotica, to name but a few. Despite some usual and ubiquitous difficulties (for example, tracing the movement of perishable goods, including self-moving items of trade such as slaves), material evidence remains our best hope for recovering the circulation and consumption of things, both tangible and intangible.

The nature of these interactions varied, of course, from period to period, and from one political formation to another. In some cases, they took the shape of serendipitous exchange, in others, of highly structured, long-distance trade. Colonial foundations opened up and nurtured new links—not least through intermarriage between colonial and indigenous populations—while imperial expansion forged entirely unprecedented unified worlds, such as the *Mare Nostrum* ("Our Sea") of the Roman empire. The complexities of living in these wider worlds in turn complicate definitions of just what we mean by "Greek," or "Roman," culture.

For all this multiplicity of connection and interaction, contact with "the other" nonetheless simultaneously provoked new perceptions of the self and of separate cultural identities (see also chapter 9). The polarity of Greek and barbarian ran profoundly deep: a fact with immense ramifications for later conceptions of "western civilization." Despite this perceived distance, ongoing, two-way exchanges between Hellenic and eastern societies are now readily documented. Similarly, Rome's frontiers are increasingly perceived as highly permeable; indeed they are better described as zones of interaction than firm barriers. Yet in antiquity they still demarcated spheres of *Romanitas* versus barbarism. These ambiguities have contributed to making the study of culture contact, as well as of frontiers and boundaries, among the most fertile topics in classical archaeology today.

10 (a)

Linking with a Wider World

Greeks and "Barbarians"

Sarah P. Morris

Greek archaeology is often monopolized by the art of classical Athens, thanks to its standing monuments, its vases made largely for export, and its historical reputation. In the context of this chapter, just how much wider was the world of Hellenism, and how can archaeology help us understand and visualize the expanded arena of classical antiquity? For the Greek culture of the *polis* flourished in hundreds of city-states, initially dispersed across the Aegean archipelago, then multiplied on the shores of the Adriatic, the Black Sea, North Africa, Europe, and eventually as far as the Indus river. Never centered on a single city or power, this expansive network of linked yet independent *poleis* gave Hellenism infinite confrontations with other cultures in local constellations, unlike the expanding and contracting frontiers of the Rome-centered world analyzed in this chapter. Moreover, the origins of this polis culture took root in a much wider Mediterranean world than ancient Greeks, or modern Europeans, have always recognized. The culture of classical Greece reached deep into prehistory and the Levant, while its ultimate expansion through Macedonian conquest extended down the Nile and up the Himalayas. Thus in its origins and its reach, Greece was always part of a wider world, and archaeology illustrates this extent and variety, beyond textual sources.

Prehistoric Prelude: Contacts East and West

The Mediterranean had enjoyed links with a wider world since the Late Bronze Age, when exotica such as Baltic amber from northern Europe and Mesopotamian seals made their way into wealthy tombs and palaces in Greece (Gale 1991; Cline and Harris-Cline 1998). As with the circulation of goods in the Roman Empire, maritime trade is richly illustrated in shipwrecks full of cargoes reflecting contacts around the Mediterranean. Archaeology has animated Near Eastern texts and images of commodities and luxuries with the contents of two ships that sank off the coast of southwest Anatolia in the Late Bronze Age (Bass 1998). Key to the wider world at the time was a network of diplomatic relations maintained between Near Eastern principalities, through gift exchange and marriage alliances (Liverani 1990). While such relations survive primarily in texts (royal correspondence from Egypt, Babylon, and the Hittite capital of Hattusas), recent analysis of luxury artifacts (ivory, faience) sees artists at royal courts such as Ugarit practicing a form of "diplomacy by design," by creating a deliberate hybridity in art (Feldman 2005). It was in such luxury arts that Aegean "Keftiu" (in Egyptians' terms), distinguished themselves in Near Eastern sources, and applied these arts to decorate palaces in the Egyptian delta (Avaris) and the Canaanite Levant (Tel Kabri).

But Aegean rulers (Minoans on Crete, then Mycenaeans of mainland Greece) remained largely on the margins of the greater world empires of the east and their power dynamics, as did classical Greeks prior to the aggressive campaigns of Alexander the Great. "Keftiu" served as artists, merchants, and mercenaries, as in later Greek contact with the Near East. Not until the Roman period did Mediterranean leaders learn to exploit power relations with Near Eastern client kings, on an equal footing and to mutual advantage. Meanwhile, in the Bronze Age western Mediterranean, Mycenaean pottery was carried to Italy, Sicily, Sardinia, and even as far as Spain, in an early prelude to later exploitation of resources by Aegean captains and entrepreneurs.

The distinctive international flavor of Greek culture proper that is the subject of this chapter belongs to the Iron Age (especially 1000–500 B.C.). Since the tenth century, Near Eastern luxury goods (faience, jewelry, ivory) had appeared in Greek tombs on Crete and Euboia, a sign of early contact probably via Phoenician traders, as well as of Greek enterprise in the Levant. Foreign craftsmen, as well, may have settled in the Aegean to produce these luxury goods (for a critical view of this hypothesis, see Hoffmann 1997). As raiders, traders, and mercenaries, "Ionians" (Iavan) found opportunities in later centuries with then world powers Assyria and Egypt, leaving their names on foreign monuments (for example, at Abu Simbel in Upper Egypt) and bringing home exotic trophies (Figure 10.1). In the lands of the Bible, poets and prophets knew "Iavan" for their metals and slaves, prior to the fall of Assyria in 612 B.C. (Ezekiel 27.13), and in Egypt, Greek mercenaries were prized as "men of bronze from the sea" (Herodotus 2.152). An Ionian who served pharaoh Psammetichus in battle was rewarded with a gold bracelet and a polis, the command of a city: he commemorated his adventure on an Egyptian basalt statue, back home near Priene (Boardman 1999:281, figure 324). As much as ancient and modern sources glamorize this era (800–500 B.C.) as one of heroic exploration and adventure, in reality, Hellenes were largely in competition with, if not often in service to, Near Eastern commercial entrepreneurs and military masters, and the prizes they brought home reflect but a small share of foreign booty.

Perhaps the most important legacy of this early exchange was the adoption of the Northwest Semitic (Phoenician) alphabet by Greeks in the eighth century B.C.,

Figure 10.1 Syrian horse frontlet, ninth century B.C., found at sanctuary of Hera, Samos. H. = 27.3 cm. Inscribed as booty from Umqi seized by King Haza'el of Damascus (ninth century B.C.). Photo: Deutsches Archäologisches Institut Samos 1988/1022: Kyrieleis

a tool passed on to Rome, Europe, and most of the literate world today. So closely associated was this innovation with its Phoenician sources that a scribe on Crete was still called a *poinikastas* ("Phoenicianizer") in the sixth century B.C. (*Supplementum Epigraphicum Graecum* 27.631), and early writing was remembered as "Kadmeian letters," named for Kadmos, a mythical Phoenician who settled at Thebes (Herodotus 5.58). Its path was complicated: Semitic alphabet writing first appears on a bronze cup buried at Knossos in the tenth century B.C., but Greek versions do not materialize until two or three centuries later, and then in several locales, including Italy. In the west, Semitic letters are scratched on Greek vases found in Italy (Ischia), Cypriots are involved at many key locales but ignored the alphabet at home, Phrygians and Etruscans may have adopted Semitic writing independently from Greeks, and the entire picture suggests multiple encounters between writers of Semitic letters and the rest of the Mediterranean. An attractive model for this important step in cultural transmission remains intermarriage and its bilingual offspring (Coldstream 1993; Shepherd 1999), a natural development among mobile and migrant populations, and one that inserts the role of women as well as men into Hellenic contacts. Meanwhile, Ionian Greeks may have adopted the demotic Egyptian system for their alphabetic numerals (Chrisomalis 2003): learning to count from Egypt but writing like Phoenicians. These lessons typify the variety of simultaneous engagements with a wider world throughout the classical Mediterranean in the first millennium B.C.

More material responses to the stimulation of Near Eastern culture include the first colossal Greek statues in stone of the seventh and sixth centuries B.C., closely modeled on Egyptian types (for an example from the island of Samos, long-time partner of Egypt, see Figure 10.2). Along with monumental architecture modeled on Near Eastern traditions, Greece eventually bequeathed these arts to post-classical Europe, together with institutions like the alphabet. Invisible until later texts are the long-lived intellectual fruits of this exchange, especially in Ionia, where developments in mathematics, cosmology, and philosophy may reflect tutelage in Babylonian learning or Egyptian practices. It was in this early and fertile stage of contacts through trade and enterprise that the wider world of the eastern Mediterranean, in particular, contributed to the culture that became Greece (Burkert 1992), and these contacts are largely visible in archaeology (Morris 1992). Thus, Greece absorbed and incorporated major components of its wider world from an early age, and its natural orientation to maritime traffic and trade kept it a constant participant in the life of the ancient Mediterranean.

Famished Colonists and Thirsty Barbarians: Greeks and Others Overseas

A more deliberate stage of Greek-led expansion took the form of colonies implanted at strategic harbors and near attractive resources, all around the Mediterranean and into the Black Sea. Legends often trace these initiatives to hardship at home (as in the foundation of Cyrene in Libya: Herodotus 4.147–167), but Greeks may more often have followed the positive example and path of Phoenicians in seeking new and profitable economic niches abroad. While Greek memory celebrates heroic founders and their deeds in the textual "poetics of colonization" (Dougherty 1993), daily transactions and long-term effects may have been more closely determined by native agents and sub-elite Greek merchants, not by the

Figure 10.2 Marble statue of youth (*kouros*) found in sanctuary of Hera, Samos; dedicated by Isches. Restored H. = 4.80 m. Date: ca. 560 B.C. Photo: Deutsches Archäologisches Institut Samos 1987/908: Koppermann

aristocrats worshipped as leaders and heroes. Here the archaeological record helps restore equity across ancient lines of class and ethnicity, throughout the wider world, and demonstrates many modes of interaction and their results, not covered in literary sources.

A key recent development in understanding these relationships has been guided by new conceptualizations of the "archaeology of colonialism" (Lyons and Papadopoulos 2002), in a post-colonial age. Modern European experience has often influenced the way we view ancient sea-borne exploration, but new approaches and methods are uncovering a fresh variety of configurations in this early Greek diaspora. Recently archaeologists have moved beyond identifying Greek artifacts abroad and their local imitations, and mapping their distributions as an index of Hellenism, assumed to be a civilizing force. Instead, more interesting and informative patterns of production and consumption in terms of native agendas emerge in these encounters (Dietler 1995; Shepherd 1999; Dominguez 2002). Thanks to a major shift in archaeological attention, non-Greek populations around the ancient Mediterranean are emerging more clearly. The very word "colonization" as a concept for early Greek expansion, and the powers of archaeology to distinguish and classify different historical experiences, have been questioned (Osborne 1998). Fresh new views of Greek expansion have opened up an even wider world, transcending frameworks like Hellenization or colonization, for a bilateral view of cultural interaction.

Often no more than trading outposts (manifest in names like "Emporion") near harbors or rivers, with limited contact to the interior or up river except through indigenous partners, Greek "colonial" implantations can survive in town plans, building techniques, mortuary customs, and explicitly Greek imported goods. Moreover, within one generation of contact or settlement, local production of artifacts influenced by Greek forms displays a hybridity of culture difficult to translate into demographics, but clearly an important dimension of the way Greek culture multiplied itself across space, through time. Here archaeology allows us to compare settlements and ways of life in Iberia (at Emporion), Libya (Tocra, Cyrene), the Black Sea or Pontos (Olbia and other Milesian colonies), and Egypt, to consider the quality of life and relations with natives as a series of social experiments (Boardman 1999; Karageorghis 2003).

In many of these locales, newly arrived Greeks met vastly different social groups: strong tribal powers in proto-urban Illyria, nomads of the south Russian steppes along with semi-settled forest dwellers on the north coast of the Black Sea, Phoenician mercantile rivals in Sicily and Spain, and eventually the expansionist Persian empire in Scythia, Anatolia, and Egypt. They also encountered institutions alien to their own history, such as monarchy, and exported traditions of their own, such as athletics: soon "barbarians" like Macedonians (Herodotus 5.22) and Molossians (Pindar, Nemean 7.34–64) discovered long-lost Greek pedigrees and competed in pan-hellenic games. Local developments as well as changed conditions back in Greece encouraged new waves of expansion in the fourth century, with a shift to escalated agricultural production abroad near cheap land and labor, notably on the north coast of the Black Sea (Randsborg 1994; Saprykin

1994). Thus, the myth of an early "age of colonization" receives important correction from the archaeological record, with its long-term picture of Greek (and non-Greek) mobility and enterprise, independent of strictly political events.

Illyria, Iberia, and beyond

The earliest colony on the north shore of the Black Sea, the island of Borysthenes (Berezan in Russian), was settled by Greeks in the later seventh century B.C., according to imported ceramics. But local handmade vessels continued to be made and used, and it has been argued that before houses in fully Greek style, on an orthogonal grid plan, were implanted in the late sixth century, settlers lived in native dugout houses, enhanced by Greek techniques such as mud-brick walls on stone socles (Solovyov 1999; Tsetskhladze 2004). In striking fusions of native and Hellenic traditions in the archaeological evidence, we can imagine the growth of a hybrid culture under Greek influence, even when we cannot identify inhabitants by ethnicity, or settlements as colonies. The Berezan model of interaction observed in housing is matched in burial customs at other Greek colonies. For example, at the Corinthian colony of Apollonia in Illyria, the dead were buried in limestone sarcophagi with Greek pottery, but incorporated into the local tradition of tumuli, leaving hundreds of earth mounds in the necropolis. In death, as in life, Hellenism abroad evolved into a new culture that drew from multiple traditions.

Colonialism without colonies, or exploitation of resources without permanent, political settlements, has been explored in southeastern Iberia (Dominguez 2002). Within Greek colonies like Emporion (Empúries), Greeks and Iberians lived separately at first, although the Greek quarter shows few Hellenic features. Only with the Roman conquest, it has been argued, did Greeks assert their ethnic identity with an aggressive building program at Empúries (Kaiser 2003). But archaeology demonstrates a much wider sphere of interaction than at historical colonies such as Empúries. For example, monumental sculpture in southeastern Iberia in the fifth century was clearly inspired by Greek examples, but flourished in native settlements, especially as elite monuments in cemeteries (Dominguez 1999). That these statues were identified with a ruling elite with close ties to foreign traditions is implied by their eventual destruction, a sign of popular native resistance to this ruling elite, it has been argued. Elsewhere within the Iberian sphere, a stone statue of a warrior was reused as a door jamb in an indigenous settlement in southern France: stylistic details connect it to Etruria and Greece as well as Spain, but its original function(s) remain to be explained from local conditions (Dietler and Py 2003). The development of Greek-inspired sculpture in Iberia and Gaul, and its demise, provide a contrast with the "subversive" use of Classical-style religious sculpture in Roman-era Germania, identified as a sign of resistance rather than adaptation (Webster 1997:327; Dominguez 2002:80). Whether this reflects the striking differences between Greek and Roman interaction with their Mediterranean neighbors, or local divergences between Celtic and Iberian cultures, requires further testing of the archaeological record, but it moves inquiry beyond marking the mere presence or absence of Classical influences in the western Mediterranean, and towards understanding them.

The Greeks in Gaul: The Bride of Massalia and the Princess of Vix

Gaul was a significant arena for both Greeks and Romans abroad, beginning with Phocaean migration from Asia Minor to the mouth of the Rhône in southern France (compare Dietler 1997 and Hermary 2003, for different views of Greek colonization). Its principal Greek colony, Massalia, lies buried under modern Marseille, but new exploration reveals a constellation of satellite settlements in the hinterland of the port city, under Greek influence (Hermary 2003). In legend-ary accounts, the marriage of a Celtic princess (Gyptis) to a Greek settler of Massalia has the bride choose her consort from a selection of Greek suitors by offering him a cup of wine (Aristotle, Frag. 549=Athenaeus 13.576; cf. Justin 43.3), which helps make ceramics found at colonial sites more than mere imports but bearers of meaning in colonial-native encounters (Dietler 1995). The pairing of a native female partner with a Greek trader in this story restores female agents to processes often reduced to mercantile exchanges between men, and recalls the crucial role of intermarriage stressed above.

Gyptis is not the only Celtic woman to play an active role in encounters between Hellenes and their wider world: in the mid-sixth century B.C., a magnificent bronze krater made its way into the grave of a Celtic princess, many miles up the Rhône and Seine from Greek Massalia (Figure 10.3). Probably made in Magna Graecia and re-assembled in Gaul, the size (1.64 m. in height) and splendor of this krater recall legendary vessels exchanged as gifts in archaic Greece and dedicated in Greek sanctuaries such as Samos (Herodotus 4.152). The Vix krater also claims a smaller twin in a rich burial in Trebenishte in the Balkans (Boardman 1999:237, figure 280), suggesting that certain artifacts played a key role in Greek traffic with "barbarians," perhaps as lavish gifts establishing favorable relations. The rich variety of other imported items in the Vix tomb and at other sites in France dem-onstrates how successfully traders navigated local rivers and markets to distribute luxury goods far from the Mediterranean, and how these objects fed local elite ambitions and materialized their status. Indeed, certain classes of artifacts, most notably Attic black- and red-figure vessels found predominantly in Etruscan tombs in Central Italy, may have been produced largely for a non-Greek market, as barbarian tastes largely shaped specialized industries of early Greek art. How they were distributed, and what role natives rather than Greeks may have played in selecting as well as rejecting imports, are larger questions that open up important issues of social relations and local materialization of power, beyond mere "market" mechanics and notions of "trade" (see discussion in Arafat and Morgan 1994).

Just how Gaul negotiated its needs with Greeks can be compared with her unique relationship with Rome, in a later, imperial encounter where Gaul played the role of a crucial locale for "becoming Roman" (Woolf 1998; see the second half of this chapter). Explicit comparison between Hellenization and Romanization

Figure 10.3 Greek bronze krater found in Celtic grave at Vix, France. H. = 1.64 m. Date: ca. 530 B.C. Photo: Giraudon. Musée du Châtillonais, Châtillon-sur-Seine

in southern France (at Glanum-St. Remy: Heyn 2002, or Marseille: Lomas 2004) illustrates how archaeology can pose and answer deliberate questions about Greeks and Romans among barbarians, with long-lasting effects on what became the culture called Europe. In the case of Massalia, its Greek identity survived, and was even actively retained by Romans, as a continuing, civilizing buffer against the "barbarians" of Gaul (Lomas 2004).

One lasting legacy of this encounter that involves both Greeks and Romans, embodied in vessels such as cups and kraters (bowls for mixing wine), was the introduction of Greek vines to southern Gaul, the basis of a long relationship that Italy, as well as Greece, conducted with the western Mediterranean. Greek drinking cups and amphoras, followed by local versions, trace the path and growth of native appetites for fermented goods, commodities also introduced to local agriculture (the origin of the modern French wines). But native rituals such as feasting predated the foundation of Massalia, and modern focus has shifted from Greek distribution to native consumption of these commodities (Dietler 1989). They were also linked to other trade goods, most notably slaves, by the Roman period: natives of Gaul readily traded their own enslaved war captives to Italians for wine, and Italians put those slaves to work in their vineyards to produce more wine for thirsty barbarians (Diodorus Siculus 5.26). Thus invisible cargoes, both human and consumables, lie behind the artifacts that we analyze for history, in a process where classical containers have probably played an exaggerated role in native dramas as imagined by archaeologists.

Traditions in architecture and settled life were slower to appear in Europe, but have been posited, as at Berezan. Innovations such as urban fortifications and stone socles supporting mud-brick walls at princely seats in Celtic territory (Heuneburg) have been claimed as symptoms of Mediterranean influence (Wells 1980), when accompanied by Greek coins and pottery. But, as in the interpretation of ceramics and bronzes, other mechanisms could have inspired innovations, not merely imitation of classical forms. Are the *oppida* (hill forts) of Iron Age central Europe a native response to fortified citadels of the Mediterranean, a material sign of secondary urbanization, or a local development independent of classical cities (compare Wells 1984 and Hermary 2003 to Dietler 1989)? These early experiences on the edges of the Greek world form both a prelude and a contrast to Rome's relationship with the same area (as discussed in the second half of this chapter). In particular, the dominant role of Greece and later Rome in these local urban developments, once assumed by archaeologists, has been examined more critically in Gaul and Germania (Woolf 1993).

The same building escalation strikes Illyria and other Balkan areas where Greek-style fortifications proliferate in the wake, it is assumed, of Greek colonization and influence. Often such developments are linked by scholars to literary traditions that credit Athens with educating barbarians for a more civilized life. Tribes like the Molossians of Epirus claimed descent from Homeric heroes and sent princes to Athens for lessons in democracy (Plutarch, *Pyrrhus* 1), where some became honorary citizens (*IG* II^2 226; Davies 2000). Can one apply these testimonia to the rise of planned cities and fortified citadels in northwest Greece, or are these architectural developments independent of contact with classical Greece? Comparative analysis throughout the wider world of Hellenism helps transcend local restrictions on these questions, and so do new methods in archaeology, such as surface survey which demonstrates widespread transformation of landscapes (or its absence) as a result of Mediterranean contact. Investigating a greater range of sites, such as modest native settlements as well as elite citadels, wealthy burials, or Greek colonies, may provide more information (as at Lattes, in southern Gaul: Dietler and Py 2003). By privileging classical sites and long-term effects on Europe, we surely have lost insights into regional microcosms that contributed to the larger picture.

Ancient stories and modern views of these regional encounters often anticipate or assume native resistance to Hellenic settlers, and the "civilizing" power of Hellenism that transformed native life. These assumptions become leitmotifs in how Rome viewed her "barbarian" neighbors in the same areas, centuries later, along with the polarization of Greek and native as positive and negative, or at least unequal forces, in a hegemonic process. The variety of ancient settlements and archaeological juxtapositions suggest an infinitely more varied and complicated set of encounters at the boundaries between ancient cultures, beyond the inequalities assumed from modern colonialism.

In general, Greeks enjoyed greater freedom in the pre-Punic west, even with Phoenicians as constant rivals for markets and resources, than the Romans did once Carthage loomed as enemy number one. Yet the rise of Carthage also drove Greeks from the west as it left Rome to cope with Punic power, leaving little basis for comparing Greek and Roman contact. In areas where Romans replaced Greeks as chief foreign agents, and trading posts became provincial capitals, differences are more dramatic (Randsborg 1992). In a sense, Carthage and Rome largely diminished the visibility of Greek activity in the western Mediterranean (but see Emporion in Iberia: Kaiser 2003), and the rest of the story of their wider world belongs to the east.

The Eastern Front: Egypt

The wider world offered Greeks and Romans profoundly different challenges and opportunities in the Eastern Mediterranean, where major world powers had controlled events since the Bronze Age, unlike the western Mediterranean and the north (Europe and the Black Sea). Unlike the mother-city and colony pattern emphasized in literary sources, or the independent trading posts maintained by Greek entrepreneurs, archaic settlements in Egypt like Naukratis were established according to special regulations dictated by an Egyptian pharaoh (Herodotus 2.154, 178–182). They were restricted to the Nile Delta (i.e. coastal areas) and, unlike other Greek colonies, included representatives of many different Greek cities who maintained their own residential areas and religious cults. One of the first sites excavated by the founder of modern stratigraphic archaeology, Sir William Flinders Petrie, Naukratis has received renewed attention in several modern campaigns (for summaries, see Boardman 1999:118–133; Möller 2000). Trading settlements like these are likely locales for lessons in counting, and if the Ionians did adopt an Egyptian numerical system (see above, with Chrisomalis 2003), we imagine this developed through activity at sites like Naukratis. But did emporia like these, with their ceramic and faience factories, or did more independent Greek traffic provide the kind of cultural exchange we see reflected as

Egyptian influence on early Greek architecture and statuary (compare Figure 10.2)? How does Naukratis compare with the more independent settlement at Berenike on the Red Sea established in Ptolemaic and Roman times (below), linked as it was both to India and to Nilotic Egypt via desert trade routes (Alcock et al. 2003)? Farther west on the north coast of Africa (Libya), Greeks settled beyond Pharaonic or Punic powers in more "typical" Greek colonies at Cyrene, Tocra, and Euesperides (Barker et al. 1985; Gill 2004). Eastward up the Via Maris into the Levant, Greeks may have settled permanently after military service with Near Eastern armies, in enclaves or garrisons resembling pharaonic Tell Defenneh (Daphnae) in the Nile Delta (Niemeier 2001).

In many ways, Egypt cast a lasting spell over the Greek and Roman imagination, first struck by the tremendous scale and age of its monuments, while forever entranced by the mysteries of its royal hierarchy and religious system. From Herodotus to Plutarch, Greeks recognized or even exaggerated what was Egyptian in their own religious practices, and often attributed their own achievements in wisdom to Egyptian sources. Much of these connections transpired through traveling priests and sages attached to eastern courts, who brought eastern lore back to Greece, and Greek specialties to the east (Burkert 1992). This kind of activity is hard to document archaeologically, but had longer-lasting effects on culture.

In short, it was the archaic period or early Iron Age that first introduced Hellenism to the western Mediterranean and Europe, in ways that had profound and lasting effects on Rome's relationship with these areas, and ultimately on modern "Europe." In contrast, the greater powers of the east required negotiations that continued to challenge Greece and Rome as they did Europe, long after the end of classical antiquity. This contrast has been called "learning in the east and south, teaching in the west and north" (Boardman 1999:8, 282; cf. Coldstream 1993:105), a description that forces contacts in the wider world into a didactic, hegemonic model, disguising how much influence traveled in both directions, in more than one place.

The Classical Moment: Greeks and "Barbarians"

An extensive sphere of activity, stimulated by the movement of people and goods, and highly productive in intellectual and cultural exchange, was forever altered (largely conceptually rather than practically) by the historic encounter between eastern Greeks and the expanding Persian empire. From the fall of Lydia (546 B.C.) through the battle of Plataea (479 B.C.), Ionians, then Athenians and central Greeks, and finally most of the Greek states engaged in battle with the largest land empire of the time. It was the Hellenes involved in this encounter, and principally the Athenians, who invented the concept of the barbarian in the aftermath of their defeat of the Persians (Hall 1989), and deployed it in discourse to designate, and often denigrate, those who did not speak Greek. This established an attitude towards the wider world inherited by the Romans, who applied it largely to the cultures that became western Europe. In the Greek world, it also simplified and flattened the variety of "other" cultures on their borders, reducing them to those who did not speak Greek or live in Greek-style communities. Archaeology has recently helped to recover the tremendous variety of these cultures.

Even at the moment the term "barbarian" was invented, the concept and its ideology veiled a material world long enchanted with eastern luxury goods—from peacocks to parasols—the archaeological record betrays an appetite for the culture of the enemy (see illustrations in Miller 1997). Like the captivation Greece exercised over its Roman captors (Horace, *Epistulae* 2 1.156), Achaemenid Persia largely shaped life in the eastern Mediterranean for Greeks, Persians, and many others, before and after the Battle of Marathon. While their influence is most vivid in metalwork, seals, and ceramics, even the design and message of the Parthenon frieze—perhaps the most famous classical work of art in modern eyes— may have been inspired by royal reliefs of Achaemenid Persia, the culture whose defeat it sought to celebrate (Root 1985). Other neighbors of Greece had become part of daily life and work. The very barbarians whom Herodotus analyzed and classified in his *Histories* (4.1–82) policed the streets of Athens as Scythian archers or decorated the Parthenon frieze (horsemen in Thracian dress: see essays in Cohen 2000). Artists responsible for these vases and sculptures were often non-Athenians, who signed their works with foreign names; in building accounts, workmen on the Erechtheion frieze who were metics (resident aliens) or slaves (often foreigners) greatly outnumbered citizens as artists (Randall 1953). Thus, while rhetoric helped Athenian speakers and audiences distinguish themselves, for political purposes, from foreign enemies—Persians in the fifth century, Macedonians in the fourth century—their material world was an international one, with as many imported exotica and migrant artists as in the archaic period.

Similarly, Greek art and artists flourished in "barbarian" locales from the sixth century B.C. Most famously, the Persians themselves captured war trophies from Greece, including images of Athenian heroes like the Tyrannicides, and the statue of a woman made famous from Homeric poetry (the so-called "Mourning Penelope," was found at Persepolis: Ridgway 1970:101–104, figure 139). Their palaces were decorated by eastern Greek craftsmen, who represented eastern costume with Greek drapery folds (Nylander 1970), just as later Persians (Parthians) emulated Greek statuary (Boardman 2000). But elsewhere in the Persian empire, closer to Greece, contact and influence are also visible. Only recently has Achaemenid (rather than Greek or Anatolian) culture seen archaeological investigation in Asia Minor, with dramatic results (Bakir 2001; Dusinberre 2003). Within the borders of the Hellenized Persian world, stone carvers disseminated a distinctly "Graeco-Persian" style in gems, vessels, and funerary art (gravestones, sarcophagi), especially at locales such as Daskyleion in northwest Asia Minor, seat of a Persian satrap (Kaptan 2002). The fusion of Persian ambition with Greek style in service to a third party shows us the other side of the coin, as it were, to the non-Greek role noted above in Athenian art. Emphasis on Persia as the chief non-Greek "other" (Cohen 2000), in ancient and modern sources, also skirts the rich variety of other non-Greeks in Asia Minor: Carians adopted both Greek and

Persian traditions to forge new identities in material culture, at contact points between East and West (Linders and Hellström 1987). Other native cultures of Anatolia at the interface of Greek and Persian spheres include Lydians and Phrygians (see essays in Cohen 2000 and in Sancisi-Weerdenburg and Kuhrt 1991), or the Lycian elite who affected Achaemenid styles in their tomb paintings and sculpture (Childs 1981; Miller 1997: figure 29).

Cultural encounters between Greeks and Persians transcended their own political boundaries and outlasted the fifth century. In a striking example of ethnic and aesthetic triangulation, one Greek artist signed a red-figured relief lekythos, depicting Persians hunting creatures both real and imaginary in an Oriental *paradeisos*, as "Xenophantos the Athenian." But he made it for a Crimean customer in the early fourth century: the vessel was found in a grave at ancient Pantikapaion on the north-eastern shore of the Black Sea (Miller 2003). Beyond its fascinating incorporation into Greek art of Achaemenid hunting iconography (probably borrowed from imported stone seals), this vase also demonstrates the widened horizons of Graeco-Persian artistic activity that anticipates the cultural expansion enacted by Macedon. These experiences wove barbarian tastes and talents into "Greek" art in many locales over the centuries, in a way that challenges us to define Hellenism, in cultural and material terms, separately from its wider world.

Hellenism Abroad: Macedon and After

The political limits of the Greek world were changed dramatically with the expeditions of Alexander (the Great) of Macedon, whose ten years of campaigns brought Greek culture through conquest to Syria, India, and Egypt by 323 B.C. For the second but not final time, classical armies clashed with and triumphed over Persians, later reborn as the Parthian enemies of Rome. Short-lived as a world empire, this vast territory, combining the lands of Darius V and Philip II, soon re-consolidated itself following the death of Alexander into kingdoms based at Antioch (Syria), Alexandria (Egypt), Seleucia (Mesopotamia), and Pella in Macedon (Greece). Many of these cities lie buried under modern successors, but archaeological research in areas like Syria has produced valuable results in regions overshadowed by Roman remains. This fragmented Greek world was eventually absorbed by Rome through conquest and bequest, but the eastern Mediterranean remained profoundly Greek until the fall of Constantinople in 1453, or even the expulsion of Greeks from Asia Minor and Egypt in the 20th century. The Euphrates remained a significant frontier for the Romans as for Seleucid kings, requiring the establishment of border posts such as Dura-Europos and Ghebel el-Khalid as a bulwark against the Parthians. Like Germania in the west, Persia and its successors defined the limits of Mediterranean expansion in the east. But they also transmitted (as Parthians) a classical style in sculpture and imagery that far outlasted the political power of Greece and Rome, and spawned a new classicizing style as far as the Hindu Kush (Boardman 1994:75–153).

While historical studies of this period are dominated by conquests, kings, and cities, its economy was far more visible in archaeology, in the contents of shipwrecks, and the production of amphoras that anticipates Roman trade patterns (Archibald 2002). It was in this era that Mediterranean interests in luxury goods and specialty commodities reached the Indian Ocean, a prelude to the escalation in Roman trade with the Asian sub-continent (Salles 1996).

In the wake of Macedonian conquest, garrisons and outposts of the Greek city mushroomed across Asia (Leriche 2003). At Aï Khanoum in Afghanistan (ancient Bactria), implanted classical theaters and gymnasia hosted Hellenic cultural practices such as drama and athletics, next to Persian-style palaces and houses built in local mud-brick technique. Local rulers reinvented themselves as Greek dynasts who minted coins and promoted their own portraits on them. Meanwhile, Greek cities at home became subject to Macedon, and to the rule of monarchy: Athens herself, bastion against barbarians, experienced Macedonian rule, which left its mark on Athenian art and archaeology (Palagia and Tracy 2002). In between Greece and Afghanistan, archaeological research in the Levant reveals Hellenization on the ground, in architecture, sculpture, and mosaics at sites like Tel Dor in Israel (Stewart and Martin 2003).

At the same time, as in earlier ages, cultural influence traveled in both directions. In one lasting development in architecture, the practical and long-lived arch and its extension, the barrel vault, may have been launched in Greece as a re-creation in stone of mud-brick forms viewed by Alexander's engineers in the east (Boyd 1978). Most notoriously, the conqueror himself, Alexander, was reputed to have adopted eastern dress, promoted marriage for himself and his officers with Persian wives, and demanded eastern-style obeisance from his soldier-subjects (Plutarch, *Alexander*; Arrian 4.10.5–12.5, 7.4.4). Modern and ancient versions of these anecdotes either deplore this behavior as signs of "going native," or praise it as a vision of universal brotherhood; neither scenario may be close to ancient events. But even the legends underscore the implied or actual role of intermarriage in cultural interaction, emphasized above in considering encounters between Greeks and their neighbors in an earlier era (see above). Greek names soon proliferate in documents throughout the Hellenized Near East, without guaranteeing that we can thereby distinguish a Greek or Macedonian from a Hellenized native. Perhaps the most interesting conversions in both directions took place in the ritual sphere: Macedonian generals restored the shrine of Marduk at Babylon, even the highly Greek Aï Khanoum maintained a strictly Mesopotamian temple, and Greek kings in the east converted to Buddhism by the second century B.C. (Colledge 1987; Potter 2003). In Egypt, the new Macedonian dynasty founded by Ptolemy adopted Serapis (Osirapis: a fusion of Osiris, god of the underworld, and the bull-god, Apis), already popular among Greeks of Memphis, as the patron god of their new capital, Alexandria. Back in the Aegean, archaeological and epigraphic evidence shows a proliferation of foreign cults from Egypt, Syria, and Persia, at international places like the island of Delos.

Given the spell cast by Egypt and its relative proximity, it was no accident that the foremost of the cities founded by Alexander lay in Egypt, and ultimately replaced Naukratis as chief domain of Greek activity in coastal Egypt. The modern city has made ancient Alexandria difficult to trace archaeologically (see *Alexandria and Alexandrianism*, for a survey of material arts and culture), and recent exploration has focused on its submerged remains. Inside and outside of Alexandria, our understanding of Ptolemaic and Roman Egypt is dominated by documents, chiefly papyri, and exploration of the interaction of Egyptians, Greeks, Jews, and Romans heavily weighted towards texts (e.g., Bilde et al. 1992). Yet these texts also suggest strategies for archaeological research beyond cities and archives. For example, the most multicultural arena of Ptolemaic Egypt may have been the countryside, where Greek settlers and Macedonian veterans (and later Romans) took advantage of new land and opportunities (Rowlandson 2003). Documentary papyri suggest how regional survey might reveal such textures, and current archaeological survey (e.g. in the Fayoum lake area, drained by the Ptolemies) could restore these dimensions of Greek life in Egypt. A shift in focus away from texts and monuments towards the more ubiquitous minor arts in clay, so productive for the study of early Greek activity in the Mediterranean, offers a more informative and equitable picture of eastern life in the Hellenistic period, especially in Alexandria (Rotroff 1997). Through Antony's affiliation with Cleopatra VII, the last Ptolemaic ruler, Hellenistic Egypt took the losing side in a Roman civil war and fell to Rome as enemy territory. But a taste for Egypt long animated the world of Rome, not just in obelisk trophies or "pyramid" tombs set up in the capital, but in the widespread cult of Serapis and Isis, and in "Nilotic" landscapes decorating Roman villas.

One model for this vast new world, widely Hellenized after Alexander, derives from the ancient literary paradigm of the *oikoumene* or "inhabited," i.e., civilized, world. But this concept privileges Hellenism as it overlooks the great variety of local cultures, maps the *oikoumene* along political borders, and neglects local developments that may have transpired independently of Greek or Macedonian influence. The Bosporan kingdom on the Black Sea is one case in point where local consolidation of power took place on its own terms (Alcock et al. 2003). As in the western sphere of Mediterranean activity, regional analysis helps greatly by "breaking up the Hellenistic world" into landscapes transformed, to transcend a narrow focus on cities and temples, statues, and coins as measures of Hellenism exported. A striking variety of regional identities was expressed in material culture, beyond strictly Greek and Persian styles. For example, a new style of column capital developed by Pergamum, deliberately recalling earlier local forms, was featured in buildings they donated to cities like Athens. The fate of those identities in transition to more uniform Roman rule, and ultimately into the shadow of a new pair of superpowers, Romans and Parthians, has also recently come under scrutiny by archaeologists.

Beyond Greeks, Persians, and Macedonians as major players, old neighbors became new "barbarians," in particular the Celts of Gaul. Reborn as Galatians, they attacked the city of Rome, the sanctuary of Delphi in Greece, and invaded Asia Minor in the third century B.C. (Mitchell 2003). Art and literature offer one picture of their assault and defeat, but only recently has archaeology revealed

Figure 10.4 Funerary monument of Philopappos of Besa, Mouseion Hill, Athens. Date: A.D. 114–116. Photo: Marie Mauzy

dozens of sites they fortified in Asia Minor, and cemeteries (e.g., at Gordion) where they buried their dead with Celtic rites (such as horse sacrifice). Resembling or even absorbing those natives of Anatolia invisible between the literary poles of Greeks and Persians, the Galatians emerge as a major force of minor barbarians, in archaeological survey and research in regional landscapes (Strobel 2002). Their archaeological profile includes Hellenized Anatolian natives, assimilated to both Greek and Celtic ideals, and more convenient for the Romans to treat as Greeks, or *Gallograeci* (Livy 38.17.9). Like the Phoenicians, the Celts challenged both Greeks and Romans, in East and West, and during Archaic as well as Hellenistic times, as a lasting element of Europe in contact and conflict with the Mediterranean.

What was the ultimate fate of this vast panorama of local kingdoms, based on classical-style cities but ruled by "barbarians," and how did it survive in Roman terms? The eastern world obeyed no single master, but all honored the cultural magnet that was still Athens, long after its political power had disappeared and it had become, to all intents and purposes, a town of universities and museums. Eastern benefactors continued to endow the city of classical culture with monuments, notably the kings of Pergamum, sent their sons to be educated in Athens, and even took refuge there from local disasters. One of the latest and most prominent classical monuments in Athens has crowned the Mouseion hill since the second century A.D. (Figure 10.4). It commemorates Philopappos, the last member of the eastern Commagene dynasty (whose kingdom was annexed by Rome); Syrian and Seleucid by birth, he became a naturalized citizen of Rome and Athens, held office in both cities, and was buried in Athens. Until the Christian emperor Justinian banned pagan teaching of philosophy in the city in the late sixth century A.D., Athens flourished as the cultural and pedagogical capital of the international Mediterranean, and its Greek learning outlasted it for many centuries.

The ultimate European legacy of the Hellenized eastern Mediterranean, it can be argued, was a new religion, Christianity. Born in an eastern province of Augustan Rome among native speakers of Aramaic but disseminated by Hellenized Jews, it was eventually adopted by Roman emperors and their successors, East and West. Greek remained the chief language of the eastern Mediterranean for over a thousand years, not only under Byzantium but also in many cities of the Ottoman empire, just as Latin survived in the west as a theological and scholastic idiom until recent centuries. The boundaries of Christianity replaced the reach of the Greek and Roman Mediterranean in many locales, and became the most lasting legacy of ancient multicultural life.

NOTE

The references for this chapter are on pp. 416–424.

10 (b)

Linking with a Wider World

Romans and "Barbarians"

Jane Webster

The citizens of Rome regarded themselves as masters of a world they controlled as a matter of destiny and right. But where did the limits of that world lie? For the Augustan poet Ovid "the extent of Rome's city is the same as that of the world" (*Fasti* 2.684). From the fifth century B.C. to Ovid's own day, Rome had been expanding its territory though conquest. Even so, most citizens of imperial Rome would have taken Ovid's claim with a pinch of salt, being aware that a wider world existed beyond their own, and that regular interactions occurred between the empire and "other" peoples beyond.

This chapter explores Rome's understanding of "other" peoples, and highlights the kinds of information that archaeology yields concerning Rome's dealings with the wider world. Trade was the initial motor driving many of those exchanges. Conquest, for some of Rome's "neighbors," was the final outcome. Trade went hand in hand with diplomatic and cultural exchange. On the one hand, the annexation of a new Roman province was often the culmination of centuries of pre-conquest diplomatic and trading links. On the other, trade routes were lines of communication along which a wide variety of things—people and ideas, as well as goods—were able to flow. Archaeology has a pivotal role to play in the recon-struction of Roman trading patterns and routes, and in the exploration of the frontier systems that marked the physical limits of the Roman world. Archaeolo-gists have an equally important part to play in exploring wider issues of contact and culture change both within, and beyond, Rome's own frontiers.

Rome began acquiring lands in Italy in the fifth century B.C. and between the third century B.C. and the first century A.D. laid claim to a vast overseas empire. Some of the major debates in classical studies have concerned the motives driving this expansion, and the nature of Rome's dealings with the "peripheral" peoples who eventually came under Roman rule. Did the Romans acquire an empire by accident or design? What drove them to conquer other peoples, and when, how and why were the limits of conquest deemed to have been reached? Finally, to what extent did contact with Rome stimulate culture change among peoples lying—temporarily or permanently—beyond direct Roman control? These questions are crucial to an understanding of Rome and its wider world.

The Roman Republic and the Wider World

Roman territory expanded so greatly under the Republic that there can be no straightforward answer to the question "what lay beyond Rome?" But some things did not change, and among those immutables was Rome's privileged sense of itself as the center of both the known and the "civilized" world.

The known world

The Greek worldview—perpetuated by the Romans—enshrined the concept that "civilization" declined with distance from the Mediterranean. This idea remains even today deeply rooted in western archaeological thinking (Rowlands et al. 1987; Champion 1989, Ascherson 1995). Even so, it is gradually coming to be realized that archaeologists do the northern peoples a fundamental disservice by perpetuating the concept of the "barbarian periphery" (Champion 1989; Webster 1999; Wells 1999).

Roman expansion began in the fifth century B.C. with the conquest of southern Latium and the establishment of the first Roman colonies there. From 340–270 B.C., Rome engaged in conquest south of the Po Valley, quickly becoming the principal power in Italy. Overseas conquest began in 261–241 B.C. with the First Punic War against Carthage, which resulted in the acquisition of Sicily, Rome's first formally administered overseas territory, or province (*provincia*). The late third and second centuries brought expansion in the Po Valley and southern Spain, after which Roman attention shifted to the Greek East. A new province was won in Illyria in 168–167 B.C. and Macedonia was conquered in 146 B.C., with the city-states of Greece falling to Rome at the same time. In that same year Rome finally destroyed Carthage, and established the province of Africa. In 133 B.C., Pergamum was bequeathed to Rome, becoming the province of Asia. Gallia Narbonensis (Southern France) was annexed in 121 B.C., and Syria in 62 B.C. From 58–51 B.C., Julius Caesar conquered Gaul up to the Rhine, and took his legions to southern Britain too. Finally, the victory at Actium that gave Octavian (soon to be Augustus) mastery over the Roman world in 31 B.C. brought Egypt under Roman control.

Having become Emperor, Augustus annexed the remainder of the Iberian peninsula, and his armies made further forays into Germany. In A.D. 9, three legions perished in the Teutoberg Forest, deep inside northern Germany, and these new gains were lost. This reversal by no means extinguished Roman efforts to expand the *imperium* (Whittaker 1994:31–59; Hanson 2002), but the disaster marked a "sea change" in attitudes to further expansion. In his will, Augustus advised his successor Tiberius that the empire "should be kept within its boundary stones" (Whittaker 1994:25–30), and after this, the brake on territorial advance began to be applied.

Among ancient historians, debate has gone on for decades concerning the motivation underlying the rapid expansion of Rome. The dominant paradigm for many years was "defensive imperialism": the notion that Rome made territorial advances in an *ad hoc* and largely accidental way, whenever its own borders were perceived to be threatened. Harris (1979) challenged this idea, arguing that Roman expansion was actively motivated by greed (the desire for war booty, foreign resources, and wealth) and by belligerence (the desire to subdue and control "other" peoples). The defensive imperialism debate is far from settled, though many ancient historians today follow the lead set by North (1981), who tempered Harris' portrait of "Rome the aggressor" by relating the bellicosity of both the state and its elites to underlying characteristics of the Roman political system (Champion 2004).

Archaeologists do have an important part to play in this debate. Archaeological fieldwork is unlocking vital information about contact and culture change in key frontier zones, and about the mutable, and surprisingly permeable, nature of the frontiers themselves. These details are in turn helping classical scholars to come to a better understanding of the varied approaches that Roman emperors and administrators took to territorial expansion, and to the delineation of the Roman Empire.

In spite of the vast Republican territorial gains and the vast increase in knowledge of "other" peoples that resulted from them (Austin and Rankov 1995), the Mediterranean—which the Romans thought of as *mare nostrum* ("our sea")—remained the spiritual and physical heart of the Classical world. Crucially, the Romans saw the *orbis terrarum* as having two parts: the organized territory of Roman administration (the imperium, with metropolitan Rome at its center), and the *externae gentes* (the peoples dwelling in the so-called "barbarian periphery" that ringed the oikumene but was not under formal Roman administration). The Romans regarded almost all the *gentes* (outer peoples) with whom they came into contact as subject peoples falling within the imperium (Isaac 1992:14; Whittaker 1994:16–18). Varying degrees of loyalty, and in some cases even tribute and taxation, were demanded of these peoples, who were invariably regarded as ripe for economic exploitation, too. For much of Roman history, moreover, it was possible to envisage, and achieve, expansion into the lands of these neighbouring *gentes*.

Looking east I: friends, allies, clients and indirect hegemony

By late Republican times, Rome's principal neighbors in this region were the Seleucid and Parthian empire, whose borders marched with those of Rome along the Euphrates in Mesopotamia. Under Mithradates I and his successors, the Parthians had become the dominant power in the Near East, creating an empire that inevitably came to oppose that of Rome (Kennedy 1996a; 1996b). In 56 and

36 B.C., the Parthians defeated Roman attacks. Under Augustus, both empires tacitly accepted the Euphrates as their shared boundary line. This arrangement lasted down to the time of Trajan.

Between Parthia and Rome lay the many small kingdoms of Asia Minor, the Levant and Armenia. Those west of the Euphrates would over time become incorporated into the Roman Empire: Syria, Egypt, Bithynia, Galatia and Cyrene had all been annexed by the start of the Augustan era. Egypt fell to Augustus (Kennedy 1996b; Butcher 2003). Rome's gradual domination of the Red Sea brought access to the Indian sub-continent. Beyond the Levant lay the Nabatean kingdom that eventually (A.D. 106) become the province of Arabia (Freeman 1996). Until this point, Arabia Felix ("happy Arabia") remained a mythical land of reputed wealth and luxury.

Despite all these territorial gains, Rome's relations with the *gentes* throughout Asia Minor and the Near East remained very fluid. The Romans defined their imperium less by reference to formal, fixed boundaries, than in terms of their ability to influence and exert control over others. Rome acquired a diverse range of "friends," "allies," and "clients" loyal to Rome, who retained a substantial degree of autonomy in return for their support. This approach—indirect hegemony as opposed to direct rule—was especially favored in the east, where there were many small, independent kingdoms with centrally devolved forms of government (Badian 1958; Braund 1984; Sullivan 1990). No formal province was established in the east until the conquest of Macedonia in 146 B.C.

Looking east II: the faraway lands

By the close of the Republican era, Roman control of the Mediterranean was so extensive that contacts began to be made with peoples far away to the east in India, Southeast Asia and China, who became reachable via long distance coastal and overland trade routes emanating from the Mediterranean. The key maritime route to western and southern India lay initially in the hands of Arab merchants, but in the later second century B.C. Greek sailors made the discovery that the Red Sea gave direct access to the Indian Ocean, and the way was open for direct Roman trade with India. Goods coming into the Roman world from India (and Arabia) often passed through African ports sited on the edge of the Red Sea, *en route* to Alexandria. Recent fieldwork at one of these, Berenike, has revealed a town occupied until the sixth century A.D., with major periods of activity occurring in the first–second and fourth–fifth centuries (Sidebotham and Wendrich 1998; 2002). Floral and faunal remains and artifacts, including examples of at least 11 different written languages, attest to commerce not simply with Rome but with the Persian Gulf, southern Arabia, India, Sri Lanka, the Kingdom of Aksum (on which, see below), central Europe, and the Near East.

Direct trade to India increased Roman access to frankincense, ivory, textiles and other exotica. The *Periplus of the Erythraean Sea*, a guide to the ports of Arabia, East Africa, and India written around A.D. 50 (Casson 1989; Romm 1992:94–109) speaks of many trade goods being acquired from India, including spices, drugs and aromatics, gems, textiles, ivory, pearls, and tortoise shell. Roman products entering India included fine pottery and amphora-borne foodstuffs such as olive oil. Recent decades have seen increasing archaeological interest in Roman trade with India (Begley and DePuma 1991; Ray 1994). At Arikamedu on the southeast coast of India, fieldwork has helped to show that a port once thought to be the work of Roman merchants was in fact already an important emporium and bead-manufacturing center by at least the second century B.C. (Begley 1996).

Rome also had access to products traveling along the Silk Road, the ancient caravan route linking China to the eastern Mediterranean. Chinese silk found its way to Rome nevertheless, and Mediterranean textiles have correspondingly been found in China (Thorley 1971). Chinese ships may even have reached the Red Sea (Greene 1986:143). China, and the Far East as a whole, however, lay largely beyond the limits of knowledge, and certainly beyond the limits of conquest.

Looking south: Africa beyond the desert

Looking southwards, the late Republican eye fell upon Carthaginian North Africa. Rome took formal control of Carthage in 146 B.C., and established its first African colony (*Africa Vetus*) in the most fertile part of Tunisia. Neighboring Numidia (Algeria/Tunisia) was subdued following war against Jugurtha in 105 B.C. (Fentress 1979). By the end of the Republic, the entirety of coastal North Africa, from Egypt and (formerly Greek) Cyrenaica in the east to Mauritania in the west, had fallen to Rome. The Sahara desert formed an effective natural divide between Roman Africa and the little-known hinterland beyond. Dominant in the Libyan Sahara were the Garamantes of the Fazzan, who were highly successful farmers and engineers, developing a complex subterranean water extraction system that allowed them to farm in the pre-desert zone (Mattingly 2003).

The Sahara was no hindrance to trade. Arab-maintained caravan routes had long crossed the desert, giving access to the interior of Sub-Saharan east Africa, and the Romans were also able to access this region via ports on the western shore of the Red Sea, such as Berenike and Adulis (in Ethiopia), the port of the kingdom of Aksum, which by the first century B.C. was in regular contact with Rome. The archaeology of the Aksumite kingdom is still in its infancy (Munro-Hay 1991; 1993), but the town of Aksum was important enough to have been noted as a metropolis in the *Periplus*. Ivory, tortoise shell, frankincense, myrrh, and cassia were all acquired from Africa: the *Periplus* refers to the port of Rhapta (probably in modern Tanzania) as a source of both ivory and tortoise shell.

Looking north and west: Rome's "barbarians"

Despite the fact that the Classical concept of the barbarian had emerged specifi-cally in the context of Greek warfare with Persia, in the Roman mind the world to the east was conceptualized as *different*, rather than as barbaric or uncivilized. One reason for this was simply Rome's detailed knowledge of the complex, state-organized, urbanized peoples living to the east. Another was that the long history of Greek interchange with the Persian and Macedonian empires had left much of the east deeply Hellenized. *Barbaroi* figured as strongly in Roman thinking as in Greek, but Rome found its "barbarians" not in the east—among the Parthians, Syrians, and Egyptians—but in the north.

To understand why barbarism and northern Europe went hand in hand in Roman thinking, we need to look at what happened as Rome began to exert control over Italy in the fourth and third centuries B.C. Throughout the "migration period" (ca. 400–200 B.C.), the Cisalpine Gauls (Gauls living on the southern side of the Alps) made incursions southwards into Roman Italy, fighting a protracted series of wars with Rome. Ultimately Rome prevailed, with colonies being established throughout the Po Valley by the 180s B.C., but these wars had begun badly for Rome, and many worrying moments followed before victory was assured. One event, in particular, had a profound effect upon Roman attitudes to the northern "barbarians." This was the infamous *dies ater* (the black day) of ca. 386 B.C., on which the Gauls sacked the city of Rome itself (Vitali 1991). Gauls similarly invaded Anatolia in the third century, and actually sacked Delphi in 278 B.C. (Mitchell 1993). For centuries to come, Rome would look upon "Celtic" peoples (among whom were bracketed the Gauls, the Britons, and the Celtiberians of Spain) as fearsome and uncivilized enemies.

The Germanic peoples living to the north and east of the Rhine evoked a similar reaction. Rome's first sustained contact with these peoples came in the late second century B.C. as the Cimbri and Teutones attempted to migrate *en masse* into Gaul (Cunliffe 1988: 53–58; King 1990: 34–62). The migrants (probably from what is today Jutland) defeated Roman armies at Noricum (113 B.C.) and at Arausio, or Orange (105 B.C.). Marius subsequently crushed the Cimbri and Teutones, and the Roman annexation of *Gallia Narbonensis* (Southern Gaul) was assured at the same time. Caesar's wars of conquest in northern Gaul (58–51 B.C.) brought Rome into direct conflict with the Suebi of southern Germany, and saw the legions advance as far as the Rhine. Caesar wrote about the *Germani* at some length in his account of the Gallic War (*BG* 6, 11–28). So it was that, well before a succession of Roman emperors turned their minds and armies to the Rhineland, Germanic peoples had come to be regarded as even less civilized than the Gauls; a way of thinking that owed at least as much to Julius Caesar's account as it did to a worldview that saw civilization declining with distance from the Mediterranean (Wells 1999: 75–85, 99–121). Tacitus' later *Germania*, which depicted the *Germani* as "noble savages," actually served to compound that stereotype; a noble savage is, after all, still a savage. And the *Germani*, unlike the Celts, remained a serious threat to Rome. As time passed, and as that threat repeatedly resurfaced (for example, during the Batavian revolt of A.D. 69–70 and the "barbarian" incursions of the third century A.D.), the Germani came, above all others, to personify barbarianism in the Roman mind. Indeed, the Roman name for "Free Germany" (the vast hinterland beyond the

Rhine) was *Barbaricum*. This name reminds that although other peoples (including the Berber peoples of desert North Africa: Mattingly 1996) were dubbed barbarians too, the Germani held a special status in Roman thinking.

Roman exchange and conquest among the barbaroi

Archaeology plays a key role in articulating aspects of Roman relationships with neighboring peoples, revealing trade, diplomacy, and culture change from the point of view of the *non*-Roman partners in these exchanges. This is especially the case for the pre-literate peoples of the north and west who have left no textual record to set beside Roman accounts (Fitzpatrick 1989; Wells 1999).

Republican Rome was a small place with an expanding population, and limited natural resources. Self-sufficiency was not an option, and from the earliest days Rome looked beyond its own borders for foodstuffs, metals, minerals, slaves, and so on. Trade was one mechanism by which to acquire these things. The formal annexation of territories blessed with those resources was another. Both strategies often went hand in hand—that is, first-hand trading knowledge of the resources of neighboring territories played a part in the decision to annex them. The late first millennium B.C. and first two centuries A.D. were periods of economic growth, fueled in part by rapid territorial expansion, provincial taxation, and trade (Hopkins 1980, Harris 1993; Mattingly and Salmon 2001). Roman expansion was not powered by the mercantilist spirit that drove, say, European colonial expansion after 1492, but the Romans were not blind to the resources on their doorstep, and were well aware of the gains that could be made both by exploiting those resources, and by taxing new provinces.

One of the most important of these material gains was foreign labor, in the form of slaves acquired through conquest. Unfortunately, slaves are the least archaeologically "visible" of all social classes in the Roman world, and the archaeology of slavery remains in its infancy (Thompson 2003). Almost continuous warfare in the later Republic impacted upon the rural poor within Italy: many never came back from the expansionary wars to which they were despatched. Rural depopulation in turn led to agrarian change at home, and many of those put to work on the huge agricultural estates (*latifundia*) that emerged in Etruria at this time were foreign slaves acquired as a result of conquest and colonization (Thompson 2003).

Rome's pre- and post-conquest relationship with the Iberian peninsula provides a good case study in provincial conquest and exploitation. Romans showed little interest in Iberia until the aftermath of the First Punic War, when the Carthaginians set about conquest there, having lost their other Mediterranean possessions to Rome. In 226 B.C., Rome went to war with the Carthaginians in Iberia following the sack of Saguntum, a city allied to Rome. This conflict (the Second Punic War) continued until 206 B.C., when Scipio defeated the Carthaginians and established Rome's first Hispanic colony at Italica, near Seville.

Scipio's victory gave Rome control of coastal southeastern Spain, and in 197 B.C. the provinces of Hispania Citerior and Hispania Ulterior were created. Rome now had control over Carthaginian silver mines near Nova Carthago (Cartagena) and in Sierra Morena, and also over copper mines at Luxia (Rio Tinto). By the mid-second century B.C., 40,000 men were at work at Carthago Nova, bringing in 257,000 drachmas a day to the Roman people (Strabo 3.147–148). The extent to which southern Spain (and its people) were exploited in this period can be gauged by noting that the activities of the Roman *propraetors* (governors) here led to the establishment at Rome of a standing commission on extortion (Rankin 1987:166–187). The documentary and material evidence give a detailed picture of the grim conditions endured by Roman mine workers (Thompson 2003).

The Augustan campaigns brought further metal resources under Roman control, including the extensive gold reserves of Tarraconensis (northwestern Iberia), where archaeological field survey has uncovered more than 230 individual mining sites (Cunliffe 2001:374–377). Gold from the region was taken to Asturica Augusta (the provincial capital), then by road to the port of Gadir, for shipment to Rome. The main gold-producing areas apparently yielded 20,000 pounds weight of gold each year (Pliny, *Naturalis Historia* 33). Spain's agricultural products were also widely exported. Spanish oil amphoras make up much of Monte Testaccio, a vast dump of broken amphoras sherds at the Roman port of Ostia. Archaeologists have calculated that the dump represents an importation to Rome of four million kilos of oil, carried in some 55,000 amphoras each year (Potter 1987:168–169). Iberian oil was also exported to Gaul and Britain, and fish sauce (*garum*), produced at many sites on the Iberian coast, was shipped to both Italy and Britain.

What impact did Roman contact, trade, and markets have upon Rome's *pre-conquest* neighbors? Archaeological debate upon these issues has been at its most vociferous in Celtic eastern Gaul and western Germany (Wells 1999).

The Roman presence in southern France (intense even before formal annexation of Narbonensis, ca.121 B.C.) brought opportunities for Roman entrepreneurs to develop trading links far into Gaul. Dressel IA wine amphoras entered Gaul in vast quantities by the late second century B.C, many of them passing through two major trading ports at Toulouse and Chalon (an estimated 24,000 amphoras were thrown into the river at Chalon, for example: Cunliffe 1997:216–221). Trade and diplomacy went hand-in-hand with Rome forging a formal alliance with the powerful Aedui of central Gaul as early as 125 B.C. The important Aeduan *oppidum* of Bibracte (Mt. Beuvray, France) provides a good case study of the impact of Rome. The evidence uncovered to date reveals that, within a few years of the conquest, a major town had arisen here. But this short-lived town (abandoned ca. 20 B.C. for nearby Augustodunum) succeeded a 135-hectare oppidum of second-century B.C. origin. Within just a few years of the conquest, Roman Bibracte boasted Mediterranean-style courtyard houses in defined residential areas, paved streets, and a central market area. None of these features, however, can be shown to have pre-conquest origins. In fact, very little is known about the pre-conquest settlement organization at Bibracte, and the density of Iron Age occupation remains a matter for guesswork. In short, a "town" in the Roman sense eludes us at Iron Age Bibracte. The pre-Roman residents of this and other *oppida* certainly had access to Mediterranean imports. They also minted coinage, and engaged in manufacturing. Yet it would be misleading to refer to the way of life within these archaic central places as "Romanized." Indeed, in comparison to Augustodunum, those living at Bibracte were notably slow to adopt literacy, urban infrastructure, and other common features of Romanized town life even *after* the conquest (Woolf 1998:10–11).

Interest in the impact of the Roman center on its Celtic periphery peaked in the 1980s. Subsequent critiques of the interpretation of the Gallic archaeological evidence, in particular, have caused this model for contact and culture change to fall from favor (Ralston 1988; Fitzpatrick 1989; Woolf 1993). In its place, we can point to a growing understanding that the Roman impact on Iron Age social change has almost certainly been overstated at the expense of a more useful focus on internal, indigenous developments (Haselgrove 1995). But it remains the case that some of the more nuanced center–periphery studies (such as that of Hedeager 1987, on the existence of a "buffer zone" between the *limes* and Free Germany) have stood the test of time, influencing the subsequent work of Whittaker (1994), Wells (1999) and others. At the very least, the center–periphery perspective has highlighted the active relationship between contact, trade, diplomacy, and conquest in the Roman north and west, reminding us that—on a number of levels— Rome *needed* its *barbaroi*. It is now widely accepted that Roman conquest was most likely to occur—and pacification most likely to succeed—in regions with well-organized urban or proto-urban structures and "compliant local elites" (Hanson 2002) onto which Rome could project her administrative system. That kind of "compliance" was built through pre-conquest diplomacy, not simply through territorial annexation (see, in this context, Creighton 2000, on Rome's relationship with the elites of pre-conquest Southern Britain).

Exchanging Things within the Roman Empire

Most provincial regions were able to supply their own basic needs, and could source their other requirements from within the wider empire. This should not be taken to mean that the long-distance trade links discussed above ended. Indeed, new ones grew up, including a trade in amber from the Baltic, which the Romans reached by the first century A.D. (Künow 1980). There were some Roman "customers," in any case (the army being one, and the metropolis of Rome being another), whose needs were so great that their immediate hinterlands could not supply them. In these cases, complex trading and support systems grew up.

Different parts of Rome's empire obviously boasted differing resources. Large-scale production of foods such as grain, wine, and olive oil went on in the provinces rich in these resources, with their products often being transported in vast quantities, and over very long distances, to other parts of the Roman world. North Africa has often been referred to as the "granary" of Rome, with much of the grain from this region being shipped to Rome via Alexandria (Mattingly and Aldrete 2000). Many now deserted North African areas were also engaged in intensive oil and wine production in the Roman period (for the seminal UNESCO Libyan Valleys survey, see Barker 1996; Mattingly 1996). Spain exported oil. Wine was mainly produced in Tuscany and Campania (western Italy), Narbonensis (the Mediterranean coast of France, Tchernia 1983; 1986), and in Spain and Crete. Other products widely exported across the empire included "consumer" goods such as marble, metal ores, timber, textiles, and mass-produced ceramics (Greene 1986:142–168). The red-glazed *terra sigillata* tablewares mass-produced in Arezzo (Etruria) and in Gaul are near ubiquitous on sites throughout the Roman west (Greene 1986:152–168, Woolf 1998:187–203).

We know a good deal about the movement of such goods around the Roman empire–road networks, aqueducts, harbors, and so on—survive for archaeologists to uncover today (Greene 1986:17–44). Water-borne trade has been brought into archaeological focus by the efforts of underwater archaeologists. Over 1,000 wrecks are known in the shallow waters of the Mediterranean alone, and many more await discovery in deeper waters too (Parker 1992). The Madrague de Giens wreck from southern France, dating to the first century B.C. (Tchernia et al. 1978; Greene 1986:25–28), is of a ship carrying wine produced near Terracina (to the south of Rome), fine tablewares, kitchenwares, and preserved fruits.

A good deal of information about trade routes and exchange networks can be obtained by studying amphoras and other ceramics (Peacock and Williams 1986; Panella and Tchernia 2002). The primary export container for Italian wine was the Dressel 1 amphora, succeeded from the end of the first century B.C. by Dressel 2–4 forms. Wine entered Italy in amphoras too, for example, in Spanish versions of Dressel 2–4. Spanish olive oil was primarily shipped in Dressel 20 globular forms, and that from North Africa in large cylindrical amphoras. Whatever their contents, amphoras reveal vital information about Roman trading routes, and about shifting trading patterns over time. For example, stamps of the Italian producer Sestius (from Cosa) have been found on amphoras on a large number of sites stretching from the port of Cosa to southern and central Gaul. Study of their distribution reveals information about the pattern of exports from Cosa, and about Gallic markets for imported wine (Figure 10.5; Greene 1986:91–92).

Documentary evidence about trade and the movement of goods also survives. Written sources include maps and itineraries, and "shopping lists" such as the writing tablets found at Vindolanda near Hadrian's Wall (Bowman 1998) and the pottery *ostraka* from Roman Egypt from the granite mining complex at Mons Claudianus have yielded detailed information about the pay and diet of the skilled workers there (Maxfield and Peacock 2001; see Figure 3.5).

All this information helps us to build up a broad general picture of the movement of staple goods around the Empire. These sources also show that the city of Rome—the metropolis at the heart of the empire—was heavily reliant upon provincial imports. But was this true of other cities and smaller urban sites elsewhere in the empire? There are still some surprising gaps in our understanding of the Roman economy, particularly concerning the relationship between urban

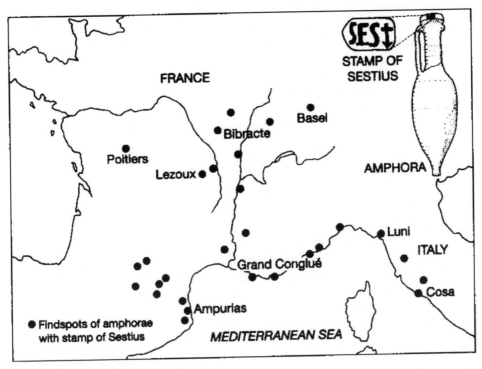

Figure 10.5 Distribution of Roman amphorae bearing the stamp of the potter Sestius, ML Design. From Renfrew and Bahn 2000:167

centers and the countryside around them. The majority of the populations of the largest urban centers could not have been directly engaged in food production, and so food at least must have been imported from elsewhere. This was certainly the case for metropolitan Rome, which by imperial times was importing a huge array of goods from the provinces. But the sheer size of Rome and the rate of its expansion make this a special case. Other Roman cities may have been both more self-reliant and more geared to export production. Leptiminus (in Tunisia) manufactured amphoras, red slipware ceramics and ironwork (Mattingly et al. 2001); Timgad produced textiles (Wilson 2001).Wine amphoras from Pompeii have been found from Carthage to Trier, and from Spain to southern Britain (Potter 1987:164–180).

Exchange and Identity on the Frontiers

Archaeologists have always shown a keen interest in "frontier studies," a branch of classical archaeology that combines information from literary sources with the results of archaeological fieldwork and the analysis of inscriptions (Isaac 1992: 14). Recent decades have seen a move away from more traditional militaristic concerns towards a broader interest in issues of contact and culture change. In short, it is now widely appreciated that the frontiers marked more than simply the physical limits of the Roman world; they were also zones of interaction within which extraordinarily cosmopolitan military and civilian communities forged a wide variety of Roman (and non-Roman) identities. Frontier studies have generated a vast and often daunting body of archaeological literature, but good entry points are Whittaker (1994), Dyson (1985), and Elton (1996), with Brun, van der Leeuw and Whittaker (1993), and Groenman-van Waateringe (1997).

Defining the frontier

The Roman word for frontier was *limes* (the same word sometimes also being used to denote roads: a rather revealing point). Debate rages as to whether it is possible to speak of any Roman "frontier policy," and it is clear that formal, linear boundaries (like the wall built for Hadrian in northern England, for example) were the exception rather than the norm (Isaac 1992; Whittaker 1994). The limits of empire were expressed in terms of power and military action, with no long-term, strategic approach to expansion (*contra* Luttwak 1976). But in the simple sense that we can find archaeological evidence for systems of fortifications, roads, and linear boundaries that mark the limit of direct Roman control on the "fringes" of the empire, "frontiers" certainly *did* exist. Roman frontier systems differed remarkably from each other, nevertheless, and many were not in any sense linear boundaries, but it makes sense to begin this brief overview, however, with those that were.

The history of Roman conquests along the Rhine and Danube is complex (Wells 1999:85–98, 122–147). Augustus pushed forward to the Elbe, but following the Teutoberg Forest disaster, fell back to the Rhine. The Rhine became, and basically remained, the permanent eastern border of Rome's two Germanic provinces. Work on the *limes*—the well-known boundary initially created to link the middle Rhine frontier with that on the upper Danube—began in the 80s A.D. and embellishments went on for centuries (King 1990:162–171). Ongoing fieldwork at the military and civilian settlements of Nijmegen (Noviomagnus) is facilitating a detailed exploration of many aspects of military/civilian interaction (Enckevort and Thijssen 2003). Archaeozoologists are beginning to build up a detailed picture of the impact of the Roman army—and its food supply needs— upon farming practices and dietary habits in the frontier zone (Lauwerier and Robeerst 2001).

The Roman emperors Trajan and Hadrian initiated a (spatially intermittent) African frontier in the pre-desert zone running from the Libyan valleys to Algeria. Large-scale survey work in Libya, in particular, has done much to extend knowledge of the permeable nature of a "frontier" which facilitated, rather than hindered, the movement of people and trade (Barker 1996; Mattingly 1995; 1996). Tripolitania (Libya) is the only part of Roman Africa boasting a truly unbroken, desert frontier, but here we also find a category of shorter linear barriers known

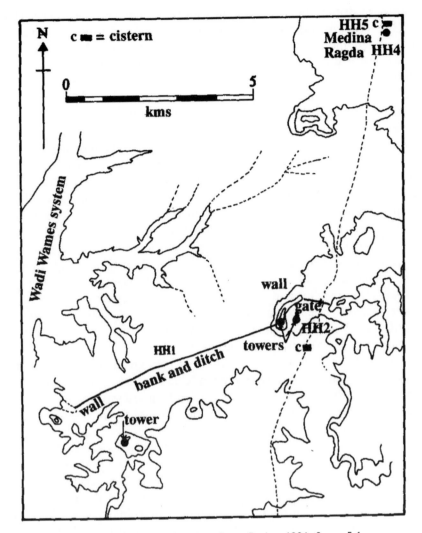

Figure 10.6 Map of the Hadd Hajar claustura. From Barker 1996: figure 5.6

as *clausturae*, erected to the south of the frontier zone (that is, some way beyond the formal Roman frontier). Survey and excavation at the recently discovered *claustura* at Hadd Hajar have brought to light associated towers, an entrance gate, and cisterns (Figure 10.6). Observation towers, monitoring ingress and egress through the gate, were located on prominent hillocks overlooking the claustura. Finds like this suggest that the *clausturae*—which were located very close to the edge of the pre-desert farming zone—were not put in place to "demarcate provincial lands from those of the 'barbarians'" (Mattingly 1996:325), but to regulate transhumance (the seasonal movement of livestock) between pastoral and sedentary zones. People, for example seasonal laborers, and trade goods would also, of course, have moved backwards and forwards through the *clausturae*.

In northern Britain the turf and stone wall constructed on the order of Hadrian in 122 B.C. (Breeze and Dobson 2000) was not the first Roman frontier in the north (see Woolliscroft 2002, on the Gask Ridge), and for a short period (A.D. 142–169) it was even usurped by the more northerly Antonine Wall (Hanson and Maxwell 1983). The forts of Hadrian's Wall and its environs remain, nevertheless, an obvious magnet for British archaeologists interested in military and civil interaction. The *vici* (the civilian settlements) of the northern forts were very extensive, with complex intra-site patterning (Biggins and Taylor 1999).

In the east, we do not encounter linear boundaries of the type described above (Whittaker 1994:49–59). Under Trajan, the limit of the imperium was marked by the *Via Nova Trajana*, a road extending from southern Syria to the Red Sea. A number of forts were constructed along this route, but the Romans on the whole preferred to station troops in existing fortified towns and cities. A key example here is Dura-Europos (Pollard 1996; James 2004). This site was typical of arrangements in the region, in that the Roman garrison was housed in a *cantonment*, a part of the town walled off for exclusive military use. In A.D. 253/254, an embankment was constructed as a siege defense against the Sasanians by sacrificing a dense occupation zone located near the city's impressive western wall. Excavation here has revealed a complex pattern of *insulae* (residential blocks), displaying Hellenistic, Roman, Parthian, Aramaic, and other cultural influences. The town was particularly closely linked with the city of Palmyra (itself a nexus of the desert caravan route though Syria), and a number of Palmyrene gods were worshipped here. Many other deities were worshipped at Dura-Europos, however. The late Roman city boasted a *mithraeum* (a temple of Mithras), a synagogue, and a church building. The latter dates to ca. A.D. 240 and is one of the earliest such buildings known.

At its height in the third century A.D., Dura-Europos underscores the astonishingly cosmopolitan nature of the communities living on the eastern fringes of the empire. Among those co-existing at Dura were Syrians (especially Palmyrenes), Mesopotamians, Steppe pastoralists, people of Greek and Iranian descent, and many other resident or visiting groups ranging from Roman provincial soldiers to the thriving Jewish community who remodeled a residential building to create a synagogue. Excavation has helped to show that the cultural repertoire of the Dura-Europos community was extraordinarily diverse, and that many of those living here did not regard "Roman" cultural values as either superior or dominant. A similar story is repeated all along the eastern frontier, and it is not hard to see why this zone has become a focal point for archaeological studies of military and civil interaction (Kennedy 1996b; Alcock 1997; Pollard 2000).

Exchange beyond the frontiers

The borders of the Roman world were rarely closed. Even the formal boundaries created in Africa and the "barbarian" north were designed not to *prevent* ingress and egress, but to facilitate and observe movement. Prehistorians of pre-contact

Figure 10.7 Roman weapons from Grave A4103, Hedegård, Denmark. Courtesy of Haderslev Museum, photo: Steen Hendriksen

and contact periods have made a sustained effort to explore the social repercussions of the permeable frontier. *Barbaricum* ("Free Germany")is a particularly interesting example in view of Roman attitudes to the German. Literary sources reveal that Roman merchants passed freely between Roman Germany and the unconquered lands beyond, acquiring clothing, amber, hides, and other items, and the provincial authorities frequently gave gifts to leaders across the Rhine, thereby oiling the wheels of commerce and diplomacy. Archaeological evidence, notably in the form of Roman objects in funerary contexts, points to the same conclusion (Figure 10.7; Whittaker 1994:113–121; Wells 1999:227–229).

The Romans were no doubt interested in trade with Free Germany both as a means to foster peace on the frontier, and for economic gain. But what did the Germanic peoples hope to gain in return? Several archaeologists have suggested that the high status Roman metal artifacts found in graves in Free Germany had primarily been sought out because gold and silver were highly desirable symbols of status among Germanic peoples (Hedeager 1978; 1987). This helps to explain why Roman pottery, brooches, bronzes, glass, coinage, and silver are found beyond the Elbe and even in Poland and Scandinavia (see also Hedeager [1992] on Roman finds in Scandinavia, and Hunter [2002] for a similar case study on Scotland). At the same time, however, it is possible to argue that acquisition of these goods exposed cross-border elites to the customs and values of the Roman world, gradually eroding social differences on either side of the frontier (Wells 1999:224–258). This brings us back once again to debates about Roman influence on the "periphery." And here there is a twist in the tale: continuing elite access to Roman prestige goods, customs, and values appears to have played its part in the emergence of new, dynamic, tribal confederations in Germany in the third century A.D. and thus to have sown the seeds of the "barbarian" crisis that marked the beginning of the end in the Roman west.

REFERENCES

Alcock, Susan, ed. 1997 The Early Roman Empire in the East. Oxford: Oxbow.
——, Jennifer E. Gates, and Jane E. Rempel 2003 Reading the Landscape: Survey Archaeology and the Hellenistic Oikoumene. In The Cambridge Companion to the Hellenistic World. Andrew Erskine, ed. Pp. 354–372. Cambridge: Cambridge University Press.
Alexandria and Alexandrianism 1996. Malibu: The J. Paul Getty Museum.
Arafat, Karim, and Catherine Morgan 1994 Athens, Etruria and the Heuneburg: Mutual Misconceptions in the Study of Greek-Barbarian Interrelations. In Classical Greece. Ancient Histories and Modern Archaeologies. I. Morris, ed. Pp. 103–134. Cambridge: Cambridge University Press.
Archibald, Zosia, ed. 2002 Hellenistic Economies. Oxford: Oxford University Press.
Ascherson, Neal 1995 The Black Sea: The Birthplace of Civilization and Barbarism. London: Jonathan Cape.

Austin, N. J. E., and Boris Rankov 1995 Exploratio: Military and Political Intelligence in the Roman World from the Second Punic War to the Battle of Adrianople. London: Routledge.

Badian, Ernst 1958 Foreign Clientelae (264–70 BC). Oxford: Clarendon Press.

Bakir, T., ed. 2001 Achaemenid Anatolia. Proceedings of the First International Symposium on Anatolia in the Achaemenid Period. Bandirma, 15–18 August 1997. Leiden: Nederlands Instituut voor Het Nabije Oosten.

Barker, Graeme, ed. 1996 Farming the Desert: The UNESCO Libyan Valleys Archaeological Survey, vol. 1. Synthesis. London: Society for Libyan Studies.

——, John A. Lloyd, and Joyce Reynolds, eds. 1985 Cyrenaica in Antiquity. British Archaeological Reports 236. Oxford: British Archaeological Reports.

Bass, George 1998 Sailing between the Aegean and the Orient in the Second Millennium B.C. In The Aegean and the Orient in the Second Millennium BC: Proceedings of the 50th Anniversary Symposium. Eric Cline and Diane Harris-Cline, eds. Pp. 183–191. Aegaeum 18 Liège: Université de Liège, Histoire de l'art et archéologie de la Grèce antique.

Begley, Vimala, ed. 1996 The Ancient Port of Arikamedu, Vol. 1. New Excavations and Researches 1989–1992. Pondicherry: L'École Française d'Extrême-Orient.

——, and Richard D. DePuma, eds. 1991 Rome and India: The Ancient Sea Trade. Madison, WI: University of Wisconsin Press.

Bémont, Colette, and Jean-Paul Jacob 1986 La Terre sigillée gallo-romaine. Paris: Maison des Sciences de l'Homme.

Biggins, J. A., and D. J. A. Taylor 1999 A Survey of the Roman Fort and Settlement at Birdoswald, Cumbria. Britannia 30:91–110.

Bilde, Per, Troels Engberg-Pedersen, Lise Hannestad, and Jan Zahle, eds. 1992 Ethnicity in Hellenistic Egypt. Aarhus: Aarhus University Press.

Boardman, John 1994 The Diffusion of Classical Art in Antiquity. Princeton: Princeton University Press.

——1999 The Greeks Overseas: Their Early Colonies and Trade. 4th edition. London: Thames and Hudson.

——2000 Persia and the West: An Archaeological Investigation of the Genesis of Achaemenid Art. London: Thames and Hudson.

Bowman, Alan K. 1998 Life and Letters on the Roman Frontier. London: British Museum Press.

Boyd, Thomas 1978 The Arch and Vault in Greek Architecture. American Journal of Archaeology 82:83–100.

Braund, David 1984 Rome and the Friendly King. London: Croom Helm.

Breeze, David, and Brian Dobson 2000 Hadrian's Wall. 3rd edition. London: Penguin.

Brun, Patrice, Sander van der Leeuw, and C. R. Whittaker, eds. 1993 Frontières d'empire: Nature et signification des frontières romaines. Mémoires du Musée de Préhistoire d'Île-de-France no. 5. Nemours: Musée de Préhistoire d'Île-de-France.

Burkert, Walter 1992 The Orientalizing Revolution. Cambridge, MA: Harvard University Press.

Butcher, Kevin 2003 Roman Syria and the Near East. London: British Museum.

Casson, Lionel 1989 The Periplus Maris Erythraei. Princeton: Princeton University Press.

Champion, Craige B., ed. 2004 Roman Imperialism: Readings and Sources. London: Blackwell.

Champion, Timothy C., ed. 1989 Centre and Periphery: Comparative Studies in Archaeology. London: Unwin Hyman.

Cherry, David 1998 Frontier and Society in Roman North Africa. Oxford: Clarendon Press.

Childs, William A. P. 1981 Lycian Relations with Persians and Greeks in the Fifth and Fourth Centuries Re-examined. Anatolian Studies 31:55–80.

Chrisomalis, Stephen 2003 The Egyptian Origin of the Greek Alphabetic Numerals. Antiquity 77:485–496.

Cline, Eric, and Diane Harris-Cline, eds. 1998 The Aegean and the Orient in the Second Millennium BC: Proceedings of the 50th Anniversary Symposium. Aegaeum 18. Liège: Université de Liège, Histoire de l'art et archéologie de la Grèce antique.

Cohen, Beth, ed. 2000 Not the Classical Ideal: Athens and the Construction of the Other in Greek Art. Leiden: Brill.

Coldstream, Nicholas 1993 Mixed Marriages at the Frontiers of the Early Greek World. Oxford Journal of Archaeology 12:89–107.

Colledge, Malcolm 1987 Greek and Non-Greek Interaction in the Art and Architecture of the Hellenistic East. In Hellenism in the East: The Interaction of Greek and Non-Greek Civilizations from Syria to Central Asia after Alexander. Amélie Kuhrt and Susan Sherman-White, eds. Pp. 134–162. Berkeley and Los Angeles: University of California Press.

Creighton, John 2000 Coins and Power in Late Iron Age Britain. Cambridge: Cambridge University Press.

Cunliffe, Barry 1988 Greeks, Romans and Barbarians: Spheres of Interaction. London: Batsford.

——1997 The Ancient Celts. Oxford: Oxford University Press.

——2001 Facing the Ocean: The Atlantic and its Peoples 8000 BC–AD 1500. Oxford: Oxford University Press.

Davies, John 2000 A Wholly Non-Aristotelian Universe: The Molossians as Ethnos, State and Monarchy. In Alternatives to Athens: Varieties of Political Organization and Community in Ancient Greece. Roger Brock and Stephen Hodkinson, eds. Pp. 234–258. Oxford: Oxford University Press.

Dietler, Michael 1989 Greeks, Etruscans and Thirsty Barbarians. In Centre and Periphery: Comparative Studies in Archaeology. Timothy Champion, ed. Pp. 124–141. London: Unwin Hyman.

——1995 The Cup of Gyptis: Rethinking the Colonial Encounter in Early-Iron-Age Western Europe and the Relevance of World-Systems Models. Journal of European Archaeology 3.2:89–111.

——1997 The Iron Age in Mediterranean France: Colonial Encounter, Entanglements and Transformations. Journal of World Prehistory 11:269–358.

Dietler, Michael, and Michel Py 2003 The Warrior of Lattes: An Iron Age Statue Discovered in Mediterranean France. Antiquity 77:780–795.

Domergue, Claude 1990 Les Mines de la peninsule ibérique dans l'antiquité romaine. Rome: L'École Française de Rome.

Dominguez, A. J. 1999 Hellenization in Iberia? The Reception of Greek Products and Influences by the Iberians. In Ancient Greeks West and East. Gocha Tsetskhladze, ed. Pp. 301–329. Leiden: Brill.

——2002 Greeks in Iberia: Colonialism without Colonization. In The Archaeology of Colonialism. Claire Lyons and John Papadopoulos, eds. Pp. 65–92. Los Angeles: The Getty Research Institute.

Dougherty, Carol 1993 The Poetics of Colonization: From City to Text in Archaic Greece. Oxford: Oxford University Press.

Dusinberre, Elspeth M. 2003 Aspects of Empire in Achaemenid Sardis. Cambridge: Cambridge University Press.

Dyson, Stephen L. 1985 The Creation of the Roman Frontier. Princeton: Princeton University Press.

Elton, Hugh 1996 Frontiers of the Roman Empire. London: Batsford.

Enckevort, Harry van, and J. Thijssen 2003 Nijmegen: A Roman Town in the Frontier Zone of Germania Inferior. *In* The Archaeology of Roman Towns. Studies in Honour of John S. Wacher. Peter Wilson, ed. Pp. 59–72. Oxford: Oxbow.

Feldman, Marian 2005 Diplomacy by Design: Luxury Arts and an "International Style" in the Ancient Near East, 1400–1200 BCE. Chicago: University of Chicago Press.

Fentress, Elizabeth 1979 Numidia and the Roman Army. British Archaeological Reports International Series 53. Oxford: British Archaeological Reports.

Fitzpatrick, Andrew 1989 The Uses of Roman Imperialism by the Celtic Barbarians. *In* Barbarians and Romans in North-West Europe: From the Late Republic to Late Antiquity. John C. Barrett, Andrew Fitzpatrick, and Leslie MacInnes, eds. Pp. 27–54. British Archaeological Reports International Series 471. Oxford: British Archaeological Reports.

Freeman, Philip 1996 The Annexation of Arabia and Imperial Grand Strategy. *In* The Roman Army in the East. David L. Kennedy, ed. Pp. 91–117. Journal of Roman Archaeology Supplementary Series 18. Ann Arbor: Journal of Roman Archaeology.

Gale, Noel, ed. 1991 Bronze Age Trade in the Mediterranean. Studies in Mediterranean Archaeology 90. Jonsered: Aströms.

Gill, David 2004 Euesperides: Cyrenaica and its Contacts with the Greek World. *In* Greek Identity in the Western Mediterranean. Papers in Honour of Brian Shefton. Kathryn Lomas, ed. Pp. 291–409. Mnesmosyne Supplement 246. Leiden: Brill.

Greene, Kevin 1986 The Archaeology of the Roman Economy. Berkeley: University of California Press.

Groenman-van Waateringe, W. 1997 Roman Frontier Studies 1995: Proceedings of the XVIth International Congress of Roman Frontier Studies. Oxford: Oxbow.

Hall, Edith 1989 Inventing the Barbarian: Greek Self-Definition through Tragedy. Oxford: Clarendon Press.

Hanson, W. S. 2002 Why Did the Roman Empire Cease to Expand? *In* Proceedings of the XVIIIth International Congress of Roman Frontier Studies held in Amman, Jordan (2000). Philip Freeman, J. Bennett, Zbigniew T. Fiema, and B. Hoffmann, eds. Pp. 23–34. British Archaeological Reports International Series 1084. Oxford: British Archaeological Reports.

——, and Gordon Maxwell 1983 Rome's North West Frontier: The Antonine Wall. Edinburgh: Edinburgh University Press.

——, and Ian P. Haynes, eds. 2004 Roman Dacia: The Making of a Provincial Society. Journal of Roman Archaeology Supplementary Series 56. Portsmouth RI: Journal of Roman Archaeology.

Harris, William V. 1979 War and Imperialism in Republican Rome, 327–70 BC. Oxford: Clarendon Press.

——, ed. 1993 The Inscribed Economy: Production and Distribution in the Roman Empire in the Light of Instrumentum Domesticum. Ann Arbor: University of Michigan Press.

Haselgrove, Colin 1995 Late Iron Age Society in Britain and North-East Europe: Structural Transformation or Superficial Change? *In* Celtic Chiefdom, Celtic State. Bettina

Arnold and D. Blair Gibson, eds. Pp. 81–87. Cambridge: Cambridge University Press.

Hedeager, Lotte 1978 A Quantitative Analysis of Roman Imports in Europe North of the Limes and the Question of Romano-Germanic Exchange. *In* New Directions in Scandinavian Archaeology. Kristian Kristiansen and Carsten Paluden-Müller, eds. Pp. 191–216. Copenhagen: National Museum.

——1987 Empire, Frontier and the Barbarian Hinterland. Rome and Northern Europe from AD 1–400. *In* Centre and Periphery in the Ancient World. Michael J. Rowlands, Mogens T. Larsen, and Kristian Kristiansen eds. Pp. 125–153. Cambridge: Cambridge University Press.

——1992 Iron Age Societies. Oxford: Blackwell.

Hermary, Antoine 2003 The Greeks in Marseille and the Western Mediterranean. *In* The Greeks Beyond the Aegean: From Marseilles to Bactria. Vassos Karageorghis, ed. Pp. 59–77. New York: Alexander S. Onassis Public Benefit Foundation.

Heyn, M. 2002 Social Relations and Material Culture Patterning in the Roman Empire: A Juxtaposition of East and West. Ph.D. thesis, University of California, Los Angeles.

Hoffman, Gail 1997 Imports and Immigrants: Near Eastern Contacts with Iron Age Crete. Ann Arbor: University of Michigan.

Hopkins, Keith 1980 Taxes and Trade in the Roman Empire (200 BC–AD 400). Journal of Roman Studies 70:101–125.

Hunter, Frasier 2002 Problems in the Study of Roman and Native. *In* Proceedings of the XVIIIth International Congress of Roman Frontier Studies held in Amman, Jordan (2000). Philip Freeman, J. Bennett, Zbigniew T. Fiema and B. Hoffmann, eds. Pp. 43–48. British Archaeological Reports International Series 1084. Oxford: British Archaeological Reports.

Isaac, Benjamin H. 1992 The Limits of Empire: The Roman Army in the East. Rev. edition. Oxford: Clarendon Press.

James, Simon 2004 Excavations at Dura-Europos. Final Report VII, The Arms and Armour, and Other Military Equipment. London: British Museum Press.

Kaiser, Alan 2003 Ethnic Identity and Urban Fabric: The Case of the Greeks of Empúries, Spain. Journal of Mediterranean Archaeology 13.2:189–203.

Kaptan, Deniz 2002 The Daskyleion Bullae: Seal Images from the Western Achaemenid Empire. Achaemenid History 12. Leiden: Nederlands Instituut voor Het Nabije Oosten.

Karageorghis, Vassos, ed. 2003 The Greeks Beyond the Aegean: From Marseilles to Bactria. New York: Alexander S. Onassis Public Benefit Foundation.

Kennedy, David L. 1996a Parthia and Rome: Eastern Perspectives. *In* The Roman Army in the East. David L. Kennedy, ed. Pp. 67–90. Journal of Roman Archaeology Supplementary Series 18. Ann Arbor: Journal of Roman Archaeology.

——, ed. 1996b The Roman Army in the East. Journal of Roman Archaeology Supplementary Series 18. Ann Arbor: Journal of Roman Archaeology.

King, Anthony 1990 Roman Gaul and Germany. London: British Museum Press.

Künow, Jürgen 1980 Negotiator et Vectura: Händler und Transport im Freien Germanien. Munich: Kleine Schriften aus dem Vorgeschichtlichen Seminar Marburg.

Lauwerier, Roel C. G. M., and J. M. M. Robeerst 2001 Horses in Roman Times in the Netherlands. *In* Animals and Man in the Past. H. Buitenhuis and W. Prummel, eds. Pp. 275–290. Groningen: ARC-Publication.

Leriche, Pierre 2003 The Greeks in the Orient: From Syria to Bactria. *In* The Greeks Beyond the Aegean: From Marseilles to Bactria. Vassos Karageorghis, ed. Pp. 78–128. New York: Alexander S. Onassis Public Benefit Foundation.

Linders, Tullia, and Pontus Hellström, eds. 1987 Architecture and Society in Hecatomnid Caria. Proceedings of the Uppsala Symposium 1987; Boreas 17. Stockholm: Almqvist & Wiksell.

Liverani, Mario 1990 Prestige and Interest: International Relations in the Ancient Near East, 1600–1100 B.C. Padua: Sargon.

Lomas, Kathryn 2004 Hellenization, Romanization, and Cultural Identity at Massalia. *In* Greek Identity in the Western Mediterranean. Papers in Honour of Brian Shefton. Kathryn Lomas, ed. Pp. 475–493. Mnesmosyne Supplement 246. Leiden: Brill.

Luttwak, Edward N. 1976 The Grand Strategy of the Roman Empire from the First Century A.D. to the Third. London: John Hopkins University Press.

Lyons, Claire, and John Papadopoulos, eds. 2002 The Archaeology of Colonialism. Los Angeles: The Getty Research Institute.

Mattingly, David J. 1995 Tripolitania. London: Batsford.

——, ed. 1996 Farming the Desert: The UNESCO Libyan Valleys Archaeological Survey. Vol. 2, Gazetteer and Pottery. London: Society for Libyan Studies.

——, ed. 2003 The Archaeology of Fazzan. Vol. 1, Synthesis. London: Society for Libyan Studies.

——, and Greg Aldrete 2000 The Feeding of Imperial Rome: The Mechanics of the Food Supply System. *In* Ancient Rome. The Archaeology of the Eternal City. Jon C. Coulston and Hazel Dodge, eds. Pp. 142–165. University of Oxford, School of Archaeology Monograph 54. Oxford: Oxford University School of Archaeology.

——, and John Salmon, eds. 2001 Economies Beyond Agriculture in the Roman World. London: Routledge.

——, David Stone, Lea Stirling, and Najib Ben Lazreg 2001 Leptiminus (Tunisia): A "Producer" City'? *In* Economies Beyond Agriculture in the Roman World. David J. Mattingly and John Salmon, eds. Pp. 66–89. London: Routledge.

Maxfield, Valerie, and David P. S. Peacock 2001 Survey and Excavation: Mons Claudianus 1987–1993. Vol. 2, Excavations, Part 1. Cairo: Institut Français d'Archéologie Orientale.

Miller, Margaret C. 1997 Athens and Persia in the Fifth Century B.C.: A Study in Cultural Receptivity. Cambridge: Cambridge University Press.

——2003 Art, Myth and Reality: Xenophantos' Lekythos Re-examined. *In* Poetry, Theory, Praxis: The Social Life of Myth, Word and Image in Ancient Greece. Essays in Honour of William J. Slater. Eric Csapo and Margaret C. Miller, eds. Pp. 19–47. Oxford: Oxbow.

Mitchell, Stephen 1993 Anatolia: Land, Men and Gods in Asia Minor. Oxford: Clarendon Press.

——2003 The Galatians: Representation and Reality. *In* The Cambridge Companion to the Hellenistic World. Andrew Erskine, ed. Pp. 280–293. Cambridge: Cambridge University Press.

Möller, Astrid 2000 Naukratis: Trade in Archaic Greece. Oxford: Oxford University Press.

Morris, Sarah 1992 Daidalos and the Origins of Greek Art. Princeton: Princeton University Press.

Munro-Hay, Stuart C. 1991 Aksum: An African Civilization of Late Antiquity. Edinburgh: Edinburgh University Press.

——1993 State Development and Urbanism in Northern Ethiopia. *In* The Archaeology of Africa: Food, Metals and Towns. Thurstan Shaw, Paul Sinclair, Bassey Andah, and Alex Okpoko, eds. Pp. 609–621. London: Routledge.

Nash, Daphne 1985 Celtic Territorial Expansion and the Mediterranean World. *In* Settlement and Society: Aspects of West European Prehistory in the First Millennium AD. Timothy C. Champion and J. V. S. Megaw, eds. Pp. 45–67. Leicester: Leicester University Press.

Niemeier, Wolf-Dietrich 2001 Archaic Greeks in the Orient: Textual and Archaeological Evidence. Bulletin of the American Schools of Oriental Research 322:11–32.

North, John 1981 The Development of Roman Imperialism. Journal of Roman Studies 71:1–9.

Nylander, Carl 1970 Ionians at Pasargadae: Studies in Persian Architecture. Uppsala: Universitetet.

Osborne, Robin 1998 Early Greek Colonization? The Nature of Greek Settlement in the West. *In* Archaic Greece: New Approaches and New Evidence. Nick Fisher and Hans van Wees, eds. Pp. 251–269. London: Duckworth.

Palagia, Olga, and Stephen V. Tracy 2002 The Macedonians in Athens, 322–239 B.C. Proceedings of an International Conference held at the University of Athens, May 24–26 2001. Oxford: Oxbow Books.

Panella, Clementina, and André Tchernia 2002 Agricultural Products Transported in Amphorae: Oil and Wine. *In* The Ancient Economy. Walter Scheidel and Sitta von Reden, eds. Pp. 173–189. Edinburgh: Edinburgh University Press.

Parker, Anthony J. 1992 Ancient Shipwrecks of the Mediterranean and the Roman Provinces. British Archaeological Reports International Series 580. Oxford: British Archaeological Reports.

Peacock, D. P. S. and D. F. Williams 1986 Amphorae and the Roman Economy: An Introductory Guide. London: Longman.

Pollard, Nigel 1996 The Roman Army as "Total Institution" in the Near East? Dura-Europos as a Case Study. *In* The Roman Army in the East. David L. Kennedy, ed. Pp. 211–227. Journal of Roman Archaeology Supplementary Series 18. Ann Arbor: Journal of Roman Archaeology.

——2000 Soldiers, Cities, and Civilians in Roman Syria. Ann Arbor: University of Michigan Press.

Potter, David 2003 Hellenistic Religion. *In* The Cambridge Companion to the Hellenistic World. Andrew Erskine, ed. Pp. 407–430. Cambridge: Cambridge University Press.

Potter, Timothy W. 1987 Roman Italy. London: British Museum Press.

Ralston, Iain B. M. 1988 Central Gaul at the Roman Conquest: Conceptions and Misconceptions. Antiquity 62(237):786–794.

Randall, R. H. 1953 The Erechtheum Workmen. American Journal of Archaeology 57:199–210.

Randsborg, Klaus 1992 Barbarians, Classical Antiquity and the Rise of Western Europe: An Archaeological Essay. Past and Present 137:8–24.

——1994 A Greek Episode: The Hellenistic North in the Black Sea Region. Acta Archaeologica 65:171–196.

Rankin, H. D. 1987 Celts and the Classical World. London: Croom Helm.

Ray, Himanshu P. 1994 The Winds of Change: Buddhism and the Maritime Links of Early South Asia. Delhi: Oxford University Press.

Renfrew, Colin, and Paul Bahn 2000 Archaeology: Theories, Methods and Practice. 3rd edition. London: Thames and Hudson.

Ridgway, Brunilde 1970 The Severe Style in Greek Sculpture. Princeton: Princeton University Press.

Romm, James S. 1992 The Edges of the Earth in Ancient Thought. Princeton: Princeton University Press.

Root, Margaret Cool 1985 The Parthenon Frieze and the Apadana Reliefs at Persepolis: Reassessing a Programmatic Relationship. American Journal of Archaeology 89:103–120.

Rotroff, Susan 1997 The Greeks and the Other in the Age of Alexander. *In* Greeks and Barbarians: Essays on the Interactions between Greeks and Non-Greeks in Antiquity and the Consequences of Eurocentrism. John Coleman and Clark Walz, eds. Pp. 221–235. Bethesda: CDL Press.

Rowlands, Michael, Mogens Larsen, and Kristian Kristiansen, eds. 1987 Centre and Periphery in the Ancient World. Cambridge: Cambridge University Press.

Rowlandson, Jane 2003 Town and Country in Ptolemaic Egypt. *In* The Cambridge Companion to the Hellenistic World. Andrew Erskine, ed. Pp. 249–263. Cambridge: Cambridge University Press.

Salles, Jean-Paul 1996 Achaemenid and Hellenistic trade in the Indian Ocean. *In* The Indian Ocean in Antiquity. Julian Reade, ed. Pp. 215–267. London: Kegan Paul International.

Sancisi-Weerdenburg, Heleen, and Amélie Kuhrt, eds. 1991. Asia Minor and Egypt: Old Cultures in a New Empire. Achaemenid History 6. Leiden: Nederlands Instituut voor Het Nabije Oosten.

Saprykin, Sergei 1994 Ancient Farms and Land-Plots on the Khora of Khersonesos Taurike: Research in the Herakleian Peninsula 1974–1990. Amsterdam: Gieben.

Shepherd, Gillian 1999 Fibulae and Females: Intermarriage in the Western Greek Colonies and the Evidence from Cemeteries. *In* Ancient Greeks West and East. Gocha Tsetskhladze, ed. Pp. 267–300. Leiden: Brill.

Sidebotham, Steven E., and Willemina Z. Wendrich 1998 Berenike: Archaeological Fieldwork at a Ptolemaic-Roman Port on the Red Sea Coast of Egypt 1994–1998. Sahara 10:85–96.

——2002 Berenike: Archaeological Fieldwork at a Ptolemaic-Roman Port on the Red Sea Coast of Egypt 1999–2001. Sahara 13:31–44.

Solovyov, S. L. 1999 Ancient Berezan: The Architecture, History and Culture of the First Greek Colony in the Northern Black Sea. John Boardman and Gocha Tsetskhladze, eds. Colloquia Pontica 4. Leiden: Brill.

Stewart, Andrew and S. Rebecca Martin 2003 Hellenistic Discoveries at Tel Dor, Israel. Hesperia 72:121–145.

Strobel, Karl 2002 State Formation by the Galatians of Asia Minor: Politico-historical and Cultural Processes in Hellenistic Central Anatolia. Anatolica 28:1–46.

Sullivan, Richard D. 1990 Near Eastern Royalty and Rome. Toronto: Toronto University Press.

Tchernia, André 1983 Italian Wine in Gaul at the End of the Republic. *In* Trade in the Ancient Economy. Peter Garnsey, Keith Hopkins, and C.R. Whittaker, eds. Pp. 87–104. London: Chatto and Windus.

——1986 Le Vin de l'Italie romaine: essai d'histoire économique d'après les amphores. Rome: L'Ecole Française de Rome.

——, Patrice Pompey, and Antoinette Hesnard, 1978 L'épave romaine de la Madrague de Giens (Var). Gallia Supplement 34. Paris: Editions du Centre National de la Recherche Scientifique.

Thompson, Frederick H. 2003 The Archaeology of Greek and Roman Slavery. London: Duckworth.

Thorley, J. 1971 The Silk Trade between China and the Roman Empire at its Height, circa AD 90–130. Greece and Rome 18:71–80.

Todd, Malcolm 1987 The Northern Barbarians, 100 BC–AD 300. Oxford: Blackwell.

Tsetskhladze, Gocha 2004 On the Earliest Greek Colonial Architecture in the Pontus. *In* Pontus and the Outside World. Studies in Black Sea History, Historiography and Archaeology. C. J. Tuplin, ed. Pp. 225–278. Colloquia Pontica 9. Leiden: Brill.

Vitali, Daniele 1991 The Celts in Italy. *In* The Celts. Sabatino Moscati, ed. Pp. 220–235. London: Thames and Hudson.

Webster, Jane 1997 Necessary Comparisons: A Post-colonial Approach to Religious Syncretism in the Roman Provinces. World Archaeology 28.3:324–338.

——1999 Here Be Dragons! Roman Attitudes to Northern Britain. *In* Northern Exposure: Interpretative Devolution and the Iron Ages of Britain. Bill Bevan, ed. Pp. 1–20. Leicester Archaeology Monographs 5. Leicester: School of Archaeological Studies, University of Leicester.

Wells, Peter 1980 Culture Contact and Culture Change: Early Iron Age Central Europe and the Mediterranean. Cambridge, MA: Harvard University Press.

——1984 Farms, Villages and Cities: Commerce and Urban Origins in Late Prehistoric Europe. Ithaca: Cornell University Press.

——1999 The Barbarians Speak. How the Conquered Peoples Shaped Roman Europe. Princeton: Princeton University Press.

Whittaker, Charles R. 1994 Frontiers of the Roman Empire: A Social and Economic Study. Baltimore: Johns Hopkins University Press.

Wilson, Andrew 2001 Timgad and Textile Production. *In* Economies Beyond Agriculture in the Roman World. David J. Mattingly and John Salmon, eds. Pp. 271–296. London: Routledge.

Woolf, Greg 1993 Rethinking the Oppida. Oxford Journal of Archaeology 12.2: 223–234.

——1998 Becoming Roman: The Origins of Provincial Civilization in Gaul. Cambridge: Cambridge University Press.

Woolliscroft, David J. 2002 The Roman Frontier on the Gask Ridge. Oxford: Archeopress.

Prospective

Susan E. Alcock and Robin Osborne

Google reports, in 0.03 seconds, the existence of some 6,110,000 links (at the time of writing) for "classical archaeology." Not surprisingly the vast majority of these relate to university instruction, field projects, museum exhibits, or other forms of the academic enterprise. But punctuating the list (not least in its "sponsored links"), other facets of the field emerge: the ability to purchase "fragments of time" (Great Deals on the Ancient World!), the existence of blogs in which people react personally to the debate over the Elgin Marbles or wail over having to attend an archaeology class, the opportunity for "real people" to volunteer in archaeological fieldwork in the Mediterranean world.

This Internet barometer points to an unquestionable level of general interest in and awareness of classical archaeology. This can be reinforced through a more old-fashioned form of data search. If one simply asks people what they know of the subject, the range of responses normally revolves around "Greeks and Romans," "Athens and Rome," "digging and temples," "the Parthenon and the Colosseum"—all perfectly good answers. What is perhaps most remarkable, for such an apparently recherché and remote topic, is how rarely those questioned have no idea of how to respond, and how frequently they react with infectious enthusiasm.

At some point along the way, then, people learn something of the discipline of classical archaeology. This acquaintance no doubt varies considerably from nation to nation, with the Roman heritage of Great Britain, for example, providing a day-to-day familiarity with the classical past that others can only envy. Generational differences too play a part in what people know, and what they don't know. The foundational character of ancient studies in the evolution of western civilization has become, as our Introduction makes clear, an increasingly problematic zone; coupled with that development are issues of educational practicalities and priorities. Latin is no longer regularly taught at the secondary level (and Greek is vanishingly rare) in Great Britain and North America, and curricular reforms often (if not always) trend in the direction of reducing the amount of ancient history or classical civilization presented in the secondary school classroom or required (or even offered) at university level.

Yet, despite such developments, classical archaeology obviously remains on the popular radar. The sources behind this phenomenon are myriad, and surely vary from individual to individual. For some people, the pull comes from the movies. After a decline in the "sword and sandals" genre of the 1950s and 1960s (the era of *Ben-Hur* and *Cleopatra*), ancient epics have recently made something of a comeback with such features as *Troy* (2004), *Alexander* (2004), *300 Spartans* and—most successfully—*Gladiator* (2000). Cable television, with the Discovery and History Channels, is another benefactor; made-for-television series (such as *Empire* or *Rome*) have also garnered acceptable ratings. Contemporary news or sporting events pack their own punch, such as the spectacle of the 2004 Olympics in Athens with its constant use of the Parthenon as a backdrop and of ancient sites, such as Olympia, as dramatic sets for performance. Through these and numerous other electronic and digital means, the "look" of the ancient world has been readily available for those who chose to view it.

As for print media, there are the classics of fiction set in the ancient world—the novels of Robert Graves, Mary Renault, Marguerite Youcenar, and Gore Vidal, to name but a few which still sell well. Recent #1 bestsellers have included Robert Harris' *Pompeii: A Novel* (2003). On Amazon.com, at the time of writing, just one of Colleen McCullough's *Masters of Rome* series had 109 online reviews, Stephen Pressfield's *Gates of Fire: An Epic Novel of the Battle of Thermopylae* a whopping 488: both can be compared to three and two reviews, respectively, for books by this volume's editors. Intriguingly, antiquity has proved a fertile ground for the mystery novel, from the fourth-century B.C. settings of "murders in Macedon," to the detectives of Republican Rome, P. Didius Falco and Gordianus the Finder (the work of Anna Apostolou, Lindsay Davies and Stephen Saylor, respectively). This list—of books, movies, video games, beer advertisements, and so on—could go on and on, and other prime favorites (or stinkers) mooted. The basic point is that the classical past remains an active ingredient in the popular, and not simply the scholarly, imagination.

But what version of that past do people receive from these sources, and how does it measure up against the spectrum of perspectives offered in this volume? Even in the cursory review above, some centers of gravity are clear: Alexander, Athens, games, gladiators, politics, Pompeii, Rome, war . . . This construction of antiquity, with its focus on great men, disasters, cosmopolitan cities and violent or salacious activities, is by no means to be despised, and indeed should (within reason) be enjoyed with gusto. Moreover, it is, in itself, a rich topic for analysis, as the burgeoning study (and teaching) of the classics in film, or of the role of classics in modern popular culture, amply testifies. For all that, this particular construction must also be recognized as an exceptionally partial view of the past.

Two things could be said to connect the various themes mentioned above. First, each possesses distinct material correlates—portraits, architectural spaces, graffiti, cities, houses, burials, implements. Indeed, without these material traces, it would be impossible to envision and represent the subjects that fascinate us so; such illustrations are the very stuff of long-established traditions in classical archaeology. Yet, and second, investigation of these topics has only occasionally, and only recently, taken advantage of the more interrogative approaches to material culture presented in this volume. In other words, there is more than a little disconnect between the popular image of the past and what classical archaeology can actually offer by way of augmenting, illuminating, and even enlivening antiquity.

Some areas of amplification and improved accuracy are easily identified: the close juxtaposition of Greek and Roman (as here broadly defined) phenomena; the balanced use of material versus textual sources, with critical assessment and respect for both domains; the discussion of non-elite lives (the so-called "people without history") and of cities and territories apart from the core regions of Athens and Rome. Beyond such (to our eyes) admirable attributes, however, we would identify three broader themes that swim throughout, and underpin, the volume: themes that can and should appeal to those thinking, imagining, or dreaming of the ancient world in any fashion, at any level, and to any purpose. The three themes are dirt, space and choice.

Dirt, real and metaphorical, plays a variety of roles in this volume. On the one hand, it can be taken to sum up the emphasis (in chapters 1 and 2) on the ever-changing way of "doing" classical archaeology. Dirt means more in that context, however, than any obvious connection with excavation and stratigraphy. Accepting the grit in the system—that archaeological research in the Mediterranean world has politics (big and small), and that precise scientific goals and results do not always reign supreme—is a salutary, if occasionally painful, advance in understanding. More "real" dirt comes into play with the situation of ancient life in its physical environment (chapter 3). The historical interplay of humanity and nature has attracted attention in many periods or places, not least as a way to ponder past attitudes toward environmental caretaking, or its opposite. The Mediterranean landscape, too long viewed as idyllic and pristine by authorities informed by poetry rather than personal autopsy, has begun to be studied from this, more critical perspective. Evaluating the impact of human exploitation on the environment, as well as reviewing the essential agricultural basis of ancient society (chapter 4) underscores the sheer human effort that went into everyday survival and the production of surplus. Uncertainty and fear—of hunger, of want—were an endemic condition for many members of civilizations routinely and automatically perceived as cultivated, glorious, and powerful. One contribution of this volume to all audiences, then, is to ground an often-romanticized understanding of the past in its actual messiness, both by acknowledging past sweat and present complications.

Awareness of the significance of space is another impulse at work throughout the volume. Classical archaeology has always paid due attention to individual structures and monuments (public buildings, temples, treasuries and tombs), in many cases lavishly describing their organization and decoration. Emphasized in this volume, instead, are the linkages and relationships between such separate elements, be it within wider landscapes (chapter 4), cities (chapter 5), or sanctuaries (chapter 7). Spaces of action and interaction are thus created, for example, in the various agoras of Greek cities or in Roman fora, with human movement and visual perspectives, as well as individual and collective decision-taking about their design and perception, very much a part of the interpretation. Considering the ancient house (chapter 6), not as a two-dimensional assemblage of rooms, but as a household with mobile traffic patterns and endlessly revolving activities, is another example of this new mode of conceptualizing people in space. This development in classical archaeology echoes change in the discipline at large, as well as in numerous other academic fields. At a different level, an early 21st-century concern with spatial linkages and connectivity also explains the inclusion of chapter 10, with its stress on the far-from-isolated, global position of Greek and Roman polities and cultures within a far-from-passive "wider world."

Finally, choice. Everywhere the chapters in this volume make clear the contingent quality of life in antiquity. The inhabitants of cities had to, and did, make choices about communal organization and embellishment; patrons about monuments to dedicate; families about their economic options and resources; household heads about management and decoration of the home; rulers about their self-representation in portraiture; "barbarians" about their interaction with Mediterranean powers. Choice abounded about how to create and express identity through language, religion, dress, diet, and behavior (chapter 9). This may appear a basic point, but it is a vital one. Armed only with knowledge from hindsight, and too often burdened with essentialized notions of what the categories of "Greek," "Roman," and "barbarian" represent, scholarly interpretations sometimes found it easy to assume that peoples in the past lived a simpler, more constrained life, and to limit the range of options open in antiquity for individual and collective expression and action.

Such assumptions, though rarely articulated fully, are both patronizing and deceptive. Worse still, they can take much of the spontaneity, and the fun, out of studying the classical past—one reason, perhaps, why fiction and cinema are so much more powerful in the popular sphere. Yet inventiveness, surprise, and the fascination of human choice are there to be wondered at in our academic data as well. As this collection of chapters argues, that distinction of "popular" and "scholarly" need not be as wide as at present—a resolution that would benefit the entire spectrum of those intrigued by what classical archaeology can reveal about the ancient world.

Index

Note: Page numbers in *italics* refer to figures.